CCSP Self-Study: Cisco Secure PIX Firewall Advanced (CSPFA)
Second Edition

Behzad Behtash

Cisco Press

800 East 96th Street
Indianapolis, IN 46240 USA

CCSP Self-Study: Cisco Secure PIX Firewall Advanced (CSPFA)

Second Edition

Behzad Behtash

Copyright© 2004 Cisco Systems, Inc.

Cisco Press logo is a trademark of Cisco Systems, Inc.

Published by:

Cisco Press

800 East 96th Street

Indianapolis, IN 46240 USA

Printed in the United States of America 2 3 4 5 6 7 8 9 0

Second Printing August 2004

Library of Congress Cataloging-in-Publication Number: 2003107973

ISBN: 1-58705-149-4

Warning and Disclaimer

This book is designed to provide information about Private Internet Exchange (PIX) Firewall topics related to CCSP certification. Every effort has been made to make this book as complete and as accurate as possible, but no warranty or fitness is implied.

The information is provided on an "as is" basis. The authors, Cisco Press, and Cisco Systems, Inc. shall have neither liability nor responsibility to any person or entity with respect to any loss or damages arising from the information contained in this book or from the use of the discs or programs that might accompany it.

The opinions expressed in this book belong to the author and are not necessarily those of Cisco Systems, Inc.

The Cisco Press self-study book series is as described, intended for self-study. It has not been designed for use in a classroom environment. Only Cisco Learning Partners displaying the following logos are authorized providers of Cisco curriculum. If you are using this book within the classroom of a training company that does not carry one of these logos, then you are not preparing with a Cisco trained and authorized provider. For information on Cisco Learning Partners please visit: www.cisco.com/go/authorizedtraining. To provide Cisco with any information about what you may believe is unauthorized use of Cisco trademarks or copyrighted training material, please visit: http://www.cisco.com/logo/infringement.html.

Trademark Acknowledgments

All terms mentioned in this book that are known to be trademarks or service marks have been appropriately capitalized. Cisco Press or Cisco Systems, Inc. cannot attest to the accuracy of this information. Use of a term in this book should not be regarded as affecting the validity of any trademark or service mark.

Corporate and Government Sales

Cisco Press offers excellent discounts on this book when ordered in quantity for bulk purchases or special sales.

For more information, please contact:

U.S. Corporate and Government Sales 1-800-382-3419 corpsales@pearsontechgroup.com

For sales outside of the U.S. please contact:

International Sales at international@pearsontechgroup.com

Feedback Information

At Cisco Press, our goal is to create in-depth technical books of the highest quality and value. Each book is crafted with care and precision, undergoing rigorous development that involves the unique expertise of members from the professional technical community.

Readers' feedback is a natural continuation of this process. If you have any comments regarding how we could improve the quality of this book, or otherwise alter it to better suit your needs, you can contact us through e-mail at feedback@ciscopress.com. Please make sure to include the book title and ISBN in your message.

We greatly appreciate your assistance.

Publisher	John Wait
Editor-in-Chief	John Kane
Executive Editor	Brett Bartow
Cisco Representative	Anthony Wolfenden
Cisco Press Program Manager	Nannette M. Noble
Acquisitions Editor	Michelle Grandin
Production Manager	Patrick Kanouse
Development Editor	Betsey Henkels
Project Editors	San Dee Phillips and Keith Cline
Copy Editor	Kris Simmons
Technical Editors	Nairi Adamian, Andy Fox, Izak Karmona
Team Coordinator	Tammi Barnett
Book Designer	Gina Rexrode
Cover Designer	Louisa Adair
Composition	Mark Shirar
Indexer	Tim Wright

CISCO SYSTEMS

Corporate Headquarters
Cisco Systems, Inc.
170 West Tasman Drive
San Jose, CA 95134-1706
USA
www.cisco.com
Tel: 408 526-4000
800 553-NETS (6387)
Fax: 408 526-4100

European Headquarters
Cisco Systems International BV
Haarlerbergpark
Haarlerbergweg 13-19
1101 CH Amsterdam
The Netherlands
www-europe.cisco.com
Tel: 31 0 20 357 1000
Fax: 31 0 20 357 1100

Americas Headquarters
Cisco Systems, Inc.
170 West Tasman Drive
San Jose, CA 95134-1706
USA
www.cisco.com
Tel: 408 526-7660
Fax: 408 527-0883

Asia Pacific Headquarters
Cisco Systems, Inc.
Capital Tower
168 Robinson Road
#22-01 to #29-01
Singapore 068912
www.cisco.com
Tel: +65 6317 7777
Fax: +65 6317 7799

Cisco Systems has more than 200 offices in the following countries and regions. Addresses, phone numbers, and fax numbers are listed on the
Cisco.com Web site at www.cisco.com/go/offices.

Argentina • Australia • Austria • Belgium • Brazil • Bulgaria • Canada • Chile • China PRC • Colombia • Costa Rica • Croatia • Czech Republic
Denmark • Dubai, UAE • Finland • France • Germany • Greece • Hong Kong SAR • Hungary • India • Indonesia • Ireland • Israel • Italy
Japan • Korea • Luxembourg • Malaysia • Mexico • The Netherlands • New Zealand • Norway • Peru • Philippines • Poland • Portugal
Puerto Rico • Romania • Russia • Saudi Arabia • Scotland • Singapore • Slovakia • Slovenia • South Africa • Spain • Sweden
Switzerland • Taiwan • Thailand • Turkey • Ukraine • United Kingdom • United States • Venezuela • Vietnam • Zimbabwe

About the Author

Behzad Behtash, CCNP, CCDP, MCSE, is an IT consultant with more than 9 years of experience in networking and security. He holds a bachelor's degree in chemical engineering from the University of Wisconsin-Madison. Behzad resides in Oakland, California.

About the Technical Reviewers

Nairi Adamian, CCIE Security No. 10294, CISSP, is currently working as a security and virtual private network (VPN) engineer in the Technical Assistance Centre (TAC) at Cisco Systems in Australia. She provides support on multiple Cisco security products such as the PIX Firewall, VPN Concentrator, Intrusion Detection System, and other related technologies. She holds a bachelor's degree in computer science from the University of Technology, Sydney, and is currently pursuing an MBA at Macquarie Graduate School of Management.

Andy Fox, CCNA, CCDA, CSS-1, is a certified Cisco Systems instructor with Global Knowledge. Andy has been teaching Cisco Certified classes for more than 6 years and is the course director for the Managing Cisco Network Security course. Andy is the author of the first edition of this book, *Cisco Secure PIX Firewalls*. Andy began his career in computer science as a computer operator in the U.S. Air Force.

Izak Karmona is a network security consultant for Hewlett-Packard in Israel. He is a CCSP and is currently working toward his CCIE Security certification. Izak has more than 15 years of experience in the networking industry. As part of his job, he provides network design, security, and implementation services for customers of HP. Izak holds a bachelor's degree in computer science from the Technion Institute of Technology at Haifa, Israel.

Dedications

I dedicate this book to my daughter, Tiana; my son, Daryan; and my loving wife, Anita, who always come first in my book.

I further dedicate this book to my parents for their unconditional love and for always being there for me. And to Ramin, Kaveh, and Saman, great brothers and greater friends.

I would also like to acknowledge two great individuals who have a lot to do with the person that I am today: Professors Glenn Sather and Thatcher Root of the University of Wisconsin-Madison. Thank you for believing in me.

Acknowledgments

I would like to thank Michelle Grandin, Christopher Cleveland, Tammi Barnett, Kris Simmons, San Dee Phillips, Keith Cline, and the rest of the Cisco Press team for the opportunity to write this book and for their support and guidance throughout the writing process. In particular, I would like to thank Betsey Henkels, who has been simply wonderful to work with throughout. She is a superb
professional, and her efforts as the development editor have improved the quality of this book immensely.

I would also like to thank the reviewers, Nairi Adamian, Andy Fox, and Izak Karmona, for their dedication and constructive suggestions. Their contributions are very much appreciated.

My thanks also goes to my colleague and friend, Grant Moerschel, for introducing me to Cisco Press and for his continued friendship and insight.

Finally, I would like to thank Matt Krieg at Cisco Systems for providing me with timely information on PIX Firewall developments.

Contents at a Glance

Contents

Icons Used in This Book

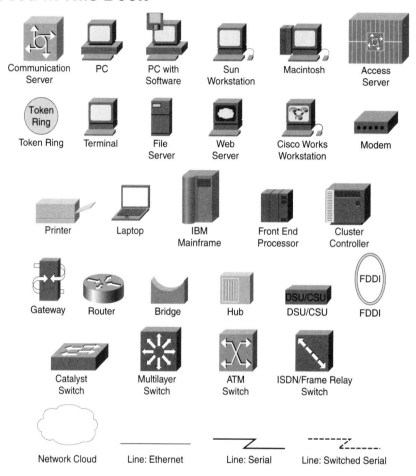

Command Syntax Conventions

The conventions used to present command syntax in this book are the same conventions used in the IOS Command Reference. The Command Reference describes these conventions as follows:

- **Boldface** indicates commands and keywords that are entered literally as shown. In actual configuration examples and output (not general command syntax), boldface indicates commands that are manually input by the user (such as a **show** command).

- *Italics* indicate arguments for which you supply actual values.

- Vertical bars (l) separate alternative, mutually exclusive elements.

- Square brackets [ ] indicate optional elements.

- Braces { } indicate a required choice.

- Braces within brackets [{ }] indicate a required choice within an optional element.

Foreword

CCSP Self-Study: Cisco Secure PIX Firewall Advanced (CSPFA) Second Edition, is a Cisco-authorized, self-paced learning tool that helps you understand foundation concepts covered on the Cisco Secure PIX Firewall Advanced (CSPFA) exam. This book was developed in cooperation with the Cisco Internet Learning Solutions group, the team within Cisco responsible for the development of the CSPFA exam. As an early-stage exam preparation product, this book presents detailed and comprehensive coverage of the tasks that network and security engineers need to configure, verify, and manage the PIX Firewall product family. Whether you are studying to become CCSP certified or to achieve your PIX specialization, or you are simply seeking to gain a better understanding of the products, services, and policies that enable you to implement the products in the PIX Firewall product family, you will benefit from the information presented in this book.

Cisco Systems and Cisco Press present this material in text-based format to provide another learning vehicle for our customers and the broader user community in general. Although a publication does not duplicate the instructor-led or e-learning environment, we acknowledge that not everyone responds in the same way to the same delivery mechanism. It is our intent that presenting this material via a Cisco Press publication will enhance the transfer of knowledge to a broad audience of networking professionals.

Cisco Press will present other books in the Certification Self-Study Series on existing and future exams to help achieve Cisco Internet Learning Solutions Group's principal objectives: to educate the Cisco community of networking professionals and to enable that community to build and maintain reliable, scalable networks. The Cisco Career Certifications and classes that support these certifications are directed at meeting these objectives through a disciplined approach to progressive learning.

For you to succeed with Cisco Career Certifications and in your daily job as a Cisco certified professional, we recommend a blended learning solution that combines instructor-led training with hands-on experience, e-learning, and self-study training. Cisco Systems has authorized Cisco Learning Partners worldwide, which can provide you with the most highly qualified instruction and invaluable hands-on experience in lab and simulation environments. To learn more about Cisco Learning Partner programs available in your area, go to http://www.cisco.com/go/authorizedtraining.

The books Cisco Press creates in partnership with Cisco Systems will meet the same standards for content quality demanded of our courses and certifications. It is our intent that you will find this and subsequent Cisco Press certification self-study publications of value as you build your networking knowledge base.

Thomas M. Kelly
Vice-President, Internet Learning Solutions Group
Cisco Systems, Inc.
January 2004

Introduction

Network security has garnered a great deal of attention over the last several years. The current geopolitical climate and spotlight on security in general has only intensified the focus on network security technologies and products. This focus on security is reflected in the increased spending on network security products and services by public and private organizations alike and the growing demand for network security professionals and experts.

Responding to market demand for increased security, Cisco Systems provides a wide range of network security products, innovative technologies, and services. The Cisco PIX Firewall security appliance series is a market-leading firewall platform used by network engineers and security professionals to protect networks of all sizes and complexities.

Who Should Read This Book?

This book targets network engineers, security professionals, and support engineers looking for detailed information on the installation, configuration, and maintenance of PIX firewalls. It can also be used by CCSP certification candidates who want to augment their exam preparation material with additional PIX-related topics. To make full use of the information presented, readers should have a solid knowledge of networking essentials and be familiar with basic network security concepts.

Motivation for the Book

The first edition of the *Cisco Secure PIX Firewalls* book, published by Cisco Press in 2001, filled the market need for a book covering the operations and advanced features of the PIX Firewall. Since the publication of that book, the PIX Firewall has been significantly modified and improved, and several new models, including a module designed for the Catalyst 6500 Series Switch and the Cisco 7600 Series Internet Router, have been introduced. Cisco Systems has also introduced a new graphical user interface (PIX Device Manager [PDM]) and has revamped the enterprise management and maintenance tools for the PIX Firewall.

This book provides updated information and covers the new PIX Firewall models and technologies introduced since the publication of the first edition of the CSPFA book. Coverage includes features of the PIX Firewall Software Version 6.3 including Open Shortest Path First (OSPF), 802.1Q VLANs and logical interfaces, and network address translation (NAT) Traversal. Also, greater emphasis is placed on coverage of the PDM as a primary management and configuration tool for the PIX Firewall.

How to Use This Book

This book consists of 22 chapters. The chapters are presented in a logical order, but you can easily read chapters in the order that fits your specific needs. Several scenarios are presented in Chapter 4, "Implementing Cisco PIX Firewall in the Network," to allow you to review typical network layouts and complete PIX Firewall configurations. You can review the material in that chapter to determine the basic layout appropriate for your implementation and proceed with the remaining chapters. Alternatively, you may want to read Chapter 4 after you have read the other chapters and are familiar with the topics covered in those chapters.

The chapters present the following topics:

Chapter 1, "The Cisco Role in Network Security"—This chapter provides an overview of network security essentials and presents an outline of the Cisco Architecture for Voice, Video, and Integrated Data (AVVID) and Secure Architecture for Enterprises (SAFE) framework.

Chapter 2, "Cisco PIX Firewall Technology and Features"—This chapter provides an overview of the PIX Firewall technologies and capabilities, including an introduction to the Adaptive Security Algorithm (ASA).

Chapter 3, "The Cisco PIX Firewall Family"—This chapter covers the PIX Firewall Security Appliance series and provides information on features and capabilities of each model.

Chapter 4, "Implementing Cisco PIX Firewall in the Network"—Chapter 4 presents several scenarios for the implementation of the PIX Firewall in networks of different sizes and complexities.

Chapter 5, "Getting Started with the Cisco PIX Firewall"—Basic PIX Firewall configuration procedures and commands are presented in this chapter. You can use the information in this chapter to bring up and run the PIX Firewall.

Chapter 6, "Cisco PIX Device Manager"—This chapter covers the operation of the PDM and the procedures for the configuration of the PIX Firewall using the PDM.

Chapter 7, "Translations and Connections"—Chapter 7 details how the PIX Firewall processes inbound and outbound transmissions. Information on NAT and port address translation (PAT) is also provided in this chapter.

Chapter 8, "Access Control Lists and Content Filtering"—This chapter explains the use of access control lists (ACLs) to control the flow of traffic through the PIX Firewall.

Chapter 9, "Object Grouping"—This chapter covers the object grouping function in the PIX Firewall to simplify the creation and application of ACLs.

Chapter 10, "Routing"—Chapter 10 covers the routing functions supported by the PIX Firewall.

Chapter 11, "Advanced Protocol Handling"—This chapter provides information on the PIX Firewall's fixup protocol function and advanced protocol-handling capabilities.

Chapter 12, "Attack Guards, Intrusion Detection, and Shunning"—The PIX Firewall's inline intrusion detection and shunning capabilities and related configuration procedures are presented in this chapter.

Chapter 13, "Authentication, Authorization, and Accounting"—This chapter includes an overview of PIX Firewall's authentication, authorization, and accounting (AAA) procedures. Downloadable ACLs are also discussed in this chapter.

Chapter 14, "Failover"—This chapter details the PIX Firewall's high availability capabilities and related configuration procedures.

Chapter 15, "Virtual Private Networks"—Chapter 15 provides an overview of VPN basics and describes IP Security (IPSec) and Internet Key Exchange (IKE) implementations in PIX Firewall.

Chapter 16, "Site-to-Site VPNs"—This chapter provides detailed configuration procedures for building site-to-site VPN connections using the PIX Firewall.

Chapter 17, "Client Remote Access VPNs"—Configuration procedures for building client remote access VPN connections using the PIX Firewall are included in this chapter.

Chapter 18, "System Maintenance"—Chapter 18 details system management protocols and configuration tasks for the PIX Firewall, including image upgrade and password recovery procedures.

Chapter 19, "PIX Firewall Management in Enterprise Networks"—This chapter covers the Cisco Management Center for Firewalls (Firewall MC) operations and capabilities.

Chapter 20, "PIX Firewall Maintenance in Enterprise Networks"—Chapter 20 provides information on the use of the Firewall Auto Update Server for enterprise maintenance operations.

Chapter 21, "Firewall Services Module"—This chapter provides detailed information on the PIX Firewall Services Module (FWSM) for the Cisco Catalyst 6500 Series Switch and the Cisco 7600 Series Internet Router.

Chapter 22, "PIX Firewall in SOHO Networks"—This chapter provides an overview of PIX Firewall capabilities and technologies that address the needs of small office/home office (SOHO) networks.

Appendix A, "Answers to Chapter Review Questions"—This appendix provides the answers to the review questions at the end of each chapter.

Appendix B, "Security Resources"—This appendix provides a list of useful security resources available in print and on the Internet.

Introduction and Overview

On completion of this chapter, you will be able to perform the following tasks:

- State the reasons for securing computer networks.
- Define the four primary security threats.
- Describe different types of network attacks.
- Explain the major steps for implementing network security.
- Identify the Cisco Architecture for Voice, Video, and Integrated Data (AVVID) framework and Secure Architecture for Enterprises (SAFE) Blueprint components and benefits.
- Describe the approaches that attackers use to attack networks.
- Identify the common network attack points and security weaknesses in networks.
- Explain the functions of common attack tools.

CHAPTER 1

The Cisco Role in Network Security

Networks transform computers from islands of information to powerful tools of communication, collaboration, and productivity. Private networks have been in use by the government, universities, and businesses for many years. With the explosion of the Internet in the mid 1990s, more private networks and individuals are now connected in the global public network.

The Internet has become a vital resource for millions of computer users in the United States and around the world, and reliance on Internet services will only increase with time. Corporations, academic institutions, organizations, and governments, large and small, are finding the Internet the most accessible, efficient, and cost-effective means of providing services and disseminating information.

There is, however, a negative aspect to the unprecedented connectivity made possible by the Internet and new networking technologies. Although it is easier and cheaper than in the past to connect to partners and customers across the public network, risks of exposure to unscrupulous activity from inside and outside the network have increased significantly.

Why Network Security Is Necessary

Today, the Internet consists of tens of thousands of networks that are interconnected without boundaries. Network security is essential in this environment because Internet-connected organizational networks are accessible from any computer in the world and, therefore, are potentially vulnerable to threats from individuals even without physical access. The unfortunate events of September 11, 2001, and the emphasis on homeland security increase the importance of network security in the United States, as demonstrated by the creation of the National Strategy to Secure Cyberspace.

In a recent survey conducted by the Computer Security Institute (CSI), 70 percent of the organizations polled stated that their network security defenses had been breached and that 60 percent of the incidents came from within the organizations themselves.

Although it is difficult to measure how many companies have had Internet-related security problems and to estimate the financial losses caused by those problems, it is clear that the problems are significant. Several high-profile denial-of-service (DoS) attacks and virus and worm outbreaks in recent years serve as examples of Internet-related threats and security problems and the tremendous impact they can have on targeted companies and the economy in general.

Types of Security Threats

There are four primary types of threats to network security:

- Unstructured
- Structured
- External
- Internal

Unstructured threats come mainly from inexperienced individuals using hacking tools that are easily available from the Internet. Some people in this category are motivated by malicious intent, but most are eager for intellectual challenge. The latter are commonly known as *script kiddies*. They are not the most talented or experienced hackers, but they are motivated, which is all that matters. These individuals are looking for easy prey and typically have no specific target in mind.

Structured threats come from hackers who are more highly motivated and technically competent. They usually understand network system designs and vulnerabilities, and they can understand as well as create hacking scripts to penetrate those network systems. Structured threats are often directed at a specific target, such as a server or specific application.

External threats come from individuals or organizations working outside a company who do not have authorized access to computer systems or network. They work their way into a network mainly from the Internet or dialup access servers.

Internal threats come from people who have authorized access to an organization's network and, therefore, have either an account on a server or physical access to the wire. Internal threats typically result from malicious conduct by disgruntled current or former employees or contractors, but these threats can also result from unintentional acts, such as employees downloading viruses, accidentally accessing unauthorized information, using weak passwords, or sharing their passwords with others.

Network Attacks

Network attacks take many different shapes, but they can generally fit into one of the following three main categories:

- **Reconnaissance attacks**—An intruder attempts to discover and map systems, services, and vulnerabilities.
- **Access attacks**—Intruders attack networks or systems to retrieve data, gain access, or escalate their access privileges.
- **DoS attacks**—An intruder attacks a network in a way that damages or corrupts a computer system or denies users access to networks, systems, or services.

Each attack type is further discussed in the following subsections.

Reconnaissance Attacks

Reconnaissance attacks (also known as information gathering or reconnaissance) are the unauthorized discovery and mapping of systems, services, or vulnerabilities. In most cases, reconnaissance precedes an actual access or DoS attack. The malicious intruder typically ping sweeps the target network first to determine what IP addresses are alive. After this step, the intruder determines what services or ports are active on the live IP addresses. From this information, the intruder queries the ports to determine the application type and version, as well as the type and version of the operating system running on the target host.

Reconnaissance is somewhat analogous to a thief scoping out a neighborhood for vulnerable homes that can easily be broken into, such as an unoccupied residence, an easy-to-open door or window, and so on. In many cases, the intruders go as far as "rattling the door handle," not to enter immediately, but to discover vulnerable entries that they can exploit later, when there is less likelihood of being "seen."

Access Attacks

Access is an all-encompassing term that refers to unauthorized data manipulation, system access, or privilege escalation. Attackers can also use access attacks to gain control of a system and install and hide software that they will use later.

Unauthorized Data Retrieval

Unauthorized data retrieval is simply reading, writing, copying, or moving files that are not intended to be accessible to the intruder. Sometimes, this retrieval is as easy as finding wide-open shared folders in Windows or Network File System (NFS)–exported directories in UNIX systems with read-and-write access for everyone. The intruder has no problem getting to such files, and more often than not, the easily accessible information is highly confidential and completely unprotected from prying eyes, especially if the attacker is already an internal user.

Unauthorized System Access

Unauthorized system access is the ability of an intruder to gain access to a machine that the intruder is not authorized to access through an account or password. Entering or accessing systems without authorization usually involves running a hack, script, or tool that exploits a known vulnerability of the system or application being attacked.

Unauthorized Privilege Escalation

Another form of access attacks involves *privilege escalation*. This escalation happens when legitimate users use higher levels of access privileges than their authorization permits or when intruders gain privileged access. The intent of these intrusions is to gain information or execute procedures that are beyond the intruder's current authorization level. In many cases in a UNIX system, it involves gaining root access to install a network-monitor application to record network traffic, such as usernames and passwords that can be used to access another target.

In some cases, intruders want only to gain access with no intent to steal information— especially when the motive is intellectual challenge or curiosity or when the intruders are merely making a mistake.

DoS Attacks

DoS occurs when an attacker disables or corrupts networks, systems, or services with the intent to deny the service to legitimate users. A DoS attack typically crashes the system, slows it down to the point that it is unusable, or overloads the network with useless traffic. However, a DoS can also be as simple as wiping out or corrupting information necessary for business. In most cases, carrying out the attack simply involves running a hack, script, or tool. The attacker does not need prior access to the target because all that is usually required is a way to reach the network or system. For these reasons and because of the great damage potential, DoS attacks are the most feared intrusions—especially by e-commerce website operators.

NOTE	In recent years, a number of high-profile DoS attacks have occurred against several of the largest e-commerce companies. In those cases, the attackers used an army of zombies (unprotected systems compromised by the attackers for use in DoS attacks against other systems) to launch coordinated attacks against targeted servers. These types of attacks are commonly referred to as distributed denial-of-service (DDoS) attacks.

Implementing Network Security

Maintaining network security should be a continuous process built around a security policy. A security policy that is continuously in revision is most effective because it promotes retesting and reapplying updated security measures on a continuous basis. This continuous security process is represented by the security wheel, as shown in Figure 1-1.

Figure 1-1   *Network Security as a Continuous Process*

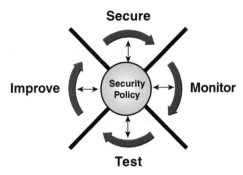

As shown on the security wheel, to begin this continuous process, you should create a security policy that enables the application of security measures. A security policy should accomplish the following tasks:

- Identify the organization's security objectives.
- Document the resources to be protected.
- Identify the network infrastructure with current maps and inventories.

To create or implement an effective security policy, you must determine what to protect, how to protect it, and the level or risk that is acceptable to your organization. You should know and understand your network's weak points and how they can be exploited. You should also understand how your system normally functions so that you know what to expect and are familiar with how the devices are normally used. Finally, consider the physical security of your network and how to protect it. Physical access to a computer, router, or firewall can give a user total control over that device.

After you develop the security policy, it becomes the hub around which the next four steps of the security wheel are based:

Step 1   **Secure the system**. This step involves implementing security devices such as firewalls, identification of authentication systems, and encryption with the intent to prevent unauthorized access to network systems. This point is where the Cisco Private Internet Exchange (PIX) Firewall is effective.

Step 2   **Monitor the network for violations and attacks against the corporate security policy**. Violations can occur within the secured perimeter of the network from a disgruntled employee or from outside the network from a hacker. Monitoring the network with a real-time intrusion detection system, such as the Cisco Secure Intrusion Detection System (IDS), can ensure that you properly configured the security devices in Step 1. These systems can also maintain detailed logs of network activity, which you can use to identify unsuccessful attacks against the network or to assist forensics if a successful attack occurs.

Step 3   **Test the effectiveness of existing security safeguards**. Use a security vulnerability assessment tool to identify the security posture of the network with respect to the security procedures that form the hub of the security wheel.

Step 4   **Improve corporate security**. Collect and analyze information from the monitoring and testing phases to make security improvements.

All four steps—secure, monitor, test, and improve—should be repeated on a continuous basis and should be incorporated into updated versions of the corporate security policy. Each step is discussed in further detail in the sections that follow.

Securing the System

You can secure the network by applying the security policy and implementing the following security solutions:

- **Firewalls**—Monitor network activity and permit or deny traffic based on configured policies.

- **IDSs**—Monitor network traffic and identify suspicious patterns using a periodically updated database of attack signatures. You can configure IDS devices to use a firewall or a router and actively block suspicious activity by modifying their access rules.

- **Identification authentication systems**—Services such as RADIUS, TACACS+, and Windows Active Directory can identify authorized users and provide appropriate access. Higher levels of security are available through hardware tokens, one-time passwords, and two-factor authentication systems such as SecurID. Authentication systems are covered in more detail in Chapter 13, "Authentication, Authorization, and Accounting."

- **Encryption**—Use encryption standards such as IP Security (IPSec), Data Encryption Standard (DES), or Advanced Encryption Standard (AES) to conceal the contents of data streams from prying eyes. Encryption technologies are covered in more detail in Chapter 15, "Virtual Private Networks."

- **Vulnerability patching**—Apply fixes or measures to stop the exploitation of known system vulnerabilities. This area includes disabling services that are not needed on every system. Systems with fewer enabled services are more difficult to exploit.

- **Physical security**—Limit unauthorized physical access to the network. This area is an important and often overlooked aspect of securing the system. If someone is able to walk away with system hardware, all other security might be useless. It is also important to protect against the unauthorized installation of promiscuous-mode devices that can capture sensitive data.

Monitoring the Network

In this step, you monitor the network for violations and attacks against the corporate security policy. These attacks can occur within the secured perimeter of the network (from a disgruntled employee or contractor) or from a source outside your trusted network. You should monitor the network with a real-time intrusion-detection device such as the Cisco Secure IDS. Proper monitoring assists you in discovering unauthorized entries and also serves as a check-and-balance system for ensuring that devices implemented in Step 1 of the security wheel are configured and working properly.

Testing Security

You need to validate the effectiveness of the security policy through system auditing and vulnerability scanning. Validation is a must. You can have the most sophisticated network security system, but if it is not working properly, your network can be compromised. This is the reason why you should test the devices and systems you implemented in Steps 1 and 2 to make sure they are functioning properly.

Improving Security

The improvement phase of the security wheel involves analyzing the data collected during the monitoring and testing phases and developing and implementing improvement mechanisms that feed into your security policy and the securing phase in Step 1. Specifically, you should

- Use the information gathered from the monitoring and testing phases to improve the security implementation.

- Adjust the security policy as new security vulnerabilities and risks are identified.

To keep your network as secure as possible, you must keep repeating the cycle of the security wheel because new network vulnerabilities and risks are discovered every day.

Cisco AVVID and SAFE

This section discusses the Cisco AVVID and its secure blueprint for enterprise networks, SAFE. Together, the AVVID framework and SAFE Blueprint present the Cisco vision of the combination of new technologies and services that enables a secure and robust infrastructure to serve enterprise businesses.

Cisco AVVID Framework

Cisco AVVID can be viewed as a framework for describing a network optimized for supporting Internet business solutions and as a best practice or roadmap for network implementation. This section discusses the various layers of the Cisco AVVID framework, shown in Figure 1-2.

Figure 1-2   *Cisco AVVID Framework Layers*

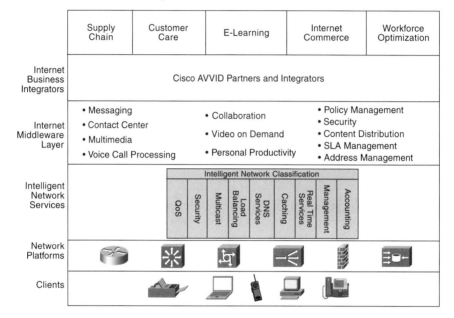

Following are the different parts of the Cisco AVVID architecture:

- **Clients**—These are the wide variety of devices that you can use to access the Internet business solutions through the network. Clients can include traditional access devices such as PCs as well as phones, personal digital assistants (PDAs), and other wired and wireless access devices. Unlike traditional telephony and video solutions, proprietary access devices are not necessary. Instead, functionality is added through the intelligent network services provided in the infrastructure.

- **Network platforms**—The network infrastructure provides the physical and logical connection for devices and brings them into the network. Network platforms are the LAN switches, routers, gateways, and other equipment that interconnect users and servers. This layer of Cisco AVVID is the foundation for all applications to be integrated to solve business problems.

- **Intelligent network services**— From quality of service (QoS) through security, accounting, and management, intelligent network services reflect the enterprise's business rules and policies in network performance. A consistent set of the services end-to-end through the network is important if the infrastructure is to be reliable as a network utility. These consistent services enable each new Internet business application and e-business initiative to roll out quickly without major re-engineering of the network.

- **Internet middleware layer**—This component, including service control and communication services, is a key part of any networking architecture, providing the software and tools to break down the barriers of complexity posed by new technology. These combined layers provide the tools for integrators and customers to tailor their network infrastructure and customize intelligent network services to meet application needs. These layers manage access, call setup and teardown, perimeter security, prioritization and bandwidth allocation, and user privileges. Software such as distributed customer contact suites, messaging solutions, and multimedia and collaboration provide capabilities and communication foundations that enable interaction between users and a variety of application platforms.

- **Internet business integrators**—As part of the open ecosystem, it is imperative to enable partners with Cisco AVVID. Cisco AVVID offers a guide for these interactions by describing a consistent set of services and capabilities that form a basis for many types of partner relationships.

- **Internet business solutions**—Enterprise customers are deploying Internet business solutions to re-engineer their organizations. The applications associated with Internet business solutions are not provided by Cisco but are enabled, accelerated, and delivered through Cisco AVVID.

The Internet is creating tremendous business opportunities. Internet business solutions such as e-commerce, supply-chain management, e-learning, and customer care are dramatically increasing productivity and efficiency. Cisco AVVID is an enterprise architecture that provides the intelligent network infrastructure for today's Internet business solutions.

SAFE Blueprint Overview

The Cisco SAFE Blueprint is a comprehensive framework for securing today's enterprise network from the ground up. Detailed discussion of the SAFE Blueprint is beyond the scope of this book, but a brief overview is provided. You can get additional and updated information on the Cisco SAFE Blueprint on Cisco.com (http://www.cisco.com/go/safe).

The SAFE Blueprint provides a robust security blueprint that builds on Cisco AVVID. SAFE layers are incorporated throughout the Cisco AVVID infrastructure:

- **Infrastructure layer**—Intelligent, scalable security services in Cisco platforms, such as routers, switches, firewalls, IDSs, and other devices

- **Appliances layer**—Incorporation of key security functionality in mobile hand-held devices and remote PC clients

- **Service control layer**—Critical security protocols and application programming interfaces (APIs) that enable security solutions to work together cohesively
- **Applications layer**—Host and application-based security elements that ensure the integrity of critical e-business applications

To facilitate rapidly deployable, consistent security throughout the enterprise, SAFE consists of modules that address the distinct requirements of each network area. By adopting a SAFE Blueprint, security managers do not need to redesign the entire security architecture each time they add a new service to the network. With modular templates, it is easier and more cost-effective to secure each new service as it is needed and to integrate it with the overall security architecture.

One of the unique characteristics of the SAFE Blueprint is that it is the first industry blueprint that recommends exactly which security solutions should be included in which sections of the network and why they should be deployed. Each module in the SAFE Blueprint is designed specifically to provide maximum performance for e-business while at the same time enabling enterprises to maintain security and integrity.

NOTE   Although SAFE is primarily aimed at the enterprise network, it serves as a useful blueprint for securing smaller networks. The white paper "SAFE: Extending the Security Blueprint to Small, Midsize, and Remote-User Networks" provides useful information on security best practices for smaller networks. This document and other white papers about the Cisco SAFE Blueprint are available on Cisco.com.

SAFE Benefits

There are several major benefits to implementing the SAFE Blueprint for secure e-business:

- SAFE provides the foundation for migrating to secure, affordable, converged networks.
- SAFE enables companies to cost-effectively deploy a modular, scalable security framework in stages.
- SAFE delivers integrated network protection via high-level security products and services.

In addition, Cisco has opened its Cisco AVVID architecture and SAFE Blueprint to key third-party vendors to create a security solution ecosystem and spur development of best-in-class multiservice applications and products. The Cisco AVVID architecture and SAFE Blueprint provide interoperability for third-party hardware and software using standards-based media interfaces, APIs, and protocols.

NOTE   For more comprehensive and updated information on the Cisco AVVID framework, SAFE Blueprint, and AVVID and security partners, visit the following URLs at Cisco.com:

http://www.cisco.com/go/avvid

http://www.cisco.com/go/safe

http://www.cisco.com/go/avvidpartners

http://www.cisco.com/go/securitypartners

Summary

This section summarizes the information you learned in this chapter:

- Network security is essential because networked computers that are connected to the Internet are accessible and vulnerable from any computer in the world.

- There are four primary types of threats to network security: unstructured, structured, external, and internal.

- There are three types of network attacks: reconnaissance, access, and DoS.

- The security wheel is the graphical representation of security as a continuous process and includes the following four steps:

  — Secure the network.

  — Monitor the network.

  — Test security.

  — Improve security.

- Cisco AVVID is a standards-based enterprise architecture that accelerates the integration of business and technology strategies.

- Cisco SAFE, which is based on Cisco AVVID, is a flexible, dynamic, security blueprint for networks.

Chapter Review Questions

To test what you have learned in this chapter, answer the following questions and then refer to Appendix A, "Answers to Chapter Review Questions," for the answers:

1 What are the three types of network attacks?

2 List the four primary threats to network security.

3 What kind of threat do script kiddies pose to network security?

4 What are the four steps in the security wheel?

5 What are the two main components of the Cisco vision for secure enterprise networking?

On completion of this chapter, you will be able to perform the following tasks:

- Describe firewall technologies.
- Define the three types of firewalls commonly used to secure computer networks.
- Describe Private Internet Exchange (PIX) Firewall technologies and features.

CHAPTER 2

Cisco PIX Firewall Technology and Features

By conventional definition, a firewall is a partition made of fireproof material designed to prevent the spread of fire from one part of a building to another.

When applied to computer networks, the term *firewall* means a system or group of systems that enforces an access control policy between two or more networks. Firewalls are typically used on the edge or perimeter of the network to secure the network against external threats. However, they can also be used internally to secure the network against internal threats.

There are now personal firewalls—software applications that run on individual PCs and protect the system against unauthorized access and malicious activities.

Types of Firewalls

Firewall systems available on the market today operate using one of three technologies:

- **Packet filtering**—Limits information transmittal into a network based on static packet-header information

- **Proxy server**—Requests connections between a client on the inside of the firewall and the Internet

- **Stateful packet filtering**—Combines the best of packet-filtering and proxy-server technologies

Each of these firewall technologies is discussed in further detail in the following sections.

Packet Filters

Packet-filtering firewalls analyze network traffic, typically at the network or transport layer of the Open System Interconnection (OSI) model, and limit information entering or leaving a network or information moving from one segment of a network to another based on predetermined policies. Packet filtering uses access control lists (ACLs), which allow a firewall to permit or deny access based on packet types and other variables.

This method is effective when a protected network receives a packet from an unprotected network. Any packet that is sent to the protected network and does not fit the criteria defined by the ACL is dropped.

Typically, packet-filtering firewalls can deny or permit traffic based on the following criteria:

- Protocol (IP, User Datagram Protocol [UDP], TCP, Internet Control Message Protocol [ICMP], and others)
- Source IP address
- Source port
- Destination IP address
- Destination port

NOTE   Packet-filtering firewalls can also deny or permit traffic based on specific settings in the TCP packet header. By looking at the SYN bit in the TCP header, the firewall can determine whether the incoming packet is initiating a new session or is part of an existing session initiated by internal hosts. (The SYN bit is on for new sessions.) Depending on the rules running on the firewall, it can then allow incoming packets that are part of an existing session while denying packets that are initiating new sessions.

Packet-filtering firewalls have been around for a number of years and provide a measure of security, but they also have shortcomings. Specifically, packet-filtering firewalls have the following disadvantages:

- Someone can send arbitrary packets that fit the ACL criteria and, therefore, pass through the filter.
- Fragmented packets can pass through the filter.
- Complex ACLs are difficult to implement and maintain correctly.
- You cannot filter some services, such as multimedia applications using dynamic ports.

Most modern firewalls, including the PIX, rely on technologies other than packet filtering. A Cisco router configured with an ACL is an example of a packet-filtering firewall.

NOTE   Cisco routers running the IOS Firewall Feature Set and Context-Based Access Control (CBAC) are not simple packet-filtering firewalls. Utilizing the IOS Firewall Feature Set and CBAC, Cisco routers can secure the network through stateful packet inspection.

Proxy Server

Recall that packet-filtering firewalls operate on Layers 3 and 4 of the OSI model (the network and transport layers). In contrast, a *proxy-server* firewall examines packets at higher layers of the OSI model, typically Layers 4 through 7. Peeking into higher layers of the OSI model allows proxy servers to better protect the network but at a much higher overhead relative to that of packet-filtering devices.

Proxy-server firewalls hide valuable data by requiring users to communicate with a secure system by means of a proxy. Users gain access to the network by going through a process that establishes session state, user authentication, and authorized policy. Users connect to outside services via application programs (proxies) running on the gateway connecting to the outside, unprotected zone.

Proxy-server firewalls typically provide better security than packet-filtering devices. However, there are several disadvantages to using a proxy firewall:

- Proxy-server firewalls create a single point of failure, which means that if the entrance to the network is compromised, the entire network is compromised.

- It is difficult to add new services to the firewall.

- Proxy-server firewalls perform more slowly under stress.

Stateful Packet Filters

A third firewall technology, *stateful packet filtering*, combines the benefits of proxy-server and packet-filtering devices while eliminating many of their disadvantages. This technology maintains complete session state. Each time a TCP or UDP connection is established for inbound or outbound connections, the information is logged in a stateful session flow table. Stateful packet filtering is the method that the Cisco PIX Firewall uses.

The stateful session flow table contains the source and destination addresses, port numbers, TCP sequencing information, and additional flags for each TCP or UDP connection associated with that particular session. This information creates a connection object, and consequently, all inbound and outbound packets are compared against session flows in the stateful session flow table. Data is permitted through the firewall only if an appropriate connection exists to validate its passage.

This method is effective because it

- Works on packets and connections.

- Operates at a higher performance level than packet filtering or proxy servers.

- Records data in a table for every connection or connectionless transaction. This table serves as a reference point to determine whether packets belong to an existing connection or are from an unauthorized source.

PIX Firewall Overview

The PIX Firewall is a key element in the overall Cisco end-to-end security solution. The PIX Firewall is a dedicated hardware and software security solution that delivers high-level security without impacting network performance. It is a hybrid system because it uses features from both the packet-filtering and proxy-server technologies.

Unlike typical CPU-intensive, full-time proxy servers that perform extensive processing on each data packet at the application level, the PIX Firewall uses a proprietary operating system that is a secure, real-time, embedded system.

The PIX Firewall features the following technologies and benefits:

- **Nongeneral-purpose, secure, real-time, embedded system**—Unlike typical CPU-intensive proxy servers that perform extensive processing on each data packet, the PIX Firewall uses a secure, real-time, embedded system, which enhances the security of the network.

- **Adaptive Security Algorithm (ASA)**—This algorithm implements stateful connection control through the PIX Firewall.

- **Cut-through proxy**—This type of proxy is a user-based authentication method of both inbound and outbound connections, providing better performance than that of a proxy server.

- **Stateful packet filtering**—This method is a secure way to analyze data packets that places extensive information about a data packet into a table. For a session to be established, information about the connection must match the information in the table.

- **High availability**—You can deploy two Cisco firewalls in a fully redundant configuration to provide stateful failover capabilities.

Each technology component is discussed in further detail in the sections that follow.

Finesse Operating System

Finesse, a Cisco proprietary operating system, is a non-UNIX, non-Windows NT, IOS-like operating system. Using Finesse eliminates the risks associated with the general-purpose operating systems. It enables the PIX Firewall to deliver outstanding performance with up to 500,000 simultaneous connections—a level that is dramatically higher than any UNIX-based firewall.

NOTE The stated performance numbers exclude the Firewall Services Module (FWSM), discussed later in this book. FWSM utilizes PIX technology and the same Finesse operating system. It is currently capable of delivering up to 1 million concurrent connections.

ASA

The heart of the PIX Firewall is the *ASA*. The ASA maintains the secure perimeters between the networks controlled by the firewall. The stateful, connection-oriented ASA design creates session flows based on source and destinations addresses. It randomizes the initial TCP sequence number and tracks port numbers and additional TCP flags before completion of the connection. This function is always in operation, monitoring return packets to ensure they are valid, and allows one-way (inside to outside) connections without an explicit configuration for each internal system and application. The randomizing of the initial TCP sequence numbers minimizes the risk of a TCP sequence number attack. Because of the ASA, the PIX Firewall is less complex and more robust than a packet-filtering firewall.

Features and benefits of ASA follow:

- ASA provides "stateful" connection security:
    - It tracks source and destination ports and addresses, TCP sequence numbers, and additional TCP flags.
    - It randomizes initial TCP sequence numbers.
- By default, ASA allows connections originating from hosts on inside (higher security level) interfaces destined for hosts on the outside (or other interfaces with a lower security level).
- By default, ASA drops connection attempts originating from hosts on outside (lower security level) interfaces destined for hosts on the inside (a higher security level).
- ASA supports authentication, authorization, and accounting (AAA).

Cut-Through Proxy

Cut-through proxy is a method of transparently verifying the identity of the users at the firewall and permitting or denying access to any TCP- or UDP-based applications. It is also known as user-based authentication of inbound or outbound connections. Unlike a proxy server that analyzes every packet at the application layer of the OSI model, the PIX Firewall first challenges a user at the application layer. After the user is authenticated and the policy is checked, the PIX Firewall shifts the session flow to a lower layer of the OSI model for dramatically faster performance. This process lets you enforce security policies on a per-user-identification basis. Figure 2-1 illustrates the operation steps for cut-through proxy.

Figure 2-1   *Cut-Through Proxy Operation*

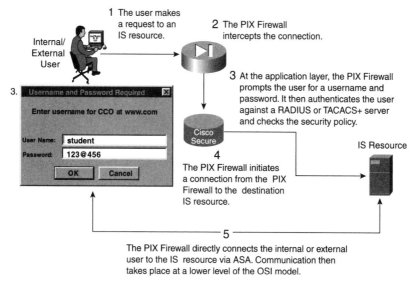

Connections must be authenticated with a user identification and password before they can be established. A user enters the identification and password via an initial HTTP, Telnet, or FTP connection. This method eliminates the price-performance impact that UNIX system-based firewalls impose in similar configurations and allows a finer level of administrative control over connections. The cut-through proxy method of the PIX Firewall also leverages the AAA services of the Cisco Secure Access Control Server (CSACS).

Stateful Packet Filtering

Stateful packet filtering is a secure method of analyzing data packets that places extensive information about a data packet into a table. Each time a TCP connection is established for inbound or outbound connections through the PIX Firewall, the information about the connection is logged in a stateful session flow table. For a session to be established, information about the connection must match information stored in the table. With this methodology, the stateful filters work on the connections and not the packets, making it a more stringent security method with its sessions immune to hijacking.

Stateful packet filtering

- Obtains the session identifying parameters, IP addresses, and ports for each TCP connection.

- Logs the data in a stateful session flow table and creates a session object.

- Compares the inbound and outbound packets against session flows in the connection table.

- Allows data packets to flow through the PIX Firewall only if an appropriate connection exists to validate their passage.
- Temporarily sets up a connection object until the connection is terminated.

Failover

Failover provides a mechanism for the PIX Firewall to be redundant by allowing two identical firewalls to serve the same function. The *active* firewall performs normal security functions, whereas the *standby* firewall monitors and remains ready to take control should the active firewall fail. You can configure the PIX Firewall for stateful failover so that active connections remain when failover occurs. With its failover capabilities, the PIX Firewall is well-suited for high-availability implementations.

NOTE   PIX Firewall 500 Series models that support failover include legacy models 515 and 520, which are not covered in this book, as well as current models 515E, 525, and 535. PIX Firewall 501 and 506E models do not support failover functionality.

Summary

This section summarizes the information you learned in this chapter:

- There are three firewall technologies:
  - **Packet filtering**—Provides basic security and adequate performance but is limited by the following drawbacks: It is hard to maintain, fragmented packets can compromise security, and it cannot support newer multimedia applications.
  - **Proxy server**—Provides better security than packet filtering but is limited by the following drawbacks: It is slow, it can be a single point of failure on the network, and new services are difficult to add.
  - **Stateful packet filtering**—Combines the benefits of packet-filtering and proxy-server firewalls to provide high security, fast performance, and good compatibility with most applications.
- The PIX Firewall features include the following technologies:
  - **Finesse operating system**—An IOS-like proprietary Cisco operating system, which is non-UNIX and non-Windows NT. Use of Finesse eliminates the risks associated with the general-purpose operating systems and provides superior performance.

— **ASA**—Provides "stateful" connection security and tracks the following: source and destination ports and addresses, TCP sequence numbers, and additional TCP flags. It also randomizes initial TCP sequence numbers for increased security.

— **Cut-through proxy**—A method of transparently verifying the identity of the users at the firewall and permitting or denying access to any TCP- or UDP-based applications.

— **Stateful packet filtering**—A secure method of analyzing data packets that places extensive information about a data packet into a table.

— **Stateful failover**—A mechanism for the PIX Firewall to be redundant by allowing two identical firewalls to serve the same function. If the active unit fails, the standby unit assumes control.

Chapter Review Questions

To test what you learned in this chapter, answer the following questions and then refer to Appendix A, "Answers to Chapter Review Questions," for the answers:

1 What are the three types of firewall technologies?

2 Which type of firewall technology provides the best overall security?

3 Which type of firewall technology does the Cisco PIX Firewall use?

4 What are the main technologies and benefits on the PIX Firewall?

5 What are the main disadvantages of proxy servers?

On completion of this chapter, you will be able to perform the following tasks:

- Identify the Private Internet Exchange (PIX) Firewall models.

- Describe the key features of the PIX Firewall models 501, 506E, 515E, 525, and 535.

- Identify the interfaces, controls, connectors, and status lights of PIX Firewall models 501, 506E, 515E, 525, and 535.

- Describe the key features of the Firewall Services Module (FWSM) for the Cisco Catalyst 6500 switch and the Cisco 7600 series Internet router.

- Identify the switch and router slots in which the FWSM can be installed.

- Identify and describe the LEDs, which display the status of the FWSM.

- Describe the PIX Firewall licensing options.

CHAPTER 3

The Cisco PIX Firewall Family

Since its introduction in 1996, the industry-leading Cisco Secure PIX family of firewalls has been expanded to include five different models to meet the security needs of customers with small and large networks alike. This chapter presents descriptions of the Cisco Secure PIX Firewall family of products, including the 500 series models and the PIX technology-based FWSM for the Cisco Catalyst 6500 switch and the Cisco 7600 router.

PIX Firewall 500 Series Models

The Cisco PIX Firewall 500 series scales to meet a range of requirements and network sizes and currently consists of five models:

- **PIX Firewall 501**—The smallest of the five models, the PIX Firewall 501 aims at the telecommuter and small office/home office (SOHO) markets and has an integrated 10/100 Fast Ethernet outside port and an integrated four-port 10/100 switch.

- **PIX Firewall 506E**—The PIX Firewall 506E has dual integrated 10/100 Fast Ethernet interfaces and is designed for small and remote office applications.

- **PIX Firewall 515E**—The PIX Firewall 515E supports up to six 10/100 Ethernet interfaces and is designed for small to medium businesses.

- **PIX Firewall 525**—The PIX Firewall 525 supports up to eight 10/100 Fast Ethernet and Gigabit Ethernet interfaces and is designed for large business and enterprise customers.

- **PIX Firewall 535**—The most powerful 500 series model, the PIX Firewall 535 supports up to ten 10/100 Fast Ethernet and Gigabit Ethernet interfaces and is designed for enterprise and service provider customers.

Figure 3-1 shows the relative market position for each of the PIX 500 series models.

Figure 3-1 *PIX Firewall 500 Series Family*

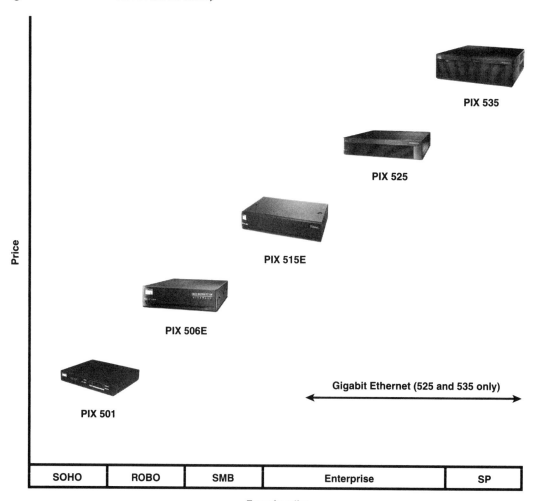

Table 3-1 lists the basic specifications for the PIX Firewall 500 series models.

Table 3-1   *PIX Firewall 500 Series Specifications*

PIX Firewall Model	PIX 501	PIX 506E	PIX 515E	PIX 525	PIX 535
Size (Rack Units)	N/A	1	1	2	3
Processor MHz	133	300	433	600	1 GHz
Maximum Interfaces	2^1	2	6	8	10
Failover Support	No	No	Yes	Yes	Yes
Maximum Connections[2]	7500	25,000	130,000	280,000	500,000
Throughput[2] (Mbps)	60	100	188	330	1.7 Gbps
IP Security (IPSec) Throughput (Mbps)[3]	3 Triple Data Encryption Standard (3DES) 4.5 128-bit Advanced Encryption Standard (AES)[4]	17 3DES 30 128-bit AES[4]	140 3DES 140 256-bit AES[4]	155 3DES 170 256-bit AES[4]	440 3DES 440 256-bit AES[4]
Maximum IPSec Tunnels	10^5	25	2000	2000	2000

[1] PIX Firewall 501 includes a four-port switch for use by internal hosts.

[2] Performance specifications listed apply to PIX Firewall Software Version 6.3. Performance numbers might vary if you use a different version of the PIX Firewall software.

[3] IPSec throughput figures listed apply to PIX Firewall Software Version 6.3. Figures listed for PIX Firewall 515E, 525, and 535 models are valid only for hardware-based encryption. Software-based encryption yields lower throughput on these models.

[4] AES support is available only with PIX Firewall Software Version 6.3 or higher. AES throughput figures listed for PIX Firewall 515E, 525, and 535 are based on the new virtual private network (VPN) Acceleration Card Plus (VAC+), which also requires PIX Firewall Software Version 6.3 or later.

[5] The maximum number of IPSec tunnels listed for PIX Firewall 501 applies to Software Version 6.3.

PIX Firewall 501

The PIX 501 is ideal for securing high-speed, "always-on" broadband environments in SOHO and telecommuter installations. It provides small-office networking features and powerful remote management capabilities in a compact, all-in-one solution.

The PIX Firewall 501 provides a convenient way for multiple computers to share a single broadband connection. In addition to its RS-232 (RJ-45) 9600 baud console port and its integrated 10/100 Fast Ethernet port for the outside interface, it features an integrated autosensing, auto–medium dependent interface crossover (MDIX) four-port 10/100 switch for the inside interface. Auto-MDIX support eliminates the need to use crossover cables with devices connected to the switch.

The PIX Firewall 501 can also secure all network communications from remote offices to corporate networks across the Internet using its standards-based Internet Key Exchange (IKE)/IPSec VPN capabilities. Users can also enjoy plug-and-play networking by taking advantage of the built-in Dynamic Host Configuration Protocol (DHCP) server within the PIX Firewall, which automatically assigns network addresses to the computers when they are powered on.

The PIX Firewall 501 comes with an integrated security lock slot for improved physical security and contains 8 MB of Flash memory.

NOTE   The Cisco PIX Firewall 501 requires Software Version 6.1(1) or higher.

The PIX 501 has the following LEDs on the front panel, as shown on Figure 3-2:

- **Power**—On when the device is powered on.

- **Link/Act**—On when the correct cable is in use and the connected equipment has power and is operational. Off when no link is established. Flashing green light indicates network activity (such as Internet access).

- **VPN Tunnel**—On indicates one or more IKE/IPSec VPN tunnels are established. Off indicates no established tunnels are present. If you have not modified the standard configuration to support VPN tunnels, the LED does not light up because it is disabled by default.

- **100 Mbps**—On indicates the interface is enabled at 100 Mbps (autonegotiated). Off indicates 10-Mbps operation.

Figure 3-2 *PIX Firewall 501 Front-Panel LEDs*

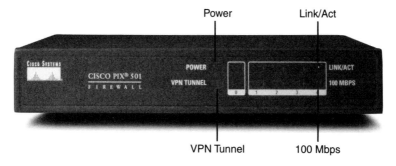

NOTE   The VPN Tunnel LED does not light up when Point-to-Point Tunneling Protocol (PPTP) or Layer 2 Tunneling Protocol (L2TP) tunnels are established.

The back panel of the PIX 501 is shown in Figure 3-3. The following are the PIX Firewall 501 features:

- **10/100 switch ports**—Private ports in the autosensing, auto-MDIX switch used for the inside interface. Connect your PC or other network devices to one of the four switched ports, which are numbered 1 through 4.

- **Public network port (Port 0)**—A 10/100 Fast Ethernet port for the public network. Unlike the private ports, this port is not auto-MDIX, and you should use the correct type of cable for connectivity. Use a straight cable to connect the device to a switch or hub. Use a crossover cable to connect the device to a DSL modem, cable modem, or router.

- **Console port**—RS-232 (RJ-45) 9600 baud port used to connect a computer to the PIX Firewall for console, out-of-band management.

- **Power connector**—Used to attach the power-supply cable to the PIX Firewall. The PIX Firewall 501 does not have a power switch.

- **Security lock slot**—A slot that accepts standard desktop cable locks to provide physical security.

Figure 3-3   *PIX Firewall 501 Back Panel*

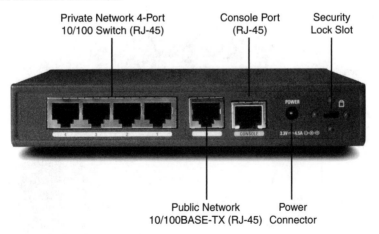

NOTE When installing the PIX Firewall 501, place the chassis on a flat, stable surface. The chassis is not rack mountable.

PIX Firewall 506E

The PIX Firewall 506E is designed for remote/branch office environments. It delivers full firewall protection and IPSec VPN capabilities. The PIX Firewall 506E can connect with up to 25 VPN peers simultaneously and provides a complete implementation of IPSec standards, including 56-bit DES, 168-bit 3DES, and up to 256-bit AES encryption. It comes with a 300-MHz processor, 32 MB of SDRAM, 8 MB of Flash memory, and two integrated 10/100BASE-TX ports in a compact enclosure (8 by 12 by 1.7 inches). The PIX 506E has no failover capabilities.

The PIX 506E has the following LEDs on the front panel, as shown in Figure 3-4:

- **Power**—On when the device is powered on.
- **Act**—On when the software image has been fully loaded on the 506E unit and the system is active.
- **Network**—On when at least one network interface is passing traffic.

Figure 3-4 *PIX Firewall 506E Front-Panel LEDs*

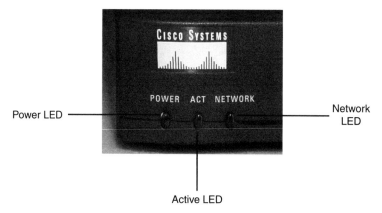

The back panel of the PIX 506E is shown in Figure 3-5. On the unit, Ethernet 1 connects the inside (private) network and Ethernet 0 is for the outside (public) network. You use the console port to connect a computer directly to the PIX 506E and enter configuration commands. The USB port to the left of the console port is not currently used. The power connection is directly beneath the power switch. The PIX Firewall 506E uses an external power supply.

Figure 3-5 *PIX Firewall 506E Back Panel*

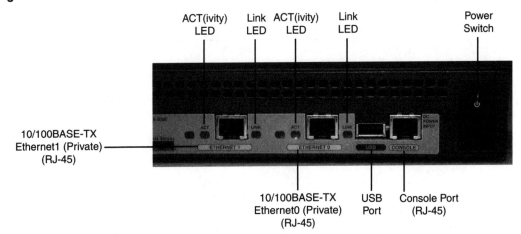

The LEDs on the back panel display the following transmission states:

- **Act**—Shows network activity
- **Link**—Shows that data is passing on the network to which the connector is attached

PIX Firewall 515E

The PIX Firewall 515E is designed for small- and medium-sized businesses. It delivers full firewall protection and IPSec VPN capabilities with complete implementation of IPSec standards, including 56-bit DES, 168-bit 3DES, and up to 256-bit AES encryption. You can create and terminate VPN tunnels between two PIX Firewalls. You can also create and terminate VPN tunnels between a PIX Firewall and the following:

- Any Cisco VPN-enabled router
- Cisco 3000 VPN concentrator
- Cisco (VPN) Client
- Any other IPSec standard-compliant device
- Any standard PPTP- or L2TP-compliant client or device

The PIX Firewall 515E is also ideal for remote sites that require only two-way communication with their corporate network.

The PIX Firewall 515E supports up to six 10/100 Ethernet ports. This setup allows for more robust traffic configurations and establishing a protected demilitarized (DMZ) for hosting a website and other publicly accessible services or performing URL filtering and virus detection.

NOTE   A PIX Firewall 515E-UR license is required for the support of six interfaces. The 515E-R license supports up to three interfaces.

The PIX Firewall 515E supports hardware-based IPSec acceleration, delivering VPN performance of up to 140 Mbps while freeing system resources for other mission-critical security functions. IPSec acceleration is provided by an optional PIX Firewall VAC or the higher-performance VAC+. When neither a VAC nor a VAC+ is installed, PIX Firewall 515E performs software-based encryption with reduced throughput.

NOTE   Several unrestricted and failover bundle configurations of the PIX Firewall 515E include the VAC+ card at no additional cost. You can check Cisco.com for the current bundle configurations and the specific components included with each bundle.

The PIX Firewall 515E is rack mountable and comes with a 433-MHz processor, 32 or 64 MB of SDRAM, and 16 MB of Flash memory. You can order it with either an AC or a 48-volt DC power supply.

The PIX 515E has the following LEDs on the front panel, as shown on Figure 3-6:

- **Power**—On when the PIX Firewall has power.
- **Act**—When the PIX Firewall is used in a standalone configuration, the light shines. When the PIX Firewall is configured for failover operations, the light shines on the active PIX Firewall. (Failover is discussed in Chapter 14, "Failover.")
- **Network**—On when at least one network interface is passing traffic.

Figure 3-6   *PIX Firewall 515E Front-Panel LEDs*

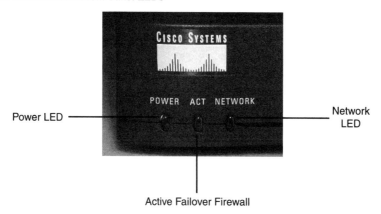

Figure 3-7 shows the back panel of the PIX Firewall 515E. The main features on the back panel of the system include the following:

- **Ethernet connections**—With software versions 5.2 and higher, any port—whether fixed or a Peripheral Component Interconnect (PCI) expansion port—and any interface type—Fiber Distributed Data Interface (FDDI), Token Ring, Fast Ethernet, or Gigabit Ethernet—can be assigned to be the inside or outside network port.

- **Console port**—Connects a computer to the PIX Firewall for console operations.

- **Failover connection**—Attaches a serial failover cable between two PIX Firewalls.

- **100-Mbps LED**—A 100-Mbps, 100BASE-TX communication LED for the respective connector. If the light is off, the PIX Firewall 515E uses 10-Mbps data exchange.

- **Link LED**—Indicates that data is passing on the network to which the connector is attached.

- **FDX LED**—Indicates that the connection uses full-duplex data exchange. (Data can be transmitted and received simultaneously.) If the light is off, half duplex is in effect.

- **Power switch**—Controls the power to the PIX Firewall.

Figure 3-7 *PIX Firewall 515E Back Panel*

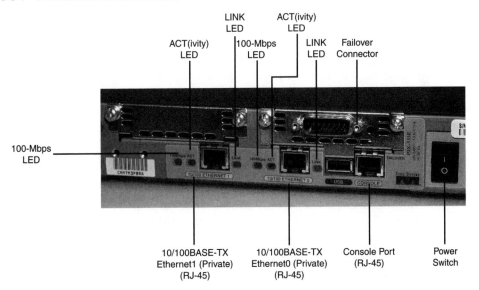

NOTE The USB port to the left of the console port and the detachable plate above the Ethernet 1 connector are for future PIX Firewall enhancements.

There are two expansion slots available on the PIX Firewall 515E. You can use these slots to add Ethernet interfaces or increase VPN throughput by using a VAC or VAC+. The PIX Firewall 515E can support up to six Ethernet interfaces when a four-port Ethernet card (quad card) is installed in one of the expansion slots, as shown on Figure 3-8.

Figure 3-8 *PIX Firewall 515E Quad Card*

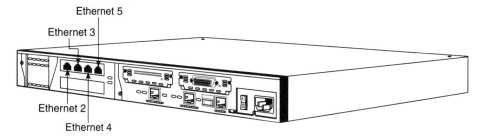

NOTE Using the quad card requires the PIX Firewall 515E-UR license. You can use up to three interfaces with the basic restricted license. Use of more advanced features such as failover and any configuration with more than three interfaces requires an upgrade to the unrestricted license.

NOTE The maximum number of interfaces allowed on a PIX Firewall 515E is six. Additional cards are not recognized.

When you connect the perimeter network cables to the quad card, you begin with the far-left connector and move to the right. For example, Ethernet 2 goes in the far-left connector, Ethernet 3 in the second connector from the left, and so on.

You can also add interfaces to the PIX 515E using single-port Ethernet cards. When you install two single-port interfaces, the cards are numbered top to bottom so that the top card is Ethernet 2 and the bottom card is Ethernet 3.

NOTE Using two single-port Ethernet cards requires the removal of the VAC or VAC+ from the PIX 515E, resulting in software-based encryption and reduced VPN throughput.

PIX Firewall 525

The PIX Firewall 525 is intended for large businesses and enterprises. Ideal for protecting the perimeter of the enterprise headquarters, the PIX Firewall 525 delivers full firewall protection and robust IPSec VPN capabilities.

The PIX Firewall 525 supports a broad range of network interface cards. Standard cards include single-port or four-port 10/100 Fast Ethernet and Gigabit Ethernet (with unrestricted license). The restricted license supports up to six interfaces. The unrestricted license supports up to eight total interfaces.

The PIX Firewall 525 comes with a 600 MHz processor, 128- or 256-MB SDRAM, 16-MB Flash memory, dual integrated 10/100BASE-T Fast Ethernet interfaces, and three expansion slots. It also offers multiple power-supply options. You can choose between AC and a 48-volt DC power supply. You can pair either option with a second power supply for redundancy and high availability.

You can upgrade the PIX Firewall 525 with an optional VAC or the higher-performing VAC+, delivering VPN performance of up to 150 Mbps while freeing system resources for other mission-critical security functions.

NOTE   Unrestricted and failover bundle configurations of the PIX Firewall 525 include the VAC+ at no additional cost. You can check Cisco.com for the current bundle configurations and the specific components included with each bundle.

There are two LEDs on the front panel of the PIX Firewall 525, as shown on Figure 3-9. The LEDs function as follows:

- **Power**—On when the firewall has power.
- **Act**—On when the firewall is the active failover firewall. If failover is present, the light is on when the firewall is the active firewall and off when the firewall is in standby mode.

Figure 3-9 *PIX Firewall 525 Front-Panel LEDs*

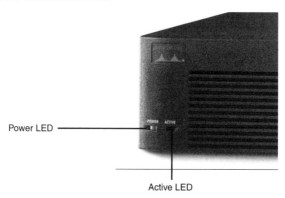

On the back of the PIX Firewall 525 are three LEDs for each Ethernet interface port and three types of fixed interface connectors, as shown on Figure 3-10. The LEDs display the following transmission states:

- **100 Mbps**—On indicates 100-Mbps, 100BASE-TX communication. If the light is off during network activity, that port is using 10-Mbps data exchange.

- **Act**—Shows network activity.

- **Link**—Shows that data is passing through that interface.

Figure 3-10 *PIX Firewall 525 Back Panel*

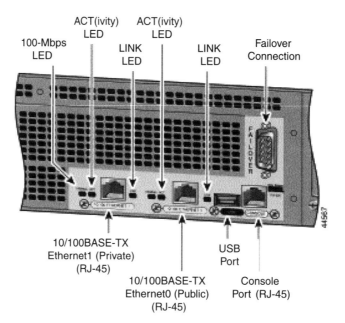

The following are fixed connectors on the back of the PIX Firewall 525:

- **RJ-45**—10/100 Fast Ethernet and console connectors
- **DB-15**—Failover cable connector
- **USB**—Not used at the present time

You can make the inside, outside, or perimeter network connections to any available interface port on the PIX Firewall 525. If you are using only the Ethernet 0 and Ethernet 1 ports, connect the inside network cable to the interface connector marked Ethernet 0 or Ethernet 1. Connect the outside network cable to the remaining Ethernet port.

The following are the PIX Firewall 525 restricted interface options:

- 3 Fast Ethernet
- 2 Fast Ethernet + 1 VPN Accelerator
- 1 Gigabit Ethernet + 1 Fast Ethernet
- 1 Gigabit Ethernet + 1 Fast Ethernet + 1 VPN Accelerator
- 3 Gigabit Ethernet
- 2 Gigabit Ethernet + 1 VPN Accelerator
- 1 four-port Fast Ethernet
- 1 four-port Fast Ethernet + 1 VPN Accelerator

The following are the PIX Firewall 525 unrestricted interface options:

- 3 Fast Ethernet
- 2 Fast Ethernet + 1 VPN Accelerator
- 1 Gigabit Ethernet + 2 Fast Ethernet
- 1 Gigabit Ethernet + 1 Fast Ethernet + 1 VPN Accelerator
- 3 Gigabit Ethernet
- 2 Gigabit Ethernet + 1 VPN Accelerator
- 1 four-port Fast Ethernet
- 1 four-port Fast Ethernet + 2 Fast Ethernet
- 2 four-port Fast Ethernet
- 1 four-port Fast Ethernet + 2 Gigabit Ethernet
- 1 four-port Fast Ethernet + 1 VPN Accelerator
- 1 four-port Fast Ethernet + 1 VPN Accelerator + FE
- 1 four-port Fast Ethernet + 1 VPN Accelerator + Gigabit Ethernet

When connecting the network cables to the expansion interface ports, the first expansion port number, at the top left, is interface 2. Starting from that port and going from left to right and top to bottom, the next port is interface 3, the next is interface 4, and so on.

PIX Firewall 535

The PIX Firewall 535 is intended for enterprise and service provider use. It has a throughput of 1.7 Gbps with the ability to handle up to 500,000 concurrent connections. Supporting both site-to-site and remote-access VPN applications via 56-bit DES, 168-bit 3DES, 128-bit AES, and 256-bit AES, the PIX Firewall 535 can deliver up to 440 Mbps of 3DES and 256-bit AES throughput and 2000 IPSec tunnels.

The PIX Firewall 535 supports both Fast Ethernet and Gigabit Ethernet interfaces and comes with an integrated VAC (unrestricted license only).

NOTE   PIX Firewall software versions earlier than 6.1 required the monitor mode to perform activation key upgrades for all systems. The monitor mode does not support Gigabit interfaces. If you are upgrading a PIX Firewall 535 with software version 6.0 or earlier and Gigabit interfaces only, you must install a Fast Ethernet interface to use the monitor mode and upgrade the activation key.

NOTE   If, after configuring a PIX Firewall for Gigabit Ethernet cards, you replace the cards with 10/100 Ethernet cards, the order of the cards in the configuration changes from what you originally configured. For example, if you configure Ethernet 2 for a Gigabit Ethernet card assigned to the inside interface and replace this card with a 10/100 Ethernet card, the card might no longer appear as Ethernet 2.

The PIX Firewall 535 comes with a 1 GHz processor, 512 MB or 1 GB of SDRAM, and 16 MB of Flash memory and supports the PIX Firewall Software Version 5.3 or later.

There are two LEDs on the front panel of the PIX Firewall 535, as shown on Figure 3-11. The LEDs function as follows:

- **Power**—On when the PIX Firewall has power.
- **Act**—On when the PIX Firewall is the active failover firewall. If failover is present, the light is on when the PIX Firewall is the active firewall and off when the PIX Firewall is in standby mode.

Figure 3-11 *PIX Firewall 535 Front-Panel LEDs*

There are three separate buses for the nine interface slots in the PIX Firewall 535. Figure 3-12 is a reference for the interface slot configuration on the PIX Firewall 535. The slots and buses are configured as follows:

- **Slots 0 and 1**—64-bit, 66-MHz Bus 0
- **Slots 2 and 3**—64-bit, 66-MHz Bus 1
- **Slots 4 to 8**—32-bit, 33-MHz Bus 2

Figure 3-12 *PIX Firewall 535 Interface Slot Configuration*

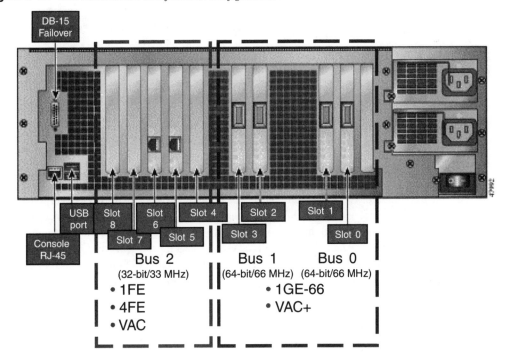

You must follow the following practices to achieve the best possible system performance on the PIX Firewall 535:

- PIX-1GE-66 and VAC+ cards should be installed in 64-bit, 66-MHz bus slots. Installing these cards in the 32-bit, 33-MHz bus will result in degraded performance.

- PIX-1GE and PIX-1FE are 32-bit cards and should be installed in the 32-bit, 33-MHz bus before they are installed in the 64-bit, 66-MHz buses. If you need more than five 32-bit cards (PIX-1GE or PIX-1FE), you can install them in a 64-bit, 66-MHz bus, but doing so lowers the speed on the bus and limits the potential throughput of any PIX-1GE-66 card installed in that bus.

The PIX-1GE or VAC+ Gigabit Ethernet adapter is supported in the PIX Firewall 535; however, its use is strongly discouraged because maximum system performance with the PIX-1GE card is much lower than that with the PIX-1GE-66 card. The PIX operating system (OS) displays a warning at boot time if a PIX-1GE is detected.

Table 3-2 summarizes the performance considerations of the different interface card combinations.

Table 3-2 *PIX 535 Performance Considerations*

Interface Card Combination	Installed in Interface Slot Numbers	Potential Throughput
Two to four PIX-1GE-66s or VAC+	0 through 3	Best
PIX-1GE-66 or VAC+ combined with PIX-1GE or just PIX-1GE cards	0 through 3	Degraded
Any PIX-1GE-66 or PIX-1GE	4 through 8	Severely degraded

NOTE The PIX-4FE and VAC cards can be installed only in the 32-bit, 33-MHz bus and must never be installed in a 64-bit, 66-MHz bus. Installing these cards in a 64-bit, 66-MHz bus can cause the system to hang at boot time.

If stateful failover is enabled, the interface card and bus used for the stateful failover LAN port must be equal to or faster than the fastest card used for the network interface ports. For example, if the inside and outside interfaces are PIX-1GE-66 cards installed in bus 0, the stateful failover interface must be a PIX-1GE-66 card installed in bus 1. You cannot use a PIX-1GE or PIX-1FE card in this case, nor can you install a PIX-1GE-66 card in bus 2. In addition, sharing bus 1 with a slower card is not possible.

Depending on the type of interface, there are four possible LEDs for each network interface port. The LEDs for the network interface ports display the following transmission states, as shown on Figure 3-13:

- **100 Mbps**—On indicates 100-Mbps 100BASE-TX communication. If the light is off during network activity, that port is using 10-Mbps data exchange.

- **Act**—Shows network activity.

- **Link**—Shows that data is passing through that interface.

- **FDX**—Shows that the connection uses full-duplex data exchange in which data can be transmitted and received simultaneously. If this light is off, half duplex is in effect.

Figure 3-13   *PIX Firewall 535 Back Panel*

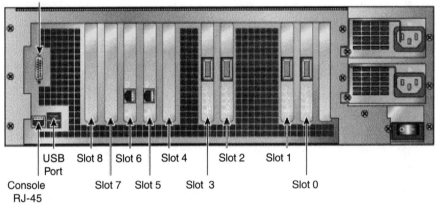

When connecting the inside, outside, or perimeter network cables to the interface ports on the PIX Firewall 535, starting from the right and moving left, the connectors are Ethernet 0, Ethernet 1, Ethernet 2, and so forth.

NOTE   The PIX Firewall 535 is equipped with hot-swappable power supplies. Should a power supply fail, you can remove the power supply without powering off the PIX Firewall 535.

FWSM

The FWSM is a multigigabit integrated firewall module for the Cisco Catalyst 6500 series switch and the Cisco 7600 series Internet router. It is a high-performance platform designed for high-end enterprise and service-provider installations. It is fabric-enabled and capable of interacting with the bus and the switch fabric. Based on PIX Firewall technology, FWSM provides stateful firewall functionality in these switches and routers.

The following are the key features of FWSM:

- High-performance, 5-Gbps throughput, full-duplex firewall functionality
- Entire PIX Firewall 6.0 software feature set and the following PIX Firewall 6.2 software features:
  - Command authorization
  - Object grouping
  - Internet Locator Service (ILS)/NetMeeting fixup
  - URL filtering enhancement
- 3 million packets per second (pps) throughput
- Support for 100 VLANs
- 1 million concurrent connections
- LAN failover—active or standby, interchassis or intrachassis
- Dynamic routing with Open Shortest Path First (OSPF) and passive Routing Information Protocol (RIP)
- Multiple modules per chassis supported

Table 3-3 shows the major differences between the PIX Firewall and FWSM. Similarities and differences are explored in depth later in the book.

Table 3-3 *FWSM and PIX Firewall Comparison*

	FWSM	**PIX Firewall**
Interfaces Supported	100 (via VLANs)	24 (including logical interfaces avaiable with PIX Firewall Software Version 6.3)
Failover License	Not required	Required
VPN Functionality	Not present	Present
Routing	Supports static routing and dynamic routing via OSPF and passive RIP	Supports static routing and dynamic routing via OSPF and passive RIP (OSPF support only available in PIX Firewall Software Version 6.3 or later)

The FWSM comes with 128 MB of Compact Flash memory and 1 GB of DRAM memory. Memory is not field upgradeable.

Figure 3-14 shows the FWSM installed in slot 9 of a Catalyst 6500 nine-slot chassis. Slot 1 is reserved for the supervisor engine. The supervisor engine is the control module that defines and drives all operational capabilities of the switch. Slot 2 can contain an additional redundant supervisor engine in case the supervisor engine in slot 1 fails. If you do not use a redundant supervisor engine, slot 2 is available for switching modules.

Figure 3-14   *FWSM in the Catalyst 6500 Switch*

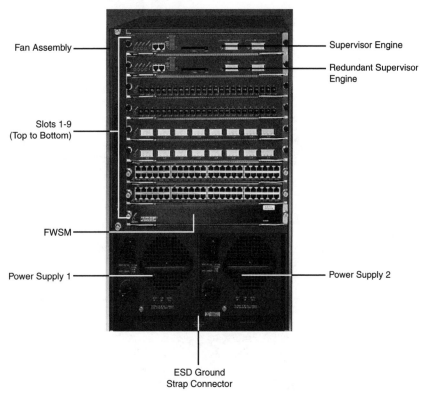

You can install a Switch Fabric Module to work with the supervisor engine 2 to deliver an increase in available system bandwidth. Using a Switch Fabric Module restricts the slot in which you can install the FWSM by taking up an available slot. If you install a Switch Fabric Module, you must install it in slot 5 of the Catalyst 6500 switch. For redundancy, you can install an additional Switch Fabric Module in slot 6. If you do not install a redundant Switch Fabric Module, slot 6 is available for other supported modules, such as the FWSM. If you do not install any Switch Fabric Modules, slot 5 and slot 6 are available for the FWSM.

NOTE   Detailed instructions on installing FWSM in a Catalyst 6500 switch are provided in Chapter 21, "Firewall Services Module."

Figure 3-15 shows the FWSM installed in slot 9 of a Cisco 7609 Internet router. As with the Catalyst 6500 switch, you must install the supervisor engine in slot 1. You can install a redundant supervisor engine in slot 2. If you do not install a redundant supervisor engine 2 module, slot 2 is available for Optical Services Modules (OSMs) or other supported modules, such as the FWSM.

Figure 3-15   *FWSM in the 7609 Internet Router*

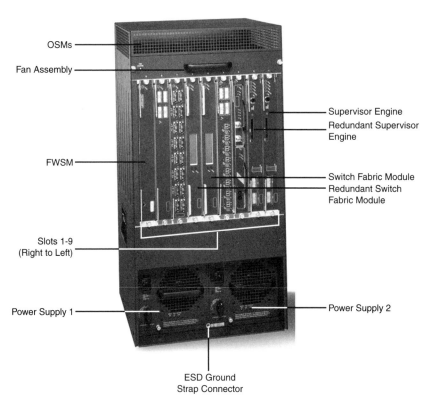

You can install a Switch Fabric Module to work with the supervisor engine 2 module to deliver an increase in available system bandwidth. The use of a Switch Fabric Module restricts the slot in which you can install the FWSM by taking up a slot. If you install a Switch Fabric Module, you must install it in slot 5 of the Cisco 7606 or the 7609 Internet router. For redundancy, you can install an additional Switch Fabric Module in slot 6. If you do not use a redundant Switch Fabric Module, slot 6 is available for OSMs or other supported modules, such as the FWSM. If you do not install any Switch Fabric Modules, slot 5 and slot 6 are available for OSMs or the FWSM.

NOTE   The OSMs provide high-speed, high-density WAN connectivity. These modules allow service providers to increase network bandwidth and performance while offering a wide range of IP services.

NOTE   Detailed instructions on installing FWSM in a 7600 series Internet router are provided in Chapter 21.

PIX Firewall Licensing

This section explains the various licensing options and VPN upgrades for the PIX Firewall.

Basic License Options

The PIX Firewall license determines the level of service it provides, its functions in a network, and the maximum number of interfaces and memory it can support. For all PIX Firewall models, except the PIX Firewall 506E, several license options are available. The PIX Firewall 506E is available in a single, unlimited mode.

The PIX Firewall 501 comes with a 10-user license, which allows up to 10 concurrent source IP addresses from your internal network to traverse the firewall. The 10-user license is upgradeable to a 50-user license or an unlimited user, allowing up to 50 or an unlimited number of concurrent source IP addresses from your internal network to traverse the firewall. For all other PIX Firewall models, the following basic license types are available:

- **Unrestricted**—PIX Firewall platforms in an unrestricted (UR) license mode allow installation and use of the maximum number of interfaces and RAM supported by the platform. The unrestricted license supports failover.

- **Restricted**—PIX Firewall platforms in a restricted (R) license mode limit the number of interfaces supported and the amount of RAM available within the system. A restricted licensed firewall does not support a redundant system for failover configurations.

- **Failover**—The failover (FO) software license places the PIX Firewall in a failover mode for use alongside another PIX Firewall with an unrestricted license.

NOTE	A PIX Firewall with failover licensing should not be operated in standalone mode. If run in standalone mode, the system reboots once every 24 hours and reports the following error message:

```
This machine is running in secondary mode without
a connection to an active primary PIX. Please
check your connection to the primary system.
REBOOTING....
```

License keys are not specific to a particular PIX Firewall software version.

VPN License Options

In addition to upgrading your license, you might want to add data encryption services or increase the level of data encryption your PIX Firewall can provide. You can fill out an online form at the PIX Firewall Software home page at Cisco.com to obtain a free 56-bit DES or 168-bit 3DES and AES activation key. For failover configurations, the unrestricted and failover firewalls each require their own unique corresponding DES or 3DES/AES license for failover functionality.

Adding cryptographic services, which are discussed in depth in later chapters, and upgrading your PIX Firewall license both require obtaining and installing an activation key. Log on to Cisco.com for current information about obtaining activation keys. The installation of activation keys is discussed in Chapter 18, "System Maintenance."

NOTE	AES encryption is supported with VAC+ and PIX OS v6.3 or later. A PIX Firewall licensed for 3DES encryption can also use 128-bit and 256-bit AES encryption.

NOTE	Licensing policies and information tend to change frequently. For the latest information on PIX Firewall licensing, refer to the following URL at Cisco.com:

http://www.cisco.com/univercd/cc/td/doc/product/iaabu/pix/pix_sw/license/license.htm.

Because URLs often change, the link listed here might not be available. In that case, try searching for "pix licensing" at Cisco.com. You should see updated links to the latest information about licensing.

Summary

This section summarizes the information you learned in this chapter:

- There are currently five PIX Firewall models in the 500 series: 501, 506E, 515E, 525, and 535.

- The PIX Firewall models 501, 506E, 515E, 525, and 535 come equipped with Ethernet connections, console connections, and intuitive LEDs.

- PIX Firewall models 515E, 525, and 535 support failover.

- Your PIX Firewall license determines its level of service in your network and the number of interfaces it supports.

- Restricted, unrestricted, and failover licenses are available for PIX Firewall models 515E, 525, and 535.

- Based on PIX Firewall technology, the FWSM for the Cisco Catalyst 6500 Switch and Cisco 7600 series Internet routers provides an alternative to the PIX Firewall appliance.

- FWSM supports the PIX Firewall Software Version 6.0 feature set and some of the 6.2 feature set.

- FWSM delivers 5-Gbps throughput and 1 million concurrent connections.

Chapter Review Questions

To test what you have learned in this chapter, answer the following questions and then refer to Appendix A, "Answers to Chapter Review Questions," for the answers:

1 What is the maximum number of physical interfaces supported on the PIX Firewall 515E with a restricted license?

2 Which model of the PIX Family has only a single option for licensing?

3 Which models of the PIX family support failover?

4 What is the maximum number of physical interfaces supported on a PIX Firewall 535 with an unrestricted license?

5 How many VPN tunnels can you establish on a PIX Firewall 506E?

6 What is the maximum 3DES throughput on a PIX Firewall 535 with VAC+?

7 What is the maximum throughput on the FWSM?

8 How many interfaces are supported on the FWSM via VLANs?

Getting Started with Cisco PIX Firewall

On completion of this chapter, you will be able to perform the following tasks:

- Describe layered security concepts and benefits.
- Identify security measures typically used to make up overall network security.
- Define the demilitarized zone (DMZ) as it applies to network security.
- Identify DMZ schemes and benefits.
- Identify common PIX Firewall implementation scenarios for small and large networks.
- Choose an appropriate PIX Firewall model for your implementation requirements.

CHAPTER 4

Implementing Cisco PIX Firewall in the Network

One of the most important aspects of implementing a PIX Firewall, or any other networking device, for that matter, is proper planning. Before you begin configuring the PIX Firewall, you need to determine your security goals and policies, how you plan to implement those policies, and how the PIX Firewall or other security devices can help you achieve your security goals.

This chapter provides several scenarios for implementing the PIX Firewall in different networks. The aim is to illustrate how large and small networks use the PIX Firewall and describe best practices. You can use this information to determine the best way to use the PIX Firewall in your network to achieve your security goals.

Design Considerations

General discussions on the development of security policies and plans and how they relate to business requirements appear in Chapter 1, "The Cisco Role in Network Security." Additional information on network security and planning is available in numerous Cisco Role in Network Security written on this topic and on the Internet. (Appendix B, "Security Resources," lists some of the security-related resources available on the Internet and in print.) As discussed in Chapter 1, it is extremely important that security be viewed as an overall process and not merely a shopping list of devices. You must develop (and periodically review and modify if necessary) a sound security plan that is aligned with your business goals and requirements. Only then can you best utilize security devices such as the PIX Firewall.

NOTE	The security wheel, which was discussed in Chapter 1, promotes continuous evaluation and improvement of security policies and procedures.

NOTE	You can look at several Cisco Security Architecture for Enterprises (SAFE) Blueprint white papers on Cisco.com that provide tips and best-practice information to help with the design and implementation of secured networks.

In general, you should aim to provide several layers of security in your network. The types of security measures that make up the overall security of a network might include any of the following:

- Authentication, authorization, and accounting (AAA)
- Virtual private networks (VPNs)
- Secure Socket Layer (SSL) encryption of web traffic
- Secure Shell (SSH) for secure remote management of network devices and servers
- Firewalls
- Intrusion detection systems (IDSs)
- Cisco IOS routers with access control lists (ACLs) or firewall feature sets
- DMZs

You might choose to add security measures not included in the preceding list to your security plan as necessary. With the right combination of security measures, a layered approach ensures greater security because if one measure fails, the resulting damage is limited.

DMZs

By placing your hosted services, such as web servers, SMTP servers, and VPN concentrators, on a DMZ (a separate, isolated network), you can prevent hosts on the Internet from directly accessing your internal hosts. If the devices on the DMZ are compromised, security policies governing the traffic flow between the DMZ and your internal network can still prevent your internal hosts from being compromised as well.

The particular DMZ design that might best match your needs depends on your business requirements and network layout. The PIX Firewall provides hardware and software capabilities that can accommodate most DMZ design requirements, regardless of how simple or complex they might be.

The following PIX Firewall models support DMZ implementations:

- **PIX Firewall 515E**—Supports up to 6 separate DMZs when using logical interfaces
- **PIX Firewall 525**—Supports up to 8 separate DMZs when using logical interfaces
- **PIX Firewall 535**—Supports up to 22 separate DMZs when using logical interfaces

---

NOTE   Logical interfaces are supported only on PIX Firewall Software Version 6.3 or higher.

Choosing the Appropriate PIX Firewall Model

One of the first decisions to make when implementing a PIX Firewall is choosing the appropriate model for your network. An obvious criterion for selecting one model over another is performance. However, the model choice is also highly dependent on your security goals and requirements. For example, a PIX Firewall 515E might provide more than adequate performance for the connections on your network. But if it cannot accommodate the number of interfaces required for implementing a particular DMZ design, it's not appropriate for your security goals.

You should consider the following factors to determine the best model to implement:

- **Performance specification**—Includes the following:
  - Cleartext throughput
  - Concurrent connections
  - IP Security (IPSec) throughput (168-bit Triple Data Encryption Standard [3DES] and 128-bit, 192-bit, and 256-bit Advanced Encryption Standard [AES] IPSec VPN)
  - Simultaneous VPN tunnels supported
- **Expandability (scalability)**—Available Peripheral Component Interconnect (PCI) slots to add network interface or VPN acceleration cards (VACs). The maximum number of physical and logical interfaces is supported.
- **High availability**—Support for failover.
- **Features supported**—Certain models do not support all features.

Table 4-1 lists the PIX Firewall 500 series models, lists basic capabilities and specifications for each model, and provides a suggestion for appropriate use. You can use the information in this table to assist you in choosing the appropriate PIX Firewall model for your network.

Table 4-1   *PIX Firewall 500 Series Model Comparison*

PIX Firewall Model	Features and Specifications	Appropriate Use
PIX 501	-Small desktop unit -Built-in four-port switch -133 MHz processor -Two physical interfaces -No failover support -7500 connections -60 Mbps throughput -3 Mbps 168-bit 3DES 4.5 Mbps 128-bit AES IPSec throughput -10 IPSec tunnels	Home office users or small office requiring basic protection and VPN capability

continues

Table 4-1   *PIX Firewall 500 Series Model Comparison (Continued)*

PIX Firewall Model	Features and Specifications	Appropriate Use
PIX 506E	-Small desktop unit -300 MHz processor -Two physical interfaces -No failover support -25,000 connections -100 Mbps throughput -17 Mbps 168-bit 3DES, 30 Mbps 128-bit AES IPSec throughput -25 IPSec tunnels	Small-to-medium size networks that are not hosting services
PIX 515E	-1U rack-mount unit -433 MHz processor -Six physical interfaces -Eight logical interfaces -Failover support -130,000 connections -188 Mbps throughput -140 Mbps 168-bit 3DES, 140 Mbps 256-bit AES IPSec throughput -2000 IPSec tunnels	Medium-to-large networks requiring high availability and performance
PIX 525	-2U rack-mount unit -600 MHz processor -Eight physical interfaces -10 logical interfaces -Failover support -280,000 connections -330 Mbps throughput -155 Mbps 168-bit 3DES, 170 Mbps 256-bit AES IPSec throughput -2000 IPSec tunnels	Large- to enterprise-size networks requiring high availability, expandability, and performance
PIX 535	-3U rack-mount unit -1 GHz processor -10 physical interfaces -24 logical interfaces -Failover support -500,000 connections -1.7 Gbps throughput -440 Mbps 168-bit 3DES, 440 Mbps 256-bit AES IPSec throughput -2000 IPSec Tunnels	Internet service provider (ISP) or enterprise networks requiring maximum performance

Implementation Scenarios

This section presents several scenarios to demonstrate the use of PIX Firewalls to secure large and small networks alike. Each scenario includes a basic network diagram, network connection and equipment list, task list, list of features and technologies used (and the PIX Firewall Software Version required), and PIX Firewall sample configurations along with explanations. The task list includes the following:

- Choosing the right PIX Firewall model
- Choosing the network layout as it pertains to the PIX Firewall
- Configuring the PIX Firewall

These scenarios include complete configurations and current topics and technologies that are covered in later chapters of this book. Although these scenarios include yet-to-be covered topics, they can give you a better feel for the proper placement of PIX Firewalls in the network and associated security considerations. You might find this chapter a useful reference and worth a second look after you read through the rest of the book. Configurations include descriptive comments and identify the chapter covering the topic or command usage.

Enterprise Network Scenario

Enterprise networks are complex and demanding. Typically, enterprise networks are not the result of organic growth. Mergers and acquisitions might force design compromises, and different business units or divisions might have conflicting preferences. So, the chances of finding the relatively simple network design shown on Figure 4-1 are low. However, this scenario demonstrates the use of PIX Firewall models and technologies that are likely to be used in large, enterprise networks.

Figure 4-1 *Enterprise Network Scenario*

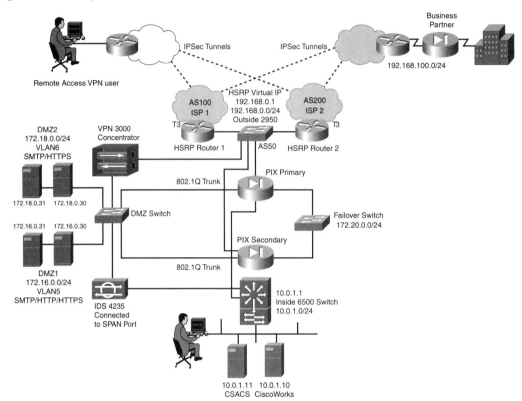

Connections and Equipment List for the Enterprise Network

The network in this scenario consists of the following connections and devices:

- Redundant T3 links to the Internet
- Cisco 3700 routers
- Cisco 6500 Switch
- Cisco 2950 Switch
- Cisco Secure Access Control Server (CSACS)
- Cisco VPN 3000 Concentrator
- Cisco Secure IDS 4235
- Cisco PIX 525 Failover Bundle
- CiscoWorks Server

Task List for the Enterprise Network

For the enterprise network scenario, the following tasks are required:

- Provide redundant links to the Internet.
- Configure the PIX Firewall with stateful, LAN-based failover.
- Create two DMZs to host servers, one physical, one logical.
- Monitor DMZ traffic with Cisco Secure IDS 4235.
- Permit port 25 (Simple Mail Transfer Protocol [SMTP]), port 80 (HTTP), and Port 443 (Secure HTTP [HTTPS]) to DMZ1 hosts.
- Permit Port 25 and 443 to DMZ2 hosts.
- Create a site-to-site VPN connection to partner.
- Configure remote access VPN using CSACS for extended authentication (XAUTH).
- Create a global network address translation (NAT) pool of 50 IP address for all inside hosts.
- Assign a single address for port address translation (PAT).
- Configure Open Shortest Path First (OSPF) on the PIX.
- Enable the PIX IDS.
- Set the CiscoWorks Server as the syslog server.

Features Used for the Enterprise Network

The enterprise network uses the following features:

- OSPF (PIX Firewall Version 6.3)
- 802.1Q VLAN (PIX Firewall Version 6.3)
- ACLs
- Object groups
- NAT and PAT
- Intrusion detection
- CSACS and AAA
- Failover
- VPN support

Configuration for the Enterprise Network

Figure 4-1 shows the layout for this network design scenario. The network is configured as follows:

- Two Cisco 3700 routers with T3 network modules provide connectivity to the Internet in a multihomed Border Gateway Protocol (BGP) network:
  - Routers configured as a Hot Standby Router Protocol (HSRP) pair
  - BGP configured
  - Connected to an external 2950 switch

  Configuring the BGP routers as an HSRP pair as shown in Figure 4-1 simplifies the required DMZ design and meets the connection and device redundancy requirements of this scenario. The two BGP routers provide device and connection redundancy and provide a single default gateway for use by the PIX Firewall failover pair.

  Other network designs can also provide redundant links to the Internet using BGP. For example, Cisco.com includes a sample configuration ("Sample Configuration of BGP Across a PIX Firewall") that deploys a separate PIX Firewall behind each BGP router connected to the Internet. That design requires a more complicated DMZ implementation across two separate PIX Firewalls but it provides a greater level of device redundancy.

- The PIX Firewall 525 failover set is configured as follows:
  - Interface ethernet0 on both firewalls connected to the outside 2950 switch
  - Interface ethernet1 on both firewalls connected to the inside 6500 switch
  - Interface ethernet2 on both firewalls connected to 802.1Q trunk ports on the DMZ 2950
  - Interface ethernet5 on both firewalls connected to a dedicated failover 2950 switch

- The DMZ 2950 Switch is configured:
  - Configured with two VLANS:
    - DMZ1(VLAN5)—Hosting SMTP, HTTP, and HTTPS services
    - DMZ2(VLAN6)—Hosting SMTP and HTTPS services
  - Configured ports for 802.1Q trunk
  - Configured Switched Port Analyzer (SPAN) port for Cisco IDS 4235

- The Cisco Secure IDS 4235 has the following connections:
  - Sniffing port connected to SPAN port on DMZ 2950 switch
  - Management port connected to the 6500 inside switch

- CSACS and CiscoWorks are attached to the 6500 inside switch.
- The 6500 switch is the default gateway for internal hosts and runs OSPF:
  - Connected to other networks through a WAN module (hence the requirement to run OSPF)

Example 4-1 lists the PIX Firewall configuration for this scenario.

Example 4-1   *Enterprise Network Configuration*

```
pixfirewall(config)# show config
Building configuration...
: Saved
:
PIX Version 6.3(1)
!--- Physical and logical interfaces are configured.
!--- Interface speeds and duplex settings should be specified for LAN-based
!--- and stateful failover. Using the auto setting is not supported.
!--- Interface configuration is covered in Chapter 5, "Getting Started with
!--- the Cisco PIX Firewall"
interface ethernet0 100full
interface ethernet1 100full
interface ethernet2 100full
interface ethernet2 vlan5 physical
interface ethernet2 vlan6 logical
interface ethernet3 auto shutdown
interface ethernet4 auto shutdown
interface ethernet5 100full
nameif ethernet0 outside security0
nameif ethernet1 inside security100
nameif ethernet2 DMZ1 security50
nameif vlan6 DMZ2 security30
nameif ethernet3 intf3 security0
nameif ethernet4 intf4 security0
nameif ethernet5 pix_failover security90
enable password 8Ry2YjIyt7RRXU24 encrypted
passwd 2KFQnbNIdI.2KYOU encrypted
hostname pixfirewall
domain-name cisco.com
!--- Fixup protocols are covered in Chapter 11, "Advanced Protocol Handling"
fixup protocol ftp 21
fixup protocol h323 h225 1720
fixup protocol h323 ras 1718-1719
fixup protocol http 80
fixup protocol ils 389
fixup protocol rsh 514
fixup protocol rtsp 554
fixup protocol sip 5060
fixup protocol sip udp 5060
fixup protocol skinny 2000
fixup protocol smtp 25
fixup protocol sqlnet 1521
!--- You can assign common names to hosts or networks to make configurations
!--- easier to read, understand, and maintain.
```

continues

Example 4-1 *Enterprise Network Configuration (Continued)*

```
names
name 192.168.100.0 bizpartner
!--- Object groups are created here to improve the configuration and management
!--- of ACLs. Object groups are covered in detail in Chapter 9, "Object Grouping"
object-group service DMZ1 tcp
  description Object Group for DMZ1 Services
  port-object eq www
  port-object eq https
  port-object eq smtp
object-group service DMZ2 tcp
  description Object Group for DMZ2 Services
  port-object eq https
  port-object eq smtp
!--- ACLs are covered in Chapter 8, "Access Control Lists and Content Filtering."
!--- The first four ACL statements define traffic that is subject to IPSec
encryption.
access-list inside_outbound_nat0_acl permit ip 10.0.1.0 255.255.255.0 bizpartner
  255.255.255.0
access-list inside_outbound_nat0_acl permit ip 10.0.1.0 255.255.255.0 10.0.20.0
  255.255.255.128
access-list outside_cryptomap_20 permit ip 10.0.1.0 255.255.255.0 bizpartner
  255.255.255.0
access-list outside_cryptomap_dyn_20 permit ip any 10.0.20.0 255.255.255.128
!--- The next two ACLs allow inbound traffic to DMZ hosts for services that were
!--- previously defined with the object-group command.
access-list outside_access_in permit tcp any 192.168.0.0 255.255.255.0 object-group
  DMZ1
access-list outside_access_in permit tcp any 192.168.0.0 255.255.255.0 object-group
  DMZ2
!--- The pager command defines the number of lines per page that the PIX Firewall
!--- should display in console or Telnet sessions.
pager lines 24
!--- Syslog configuration follows. Logging options are discussed in Chapter 5.
logging on
logging standby
logging host inside 10.0.1.12
!--- Default MTU settings work well in most situations. You can use the MTU command
!--- to modify them here if required, such as for certain VPN scenarios.
mtu outside 1500
mtu inside 1500
mtu DMZ1 1500
!--- IP address for each interface is configured. Refer to Chapter 5
!--- for information on this command.
ip address outside 192.168.0.2 255.255.255.0
ip address inside 10.0.1.1 255.255.255.0
ip address DMZ1 172.16.0.2 255.255.255.0
ip address DMZ2 172.18.0.2 255.255.255.0
ip address pix_failover 172.20.0.2 255.255.255.0
!--- PIX Firewall IDS capabilities and configuration procedures are presented in
!--- Chapter 12, "Attack Guards, Intrusion Detection, and Shunning."
!--- PIX Firewall IDS rules are defined in the next two statements.
ip audit name attack-rule attack action alarm drop reset
ip audit name info-rule info action alarm
!--- Defined IDS rules are then applied to the interfaces.
```

Example 4-1 *Enterprise Network Configuration (Continued)*

```
ip audit interface outside info-rule
ip audit interface outside attack-rule
ip audit interface inside info-rule
ip audit interface inside attack-rule
ip audit interface DMZ1 info-rule
ip audit interface DMZ1 attack-rule
ip audit interface DMZ2 info-rule
ip audit interface DMZ2 attack-rule
ip audit info action alarm
ip audit attack action alarm
!--- Remote access VPN is covered in Chapter 17, "Client Remote Access VPNs."
!--- Local IP address pool is defined for remote access VPN users.
ip local pool MYPOOL 10.0.20.50-10.0.20.100
!--- Ip verify reverse-path statements protect against IP spoofing attacks.
ip verify reverse-path interface outside
ip verify reverse-path interface DMZ1
ip verify reverse-path interface DMZ2
!--- PIX Firewall failover capabilities are discussed in Chapter 14, "Failover."
!--- LAN-based, stateful failover is configured and enabled.
failover
failover timeout 0:00:00
failover poll 4
!--- Enable stateful replication of HTTP sessions.
failover replication http
failover ip address outside 192.168.0.3
failover ip address inside 10.0.1.3
failover ip address DMZ1 172.16.0.3
failover ip address DMZ2 172.18.0.3
no failover ip address intf3
no failover ip address intf4
failover ip address pix_failover 172.20.0.3
failover link pix_failover
failover lan unit primary
!--- The same interface is used for LAN-based and stateful failover transmissions.
!--- You might need to use seperate interfaces in high utilization scenarios.
failover lan interface pix_failover
failover lan key ********
failover lan enable
!--- PDM adds host information automatically.
pdm location 10.0.1.10 255.255.255.255 inside
pdm location 10.0.1.11 255.255.255.255 inside
pdm location bizpartner 255.255.255.0 outside
pdm location 172.16.0.30 255.255.255.255 DMZ1
pdm location 172.16.0.31 255.255.255.255 DMZ1
pdm location 172.18.0.40 255.255.255.255 DMZ2
pdm location 172.18.0.41 255.255.255.255 DMZ2
pdm history enable
arp timeout 14400
!--- NAT and PAT are covered in Chapter 7, "Translations and Connections."
!--- Global address pools are defined. The first statement defines the pool
!--- used for NAT. The second statement is used for PAT.
```

continues

Example 4-1   *Enterprise Network Configuration (Continued)*

```
global (outside) 1 192.168.0.200-192.168.0.250 netmask 255.255.255.0
global (outside) 1 192.168.0.251
!--- NAT 0 statement excludes traffic defined by the ACL. This is used to
!--- avoid translation of addresses for IPSec-bound traffic.
nat (inside) 0 access-list inside_outbound_nat0_acl
!--- Hosts in the 10.0.1.0 network are translated with global address pool 1.
nat (inside) 1 10.0.1.0 255.255.255.0 0 0
!--- Static translations are defined for inside hosts accessing services on DMZ1
!--- and DMZ2 and DMZ1 and DMZ2 hosts providing services to the outside.
static (inside,DMZ1) 10.0.1.0 10.0.1.0 netmask 255.255.255.0 0 0
static (inside,DMZ2) 10.0.1.0 10.0.1.0 netmask 255.255.255.0 0 0
static (DMZ1,outside) 192.168.0.30 172.16.0.30 netmask 255.255.255.255 0 0
static (DMZ1,outside) 192.168.0.31 172.16.0.31 netmask 255.255.255.255 0 0
static (DMZ2,outside) 192.168.0.40 172.18.0.40 netmask 255.255.255.255 0 0
static (DMZ2,outside) 192.168.0.41 172.18.0.41 netmask 255.255.255.255 0 0
!--- ACLs previously defined are enabled using the access-group command.
access-group outside_access_in in interface outside
!--- Routing features and configuration are covered in Chapter 10, "Routing."
!--- One OSPF process is configured and the prefix list command is used to filter
!--- Type 3 LSAs, preventing propagation of internal routes to the outside.
!--- OSPF is only supported on PIX Firewall Software Version 6.3 or higher.
prefix-list secure-ospf seq 1 deny 10.0.1.0/24
prefix-list secure-ospf seq 2 deny 172.16.0.0/24
prefix-list secure-ospf seq 3 deny 172.18.0.0/24
routing interface outside
  ospf message-digest-key 1 md5 cisco
  ospf authentication message-digest
routing interface inside
  ospf message-digest-key 1 md5 cisco
  ospf authentication message-digest
routing interface dmz
  ospf message-digest-key 1 md5 cisco
  ospf authentication message-digest
router ospf 1
network 10.0.1.0 255.255.255.0 area 0
network 172.16.0.0 255.255.255.0 area 1
network 172.18.0.0 255.255.255.0 area 2
network 192.168.0.0 255.255.255.0 area 3
area 0 authentication message-digest
area 1 authentication message-digest
area 2 authentication message-digest
area 3 authentication message-digest
area 3 filter-list prefix secure-ospf in
log-adj-changes
timeout xlate 3:00:00
timeout conn 1:00:00 half-closed 0:10:00 udp 0:02:00 rpc 0:10:00 h225 1:00:00
timeout h323 0:05:00 mgcp 0:05:00 sip 0:30:00 sip_media 0:02:00
timeout uauth 0:05:00 absolute
!--- AAA configurations are covered in Chapter 13, "Authentication, Authorization,
!--- and Accounting." Server groups are defined here.
```

Example 4-1 *Enterprise Network Configuration (Continued)*

```
aaa-server TACACS+ protocol tacacs+
aaa-server RADIUS protocol radius
aaa-server LOCAL protocol local
aaa-server MYTACACS protocol tacacs+
!--- AAA server is configured as part of server group MYTACACS
aaa-server MYTACACS (inside) host 10.0.1.11 tacacskey timeout 5
!--- PDM is enabled for hosts on the inside interface. Chapter 6, "Cisco PIX Device
!--- Manager," covers PDM features and configuration procedures.
http server enable
http 10.0.1.0 255.255.255.0 inside
no snmp-server location
no snmp-server contact
snmp-server community public
no snmp-server enable traps
floodguard enable
!--- VPN configuration for site-to-site connection to business partner and
!--- remote access connection for client access are included here.
!--- VPN overview and configuration procedures for site-to-site and client
!--- remote access are presented in Chapter 15, "Virtual Private Networks," Chapter
16, "Site-to-Site VPNS," and Chapter 17, "Client Remote Access VPNs."
sysopt connection permit-ipsec
!--- Transform sets are defined.
crypto ipsec transform-set ESP-3DES-MD5 esp-3des esp-md5-hmac
crypto dynamic-map outside_dyn_map 20 match address outside_cryptomap_dyn_20
crypto dynamic-map outside_dyn_map 20 set transform-set ESP-3DES-MD5
crypto map outside_map 20 ipsec-isakmp
crypto map outside_map 20 match address outside_cryptomap_20
crypto map outside_map 20 set peer 192.168.100.2
crypto map outside_map 20 set transform-set ESP-3DES-MD5
crypto map outside_map 65535 ipsec-isakmp dynamic outside_dyn_map
crypto map outside_map client authentication MYTACACS
crypto map outside_map interface outside
!--- Site-to-site IKE settings are configured for business partner.
isakmp enable outside
isakmp key ******** address 192.168.100.2 netmask 255.255.255.255 no-xauth no-
  config-mode
isakmp policy 20 authentication pre-share
isakmp policy 20 encryption 3des
isakmp policy 20 hash md5
isakmp policy 20 group 2
isakmp policy 20 lifetime 86400
!--- Client remote access settings are configured for MYVPNGROUP.
vpngroup MYVPNGROUP address-pool MYPOOL
vpngroup MYVPNGROUP dns-server 10.0.1.20 10.0.1.21
vpngroup MYVPNGROUP wins-server 10.0.1.22 10.0.1.23
vpngroup MYVPNGROUP default-domain cisco.com
vpngroup MYVPNGROUP idle-time 1800
vpngroup MYVPNGROUP password ********
telnet 10.0.1.0 255.255.255.0 inside
telnet timeout 5
ssh 10.0.1.0 255.255.255.0 inside
ssh timeout 5
```

continues

Example 4-1 *Enterprise Network Configuration (Continued)*

```
management-access inside
console timeout 0
terminal width 80
Cryptochecksum:dceddd712577d5ffdf870fb8d1312619
: end
[OK]
```

Large Company Network Scenario

The network layout for a large company deployment appears in Figure 4-2. In this scenario, a single T3 connection to the Internet provides connectivity for the network. This layout does not provide the same level of redundancy as the layout shown on Figure 4-1.

Figure 4-2 *Large Company Network Scenario*

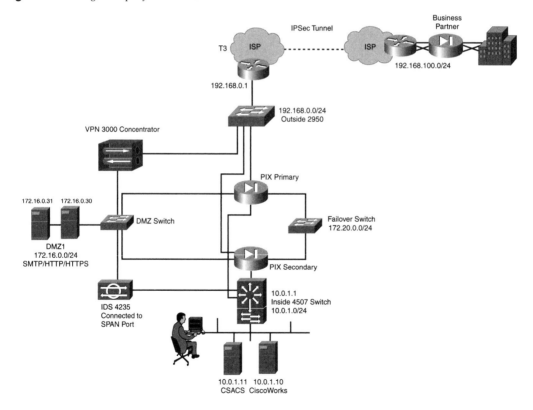

Connections and Equipment List for the Large Company Network

The large company network in this scenario consists of the following connections and devices:

- T3 link to the Internet
- Cisco 3700 Router
- Cisco 4507 Switch
- Cisco 2950 Switch
- Cisco VPN 3000 Concentrator
- Cisco Secure IDS 4215
- Cisco PIX 515E Failover Bundle

Task List for the Large Company Network

For the large company network scenario, the following tasks are required:

- Set up a single link to the Internet.
- Configure the PIX Firewall with stateful, LAN-based failover.
- Create a DMZ to host servers.
- Permit Port 25 (SMTP), Port 80 (HTTP), and Port 443 (HTTPS) to DMZ hosts.
- Create a site-to-site VPN connection to partners.
- Create a global NAT pool of 20 IP address for all inside hosts.
- Assign a single address for PAT.
- Enable the PIX IDS.

Features Used for the Large Company Network

The large company network uses the following features:

- ACLs
- Object groups
- NAT and PAT
- Intrusion detection
- Failover
- VPN support

Sample Configuration for the Large Company Network

The layout for this network appears in Figure 4-2. The network is configured as follows:

- The Cisco 3700 Router with T3 network module provides connectivity to the Internet:
  - Connected to an external 2950 switch
- The PIX Firewall 515E failover set is configured as follows:
  - Interface ethernet0 on both firewalls connected to the outside 2950 switch
  - Interface ethernet1 on both firewalls connected to the inside 4507 switch
  - Interface ethernet2 on both firewalls connected to the DMZ 2950 switch
  - Interface ethernet5 on both firewalls connected to a dedicated failover 2950 switch
- The DMZ 2950 Switch is configured:
  - Configured SPAN for IDS monitoring
- The 4507 Switch is the default gateway for internal hosts.

Example 4-2 lists the PIX Firewall configuration for this scenario.

Example 4-2   *Large Company Network Configuration*

```
pixfirewall(config)# show config
Building configuration...
: Saved
:
PIX Version 6.3(1)
!--- Physical interfaces are configured.
!--- Interface speeds and duplex settings should be specified for LAN-based
!--- and stateful failover. Using the auto setting is not supported.
!--- Interface configuration is covered in Chapter 5.
interface ethernet0 100full
interface ethernet1 100full
interface ethernet2 100full
interface ethernet3 auto shutdown
interface ethernet4 auto shutdown
interface ethernet5 100full
nameif ethernet0 outside security0
nameif ethernet1 inside security100
nameif ethernet2 DMZ security50
nameif ethernet3 intf3 security0
nameif ethernet4 intf4 security0
nameif ethernet5 pix_failover security90
enable password 8Ry2YjIyt7RRXU24 encrypted
passwd 2KFQnbNIdI.2KYOU encrypted
hostname pixfirewall
domain-name cisco.com
!--- Fixup protocols are covered in Chapter 11.
fixup protocol ftp 21
fixup protocol h323 h225 1720
fixup protocol h323 ras 1718-1719
```

Example 4-2 *Large Company Network Configuration (Continued)*

```
fixup protocol http 80
fixup protocol ils 389
fixup protocol rsh 514
fixup protocol rtsp 554
fixup protocol sip 5060
fixup protocol sip udp 5060
fixup protocol skinny 2000
fixup protocol smtp 25
fixup protocol sqlnet 1521
!--- You can assign common names to hosts or networks to make configurations
!--- easier to read, understand, and maintain.
names
name 192.168.100.0 bizpartner
!--- Object groups are created here to improve the configuration and management
!--- of ACLs. Object groups are covered in detail in Chapter 9.
object-group service DMZ tcp
  description Object Group for DMZ Services
  port-object eq https
  port-object eq www
  port-object eq smtp
!--- ACLs are covered in Chapter 8.
!--- The next ACL allows inbound traffic to DMZ hosts for services that were
!--- previously defined with the object-group command.
access-list outside_access_in permit tcp any 192.168.0.0 255.255.255.0 object-group
  DMZ
!--- The next two ACL statements define traffic that is subject to IPSec encryption.
access-list inside_outbound_nat0_acl permit ip 10.0.1.0 255.255.255.0 bizpartner
255.255.255.0
access-list outside_cryptomap_20 permit ip 10.0.1.0 255.255.255.0 bizpartner
255.255.255.0
pager lines 24
logging on
logging host inside 10.0.1.12
!--- Default MTU settings work well in most situations. You can use the MTU command
!--- to modify them here if required, such as for certain VPN scenarios.
mtu outside 1500
mtu inside 1500
mtu DMZ 1500
!--- The IP address for each interface is configured. Refer to Chapter 5
!--- for information on this command.
ip address outside 192.168.0.2 255.255.255.0
ip address inside 10.0.1.1 255.255.255.0
ip address DMZ 172.16.0.2 255.255.255.0
ip address pix_failover 172.20.0.2 255.255.255.0
!--- PIX Firewall IDS capabilities and configuration procedures are presented in
!--- Chapter 12. PIX Firewall IDS rules are defined in the next two statements.
ip audit name attack-rule attack action alarm drop reset
ip audit name info-rule info action alarm
!--- Defined IDS rules are then applied to the interfaces.
ip audit interface outside info-rule
ip audit interface outside attack-rule
ip audit interface inside info-rule
ip audit interface inside attack-rule
```

continues

Example 4-2 *Large Company Network Configuration (Continued)*

```
ip audit interface DMZ info-rule
ip audit interface DMZ attack-rule
ip audit info action alarm
ip audit attack action alarm
!--- Ip verify reverse-path statements protect against IP spoofing attacks.
ip verify reverse-path interface outside
ip verify reverse-path interface DMZ
!--- PIX Firewall failover capabilities are discussed in Chapter 14.
!--- LAN-based, stateful failover is configured and enabled.
failover
failover timeout 0:00:00
failover poll 4
!--- Enable stateful replication of HTTP sessions.
failover replication http
failover ip address outside 192.168.0.3
failover ip address inside 10.0.1.3
failover ip address DMZ 172.16.0.3
no failover ip address intf3
no failover ip address intf4
failover ip address pix_failover 172.20.0.3
failover link pix_failover
failover lan unit primary
!--- The same interface is used for LAN-based and stateful failover transmissions.
!--- You may need to use separate interfaces in high utilization scenarios.
failover lan interface pix_failover
failover lan key ********
failover lan enable
!--- PDM adds host information automatically.
pdm location 172.16.0.30 255.255.255.255 DMZ
pdm location 172.16.0.31 255.255.255.255 DMZ
pdm location bizpartner 255.255.255.0 outside
pdm history enable
arp timeout 14400
!--- NAT and PAT are covered in Chapter 7.
!--- Global address pools are defined. The first statement defines the pool
!--- used for NAT. The second statement is used for PAT.
global (outside) 1 192.168.0.200-192.168.0.220 netmask 255.255.255.0
global (outside) 1 192.168.0.221
!--- NAT 0 statement excludes traffic defined by the ACL. This is used to
!--- avoid translation of addresses for IPSec-bound traffic.
nat (inside) 0 access-list inside_outbound_nat0_acl
!--- Hosts in the 10.0.1.0 network are translated with global address pool 1.
nat (inside) 1 10.0.1.0 255.255.255.0 0 0
!--- Static translations are defined for inside hosts accessing services on DMZ
!--- and DMZ hosts providing services to the outside.
static (inside,DMZ) 10.0.1.0 10.0.1.0 netmask 255.255.255.0 0 0
static (DMZ,outside) 192.168.0.30 172.16.0.30 netmask 255.255.255.255 0 0
static (DMZ,outside) 192.168.0.31 172.16.0.31 netmask 255.255.255.255 0 0
!--- ACLs previously defined are enabled using the access-group command.
access-group outside_access_in in interface outside
timeout xlate 3:00:00
```

Example 4-2 *Large Company Network Configuration (Continued)*

```
timeout conn 1:00:00 half-closed 0:10:00 udp 0:02:00 rpc 0:10:00 h225 1:00:00
timeout h323 0:05:00 mgcp 0:05:00 sip 0:30:00 sip_media 0:02:00
timeout uauth 0:05:00 absolute
aaa-server TACACS+ protocol tacacs+
aaa-server RADIUS protocol radius
aaa-server LOCAL protocol local
!--- PDM is enabled for hosts on the inside interface. Chapter 6
!--- covers PDM features and configuration procedures.
http server enable
http 10.0.1.0 255.255.255.0 inside
no snmp-server location
no snmp-server contact
snmp-server community public
no snmp-server enable traps
floodguard enable
!--- VPN configuration for site-to-site connection to business partner is included
    here.
!--- VPN overview and configuration procedures for site-to-site and client
!--- remote access are presented in Chapter 15, Chapter 16, and Chapter 17.
sysopt connection permit-ipsec
!--- Transform sets are defined.
crypto ipsec transform-set ESP-3DES-MD5 esp-3des esp-md5-hmac
crypto map outside_map 20 ipsec-isakmp
crypto map outside_map 20 match address outside_cryptomap_20
crypto map outside_map 20 set peer 192.168.100.2
crypto map outside_map 20 set transform-set ESP-3DES-MD5
crypto map outside_map interface outside
!--- Site-to-site IKE settings are configured for business partner.
isakmp enable outside
isakmp key ******** address 192.168.100.2 netmask 255.255.255.255 no-xauth no-
config-mode
isakmp policy 20 authentication pre-share
isakmp policy 20 encryption 3des
isakmp policy 20 hash md5
isakmp policy 20 group 2
isakmp policy 20 lifetime 86400
telnet 10.0.1.0 255.255.255.0 inside
telnet timeout 5
ssh 10.0.1.0 255.255.255.0 inside
ssh timeout 5
console timeout 0
terminal width 80
Cryptochecksum:d7cac0c1f0dd23e8108e7beef67c6df4
: end
[OK]
```

Medium and Small Business Network Scenario

Medium and small businesses typically have more modest requirements than large and enterprise networks. Figure 4-3 shows a typical PIX Firewall implementation for a medium or small company.

Figure 4-3 *Medium and Small Business Network Scenario*

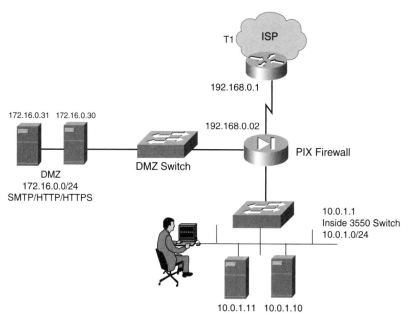

In this scenario, the configuration is based on a business that is hosting its own e-mail and web servers. Because this configuration requires three interfaces (with a DMZ design), the use of the PIX Firewall 506E was ruled out. If hosting was not a requirement in this scenario, a PIX Firewall 506E would have been sufficient.

Network Connections and Equipment List for Medium and Small Business Networks

The network in this scenario consists of the following connections and devices:

- Single T1 link to the Internet
- Cisco 2600 router
- Cisco 2950 DMZ Switch
- Cisco 3550 inside Switch
- Cisco PIX Firewall 515E

Task List for Medium and Small Business Networks

For this scenario, the following tasks are required:

- Provide a single link to the Internet.
- Create a DMZ to host servers.
- Permit Port 25 (SMTP), Port 80 (HTTP), and Port 443 (HTTPS) to DMZ hosts.
- Create a global NAT pool of 5 IP address for all inside hosts.
- Assign a single address for PAT.
- Enable the PIX IDS.

Features Used for Medium and Small Business Networks

Medium and small business networks use the following features:

- ACLs
- Object groups
- NAT and PAT
- Intrusion detection

Sample Configuration for Medium and Small Business Networks

The layout for this network appears in Figure 4-3. The network is configured as follows:

- The Cisco 2600 Router with T1 WAN interface card is configured:
  - Connected to the outside interface of the PIX Firewall
- The PIX Firewall 515E is configured:
  - Interface ethernet0 connected to the 2600 Router
  - Interface ethernet1 connected to the 3550 inside switch
  - Interface ethernet2 connected to the 2950 DMZ switch
- The inside interface (ethernet1) is the default gateway for internal hosts.
- The 2950 DMZ Switch is configured:
  - Connected to ethernet2 interface of the PIX Firewall
- The 3550 inside Switch is configured:
  - Connected to internal hosts

Example 4-3 lists the PIX Firewall configuration for this scenario.

Example 4-3 *Medium and Small Company Network Configuration*

```
pixfirewall(config)# show config
Building configuration...
: Saved
:
PIX Version 6.3(1)
!--- Physical interfaces are configured and speed and duplex settings are explicitly
!--- defined. While the auto setting usually works, explicit settings are more
 reliable.
!--- Interface configuration is covered in Chapter 5.
interface ethernet0 100full
interface ethernet1 100full
interface ethernet2 100full
nameif ethernet0 outside security0
nameif ethernet1 inside security100
nameif ethernet2 DMZ security50
enable password 8Ry2YjIyt7RRXU24 encrypted
passwd 2KFQnbNIdI.2KYOU encrypted
hostname pixfirewall
domain-name cisco.com
!--- Fixup protocols are covered in Chapter 11.
fixup protocol ftp 21
fixup protocol h323 h225 1720
fixup protocol h323 ras 1718-1719
fixup protocol http 80
fixup protocol ils 389
fixup protocol rsh 514
fixup protocol rtsp 554
fixup protocol sip 5060
fixup protocol sip udp 5060
fixup protocol skinny 2000
fixup protocol smtp 25
fixup protocol sqlnet 1521
names
!--- Object groups are created here to improve the configuration and management
!--- of ACLs. Object groups are covered in detail in Chapter 9.
object-group service DMZ tcp
  description Object Group for DMZ Services
  port-object eq https
  port-object eq www
  port-object eq smtp
!--- ACLs are covered in Chapter 8.
!--- The ACLs allow inbound traffic to DMZ hosts for services that were previously
!--- defined with the object-group command.
access-list outside_access_in permit tcp any 192.168.0.0 255.255.255.0 object-group
DMZ
pager lines 24
logging on
logging host inside 10.0.1.12
!--- Default MTU settings work well in most situations. You can use the MTU command
!--- to modify them here if required, such as for certain VPN scenarios.
```

Example 4-3 *Medium and Small Company Network Configuration (Continued)*

```
mtu outside 1500
mtu inside 1500
mtu DMZ 1500
!--- IP address for each interface is configured. Refer to Chapter 5
!--- for information on this command.
ip address outside 192.168.0.2 255.255.255.0
ip address inside 10.0.1.1 255.255.255.0
ip address DMZ 172.16.0.2 255.255.255.0
!--- PIX Firewall IDS capabilities and configuration procedures
!--- are presented in Chapter 12.
!--- PIX Firewall IDS rules are defined in the next two statements.
ip audit name attack-rule attack action alarm drop reset
ip audit name info-rule info action alarm
!--- Defined IDS rules are then applied to the interfaces.
ip audit interface outside info-rule
ip audit interface outside attack-rule
ip audit interface inside info-rule
ip audit interface inside attack-rule
ip audit interface DMZ info-rule
ip audit interface DMZ attack-rule
ip audit info action alarm
ip audit attack action alarm
!--- Ip verify reverse-path statements protect against IP spoofing attacks.
ip verify reverse-path interface outside
ip verify reverse-path interface DMZ
!--- PDM adds host information automatically.
pdm location 172.16.0.30 255.255.255.255 DMZ
pdm location 172.16.0.31 255.255.255.255 DMZ
pdm history enable
arp timeout 14400
!--- NAT and PAT are covered in Chapter 7.
!--- Global address pools are defined. The first statement defines the pool
!--- used for NAT. The second statement is used for PAT.
global (outside) 1 192.168.0.200-192.168.0.205 netmask 255.255.255.0
global (outside) 1 192.168.0.206
!--- Hosts in the 10.0.1.0 network are translated with global address pool 1.
nat (inside) 1 10.0.1.0 255.255.255.0 0 0
!--- Static translations are defined for inside hosts accessing services on DMZ
!--- and DMZ hosts providing services on the outside.
static (inside,DMZ) 10.0.1.0 10.0.1.0 netmask 255.255.255.0 0 0
static (DMZ,outside) 192.168.0.30 172.16.0.30 netmask 255.255.255.255 0 0
static (DMZ,outside) 192.168.0.31 172.16.0.31 netmask 255.255.255.255 0 0
!--- ACLs previously defined are enabled using the access-group command.
access-group outside_access_in in interface outside
timeout xlate 3:00:00
timeout conn 1:00:00 half-closed 0:10:00 udp 0:02:00 rpc 0:10:00 h225 1:00:00
timeout h323 0:05:00 mgcp 0:05:00 sip 0:30:00 sip_media 0:02:00
timeout uauth 0:05:00 absolute
aaa-server TACACS+ protocol tacacs+
aaa-server RADIUS protocol radius
aaa-server LOCAL protocol local
!--- PDM is enabled for hosts on the inside interface. Chapter 6,
```

continues

Example 4-3 *Medium and Small Company Network Configuration (Continued)*

```
!--- covers PDM features and configuration procedures.
http server enable
http 10.0.1.0 255.255.255.0 inside
no snmp-server location
no snmp-server contact
snmp-server community public
no snmp-server enable traps
floodguard enable
telnet 10.0.1.0 255.255.255.0 inside
telnet timeout 5
ssh 10.0.1.0 255.255.255.0 inside
ssh timeout 5
console timeout 0
terminal width 80
Cryptochecksum:a3b3fd99630a4a698b6c41c64ce5ced9
: end
[OK]
```

SOHO Network Scenario

The simple network layout for a small office/home office (SOHO) user appears in Figure 4-4. In this scenario, a home-office worker is utilizing a PIX Firewall 501 to securely connect to corporate resources using a DSL line with Point-to-Point Protocol over Ethernet (PPPoE).

Figure 4-4 *Home Office Network Scenario*

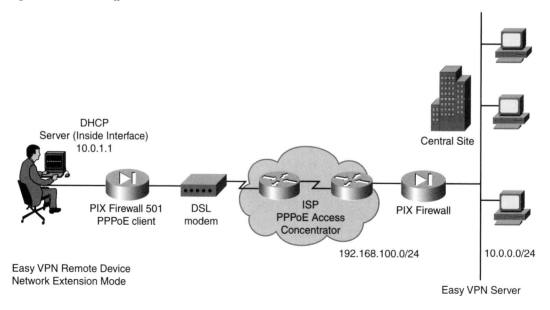

Network Connections and Equipment List for a SOHO Network

The network in this scenario consists of the following connections and devices:

- DSL link to the Internet
- ISP-provided DSL router
- PIX Firewall 501

Task List for a SOHO Network

For this scenario, the following tasks are required:

- Configure PPPoE on the PIX Firewall.
- Configure a Dynamic Host Configuration Protocol (DHCP) client on the outside interface.
- Configure the PIX Firewall as an Easy VPN remote device in network extension mode.
- Configure split tunneling so that normal Internet traffic is not encrypted.
- Configure a DHCP server on the inside interface.
- Create a global NAT pool using the interface address.
- Enable the PIX IDS.

Features Used for a SOHO Network

The SOHO network uses the following features:

- PPPoE
- DHCP server and client
- Easy VPN remote device
- NAT and PAT
- Intrusion detection
- Split tunneling

Sample Configuration for SOHO Network

The layout for this network appears in Figure 4-4. The network is configured as follows:

- An ISP-provided DSL router provides a DSL link to the Internet.
    - Connected to the outside interface of the PIX Firewall
- The PIX Firewall 501 is configured:

— Interface ethernet0 connected to the DSL Router

— Outside interface running PPPoE and DHCP client

— Interface ethernet1 (four-port switch) connected to internal hosts

— Inside interface running DHCP server

— Configured as Easy VPN remote device in network extension mode

Example 4-4 lists the PIX Firewall configuration for this scenario.

Example 4-4 *Home Office Network Configuration*

```
pixfirewall(config)# show config
Building configuration...
: Saved
:
PIX Version 6.3(1)
!--- Physical interfaces are configured and speed and duplex settings are explicitly
!--- defined. While the auto setting usually works, explicit settings are more
  reliable.
!--- Interface configuration is covered in Chapter 5.
interface ethernet0 10baset
interface ethernet1 10full
nameif ethernet0 outside security0
nameif ethernet1 inside security100
enable password 8Ry2YjIyt7RRXU24 encrypted
passwd 2KFQnbNIdI.2KYOU encrypted
hostname pixfirewall
domain-name cisco.com
!--- Fixup protocols are covered in Chapter 11.
fixup protocol ftp 21
fixup protocol h323 h225 1720
fixup protocol h323 ras 1718-1719
fixup protocol http 80
fixup protocol ils 389
fixup protocol rsh 514
fixup protocol rtsp 554
fixup protocol sip 5060
fixup protocol sip udp 5060
fixup protocol skinny 2000
fixup protocol smtp 25
fixup protocol sqlnet 1521
names
pager lines 24
mtu outside 1500
mtu inside 1500
!--- The outside interface is configured for PPPoE. Refer to Chapter 5
!--- for information on this command.
ip address outside pppoe setroute
ip address inside 10.0.1.1 255.255.255.0
!--- PIX Firewall IDS capabilities and configuration procedures are presented in
!--- Chapter 12 PIX Firewall IDS rules are defined in the next two statements.
ip audit name attack-rule attack action alarm drop reset
ip audit name info-rule info action alarm
!--- Defined IDS rules are then applied to the interfaces.
```

Example 4-4   *Home Office Network Configuration (Continued)*

```
ip audit interface outside info-rule
ip audit interface outside attack-rule
ip audit interface inside info-rule
ip audit interface inside attack-rule
ip audit info action alarm
ip audit attack action alarm
!--- Ip verify reverse-path statements protect against IP spoofing attacks.
ip verify reverse-path interface outside
!--- PDM adds host information automatically.
pdm location 10.0.1.215 255.255.255.255 inside
pdm history enable
arp timeout 14400
!--- NAT and PAT are covered in Chapter 7.
!--- Global address pool is defined for PAT using the IP address of the interface.
global (outside) 10 interface
!--- All hosts behind the PIX are translated using the global address pool 10.
nat (inside) 10 0.0.0.0 0.0.0.0 0 0
timeout xlate 3:00:00
timeout conn 1:00:00 half-closed 0:10:00 udp 0:02:00 rpc 0:10:00 h225 1:00:00
timeout h323 0:05:00 mgcp 0:05:00 sip 0:30:00 sip_media 0:02:00
timeout uauth 0:05:00 absolute
aaa-server TACACS+ protocol tacacs+
aaa-server RADIUS protocol radius
aaa-server LOCAL protocol local
!--- PDM is enabled for hosts on the inside interface. Chapter 6
!--- covers PDM features and configuration procedures.
http server enable
http 10.0.1.0 255.255.255.0 inside
no snmp-server location
no snmp-server contact
snmp-server community public
no snmp-server enable traps
floodguard enable
telnet timeout 5
ssh timeout 5
!--- The inside interface is configured for management. This allows remote
  management of
!--- the PIX 501 by administrators at the central site. This is a PIX Firewall
  software
!--- version 6.3 feature.
management-access inside
console timeout 0
!--- PPPoE settings are configured here. Refer to Chapter 5
!--- for details on PPPoE configuration.
vpdn group pppoe_group request dialout pppoe
!--- Username, password, and the PPP authentication protocol are defined.
vpdn group pppoe_group localname MYUSERNAME
vpdn group pppoe_group ppp authentication pap
vpdn username MYUSERNAME password *********
!--- DHCP configuration follows. Chapter 5 covers DHCP-related commands.
!--- The DHCP address range is defined
dhcpd address 10.0.1.200-10.0.1.225 inside
```

continues

Example 4-4 *Home Office Network Configuration (Continued)*

```
!--- Client settings for DNS and WINS are set (pointing back to central site)
dhcpd dns 192.168.100.10 192.168.100.11
dhcpd wins 1192.168.100.20 192.168.100.21
dhcpd lease 3600
dhcpd ping_timeout 750
dhcpd domain cisco.com
dhcpd enable inside
!--- The PIX is configured as an Easy VPN client connecting to a server at
  192.168.100.2
vpnclient server 192.168.100.2
!--- Network extension mode is specified. This allows administrators at a central
  site
!--- to access hosts behind the PIX Firewall for management.
vpnclient mode network-extension-mode
vpnclient vpngroup MYGROUP password ********
vpnclient username MYUSER password ********
vpnclient enable
terminal width 80
Cryptochecksum:7fe4a3b41876dcc126cbdb8e4c00adfd
: end
[OK]
```

Summary

This section summarizes the information you learned in this chapter:

- Network security begins with using a sound security plan and policy that correspond to your business requirements.

- The security plan should be living document. You should review and revise the plan as necessary, at least on an annual basis.

- You should implement a layered security plan that deploys several security measures, such as
  - AAA
  - VPNs
  - SSL encryption of web traffic
  - SSH for secure remote management of network devices and servers
  - Firewalls
  - IDSs
  - Cisco IOS routers with ACLs or a firewall feature set
  - DMZs

- You should use DMZs to host services accessible on the Internet.

- You should select the appropriate devices, including PIX Firewalls, based on the specific requirements of your security plan.

Chapter Review Questions

To test what you have learned in this chapter, answer the following questions and then refer to Appendix A, "Answers to Chapter Review Questions," for the answers:

1 How often should you review and revise your security plan?

2 What does *layered security* mean?

3 What types of security measures can you use in a layered security plan?

4 If your security plan requires high-availability firewalls, which models of the PIX Firewall should you not use?

5 What is the function of a DMZ?

PART III

Firewall Configuration Topics

On completion of this chapter, you will be able to perform the following tasks:

- Describe the PIX Firewall access modes.
- Navigate the PIX Firewall's user interface and examine the PIX Firewall's status.
- Describe the Adaptive Security Algorithm (ASA) security levels.
- Describe and execute the basic configuration commands.
- Configure the PIX Firewall to send syslog messages to a syslog server.
- Configure the PIX Firewall as a Dynamic Host Configuration Protocol (DHCP) client.
- Describe the PIX Firewall's DHCP server feature.
- Configure the PIX Firewall's Point-to-Point Protocol over Ethernet (PPPoE) client.

CHAPTER 5

Getting Started with the Cisco PIX Firewall

Previous chapters provided information on the PIX Firewall technologies, the benefits they provide, and the specific capabilities of each PIX Firewall model. This chapter presents basic command-line interface (CLI) configuration procedures and commands. You also learn about the basic tasks for configuring and monitoring PIX Firewalls.

CLI

The PIX Firewall contains a command set based on the Cisco IOS and provides four administrative access modes:

- **Unprivileged mode**—This mode, also referred to as the user mode, is available when you first access the PIX Firewall. It displays the > prompt. This mode enables you to view restricted settings.

- **Privileged mode**—This mode displays the # prompt and enables you to change the current settings. Any unprivileged command also works in privileged mode.

- **Configuration mode**—This mode displays the **(config)#** prompt and enables you to change system configurations. All privileged, unprivileged, and configuration commands work in this mode.

- **Monitor mode**—This special mode enables you to update the image over the network. While in the monitor mode, you can enter commands specifying the location of the Trivial File Transfer Protocol (TFTP) server and the binary image to download.

Within each access mode, you can abbreviate most commands down to the fewest unique characters for a command. For example, you can enter **write t** to view the configuration instead of entering the full command **write terminal**. You can enter **en** instead of **enable** to start privileged mode and **co t** instead of **configuration terminal** to start configuration mode.

You can obtain help information from the PIX Firewall command line by entering **help** or **?** to list all commands. If you enter **?** after a command (for example, **route?**), the command syntax is listed. If you enter **help** before a command (for example, **help nameif**), the command description and syntax is listed. The number of commands listed when you use the question mark or help command differs by access mode so that unprivileged mode offers the least commands and configuration mode offers the greatest number of commands. In addition, you can enter any command by itself on the command line and then press **Enter** to view the command syntax.

NOTE	A nice feature of the PIX Firewall CLI environment relative to Cisco IOS routers is that you can perform all functions while in the configuration mode. So unlike IOS routers, you don't need to exit from the configuration mode to list the running or currently saved configuration. You can also use all the show and debug commands while in configuration mode.

NOTE	You can create your configuration on a text editor and then cut and paste it into the configuration. You can paste the configuration in a line at a time or the entire configuration at once. Always check your configuration after pasting large blocks of text to be sure everything was copied correctly.

Basic Commands

To get started with the PIX Firewall, the first command you need to know is the **enable** command. It provides entrance to the privileged access modes. After you enter **enable**, the PIX Firewall prompts you for your privileged mode password. By default, a password is not required, so you can press **Enter** at the password prompt, or you can create a password of your choice. When you are in privileged mode, notice that the prompt changes to **#**.

The **enable password** command sets the privileged mode password. The password is case sensitive and can be from 3 to 16 alphanumeric characters long. You can use any character except the question mark, space, and colon.

If you create a password, write it down and store it in a manner consistent with your site's security policy. After you create this password, you cannot view it again because it is encrypted. The **show enable password** command lists the encrypted form of the password. After passwords are encrypted, they cannot be reversed back to plaintext.

The syntax for the **enable** commands is as follows:

```
enable [priv_level]
enable password pw [level priv_level] [encrypted]
```

Table 5-1 describes the **enable** command arguments.

Table 5-1   enable *Command Arguments*

Argument	Definition
priv_level	The privilege level, from 0 to 15
pw	A case-sensitive password of 3 to 16 alphanumeric characters
encrypted	Specifies that the password you entered is already encrypted

NOTE   An empty password is also changed into an encrypted string.

Use the **configure terminal** command to move from privileged mode to configuration mode. As soon as you enter the command, the prompt changes to **(config)#**, as shown in Example 5-1. Use the **exit** or **quit** command to exit and return to the previous mode.

Example 5-1   **configure terminal** *Command*

```
pixfirewall# configure terminal
pixfirewall(config)# exit
pixfirewall# exit
pixfirewall>
```

The **hostname** command changes the host-name label on the prompts. The host name can be up to 16 alphanumeric uppercase and lowercase characters. The default host name is pixfirewall.

The syntax for the **hostname** command is as follows:

hostname *newname*

Configuring the PIX Firewall

When a nonconfigured PIX Firewall boots up, it prompts you to preconfigure it through interactive prompts. If you press **Enter** to accept the default answer of yes, you see a series of prompts that lead you through the basic configuration steps. Example 5-2 demonstrates a typical interactive session and how to respond to the prompts.

Example 5-2   *Setup Interactive Dialog*

```
pixfirewall (config)# setup
Pre-configure PIX Firewall now through interactive prompts [yes]? <Enter>
Enable Password [<use current password>]: ciscopix
Clock (UTC)
  Year [2003]: <Enter>
  Month [Aug]: <Enter>
  Day [27]: 12
  Time [22:47:37]: 14:22:00
Inside IP address: 10.0.1.1
Inside network mask: 255.255.255.0
Host name: pixfirewall
Domain name: cisco.com
IP address of host running PIX Device Manager: 10.0.1.11
Use this configuration and write to flash? Y
```

The setup dialog was designed to preconfigure the PIX Firewall to interact with the PIX Device Manager (PDM). PDM is a GUI that you can use to configure and monitor the PIX Firewall, and Chapter 6, "Cisco PIX Device Manager," discusses it in detail.

NOTE   With the exception of a few unsupported commands (which are seldom used), the PDM provides an easy-to-use interface and ample capability to configure and manage a single PIX Firewall. You might want to consider the PDM as the primary management tool for your PIX Firewall installation.

You can also access the setup dialog by entering the **setup** command. The following are the prompts in the setup dialog:

- **Enable password**—Specifies an enable password for this PIX Firewall.
- **Clock (UTC)**—Sets the PIX Firewall clock to universal coordinated time (also known as Greenwich mean time).
- **Year**—Specifies the current year, or defaults to the year stored in the host computer.
- **Month**—Specifies the current month, or defaults to the month stored in the host computer.
- **Day**—Specifies the current day, or defaults to the day stored in the host computer.
- **Time**—Specifies the current time in hh:mm:ss format, or defaults to the time stored in the host computer.
- **Inside IP address**—Network interface IP address of the PIX Firewall.
- **Inside network mask**—A network mask that applies to the inside IP address.
- **Host name**—The host name you want to display in the PIX Firewall CLI prompt.
- **Domain name**—The Domain Name System (DNS) domain name of the network on which the PIX Firewall runs (for example, example.com).
- **IP address of host running PIX Device Manager**—IP address on which PDM connects to the PIX Firewall.

At the end of the setup dialog, you are asked whether you want to write the configuration to Flash memory. If you answer yes, the configuration you just entered is saved to Flash memory. If you answer no, the setup dialog repeats, using the values already entered as the defaults for the questions.

NOTE   You can escape the setup dialog by pressing **Ctrl-Z**.

Viewing and Saving Your Configuration

The **show running-config** command displays the current configuration in the PIX Firewall's RAM on the terminal. You can also display the current running configuration with the **write terminal** command.

The **show running-config** and **show startup-config** commands are available on PIX Firewalls running Software Version 6.2 or later.

The **write memory** command saves the current running configuration to Flash memory. It is the same as answering yes to the setup dialog prompt that asks whether you want to save the current configuration to Flash memory. When the configuration is written to Flash memory, you can view it with either the **show startup-config** or **show configure** command.

Another useful command is **show history**, which displays previously entered commands. You can examine commands individually with the up and down arrows or by entering **^p** to view previously entered lines or **^n** to view the next line.

write erase and tftp-server Commands

The **write erase** command clears the Flash memory configuration. When you issue this command, you are prompted to confirm whether you want to erase the configuration:

```
pixfirewall(config)# write erase
Erase PIX configuration in Flash memory? [confirm]
```

The **tftp-server** command enables you to specify the IP address of a TFTP server that you use to propagate PIX Firewall configuration files to your PIX Firewalls. Use the **tftp-server** command with the **configure net** command to read from the configuration or with the **write net** command to store the configuration in the file you specify.

The path name you specify in **tftp-server** is appended to the end of the IP address you specify in the **configure net** and **write net** commands. The more you specify of a file and path name with the **tftp-server** command, the less you need to specify with the **configure net** and **write net** commands. If you specify the full path and filename in the **tftp-server** command, the IP address in the **configure net** and **write net** commands can be represented with a colon (**:**).

The **no tftp server** command disables access to the server, and the **clear tftp-server** command removes the **tftp-server** command from your configuration. The **show tftp-server** command lists the **tftp-server** command statements in the current configuration.

The syntax for the **tftp-server** command is as follows:

```
tftp-server [if_name] ip_address path
```

Table 5-2 describes the **tftp-server** command arguments.

Table 5-2   **tftp-server** *Command Arguments*

Argument	Definition
if_name	Interface name on which the TFTP server resides. If not specified, an internal interface is assumed. If you specify the outside interface, a warning message informs you that the outside interface is unsecure.
ip_address	The IP address or network of the TFTP server.
path	The path and filename of the configuration file. The format for path differs by the type of operating system on the server. The contents of path are passed directly to the server without interpretation or checking. The configuration file must exist on the TFTP server. Many TFTP servers require the configuration file to be world-writable to write to it and world-readable to read from it.

NOTE   The PIX Firewall supports only one TFTP server.

NOTE   If you erase the configuration, you must re-enable and set an IP address on the interface connected to the TFTP server before the PIX Firewall can read a new configuration from the TFTP server.

write net and configure net Commands

The **write net** command enables you to store the current configuration to a file on a TFTP server elsewhere in the network. The **configure net** command merges the current running configuration with the TFTP configuration stored at the IP address you specify and from the file you name. If you specify both the IP address and full path in the **tftp-server** command, the *server_ip* and filename in the **configure net** and **write net** commands can be omitted or represented with a colon (**:**).

If you have an existing PIX Firewall configuration on a TFTP server and store a shorter configuration with the same filename on the TFTP server, some TFTP servers leave some of the original configuration after the first "end" mark. This does not affect the PIX Firewall because the **configure net** command stops reading when it reaches the first "end" mark. However, it might cause confusion if you view the configuration and see extra text at the end of the configuration. This issue does not arise if you are using Cisco TFTP Server Version 1.1 for Windows NT.

Example 5-3 shows the commands required to specify the TFTP server address as 10.0.0.11 and the path to the file test_config as **pixfirewall/config**. Because the interface where the

TFTP server resides is not specified, the inside interface is assumed. The **configure net** command tells the PIX to read the configuration file named **test_config** and merge it with the current running configuration. The **write net** command tells the PIX Firewall to store the resulting configuration in the **test_config** file. (The file is overwritten in this case.)

Example 5-3   write net *Command Example*

```
pixfirewall(config)# tftp-server 10.0.0.11 pixfirewall/config/test_config
pixfirewall(config)# Configure net :
pixfirewall(config)# write net :
```

NOTE   To view the saved configuration file more easily, name the configuration file with an **.rtf** extension. You can then open the file using Microsoft Word or WordPad application by default, displaying the configuration file properly.

The syntax for the **write net** and **configure net** commands is as follows:

```
write net [server_ip]:[filename]
configure net [server_ip]:[filename]
```

Table 5-3 describes the **write net** and **configure net** command arguments.

Table 5-3   write net *and* configure net *Command Arguments*

Argument	Definition
server_ip	The IP address of a TFTP host available across the network. If you specify a server with the **tftp-server** command, do not specify it in the **write** command; instead use only a colon (**:**) without a server IP address.
filename	A filename you specify to qualify the location of the configuration file on the TFTP server named in *server_ip*. If you set a filename with the **tftp-server** command, do not specify it in the **write** command; instead use only a colon (**:**) without a filename.

name Command

The **name** command enables you to configure a list of name-to-IP-address mappings on the PIX Firewall. This process lets you use names in the configuration instead of IP addresses.

The syntax for the **name** command is as follows:

```
name ip_address name
```

Table 5-4 describes the **name** command arguments.

Table 5-4   **name** *Command Arguments*

Argument	Definition
ip_address	The IP address of the host being named
name	The name assigned to the IP address

Allowable characters for the name are a to z, A to Z, 0 to 9, a dash (-), and an underscore (_). The name cannot start with a number. If the name is more than 16 characters long, the **name** command fails. After the name is defined, you can use it in any PIX Firewall command reference in place of an IP address. The **names** command enables the use of the **name** command. You must first use the **names** command before using the **name** command. The **clear names** command clears the list of names from the PIX Firewall configuration. The **no names** command disables the use of the text names but does not remove them from the configuration. The **show names** command lists the **name** command statements in the configuration.

For example, to assign the name mailserver to host 172.16.0.2, you issue the following command:

```
pixfirewall(config)# name 172.16.0.2 mailserver
```

You can remove or disable most commands by placing the word **no** in front of the command. For example, the **no** form of the **names** command shown previously disables the use of names. Another method for removing a configured command is the **clear** command. The **clear** command typically removes all commands that begin with the same command. For example, if there are five **name** commands in a configuration, the **clear name** command remove all five **name** commands.

reload Command

The **reload** command reboots the PIX Firewall and reloads the configuration from Flash memory. You are prompted for confirmation before the reload process begins with the prompt "Proceed with reload?" Any response other than **Y** causes the reload to be canceled.

Configuration changes not written to Flash memory are lost after reload. Before rebooting, store the current configuration in Flash memory with the **write memory** command.

The **noconfirm** option permits the PIX Firewall to reload without user confirmation. The PIX Firewall does not accept abbreviations to the keyword **noconfirm**.

Examining the PIX Firewall Status

The **show** command enables you to view command information. Several **show** commands display system information. You can enter either **show** or **?** to view the names of the **show** commands and their descriptions.

show memory

The **show memory** command displays a summary of the maximum physical memory and current free memory available to the PIX Firewall operating system.

NOTE   Unlike with the Cisco IOS CLI environment, you can issue any of the **show** commands while you are still in the configuration mode of the PIX Firewall. This option is a useful way to verify settings as you configure the PIX Firewall.

---

show version

Use the **show version** command to display the PIX Firewall's software version, operating time since the last reboot, processor type, Flash memory type, interface boards, serial number (BIOS identification), and activation key value.

The serial number listed with the **show version** command in PIX Firewall Software Version 5.3 and higher is for the Flash memory BIOS. This number is different from the serial number on the chassis. To obtain a software upgrade, you need the serial number that appears in the **show version** command, not the chassis number.

Example 5-4 demonstrates the output of the **show version** command for PIX Firewall Software Version 6.2 and higher.

Example 5-4   **show version** *Command Output*

```
pixfirewall# sh ver

Cisco PIX Firewall Version 6.3(3)
Cisco PIX Device Manager Version 3.0(1)

Compiled on Wed 13-Aug-03 13:55 by morlee
pixfirewall up 21 days 4 hours

Hardware:   PIX-506E, 32 MB RAM, CPU Pentium II 300 MHz
Flash E28F640J3 @ 0x300, 8MB
BIOS Flash AM29F400B @ 0xfffd8000, 32KB

0: ethernet0: address is 0009.438a.8096, irq 10
1: ethernet1: address is 0009.438a.8097, irq 11
Licensed Features:
```

continues

Example 5-4   **show version** *Command Output (Continued)*

```
Failover:           Disabled
VPN-DES:            Enabled
VPN-3DES-AES:       Enabled
Maximum Interfaces: 2
Cut-through Proxy:  Enabled
Guards:             Enabled
URL-filtering:      Enabled
Inside Hosts:       Unlimited
Throughput:         Unlimited
IKE peers:          Unlimited

This PIX has a Restricted (R) license.

Serial Number: 444444444 (0x18351565)
Running Activation Key: 0x44251663 0x93bb73e2 0x118a6aa7 0xcce0fdd9
Configuration last modified by enable_15 at 22:25:20.885 UTC Sun Jul 13 2003
```

show ip address

The **show ip address** command enables you to view which IP addresses are assigned to the network interfaces. The current IP addresses are the same as the system IP addresses on the failover active firewall. When the active firewall fails, the current IP addresses become that of the standby firewall.

Example 5-5 shows the output of the **show ip address** command for a PIX Firewall with five interfaces.

Example 5-5   **show ip address** *Command Output*

```
pixfirewall# show ip address
System IP Addresses:
        ip address outside 192.168.0.2 255.255.255.0
        ip address inside 10.0.1.1 255.255.255.0
        ip address DMZ1 172.16.0.2 255.255.255.0
        ip address DMZ3 172.20.0.2 255.255.255.0
        ip address DMZ2 172.18.0.2 255.255.255.0
Current IP Addresses:
        ip address outside 192.168.0.2 255.255.255.0
        ip address inside 10.0.1.1 255.255.255.0
        ip address DMZ1 172.16.0.2 255.255.255.0
        ip address DMZ3 172.20.0.2 255.255.255.0
        ip address DMZ2 172.18.0.2 255.255.255.0
```

show interface Command

The **show interface** command enables you to view network interface information and is useful for determining physical connectivity problems such as duplex mismatches. This command is one of the first commands you should use when trying to establish connectivity. Example 5-6 shows the output of the **show interface** command for a physical (DMZ1) and a logical (DMZ2) interface:

NOTE   PIX Firewall Versions 6.3 or higher support logical interfaces using the 802.1Q VLAN
protocol.

Example 5-6 show interface *Command Output*

```
interface ethernet2 "DMZ1" is up, line protocol is up
  Hardware is i82559 ethernet, address is 0002.b31f.74b5
  IP address 172.16.0.2, subnet mask 255.255.255.0
  MTU 1500 bytes, BW 100000 Kbit full duplex
        91 packets input, 5937 bytes, 0 no buffer
        Received 91 broadcasts, 0 runts, 0 giants
        0 input errors, 0 CRC, 0 frame, 0 overrun, 0 ignored, 0 abort
        3 packets output, 180 bytes, 0 underruns
        0 output errors, 0 collisions, 0 interface resets
        0 babbles, 0 late collisions, 0 deferred
        0 lost carrier, 0 no carrier
        input queue (curr/max blocks): hardware (128/128) software (0/1)
        output queue (curr/max blocks): hardware (0/1) software (0/1)
        0 aggregate VLAN packets input, 0 bytes
        2 aggregate VLAN packets output, 92 bytes
        91 native VLAN packets input, 5937 bytes
        1 native VLAN packets output, 42 bytes
        0 invalid VLAN ID errors
interface vlan5 "DMZ2" is up, line protocol is up
  Hardware is i82559 ethernet, address is 0002.b31f.74b5
  IP address 172.18.0.2, subnet mask 255.255.255.0
  MTU 1500 bytes, BW 100000 Kbit full duplex
        0 packets input, 0 bytes
        1 packets output, 46 bytes
```

The following are explanations of the information that appears after you enter the **show
interface** command:

- **Interface**—Identifies the interface and the name assigned to the interface. In Example
  5-6, the first interface is ethernet2 (a physical interface) with an assigned name of
  DMZ1, and the second interface is vlan5 (a logical interface) with an assigned name
  of DMZ2. Status of each interface is also displayed as available ("up") or not available
  ("down").

- **Line protocol up**—A working cable is plugged into the network interface.

- **Line protocol down**—Either the cable plugged into the network interface is
  incorrect, or it is not plugged into the interface connector.

- **Network interface type**—Identifies the network interface. In this example, the
  interface type is Ethernet. The type of network card is also identified (i82559 in this
  case). Intel cards begin with "i" and 3Com cards begin with "3c."

- **MAC address**—Displays the MAC address of the physical card. Note that logical interfaces have the same MAC address as the physical interface they are configured on.

- **MTU (maximum transmission unit)**—The size in bytes that data can best be sent over the network.

- **Packets input**—Indicates that packets are being received in the PIX Firewall.

- **Packets output**—Indicates that packets are being sent from the PIX Firewall.

- **VLAN packet input**—Displays aggregate or native VLAN (802.1Q tagged) packets coming into the interface.

- **VLAN packet output**—Displays aggregate or native VLAN (802.1Q tagged) packets coming out of the interface.

- **Line duplex status**—Indicates whether the PIX Firewall is running either full duplex (simultaneous packet transmission) or half duplex (alternating packet transmission).

- **Line speed**—10BASE-T is listed as 10,000 kilobits (Kb). 100BASE-TX is listed as 100,000 Kb.

As shown in Example 5-6, logical interfaces display an abbreviated output for the **show interface** command. The packet input and packet output counters on logical interfaces are based on the native VLAN traffic on that interface.

The following are explanations of **show interface** command output that can indicate interface problems:

- **No buffer**—Indicates the PIX Firewall is out of memory or slowed down due to heavy traffic and cannot keep up with the received data.

- **Runts**—Packets with less information than expected.

- **Giants**—Packets with more information than expected.

- **CRC (cyclic redundancy check)**—Packets that contain corrupted data (checksum error).

- **Frame errors**—Indicates framing errors.

- **Ignored and aborted errors**—This information is provided for future use but is not currently checked; the PIX Firewall does not ignore or abort frames.

- **Underruns**—Occurs when the PIX Firewall is overwhelmed and cannot get data fast enough to the network interface card (NIC).

- **Overruns**—Occurs when the NIC is overwhelmed and cannot buffer received information before more needs to be sent.

- **Unicast rpf drops**—Occurs when packets sent to a single network destination using reverse path forwarding are dropped.

- **Output errors**—(Maximum collisions.) The number of frames not transmitted because the configured maximum number of collisions was exceeded. This counter should increment only during heavy network traffic.

- **Collisions**—(Single and multiple collisions.) The number of messages retransmitted due to an Ethernet collision. This retransmission usually occurs on an overextended LAN when the Ethernet or transceiver cable is too long, there are more than two repeaters between stations, or there are too many cascaded multiport transceivers. A packet that collides is counted only once by the output packets.

- **Interface resets**—The number of times an interface has been reset. If an interface is unable to transmit for 3 seconds, the PIX Firewall resets the interface to restart transmission. During this interval, the connection state is maintained. An interface reset can also happen when an interface is looped back or shut down.

- **Babbles**—The transmitter has been on the interface longer than the time taken to transmit the largest frame. This counter is unused.

- **Late collisions**—The number of frames that were not transmitted because a collision occurred outside the normal collision window. A late collision is a collision that is detected late in the transmission of the packet. Normally, these should never happen. When two Ethernet hosts try to talk at once, they should collide early in the packet and both back off, or the second host should see that the first one is talking and wait.

  If you get a late collision, a device is jumping in and trying to send on the Ethernet while the PIX Firewall is partly finished sending the packet. The PIX Firewall does not resend the packet because it might have freed the buffers that held the first part of the packet. This scenario is not a real problem because networking protocols are designed to cope with collisions by resending packets. However, late collisions indicate that a problem exists in your network. Common problems are large repeated networks and Ethernet networks running beyond the specification:

- **Deferred**—The number of frames that were deferred before transmission due to activity on the link.

- **Lost carrier**—The number of times the carrier signal was lost during transmission.

- **No carrier**—This counter is unused.

- **Input queue**—The input (receive) hardware and software queue.

- **Hardware**—(Current and maximum blocks.) The number of blocks currently present on the input hardware queue and the maximum number of blocks previously present on that queue.

- **Software**—(Current and maximum blocks.) The number of blocks currently present on the input software queue and the maximum number of blocks previously present on that queue.

- **Output queue**—The output (transmit) hardware and software queue.

- **Hardware**—(Current and maximum blocks.) The number of blocks currently present on the output hardware queue and the maximum number of blocks previously present on that queue.

- **Software**—(Current and maximum blocks.) The number of blocks currently present on the output software queue and the maximum number of blocks previously present on that queue.

NOTE   The following counters are only valid for Ethernet interfaces: output errors, collisions, interface resets, babbles, late collisions, deferred, lost carrier, and no carrier.

NOTE   Starting with PIX Firewall Software Version 6.0(1), Fiber Distributed Data Interface (FDDI), Private Link 2 (PL2), and Token Ring interfaces are no longer supported.

---

show cpu usage Command

The **show cpu usage** command displays CPU use. In the following sample output for the **show cpu usage** command, **p1** is the percentage of CPU used for 5 seconds, **p2** is the average percentage of CPU use for 1 minute, and **p3** is the average percentage utilization for 5 minutes:

```
CPU utilization for 5 seconds: p1%; 1 minute: p2%; 5 minutes: p3%
```

The percentage of usage is shown as NA (not available) if the usage is not available for any of the time intervals. This can happen if the user asks for CPU usage before the 5-second, 1-second, or 5-minute time interval has elapsed.

ping Command

The **ping** command determines whether the PIX Firewall has connectivity or whether a host is available (visible to the PIX Firewall) on the network. The command output shows whether the ping was received. If the ping was received, then the host exists on the network. If the ping was not received, the command output displays "No response received." (At this time, you would use the **show interface** command to ensure that the PIX Firewall is connected to the network and is passing traffic.) By default, the **ping** command makes three attempts to reach an IP address, as shown in Example 5-7.

Example 5-7   **ping** *Output*

```
pixfirewall(config)# ping 10.0.0.11
10.0.0.11 response received -- 0Ms
10.0.0.11 response received -- 0Ms
10.0.0.11 response received -- 0Ms
```

If you want internal hosts to be able to ping external hosts, you must create an Internet Control Message Protocol (ICMP) conduit or access list for echo-reply. If you are pinging through the PIX Firewall between hosts or routers and the pings are not successful, use the **debug icmp trace** command to monitor the success of the ping.

After your PIX Firewall is configured and operational, you will not be able to ping the inside interface of the PIX Firewall from the outside network or from the outside interfaces of the PIX Firewall. If you can ping the inside networks from the inside interface and if you can ping the outside networks from the outside interface, the PIX Firewall is functioning normally and your routes are correct.

The syntax for the **ping** command is as follows:

```
ping [if_name] host
```

Table 5-5 describes the **ping** command arguments.

Table 5-5   **ping** *Command Arguments*

Argument	Definition
if_name	The network interface name. The address of the specified interface is used as the source address of the ping.
host	The name or IP address of the host being pinged.

Time Setting and NTP Support

The **clock** command sets the PIX Firewall clock. It enables you to specify the time, month, day, and year. The clock setting is retained in memory when the power is off by a battery on the PIX Firewall's motherboard. The PIX Firewall generates syslog messages for system events and can log these messages to a syslog server. If you want the messages to contain a timestamp value, you must enter the **logging timestamp** command. The **logging timestamp** command requires that the **clock set** command be used to ensure that the correct time appears on the syslog messages. Syslog and its corresponding commands are explained in another chapter.

It is also important to ensure that the clock is correctly set if you use Public Key Infrastructure (PKI), which uses digital certificates for authentication of virtual private network (VPN) peers. The Cisco PKI protocol uses the clock to make sure that a certificate revocation list (CRL) is not expired. Otherwise, the certificate authority (CA) might reject or allow certificates based on an incorrect timestamp. The lifetimes of certificates and CRLs are checked in UTC. If you are using certificates with IPSec for VPNs, set the PIX Firewall clock to UTC time zone to ensure that CRL checking works correctly. VPNs are discussed in greater detail in Chapter 15, "Virtual Private Networks."

You can view the time with the **show clock** command, which displays the time, time zone, day, and full date. You can remove the **clock set** command with the **clear clock** command.

The syntax for the **clock set** command is as follows:

```
clock set hh:mm:ss month day year
```

Table 5-6 describes the **clock set** command arguments.

Table 5-6   **clock set** *Command Arguments*

Argument	Definition
day	The day of the month to start, from 1 to 31.
hh:mm:ss	The hour:minutes:seconds expressed in 24-hour time (for example, 20:54:00 for 8:54 p.m.). Zeros can be entered as a single digit (for example, 21:0:0).
month	The month expressed as the first three characters of the month (for example, apr for April).
year	The year expressed as four digits (for example, 2000).

For example, to set the time and date on a PIX Firewall to 9:00 p.m. on August 10, 2003, you issue the following command:

```
pixfirewall(config)# clock set 21:0:0 aug 10 2003
```

Setting Daylight Savings Time and Time Zones

Although the PIX Firewall clock does not adjust itself for daylight savings time changes, you can configure it to display daylight savings time by using the **clock summer-time** command. The **summer-time** keyword causes the PIX Firewall to automatically switch to summer time (for display purposes only). The **recurring** keyword indicates that summer time should start and end on the days specified by the values that follow it. If no values are specified, the summer time rules default to United States rules.

You can also specify the exact date and times with the **date** version of the **clock summer-time** command. In the following example, daylight savings time (summer time) is configured to start on April 7, 2002 at 2 a.m. and end on October 27, 2002 at 2 a.m.:

```
pixfirewall (config)# clock summer-time PDT date 7 April 2002 2:00 27 October
   2002 2:00
```

Use the **clock timezone** command to set the time zone. The **clock timezone** command sets the time zone for display purposes only. Internally, the time is kept in UTC. The **no** form of the command is used to set the time zone to UTC. The **clear clock** command removes summer time settings and sets the time zone to UTC.

The syntax for the **clock** commands is as follows:

```
clock summer-time zone recurring [week weekday month hh:mm week weekday month hh:mm]
   [offset]
clock summer-time zone date {day month | month day} year hh:mm {day month | month day}
   year hh:mm [offset]
clock timezone zone hours [minutes]
show clock [detail]
```

Table 5-7 describes the **clock** command arguments.

Table 5-7   **clock** *Command Arguments*

Argument	Definition
summer-time	The **clock summer-time** command displays summertime hours during the specified summertime date range. This command affects the clock display time only.
zone	The name of the time zone.
recurring	Specifies the start and end dates for local summer "daylight savings" time. The first date entered is the start date and the second date entered is the end date. (The start date is relative to UTC and the end date is relative to the specified summer time zone.) If no dates are specified, United States daylight savings time is used. If the start date month is after the end date month, the summer time zone is accepted and assumed to be in the Southern Hemisphere.
week	Specifies the week of the month. Enter 1, 2, 3, or 4 to specify the first, second, third, or fourth week of the month. Use first or last to specify a partial week at the beginning or end of a month. For example, you specify week 5 of any month by using **last**.
weekday	Specifies the day of the week. Enter **Monday, Tuesday, Wednesday, Thursday, Friday, Saturday**, or **Sunday**.
month	Specifies the month. Enter the first three characters of the month (for example, **apr** for April).
hh:mm	The hour and minutes expressed in 24-hour time (for example, 20:54 for 8:54 p.m.). Zeros can be entered as a single digit (for example, 21:0).
offset	The number of minutes to add during summertime. The default is 60 minutes.
date	Used as an alternative to the recurring form of the **clock summer-time** command. It specifies that summertime should start on the first date entered and end on the second date entered. If the start date month is after the end date month, the summer time zone is accepted and assumed to be in the Southern Hemisphere.
day	The day of the month to start. Enter a number from 1 to 31.
year	The year expressed as 4 digits (for example, 2000). The year range supported for the **clock** command is 1993 to 2035.
timezone	The **clock timezone** command sets the clock display to the time zone specified. It does not change internal PIX Firewall time, which remains UTC.
hours	The hours of offset from UTC.
minutes	The minutes of offset from UTC.
detail	Displays the clock source and current summertime settings.

ntp Command

The **ntp server** command synchronizes the PIX Firewall with the network time server you specify. You can configure the PIX Firewall to require authentication before synchronizing with the NTP server. To enable and support authentication, several forms of the **ntp** command work with the **ntp server** command. The following are the **ntp** command forms and their uses:

- **ntp server**—Specifies an NTP server. The PIX Firewall listens for NTP packets (port 123) only on interfaces that have an NTP server configured. NTP packets that are not responses from a request by the PIX Firewall are dropped.

- **ntp authenticate**—Enables NTP authentication.

- **ntp authentication-key**—Defines the authentication keys for the **ntp** commands. If you use authentication, you must configure the PIX Firewall and NTP server with the same key.

- **ntp trusted-key**—Defines one or more key numbers that the NTP server needs to provide in its NTP packets for the PIX Firewall to accept synchronization with the NTP server. Use this command if NTP authentication is enabled.

You can use the **show ntp** command to display the current NTP configuration and the **show ntp status** command to display the NTP clock information. The **clear ntp** command removes the NTP configuration, including disabling authentication and removing all authentication keys and NTP server designations.

The syntax for the **ntp** commands is as follows:

```
ntp authenticate
ntp authentication-key number md5 value
ntp server ip_address [key number] source if_name [prefer]
ntp trusted-key number
```

Table 5-8 describes the **ntp** command arguments.

Table 5-8   **ntp** *Command Arguments*

Argument	Definition
authenticate	Enables NTP authentication. If enabled, the PIX Firewall requires authentication before synchronizing with an NTP server.
authentication-key	Defines the authentication keys for use with other NTP commands.
if_name	Specifies the interface to use to send packets to the network time server.
ip_address	The IP address of the network time server with which to synchronize.
key	Specifies the authentication key.
md5	The authentication algorithm.
number	The authentication key number (1 to 4,294,967,295).

Table 5-8   **ntp** *Command Arguments (Continued)*

Argument	Definition
prefer	Designates the network time server specified as the preferred server with which to synchronize time.
server	The network time server.
source	Specifies the network time source.
trusted-key	Specifies the trusted key against which to authenticate.
value	The key value, an arbitrary string of up to 32 characters. The key value appears as "***********" when you view the configuration with **write terminal** or **show tech-support**.

The following example specifies the NTP server at 10.0.0.12 on the inside interface as the preferred network time source for the PIX Firewall. An authentication key of 1234 is also specified:

```
pixfirewall(config)# ntp server 10.0.0.12 key 1234 source inside prefer
```

ASA Security Levels

The ASA is a stateful approach to security. Every inbound packet (the packet originating from a host on a less-protected network and destined for a host on a more-protected network) is checked against the ASA and against connection state information in the PIX Firewall's memory. Knowledge of the ASA is fundamental to implementing Internet access security because it performs the following tasks:

- Implements stateful connection control through the PIX Firewall.
- Allows one-way (outbound) connections without an explicit configuration for each internal system application. An outbound connection is a connection originating from a host on a more-protected interface and destined for a host on a less-protected network.
- Monitors return packets to ensure they are valid.
- Randomizes the initial TCP sequence number to minimize the risk of attack.

ASA maintains the secure perimeters between the networks controlled by the PIX Firewall. The stateful connection-oriented ASA design creates session flows based on source and destination addresses. ASA randomizes TCP sequence numbers, port numbers, and TCP flags before the completion of the connection. This function is always running and monitors return packets to ensure that they are valid.

The security level designates whether an interface is trusted (and more protected) or untrusted (and less protected) relative to another interface. An interface is considered trusted (and more protected) in relation to another interface if its security level is higher than the other interface's security level and is considered untrusted (and less protected) in relation to another interface if its security level is lower than the other interface's security level. This concept is demonstrated in Figure 5-1.

Figure 5-1 *ASA Security Levels*

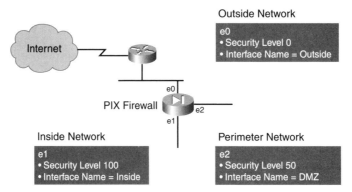

The primary rule for security levels is that an interface with a higher security level can access an interface with a lower security level. Conversely, an interface with a lower security level cannot access an interface with a higher security level without a conduit or an access control list (ACL), which is discussed later in the chapter. Security levels range from 0 to 100, and the following are more specific rules for these security levels:

- **Security level 100**—This level is the highest security level for the inside interface of the PIX Firewall. This setting is the default setting for the PIX Firewall and cannot be changed. Because 100 is the most trusted interface security level, you should set up your corporate network behind it so that no one else can access it unless they are specifically given permission and so that every device behind this interface can have access outside the corporate network.

- **Security level 0**—This level is the lowest security level for the outside interface of the PIX Firewall. This setting is the default setting for the PIX Firewall and cannot be changed. Because 0 is the least-trusted interface security level, you should set your most untrusted network behind this interface so that it does not have access to other interfaces unless it is specifically given permission. This interface is usually used for your Internet connection.

- **Security levels 1–99**—These are the security levels that you can assign to the perimeter interfaces connected to the PIX Firewall. You assign the security levels based on the type of access you want each device to have.

The following are examples of different interface connections between the PIX Firewall and other perimeter devices:

- **More secure interface (the higher security level) to a less secure interface (the lower security level)**—Traffic originating from the inside interface of the PIX Firewall with a security level of 100 to the outside interface of the PIX Firewall with a security level of 0 follows this rule: allow all IP-based traffic unless restricted by ACLs, authentication, or authorization.

NOTE	Although default security settings on the PIX Firewall allow traffic from higher-security-level interfaces to lower-security interfaces, you must configure translation to allow traffic through the PIX. To do so, you can use the **global** and **nat** commands, the **static** command, or the **nat 0** (to allow traffic without address translation) command.

- **Less secure interface (lower security level) to a more secure interface (higher security level)**—Traffic originating from the outside interface of the PIX Firewall with a security level of 0 to the inside interface of the PIX Firewall with a security level of 100 follows this rule: drop all packets unless specifically allowed by the **conduit** or **access list** command. Further restrict the traffic if authentication and authorization is used.
- **Same secure interface to a same secure interface**—No traffic flows between two interfaces with the same security level.

Table 5-9 explains the diagram in Figure 5-1.

Table 5-9   *ASA Security Level Example*

Interface Pair	Relative Interface Relationship for Ethernet 2 (Demilitarized Zone [DMZ]) Interface	Configuration Guidelines
Outside security 0 to DMZ security 50	DMZ is considered trusted	**Statics** and **ACLs** must be configured to enable sessions originating from the outside interface to the DMZ interface.
Inside security 100 to DMZ security 50	DMZ is considered untrusted	**Globals** and **nat** are configured to enable sessions originating from the inside interface to the DMZ interface. **Statics** may be configured for the DMZ interface to ensure service hosts have the same source address.

Basic PIX Firewall Configuration

You can use the PDM or the CLI interface to perform basic configuration of the PIX Firewall. Configuration procedures using the PDM are covered in detail in Chapter 6. This section covers the basic configuration commands and procedures using the CLI interface.

The following are some of the primary configuration commands for the PIX Firewall:

- **nameif**—Assigns a name to each perimeter interface and specifies its security level
- **interface**—Configures the type and capability of each perimeter interface
- **ip address**—Assigns an IP address to each interface
- **nat**—Shields IP addresses on the inside network from the outside network
- **global**—Shields IP addresses on the inside network from the outside network using a pool of IP addresses
- **route**—Defines a static or default route for an interface

nameif Command

The command **nameif** assigns a name to each perimeter physical or logical interface on the PIX Firewall and specifies its security level (except for the inside and outside PIX Firewall interfaces, which are named by default). The syntax for the **nameif** commands is as follows:

```
nameif {hardware_id | vlan_id} if_name security_level
clear nameif
show nameif
```

Table 5-10 describes the **nameif** command arguments.

Table 5-10   **nameif** *Command Arguments*

Argument	Definition
hardware_id	Specifies a perimeter interface and its slot location on the PIX Firewall.
	There are 3 interfaces that you can enter here: Ethernet, FDDI, or Token Ring. Each interface is represented by an alphanumeric identifier based on which interface it is and what numeric identifier you choose to give it. For example, an Ethernet interface is represented as e1, e2, e3, and so on; a FDDI interface is represented as fddi1, fddi2, fddi3, and so on; and a Token Ring interface is represented as token-ring1, token-ring2, and token-ring3, and so on.
vlan_id	The VLAN identifier. For example: vlan10, vlan20, and so on. (*vlan_id* is configured with the **interface** command, discussed in the next subsection.)
if_name	Describes the perimeter interface. This name is assigned by you and must be used in all future configuration references to the perimeter interface.
security_level	Indicates the security level for the perimeter interface. Enter a security level of 1–99.

NOTE	Depending on the model and license, PIX Firewalls running Version 6.3 or higher can have up to 22 perimeter networks for a total of 24 interfaces. This number includes physical and logical (802.1Q VLAN) interfaces.

NOTE	PIX Firewall 501 and 501E models do not provide support for logical interface and VLANS.

For example, the following command assigns a name of "dmz" and a security level of 50 to interface ethernet2:

```
pixfirewall(config)# nameif ethernet2 dmz sec50
```

interface Command

The **interface** command identifies hardware, sets its hardware speed, and enables the interface. The **shutdown** option disables an interface. When you first install the PIX Firewall, all interfaces are shut down by default. You must explicitly enable them by entering the **interface** command without the **shutdown** option.

The syntax for the **interface** commands is as follows:

```
interface hardware_id [hardware_speed] [shutdown]
interface hardware_id vlan_id [logical | physical] [shutdown]
interface hardware_id change-vlan old_vlan_id new_vlan_id
clear interface
```

Table 5-11 describes the **interface** command arguments.

Table 5-11   **interface** *Command Arguments*

Argument	Definition
change-vlan	Keyword to change the VLAN identifier for an interface.
hardware_id	Specifies an interface and its slot location on the PIX Firewall. This variable is the same variable that was used during the **nameif** command.

continues

Table 5-11   **interface** *Command Arguments (Continued)*

Argument	Definition
hardware_speed	Determines the connection speed. Possible Ethernet values are as follow:
	10baset—Set for 10-Mbps Ethernet half-duplex communication.
	10full—Set for 10-Mbps Ethernet full-duplex communication.
	100basetx—Set for 100-Mbps Ethernet half-duplex communication.
	100full—Set for 100-Mbps Ethernet full-duplex communication.
	1000sxfull—Set for 1000-Mbps Gigabit Ethernet full-duplex operation.
	1000basesx—Set for 1000-Mbps Gigabit Ethernet half-duplex operation.
	1000auto—Set for 1000-Mbps Gigabit Ethernet to auto-negotiate full or half duplex. It is recommended that you do not use this option to maintain compatibility with switches and other devices in your network. **aui**—Set 10 for Mbps Ethernet half-duplex communication with an attachment unit interface (AUI) cable interface.
	auto—Set Ethernet speed automatically. You can only use the **auto** keyword with the Intel 10/100 automatic speed-sensing NIC.
	bnc—Set for 10-Mbps Ethernet half-duplex communication with a (BNC) cable interface.
	Possible Token Ring values are as follow (not available with PIX Firewall Version 6.0 or higher):
	4mbps—4-Mbps data transfer speed. You can specify this as 4.
	16mbps—(Default) 16-Mbps data transfer speed. You can specify this as 16.
logical	Creates a logical interface and applies the VLAN.
new_vlan_id	The new VLAN identifier.
old_vlan_id	The current VLAN identifier.
physical	Applies VLAN to physical interface.
vlan_id	The VLAN identifier. For example: vlan10, vlan20, and so on.
shutdown	Administratively shuts down the interface.

NOTE   Logical interfaces and VLAN configuration are available only on supported models with PIX Firewall Version 6.3 or higher. Firewall Services Module (FWSM) also supports logical interfaces. FWSM is covered in Chapter 21, "Firewall Services Module."

Although the hardware speed is set to automatic speed sensing by default, that you should specify the speed of the network interfaces. This setting enables the PIX Firewall to operate in network environments that might include switches or other devices that do not handle autosensing correctly.

When you install a FDDI or Token Ring interface card using the **interface** command, you must define the FDDI or Token Ring interface card because the PIX Firewall does not automatically recognize it. Starting with PIX Firewall Software Version 6.0(1), FDDI, PL2, and Token Ring interfaces are not supported.

Example 5-8 demonstrates the use of the **interface** command to configure physical and logical interfaces. The first statement configures physical interface ethernet4 for 100-Mbps Ethernet full-duplex communications. The next two statements create physical and logical VLAN interfaces on interface ethernet4 and specify the VLAN identifier for each interface.

Example 5-8 **interface** *Command*

```
pixfirewall(config)# interface ethernet4 100full
pixfirewall(config)# interface ethernet4 vlan1 physical
pixfirewall(config)# interface ethernet4 vlan5 logical
```

ip address Command

After an interface is configured and named using the **interface** and **nameif** commands, you must then assign an IP address to the interface using the **ip address** command. If you make a mistake while entering this command, re-enter it with the correct information. The **clear ip** command resets all interface IP addresses to 127.0.0.1.

Instead of manually configuring an IP address on the PIX Firewall's outside interface, you can enable the PIX Firewall's DHCP client feature to have the PIX Firewall dynamically retrieve an IP address from a DHCP server. With the PIX Firewall configured as a DHCP client, a DHCP server can configure the PIX Firewall's outside interface with an IP address, subnet mask, and optionally a default route. Use the **ip address outside dhcp** command to enable this feature.

Use the **show ip address dhcp** command to view current information about your DHCP lease. Re-entering **ip address outside dhcp** enables you to release and renew a DHCP lease from the PIX Firewall. You can also use the **clear ip** command to release and renew the DHCP lease, but it clears the configuration of every PIX Firewall interface. To delete the DHCP leased IP address from the outside interface only, use the command **clear ip address outside dhcp**. The **debug dhcpc packet | detail | error** command provides debugging tools for the DHCP client feature.

The syntax for the **ip address** commands is as follows:

```
ip address if_name ip_address [netmask]
ip address outside dhcp [setroute] [retry retry_cnt]
show ip address outside dhcp
clear ip
clear ip address outside dhcp [setroute] [retry retry_cnt]
```

Table 5-12 describes the **ip address** command arguments.

Table 5-12   **ip address** *Command Arguments*

Argument	Definition
dhcp	Specifies that the PIX Firewall will use DHCP to obtain an IP address.
if_name	Describes the interface. This name is assigned by you and must be used in all future configuration references to the interface.
ip_address	Specifies the IP address of the interface.
netmask	Specifies the network mask of *ip_address*. If a network mask is not specified, the default network mask is assumed.
outside	Specifies the interface from which the PIX Firewall will poll for information.
retry	Enables the PIX Firewall to retry a poll for DHCP information.
retry_cnt	Specifies the number of times the PIX Firewall will poll for DHCP information. The values available are 4 to 16. If no value is specified, the default is 4.
setroute	Tells the PIX Firewall to set the default route using the default gateway parameter the DHCP server returns.

NOTE   The PIX Firewall DHCP client does not support failover configurations.

In Example 5-9, the first statement specifies that the IP address for the outside interface is obtained from a DHCP server. The second statement sets the interface named dmz with an IP address of 172.16.0.1 and a subnet mask of 255.255.255.0.

Example 5-9   **ip address** *Command*

```
pixfirewall(config)# ip address outside dhcp
pixfirewall(config)# ip address dmz 172.16.0.1 255.255.255.0
```

nat Command

Network address translation (NAT) enables you to keep your internal IP addresses—those behind the PIX Firewall—unknown to external networks. NAT accomplishes this task by translating the internal IP addresses, which are not globally unique, into globally accepted IP addresses before packets are forwarded to the external network. You implement NAT in the PIX Firewall with the **nat** and **global** commands.

When an outbound IP packet that is sent from a device on the inside network reaches a PIX Firewall with NAT configured, the source address is extracted and compared to an internal table of existing translations. If the device's address is not already in the table, it is then translated. A new entry is created for that device, and it is assigned an IP address from a pool of global IP addresses. You configure this global pool with the **global** command. After this translation occurs, the table is updated and the translated IP packet is forwarded. After a user-configurable timeout period (or the default of 3 hours), during which there have been no translated packets for that particular IP address, the entry is removed from the table, and the global address is freed for use by another inside device.

In the example shown in Figure 5-2, host 10.0.0.11 starts an outbound connection. The PIX Firewall translates the source address to 192.168.0.20 so that packets from host 10.0.0.11 are seen on the outside as having a source address of 192.168.0.20.

Figure 5-2   *NAT*

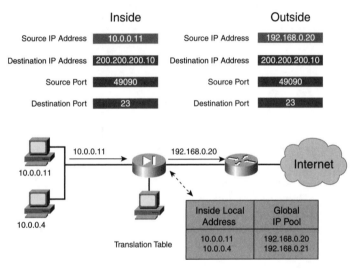

The first step in enabling NAT on your PIX Firewall is entering the **nat** command. The **nat** command can specify translation for a single host or a range of hosts. You can also enable translation for all inside hosts making outbound connections with the **nat 1 0.0.0.0 0.0.0.0** command.

NOTE   To simplify entry of the **nat** command, you can use a 0 in place of 0.0.0.0.

The syntax for the **nat** command is as follows:

```
nat [(if_name)] nat_id address [netmask] [timeout hh:mm:ss]
```

Table 5-13 describes the **nat** command arguments.

Table 5-13 **nat** *Command Arguments*

Argument	Definition
if_name	The name of the interface attached to the network to be translated.
nat_id	A number greater than zero (0) that specifies the global address pool you want to use for dynamic address translation.
address	The IP address to be translated. You can use 0.0.0.0 to allow all hosts to start outbound connections. The 0.0.0.0 can be abbreviated as 0.
netmask	Network mask for the address. You can use 0.0.0.0 to allow all outbound connections to translate with IP addresses from the global pool.
timeout	Used to modify the default **xlate** timeout value of 3 hours.
hh:mm:ss	The timeout interval for the translation slot. However, timeout only occurs if no TCP or User Datagram Protocol (UDP) connection is actively using the translation.

Using private IP addresses inside the network and translating them into globally accepted IP addresses before packets are forwarded to the external network provides added security and dramatically reduces the required number of public IP addresses. Although this configuration is recommended and typically deployed, sometimes you might not want to translate addresses as packets flow through the PIX Firewall (for example, when the PIX Firewall is operating behind another NAT device). In such cases, you can use the **nat 0** command to disable the translation of addresses across the PIX Firewall.

Example 5-10 demonstrates the use of the **nat 0** command to disable address translation for specific hosts. In this example, hosts in the 10.0.0.0 network are translated as they initiate outbound connections. However, hosts in the 192.168.0.0 network traverse the PIX Firewall without address translation.

Example 5-10 **nat 0** *Command*

```
pixfirewall(config)# nat (inside) 1 10.0.0.0 255.0.0.0
pixfirewall(config)# nat (inside) 0 192.168.0.0 255.255.255.0
```

global Command

You use the **global** command with the **nat** command to assign a registered or public IP address to an internal host when accessing the outside network through the firewall. If you use the **nat** command, you must configure the companion command, **global**, to define the pool of translated IP addresses.

Use the **no global** command to delete a global entry (for example, **no global (outside) 1 192.168.1.20-192.168.1.254 netmask 255.255.255.0**).

The syntax for the **global** command is as follows:

```
global [(if_name)] nat_id {global_ip [-global_ip] [netmask global_mask]} | interface
```

Table 5-14 describes the **global** command arguments.

Table 5-14   **global** *Command Arguments*

Argument	Definition
if_name	Describes the external network interface name where you will use the global addresses.
nat_id	Identifies the global pool and matches it with its respective **nat** command.
global_ip	Single IP addresses or the beginning IP address for a range of global IP addresses.
-global_ip	The ending IP address for a range of global IP addresses.
global_mask	The network mask for the *global_ip* address. If subnetting is in effect, use the subnet mask (for example, 255.255.255.128). If you specify an address range that overlaps subnets with the **netmask** command, this command does not use the broadcast or network address in the pool of global addresses. For example, if you use 255.255.255.128 and an address range of 192.150.50.20–192.150.50.140, the 192.150.50.127 broadcast address and the 192.150.50.128 network address are not included in the pool of global addresses.
interface	Specifies PAT using the IP address at the interface. PAT is discussed in greater detail in Chapter 7, "Translations and Connections."

For example, to enable NAT for all internal hosts and translate their private addresses to publicly assigned addressed in the 192.168.0.20 to 192.168.0.254 range, enter the following commands:

```
pixfirewall(config)# nat (inside) 1 0.0.0.0 0.0.0.0
pixfirewall(config)# global (outside) 1 192.168.0.20-192.168.0.254
```

NOTE   The PIX Firewall assigns addresses from the global pool starting from the low end to the high end of the range specified in the **global** command.

NOTE   The PIX Firewall uses the global addresses to assign a virtual IP address to an internal NAT address. After adding, changing, or removing a global statement, use the **clear xlate** command to make the IP addresses available in the translation table.

route Command

The **route** command is required for any basic PIX Firewall configuration and defines a static or default route for an interface.

The syntax for the **route** command is as follows:

```
route if_name ip_address netmask gateway_ip [metric]
```

Table 5-15 describes the **route** command arguments.

Table 5-15   **route** *Command Arguments*

Argument	Definition
if_name	Describes the internal or external network interface name.
ip_address	Describes the internal or external network IP address. Use 0.0.0.0 to specify a default route. The 0.0.0.0 IP address can be abbreviated as 0.
netmask	Specifies a network mask to apply to *ip_address*. Use 0.0.0.0 to specify a default route. The 0.0.0.0 netmask can be abbreviated as 0.
gateway_ip	Specifies the IP address of the gateway router (the next-hop address for this route).
metric	Specifies the number of hops to *gateway_ip*. If you are not sure, enter **1**. Your WAN administrator can supply this information or you can use a **traceroute** command to obtain the number of hops. The default is 1 if a metric is not specified.

For example, to route all outgoing packets (outside interface) through a router with the IP address of 192.168.1.1, issue the following command:

```
pixfirewall(config)# route outside 0.0.0.0 0.0.0.0 192.168.1.1 1
```

NOTE   You can issue the same command as follows:

```
pixfirewall(config)# route outside 0 0 192.168.1.1
```

The IP address and netmask combination of 0.0.0.0 0.0.0.0 can be abbreviated as 0 0 and a metric value of 1 is assigned by default when a different value is not configured.

You can include as many **route** statements as necessary on the PIX Firewall to configure static routes for all reachable networks. For example, if two networks, 10.0.1.0 and 10.0.2.0, are connected to a router at 10.0.0.1 on the interface named dmz, you can configure static routes for both networks as follows:

```
pixfirewall(config)# route dmz 10.0.1.0 255.255.255.0 10.0.0.1 1
pixfirewall(config)# route dmz 10.0.2.0 255.255.255.0 10.0.0.1 1
```

NOTE	You can have multiple route statements to configure static routes for different networks. However, you can only have one default route (**route** *if_name* **0 0** *gateway_ip*), and you cannot configure multiple routes to the same network. (Remember that the PIX is not a router.)

You can use the IP address of one of the PIX Firewall's interfaces as the gateway address. If you do, the PIX Firewall broadcasts an Address Resolution Protocol (ARP) request for the MAC address of the destination IP address in the packet instead of broadcasting a request for the MAC address of the gateway IP address.

Syslog Configuration

The PIX Firewall generates syslog messages for system events, such as alerts and resource depletion. You can use syslog messages to create e-mail alerts and log files or display them on the console of a designated syslog host. If you do not already have a syslog server, you can download a copy of the software from Cisco.com.

The PIX Firewall can send syslog messages to any syslog server. In the event that all syslog servers or hosts are offline, the PIX Firewall stores up to 100 messages in its memory. Subsequent messages that arrive overwrite the buffer starting from the first line.

The PIX Firewall sends syslog messages to document the following events:

- **Security**—Dropped UDP packets and denied TCP connections
- **Resources**—Notification of connection and translation slot depletion
- **System**—Console and Telnet logins and logouts and rebooting of the PIX Firewall
- **Accounting**—Bytes transferred per connection

To generate syslog message, you must first enable logging on the PIX Firewall using the **logging on** command. After enabling logging, use the **logging console** command to specify what syslog messages appear on the PIX Firewall console as each message occurs. The level parameter of the **logging console** command enables you to limit the types of messages that appear on the console.

NOTE	You should use caution when using the **logging console** command on a production device because its use can degrade the performance of the PIX Firewall. If you do enable **logging console** on a production PIX Firewall, you should configure it so that only critical messages are logged, minimizing the impact of logging on normal operation.

You can use the **logging buffered** command to store up to 100 syslog messages in a memory buffer on the PIX Firewall. This process is useful for quickly checking the most recent syslog message generated by the PIX Firewall, which is useful for troubleshooting purposes. To view a list of the current messages on the buffer, you can use the **show logging** command. You can use the **clear logging** command to clear the message buffer. New messages append to the end of the buffer.

Use the **logging message** command to specify a message to be allowed. Use it with the **no** command to suppress a message. All syslog messages are permitted unless explicitly disallowed. To block a specific message, use its message number to disallow or allow. For example, if a message is listed in the syslog as %PIX-1-101001, use "101001" as the *syslog_id* to block.

NOTE   You cannot block the "PIX Startup begin" message, and you can block only one message per command statement.

NOTE   Refer to the *System Log Messages for the Cisco Secure PIX Firewall Version 6.3* guide (or the version you are running) for message numbers. PIX Firewall documentation is available online at http://www.cisco.com/univercd/cc/td/doc/product/iaabu/pix.

You use the **logging standby** command to allow a failover standby PIX Firewall to send syslog messages. This option is disabled by default. Enabling it ensures that the standby PIX Firewall's syslog messages stay synchronized if failover occurs; however, it doubles the amount of traffic on the syslog server. You can disable this feature with the **no logging standby** command.

The syntax for **logging** commands is as follows:

```
logging buffered level
logging console level
logging device-id {hostname | ipaddress if_name | string text}
logging history level
logging host [in_if_name] ip_address [protocol/port] [format emblem]
logging message syslog_id [level level]
logging monitor level
logging queue queue_size
logging standby
logging timestamp
logging trap level
clear logging [disable]
show logging [message {syslog_id | all} | level | disabled]
show logging queue
```

Table 5-16 describes the **logging** command arguments.

Table 5-16   **logging** *Command Arguments*

Argument	Definition
buffered	Sends syslog messages to an internal buffer that you can view with the **show logging** command.
level	Specifies the syslog message level as a number or string. Levels up to the number you specify are logged. For example, if you specify level 3, syslog message levels 0, 1, 2, and 3 are generated. Possible number and string *level* values are as follows: • **0–emergencies**—System unusable messages • 1–**alerts**—Take immediate action • **2–critical**—Critical condition • **3–errors**—Error message • **4–warnings**—Warning message • **5–notifications**—Normal but significant condition • **6–informational**—Information message • **7–debugging**—Debug messages and log FTP commands and WWW URLs
console	Sends syslog messages to the PIX Firewall console as each message occurs. You can limit the types of messages that appear on the console with *level*. Use of this option on production firewalls is not recommended because its use degrades the performance of PIX Firewalls.
device-id	The device ID of the PIX Firewall to include in the syslog message.
history	Sets the Simple Network Management Protocol (SNMP) message level for sending syslog traps.
host	Specifies a syslog server that will receive the messages sent from the PIX Firewall. You can use multiple **logging host** commands to specify additional servers that would all receive the syslog messages. However, a server can only be specified to receive either UDP or TCP, not both. The PIX Firewall sends TCP syslog messages only to the PIX Firewall syslog server (PFSS).
hostname	Specifies that the host name of the PIX Firewall should be used to uniquely identify the syslog messages from the PIX Firewall.
if_name	Specifies the name of the interface whose IP address is used to uniquely identify the syslog messages from the PIX Firewall.
in_if_name	Specifies the interface on which the syslog server resides.
ip_address	IP address of the syslog server.
ipaddress	Specifies that the IP address of the PIX Firewall interface specified with *if_name* should be used to uniquely identify the syslog messages from the PIX Firewall.

continues

Table 5-16 logging *Command Arguments (Continued)*

Argument	Definition
protocol	The protocol over which the syslog message is sent: either **tcp** or **udp**. TCP syslog messages are only supported with the PIX Firewall syslog server. You can only view the port and protocol values you previously entered by using the **write terminal** command and finding the command in the listing. The TCP protocol is listed as 6 and the UDP protocol is listed as 17.
port	The port from which the PIX Firewall sends either UDP or TCP syslog messages. It must be same port at which the syslog server listens. For the UDP port, the default is 514 and the allowable range for changing the value is 1025 through 65,535. For the TCP port, the default is 1470, and the allowable range is 1025 through 65,535. TCP ports work only with the PIX Firewall syslog server.
format emblem	This option enables EMBLEM format logging on a per-syslog-server basis. EMBLEM format logging is available for UDP syslog messages only and is disabled by default.
message	Specifies a message to be allowed. Use the **no logging message** command to suppress a syslog message. Use the **clear logging disabled** command to reset the disallowed messages to the original set. Use the **show message disabled** command to list the suppressed messages. All syslog messages are permitted unless explicitly disallowed. You cannot block the "PIX Startup begin" message and or more than one message per command statement.
syslog_id	Specifies a message number to disallow or allow. If a message is listed in syslog as %PIX-1-101001, use 101001 as the *syslog_id*. Refer to *Cisco PIX Firewall System Log Messages* for message numbers.
monitor	Specifies that syslog messages appear on Telnet sessions to the PIX Firewall console. You can limit the types of messages that are sent to the Telnet sessions with *level*.
queue *queue_size*	Specifies the size of the queue for storing syslog messages. Use this parameter before the syslog messages are processed. The queue parameter defaults to 512 messages, 0 (zero) indicates unlimited (subject to available block memory), and the minimum is 1 message. When traffic is heavy, messages might be discarded if they are generated faster than the PIX Firewall can process them and the queue is full.
standby	Allows the failover standby PIX Firewall to send syslog messages. This option is disabled by default. You can enable it to ensure that the standby PIX Firewall's syslog messages stay synchronized if failover occurs. However, this option creates twice as much traffic on the syslog server. You can disable this feature with the **no logging standby** command.
timestamp	Specifies that syslog messages sent to the syslog server should have a timestamp value on each message.
trap	Sets the logging level only for syslog messages.

Table 5-16   logging *Command Arguments (Continued)*

Argument	Definition
show	Lists which logging options are enabled. If the **logging buffered** command is in use, the **show logging** command lists the current message buffer.
clear	Clears the buffer for use with the **logging buffered** command.
all	All syslog message IDs.
disabled	Clear or display messages suppressed with the **no logging** message command.

To configure the PIX Firewall to send syslog messages to a syslog server, complete the following steps:

Step 1   Enable logging with the **logging on** command. Use the **no logging on** command to disable sending messages.

Step 2   Designate a host to receive the messages with the **logging host** command:

```
logging host [in_if_name] ip_address [protocol/port]
```

Replace *in_if_name* with the interface on which the server exists and *ip_address* with the IP address of the host. If the syslog server is receiving messages on a nonstandard port, you can replace *protocol* with UDP and *port* with the new port value. The default protocol is UDP with a default port of 514, and the allowable range for changing the value is 1025 through 65,535. You can also specify TCP with a default of 1470, and the allowable range is 1025 through 65,535.

Step 3   Specify the logging levels that will be forwarded to the syslog server with the **logging trap** command:

```
logging trap level
```

Step 4   Specify the logging facility to which the PIX Firewall will assign the syslog messages with the **logging facility** command:

```
logging facility facility
```

Because network devices share the eight facilities, the **logging facility** command enables you to set the facility marked on all messages.

Step 5   If you want to send timestamped messages to a syslog server, use the **logging timestamp** command to enable timestamping. Use the **no logging timestamp** command to disable timestamp logging.

DHCP Server Configuration

DHCP provides automatic allocation of reusable network addresses on a TCP/IP network. This process eases network administration and dramatically reduces the margin of human error. Without DHCP, you must manually enter IP addresses at each computer or device that requires an IP address.

DHCP can also distribute other configuration parameters, such as the addresses and domain names of DNS and Windows Internet Name Service (WINS) server. The host that distributes the addresses and configuration parameters to DHCP clients is called a *DHCP server*. A *DHCP client* is any host using DHCP to obtain configuration parameters.

Because DHCP traffic consists of broadcasts and a significant goal of router configuration is to control the unnecessary proliferation of broadcast packets, it might be necessary to enable forwarding of DHCP broadcast packets on routers that lie between your DHCP server and its clients. Use the **ip helper-address** interface configuration command to have the Cisco IOS Software forward these broadcasts. The address specified in the command should be that of the DHCP server.

NOTE   WINS registers Network Basic Input/Output System (NetBIOS) computer names and resolves them to IP addresses.

Any PIX Firewall that runs Version 5.2 or higher supports a DHCP server and client. In a network environment secured by a PIX Firewall, PC clients connect to the PIX Firewall and establish network connections to access an enterprise or corporate network. As a DHCP server, the PIX Firewall provides these PCs (its DHCP clients) the networking parameters necessary for accessing the enterprise or corporate network, and once inside the network, the PIX Firewall provides the network services to be used, such as the DNS server. As a DHCP client, the PIX Firewall is able to obtain an IP address, subnet mask, and, optionally, a default route from a DHCP server.

Currently, the PIX Firewall can distribute configuration parameters only to clients that are physically connected to the subnet of its inside interface.

DHCP Basics

DHCP communication consists of several broadcast messages passed between the DHCP client and DHCP server. The following events occur during this exchange, as shown in Figure 5-3:

1 The client broadcasts a DHCPDISCOVER message on its local physical subnet to locate available DHCP servers.

2 Any reachable DHCP server can respond with a DHCPOFFER message that includes an available network address and other configuration parameters.

3 Based on the configuration parameters offered in the DHCPOFFER messages, the client chooses one server from which to request configuration parameters. The client broadcasts a DHCPREQUEST message requesting the offered parameters from one server and implicitly declining offers from all others.

4 The server selected in the DHCPREQUEST message responds with a DHCPACK message containing the configuration parameters for the requesting client. If the selected server has since become unable to satisfy the DHCPREQUEST (for example, in case the requested network address has already been allocated), the server responds with a DHCPNAK message. The client receives either the DHCPNAK or the DHCPACK containing the configuration parameters.

Figure 5-3   *DHCP Communications*

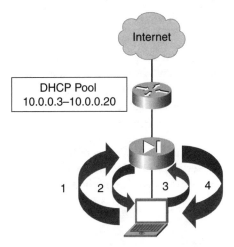

1. DHCPDISCOVER—The client seeks an address

2. DHCPOFFER—The server offers 10.0.0.3

3. DHCPREQUEST—The client requests 10.0.0.3

4. DHCPACK—The server acknowledges the assignment of 10.0.0.3

NOTE   The PIX Firewall DHCP server does not support BOOTP requests and failover configurations.

Configuring a PIX Firewall DHCP Server

You use several **dhcpd** commands to configure DHCP server support on the PIX Firewall. The **dhcpd address** command specifies the range of IP addresses for the server to distribute. The address pool of a PIX Firewall DHCP server must be within the same subnet as the PIX Firewall interface that is enabled. In other words, the client must be physically connected to the subnet of a PIX Firewall interface. The **no dhcpd address** command removes the DHCP server address pool.

NOTE PIX Firewalls Version 6.3 or higher support DHCP server on multiple interfaces. Earlier versions of the PIX Firewall support DHCP service only on the inside interface.

The syntax for the **dhcpd address** command is as follows:

```
dhcpd address ip1 [-ip2] [if_name]
```

Table 5-17 describes the **dhcpd address** command arguments.

Table 5-17 **dhcpd address** *Command Arguments*

Argument	Definition
address *ip1* [*-ip2*]	The IP pool address range. The size of the pool is limited to 32 addresses with a 10-user license and 128 addresses with a 50-user license on the PIX 501. The unlimited user license on the PIX 501 and all other PIX Firewall platforms support 256 addresses.
if_name	Name of the PIX Firewall interface.

NOTE If the address pool range is more than 253 addresses (254 to 256 addresses), the netmask of the PIX Firewall interface cannot be a Class C address (for example, 255.255.255.0) and hence needs to be something smaller, such as 255.255.254.0.

The **dhcpd dns** command optionally specifies the IP address of the DNS server for DHCP clients. You can specify up to two DNS servers with this command. Use the **no dhcpd dns** command to remove the DNS IP addresses from your configuration.

The syntax for the **dhcpd dns** command is as follows:

```
dhcpd dns dns1 [dns2]
```

Argument	Definition
dns *dns1* [*dns2*]	The IP addresses of the DNS servers for the DHCP client. The second server address is optional.

You can optionally use the **dhcpd wins** command to specify up to two WINS servers for DHCP clients to use. The **no dhcpd wins** command removes the WINS server IP addresses from your configuration.

The syntax for the **dhcpd wins** command is as follows:

```
dhcpd wins wins1 [wins2]
```

Argument	Definition
wins *wins1* [*wins2*]	The IP addresses of the Microsoft NetBIOS name servers (WINS servers). The second server address is optional.

The **dhcpd option** commands enable the PIX Firewall's DHCP server to distribute the IP address of a TFTP server to serve DHCP clients. These options are useful for IP phones, which might need to obtain configuration files from a TFTP server. With the **dhcpd option 66** command, the PIX Firewall distributes the IP address of a single TFTP server. With the **dhcpd option 150** command, it distributes a list of TFTP servers. You can remove the **dhcpd option** commands by using their **no** forms.

The syntax for the **dhcpd option** commands is as follows:

```
dhcpd option 66 ascii {server_name | server_ip_str}
dhcpd option 150 ip server_ip1 [server_ip2]
```

Table 5-18 describes the **dhcpd option** command arguments.

Table 5-18   **dhcpd option** *Command Arguments*

Argument	Definition
server_ip(1,2)	Specifies the IP addresses of a TFTP server.
server_ip_str	Any combination of characters used to identify the server. For example, it could have the form of an IP address, such as 1.1.1.1, but is treated as a character string.
server_name	Specifies an ASCII character string representing the TFTP server.

The **dhcpd lease** command specifies the amount of time in seconds that the client can use the assigned IP address. The default is 3600 seconds. The minimum lease length is 300 seconds, and the maximum lease length is 2,147,483,647 seconds.

The syntax for the **dhcpd lease** command is as follows:

```
dhcpd lease lease_length
```

lease *lease_length*	The length of the lease in seconds granted to the DHCP client from the DHCP server.

The DHCP server in the PIX Firewall pings an address before issuing it to a client to avoid IP address conflicts. If it receives a response to the ping, the PIX Firewall removes the address from its pool of DHCP addresses. In PIX Firewall Software Versions 5.3 and higher, the amount of time in milliseconds (ms) that the DHCP server waits for a response is configurable using the **dhcpd ping_timeout** command. The default value is 750 ms. The minimum value is 100, and the maximum is 10,000. You can use the **no dhcpd ping_timeout** command to reset the timeout value to the default.

The syntax for the **dhcpd ping_timeout** command is as follows:

```
dhcpd ping_timeout timeout
```

ping_timeout *timeout*	Specifies the amount of time the DHCP server waits before allocating an address to a client.

You can configure the domain name the client uses with the **dhcpd domain** command. This step is optional in configuring the PIX Firewall as a DHCP server. Use the **no** form of the command to remove a configured domain name.

The syntax for the **dhcpd domain** command is as follows:

```
dhcpd domain domain_name
```

domain *domain_name*	The DNS domain name (for example, example.com)

After you configure the IP address ranges and appropriate options, you can use the **dhcpd enable** command for each configured interface to enable the DHCP daemon on the PIX Firewall. Use the **no** form of the command and specify an interface name to disable the DHCP daemon on that interface.

The syntax for the **dhcpd enable** command is as follows:

```
dhcpd enable [if_name]
```

if_name	Name of the PIX Firewall interface

The **debug dhcpd** command displays information associated with the DHCP server. Use the **debug dhcpd event** command to display event information about the DHCP server, and use the **debug dhcpd packet** command to display packet information about the DHCP server. Use the **no** form of the **debug dhcpd** command to disable debugging.

The syntax for the **debug dhcpd** command is as follows:

```
debug dhcpd event | packet
```

Table 5-19 describes the **debug dhcpd** command arguments.

Table 5-19   **debug dhcpd** *Command Arguments*

Argument	Definition
dhcpd event	Displays event information associated with the DHCP server
dhcpd packet	Displays packet information associated with the DHCP server

You can use the **clear dhcpd** command to clear all **dhcpd** commands and binding and statistics information. Use the **clear dhcpd** command with no options to remove all **dhcpd** command statements from the configuration.

The syntax for the **clear dhcpd** command is as follows:

```
clear dhcpd [binding | statistics]
```

Table 5-20 describes the **clear dhcpd** command arguments.

Table 5-20   **clear dhcpd** *Command Arguments*

Argument	Definition
bindings	The binding information for a given server IP address and its associated client hardware address and lease length
statistics	Statistical information, such as address pool, number of bindings, malformed messages, sent messages, and received messages

The PIX Firewall can be a DHCP server, a DHCP client, or a DHCP server and client simultaneously. DHCP server and client support enables you to automatically leverage the DNS, WINS, and domain name values obtained by the PIX Firewall DHCP client for use by the hosts served by the PIX Firewall's DHCP server.

Use the **dhcpd auto_config** command to enable the PIX Firewall to automatically pass configuration parameters it receives from a DHCP server to its own DHCP clients. You must enable DHCP with the **dhcpd enable** command to use the **dhcpd auto_config** command. Use the **no dhcpd auto_config** command to disable the **auto_config** feature.

The syntax for the **dhcp auto_config** command is as follows:

```
dhcpd auto_config [client_ifx_name]
no dhcpd auto_config [client_ifx_name]
```

Table 5-21 describes the **dhcp auto_config** command arguments.

Table 5-21   **dhcp auto_config** *Command Arguments*

Argument	Definition
auto_config	Enables the PIX Firewall to automatically configure DNS, WINS, and domain name values from the DHCP client to the DHCP server.
client_ifx_name	Supports only the outside interface at this time. When more interfaces are supported, this argument specifies which interface supports the DHCP **auto_config** feature.

You are now familiar with the **dhcpd** commands and can complete the following steps to enable DHCP server support on the PIX Firewall:

Step 1   Assign a static IP address to the inside interface by using the **ip address** command.

Step 2   Specify a range of addresses for the DHCP server to distribute by using the **dhcpd address** command.

Step 3   Specify the IP address of the DNS server that the client uses by issuing the **dhcpd dns** command. This step is optional.

Step 4 Specify the IP address of the WINS server the client uses by issuing the
dhcpd wins command. This step is also optional.

Step 5 Specify the IP address of the TFTP server. This step is also optional.

Step 6 Specify the lease length to grant the client by using the **dhcpd lease**
command.

Step 7 Specify the ping timeout value using the **dhcpd ping timeout** command.
This step is optional.

Step 8 Configure the domain name the client uses by issuing the **dhcpd domain**
command. This step is optional.

Step 9 Enable the DHCP daemon within the PIX Firewall to listen for DHCP
client requests on the enabled interface by using the **dhcpd enable**
command.

Example 5-11 demonstrates the use of the **dhcpd** command to configure the PIX Firewall
as a DHCP server. The first statement in the example configures DNS servers that will be
used by the clients. The second statement configures the WINS option, and the third
statement configures the default domain, which is Cisco.com in this example. The next four
statements specify the IP address ranges for the inside and dmz1 interfaces and enable
DHCP service on each interface.

Example 5-11 *DHCP Server Configuration*

```
pixfirewall(config)# dhcpd dns 10.0.1.10 10.0.1.11
pixfirewall(config)# dhcpd wins 10.0.1.10 10.0.1.11
pixfirewall(config)# dhcpd domain cisco.com
pixfirewall(config)# dhcpd address 10.0.1.50-10.0.1.100 inside
pixfirewall(config)# dhcpd enable inside
pixfirewall(config)# dhcpd address 172.16.0.50-172.16.0.100 dmz1
pixfirewall(config)# dhcpd enable dmz1
```

DHCP Relay

You can configure the PIX Firewall to function as a DHCP relay agent using the **dhcprelay**
command introduced with PIX Firewall Version 6.3 software. The DHCP functionality can
assist in dynamic configuration of IP hosts on any of the PIX Firewall's interfaces. With this
option enabled, DHCP requests received from hosts on a given interface are forwarded to
a user-configured DHCP server on another interface. The DHCP relay option can work in
conjunction with site-to-site or Easy VPN, enabling businesses to centrally manage their IP
addresses.

NOTE The DHCP relay option using the **dhcprelay** command is available only on PIX Firewall
Version 6.3 or higher.

DHCP relay is disabled by default. To enable DHCP relay, you must first configure the server to which the requests should be forwarded. You specify the server using the **dhcprelay server** command. With the server configured, you can enable DHCP relay on the desired interface using the **dhcprelay enable** command. By default, DHCP negotiations time out after 60 seconds. You change this timeout period using the **dhcprelay timeout** command.

You use the **dhcprelay setroute** command to change the default router address in packets sent from the DHCP server to the address of the PIX Firewall interface where the client is located. If there is no default router option in the packet, the firewall adds one containing the address of the PIX Firewall interface where the client is located. This step allows the client to set its default route to point to the firewall.

Use the **show dhcprelay** command to display the current DHCP relay settings. You can use **no dhcprelay enable** to remove a specific instance or use **clear dhcprelay** to clear all DHCP relay configurations.

The syntax for **dhcprelay** commands is as follows:

```
dhcprelay enable client_ifc
dhcprelay server dhcp_server_ip server_ifc
dhcprelay setroute client_ifc
dhcprelay timeout seconds
[clear|show] dhcprelay [statistics]
```

Table 5-22 describes the **dhcprelay** command arguments.

Table 5-22 **dhcprelay** *Command Arguments*

Argument	Definition
client_ifc	The name of the interface on which the DHCP relay agent accepts client requests.
dhcp_server_ip	The IP address of the DHCP server to which the DHCP relay agent forwards client requests.
enable	Enables the DHCP relay agent to accept DHCP requests from clients on the specified interface.
seconds	The number of seconds allowed for DHCP relay address negotiation.
server_ifc	The name of the firewall interface on which the DHCP server resides.
statistics	The DHCP relay statistics, incremented until a **clear dhcprelay statistics** command is issued.

Example 5-12 demonstrates the use of **dhcprelay** commands to configure the PIX Firewall as a DHCP relay agent. The first statement in the example specifies a DHCP server at 10.1.1.1 on the outside interface. The second statement modifies the default timeout to 80 seconds. DHCP relay is then enabled on the inside interface using the **dhcprelay enable** command. The output of the **show dhcprelay** command is also included.

Example 5-12 *DHCP Relay Configuration*

```
pixfirewall(config)# dhcprelay server 10.1.1.1 outside
pixfirewall(config)# dhcprelay timeout 80
pixfirewall(config)# dhcprelay enable inside
pixfirewall(config)# show dhcprelay
dhcprelay server 10.1.1.1 outside
dhcprelay enable inside
dhcprelay timeout 80
```

PPPoE and the PIX Firewall

Beginning with Software Version 6.2, the PIX Firewall can be configured as a PPPoE client. This addition makes it compatible with broadband offerings that require PPPoE. Many Internet service providers (ISPs) deploy PPPoE because it supports high-speed broadband access using their existing remote access infrastructure and because it is easy for customers to use.

Broadband connections such as DSL, cable modem, and fixed wireless deliver high-speed, "always-on" connections at a low cost. The PIX Firewall enables you to secure these broadband Internet connections. Figure 5-4 shows a typical installation utilizing the PPPoE feature available on the PIX Firewall.

Figure 5-4 *PIX Firewall as a PPPoE Client*

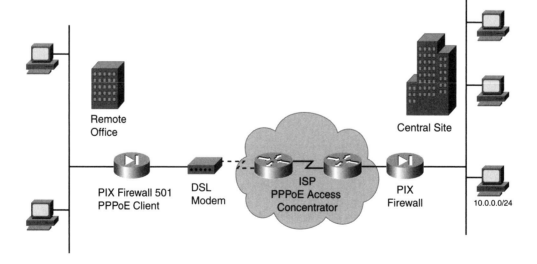

PPPoE combines two widely accepted standards, Ethernet and Point-to-Point Protocol (PPP), to provide an authenticated method of assigning IP addresses to client systems. PPPoE consists of two main phases:

- **Active discovery phase**—In this phase, the PPPoE client locates a PPPoE server, called an access concentrator (AC). A session identification is assigned and the PPPoE layer is established.

- **PPP session phase**—In this phase, PPP options are negotiated and authentication is performed. After the link setup is completed, PPPoE functions as a Layer 2 encapsulation method, allowing data to be transferred over the PPP link within PPPoE headers.

After it is configured, the PIX Firewall's PPPoE client automatically connects to a service provider's AC without user intervention. The MTU size is automatically set to 1492 bytes, the correct value to allow PPPoE to be transmitted in an Ethernet frame. All traffic flowing to, from, and through the interface is then encapsulated with PPPoE/PPP headers. The PIX Firewall also detects session termination and automatically attempts to reconnect.

The PIX Firewall PPPoE client can operate in environments where other PIX Firewall features are being used. For example, the following features function as usual:

- NAT on traffic to or from the outside interface or over a VPN

- URL and content filtering before transmission to or from the outside interface

- Application of firewall rules on traffic before transmission to or from the outside interface or over a VPN

If your ISP's PPPoE server distributes configuration parameters such as DNS and WINS addresses along with the IP addresses it assigns to its clients, the PIX Firewall's PPPoE client can retrieve these parameters and automatically pass them along to its DHCP clients. You must configure the PIX Firewall with the **dhcpd auto_config** option for it to work. Although the PIX Firewall's DHCP server feature functions normally with the PPPoE client enabled, its DHCP and PPPoE client features are mutually exclusive. When you configure the DHCP client on the outside interface, the PPPoE client is automatically disabled. The converse of this configuration statement is also true; when the PPPoE client is configured, the DHCP client is automatically disabled.

With PPPoE support, the PIX Firewall is able to provide telecommuters, branch offices, and small businesses with firewall, VPN, and intrusion protection.

NOTE   The PIX Firewall's PPPoE client is not interoperable with failover, Layer 2 Tunneling Protocol (L2TP), or Point-to-Point Tunneling Protocol (PPTP).

Configuring PPPoE on the PIX Firewall

You configure PPPoE on the PIX Firewall using the **vpdn** and **ip address pppoe** commands. You first enter the PPPoE configuration using the **vpdn** commands before enabling PPPoE with the **ip address pppoe** command.

The syntax for the **vpdn** commands is as follows:

```
vpdn group group_name request dialout pppoe
vpdn group group_name ppp authentication PAP | CHAP | MSCHAP
vpdn group group_name localname username
vpdn username name password pass
clear vpdn [group | username ]
```

Table 5-23 describes the **vpdn** command arguments.

Table 5-23   **vpdn** *Command Arguments*

Argument	Definition
request dialout pppoe	Allows dialout PPPoE requests.
group_name	Descriptive name for the group.
local name *username*	Username assigned by the ISP.
username *name*	Local username. However, when used as a **clear** command option, username removes all **vpdn username** commands from the configuration.
ppp authentication PAP | CHAP | MSCHAP	Specifies the Point-to-Point Protocol (PPP) authentication protocol. The Windows client dial-up networking supports Password Authentication Protocol (PAP), Challenge Handshake Authentication Protocol (CHAP), or the Microsoft derivation of CHAP (MS-CHAP) authentication protocols. Settings specified on the client must match the settings on the PIX Firewall. PAP passes the host name or username in cleartext and should ideally be avoided. CHAP and MS-CHAP provide authenticated access through interaction with an access server. PIX Firewall supports MS-CHAP Version 1 only (not Version 2.0). If an authentication protocol is not specified on the host, do not specify the **ppp authentication** option in the configuration.
pass	Password assigned by the ISP.
group	Removes all **vpdn group** commands from the configuration.

After you set PPPoE configuration using the **vpdn** command, the **ip address pppoe** command enables the PPPoE session. The **setroute** option of the **ip address pppoe** command causes the PIX Firewall to assume the IP address of the AC as its default route if no default route exists. If you use the **setroute** option when a default route is already set in the configuration, the PIX Firewall does not establish PPPoE. It cannot overwrite an existing default gateway with one supplied by PPPoE. If you want to use the default route from a PPPoE server, erase the default route in the configuration.

NOTE   Do not configure the PIX Firewall with a default route when using the **setroute** argument of the **ip address dhcp** or **ip address pppoe** commands.

The PPPoE client is supported only on the outside interface of the PIX Firewall. PPPoE is not supported in conjunction with DHCP because with PPPoE, the IP address is assigned by PPP. You can, however, use the **ip address pppoe** command to specify an IP address for your PIX Firewall instead of having it retrieve one from a PPPoE server. You can remove the **ip address pppoe** command with the **clear ip** command.

The syntax for the **ip address pppoe** commands is as follows:

```
ip address if_name pppoe [setroute]
ip address if_name ip_address netmask pppoe [setroute]
```

Table 5-24 describes the **ip address pppoe** command arguments.

Table 5-24   **ip address pppoe** *Command Arguments*

Argument	Definition
if_name	The name of the outside interface of the PIX Firewall
setroute	Tells the PIX Firewall to set the default route using the default gateway parameter the DHCP or PPPoE server returns
ip_address	The IP address assigned to the PIX Firewall's outside interface
netmask	The subnet mask assigned to the PIX Firewall's outside interface

NOTE   Do not use the following **ip address** commands after a PPPoE session is initiated because they terminate the PPPoE session:

- **ip address outside pppoe**—This command attempts to initiate a new PPPoE session.

- **ip address outside dhcp**—This command disables the interface until the interface obtains a DHCP configuration.

- **ip address outside address netmask**—This command brings up the interface as a normally initialized interface.

Follow these five steps to configure the PIX Firewall PPPoE client. The first four steps require use of the **vpdn** command. You then use the **ip address pppoe** command in Step 5 to complete the configuration as follows:

Step 1   Use the **vpdn group** command to define a virtual private dialup network (VPDN) group to be used for PPPoE.

Step 2 If your ISP requires authentication, use the **vpdn group** command to
select one of the following authentication protocols:

— **PAP**

— **CHAP**

— **MS-CHAP**

NOTE ISPs that use CHAP or MS-CHAP might refer to the username as the remote system name
and might refer to the password as the CHAP secret.

Step 3 Use the **vpdn group** command to associate the username assigned by
your ISP to the VPDN group.

Step 4 Use the **vpdn username** command to create a username and password
pair for the PPPoE connection. This username and password
combination is used to authenticate the PIX Firewall to the AC. The
username must be a username that is already associated with the VPDN
group specified for PPPoE.

The **clear vpdn** command removes all **vpdn** commands from the
configuration. The **clear vpdn group** command removes all **vpdn group**
commands from the configuration, and the **clear vpdn username**
command removes all **vpdn username** commands from the
configuration.

Step 5 Use the **ip address pppoe** command to enable PPPoE on the PIX
Firewall. PPPoE client functionality is disabled by default. Re-enter the
ip address pppoe command to clear and restart a PPPoE session. This
step shuts down the current session and starts a new one.

Example 5-13 shows the use of **vpdn** and **ip address pppoe** commands
to enable PPPoE on the PIX Firewall.

Example 5-13 *PPPoE Configuration*

```
pixfirewall(config)# vpdn group PPPOEGROUP request dialout pppoe
pixfirewall(config)# vpdn group PPPOEGROUP ppp authentication pap
pixfirewall(config)# vpdn group PPPOEGROUP localname MYUSERNAME
pixfirewall(config)# vpdn username MYUSERNAME password mypassword
pixfirewall(config)# ip address outside pppoe setroute
```

This example creates a VPDN group named PPPOEGROUP. The second statement species PAP as the authentication protocol for this group. The third statement adds a local user MYUSERNAME to the VPDN group PPPOEGROUP. The fourth statement sets the password for MYUSERNAME and completes the VPDN configuration portion. Finally, the last statement enables PPPoE on the outside interface using the **ip address pppoe** command with the **setroute** option.

Monitoring the PPPoE Client

The **show vpdn** command displays PPPoE tunnel and session information. To view only session information, use the **show vpdn session** command. To view only tunnel information, use the **show vpdn tunnel** command.

You can use the **show vpdn pppinterface** command when a PPPoE session is established to view the address of the AC. When the PIX Firewall is unable to find an AC, the address of the AC appears as 0.0.0.0.

You use the **show vpdn username** command to view local usernames, and the **show vpdn group** command allows you to view your configured VPDN groups.

When a PPPoE session is established, you can also use the **show ip address outside pppoe** command to view the IP address assigned by the PPPoE server.

The syntax for the **show vpdn** commands is as follows:

```
show vpdn
show vpdn session [id session_id | packets | state | window]
show vpdn tunnel [id tunnel_id | packets | state | summary | transport]
show vpdn username [name]
show vpdn group [groupname]
```

Table 5-25 describes the **show vpdn** command arguments.

Table 5-25   show vpdn *Command Arguments*

Argument	Definition
session_id	A unique session identifier.
tunnel_id	A unique tunnel identifier.
name	The local username.
group_name	The VPDN group name, an ASCII string denoting a VPDN group. The maximum length is 63 characters.

The syntax for the **show ip address pppoe** command is as follows:

```
show ip address if_name pppoe
```

| if_name | The internal or external interface name designated by the **nameif** command. |

Example 5-14 shows sample output provided by the **show vpdn** commands.

Example 5-14 *PPPoE Monitoring*

```
pixfirewall# sh vpdn
Tunnel id 0, 1 active sessions
     time since change 65862 secs
     Remote Internet Address 172.31.31.1
   Local Internet Address 192.168.10.2
     6 packets sent, 6 received, 84 bytes sent, 0 received
Remote Internet Address is 10.0.0.1
     Session state is SESSION_UP
       Time since event change 65865 secs, interface outside
       PPP interface id is 1
       6 packets sent, 6 received, 84 bytes sent, 0 received
pixfirewall# sh vpdn session
PPPoE Session Information (Total tunnels=1 sessions=1)
Remote Internet Address is 172.31.31.1
   Session state is SESSION_UP
     Time since event change 65887 secs, interface outside
     PPP interface id is 1
     6 packets sent, 6 received, 84 bytes sent, 0 received
pixfirewall# sh vpdn tunnel
PPPoE Tunnel Information (Total tunnels=1 sessions=1)
Tunnel id 0, 1 active sessions
   time since change 65901 secs
   Remote Internet Address 172.31.31.1
   Local Internet Address 192.168.10.2
   6 packets sent, 6 received, 84 bytes sent, 0 received
```

Summary

This section summarizes the information you learned in this chapter:

- The PIX Firewall has four administrative access modes: unprivileged, privileged, configuration, and monitor.

- Interfaces with a higher security level can access interfaces with a lower security level, whereas interfaces with a lower security level cannot access interfaces with a higher security level unless given permission.

- Using the PIX Firewall general maintenance commands helps you manage the PIX Firewall. The commands include **enable**, **write**, **show**, and **reload**.

- The basic commands necessary to configure the PIX Firewall are **nameif**, **interface**, **ip address**, **nat**, **global**, and **route**.

- The **nat** and **global** commands work together to translate IP addresses.

- The PIX Firewall can send syslog messages to a syslog server.
- The PIX Firewall can function as a DHCP client and DHCP server.
- Configuring the PIX Firewall as a PPPoE client enables it to secure broadband Internet connections such as DSL.

Chapter Review Questions

To test what you have learned in this chapter, answer the following questions and then refer to Appendix A, "Answers to Chapter Review Questions," for the answers:

1 What are the six basic configuration commands for the PIX Firewall?

2 What commands do you use to configure IP address translation?

3 Which command do you use to disable NAT?

4 Which logging command can adversely affect the performance of the PIX Firewall?

5 On which interface does the PIX Firewall support DHCP server functionality?

Lab Exercise—Get Started with the Cisco PIX Firewall

Complete the following lab exercise to practice what you learned in this chapter.

Objectives

In this lab exercise, you complete the following tasks:

- Execute general commands.
- Configure PIX Firewall interfaces.
- Configure global addresses, NAT, and routing for inside and outside interfaces.
- Test the inside, outside, and DMZ interface connectivity.
- Configure syslog output.
- Configure syslog output to a syslog server.

Lab Topology

Figure 5-5 displays the topology you need for the lab exercises in this chapter.

Figure 5-5 *Lab Visual Objective*

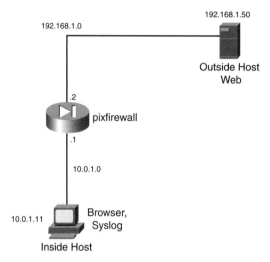

Equipment required to perform the lab includes the following:

- A PIX Firewall with two interfaces
- Category 5 patch cables
- PC host for the outside subnet with a web server (outside host)
- PC host for the inside subnet running Kiwi Syslog

Task 1—Execute General Commands

Complete the steps in this task to familiarize yourself with the general maintenance commands. Carefully observe the output of the commands. After you access the PIX Firewall console port, the PIX Firewall prompt appears:

Step 1 Erase the PIX Firewall's default configuration. When prompted to confirm, press **Enter**.

```
pixfirewall(config)# write erase
Erase PIX configuration in flash memory? [confirm] <Enter>
```

Step 2 Reboot the PIX Firewall. When prompted to confirm, press **Enter:**

```
pixfirewall(config)# reload
Proceed with reload? [confirm} <Enter>
```

Step 3   The PIX Firewall prompts you to bootstrap it through interactive prompts. Press **Control > Z** to escape. The unprivileged mode prompt appears:

```
Pre-configure PIX Firewall through interactive prompts [yes]?
<Control>Z]
pixfirewall>
```

Step 4   Display the list of help commands:

```
pixfirewall> ?
```

Step 5   Enter the privileged mode of the PIX Firewall. When prompted for a password, press **Enter**:

```
pixfirewall> enable
password:
pixfirewall#
```

Step 6   Display the list of help commands:

```
pixfirewall# ?
```

Step 7   Use the **write terminal** command to display the PIX Firewall configuration on the terminal screen:

```
pixfirewall# write terminal
Building configuration...
: Saved
:
PIX Version 6.3(3)
interface ethernet0 auto shutdown
interface ethernet1 auto shutdown
nameif ethernet0 outside security0
nameif ethernet1 inside security100
enable password 8Ry2YjIyt7RRXU24 encrypted
passwd 2KFQnbNIdI.2KYOU encrypted
hostname pixfirewall
fixup protocol dns maximum-length 512
fixup protocol ftp 21
fixup protocol h323 h225 1720
fixup protocol h323 ras 1718-1719
fixup protocol http 80
fixup protocol rsh 514
fixup protocol rtsp 554
fixup protocol sip 5060
fixup protocol sip udp 5060
fixup protocol skinny 2000
fixup protocol smtp 25
fixup protocol sqlnet 1521
```

```
               fixup protocol tftp 69
               names
               pager lines 24
               mtu outside 1500
               mtu inside 1500
               mtu intf2 1500
               no ip address outside
               no ip address inside
               no ip address intf2
               ip audit info action alarm
               ip audit attack action alarm
               pdm history enable
               arp timeout 14400
               timeout xlate 3:00:00
               timeout conn 1:00:00 half-closed 0:10:00 udp 0:02:00 rpc 0:10:00 h225
               1:00:00
               timeout h323 0:05:00 mgcp 0:05:00 sip 0:30:00 sip_media 0:02:00
               timeout uauth 0:05:00 absolute
               aaa-server TACACS+ protocol tacacs+
               aaa-server RADIUS protocol radius
               aaa-server LOCAL protocol local
               no snmp-server location
               no snmp-server contact
               snmp-server community public
               no snmp-server enable traps
               floodguard enable
               telnet timeout 5
               ssh timeout 5
               console timeout 0
               terminal width 80
               Cryptochecksum:1fc191ccbc1b517c55033e227bf129b5
               : end
               [OK]
```

Step 8 Enter the **show memory** command:

```
               pixfirewall# show memory
               Free memory:        111667240 bytes
               Used memory:         56104920 bytes
               ------------        ----------------
               Total memory:       167772160 bytes
```

Step 9 Enter the **show version** command:

```
               pixfirewall# show version
               Cisco PIX Firewall Version 6.3(1)
               Cisco PIX Device Manager Version 3.0(1)
```

```
Compiled on Wed 13-Aug-03 13:55 by morlee
pixfirewall up 11 mins 46 secs

Hardware:    PIX-515E, 160 MB RAM, CPU Pentium II 433 MHz
Flash E28F128J3 @ 0x300, 16MB
BIOS Flash AM29F400B @ 0xfffd8000, 32KB

0: ethernet0: address is 0003.e300.483a, irq 10
1: ethernet1: address is 0003.e300.483b, irq 7
Licensed Features:
Failover:            Enabled
VPN-DES:             Enabled
VPN-3DES-AES:        Enabled
Maximum Interfaces: 6
Cut-through Proxy:   Enabled
Guards:              Enabled
URL-filtering:       Enabled
Inside Hosts:        Unlimited
Throughput:          Unlimited
IKE peers:           Unlimited

This PIX has an Unrestricted (UR) license.

Serial Number: 480430947 (0x1ca2cb63)
Running Activation Key: 0xdf113ba2 0x0afa876e 0xc7df24c3 0x2ae185bc
Configuration last modified by enable_15 at 23:22:18.770 UTC Sun Oct 5
2003
```

Step 10 Enter the **show history** command:

```
pixfirewall# show history
enable
write terminal
sh memory
show version
show history
```

Step 11 Enable the use of names rather than IP addresses:

```
pixfirewall(config)# names
```

Step 12 Assign the name **insidehost** to your computer:

```
pixfirewall(config)# name 10.0.1.11 insidehost
```

Step 13 Save your configuration to Flash memory:

```
pixfirewall(config)# write memory
Building configuration.
Cryptochecksum: e901c202 27a9db19 7e3c2878 0fc0966b
[OK]
```

Task 2—Configure PIX Firewall Interfaces

Complete the following steps to configure PIX Firewall Ethernet interfaces:

Step 1   Enable the Ethernet 0 and Ethernet 1 interfaces for 100-Mbps Ethernet full-duplex communication:

NOTE   By default the interfaces are disabled. You must enable all interfaces you intend to use.

```
pixfirewall(config)# interface e0 100full
pixfirewall(config)# interface e1 100full
pixfirewall(config)# show interface
interface ethernet0 "outside" is up, line protocol is up
  Hardware is i82558 ethernet, address is 0090.2724.fd0f
  IP address 127.0.0.1, subnet mask 255.255.255.255
  MTU 1500 bytes, BW 100000 Kbit full duplex
        6 packets input, 360 bytes, 0 no buffer
        Received 6 broadcasts, 0 runts, 0 giants
        0 input errors, 0 CRC, 0 frame, 0 overrun, 0 ignored, 0 abort
        0 packets output, 0 bytes, 0 underruns
        0 output errors, 0 collisions, 0 interface resets
        0 babbles, 0 late collisions, 0 deferred
        0 lost carrier, 0 no carrier
      input queue (curr/max blocks): hardware (128/128) software (0/0)
      output queue (curr/max blocks): hardware (0/0) software (0/0)
interface ethernet1 "inside" is up, line protocol is up
  Hardware is i82558 ethernet, address is 0090.2716.43dd
  IP address 127.0.0.1, subnet mask 255.255.255.255
  MTU 1500 bytes, BW 100000 Kbit full duplex
        22811 packets input, 3365905 bytes, 0 no buffer
        Received 22811 broadcasts, 0 runts, 0 giants
        0 input errors, 0 CRC, 0 frame, 0 overrun, 0 ignored, 0 abort
        0 packets output, 0 bytes, 0 underruns
        0 output errors, 0 collisions, 0 interface resets
        0 babbles, 0 late collisions, 0 deferred
        0 lost carrier, 0 no carrier
      input queue (curr/max blocks): hardware (128/128) software (0/1)
      output queue (curr/max blocks): hardware (0/0) software (0/0)
```

Step 2   Assign IP addresses to the inside and outside network interface cards:

```
pixfirewall(config)# ip address inside 10.0.1.1 255.255.255.0
pixfirewall(config)# ip address outside 192.168.1.2 255.255.255.0
```

Step 3   Ensure that the IP addresses are correctly configured and are associated with the proper network interface:

```
pixfirewall(config)# show ip address
System IP Addresses:
        ip address outside 192.168.1.2 255.255.255.0
        ip address inside 10.0.1.1 255.255.255.0
Current IP Addresses:
        ip address outside 192.168.1.2 255.255.255.0
        ip address inside 10.0.1.1 255.255.255.0
```

Step 4   Allow Telnet sessions from the inside interface:

```
pixfirewall(config)# telnet 10.0.1.0 255.255.255.0 inside
```

Step 5   Write the configuration to the Flash memory:

```
pixfirewall(config)# write memory
```

Task 3—Configure Global Addresses, NAT, and Routing for Inside and Outside Interfaces

Complete the following steps to configure a global address pool, NAT, and routing:

Step 1   Assign one pool of NIC-registered IP addresses for use by outbound connections:

```
pixfirewall(config)# global (outside) 1 192.168.1.100-192.168.1.254
netmask 255.255.255.0
pixfirewall(config)# show global
global (outside) 1 192.168.1.100-192.168.1.254 netmask 255.255.255.0
```

Step 2   Configure the PIX Firewall to allow inside hosts to use NAT for outbound access:

```
pixfirewall(config)# nat (inside) 1 10.0.1.0 255.255.255.0
```

Step 3   Display the currently configured NAT:

```
pixfirewall(config)# show nat
nat (inside) 1 10.0.1.0 255.255.255.0 0 0
```

Step 4   Create a static route to the 10.1.1.0 network (for practice only; the actual route is not necessary for this exercise):

```
pixfirewall(config)# route inside 10.1.1.0 255.255.255.0 10.0.1.102
```

Step 5   Assign a default route (for practice only; the actual route is not necessary for this exercise):

```
pixfirewall(config)# route outside 0 0 192.168.1.1
```

Step 6   Display the currently configured routes:

```
pixfirewall(config)# show route
outside 0.0.0.0 0.0.0.0 192.168.1.1 1 OTHER static
inside 10.0.1.0 255.255.255.0 10.0.1.1 1 CONNECT static
inside 10.1.1.0 255.255.255.0 10.0.1.102 1 OTHER static
outside 192.168.1.0 255.255.255.0 192.168.1.2 1 CONNECT static
```

Step 7   Write the current configuration to Flash memory:

```
pixfirewall(config)# write memory
```

Step 8   Display a list of the most recently entered commands.

Your history inputs should be similar to the following:

```
pixfirewall(config)#  show history
interface e0 100full
interface e1 100full
show interface
ip address inside 10.0.1.1 255.255.255.0

ip address outside 192.168.1.2 255.255.255.0
show ip address
telnet 10.0.1.0 255.255.255.0 inside
write memory
exit
configure terminal
global (outside) 1 192.168.1.100-192.168.1.254 netmask 255.255.255.0
show global
nat (inside) 1 10.0.1.0 255.255.255.0
show nat
route inside 10.1.1.0 255.255.255.0 10.0.1.102
route outside 0 0 192.168.1.1
show route
write memory
show history
```

NOTE   You can use the up and down cursor keys on your keyboard to recall commands.

Step 9   Write the current configuration to the terminal and verify that you have entered the previous commands correctly:

```
pixfirewall(config)# write terminal
Building configuration...
: Saved
```

```
:
PIX Version 6.3(3)
interface ethernet0 100full
interface ethernet1 100full
nameif ethernet0 outside security0
nameif ethernet1 inside security100
enable password 8Ry2YjIyt7RRXU24 encrypted
passwd 2KFQnbNIdI.2KYOU encrypted
hostname pixfirewall
fixup protocol dns maximum-length 512
fixup protocol ftp 21
fixup protocol h323 h225 1720
fixup protocol h323 ras 1718-1719
fixup protocol http 80
fixup protocol rsh 514
fixup protocol rtsp 554
fixup protocol sip 5060
fixup protocol sip udp 5060
fixup protocol skinny 2000
fixup protocol smtp 25
fixup protocol sqlnet 1521
fixup protocol tftp 69
names
name 10.0.1.11 insidehost
pager lines 24
mtu outside 1500
mtu inside 1500
ip address outside 192.168.1.2 255.255.255.0
ip address inside 10.0.1.1 255.255.255.0
ip audit info action alarm
ip audit attack action alarm
pdm history enable
arp timeout 14400
global (outside) 1 192.168.1.100-192.168.1.254 netmask 255.255.255.0
nat (inside) 1 10.0.1.0 255.255.255.0 0 0
route outside 0.0.0.0 0.0.0.0 192.168.1.1 1
route inside 10.1.1.0 255.255.255.0 10.0.1.102 1
timeout xlate 3:00:00
timeout conn 1:00:00 half-closed 0:10:00 udp 0:02:00 rpc 0:10:00 h225
1:00:00
timeout h323 0:05:00 mgcp 0:05:00 sip 0:30:00 sip_media 0:02:00
timeout uauth 0:05:00 absolute
aaa-server TACACS+ protocol tacacs+
aaa-server RADIUS protocol radius
aaa-server LOCAL protocol local
```

```
no snmp-server location
no snmp-server contact
snmp-server community public
no snmp-server enable traps
floodguard enable
telnet 10.0.1.0 255.255.255.0 inside
telnet timeout 5
ssh timeout 5
console timeout 0
terminal width 80
Cryptochecksum:1fc191ccbc1b517c55033e227bf129b5
: end
[OK]
```

Step 10 Complete the following substeps to test the operation of the globals and NAT statements you configured by originating connections through the PIX Firewall:

    (1) Open a web browser on the inside host.

    (2) Use the web browser to access the outside host at IP address 192.168.1.50 by entering **http://192.168.1.50**.

Step 11 Observe the translation table:

```
pixfirewall(config)# show xlate
```

Your display should appear similar to the following:

```
1 in use, 1 most used
Global 192.168.1.100 Local insidehost
```

A global address chosen from the low end of the global range has been mapped to your inside host.

Task 4—Test the Inside and Outside Interface Connectivity

Complete the following steps to test and troubleshoot interface connectivity using the PIX Firewall **ping** command:

Step 1 Ping the inside interface:

```
pixfirewall(config)# ping 10.0.1.1
10.0.1.1 response received-0ms
10.0.1.1 response received-0ms
10.0.1.1 response received-0ms
```

Step 2 Ping the inside host:

```
pixfirewall(config)# ping insidehost
insidehost response received —— 0ms
insidehost response received —— 0ms
insidehost response received —— 0ms
```

Step 3 Ping the outside interface:

```
pixfirewall(config)# ping 192.168.1.2
192.168.1.2 response received —— 0ms
192.168.1.2 response received —— 0ms
192.168.1.2 response received —— 0ms
```

Task 5—Configure Syslog Output

Complete the following steps and enter the commands as directed to configure syslog output:

Step 1 Enable syslog logging:

```
pixfirewall(config)# logging on
```

Step 2 Begin storing messages to the PIX Firewall message buffer and set the logging level to debugging:

```
pixfirewall(config)# logging buffered debugging
```

Step 3 From your inside host command line, Telnet to the PIX Firewall:

```
C:\> telnet 10.0.1.1
Password: cisco
Pixfirewall> enable
Password:
Pixfirewall# exit
Logoff


Connection to host lost.
```

Step 4 View the syslog messages with the **show logging** command. New messages appear at the end of the display:

```
pixfirewall(config)# show logging
Syslog logging: enabled
    Facility: 20
    Timestamp logging: disabled
    Standby logging: disabled
    Console logging: disabled
    Monitor logging: disabled
    Buffer logging: level debugging, 25 messages logged
    Trap logging: disabled
    History logging: disabled
    Device ID: disabled
111008: User 'enable_15' executed the 'clear logging' command.
710001: TCP access requested from 10.0.1.11/2345 to inside:10.0.1.1/
telnet
710002: TCP access permitted from 10.0.1.11/2345 to inside:10.0.1.1/
telnet
```

```
605005: Login permitted from 10.0.1.11/2345 to inside:10.0.1.1/telnet
for user ""
502103: User priv level changed: Uname: enable_1 From: 1 To: 15
111008: User 'enable_1' executed the 'enable' command.
611103: User logged out: Uname: enable_15
302010: 0 in use, 0 most used
```

Step 5 Clear messages in the buffer and verify they are cleared:

```
pixfirewall(config)# clear logging
pixfirewall(config)# show logging
```

Step 6 Set the **logging buffered** command back to a minimal level:

```
pixfirewall(config)# logging buffered alerts
```

Task 6—Configure Syslog Output to a Syslog Server

NOTE   Verify that the syslog server or host is turned on and that the syslog service is installed and started.

You will now configure syslog to the inside host running Kiwi Syslog:

Step 1 Designate a host to receive the messages with the **logging host** command. For normal syslog operations to any syslog server, use the default message protocol:

```
pixfirewall(config)# logging host inside insidehost
```

Step 2 Set the logging level to the syslog server or host with the **logging trap** command. You use this command to start sending messages to the syslog server or host. For definition of levels, refer to Table 5-16.

```
pixfirewall(config)# logging trap debugging
```

Step 3 Open the Kiwi Syslog Daemon on the inside host.

Step 4 From the inside host, Telnet to the PIX Firewall:

```
C:\> telnet 10.0.1.1
Password: cisco
Pixfirewall> enable
Password:
Pixfirewall# exit
Logoff

Connection to host lost.
```

Step 5 Observe the messages logged to the Kiwi Syslog Daemon display screen:

```
%PIX-5-611103: User logged out: Uname: enable_15
%PIX-5-111008: User 'enable_1' executed the 'enable' command.
%PIX-5-502103: User priv level changed: Uname: enable_1 From: 1 To: 15
%PIX-6-605005: Login permitted from 10.0.1.11/2347 to inside:10.0.1.1/
telnet for user ""
%PIX-7-710002: TCP access permitted from 10.0.1.11/2347 to
inside:10.0.1.1/telnet
%PIX-7-710001: TCP access requested from 10.0.1.11/2347 to
inside:10.0.1.1/telnet
%PIX-5-111008: User 'enable_15' executed the 'logging trap debugging'
command.
```

On completion of this chapter, you will be able to perform the following tasks:

- Describe the PIX Device Manager (PDM) and its capabilities.
- Describe PDM's browser and PIX Firewall requirements.
- Install PDM and prepare the PIX Firewall to use PDM.
- Navigate the PDM configuration windows.
- Perform basic configuration of the PIX Firewall using PDM.
- Test and verify PDM functionality.

CHAPTER 6

Cisco PIX Device Manager

The Cisco PIX Device Manager, or PDM, is a browser-based configuration and monitoring tool that allows you to easily configure and manage a single PIX Firewall without extensive knowledge of the command-line interface (CLI). The first version of PDM, introduced with PIX Firewall Version 6.0, had limited capabilities and was suitable for basic configurations.

With each new release of the software, however, Cisco has improved and expanded the capabilities of PDM. The latest release, Version 3.0, is the most capable version of the PDM to date and adds support for many of the new features introduced in PIX Firewall Version 6.3. This chapter provides an overview of PDM, system requirements, and configuration guidelines.

PDM Overview

PDM provides a graphical console for monitoring and configuring a single PIX Firewall. The PDM software image must be installed and executed on each individual PIX Firewall that you intend to configure and monitor using PDM. However, after the software is properly installed, you can point your browser to more than one PIX Firewall and administer several PIX Firewalls from a single workstation.

NOTE   If you are interested in a GUI-based management console to manage a large number of Cisco PIX Firewalls, you should consider the Cisco Management Center for Firewalls (Firewall MC), which is covered in Chapter 19, "PIX Firewall Management in Enterprise Networks."

PDM is secure, versatile, and easy to use. It works with PIX Firewall 500 series models and runs on a variety of platforms.

NOTE   You can also use PDM to configure and monitor the Firewall Services Module (FWSM) on a Cisco Catalyst 6500 switch. This use of PDM is discussed later in Chapter 21, "Firewall Services Module."

PDM enables you to securely configure and monitor your PIX Firewall remotely. Its ability to work with the Secure Socket Layer (SSL) protocol ensures that communication with the PIX Firewall is secure, and because it is implemented in Java, it offers robust, real-time monitoring.

PDM works with PIX Firewall Software Versions 6.0 and higher and comes preloaded into Flash memory on new PIX Firewalls running Software Versions 6.0 and higher. If you are upgrading from a previous version of the PIX Firewall, you can download PDM from Cisco and then copy it to the PIX Firewall via Trivial File Transfer Protocol (TFTP).

NOTE   The specific version of the PDM that you use depends on the version of PIX Firewall you are running. PIX Firewall Versions 6.0 and 6.1 work with PDM Versions 1.0 or 1.1. If you are running PIX Firewall Version 6.2, you should use PDM 2.0 or 2.1. PDM Version 3.0 is specifically designed for use with PIX Firewall Version 6.3.

PDM runs on Windows, Sun Solaris, and Linux platforms and requires no plug-ins or complex software installations. The PDM applet uploads to your workstation when you access the PIX Firewall from your browser.

Using the PIX Firewall CLI, Firewall MC, or even legacy Cisco Secure Policy Manager (CSPM) systems, you can use PDM to create a new configuration or view, alter, and maintain configurations you previously created.

In its current release (Version 3.0), PDM is a robust, capable, and powerful management and monitoring tool that deserves consideration as the primary management tool for your PIX Firewall. Whether you choose to use PDM or other tools such as the CLI or Firewall MC depends largely on your preference. However, you might want to avoid using the PDM if

- You are managing a large number of PIX Firewalls. Firewall MC and even CLI are better suited for managing large numbers of PIX Firewalls.

- You have a large number of access; authentication, authorization, and accounting (AAA); filter; or translation rules, which are typically created more efficiently using CLI.

- You are using commands that are not yet supported in PDM such as the **alias** command.

- You are creating a configuration file that is significantly larger than 100 KB.

<table>
<tr><td>NOTE</td><td>Always check Cisco.com for the latest version of the PIX Firewall image, PDM image, and documentation to determine which commands are supported. The list of commands supported by the PDM has increased significantly since the first release, and support for additional commands in future versions of PDM is expected.</td></tr>
</table>

If your project does not involve any of the items in the preceding list and you prefer a GUI-based management console to a CLI-based one, PDM is for you, and it can serve as your primary management and monitoring tool for PIX Firewall implementations.

You can also use the PDM as a learning tool by viewing the CLI commands that it generates when you configure various components of the PIX Firewall. For example, virtual private network (VPN) commands tend to be somewhat cryptic, and PDM greatly simplifies the process of creating VPN configurations. (VPN topics are discussed in detail in Chapters 15, 16, and 17.) You can then view the generated CLI commands to better understand VPN configurations and proper CLI techniques for configuring site-to-site and remote access VPN connections.

PDM Operational Requirements

New PIX Firewalls that contain Version 6.0 also have a pre-installed Data Encryption Standard (DES) activation key. If you are using a new PIX Firewall with PIX Firewall Version 6.0 or higher pre-installed, you have all the requirements discussed in this section and you can continue to the next section, "Preparing for PDM."

A PIX Firewall must meet the following requirements to run PDM:

- You must have an activation key that enables DES or the more secure Triple DES (3DES) and Advanced Encryption Standard (AES), which PDM requires for support of the SSL protocol. If your PIX Firewall is not enabled for DES or 3DES/AES encryption, you can receive a new activation key by completing the appropriate form available on Cisco.com.

<table>
<tr><td>NOTE</td><td>You can request a free DES or 3DES/AES encryption license using the Customer Registration site at Cisco.com. You might need a Cisco Connection Online (CCO) account to access and complete the online request form for a new license and activation key.</td></tr>
</table>

- Verify that the PIX Firewall meets all requirements listed in the release notes for the PIX Firewall software version in use.

- Verify that your PIX Firewall hardware model, PIX Firewall software version, and PDM version are compatible. Refer to the Table 6-1 to ensure compatibility. If you need to update the software on the PIX Firewall, download PIX Firewall and PDM software from the following URL on Cisco.com: http://www.cisco.com/cgi-bin/tablebuild.pl/pix.

NOTE   You might need a CCO account to access and download PIX Firewall and PDM software from Cisco.com.

- You must have at least 8 MB of Flash memory on the PIX Firewall.
- Ensure that your configuration is less than 100 KB (approximately 1500 lines). Configurations over 100 KB cause PDM performance degradation.

NOTE   You can determine the size of your configuration by using the **show flashfs** command at the PIX Firewall CLI console. When you issue this command, the PIX Firewall displays several lines of output. The configuration file size is specified as "file 1" within the output of the **show flashfs** command.

Table 6-1   *Valid PIX Firewall and PDM Version Combinations*

PDM Version	Supported PIX Firewall Version	Supported PIX Firewall Model
1.0	6.0 or 6.1	506, 515, 520, 525, 535
1.1	6.0 or 6.1	506, 515, 520, 525, 535
2.0	6.2	501, 506/506E, 515/515E, 520, 525, 535
2.1	6.2	501, 506/506E, 515/515E, 520, 525, 535
2.1	FWSM 1.1	FWSM
3.0	6.3	501, 506/506E, 515/515E, 520, 525, 535

To access PDM from a browser, the system must meet the following requirements:

- JavaScript and Java must be enabled. If you are using Microsoft Internet Explorer, the native Java Virtual Machine (JVM) is supported. You can also use Java Runtime Environment (JRE) Version 1.3.1, 1.4.0, or 1.4.1. These requirements are for PDM Version 3.0. Earlier versions of the PDM also work with the latest versions of the

Microsoft JVM or Sun Microsystems JRE. If you have an older version of these environments, you can download the latest version of the JVM for Internet Explorer and the latest version of the JRE from the Microsoft and Sun Microsystems websites, respectively.

- Browser support for SSL must be enabled. The supported versions of Internet Explorer and Netscape Navigator support SSL without requiring additional configuration.

PDM can operate in browsers running on Windows, Sun Solaris, or Linux operating systems. The requirements for running PDM 3.0 on each operating system appear in the following subsections.

Windows Requirements

PDM 3.0 is supported on Windows 98, ME, NT 4.0 (Service Pack 4 [SP4] or higher), Windows 2000 (SP3), and Windows XP. Windows 3.1 and Windows 95 are not supported. Windows XP and Windows 2000 with SP3 are the preferred and recommended Windows platforms for PDM 3.0. Specific browser and Java requirements for PDM 3.0 appear in Table 6-2.

NOTE Hardware and software requirements listed in this chapter refer to Version 3.0 of the PDM. Check Cisco.com for specific requirements for running earlier or later versions of PDM.

Table 6-2 *Browser and Java Requirements for Windows Platforms Using PDM 3.0*

Operating System	Browser	JAVA Environment
Windows 98 Windows ME Windows NT 4.0 (SP4 or higher) Windows 2000 (SP3) Windows XP	Internet Explorer 5.5 or 6.0 (6.0 recommended)	Built-in JVM (VM 3167 or higher, VM 3809 recommended)
	Internet Explorer 5.5 or 6.0 (6.0 recommended)	JRE plug-in 1.3.1, 1.4.0, or 1.4.1 (1.4.1_02 recommended)
	Netscape 4.7x	Built-in JVM 1.1.5
	Netscape 7.0x (recommended)	JRE plug-in 1.4.0 or 1.4.1 (1.4.1_02 recommended)

In addition to the software requirements in Table 6-2, the following hardware requirements apply for Windows systems using PDM 3.0:

- Pentium III or compatible processor running at 450 MHz or higher
- 256 MB of RAM
- 1024-by-768 pixel display with at least 256 colors (16-bit color is recommended)

Sun Solaris Requirements

PDM 3.0 is supported on Sun Solaris 2.8 or 2.9 running CDE window manager. The following requirements apply to the use of PDM 3.0 on Solaris-based systems:

- Sun Solaris 2.8 or 2.9 running CDE window manager. Sun Solaris 2.8 is recommended.
- Netscape 4.78 with built-in JVM.

NOTE	Netscape Communicator 4.79 is not supported with PDM 3.0.

- Sparc microprocessor.
- At least 128 MB of RAM.
- A 1024-by-768 pixel display with at least 256 colors.

Linux Requirements

You can also use PDM 3.0 on Linux systems. Table 6-3 lists the operating system and browser requirements for Linux systems using PDM 3.0.

Table 6-3 *Browser and Java Requirements for Linux Platforms Using PDM 3.0*

Operating System	Browser	Java Environment
Red Hat Linux 7.0, 7.1, 7.2, 7.3, or 8.0 running GNOME or KDE (Red Hat Linux 8.0 is recommended)	Netscape 4.7x on Red Hat Version 7.x	Built-in JVM
	Mozilla 1.0.1 on Red Hat Linux 8.0 (recommended)	JRE plug-in 1.4.1 (1.4.1_02 recommended)

In addition to the software requirements listed in Table 6-3, the following hardware requirements apply for Linux systems using PDM 3.0:

- Pentium III or compatible processor running at 450 MHz or higher
- At least 128 MB of RAM
- 1024-by-768 pixel display with at least 256 colors (16-bit color is recommended)

General Guidelines

The following are a few general guidelines for workstations running PDM:

- You can run several PDM sessions on a single workstation. The maximum number of PDM sessions depends on workstation's resources, such as memory, CPU speed, and browser type.
- The time required to download the PDM applet can be greatly affected by the speed of the link between the workstation and the PIX Firewall. A minimum of 56 Kbps link speed is required; however, 1.5 Mbps or higher is recommended. After you load the PDM applet on the workstation, the link speed impact on PDM operation is negligible.
- The use of virus-checking software might dramatically increase the time required to start PDM, especially for Netscape Communicator on any Windows platform or Windows 2000 and Windows XP running any type of browser.
- Accessing the PDM using fully qualified domain names (FQDNs) is recommended. This process does require appropriate Domain Name System (DNS) entries or the use of a hosts file on the workstation. With some JVMs, you can experience degraded performance when using the IP address of the PIX to access PDM.

If a workstation's resources are running low, close and re-open the browser before launching PDM.

Preparing for PDM

As mentioned earlier, new PIX Firewalls with PIX Firewall Version 6.0 or higher are preloaded with PDM. If your PIX Firewall has PDM 2.0 or higher, you can use PDM's Startup Wizard for the initial configuration. Simply connect the PC to the inside interface (Ethernet 1) of the PIX Firewall and use Dynamic Host Configuration Protocol (DHCP) or specify an address in the range 192.168.1.2 to 192.168.1.254. Then, access the PIX Firewall through PDM using the URL https://192.168.1.1/startup.html. PIX Firewalls with default factory settings have an IP address of 192.168.1.1 for their inside interfaces.

You must configure the PIX Firewall with the following information before you can install or use PDM. You can either preconfigure a new PIX Firewall through the interactive prompts, which appear after the PIX Firewall boots, or you can enter the commands shown here for each information item:

- **Enable password**—Enter an alphanumeric password to protect the PIX Firewall privileged mode. The alphanumeric password can be up to 16 characters in length. You must use this password to log in to PDM. The command syntax for enabling a password is as follows:

  `enable password` *password* `[encrypted]`

- **Time**—Set the PIX Firewall clock to Universal Coordinated Time (UTC, also known as Greenwich Mean Time, or GMT). For example, if you are in the Pacific Daylight Savings time zone, set the clock 7 hours ahead of your local time to set the clock to UTC. Enter the year, month, day, and time. Enter the UTC time in 24-hour time as hour:minutes:seconds. The command syntax for setting the clock is as follows:

  `clock set` *hh:mm:ss {day month | month day} year*

- **Inside IP address**—Specify the IP address of the PIX Firewall's inside interface. Ensure that this IP address is unique on the network and not used by any other computer or network device, such as a router. The command syntax for setting an inside IP address is as follows:

  `ip address` *if_name ip_address* `[`*netmask*`]`

- **Inside network mask**—Use the **ip address** command to specify the network mask for the inside interface. An example is 255.255.255.0. You can also specify a subnetted mask (for example, 255.255.255.224). Do not use all 255s, such as 255.255.255.255; this prevents traffic from passing on the interface. If a network mask is not specified, the default major network mask is applied (255.0.0.0 for Class A addresses, 255.255.0.0 for Class B addresses, and 255.255.255.0 for Class C addresses).

- **Host name**—Specify up to 16 characters as a name for the PIX Firewall. The command syntax for setting a host name is as follows:

  `hostname` *newname*

- **Domain name**—Specify the domain name for the PIX Firewall. The command syntax for enabling the domain name is as follows:

  `domain-name` *name*

- **IP address of the host running PDM**—Specify the IP address of the workstation that accesses PDM from its browser. The command syntax for granting permission for a host to connect to the PIX Firewall with SSL is as follows:

  `http` *ip_address* `[`*netmask*`]` `[`*if_name*`]`

- **HTTP Server**—Enable the HTTP server on the PIX Firewall with the **http server enable** command.

If you are installing PDM on a PIX Firewall with an existing configuration, you might need to restructure your configuration from the PIX Firewall CLI before installing PDM to obtain full PDM capability. There are certain commands that PDM does not support in a configuration. If these commands are present in your configuration, you have access to only the Monitoring tab. PDM handles each PIX Firewall command in one of the following ways:

- Parse and allow changes (supported commands)
- Parse and only permit access to the Monitoring tab (unsupported commands)
- Parse without allowing changes (partially supported commands that PDM handles transparently without preventing further configuration)
- Only display in the unparseable command list (partially supported commands that PDM handles transparently without preventing future configuration)

NOTE   The different modes with which PDM handles each command and the list of commands in each mode are explained in detail in the document "PDM Support for PIX Firewall CLI Commands," available on Cisco.com.

An unconfigured PIX Firewall starts in an interactive setup dialog to enable you to perform the initial configuration required to use PDM. You can also access the setup dialog by entering **setup** at the configuration mode prompt.

NOTE   You can also use PDM's Startup Wizard for the initial configuration of a new PIX Firewall with PDM 2.0 or higher. Simply connect the PC to the inside interface (Ethernet 1) of the PIX Firewall and use DHCP or specify an address in the range 192.168.1.2 to 192.168.1.254. You can then access the PIX Firewall through PDM using the URL https://192.168.1.1/startup.html.

The dialog asks for several responses, including the inside IP address, network mask, host name, domain name, and PDM host. The host name and domain name are used to generate the default certificate for the SSL connection.

Pressing the **Enter** key instead of entering a value at the prompt causes the default value within the brackets to be accepted. You must fill in any fields that show no default values and change default values as necessary. After the configuration is written to Flash memory, the PIX Firewall is ready to start PDM.

CAUTION You must set the clock for PDM to generate a valid certification. Set the PIX Firewall clock to UTC (also known as GMT).

Table 6-4 lists the prompts in the setup dialog.

Table 6-4 *PIX Firewall Interactive Setup Dialog*

Prompt	Definition	Sample Value
Enable password	Enable password for this PIX Firewall, up to 16 characters.	cisco123
Clock (UTC)	Enables you to set the PIX Firewall clock to UTC (also known as GMT).	N/A
Year [system year]	Enables you to specify the current year or return to the default year stored in the host computer.	2003
Month [system month]	Enables you to specify the current month or return to the default month stored in the host computer.	June
Day [system day]	Enables you to specify the current day or return to the default day stored in the host computer.	4
Time [system time]	Enables you to specify the current time in hh:mm:ss format or return to the default time stored in the host computer.	20:30:00
Inside IP address	The network interface IP address of the PIX Firewall.	10.0.0.1
Inside network mask	A network mask that applies to the inside IP address. Use 0.0.0.0 to specify a default route. The 0.0.0.0 netmask can be abbreviated as 0.	255.255.255.0
Host name	The host name you want to display in the PIX Firewall command-line prompt.	pixfirewall
Domain name	The DNS domain name of the network on which the PIX Firewall runs.	Cisco.com
IP address of host running PIX Device Manager	IP address on which PDM connects to the PIX Firewall.	10.0.0.11
Use this configuration and write to flash?	Enables you to store the new configuration to Flash memory. It is the same as the **write memory** command. If the answer is yes, the inside interface is enabled and the requested configuration is written to Flash memory. If the user answers anything else, the setup dialog repeats, using the values already entered as the defaults for the questions.	Yes or No

Using PDM to Configure the PIX Firewall

You access the PDM using an SSL-encrypted connection (HTTPS) to the PIX Firewall. For example, to access the PDM on a PIX Firewall with an IP address of 10.0.0.1, you use the URL https://10.0.0.1.

The PDM Startup Wizard (available with PDM 2.0 and higher) is an easy way to begin the process of configuring your PIX Firewall. The wizard steps you through such tasks as

- Enabling the PIX Firewall interfaces
- Assigning IP addresses to the interfaces
- Configuring a host name and password
- Configuring Point-to-Point Protocol over Ethernet (PPPoE)
- Configuring Easy VPN Remote
- Configuring Auto Update
- Configuring network address translation (NAT) and port address translation (PAT)
- Configuring the DHCP server

You can run the Startup Wizard at any time by choosing **Tools > Startup Wizard**, and it automatically starts if you are accessing a PIX Firewall with PDM 2.0 or higher for the initial configuration.

Figure 6-1 *PDM 3.0 Home Screen*

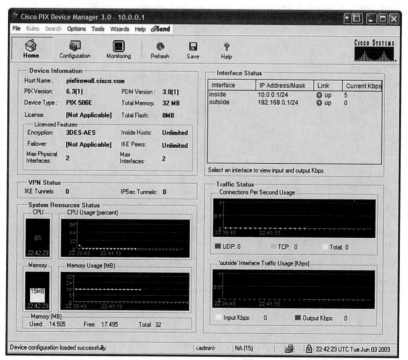

When you first start PDM, you see the home screen shown in Figure 6-1. This screen provides a quick snapshot of the firewall's status and includes five specific areas:

- **Device Information**—Information about the PIX Firewall model, PIX version, PDM version, memory, and available licenses

- **Interface Status**—Information on interfaces, IP address, link status, and throughput

- **VPN Status**—Number of active Internet Key Exchange (IKE) and IP Security (IPSec) tunnels

- **System Resources Status**—Information on CPU and memory usage

- **Traffic Status**—Information on traffic throughput and TCP and User Datagram Protocol (UDP) connections per second

You can access other functions of the PDM from the initial screen. You access configuration and monitoring screens by clicking the **Configuration** or **Monitoring** buttons at the top of the page, as shown in Figure 6-1. Clicking the **Configuration** button brings up the configuration page of the PDM, shown in Figure 6-2.

Figure 6-2 *PDM 3.0 Configuration Screen*

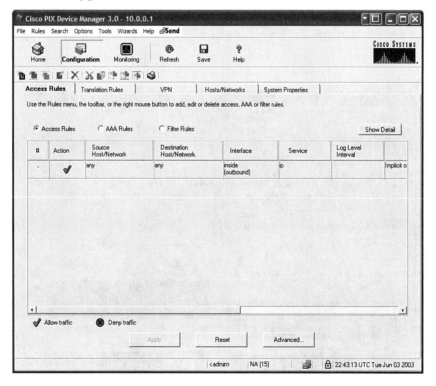

The configuration page consists of the PDM toolbar and five tabs, which enable you to configure various aspects of the product:

- **Access Rules**—Shows configured access rules for your network
- **Translation Rules**—Enables you to view all the address translation rules applied to your network
- **VPN**—Enables you to create VPNs using IPSec
- **Hosts/Networks**—Enables you to view, edit, add to, or delete from the list of hosts and networks defined for the selected interface
- **System Properties**—Enables you to configure many other aspects of the PIX Firewall, such as management protocols, logging, intrusion detection, AAA, and routing settings

You access various monitoring features of the PIX Firewall by clicking the **Monitoring** button. Figure 6-3 shows the main monitoring screen on PDM 3.0. Monitoring capabilities of the PDM are discussed later in this chapter.

Figure 6-3 *PDM 3.0 Monitoring Screen*

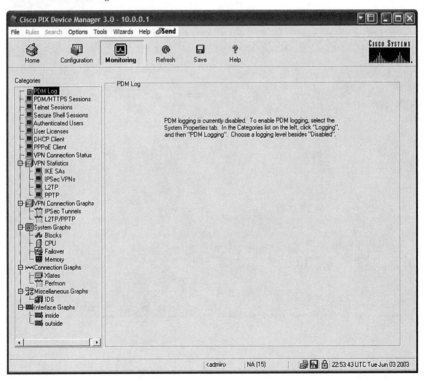

Configuration

Configuration screens and associated procedures are covered in detail in the following subsections. PDM provides excellent context-based online help, which you can utilize.

Access Rules Tab

Figure 6-4 shows the Access Rules screen (tab). It combines the concepts of access control lists (ACLs), outbound lists, and conduits to describe how an entire subnet or specific network host interacts with another to permit or deny a specific service, protocol, or both. The implicit outbound rule and any other access rules configured on the PIX Firewall appear on this screen. ACLs are covered in detail in Chapter 8, "Access Control Lists and Content Filtering."

Figure 6-4 *Access Rules Configuration Screen*

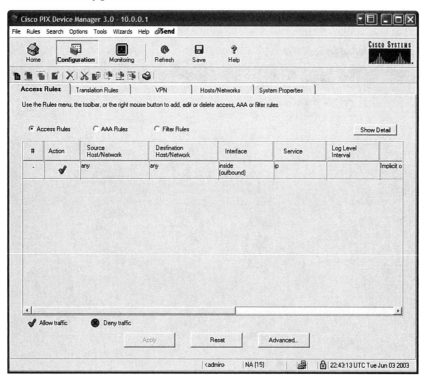

PDM does not support the use of ACLs, conduits, and outbounds together. You can use only one of the three at one time, ACLs being the preferred choice. PDM continues to use the choice you make. If you attempt to use more than one of these choices in your configuration, you will be able to only perform monitoring tasks.

NOTE	PIX Firewall Software Version 6.3 will be the last release to support the **conduit** and **outbound** commands. You should use ACLs for all new configurations and consider converting existing conduit-based configurations to ACLs.

When you work in either the Access Rules or the Translation Rules tab, you can access the task menus for creating or modifying rules in one of four ways:

- Using the PDM toolbar (the row of icons immediately above the tabs)
- Using the Rules menu
- Right-clicking anywhere in the rules table
- Double-clicking an existing rule (for inspection or modification)

Figure 6-5 shows the Add Rule screen, which enables you to perform a number of tasks:

- Define source and destination hosts and networks using the IP address and mask, previously defined names, or groups.
- Specify protocol and services that are affected by the rule.
- Use predefined service groups to simplify the access rules.
- Define new service groups by clicking **Manage Service Groups**.

Figure 6-5   *Add Rule Screen*

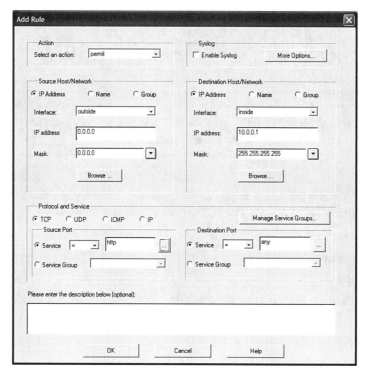

This tab also enables you to define AAA rules and filter rules for ActiveX and Java. The configuration edits you perform on the Access Rules tab are captured by PDM but are not sent to the PIX Firewall until you click **Apply**. This applies to all configurations performed with PDM, including those performed in the Translation Rules tab, the Hosts/Networks tab, and the System Properties tab. Always click **Apply** to send your configuration edits to the PIX Firewall. Also remember, it is important to save your configuration to Flash memory by choosing **File > Save Running Configuration to Flash** from the main menu or clicking the **Save** icon in the toolbar.

NOTE   You can also use the Access Rules tab to create object groups and apply them to access lists.

Translations Rules Tab

Figure 6-6 shows the Translations Rules screen. The Translations Rules tab enables you to create and view static and dynamic address translation rules for the network. Before you can designate access and translation rules for your network, you must first define each host or server for which a rule will apply. To do so, select the **Hosts/Networks** tab to define hosts and networks. Address translation concepts are presented in detail in Chapter 7, "Translation and Connections."

Figure 6-6 *Translations Rules Configuration Screen*

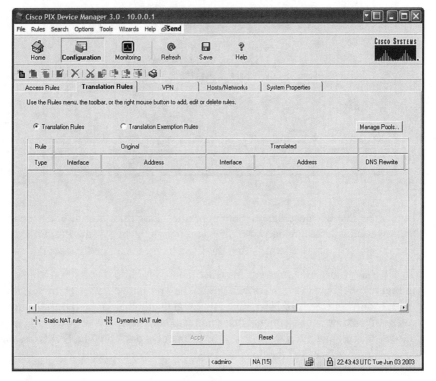

The Manage Global Address Pools window shown in Figure 6-7 enables you to configure global address pools to be used by NAT. From this window, you can edit or delete existing global pools or add new pools. You can access the Manage Global Address Pools window from the Manage Pools button on the Translation Rules tab.

Figure 6-7   *Manage Global Address Pools Window*

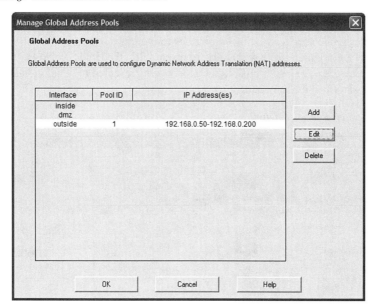

Remember that it is necessary to configure translation rules even if you have routable IP addresses on your secure networks. This is a unique feature of the PIX Firewall. You can use a routable address by translating the IP address to itself on the outside.

To add a new translation rule, you must use the Add Address Translation Rule screen shown in Figure 6-8. You access this screen within the Translation Rules tab by selecting **Rules > Add**, by clicking the **Add New Rule** button on the toolbar, or by right-clicking within the rules list window and selecting **Add** from the popup menu. As shown in Figure 6-8, you specify the original interface, original host, and network using the IP address and mask, translation interface, and the translated address (static or dynamic).

NOTE   The order in which you apply translation rules can affect the way the rules operate. PDM lists the static translations first and then the dynamic translations. When processing NAT, the PIX Firewall first translates the static translations in the order they are configured. You can use the **Insert Before** or **Insert After** commands from the Rules menu to determine the order in which static translations are processed. Because dynamically translated rules are processed on a best-match basis, the option to insert a rule before or after a dynamic translation is disabled.

Figure 6-8   *Add Translations Rules Screen*

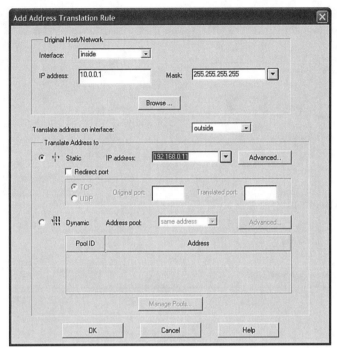

If you want to exclude a specific host or network from NAT, you can select the **Translation Exemption Rules** option on the Translation Rules tab. You use the Add Address Exemption Rule screen shown in Figure 6-9 to configure exemption rules. After activating the Translation Exemption Rules option, you can access the Add Address Exemption Rule screen by selecting **Rules > Add**, by clicking the **Add New Rule** button on the toolbar, or by right-clicking within the rules list window and selecting **Add** from the popup menu.

VPN Tab

Figure 6-10 shows the VPN configuration screen of the PDM. From the VPN tab, you can create site-to-site or remote access VPNs. You can also configure the PIX Firewall to act as an Easy VPN Remote device using the configuration options on this screen.

Figure 6-9 *Add Address Exemption Rules Screen*

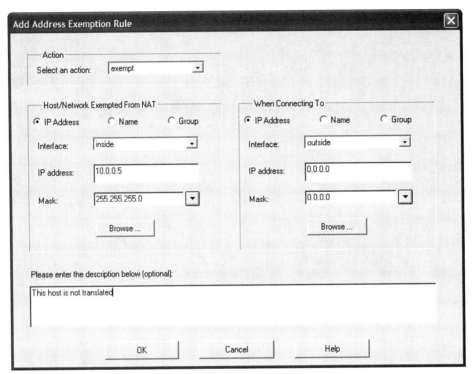

VPN topics and configuration procedures are covered in detail in Chapter 15, "Virtual Private Networks," Chapter 16, "Site-to-Site VPNs," and Chapter 17, "Client Remote Access VPNs," and are not presented here. CLI commands for configuring VPN settings tend to be somewhat complicated. PDM does an excellent job of simplifying VPN configuration tasks on the PIX Firewall and should be given strong consideration as the primary tool for VPN configurations. You are less likely to commit errors in configuration using the PDM. After you create your VPN configuration with PDM, you can view the running configuration on your PIX Firewall to see the specific CLI commands generated by the PDM.

Figure 6-10 *VPN Configuration Screen*

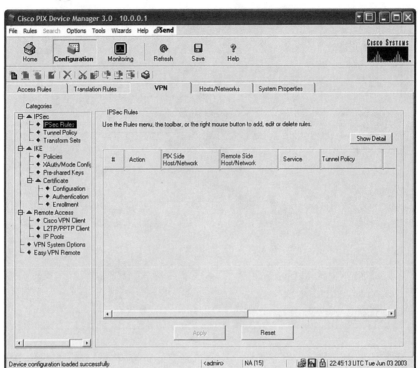

Hosts/Networks Tab

The PDM requires that you define any host or network that you intend to use in ACLs and translation rules. These hosts or networks are organized below the interface from which they are reachable. When defining either type of rule, you can reference a host or network by clicking the **Browse** button in the appropriate add or edit rule window. Additionally, you can reference the host or network by name if a name is defined for that host or network. It is recommended that you name all hosts and networks.

Figure 6-11 shows the Hosts/Networks configuration screen of the PDM. In addition to defining the basic information for these hosts or networks, you can define route settings and translation rules (NAT) for any host or network. You can also configure route settings in the Static Route panel on the System Properties tab and translation rules on the Translation Rules tab. These different configuration options accomplish the same results. The Hosts/Networks tab provides another view to modify these settings on a per-host and per-network basis. You can also define groups and add hosts and networks to a specific group. Figure 6-12 shows the Add Host/Network Group screen used to define groups and group members.

Figure 6-11 *Hosts/Networks Configuration Screen*

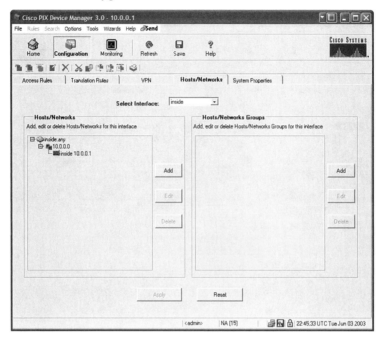

Figure 6-12 *Add Host/Network Group Screen*

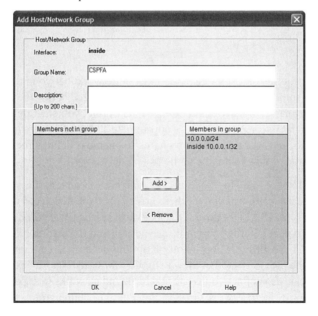

The information provided in this window enables the basic identification information for that host or network. It includes values for the IP address, netmask, interface, and name of the host or network. PDM uses the name and IP address and netmask pair to resolve references to this host or network in the source and destination conditions of access rules and in translation rules. PDM uses the interface value to apply access and translation rules that reference this host or network to the correct interface. The interface delivers network packets to the host or network; therefore, it enforces the rules that reference that host or network.

System Properties Tab

Figure 6-13 shows the System Properties configuration screen.

Figure 6-13   *System Properties Configuration Screen*

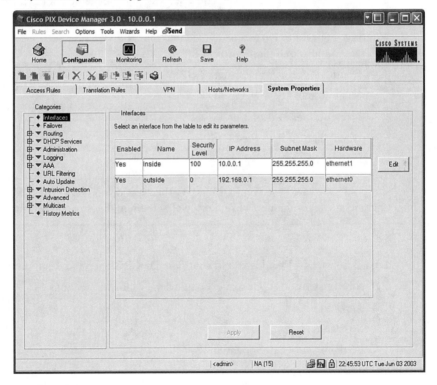

The System Properties tab enables you to configure many aspects of the PIX Firewall, including the following:

- **Interfaces**—In addition to their names, the Interfaces panel displays and enables you to edit additional configuration information required for each interface. You can configure a PIX Firewall interface with a static IP address or you can configure it to use DHCP or PPPoE.

NOTE   Your configuration edits are captured by PDM but not sent to the PIX Firewall until you click **Apply**.

- **Failover**—Enables you to enable, disable, and configure serial and LAN-based failover and stateful failover.
- **Routing**—The routing panel is divided into the following four sections dealing with different routing configurations:
    - Routing Information Protocol (RIP)
    - Static Routes
    - Proxy Address Resolution Protocols (ARPs)
    - Open Shortest Path First (OSPF)

NOTE   The categories listed are based on PDM 3.0. Earlier versions of PDM are similar, but they might not include all of the items listed or display them in the same order shown here.

- **DHCP Services**—Enables you to configure DHCP Server and Relay settings.
- **PIX Administration**—This panel contains the following sections:
    - Device
    - Password
    - Authentication/Authorization
    - User Accounts
    - Banner
    - Console
    - PDM/HTTPS
    - Telnet

- — Secure Shell
- — Management Access
- — Simple Network Management Protocol (SNMP)
- — Internet Control Message Protocol (ICMP)
- — TFTP Server
- — Clock
- — Network Time Protocol (NTP)
- **Logging**—This panel is divided into the following sections:
  - — Logging Setup
  - — PDM Logging
  - — Syslog
  - — Others
- **AAA**—This panel contains the following sections:
  - — AAA Server Groups
  - — AAA Servers
  - — Auth. Prompt
- **URL Filtering**—This panel enables you prevent users from accessing external WWW URLs that you designate using a WebSense or N2H2 URL filtering server.
- **Auto Update**—This panel enables you to specify the Auto Update server and polling parameters for image and configuration updates.
- **Intrusion Detection**—This panel is divided into the following two sections:
  - — IDS Policy
  - — IDS Signatures
- **Advanced**—This panel consists of the six panels listed here, with the Fixup panel having further selections nested beneath it:
  - — Fixup
  - — Computer Telephony Interface Quick Buffer Encoding (CTIQBE)
  - — Encapsulating Security Payload (ESP)-IKE
  - — FTP
  - — H.323 H225
  - — H.323 Registration, Admission, and Status (RAS)
  - — HTTP
  - — ICMP Error

- — Internet Locator Service (ILS)
- — Media Gateway Control Protocol (MGCP)
- — Point-to-Point Tunneling Protocol (PPTP)
- — Remote shell (RSH)
- — Real-Time Streaming Protocol (RTSP)
- — Session Initiation Protocol (SIP) over TCP
- — SIP over UDP
- — Skinny
- — Simple Mail Transfer Protocol (SMTP)
- — SQL*Net
- — Anti-Spoofing
- — Fragment
- — TCP Options
- — Timeout
- — Turbo Access Rules
- **Multicast**—This panel consists of the three panels in the list that follows, with the Internet Group Management Protocol (IGMP) panel having further selections nested beneath it:
  - — Stub Multicast Routing
  - — IGMP
  - — Protocol
  - — Access Group
  - — Join Group
  - — MRoute
- **History Metrics**—This panel enables the PIX Firewall to keep a history of many statistics, which you can display with PDM through the Monitoring tab.

NOTE   If PDM History Metrics is not enabled, the only view available in the Monitoring tab is the "real-time" view. PDM History Metrics is enabled by default.

Tools and Options

You can use CLI commands and change some of the settings on the PDM using the Tools and Options menus.

Choosing **Options** > **Preferences** > **Preview Commands Before Sending** to PIX enables you to preview commands generated by any panel before they are sent to the PIX Firewall. This choice is useful when you use PDM as a learning tool or if you simply want to verify settings before they are applied to the firewall.

Select **Tools** > **Command Line Interface** to enter CLI commands to be sent to the PIX Firewall. This option allows you to use the CLI commands without the need for a separate Telnet session. If you need to send a quick CLI command, using this tool is a time-saver. You can also access the ping tool from the tools menu by selecting **Tool** > **Ping**.

Monitoring

You access the monitoring screen in Figure 6-14 by clicking the **Monitoring** button above the toolbar.

Figure 6-14   *Monitoring Screen*

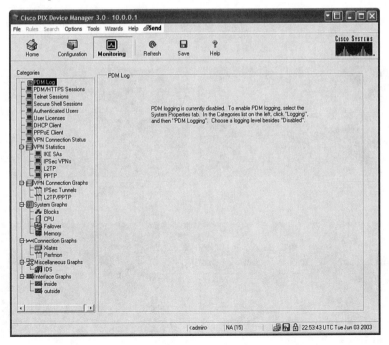

You can monitor many different items using PDM, including but not limited to the following:

- PDM Log
- PDM/HTTPS Sessions
- Secure Shell Sessions
- Telnet Console Settings
- PDM Users
- Number of Licenses in Use
- VPN Status, Statistics, and Connection Graphs
- System Performance Graphs
- Connection statistics
- Interface Graphs

The Interface Graphs panel enables you to monitor per-interface statistics, such as packet counts and bit rates, for each enabled interface on the PIX Firewall. You can select the interface and up to four variables for each graph. Figure 6-15 shows a graph for the inside interface displaying Packet Count, Packet Rate, Input Queue, and Output Queue.

Figure 6-15 *Interface Graph*

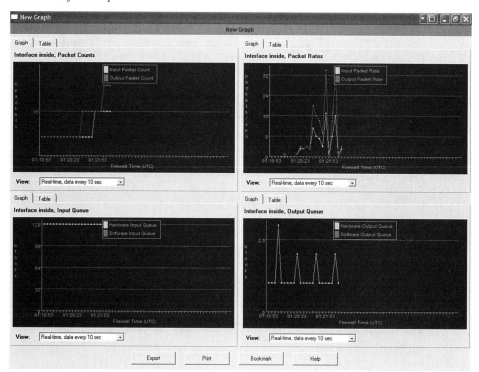

The list of graphs available is the same for every interface. You can view each graph as a line graph and in table form. You can also display each graph with different time horizons.

Summary

This section summarizes the information you learned in this chapter:

- PDM is a browser-based tool used to configure your PIX Firewall.
- To date, PDM 3.0 is the version of the tool with the greatest functionality and is suitable as the primary management and monitoring tool for many implementations.
- Minimal setup on the PIX Firewall is required to run PDM.
- PDM contains several tools in addition to the GUI to help configure your PIX Firewall.
- You can use PDM to create site-to-site and remote access VPNs.
- PDM is an excellent learning tool.

Chapter Review Questions

To test what you have learned in this chapter, answer the following questions and then refer to Appendix A, "Answers to Chapter Review Questions," for the answers:

1 What version of the PDM is supported on PIX Firewall Version 6.3?

2 Can you use conduits and ACLs concurrently with PDM?

3 Which version of the PDM is supported on the FWSM?

4 What is the minimum recommended amount of RAM for a Windows client running PDM 3.0?

5 True or False: Configuration changes made by PDM are automatically saved to the PIX Firewall.

Lab Exercise—Configure the PIX Firewall with PDM

Complete the following lab exercises to practice the PDM concepts and configuration techniques you learned in this chapter. An initial configuration is not provided for this lab because you perform an initial configuration of the PIX Firewall using the PDM.

Objectives

In this lab, you perform the following tasks:

- Clear the PIX Firewall's configuration and access the PDM Startup Wizard.
- Use the PDM Startup Wizard to configure a privileged mode password.
- Configure outbound access with NAT.
- Test connectivity through the PIX Firewall.
- Configure and test inbound access.
- Configure and test logging to a syslog server.
- Configure intrusion detection.
- Configure the PIX Firewall to monitor intrusion. Intrusion detection concepts are covered in detail in Chapter 12, "Attack Guards, Intrusion Detection, and Shunning."

Lab Topology

Figure 6-16 displays the topology for the lab exercises in this chapter.

Figure 6-16   *Topology for PDM Lab Exercises*

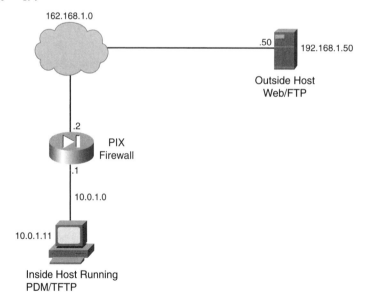

Equipment required to perform the lab includes the following:

- A PIX Firewall with two interfaces and PDM
- Category 5 patch cables

- PC host for outside subnet with web server and FTP server
- PC host for the inside subnet running TFTP and PDM

NOTE   In the following lab exercise, you bypass the initial security alert regarding the site security certificate. However, remember that when you remotely configure the PIX Firewall with PDM, you can use the security certificate for secure encrypted communication between PDM and the PIX Firewall. To do so, install the certificate by clicking **View Certificate** in the initial Security Alert window and following the prompts. Because the certificate is assigned to the PIX Firewall by name rather than by IP address, you should establish the connection with the PIX Firewall by entering its FQDN, rather than the IP address, in the browser. Using the name rather than an IP address requires that name resolution be enabled through DNS or a hosts file.

Task 1—Use the PDM Startup Wizard

The PIX Firewall used for these lab exercises should be loaded with PDM. If your PIX Firewall does not have PDM loaded on it, download the appropriate PDM image and install it on your firewall using the **copy tftp flash** command. For example, if you want to install an image file named pdm-301.bin located on a TFTP server at 10.0.1.11, issue the following command:

```
copy tftp://10.0.1.11/pdm-301.bin flash:pdm
```

If the PIX Firewall you are using has been previously configured, complete the following steps to erase the current PIX Firewall configuration and access the PDM wizard:

Step 1   In the console window, erase the current PIX Firewall configuration. When prompted to confirm, press **Enter**:

```
pixfirewall(config)# write erase
Erase PIX configuration in flash memory? [confirm] <Enter>
```

Step 2   In the console window, reload the PIX Firewall. When prompted to confirm, press **Enter**.

```
pixfirewall(config)# reload
Proceed with reload? [confirm] <Enter>
```

Step 3   When prompted to preconfigure the PIX Firewall through interactive prompts, press **Enter**.

Step 4   Agree to use the current password by pressing **Enter**:

```
Enable password [<use current password>]: <Enter>
```

Step 5   Accept the default year by pressing **Enter**:

```
Clock (UTC):
  Year [2003]: <Enter>
```

Step 6   Accept the default month by pressing **Enter**:

```
Month [Nov]: <Enter>
```

Step 7   Accept the default day by pressing **Enter:**

```
Day [14]: <Enter>
```

Step 8   Accept the default time stored in the host computer by pressing **Enter**:

```
Time [11:21:25]: <Enter>
```

Step 9   Enter the IP address of the PIX Firewall's inside interface:

```
Inside IP address: 10.0.1.1
```

Step 10   Enter the network mask that applies to the inside IP address:

```
Inside network mask: 255.255.255.0
```

Step 11   Enter the host name you want to display in the PIX Firewall command-line prompt:

```
Host name: pixfirewall
```

Step 12   Enter the DNS domain name of the network on which the PIX Firewall runs:

```
Domain name: cisco.com
```

Step 13   Enter the IP address of the host running PDM:

```
IP address of host running PIX Device Manager: 10.0.1.11
```

Step 14   Enter **y** at the prompt to save the information to the PIX Firewall's Flash memory.

Step 15   Access the PDM console by completing the following substeps:

1.   In the browser, enter **https://10.0.1.1**

2.   In the Security Alert window, click **Yes**.

3.   When prompted for the username and password, do not enter a username or password. Click **OK** to continue. The Security Warning window opens.

4.   Click **Yes**. The Update Config window opens.

5.   Click **Proceed**. If the Preview CLI Commands window opens, click **Send**. The PIX Device Manager main window opens.

Task 2—Use the PDM Startup Wizard to Configure a Privileged Mode Password

Complete the following steps to configure a privileged mode password:

Step 1   In the PIX Device Manager Startup Wizard window, click **Next**. The Startup Wizard's Basic Configuration group box appears.

Step 2   Verify that pixfirewall appears in the PIX Host Name field.

Step 3   Verify that cisco.com appears in the Domain Name field.

Step 4   Select **Change Enable Password** within the Enable Password group box.

Step 5   Enter **cisco** in the New Enable Password text box.

Step 6   Enter **cisco** in the Confirm New Enable Password text box.

Step 7   Click **Finish**. The Enter Network Password window opens.

Step 8   Leave the Username field blank, enter **cisco** in the password field, and click **OK**. The main Cisco PIX Device Manager window opens.

Task 3—Configure Outbound Access with NAT

Complete the following steps to configure the PIX Firewall inside and outside interfaces, establish a default route, enable NAT for the internal network, and create a global pool of addresses for address translation:

Step 1   Select the **System Properties** tab.

Step 2   Configure the inside interface by completing the following substeps:

1.   Select **ethernet1** in the Interfaces table and click the **Edit** button. The Edit Interface window opens.

2.   Verify that the Enable Interface check box is selected.

3.   Verify that inside appears in the Interface Name field.

4.   Verify that 10.0.1.1 appears in the IP Address field.

5.   Verify that 255.255.255.0 appears in the Subnet Mask drop-down menu.

6.   Choose **100full** from the Speed drop-down menu.

7.   Verify that 100 appears in the Security Level field.

8.   Click **OK**. You return to the Cisco PIX Device Manager main window.

Step 3 Configure the outside interface by completing the following substeps:

    1. Select **ethernet0** in the Interfaces table, and then click the **Edit** button. The Edit Interface window opens.

    2. Select the **Enable Interface** check box.

    3. Verify that outside appears in the Interface Name field.

    4. Verify that the Static IP Address radio button is selected within the IP Address group box.

    5. Enter **192.168.1.2** in the IP Address field.

    6. Choose **255.255.255.0** from the Subnet Mask drop-down menu.

    7. Choose **100full** (10baset if using a PIX Firewall 501) from the Speed drop-down menu.

    8. Verify that 0 appears in the Security Level field.

    9. Click **OK**. You return to the Cisco PIX Device Manager main window.

    10. Click **Apply**.

Step 4 Configure a global pool of addresses to be used for address translation by completing the following substeps:

    1. Select the **Translation Rules** tab.

    2. Click the **Manage Pools** button. The Manage Global Address Pools window opens.

    3. Click **Add**. The Add Global Pool Item window opens.

    4. Choose outside from the Interface drop-down menu.

    5. Enter **1** in the Pool ID field.

    6. Verify that the Range radio button is selected.

    7. Enter **192.168.1.20** in the first IP address field.

    8. Enter **192.168.1.40** in the second IP address field.

    9. Enter **255.255.255.0** in the Network Mask field.

    10. Click **OK**. You return to the Manage Global Address Pools window.

    11. Click **OK**. You return to the Cisco PIX Device Manager main window.

    12. Click **Apply**.

Step 5   Configure NAT by completing the following substeps:

1.   Verify that the Translation Rules tab is still active.

2.   Verify that the Translation Rules radio button is selected.

3.   Choose **Rules > Add** from the main menu. The Add Address Translation Rule window opens.

4.   Verify that the inside interface is chosen in the Interface drop-down menu.

5.   Click **Browse**. The Select host/network window opens.

6.   Verify that the inside interface is chosen in the drop-down menu.

7.   Select the inside network by clicking **10.0.1.0**.

8.   Click **OK**. You return to the Add Address Translation Rule window.

9.   Verify that outside is chosen in the Translate Address on Interface drop-down menu.

10.   Verify that Dynamic is selected in the Translate Address to group box.

11.   Choose **1** from the Address Pool drop-down menu.

12.   Verify that the global pool you configured earlier (192.168.1.20–192.168.1.40) appears under Address.

13.   Click **OK** in the Add Address Translation Rule window. The new rule appears on the Translation Rules tab.

14.   Click **Apply**.

Task 4—Test Connectivity Through the PIX Firewall

Complete the following steps to test interface connectivity and NAT:

Step 1   Test interface connectivity by completing the following substeps:

1.   Choose **Tools > Ping**.

2.   In the IP Address field, enter **10.0.1.1**.
Click **Ping**.

3. Observe the output in the Ping Output window. The output should appear similar to the following:

```
10.0.1.1 response received -- 0ms
10.0.1.1 response received -- 0ms
10.0.1.1 response received -- 0ms
```

4. Click **Clear Screen**.

Step 2   Repeat Step 1 for the following IP addresses. You should receive responses for all pings:

— The inside host: 10.0.1.11

— The outside interface: 192.168.1.2

Step 3   Exit the Ping window by clicking **Close**.

Test the operation of the global and NAT you configured by originating connections through the PIX Firewall. To do so, open a web browser on the inside host and access the outside host at IP address 192.168.1.50 by entering **http://192.168.1.50**.

Step 4   Observe the translation table by completing the following substeps:

1. Choose **Tools > Command Line Interface**. The Command Line Interface window opens.

2. In the Command field, enter **show xlate**.

3. Click **Send**.

4. Observe the output in the Response field. It should appear similar to the following:

```
Result of the PIX command: "show xlate"
1 in use, 1 most used
Global 192.168.1.20 Local 10.0.1.11
```

NOTE   Note that a global address chosen from the low end of the global range has been mapped to the inside host.

Step 5   Exit the Command Line Interface window by clicking **Close**.

Task 5—Configure and Test Inbound Access

Complete the following steps to configure the PIX Firewall to permit inbound access to hosts on the inside interface:

Step 1   Enable command preview by completing the following substeps:

1.   Choose **Options > Preferences** from the main menu. The Preferences window opens.

2.   Select **Preview Commands Before Sending to Firewall**.

3.   Click **OK**.

Step 2   Create a static translation for the inside host by completing the following substeps:

1.   Select the **Translation Rules** tab.

2.   Select the **Add New Rule** icon in the toolbar. The Add Address Translation Rule window opens.

3.   Verify that the inside interface is chosen in the Interface drop-down menu.

4.   Click **Browse**. The Select Host/Network window opens.

5.   Verify that the inside interface is chosen in the drop-down menu.

6.   Select the inside host: Click **10.0.1.11**.

7.   Click **OK**. You are returned to the Add Address Translation Rule window.

8.   Verify that outside is chosen in the Translate Address on Interface drop-down menu.

9.   Select **Static** in the Translate Address to group box.

10.   Enter **192.168.1.10** in the IP Address field.

11.   Click **OK**. The new rule appears on the Translation Rules tab.

12.   Click **Apply**. The Preview CLI Commands window opens.

13.   Click **Send**.

Step 3   Ping the inside host from the outside host. The ping should fail because the policy presently prevents pinging:

```
C:\> ping 192.168.1.10
Pinging 192.168.1.10 with 32 bytes of data:
Request timed out.
Request timed out.
Request timed out.
```

Step 4   Configure an ACL to allow pinging through the PIX Firewall by completing the following substeps:

1. Select the **Access** Rules tab.

2. Choose **Rules** from the main menu.

3. Click **Add**. The Add Rule window opens.

4. Verify that permit is chosen in the Select an action drop-down menu.

5. Choose outside from the Interface drop-down menu in the Source Host/Network group box.

6. Choose inside from the Interface drop-down menu in the Destination Host/Network group box.

7. Select **ICMP** in the Protocol or Service group box.

8. Verify that any is selected in the ICMP type group box.

9. Click **OK**. The new rule appears on the Access Rules tab.

10. Click **Apply**. The Preview CLI Commands window opens.

11. Observe the ACLs to be sent to the PIX Firewall.

12. Click **Send**.

Step 5   Ping the inside host again from the outside host:

```
C:\> ping 192.168.1.10
Pinging 192.168.1.10 with 32 bytes of data:
Reply from 192.168.1.10:  bytes=32 time<10ms TTL=125>
Reply from 192.168.1.10:  bytes=32 time<10ms TTL=125>
Reply from 192.168.1.10:  bytes=32 time<10ms TTL=125>
Reply from 192.168.1.10:  bytes=32 time<10ms TTL=125>
```

Step 6   Configure an ACL to allow Web access to the inside host from the outside by completing the following substeps:

1. Select the **Access Rules** tab.

2. Choose **Rules > Add**. The Add Rule window opens.

3. Verify that permit is chosen in the Select an Action drop-down menu.

4. Choose outside from the Interface drop-down menu within the Source Host/Network group box.

5. Choose inside from the Interface drop-down menu within the Destination Host/Network group box.

6. Click **Browse** in the Destination Host/Network group box. The Select Host/Network window opens.

7. Verify that inside is chosen in the Interface drop-down menu.

8. Select the IP address of the inside host: **10.0.1.11**.

9. Click **OK**. The Add Rule window becomes active.

10. Select **TCP** in the Protocol and Service group box.

11. Verify that = is chosen in the Service drop-down menu within the Source Port group box.

12. Verify that **any** appears in the Service field within the Source Port group box.

13. Verify that = is chosen in the Service drop-down menu within the Destination Port group box.

14. Click the **Ellipsis** button within the Destination Port group box. The Service window opens.

15. Choose **http** from the Service list.

16. Click **OK**. You return to the Add Rule window.

17. Click **OK**.

18. Click **Apply**. The Preview CLI Commands window opens.

19. Observe the ACLs to be sent to the PIX Firewall.

20. Click **Send**.

Step 7 Clear current translations by completing the following substeps:

1. Choose **Tools > Command Line Interface**. The Command Line Interface window opens.

2. Enter **clear xlate** in the Command field.

3. Click **Send**.

4. Verify that the output in the Response field is similar to the following:

    ```
    Result of firewall command: "clear xlate"
    The command has been sent to the firewall.
    ```

Step 8   View current translations by completing the following substeps:

1. Click **Clear Response** in the Command Line Interface window.

2. Enter **show xlate** in the Command field.

3. Click **Send**.

4. Verify that the output in the Response field is similar to the following:

    ```
    Result of firewall command: "show xlate"
    0 in use, 3 most used
    ```

5. Click **Close** in the Command Line Interface window.

6. Test web access to the inside host by opening a web browser on the outside host and entering **http:// 192.168.1.10**. You should be able to establish a web connection to the inside host if the ACL has been correctly configured.

Test FTP access to the inside host from the outside host by choosing **Start > Run > ftp 192.168.1.10**. You should be unable to access FTP.

Step 9   Observe the transactions by completing the following substeps:

1. Choose **Tools > Command Line Interface**. The Command Line Interface window opens.

2. Enter **show arp** in the Command field.

3. Click **Send**.

4. Verify that the output in the Response box is similar to the following:

    ```
    result of firewall command: "show arp"
    outside 192.168.1.50 0003.6ba4.ca60
    inside 10.0.1.11 0050.da31.6130
    ```

5. Click **Clear Response**.

6. Enter **show conn** in the Command field.

7. Click **Send**.

8. Verify that the output in the Response field is similar to the following:

```
result of firewall command: "show conn"
0 in use, 6 most used
TCP out 192.168.1.10:80 in 10.0.1.11: 3893 idle 0:00:07 Bytes
  463 flags UIO
TCP out 192.168.1.10:80 in 10.0.1.11: 3893 idle 0:00:07 Bytes
  463 flags UIO
```

9. Click **Clear Response**.

10. Enter **show xlate** in the Command field.

11. Click **Send**.

12. Verify that the output in the Response field is similar to the following:

```
result of firewall command: "show xlate"
2 in use, 3 most used
Global 192.168.1.10 Local 10.0.1.11
```

13. Click **Close**.

Task 6—Configure Intrusion Detection

Chapter 12 covers the intrusion detection features of the PIX Firewall in greater detail. It also includes CLI-based lab exercises for configuring and monitoring intrusion detection, which you can compare and contrast to this PDM-based exercise. Complete the following steps to configure the PIX Firewall to detect ICMP packet attacks, drop the packets, and send an alarm to a syslog server:

Step 1 Verify that the System Properties tab is still active.

Step 2 Expand Intrusion Detection from the Categories tree on the left of the panel. IDS Policy appears under Intrusion Detection.

Step 3 Select **IDS Policy**. The IDS Policy group box opens on the right.

Step 4 Click **Add**. The Add IDS Policy window opens.

Step 5 Enter **ATTACKPOLICY** in the Policy Name field.

Step 6 Verify that Attack is selected in the Policy Type group box.

Step 7 Select **Drop and Alarm** in the Action group box.

Step 8 Click **OK**. You return to the System Properties tab.

Step 9 Choose **ATTACKPOLICY** from the drop-down menu for the inside interface under Attack Policy.

Step 10 Click **Apply**. The Preview CLI Commands window opens.

Step 11 Click **Send**.

Task 7—Configure PDM to Monitor Intrusion Detection

Complete the following steps to configure monitoring of intrusion detection:

Step 1 Select the **Monitoring** tab.

Step 2 Expand Miscellaneous Graphs from the Categories tree on the left of the panel. IDS appears under Miscellaneous Graphs.

Step 3 Select **IDS**.

Step 4 Choose **ICMP Attacks** from the Available Graphs for: list.

Step 5 Click **Add**.

Step 6 Click **Graph It**. The New Graph window opens.

Step 7 Verify that Real-time, data very 10 sec is chosen in the View drop-down menu.

Step 8 From the Windows command line, ping the PIX Firewall's inside interface with an ICMP packet size of 10,000:

```
C:\> ping -l 10000 10.0.1.1
Pinging 10.0.1.1 with 10000 bytes of data:
Request timed out.
Request timed out.
Request timed out.
Request timed out.
```

Step 9 From the Windows command line, ping the PIX Firewall's inside interface with an increased ICMP packet size:

```
C:\> ping -l 65000 10.0.1.1
Pinging 10.0.1.1 with 65000 bytes of data:
Request timed out.
Request timed out.
Request timed out.
Request timed out.
```

Step 10 Observe the graph in the Graph tab.

Step 11 Select the **Table** tab and observe the statistics in the table view.

Step 12 Save the PIX Firewall configuration to Flash memory by clicking the **Save Running Configuration to Flash** icon in the PDM toolbar. The Save Running Configuration to Flash window opens.

Step 13 Click **Apply**. The Preview CLI Commands window opens.

Step 14 Click **Send**. The Save Successful window opens.

Step 15 Click **OK**.

On completion of this chapter, you will be able to perform the following tasks:

- Describe how TCP and User Datagram Protocol (UDP) function within the PIX Firewall.

- Describe how static and dynamic translations function.

- Configure the PIX Firewall to permit inbound connections.

- Explain the PIX Firewall's network address translation (NAT) and port address translation (PAT) features.

- Explain how to configure the PIX Firewall to perform port redirection.

- Explain how to configure the PIX Firewall to translate the IP address in a Domain Name System (DNS) A-record.

- Configure additional interfaces on the PIX Firewall.

- Test and verify correct PIX Firewall operation.

CHAPTER 7

Translations and Connections

One of the ways that firewalls protect the network is by hiding the internal network layout and addressing scheme from prying eyes on the outside. PIX Firewalls provide NAT and PAT capabilities to allow you to keep you internal network addresses hidden from the Internet, thereby providing increased security. NAT and PAT also enable the use of a few or even a single public IP address to connect hundreds or thousands of privately addressed hosts to the Internet.

This chapter describes NAT and PAT functionality and presents detailed information on how translations and connections are handled by PIX Firewalls.

Transport Protocols

For a deeper understanding of how the Cisco PIX Firewall processes inbound and outbound transmissions, a brief review of the two primary transport protocols is warranted.

Network sessions are commonly conducted over tewo transport protocols:

- **TCP**—Easy to inspect properly
- **UDP**—Difficult to inspect properly

NOTE   In the context of this textbook, the term *outbound* means connections from the more trusted side of the PIX Firewall to the less trusted side of the PIX Firewall. The term *inbound* means connections from the less trusted side of the PIX Firewall to the more trusted side of the PIX Firewall.

TCP

TCP is a connection-oriented protocol. When a session from a more secure host inside the PIX Firewall starts, the PIX Firewall creates a log in the session state filter. The PIX Firewall can extract network sessions from the network flow and actively verify their validity in real time. This stateful filter maintains the state of each network connection and checks subsequent protocol units against its expectations. When TCP initiates a session with the

PIX Firewall, the PIX Firewall records the network flow and looks for an acknowledgment from the device with which it is trying to initiate communications. The PIX Firewall then allows traffic to flow between the connections based on the three-way handshake.

Figures 7-1 and 7-2 depict what happens when a TCP session is established over the PIX Firewall.

Figure 7-1 *TCP Initialization—Inside to Outside*

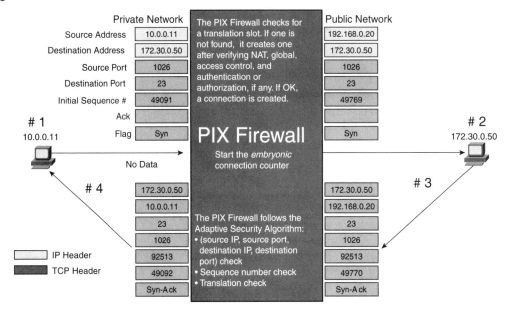

The sequence of events is as follows:

1   The first IP packet from an inside host causes a translation slot to be generated. This information is kept in memory so that it can be checked against subsequent packet flows. In the example, 10.0.0.11 is translated to 192.168.0.20. The embedded TCP information is then used to create a connection slot in the PIX Firewall.

2   The connection slot is marked as *embryonic* (not established yet).

NOTE   An *embryonic connection* is a half-open TCP session. It becomes a complete connection after the three-way handshake is completed by the inside host when it sends an acknowledge (ACK). You can limit the number of embryonic connections in a number of ways with the PIX, which can help reduce certain attacks against a network. Embryonic connections can be limited to a maximum number at a given time. Embryonic connections can also be timed for completion within a given amount of time.

---

3 The PIX Firewall randomizes the initial sequence number (ISN) of the connection, stores the delta value, and forwards the packet onto the outgoing interface.

4 At this point, the PIX Firewall expects a synchronize/acknowledge (SYN/ACK) packet from the destination host. Then, the PIX Firewall matches the received packet against the connection slot, computes the sequencing information, and forwards the return packet to the inside host.

5 The inside host completes the connection setup, the three-way handshake, with an ACK (as shown in Figure 7-2).

Figure 7-2 *TCP Initialization—Inside to Outside (Continued)*

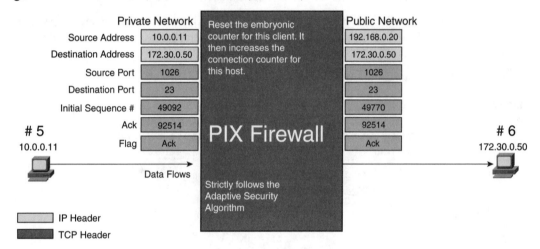

6 The connection slot on the PIX Firewall is marked as connected, or active-established, and data is transmitted. The embryonic counter is then reset for this connection.

UDP

UDP is connectionless. The PIX Firewall must therefore take other measures to ensure its security. Applications using UDP are difficult to secure properly because there is no handshaking or sequencing. It is difficult to determine the current state of a UDP transaction. It is also difficult to maintain the state of a session because it has no clear beginning, flow state, or end. However, when a UDP packet is sent from a more-secure to a less-secure interface, the PIX Firewall creates a UDP connection slot. All subsequent returned UDP packets matching the connection slot are forwarded to the inside network.

Figure 7-3 shows the sequence of events for UDP transactions on PIX Firewalls, which are as follows:

1 The first IP packet from an inside host is received by the PIX Firewall. After it verifies configured translation settings, the PIX Firewall creates a translation slot. It keeps this information in memory so that it can be checked against subsequent packet flows. In the example, 10.0.0.11 is translated to 192.168.0.20. The embedded UDP information is then used to create a UDP connection slot.

2 The PIX Firewall maintains the UDP connection slot for the duration of the user-configurable UDP timeout (2 minutes by default). When the UDP connection slot is idle for more than the configured UDP timeout, it is deleted from the connection table.

3 The PIX Firewall performs Adaptive Security Algorithm (ASA) stateful inspection of the UDP packets that are received from the destination host within the UDP timeout period.

4 The data is transmitted back to the inside host.

Figure 7-3 *UDP Sequence of Events*

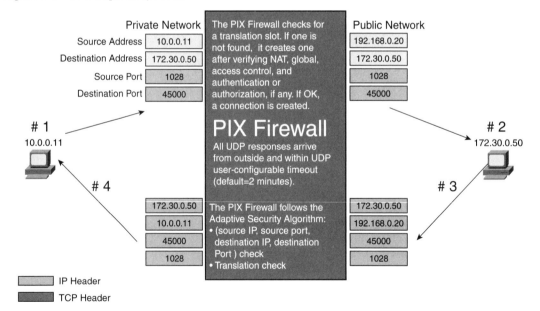

The following are some UDP characteristics:

• UDP is an unreliable (connectionless) but efficient transport protocol—unreliable in the sense that it does not provide acknowlegment of delivery.

- Spoofing UDP packets is easy because there is no handshaking or sequencing. Because there is no state machine, the initiator of the transaction or the current state usually cannot be determined.
- UDP has no delivery guarantees.
- There is no connection setup and termination.
- UDP has no congestion management or avoidance.
- Services that use UDP can be generally divided into two categories:
  - Request-reply, or ping-pong services, such as Domain Name System (DNS)
  - Flow services, such as video, Voice over IP (VoIP), and Network File System (NFS)

NAT

You can use the PIX Firewall to translate all inside IP addresses when data passes through from the inside. From a network security perspective, if a particular security policy specifies permitting only outbound traffic, translating internal addresses is a very secure action. If you use private addressing (RFC 1918) on the inside, the translated (source) addresses that connect to the Internet must be registered addresses.

If a user on the outside tries to make a connection to the inside, that outside user does not succeed. A session cannot be built from the Internet with the destination address as the private address unless it has been configured within the PIX to allow the session.

NOTE   RFC 1918 defines "Address Allocation for Private Internets."

The Internet Assigned Numbers Authority (IANA) has reserved the following three blocks of the IP address space for private internets:

10.0.0.0–10.255.255.255 (10/8 prefix)

172.16.0.0–172.31.255.255 (172.16/12 prefix)

192.168.0.0–192.168.255.255 (192.168/16 prefix)

The PIX Firewall supports the following four types of address translations:

- **Dynamic inside NAT**—Translates host addresses on more secure interfaces to a range or pool of IP addresses on a less-secure interface. This process allows internal users to share registered IP addresses and hides internal addresses from view on the public Internet.

- **Static inside NAT**—Provides a permanent, one-to-one mapping between an IP address on a more secure interface and an IP address on a less secure interface. This process allows hosts to access the inside host from the public Internet without exposing the actual IP address.

- **Dynamic outside NAT**—Translates host addresses on less secure interfaces to a range or pool of IP addresses on a more secure interface. This process is most useful for controlling the addresses that appear on inside interfaces of the PIX Firewall and for connecting private networks with overlapping addresses.

- **Static outside NAT**—Provides a permanent, one-to-one mapping between an IP address on a less-secure interface and an IP address on a more-secure interface.

Each translation type is discussed in further detail in the following subsections.

Dynamic Inside Translations

Dynamic inside translations are used for local hosts and their outbound connections and hide the host address from the Internet. With dynamic translations, you must first define which hosts are eligible for translation with the **nat** command and then define the address pool with the **global** command. The pool for address allocation is chosen on the outgoing interface based on the *nat_id* selected with the **nat** command.

The **nat** command works with the **global** command to enable NAT. The **nat** command associates a network with a pool of global IP addresses. It lets you specify lists of inside hosts that can use the PIX Firewall for address translation.

The syntax for the **nat** command is as follows:

```
nat [(if_name)] nat_id {local_ip [mask]} | {access-list acl_id} [dns] [norandomseq]
    [outside] [max_conns [emb_limit]]
```

Table 7-1 describes the **nat** command arguments.

Table 7-1   **nat** *Command Arguments*

Argument	Definition
access-list	Associates **access-list** commands to the **nat** command for policy-based translation (available with PIX Firewall Version 6.3(2) or higher) or the **nat 0** command to exempt traffic that matches the access list from NAT processing.
acl_id	The access list name.
dns	Specifies the use of the created translation to rewrite the DNS address record.
emb_limit	The maximum number of embryonic connections per host. (As stated previously, an embryonic connection is a connection request that has not finished the necessary handshake between source and destination.) Set a small value for slower systems and a higher value for faster systems. The default is 0, allowing unlimited embryonic connections.

Table 7-1   **nat** *Command Arguments (Continued)*

Argument	Definition
if_name	The name of the network interface.
local_ip	The internal network IP address to be translated. Additionally, *local_ip* determines the group of hosts or networks referred to by *nat_id*. You can use **0.0.0.0** to allow all hosts to start outbound connections. The **0.0.0.0** *local_ip* can be abbreviated as **0**.
mask	Network mask for *local_ip*. You can use **0.0.0.0** to allow all outbound connections to translate with IP addresses from the global pool. The netmask **0.0.0.0** can be abbreviated as **0**.
max_conns	The maximum number of simultaneous connections the *local_ip* hosts are to allow. (Idle connections are closed after the idle timeout specified by the **timeout conn** command.)
nat_id	The ID of the group of host or networks. This ID will be referenced by the **global** command to associate a global pool with the *local_ip*. *nat_id* values can be **0**; **0 access list** *acl_id*; any number from 1 to 2,147,483,647; or, when using PIX Firewall version 6.3(2) or higher, any number from 1 to 2,147,483,647 **access list** *acl_id*. A *nat_id* of **0** indicates that no address translation takes place for *local_ip*. A *nat_id* of **0 access list** *acl_id* specifies the traffic to exempt from NAT processing, based on the access list specified by *acl_id*. This setting is useful in a virtual private network (VPN) configuration, in which traffic between private networks should be exempted from NAT. A *nat_id* that is a number from 1 to 2,147,483,647 specifies the inside hosts for dynamic or dynamic policy-based address translation. The dynamic addresses are chosen from a global address pool created with the **global** command, so the *nat_id* number must match the *global_id* number of the global address pool you want to use for dynamic address translation.
norandomseq	Disables TCP ISN randomization protection. Only use this option if another inline firewall is also randomizing sequence numbers and the result is scrambling the data. Without this protection, inside hosts with weak self-ISN protection become more vulnerable to TCP connection hijacking.
outside	Enables outside NAT, which translates the source address of a connection coming from a lower-security interface to a higher-security interface. This feature is also called bidirectional NAT and is only available on PIX Firewall Version 6.2 or higher.

The syntax for the **global** command is as follows:

```
global [(if_name)] nat_id {global_ip [-global_ip] [netmask global_mask]} | interface
```

Table 7-2 describes the **global** command arguments.

Table 7-2   **global** *Command Arguments*

Argument	Definition
global_ip	One or more global IP addresses that the PIX Firewall shares among its connections. If the external network is connected to the Internet, each global IP address must be registered with the Network Information Center (NIC). You can specify a range of IP addresses by separating the addresses with a dash (-).
	You can create a PAT **global** command by specifying a single IP address. You can have more than one PAT **global** command per interface. A PAT can support up to 65,535 xlate objects.
global_mask	The network mask for *global_ip*. If subnetting is in effect, use the subnet mask (for example, 255.255.255.128). If you specify an address range that overlaps subnets, **global** does not use the broadcast or network addresses in the pool of global addresses. For example, if you use 255.255.255.224 and an address range of 209.165.201.0–209.165.201.30, the 209.165.201.32 broadcast address and the 209.165.201.0 network addresses are not included in the pool of global addresses.
if_name	The external network on which you use these global addresses.
interface	Specifies PAT using the IP address at the interface.
nat_id	A positive number shared with the **nat** command that groups the **nat** and **global** commands together. The valid ID numbers can be any positive number up to 2,147,483,647.
netmask	Reserved word that prefaces the network *global_mask* variable.

Example 7-1 shows the **nat** and **global** command configuration for the network shown on Figure 7-4. The global pool of addresses assigned by the **global** command is 192.168.0.20 through 192.168.0.254, enabling up to 235 individual IP addresses.

Figure 7-4   *Dynamic Inside Translations*

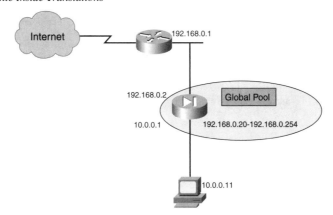

Example 7-1 *Configuring Dynamic Translations*

```
pixfirewall(config)# nat (inside) 1 0.0.0.0 0.0.0.0
pixfirewall(config)# global (outside) 1 192.168.0.20-192.168.0.254 netmask
   255.255.255.0
```

Example 7-2 shows the configuration required to enable NAT on two interfaces. The network layout for this example is shown in Figure 7-5. In this example, the first **nat** command permits all hosts on the 10.0.0.0/24 network to start outbound connections using the IP addresses from a global pool. The second **nat** command permits all hosts on the 10.2.0.0/24 network to do the same. The *nat_id* in the first **nat** command tells the PIX Firewall to translate the 10.0.0.0/24 addresses to those in the global pool containing the same *nat_id*. Likewise, the *nat_id* in the second **nat** command tells the PIX Firewall to translate addresses for hosts on network 10.2.0.0/24 to the addresses in the global pool containing *nat_id* 2.

Figure 7-5 *Two Interfaces with NAT*

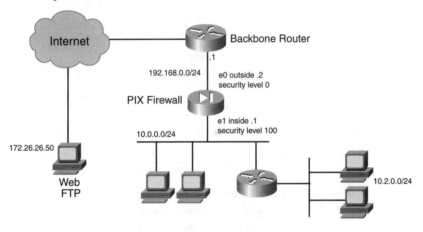

Example 7-2 *Configuring NAT with Two Interfaces*

```
pixfirewall(config)# nat(inside) 1 10.0.0.0 255.255.255.0
pixfirewall(config)# nat (inside) 2 10.2.0.0 255.255.255.0
pixfirewall(config)# global(outside) 1 192.168.0.1-192.168.0.14 netmask
   255.255.255.240
pixfirewall(config)# global(outside) 2 192.168.0.17-192.168.0.30 netmask
   255.255.255.240
```

Example 7-3 shows the configuration required to enable NAT with three interfaces. The network layout for this example is shown in Figure 7-6. In this example, the first **nat** command enables hosts on the inside interface, which has a security level of 100, to start connections to hosts on interfaces with lower security levels. In this case, that includes hosts on the outside interface and hosts on the demilitarized zone (DMZ). The second **nat** command enables hosts on the DMZ, which has a security level of 50, to start connections to hosts on interfaces with lower security levels. In this case, that includes only the outside interface.

Figure 7-6 *Three Interfaces with NAT*

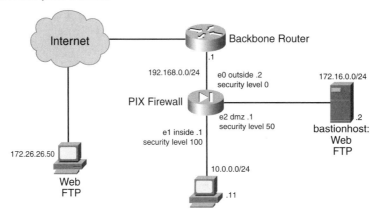

Example 7-3 *Configuring NAT with Three Interfaces*

```
pixfirewall(config)# nat(inside) 1 10.0.0.0 255.255.255.0
pixfirewall(config)# nat (dmz) 1 172.16.0.0 255.255.255.0
pixfirewall(config)# global (outside) 1 192.168.0.20-192.168.0.254 netmask
  255.255.255.0
pixfirewall(config)# global(dmz) 1 172.16.0.20-172.16.0.254 netmask 255.255.255.0
```

Because both global pools and the **nat (inside)** command use a *nat_id* of 1, addresses for hosts on the 10.0.0.0 network can be translated to those in either global pool. Therefore, when users on the inside interface access hosts on the DMZ, their source addresses are translated to addresses in the 172.16.0.20 through 172.16.0.254 range from the **global (dmz)** command. When they access hosts on the outside, their source addresses are translated to addresses in the 192.168.0.20 through 192.168.0.254 range from the **global (outside)** command.

When users on the DMZ access hosts on the outside, their source addresses are always translated to addresses in the 192.168.0.20 through 192.168.0.254 range from the **global (outside)** command. The **global (dmz)** command gives inside users access to the web server on the DMZ interface.

Static Inside Translations

You use static inside translations when you want an inside host to always appear with a fixed address on the PIX Firewall's global network. Static translations are configured using the **static** command:

- Use the **static** command for outbound connections to ensure that packets leaving an inside host are always mapped to a specific global IP address (for example, an inside DNS or Simple Mail Transfer Protocol [SMTP] host).

NOTE   In addition to the **static** command, you must also configure an appropriate access control list (ACL) to allow inbound access to the hosts providing services such as SMTP. Use of the **access-list** command is discussed in Chapter 8, "Access Control Lists and Content Filtering."

- Use the **static** command alone for outbound connections that must be mapped to the same global IP address.

The **static** command creates a permanent mapping (called a *static translation slot* or *xlate*) between a local IP address and a global IP address and can be used to create outbound and inbound translations. The syntax for the **static** command is as follows:

```
static [(prenat_interface, postnat_interface)] mapped_address | interface
    real_address [netmask mask]
```

Table 7-3 describes the **static** command arguments.

Table 7-3   static *Command Arguments*

Argument	Definition
prenat_interface	The network interface name. Usually the higher-security-level interface, in which case the translation is applied to the higher-security-level address.
postnat_interface	The lower-security-level interface when *prenat_interface* is the higher-security-level interface.
mapped_address	The address into which *real_address* is translated.
interface	Specifies to overload the global address from the interface.
real_address	The address to be mapped.
netmask	Argument used with *mask* to specify the network mask. If **netmask** is not specified, the default mask for the IP address class is used.
mask	The network mask that applies to both *mapped_address* and *real_address*.

The **static** command allows traffic to originate from an interface with a lower security value through the PIX Firewall to an interface with a higher security value. For example, you must configure a **static** and **access-list** to allow incoming sessions from the outside interface to the DMZ interface or from the outside interface to the inside interface.

NOTE   You set the security level for each interface with the **nameif** command.

In PIX Firewall Software Versions 5.2 and higher, for all inbound traffic, the PIX Firewall denies translations for destination IP addresses identified as a network address or a broadcast address. It uses the global IP and mask from a **static** command to differentiate regular IP addresses from network or broadcast addresses. If a global IP address is a valid network address with a matching network mask, the PIX Firewall disallows the xlate for network or broadcast IP addresses with inbound packets.

The following information can help you determine when to use static translations in the PIX Firewall:

- Do not create statics with overlapping IP addresses. Each IP address should be unique.
- Statics take precedence over **nat** and **global** command pairs.
- If a global IP address will be used for PAT, do not use the same global IP address for a static translation.

Example 7-4 shows the **static** command required to enable a static inside translation for the layout shown in Figure 7-7. In this example, when a packet from server 10.0.0.10 goes out through the PIX Firewall, it will have the source IP address of 192.168.0.18. The static nature of this translation is well-suited for internal service hosts such as DNS or SMTP servers.

Figure 7-7   *Static Inside Translation*

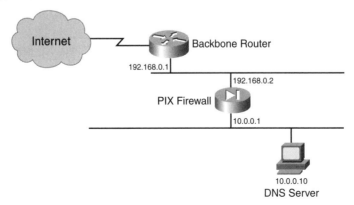

Example 7-4 *Configuring Static Inside Translation*

```
pixfirewall(config)# static (inside, outside) 192.168.0.18 10.0.0.10
```

Dynamic Outside Translations

In PIX Firewall Software Version 6.2 or higher, the **nat** command has been expanded to accommodate outside NAT. Dynamic outside NAT enables the PIX Firewall to translate a host address on a less secure interface to an address you define on a more secure interface by using the **global** command. You can specify that a single IP address, a pool or range of addresses, or the IP address of the PIX Firewall's interface be used for the translation.

The keyword **outside** in the expanded **nat** command specifies that translation applies to addresses of hosts on an outside, or lower-security-level, network. You can use the **dns** option to translate the DNS replies. Use of the **dns** option is discussed in greater detail later in this chapter.

NOTE   A DNS *A-record* is a DNS server's mapping of an IP address to a host or domain name.

Dynamic outside NAT is useful for simplifying router configuration on your internal or perimeter networks by controlling the addresses that appear on these networks. In the network shown in Figure 7-8, the outside NAT configuration eliminates the need for a route to network 172.26.26.0/24 on router C. Source addresses of packets inbound from network 172.26.26.0/24 are translated to IP addresses from the 10.0.0.20 through 10.0.0.254 range. The access list ACLIN works with the static mapping to permit hosts on the 172.26.26.0/24 network to access the FTP server at 10.0.2.2.

Figure 7-8   *Dynamic Outside Translation*

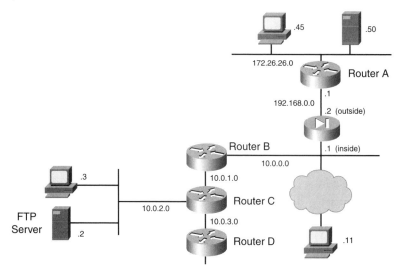

Example 7-5 shows the configuration required to enable dynamic outside translation for the network shown in Figure 7-8.

Example 7-5   *Dynamic Outside Translations*

```
pixfirewall(config)# nat (outside) 1 172.26.26.0 255.255.255.0 outside
pixfirewall(config)# global (inside) 1 10.0.0.20-10.0.0.254 netmask 255.255.255.0
pixfirewall(config)# static (inside,outside) 10.0.2.2 10.0.2.2
pixfirewall(config)# access-list ACLIN permit 172.26.26.0 255.255.255.0 host
  10.0.2.2 eq ftp
pixfirewall(config)# access-group ACLIN in interface outside
```

Static Outside Translations

The fourth type of translation supported on PIX Firewalls is static outside NAT. In PIX Firewall Version 6.2 and higher, the **static** command has been expanded to accommodate outside NAT. The **dns** option is also available in the extended **static** command. As in the **nat** command, it specifies that DNS A-records that match the static translation are rewritten. DNS rewrites are discussed in greater detail later in this chapter.

The syntax for the extended **static** command is as follows:

```
static [(prenat_interface, postnat_interface)] {mapped_address | interface}
   {real_address [netmask mask] | access-list acl_id} [dns] [norandomseq] [max_conns
   [emb_limit]]
```

Table 7-4 describes the expanded **static** command arguments.

Table 7-4   *Expanded* **static** *Command Arguments*

Argument	Definition
prenat_interface	The network interface name. Usually the higher-security-level interface, in which case the translation is applied to the higher-security-level address.
postnat_interface	The lower-security-level interface when *prenat_interface* is the higher-security-level interface.
mapped_address	The address into which *real_address* is translated.
interface	Specifies to overload the global address from the interface.
real_address	The address to be mapped.
netmask *mask*	The network mask that applies to both *mapped_address* and *real_address*.
access-list *acl_id*	Specifies the access list to use with policy-based static address translation.
dns	Specifies that DNS replies which match the xlate are translated.
norandomseq	Disables TCP ISN randomization protection. Only use this option if another inline firewall is also randomizing sequence numbers and the result is scrambling the data. Without this protection, inside hosts with weak self-ISN protection become more vulnerable to TCP connection hijacking.
emb_limit	The maximum number of embryonic connections per host. (As stated previously, an embryonic connection is a connection request that has not finished the necessary handshake between source and destination.) Set a small value for slower systems and a higher value for faster systems. The default is 0, allowing unlimited embryonic connections.
max_conns	The maximum number of simultaneous connections the *local_ip* hosts are to allow. (Idle connections are closed after the idle timeout specified by the **timeout conn** command.)

Outside static NAT (or inbound NAT) is similar to inside NAT. The only difference is that outside NAT translates addresses of hosts residing on the outer (less-secure) interfaces of the PIX Firewall. To configure static outside NAT, use the **static** command to specify a one-to-one IP address mapping.

Outside NAT simplifies the integration of two existing networks that use overlapping IP address spaces. For example, in the network shown in Figure 7-9, the PIX Firewall connects two private networks with overlapping address ranges. One of the private networks uses the range of addresses from 10.0.0.1 to 10.0.0.50 and the other network uses the range from 10.0.0.2 to 10.0.0.99. These two networks cannot communicate with each other unless outside NAT is configured. For example, inside host 10.0.0.2 cannot contact outside host 10.0.0.2 because the packet would be routed directly back to the sending host, rather than to the intended destination.

Figure 7-9 *Static Outside Translation*

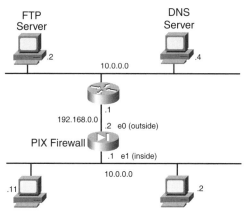

To enable hosts on the inside 10.0.0.0 network to connect to hosts on the outside 10.0.0.0 network, the following configuration is necessary:

Step 1 Enable hosts on outside network 10.0.0.0 to access inside host 10.0.0.11 by IP address 192.168.0.10:

```
static (inside, outside) 192.168.0.10 10.0.0.11 netmask 255.255.255.255
```

NOTE You also need to create ACLs to permit connections to the translated address.

Step 2 Create a permanent mapping of outside IP address 10.0.0.2 to 192.168.0.12 to enable hosts on the inside network to access outside host 10.0.0.2 by IP address 192.168.0.12:

```
static (outside,inside) 192.168.0.12 10.0.0.2 netmask 255.255.255.255
```

Step 3 Create a permanent mapping of outside IP address 10.0.0.4 to 192.168.0.14 to enable hosts on the inside network to access outside host 10.0.0.4 by IP address 192.168.0.14:

```
static (outside,inside) 192.168.0.14 10.0.0.4 netmask 255.255.255.255
```

Step 4   Send packets destined for the 10.0.0.0 network to the router's inside
interface:

```
route outside 10.0.0.0 255.255.255.128 192.168.0.1
route outside 10.0.0.128 255.255.255.128 192.168.0.1
```

NOTE   Splitting the netmask is required because an overlapping route cannot exist with a
connected route. In this example, the PIX Firewall already has a connected static route for
the inside interface network of 10.0.0.0/24. If you issue the command

```
route outside 10.0.0.0 255.255.255.0 192.168.0.1
```

you receive the error "Route already exists," and the new route is not added.

Hosts on inside network 10.0.0.0 can now communicate with hosts on outside network
10.0.0.0 by using either the statically assigned addresses or by using host names. If a host
on outside network 10.0.0.0 attempts to contact a host on inside network 10.0.0.2 by its host
name, the name must be sent to a DNS server for resolution to an IP address.

Here is an example of this process. The user at inside host 10.0.0.11 initiates a connection
to outside host 10.0.0.2 by its statically mapped IP address and the following sequence of
events occurs:

1   The user types in his browser http://192.168.0.12.

2   The PIX Firewall translates 192.168.0.12 to 10.0.0.2.

3   The PIX Firewall sends the packet to 192.168.0.1 because it has a route conveying
a message to send outbound packets destined for network 10.0.0.0 to 192.168.0.1.

4   The router has an interface on the 10.0.0.0 network, so it forwards the packet to the
host on that interface.

5   When the return packet arrives at the PIX Firewall with a destination of 192.168.0.10,
the PIX Firewall translates 192.168.0.10 back to 10.0.0.11 and forwards the packet to
inside network 10.0.0.0. The first static entered tells the PIX Firewall that
192.168.0.11 is actually 10.0.0.11 on its inside interface.

NOTE   You can implement this scenario using the **alias** command with previous versions of the
PIX Firewall. However, with PIX Firewall Version 6.2 or higher, outside NAT is the
recommended solution.

Identity NAT

Another feature that you can use to control outbound connections is the ability to control which internal IP addresses are visible on the outside. The **nat 0** command lets you disable address translation so that inside IP addresses are visible on the outside without address translation. Use this feature when you have NIC-registered IP addresses on your inside network that you want to be accessible on the outside network. Use of **nat 0** depends on your security policy. If your policy allows internal clients to have their IP addresses exposed to the Internet, then **nat 0** is the process to implement that policy.

In the network shown in Figure 7-10, the address 192.168.0.9 is not translated. When you enter a **nat 0** command for this host, the PIX Firewall displays a message to indicate that the specified host will not be translated, as shown in Example 7-6. The **nat 0** command shown in Example 7-6 allows host 192.168.0.9 to send traffic through the PIX Firewall to any lower-security interface using its nontranslated source address of 192.168.0.9.

Figure 7-10 *Identity NAT*

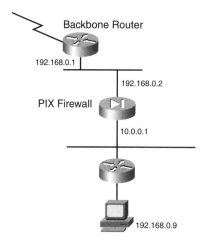

Example 7-6 *Identity NAT Configuration*

```
pixfirewall(config)# nat (inside) 0 192.168.0.9 255.255.255.255
nat 0 192.168.0.9 will be non-translated
```

Policy NAT

Policy NAT, available with PIX Firewall Version 6.3(2) or higher, provides policy-based dynamic and static address translation capabilities on the PIX Firewall. This feature lets you translate local addresses to different global addresses based on the source and destination addresses specified in an ACL. Without policy NAT, the destination address is not considered, and you can specify only a single global address for a given source address.

To configure dynamic policy NAT, you first define the source and destination addresses for traffic to be translated with an **access-list** command. (Access lists are covered in detail in Chapter 8.) You then use the **nat access-list** command and specify the access list created for policy NAT.

NOTE	You cannot use a *nat_id* value of 0 with policy NAT. Using a *nat_id* value of 0 disables translation for the host or network specified by the resulting **nat 0** command.

Configuration of static and dynamic policy NAT are similar. For static policy NAT, you define the source and destination addresses for traffic to be translated with an **access list** command. You then use the **static** command and specify the access list created for static policy NAT.

Example 7-7 shows an example of dynamic and static policy NAT configuration.

Example 7-7 *Dynamic and Static Policy NAT*

```
pixfirewall(config)# access-list policy-dynamic1 permit ip 10.0.0.0 255.255.255.0
  172.20.0.0 255.255.0.0
pixfirewall(config)# access-list policy-dynamic2 permit ip 10.0.0.0 255.255.255.0
  172.30.0.0 255.255.0.0
pixfirewall(config)# access-list policy-static1 permit ip 10.0.0.230
  255.255.255.255 172.20.0.0 255.255.0.0
pixfirewall(config)# access-list policy-static2 permit ip 10.0.0.230
  255.255.255.255 172.30.0.0 255.255.0.0
pixfirewall(config)# nat (inside) 1 access-list policy-dynamic1
pixfirewall(config)# nat (inside) 2 access-list policy-dynamic2
pixfirewall(config)# global (outside) 1 192.168.0.100-192.168.0.149
pixfirewall(config)# global (outside) 2 192.168.0.150-192.168.0.199
pixfirewall(config)# static (inside,outside) 192.168.0.230 access-list policy-
  static1
pixfirewall(config)# static (inside,outside) 192.168.0.231 access-list policy-
  static2
```

This example uses the **access-list** command to create four ACLs for use with **nat** and **static** commands. The first **nat** statement specifies dynamic address translation for traffic originating from the inside interface with source address of 10.0.0.0/24 and destined to the 172.20.0.0/16 network (traffic matching ACL named policy-dynamic1) with global address pool 1 (192.168.0.100 through 192.168.0.149). The second **nat** statement specifies dynamic address translation using a different global address pool (pool 2, 192.168.0.150 through 192.168.0.199) for the same source traffic as the first **nat** statement (inside interface with source address of 10.0.0.0/24), but with a different destination network of 172.30.0.0/16 (traffic matching ACL named policy-dynamic2).

Similarly, the **static** statements translate the same local address (10.0.0.230) to two different global addresses depending on the destination network (a global address of 192.168.0.230 when traffic is destined to 172.20.0.0/16 and 192.168.0.231 when traffic is destined to 172.30.0.0/16).

Translations and Connections

When exploring the PIX Firewall, it is important to understand the distinction between translated sessions and connected sessions. *Translations* are located at the IP layer of the TCP/IP protocol stack, and *connections* are at the transport layer. Connections are subsets of translations. You can have many connections open under one translation.

The **xlate** command allows you to show or clear the contents of the translation (xlate) slots. A translation slot is created when a session is built through the PIX. That translation slot can remain after you make configuration changes. It is good practice to use the **clear xlate** after adding, changing, or removing **alias**, **conduit**, **global**, **nat**, **route**, or **static** commands in your configuration. Although it is more invasive, a **reload** or power-cycle of the PIX also accomplishes the same goal of clearing the translation slots.

The syntax for the **clear xlate** and **show xlate** commands are as follows:

```
show xlate [global | local ip1[-ip2] [netmask mask]] lport | gport port[-port]]
  [interface if1[,if2][,ifn]] [state static [,dump] [,portmap] [,norandomseq]
  [,identity]]
clear xlate [global | local ip1[-ip2] [netmask mask]] lport | gport port[-port]]
  [interface if1[,if2][,ifn]] [state static [,dump] [,portmap] [,norandomseq]
  [,identity]]
```

Table 7-5 describes the **show xlate** and **clear xlate** command arguments.

Table 7-5   **show/clear xlate** *Command Arguments*

Argument	Definition
global	**local** *ip1*[-*ip2*] [**netmask** *mask*]	Display active translations by global IP address or local IP address using the network mask to qualify the IP addresses.
lport	**gport** *port*[-*port*]	Display active translations by local and global port specification.
interface *if*[,*if2*][,*ifn*]	Display active translations by interface.
state	Display active translations by state: static translation (**static**), **dump** (cleanup), PAT global (**portmap**), a **nat** or **static** translation with the **norandomseq** setting (**norandomseq**), or the use of the NAT 0 identity feature (**identity**).

To display all active connections, issue the **show conn** command. This command displays the number of connections as well as the source and destination IP address and port number for each connection. Table 7-6 describes the **show conn** command, which has the following syntax:

```
show conn [count] [foreign | local ip[-ip2] [netmask mask]] [protocol tcp | udp |
  protocol] [fport | lport port1[-port2]] [state up[,finin][,finout]
  [,http_get][,smtp_data][,smtp_banner][,smtp_incomplete][,nojava][,data_in]
  [,data_out][,sqlnet_fixup_data][,conn_inbound][,rpc][,h323][,dump]

show conn detail
```

Table 7-6 describes the **show conn** command arguments.

Table 7-6   **show conn** *Command Arguments*

Argument	Definition
count	Displays only the number of used connections. This feature is no longer supported and returns unreliable information.
**foreign	local** *ip*[-*ip2*] **netmask** *mask*	Displays active connections by foreign IP address or local IP address. Qualify foreign or local active connections by a network mask.
**protocol tcp	udp |** *protocol*	Displays active connections by protocol type. *protocol* is a protocol specified by number.
**fport	lport** *port1*[-*port2*]	Displays foreign or local active connections by port.
state	Displays active connections by their current state: up (**up**), FIN inbound (**finin**), FIN outbound (**finout**), HTTP get (**http_get**), SMTP mail data (**smtp_data**), SMTP mail banner (**smtp_banner**), incomplete SMTP mail connection (**smtp_incomplete**), an outbound command denying access to Java applets (**nojava**), inbound data (**data_in**), outbound data (**data_out**), SQL*Net data fixup (**sqlnet_fixup_data**), inbound connection (**conn_inbound**), Remote Procedure Call (RPC) connection (**rpc**), H.323 connection (**h323**), dump cleanup connection (**dump**).
detail	Describes connection flags.

Traffic through the PIX Firewall falls into two categories:

- **Outbound traffic**—Traffic from a higher-security interface such as the inside interface to a lower-security interface such as the outside interface. This type of traffic typically represents internal users accessing resources on the Internet or the DMZ.

- **Inbound traffic**—Traffic from a lower-security interface such as the outside or DMZ interfaces to a higher security interface such as the inside interface. This type of traffic typically results from Internet users accessing services that you host, such as DNS, SMTP, or web services.

After you perform the basic configuration on a PIX Firewall, traffic originating from higher security level interfaces and destined for lower-security-level interfaces (outbound) is permitted by default. This type of traffic is handled by the NAT policy that is required as part of the basic PIX Firewall configuration.

NOTE	As explained in Chapter 5, "Getting Started with the Cisco PIX Firewall," you must configure the six basic PIX commands, including **nat** and **global**, to get your PIX Firewall up and running.

NOTE	Although outbound traffic requires a properly configured NAT policy, that does not mean that you must translate addresses for outbound connectivity. You can use the **nat 0** command to allow your internal hosts to access networks outside the PIX Firewall without translating their addresses.

To allow inbound traffic, you enter a predefined static translation using an address or range of addresses from the global pool. You enter a conduit that defines the address, group of addresses, TCP/UDP port or range of ports, and the applications allowed to flow through the PIX Firewall.

Statics and Conduits

Although most connections occur from an interface with a high security level to an interface with a low security level, sometimes you want to allow connections from an interface with a lower security level to an interface with a higher security level. To do so, use the **static** and **conduit** commands.

NOTE	You can also enable inbound communications (connections originating from a lower-security-level interface) with a **static** and **access-list** command combination, as discussed earlier in this chapter. Access control lists are explained in great detail in Chapter 8.

NOTE	Using **static** with the **access-list** command, discussed earlier in the chapter, is now the preferred method to allow inbound traffic on PIX Firewall, and it is fully supported by various management tools such as the PIX Device Manager (PDM) and the Management Center for PIX Firewalls (PIX MC). Conduits are presented here for informational purposes, but ACLs should be your first choice for managing inbound traffic on the PIX.

The **static** command creates static mapping between an inside IP address and a global IP address. Using the **static** command enables you to set a permanent global IP address for a particular inside IP address. This process creates an entrance for the specified interfaces with the lower security level into the specified interface with a higher security level.

After you use the **static** command to create a static mapping between an inside IP address and a global IP address, the connection from the outside interface to the inside interface is still blocked by the ASA of the PIX Firewall. You use the **conduit** command to allow traffic to flow between interfaces. The **conduit** command creates the exception to the PIX Firewall's ASA.

The **conduit** command permits or denies connections from outside the PIX Firewall to access TCP or UDP services on hosts inside the network. The **conduit** statement creates an exception to the PIX Firewall ASA by permitting connections from one PIX Firewall network interface to access hosts on another.

You can have up to 8000 conduits and can remove a conduit with the **no conduit** command.

The syntax for the **conduit** command is as follows:

```
conduit permit | deny protocol global_ip global_mask [operator port [port]]
    foreign_ip foreign_mask [operator port [port]]
conduit permit | deny icmp global_ip global_mask foreign_ip foreign_mask [icmp_type]
```

Table 7-7 describes the **conduit** command arguments.

Table 7-7   conduit *Command Arguments*

Argument	Definition
permit	Permits access if the conditions are met.
deny	Denies access if the conditions are met.
protocol	Specifies the transport protocol for the connection. Possible literal values are **icmp**, **tcp**, **udp**, or an integer in the range 0 to 255 representing an IP protocol number. Use **ip** to specify all transport protocols. You can view valid protocol numbers online at http://www.iana.org/assignments/protocol-numbers.
global_ip	A global IP address previously defined by a **global** or **static** command. You can use any IP address if the *global_ip* and *global_mask* are 0.0.0.0 0.0.0.0. The **any** command applies the **permit** or **deny** to the global addresses on all interfaces. If *global_ip* is a host, you can omit *global_mask* by specifying the **host** command before *global_ip*.
icmp_type	The type of Internet Control Message Protocol (ICMP) message. Omit this option to include all ICMP types. The **conduit permit icmp any any** command permits all ICMP types and lets ICMP pass inbound and outbound.
operator	A comparison operand that enables you to specify a port or a port range. Possible values are as follows: **eq**, **lt**, **any**, **gt**, **neq**, and **range**. Not using an operator and port denotes all ports.

continues

Table 7-7   **conduit** *Command Arguments (Continued)*

Argument	Definition
global_mask	Network mask of *global_ip*. If you use 0 for *global_ip*, use 0 for the *global_mask*; otherwise, enter the *global_mask* appropriate to *global_ip*. The *global_mask* is a 32-bit, 4-part dotted decimal, such as 255.255.255.255. Use 0s to indicate bit positions to be ignored. Use subnetting if required.
port	Service you permit to be used while accessing *global_ip* or *foreign_ip*. Specify services by the ports that handles them, such as 25 for SMTP, 80 for HTTP, and so on. You can specify ports by either a literal name or as a number in the range of 0 to 65,535. You can specify all ports by not specifying a port value (for example, **conduit deny tcp any any**). This command is the default condition for the conduit command in that all ports are denied until explicitly permitted. You can view valid port numbers online at http://www.iana.org/assignments/port-numbers.
foreign_ip	An external IP address (host or network) that can access the *global_ip*. You can specify 0.0.0.0 or 0 for any host. If both the *foreign_ip* and *foreign_mask* are 0.0.0.0 0.0.0.0, you can use the shorthand **any** command, which applies to all interfaces. If *foreign_ip* is a host, you can omit *foreign_mask* by specifying the **host** command before *foreign_ip*.
foreign_mask	Network mask of *foreign_ip*. The *foreign_mask* is a 32-bit, 4-part dotted decimal, such as 255.255.255.255. Use 0s in a part to indicate bit positions to be ignored. Use subnetting if required. If you use 0 for *foreign_ip*, use 0 for the *foreign_mask*; otherwise, enter the *foreign_mask* appropriate to *foreign_ip*.

NOTE   If you want internal users to be able to ping external hosts, you must create an ICMP conduit for echo reply. For example, to give ping access to all hosts, use the **conduit permit icmp any any echo-reply** command.

The configuration on the network shown in Figure 7-11 allows FTP services via the IP address 192.168.0.10 to the inside host 10.0.0.11 from the outside. Example 7-8 shows the command that allows this traffic flow.

Figure 7-11   *Conduit Command*

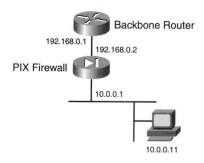

Example 7-8   *Conduit Command Configuration*

```
pixfirewall(config)# static (inside,outside) 192.168.0.10 10.0.0.11
pixfirewall(config)# conduit permit tcp host 192.168.0.10 eq ftp any
```

Configuring DNS Support

Two methods are available for configuring the PIX Firewall to translate IP addresses embedded in DNS A-records:

- Using the **alias** command
- Using the expanded **nat** or **static** command with the **dns** option

The **alias** command is the original method for configuring DNS support, and it is supported in most versions of the PIX Firewall. Use of expanded **nat** or **static** commands with the **dns** option is supported only on PIX Firewall Version 6.2 or higher.

NOTE   Avoid the **alias** command if you want to use any of the GUI-based management tools. These tools, such as the PDM or PIX MC, provide support only for the newer expanded **nat** and **static** commands.

DNS Support with the alias Command

The **alias** command has two possible functions. You can use it to perform DNS doctoring of DNS replies from an external DNS server. In DNS doctoring, the PIX Firewall translates the IP address in a DNS response from a DNS server. In this case, the address being translated is the address embedded in the A-record for the host whose name the DNS server is resolving. DNS doctoring is necessary when an internal client needs to connect to an internal server by its host name, and the DNS server is on the outside of the PIX Firewall.

You can also use the **alias** command to do destination NAT (DNAT). In DNAT, the PIX Firewall translates the destination IP address of an application call. This step is necessary when you want an application call from an internal client to a server in a perimeter network to use the server's external IP address. It does not doctor the DNS replies.

The **show alias** command displays the **alias** command in the configuration. You can remove the **alias** command with its **no** form or with the **clear alias** command.

The syntax for the **alias** command is as follows:

```
alias [(if_name)] dnat_ip foreign_ip [netmask]
```

Table 7-8 describes the **alias** command arguments.

Table 7-8 alias *Command Arguments*

Argument	Definition
dnat_ip	An IP address on the internal network that provides an alternate IP address for the external address that is the same as an address on the internal network.
foreign_ip	An IP address on the external network that has the same address as a host on the internal network.
if_name	The internal network interface name in which the *foreign_ip* overlaps.
netmask	The network mask applied to both IP addresses. Use 255.255.255.255 for host masks.

DNS Doctoring with Alias

The **alias** command translates one IP address into another. One of the main uses of this command is DNS doctoring, which is translating the IP address embedded in a DNS response.

Figure 7-12 reveals how DNS doctoring is helpful and shows how to use the **alias** command for this purpose. The internal web server in the network shown in Figure 7-12, the web server for Cisco.com, has an IP address of 10.0.0.10. For hosts on the 10.0.0.0 network to access the web server by its domain name, they must resolve the name by using the DNS server on the outside interface of the PIX Firewall. This requirement presents a problem that you can solve by using the **alias** command. To gain a better understanding of this problem and its solution, follow the sequence of events as an inside host attempts to access the web server by its host name:

1 A user at host 10.0.0.5 attempts to access Cisco.com via the user's web browser.

2 The only way the IP address of Cisco.com can be located is through the DNS server on the outside of the PIX Firewall, so the host sends the packet to the PIX Firewall.

3 Because NAT is configured for the inside network, the PIX Firewall translates the source address from 10.0.0.5 to 192.168.0.20 and forwards the message requesting the IP address of Cisco.com to the DNS server.

4 The DNS server locates its A-record for Cisco.com and sends its DNS reply to 192.168.0.20. The reply contains the response Cisco.com = 192.168.0.17.

5 When the PIX Firewall receives the DNS response, it translates 192.168.0.17 to 10.0.0.10 and forwards the packet to the originating host (10.0.0.5). Now the originating host knows that the web server is on its own network and that it can access it directly. If the **alias** command did not notify the PIX Firewall to translate the address embedded in the response, the originating host would send the next packet back through the PIX Firewall, thinking that Cisco.com resides on the outside.

Figure 7-12 *DNS Doctoring with the* **alias** *Command*

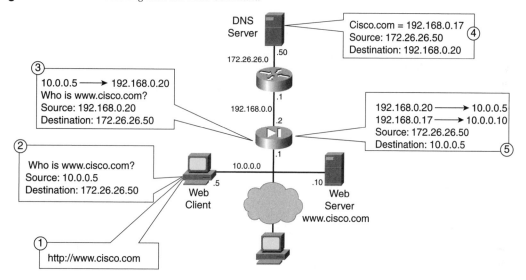

The following steps were taken to provide DNS doctoring:

1 A **static** command was configured to map the web server's internal address to 192.168.0.17, a globally routable IP address. This step is necessary because the DNS server has a static mapping of Cisco.com to 192.168.0.17. For the DNS server to resolve the name to the IP address, the IP address must always be the same. Furthermore, for users on the Internet to access the web server on the inside, a static and conduit combination must be configured.

2 A conduit was configured to give anyone on the Internet access to the web server on port 80.

3 DNS doctoring was configured. This step enables the PIX Firewall to watch for DNS replies that contain 192.168.0.17 and then replace the 192.168.0.17 address with 10.0.0.10.

When used for DNS doctoring, the **alias** command reads similar to the following:

"If a DNS packet destined for *foreign_network_address* is returned to the PIX Firewall, alter the DNS packet by changing the foreign network address to the *dnat_network_address*."

NOTE   There must be an A-record in the DNS zone file for the DNAT address in the **alias** command.

Example 7-9 shows the configuration used for the network shown in Figure 7-12.

Example 7-9   *DNS Doctoring with the **alias** Command*

```
pixfirewall(config)# nat (inside) 1 10.0.0.0 255.255.255.0
pixfirewall(config)# global (outside) 1 192.168.0.20-192.168.0.254 netmask
  255.255.255.0
pixfirewall(config)# static (inside,outside) 192.168.0.17 10.0.0.10
pixfirewall(config)# conduit permit tcp host 192.168.0.17 eq www any
pixfirewall(config)# alias (inside) 10.0.0.10 192.168.0.17 255.255.255.255
```

Destination NAT with the **alias** Command

You can also use the **alias** command to perform DNAT. This process is useful in scenarios such as the network shown in Figure 7-13. The web server in this figure resides on the PIX Firewall's DMZ and has an IP address of 172.16.0.2. Again, for hosts on the 10.0.0.0 network to access the web server by its domain name, they must resolve the name by using the DNS server on the outside interface of the PIX Firewall. This requirement presents a different problem, but one that you can solve by using the **alias** command.

Figure 7-13   *DNAT with the **alias** Command*

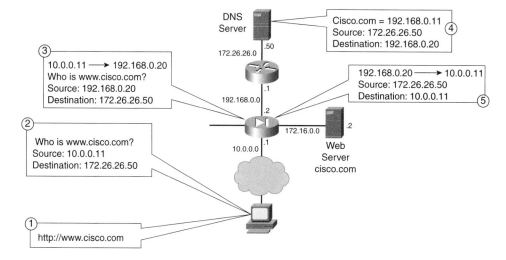

To gain a better understanding of this problem and its solution, follow the sequence of events as an inside host attempts to access the web server by its host name:

1 A user at host 10.0.0.11 attempts to access Cisco.com via the user's web browser.

2 The only way the IP address of Cisco.com can be located is through the DNS server on the outside of the PIX Firewall, so the host sends the packet to the PIX Firewall.

3 Because NAT is configured for the inside network, the PIX Firewall translates the source address from 10.0.0.11 to 192.168.0.20 and forwards the message requesting the IP address of Cisco.com to the DNS server.

4 The DNS server locates its A-record for Cisco.com and sends its DNS reply to 192.168.0.20. The reply contains the response Cisco.com = 192.168.0.11.

5 When the PIX Firewall receives the DNS response, it translates 192.168.0.20 back to 10.0.0.11 and forwards the packet to the originating host. However, this time it does not translate the address embedded in the response but instead returns the exact response sent by the DNS server. When the web client makes the actual call to the web server, the PIX Firewall translates, or DNATs, the IP address 192.168.0.11 to the web server's real address, 172.16.0.2.

The following steps are taken to provide this capability:

1 The **alias** command is configured to perform DNAT:

```
alias (inside) 192.168.0.11 172.16.0.2 255.255.255.255
```

NOTE   The IP addresses in the **alias** command are in reverse order compared with the DNS doctoring example.

2 A static translation is created for the web server:

```
static (dmz,outside) 192.168.0.11 172.16.0.2 netmask 255.255.255.255
```

3 To grant permission for access, a conduit was created:

```
conduit permit tcp host 192.168.0.11 eq www any
```

NOTE   For DNS servers on the outside, A-records for hosts behind the PIX Firewall must map host names to globally routable IP addresses.

NOTE	The interface in the **alias** command should be the interface from which the clients are calling.

When used for DNAT, the **alias** command reads similar to the following:

"If the PIX Firewall gets a packet destined for the *dnat_IP_address*, send it to the *foreign_IP_address*."

Example 7-10 shows the configuration used for the network shown in Figure 7-13.

Example 7-10   *Destination NAT with the* **alias** *Command*

```
pixfirewall(config)# nat (inside) 1 10.0.0.0 255.255.255.0
pixfirewall(config)# global (outside) 1 192.168.0.20-192.168.0.254 netmask
  255.255.255.0
pixfirewall(config)# static (dmz,outside) 192.168.0.11 172.16.0.2
pixfirewall(config)# conduit permit tcp 192.168.0.11 eq www any
pixfirewall(config)# alias (inside) 192.168.0.11 172.16.0.2 255.255.255.255
```

DNS Record Translation with Expanded NAT and Static Commands

PIX Firewall Software Version 6.2 introduced full support for NAT of DNS messages originating from either inside (more secure) or outside (less secure) interfaces.

If a client on an inside network requests DNS resolution of an inside address from a DNS server on an outside interface, the DNS A-record is translated correctly. It is no longer necessary to use the **alias** command to perform DNS doctoring. The PIX Firewall translates the DNS A-record on behalf of the **alias** command.

In the network shown in Figure 7-14, the client on the inside network issues an HTTP request to server 10.0.0.10 using its hostname, Cisco.com. The PIX Firewall translates the web client's nonroutable source address in the IP header and forwards the request to the DNS server on its outside interface. When the DNS A-record is returned, the PIX Firewall applies address translation not only to the destination address, but also to the embedded IP address of the web server. This address is contained in the user data portion of the DNS reply packet. As a result, the web client on the inside network gets the address it needs to connect to the web server on the inside network. NAT of DNS messages is implemented in both the **nat** and **static** commands by using the dns option.

Figure 7-14 *DNS Record Translation with **nat** and **static** Commands*

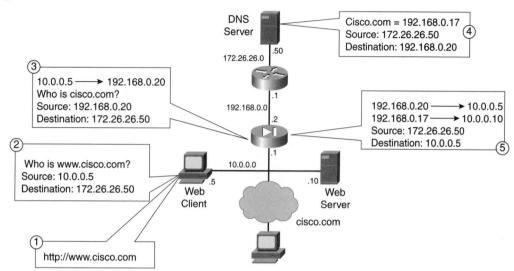

Example 7-11 shows the configuration used for DNS record translation shown on Figure 7-14.

Example 7-11 *DNS Record Translation with **nat** and **static** Commands*

```
pixfirewall(config)# nat (inside) 1 10.0.0.0 255.255.255.0 dns
pixfirewall(config)# global (outside) 1 192.168.0.20-192.168.0.254 netmask
  255.255.255.0
pixfirewall(config)# static (inside,outside) 192.168.0.17 10.0.0.10 dns
```

PAT

This section describes another way through the PIX Firewall, PAT. PAT is a combination of an IP address and a source port number, which creates a unique session. PAT uses the same IP address for all packets but a different unique source port greater than 1024. PAT provides the following advantages:

- PAT and NAT can be used together.
- The PAT address can be different from the outside interface address.
- IP address expansion is possible with PAT.
- With PAT, one outside IP address is used for up to 64,000 inside hosts.
- PAT maps port numbers to a single IP address.
- PAT secures transactions by hiding the inside source address through the use of a single IP address from the PIX Firewall.

In the example shown in Figure 7-15, two clients are requesting connectivity to the Internet. The PIX Firewall checks security rules to verify the security levels and then replaces the source IP address with the PAT IP address. To maintain accountability, the source port address is changed to a unique number greater than 1024.

Figure 7-15 *PAT*

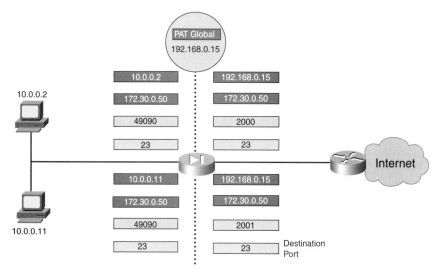

The PIX Firewall PAT feature expands a company's address pool as follows:

- One outside IP address is used for approximately 4000 inside hosts. That is the practical limit; the theoretical limit is greater than 64,000.
- PAT can be used with NAT.
- A PAT address can be a virtual address that is different from the outside address. Do not use PAT when running multimedia applications through the PIX Firewall. Multimedia applications need access to specific ports and can conflict with port mappings provided by PAT.

In the example shown in Figure 7-16, XYZ Company has only four registered IP addresses. One address is taken by the perimeter router, one by the PIX Firewall, and one by the bastion host.

The configuration for this example is shown in Example 7-12. Here, IP addresses are assigned to the internal and external interfaces. A single registered IP address is put into the global pool and is shared by all outgoing access for network 10.0.0.0.

Figure 7-16 *PAT Example*

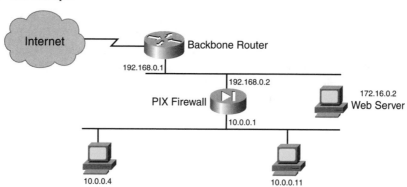

Example 7-12 *PAT*

```
pixfirewall(config)# ip address inside 10.0.0.1 255.255.255.0
pixfirewall(config)# ip address outside 192.168.0.2 255.255.255.0
pixfirewall(config)# route outside 0.0.0.0 0.0.0.0 192.168.0.1
pixfirewall(config)# nat (inside) 1 10.0.0.0 255.255.255.0
pixfirewall(config)# global (outside) 1 192.168.0.4 netmask 255.255.255.0
```

PAT Using the Outside Interface Address

You can use the IP address of the outside interface as the PAT address by using the **interface** option of the **global** command. This step is important when using the PIX Firewall's Dynamic Host Configuration Protocol (DHCP) client feature. It allows the DHCP-retrieved address to be used for PAT. DHCP support is discussed in Chapter 5.

In the network layout shown in Figure 7-16, source addresses for hosts on network 10.0.0.0 are translated to 192.168.0.2 for outgoing access, and the source port is changed to a unique number greater than 1024.

Example 7-13 shows the configuration using PAT with an outside interface address for the network shown in Figure 7-16.

Example 7-13 *PAT Using the Outside Interface Address*

```
pixfirewall(config)# ip address inside 10.0.0.1 255.255.255.0
pixfirewall(config)# ip address outside 192.168.0.2 255.255.255.0
pixfirewall(config)# route outside 0.0.0.0 0.0.0.0 192.168.0.1
pixfirewall(config)# nat (inside) 1 10.0.0.0 255.255.255.0
pixfirewall(config)# global (outside) 1 interface
```

Mapping Subnets to PAT Addresses

With PIX Firewall Software Versions 5.2 and higher, you can specify multiple PATs to track use among different subnets. For the network layout in Figure 7-17, Example 7-14 shows the commands required for mapping network 10.0.1.0 and network 10.0.2.0 to different PAT addresses. It uses a separate **nat** and **global** command pair for each network. Outbound sessions from hosts on internal network 10.0.1.0 appear to originate from address 192.168.0.8 and outbound sessions from hosts on internal network 10.0.2.0 appear to originate from address 192.168.0.9.

Figure 7-17 *Mapping Subnets to PAT Addresses*

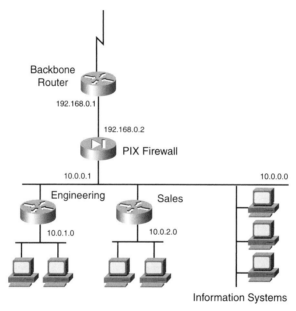

Example 7-14 *Mapping Subnets to PAT Addresses*

```
pixfirewall(config)# ip address inside 10.0.0.1 255.255.255.0
pixfirewall(config)# ip address outside 192.168.0.2 255.255.255.0
pixfirewall(config)# route outside 0.0.0.0 0.0.0.0 192.168.0.1
pixfirewall(config)# route inside 10.0.1.0 255.255.255.0 10.0.0.11
pixfirewall(config)# route inside 10.0.2.0 255.255.255.0 10.0.0.12
pixfirewall(config)# nat (inside) 1 10.0.1.0 255.255.255.0
pixfirewall(config)# nat (inside) 2 10.0.2.0 255.255.255.0
pixfirewall(config)# global (outside) 1 192.168.0.8 netmask 255.255.255.0
pixfirewall(config)# global (outside) 2 192.168.0.9 netmask 255.255.255.0
```

Backing Up PAT Addresses by Using Multiple PATs

With PIX Firewall Software Versions 5.2 and higher, you can also back up your PAT address by configuring multiple globals with the same *nat_id*.

In the network layout shown in Figure 7-17, address 192.168.0.9 is used for all outbound connections from network 10.0.1.0 when the port pool from 192.168.0.8 is at maximum capacity, using the commands shown in Example 7-15.

Example 7-15 *Backing Up PAT Addresses by Using Multiple PATs*

```
pixfirewall(config)# ip address inside 10.0.0.1 255.255.255.0
pixfirewall(config)# ip address outside 192.168.0.2 255.255.255.0
pixfirewall(config)# route outside 0.0.0.0 0.0.0.0 192.168.0.1
pixfirewall(config)# nat (inside) 1 10.0.1.0 255.255.255.0
pixfirewall(config)# global (outside) 1 192.168.0.8 netmask 255.255.255.0
pixfirewall(config)# global (outside) 1 192.168.0.9 netmask 255.255.255.0
```

Augmenting a Global Pool with PAT

You can augment a pool of global addresses with PAT. When all IP addresses from the global pool are in use, the PIX Firewall begins PAT by using the single IP address shown in the second **global** command.

Example 7-16 illustrates the use of PAT to augment a global address pool for the network shown in Figure 7-17. In the example, hosts on the 10.0.0.0 internal network are assigned addresses from the global pool 192.168.0.20 to 192.168.0.254 as they initiate outbound connections. When the addresses from the global pool are exhausted, packets from all hosts on network 10.0.0.0 appear to originate from 192.168.0.19.

Example 7-16 *Augmenting a Global Pool with PAT*

```
pixfirewall(config)# ip address inside 10.0.0.1 255.255.255.0
pixfirewall(config)# ip address outside 192.168.0.2 255.255.255.0
pixfirewall(config)# route outside 0.0.0.0 0.0.0.0 192.168.0.1
pixfirewall(config)# nat (inside) 1 10.0.0.0 255.255.255.0
pixfirewall(config)# global (outside) 1 192.168.0.20-192.168.0.254 netmask
   255.255.255.0
pixfirewall(config)# global (outside) 1 192.168.0.19 netmask 255.255.255.0
```

Port Redirection

This section explains the PIX Firewall's static PAT feature. With Software Versions 6.0 and higher, the PIX Firewall provides static PAT capability. This feature allows outside users to connect to a particular IP address or port and have the PIX Firewall redirect traffic to the appropriate inside server. You can use this capability to send multiple inbound TCP or UDP services to different internal hosts through a single global address. The shared global address can be a unique address or a shared outbound PAT address, or it can be shared with the external interface.

The **static** command was modified in PIX Firewall Software Version 6.0 to accommodate port redirection. If you specify the keyword **tcp** or **udp** in the **static** command, a static UDP or TCP port redirection is configured. If you specify the keyword interface, the outside interface address is presumed to be the global IP address.

You must configure a **conduit** or **access-list** command in addition to the **static** command to enable an inbound connection.

The syntax for the **static** command is as follows:

```
static [(internal_if_name, external_if_name)] tcp | udp global_ip | interface
   global_port local_ip local_port [netmask mask]
```

Table 7-9 describes the **static** command arguments when used for port redirection.

Table 7-9 static *Command Arguments for Port Redirection*

Argument	Definition
internal_if_name	Internal network interface name
external_if_name	External network interface name
tcp	Specifies TCP port redirection
udp	Specifies UDP port redirection
global_ip	Global IP address used for redirection
interface	Outside interface address taken to be the global address
global_port	Global TCP or UDP port for port redirection
local_ip	Local IP address from the inside network
local_port	Local TCP or UDP port for port redirection
netmask *mask*	Network mask for *global_ip* and *local_ip*

In the example shown on Figure 7-18, the external user directs a Telnet request to the PIX outside IP address 192.168.0.2. The PIX Firewall redirects the request to host 10.0.0.4. The external user then directs an HTTP port 8080 request to PAT address 192.168.0.9. The PIX Firewall redirects this request to host 172.16.0.2 port 80.

Figure 7-18   *Port Redirection Example*

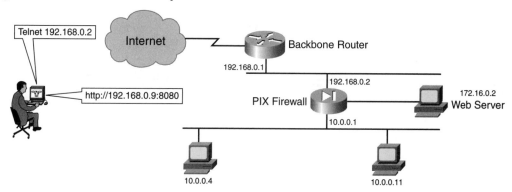

Example 7-17 shows a partial configuration for the PIX Firewall in Figure 7-18.

Example 7-17   *Port Redirections*

```
pixfirewall(config)# access-list 101 permit tcp any host 192.168.0.2 eq telnet
pixfirewall(config)# access-list 101 permit tcp any host 192.168.0.9 eq 8080
pixfirewall(config)# access-group 101 in interface outside
pixfirewall(config)# global (outside) 1 192.168.0.9
pixfirewall(config)# nat (inside) 1 0.0.0.0 0.0.0.0 0 0
pixfirewall(config)# static (inside,outside) tcp interface telnet 10.0.0.4 telnet
  netmask 255.255.255.255 0 0
pixfirewall(config)# static (dmz,outside) tcp 192.168.0.9 8080 172.16.0.2 www
  netmask 255.255.255.255 0 0
```

Configuring Multiple Interfaces

The PIX Firewall supports up to eight additional perimeter interfaces for platform extensibility and security policy enforcement on publicly accessible services. The multiple perimeter interfaces enable the PIX Firewall to protect publicly accessible web, mail, and DNS servers on the DMZ. Web-based and traditional Electronic Data Interchange (EDI) applications that link vendors and customers are also more secure and scalable when implemented using a physically separate network. As the trend toward building these extranet applications accelerates, the PIX Firewall is prepared to accommodate them.

NOTE   PIX Firewall Version 6.3 introduces 802.1Q VLAN support to the 500-series platform (excluding PIX Firewall models 501 and 506/506E). Firewall Services Module (FWSM) already supports 802.1Q and Inter-Switch Link (ISL) VLANs. Using VLANs, you can configure up to 22 additional perimeter interfaces on a PIX 535.

When configuring multiple interfaces, remember that the security level designates whether an interface is inside (trusted) or outside (untrusted) relative to another interface. An interface is considered inside in relation to another interface if its security level is higher than the other interface's security level, and it is considered outside in relation to another interface if its security level is lower than the other interface's security level. Figure 7-19 shows traffic flow and the commands that manage each type of traffic on the PIX Firewall.

Figure 7-19 *Access Through the PIX Firewall*

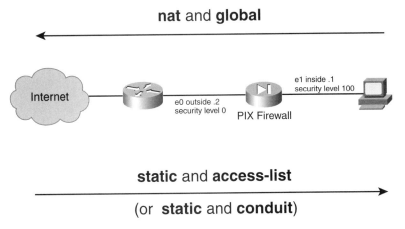

The primary rule for security levels is that an interface with a higher security level can access an interface with a lower security level. The **nat** and **global** commands work together to enable your network to use any IP addressing scheme and to remain hidden from the external network.

An interface with a lower security level cannot access an interface with a higher security level unless you specifically allow it by implementing **static** and **conduit** or **static** and **access-list** command pairs.

When your PIX Firewall is equipped with three or more interfaces, use the following guidelines to configure it while employing NAT:

- When using the interface name "outside," the security level is set to 0 and it cannot be changed.

- An interface is always outside with respect to another interface that has a higher security level. Packets cannot flow between interfaces that have the same security level.

- Use a single default route statement to the outside interface only. Set the default route with the **route** command.

- Use the **nat** command to let users on the respective interfaces start outbound connections. Associate the *nat_id* with the *global_id* in the **global** command. The valid identification numbers can be any positive number up to two billion.

- After you complete a configuration in which you add, change, or remove a **global** statement, save the configuration and enter the **clear xlate** command so that the IP addresses are updated in the translation table.

- To permit access to servers on protected networks, use the **static** and **access-list** commands (or **static** and **conduit**).

In the example shown in Figure 7-20, a PIX Firewall is configured with three interfaces. Example 7-18 shows the partial configuration for this PIX Firewall.

Figure 7-20 *Configuring Three Interfaces*

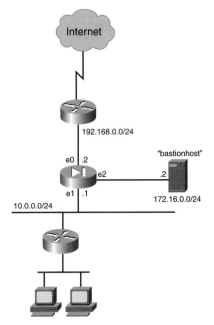

Example 7-18 *Configuring Three Interfaces*

```
pixfirewall(config)# ip address dmz 172.16.0.1 255.255.255.0
pixfirewall(config)# route outside 0.0.0.0 0.0.0.0 192.168.0.1
pixfirewall(config)# nat (inside) 1 10.0.0.0 255.255.255.0
pixfirewall(config)# global (outside) 1 192.168.0.20-192.168.0.254 netmask
  255.255.255.0
pixfirewall(config)# global (dmz) 1 172.16.0.20-172.16.0.254 netmask 255.255.255.0
pixfirewall(config)# static (dmz,outside) 192.168.0.11 172.16.0.2
pixfirewall(config)# access-list 101 permit tcp any host 192.168.0.11 eq http
pixfirewall(config)# access-group 101 in interface outside
```

In the example shown in Figure 7-21, the PIX Firewall has four interfaces. Users on all interfaces have access to all servers and hosts (inside, outside, DMZ, and Partnernet).

Figure 7-21 *Configuring Four Interfaces*

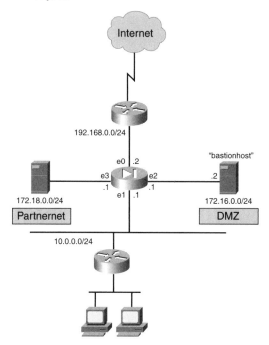

Configuring four interfaces requires more attention to detail, but you configure them with standard PIX Firewall commands. To enable users on a higher-security-level interface to access hosts on a lower-security interface, use the **nat** and **global** commands (for example, when users on the inside interface have access to the web server on the DMZ interface).

To let users on a lower-security-level interface, such as users on the Partnernet interface, access hosts on a higher-security interface (DMZ), use the **static** and **conduit** commands. As shown in the Figure 7-21, the Partnernet has a security level of 40, and the DMZ has a security level of 50. The DMZ uses **nat** and **global** commands to speak with the Partnernet and uses statics and conduits to receive traffic from the partnernet.

Example 7-19 shows the partial configuration for the PIX Firewall in Figure 7-21.

Example 7-19 *Configuring Four Interfaces*

```
pixfirewall(config)# route outside 0.0.0.0 0.0.0.0 192.168.0.1
pixfirewall(config)# nat (inside) 1 10.0.0.0 255.255.255.0
pixfirewall(config)# global (outside) 1 192.168.0.20-192.168.0.254 netmask
  255.255.255.0
pixfirewall(config)# global (dmz) 1 172.16.0.20-172.16.0.254 netmask 255.255.255.0
```

Example 7-19 *Configuring Four Interfaces (Continued)*

```
pixfirewall(config)# static (dmz,outside) 192.168.0.11 172.16.0.2
pixfirewall(config)# static (dmz,partnernet) 172.18.0.11 172.16.0.2
pixfirewall(config)# access-list 101 permit tcp any host 192.168.0.11 eq http
pixfirewall(config)# access-list 110 permit tcp any host 172.18.0.11 eq http
pixfirewall(config)# access-group 101 in interface outside
pixfirewall(config)# access-group 110 in interface partnernet
```

Summary

This section summarizes the information you learned in this chapter:

- The PIX Firewall manages the TCP and UDP protocols through the use of a translation table (for NAT sessions) and a connection table (for TCP and UDP sessions).

- Static translations assign a permanent IP address to an inside host. Mapping between local and global addresses is done dynamically with the **nat** command.

- The **nat** and **global** commands work together to hide internal IP addresses.

- You use the **static** and **access-list** commands (or **static** and **conduit**) to allow inbound communication through the PIX Firewall.

- The PIX Firewall supports PAT, port redirection, and identity NAT.

- Outside NAT provides transparent support for DNS.

- You can configure the PIX Firewall with up to 24 interfaces using the 802.1Q VLAN feature introduced in PIX Firewall Version 6.3. (PIX Firewall Versions 6.2 or earlier support up to 10 physical interfaces.)

- Configuring multiple interfaces requires more attention to detail than configuring a single interface, but you can do so with standard PIX Firewall commands.

Chapter Review Questions

To test what you have learned in this chapter, answer the following questions and then refer to Appendix A, "Answers to Chapter Review Questions," for the answers:

1 Which protocol is easier to inspect, TCP or UDP?

2 What are the four types of NAT provided by PIX Firewall?

3 How many hosts can share a single outside IP address using PAT?

4 How can you enable PAT using the IP address of the outside interface?

5 What is the maximum number of perimeter interfaces supported on a PIX Firewall 535?

6 List two methods that you can use to allow inbound connections.

7 What form of the **nat** command allows you to use nontranslated IP addresses on the outside interface of the PIX Firewall?

Lab Exercise—Configure Access Through the PIX Firewall

Complete the following lab exercise to practice the translations and connections concepts covered in this chapter. Please use the following initial configuration and continue with the lab exercises.

NOTE Many of the settings shown in this initial configuration are default values and do not need to be entered on your PIX Firewall. Specific commands that must be entered are shown in bold for your convenience.

```
:
interface ethernet0 100full
interface ethernet1 100full
interface ethernet2 100full
nameif ethernet0 outside security0
nameif ethernet1 inside security100
nameif ethernet2 dmz security50
enable password 8Ry2YjIyt7RRXU24 encrypted
passwd 2KFQnbNIdI.2KYOU encrypted
hostname pixfirewall
domain-name cisco.com
fixup protocol ftp 21
fixup protocol h323 h225 1720
fixup protocol h323 ras 1718-1719
fixup protocol http 80
fixup protocol ils 389
fixup protocol rsh 514
fixup protocol rtsp 554
fixup protocol sip 5060
fixup protocol sip udp 5060
fixup protocol skinny 2000
fixup protocol smtp 25
fixup protocol sqlnet 1521
names
pager lines 24
mtu outside 1500
mtu inside 1500
mtu dmz 1500
```

```
ip address outside 192.168.1.2 255.255.255.0
ip address inside 10.0.1.1 255.255.255.0
ip address dmz 172.16.1.1 255.255.255.0
pdm history enable
arp timeout 14400
global (outside) 1 192.168.1.150-192.168.1.200
timeout xlate 3:00:00
timeout conn 1:00:00 half-closed 0:10:00 udp 0:02:00 rpc 0:10:00 h225 1:00:00
timeout h323 0:05:00 mgcp 0:05:00 sip 0:30:00 sip_media 0:02:00
timeout uauth 0:05:00 absolute
aaa-server TACACS+ protocol tacacs+
aaa-server RADIUS protocol radius
aaa-server LOCAL protocol local
no snmp-server location
no snmp-server contact
snmp-server community public
no snmp-server enable traps
floodguard enable
telnet 10.0.1.0 255.255.255.0 inside
telnet timeout 5
ssh timeout 5
console timeout 0
terminal width 80
Cryptochecksum:aa0cc6e47d705ed128e041c2c2a8412b
: end
```

Objectives

In this lab exercise, you complete the following tasks:

- Configure a conduit to allow ICMP through the PIX Firewall.

- Configure the PIX Firewall to allow users on the inside interface to access the bastion host.

- Configure the PIX Firewall to allow users on the outside interface to access the bastion host.

- Configure the PIX Firewall to allow users on the outside interface to access the inside host.

NOTE   This lab includes **conduit** command configuration to allow you to become familiar with the **conduit** command. Keep in mind that the preferred and recommended method for allowing inbound traffic is through the use of **access-list** command. ACLs are covered in detail in Chapter 8.

Lab Topology

Figure 7-22 displays the topology you need for the lab exercises in this chapter.

Figure 7-22 *Configuring Access Through the PIX Firewall Visual Objective*

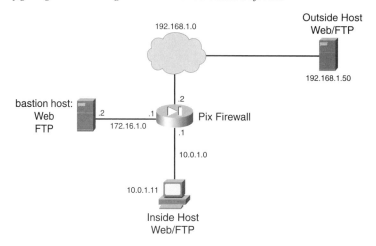

Equipment required to perform the lab includes the following:

- A PIX Firewall with three interfaces
- Category 5 patch cables
- PC host for DMZ running a web server and FTP server
- PC host for the outside subnet
- PC host for the inside subnet running a web server and FTP server

Task 1—Configure a Conduit to Allow ICMP Through the PIX Firewall

Enter the following commands to test and allow ICMP traffic through the PIX Firewall:

Step 1 From your Windows command line, ping the outside host:

```
C:\> ping 192.168.1.50
Pinging 192.168.1.50 with 32 bytes of data:
Request timed out.
Request timed out.
Request timed out.
Request timed out.
```

Step 2 Allow ICMP and ping packets through the PIX Firewall:

```
pixfirewall(config)# conduit permit icmp any any
```

Step 3 From the Windows command line, ping the outside host again:

```
C:\> ping 192.168.1.50
Pinging 192.168.1.50 with 32 bytes of data:

Reply from 192.168.1.50: bytes=32 time<10ms TTL=128
Reply from 192.168.1.50: bytes=32 time<10ms TTL=128
Reply from 192.168.1.50: bytes=32 time<10ms TTL=128
Reply from 192.168.1.50: bytes=32 time<10ms TTL=128
```

Task 2—Configure the PIX Firewall to Allow Users on the Inside Interface to Access the Bastion Host

Configure the PIX Firewall to allow access to the DMZ from the inside network:

Step 1 Assign one pool of IP addresses for hosts on the public DMZ:

```
pixfirewall(config)# global (dmz) 1 172.16.1.20-172.16.1.254
   netmask 255.255.255.0
```

Step 2 Clear the translation table so that the global IP address is updated in the table:

```
pixfirewall(config)# clear xlate
```

Step 3 Test connectivity to the bastion host from the inside host:

```
C:\> ping 172.16.1.2
```

Step 4 Test web access to your bastion host from the inside host by opening a web browser on the inside host and entering **http://172.16.1.2**.

The home page of the bastion host should appear on your web browser.

Step 5 Use the **show arp, show conn**, and **show xlate** commands to observe the transaction:

```
pixfirewall(config)# show arp
outside outsidehost 00e0.1e41.8762
inside insidehost 00e0.b05a.d509
dmz bastionhost 00e0.1eb1.78df
pixfirewall(config)# show xlate
1 in use, 1 most used
Global 172.16.1.20 Local insidehost
pixfirewall(config)# show conn
2 in use, 2 most used
TCP out bastionhost:80 in insidehost:1076 idle 0:00:07 Bytes 461 flags
UIO
TCP out bastionhost:80 in insidehost:1075 idle 0:00:07 Bytes 1441 flags
UIO
```

Step 6 Test FTP access to the bastion host from the inside host by choosing **Start > Run > ftp 172.16.1.2**. If you receive the message "Connected to 172.16.1.2," you have reached the bastion host.

Step 7 Quit the FTP session.

Task 3—Configure the PIX Firewall to Allow Users on the Outside Interface to Access the Bastion Host

Configure a static translation so that traffic originating from the bastion host always has the same source address on the outside interface of the PIX Firewall. Then, configure an ACL to allow users on the outside interface to access the bastion host.

Step 1 Create a static translation for your bastion host:

```
pixfirewall(config)# static (dmz,outside) 192.168.1.11 bastionhost
```

Step 2 Ping the bastion host from your outside host as allowed by the conduit via the static:

```
C:\> ping 192.168.1.11
```

Step 3 View current static translations:

```
pixfirewall(config)# show xlate
2 in use, 2 most used
Global 172.16.1.20 Local insidehost
Global 192.168.1.11 Local bastionhost
```

Step 4 Test web access to the bastion host by completing the following substep. You should be unable to access the IP address of the static mapped to the bastion host:

    (1) Open a web browser on the outside host and enter **http://192.168.1.11**.

Step 5 From the outside host, attempt to start an FTP session on the bastion host by choosing **Start > Run > ftp 192.168.1.11**. You should be unable to access your bastion host via FTP.

Step 6 Configure the ACL to allow web and FTP access to the bastion host and apply the ACL to the outside interface:

```
pixfirewall(config)# access-list 101 permit tcp any host 192.168.1.11 eq http
pixfirewall(config)# access-list 101 permit tcp any host 192.168.1.11 eq ftp
pixfirewall(config)# access-group 101 in interface outside
```

Step 7   Test web access to the bastion host by completing the following substeps. You should now be able to access your bastion host:

> (1) Open a web browser on the outside host and access the bastion host: **http://192.168.1.11**.

> (2) Use the **show arp**, **show conn**, and **show xlate** commands to observe the transaction.

> (3) Test FTP access to the bastion host from the outside host by choosing **Start > Run > ftp 192.168.1.11**.

> (4) Use the **show arp**, **show conn**, and **show xlate** commands to observe the transaction.

Task 4—Configure the PIX Firewall to Allow Users on the Outside Interface to Access the Inside Host

Configure a static translation so that traffic that originates from the inside host always has the same source address on the outside interface of the PIX Firewall. Then, configure a conduit to allow users on the outside interface to access the inside host.

Step 1   Create a static translation from the outside PIX Firewall interface to the internal host, and create a conduit to allow web connections from the outside to inside host on the inside:

```
pixfirewall(config)# static (inside,outside) 192.168.1.10 insidehost
pixfirewall(config)# conduit permit tcp host 192.168.1.10 eq www any
```

Step 2   Turn on ICMP monitoring at the PIX Firewall:

```
pixfirewall(config)# debug icmp trace

ICMP trace on Warning: this may cause problems on busy networks
```

Step 3   Clear the translation table:

```
pixfirewall(config)# clear xlate
```

Step 4   Ping the outside host from the inside host to test the translation. Observe the source and destination of the packets at the console of the PIX Firewall:

```
C:\> ping 192.168.1.50
```

Note the sample display for PIX Firewall:

```
Outbound ICMP echo request (len 32 id 2 seq 45056) insidehost >
192.168.1.10
 > outsidehost
Inbound ICMP echo reply (len 32 id 2 seq 45056) outsidehost >
192.168.1.10
 > insidehost
```

```
Outbound ICMP echo request (len 32 id 2 seq 45312) insidehost >
192.168.1.10
 > outsidehost
Inbound ICMP echo reply (len 32 id 2 seq 45312) outsidehost >
192.168.1.10> insidehost
Outbound ICMP echo request (len 32 id 2 seq 45568) insidehost >
192.168.1.10
 > outsidehost
Inbound ICMP echo reply (len 32 id 2 seq 45568) insidehost >
192.168.1.10> insidehost
```

Observe the source, destination, and translated addresses on the PIX
Firewall console.

Step 5   Ping the inside host from the outside host as allowed by the **conduit** via
the **static** command:

```
C:\> ping 192.168.1.10
```

Step 6   Test web access to the inside host as allowed by the **static** and **conduit**
commands configured in this task by completing the following substep:

(1) Open a web browser on the outside host and access the
inside host by entering **http://192.168.1.10**.

Step 7   Turn off debug:

```
pixfirewall(config)# no debug icmp trace
```

On completion of this chapter, you will be able to perform the following tasks:

- Configure and explain the function of access control lists (ACLs).
- Convert conduits to ACLs.
- Configure and explain the function of Turbo ACLs.
- Configure and explain the function of network address translation (NAT) 0 ACLs.
- Configure active code filtering (ActiveX and Java applets).
- Configure the PIX Firewall for URL filtering.
- Configure the PIX Firewall for long URL filtering.

CHAPTER 8

Access Control Lists and Content Filtering

Firewalls are designed to protect your network from external or internal threats. In most cases, a firewall accomplishes this goal by preventing the flow of traffic through its interfaces–for example, by disallowing traffic from its outside interface to its inside interface. Blocking all traffic into the network may improve scurity, but like a house with no doors or windows, it will have little or no utility. You can configure the PIX Firewall to selectively allow traffic through its interfaces based on source or destination address; service type; authentication, authorization, and accounting (AAA) requirements; and content or destination URL.

An ACL is a list kept by routers and the PIX Firewall to control traffic through the router or firewall. For example, an ACL can prevent packets with a certain IP address from leaving a particular interface. ACLs enable you to determine what specific traffic will be allowed or denied through the PIX Firewall.

Content filtering allows you to block the entrance of specific types of content such as Java applets and ActiveX controls into your network. Content filtering also allows you to control and prevent access to restricted websites by your internal hosts.

Access Control Lists

You implement an ACL using two commands: the **access-list** command and the **access-group** command.

Use the **access-list** command to create an ACL. The **access-group** command binds the ACL to a specific interface on the router or PIX Firewall. You can bind only one ACL to an interface using the **access-group** command.

NOTE   Unlike with Cisco IOS-based routers, the **access-group** command can be used only to bind an ACL for *inbound* traffic on any interface. You can still control *outbound* traffic on a PIX Firewall–for example, from the inside interface to the outside interface; however, you must bind the ACL to the inside interface with an **access-group** *acl_id* **in interface inside** command to control the traffic flowing into the inside interface from internal hosts.

The **access-list** and **access-group** commands are an alternative to the **outbound** or **conduit** command statements. The **access-list** and **access-group** commands also take precedence over the **outbound** or **conduit** command statements.

The **access-list** command follows the same principles and guidelines as conduits when used for permitting or denying traffic. Use the following guidelines when designing and implementing ACLs:

- Higher to lower security:
  - You use the ACL to restrict outbound traffic.
  - The source address argument of the ACL command is the actual address of the host or network.

- Lower to higher:
  - You use the ACL to restrict inbound traffic.
  - The destination address argument of the ACL command is the translated global IP address.

The **access-list** command enables you to specify whether an IP address is permitted or denied access to a port or protocol. By default, all access in an access list is denied. You must explicitly permit it.

PIX Firewall 6.3 adds support for ACL editing and including comments. You can now specify a line number for the specific ACL entry and position it anywhere within the ACL. Before Version 6.3, you had to remove the entire ACL and re-enter all the items on the list in the desired order.

When specifying the IP address of a host as a source or destination, use the **host** keyword instead of the network mask 255.255.255.255. For example, use the following ACL entry to permit FTP traffic to host 192.168.1.1:

```
access-list SAMPLEACL permit tcp any host 192.168.1.1 eq ftp
```

The **show access-list** command lists the **access-list** command statements in the configuration. The **show access-list** command also lists a hit count that indicates the number of times an element has been matched during an **access-list** command search. With PIX Firewall Version 6.3, the **show access-list** command also displays any comments that you might have added to the ACL and displays the line number for each entry.

Example 8-1 shows the output of the **show access-list** command and ACL editing on a PIX Firewall running Software Version 6.3. In this example, the PIX has an ACL named **out_in** that consists of six lines. The **show access-list** command displays each line of the ACL and corresponding hit count. Using the ACL editing feature of PIX Firewall Version 6.3, two new lines are placed after line 4 of the out_in ACL. A second **show access-list** command displays the resulting ACL.

Example 8-1   *ACL Editing and* **show access-list** *Command Output*

```
pixfirewall# show access-list
access-list cached ACL log flows: total 0, denied 0 (deny-flow-max 4096)
          alert-interval 300
access-list out_in; 6 elements
access-list out_in line 1 permit tcp any 192.168.0.0 255.255.255.0 eq smtp
 (hitcnt=0)
access-list out_in line 2 permit tcp any 192.168.0.0 255.255.255.0 eq www (hitcnt=9)
access-list out_in line 3 permit tcp any 192.168.0.0 255.255.255.0 eq https
 (hitcnt=0)
access-list out_in line 4 permit tcp any 192.168.0.0 255.255.255.0 eq ftp (hitcnt=0)
access-list out_in line 5 permit tcp any 192.168.0.0 255.255.255.0 eq telnet
 (hitcnt=3)
access-list out_in line 6 permit tcp any 192.168.0.0 255.255.255.0 eq ldap
 (hitcnt=0)
pixfirewall# config terminal
pixfirewall(config)# access-list out_in line 5 remark adding entry to allow SSH
pixfirewall(config)# access-list out_in line 6 permit tcp any 192.168.0.0
 255.255.255.0 eq 22
pixfirewall(config)# show access-list
access-list cached ACL log flows: total 0, denied 0 (deny-flow-max 4096)
          alert-interval 300
access-list out_in; 7 elements
access-list out_in line 1 permit tcp any 192.168.0.0 255.255.255.0 eq smtp
 (hitcnt=0)
access-list out_in line 2 permit tcp any 192.168.0.0 255.255.255.0 eq www (hitcnt=9)
access-list out_in line 3 permit tcp any 192.168.0.0 255.255.255.0 eq https
 (hitcnt=0)
access-list out_in line 4 permit tcp any 192.168.0.0 255.255.255.0 eq ftp (hitcnt=0)
access-list out_in line 5 remark adding entry to allow SSH
access-list out_in line 6 permit tcp any 192.168.0.0 255.255.255.0 eq ssh (hitcnt=0)
access-list out_in line 7 permit tcp any 192.168.0.0 255.255.255.0 eq telnet
 (hitcnt=3)
access-list out_in line 8 permit tcp any 192.168.0.0 255.255.255.0 eq ldap
 (hitcnt=0)
```

The **clear access-list** command removes all **access-list** command statements from the configuration. If the *acl_id* argument is specified, it clears only the corresponding ACL. If the **counters** option is specified as well, it clears the hit count for the specified ACL.

CAUTION   The **clear access-list** command also stops all traffic through the PIX Firewall on the affected **access-list** command statements.

You can use the **no access-list** command to remove a specific **access-list** command from the configuration when arguments matching an existing command are provided. For example, to remove line 2 of the ACL in Example 8-1, you can use the following command:

```
no access-list out_in permit tcp any 192.168.0.0 255.255.255.0 eq 80
```

When you use the **no access-list** command and specify only the ACL name, the entire ACL is removed. For example, to remove the ACL named **out_in** in Example 8-1, you can use the following command:

```
no access-list out_in
```

If you remove all the **access-list** command statements in an ACL group, the **no access-list** command also removes the corresponding **access-group** command from the configuration.

NOTE	The **access-list** command uses the same syntax as the Cisco IOS Software **access-list** command except that the subnet mask in the PIX Firewall **access-list** command is reversed from the Cisco IOS Software version of this command. For example, a subnet mask specified as 0.0.0.255 in the Cisco IOS **access-list** command would be specified as 255.255.255.0 in the PIX Firewall **access-list** command.

The syntax for the **access-list** commands are as follows:

```
access-list acl_ID [line line_num] deny | permit protocol source_addr  source_mask
  [operator port [port]] destination_addr destination_mask operator port [port]
access-list acl_ID [line line_num] deny | permit icmp source_addr source_mask
  destination_addr destination_mask [icmp_type]
access-list acl_ID [line line_num] remark text
show access-list
clear access-list [acl_ID] [acl_ID counters]
```

Table 8-1 describes the **access-list** command arguments.

Table 8-1 access-list *Command Arguments*

Argument	Definition
acl_ID	Name of an ACL.
line	Optional keyword to specify the line number of the ACL entry. Only supported in PIX Firewall Version 6.3 or higher.
line_num	Line number starting at 1.
deny	Does not allow a packet to travel through the PIX Firewall. By default, the PIX Firewall denies all inbound packets unless you specifically permit access.
permit	Selects a packet to travel through the PIX Firewall.
protocol	Name or number of an IP protocol. It can be one of the keywords **icmp, ip, tcp,** or **udp** or an integer in the range 1 to 254 representing an IP protocol number. To match any Internet protocol, including Internet Control Message Protocol (ICMP), TCP, and User Datagram Protocol (UDP), use the keyword **ip**.
source_addr	Address of the network or host from which the packet is being sent.

Table 8-1   **access-list** *Command Arguments (Continued)*

Argument	Definition
source_mask	Netmask bits (mask) to be applied to *source_addr*, if the source address is for a network mask.
operator	A comparison operand that lets you specify a port or a port range. Use the **access-list** command without an operator and port to indicate all ports. Valid operand keywords are **lt**, **gt**, **eq**, **neq**, and **range**.
	Use **eq** and a port to permit or deny access to a specific port. For example, to allow WWW access to host 192.168.0.10, issue the command:
	access-list acl_exmpl permit tcp any host 192.168.0.10 eq www
	Use **lt** and a port to permit or deny access to all ports less than a port you specify. For example, to allow access to host 192.168.0.10 on ports 1 through 1999, issue the command:
	access-list acl_exmpl permit tcp any host 192.168.0.10 lt 2000
	Use **gt** and a port to permit or deny access to all ports greater than a port you specify. For example, to deny access to host 192.168.0.10 on UDP ports 1025 through 65535, issue the command:
	access-list acl_exmpl deny udp any host 192.168.0.10 gt 1024
	Use **neq** and a port to permit or deny access to every port except the ports that you specify. For example, to deny access to host 192.168.0.10 on ports other than FTP, issue the command:
	access-list acl_exmpl deny tcp any host 192.168.0.10 neq ftp
	Use **range** and a port range to permit or deny access to ports specified in the range. For example, to allow access to host 192.168.0.10 on ports 1025 through 5000, issue the command:
	access-list acl_exmpl permit tcp any host 192.168.0.10 range 1025 5000
port	Services you permit or to which you deny access. Specify services by the port that handles them, such as Simple Mail Transfer Protocol (SMTP) for port 25, WWW for port 80, and so on. You can specify ports by either a literal name or a number in the range of 0 to 65,535.
destination_addr	IP address of the network or host to which the packet is being sent.
destination_mask	Netmask bits (mask) to be applied to *destination_addr*, if the destination address is a network mask.
icmp_type	Permits or denies access to ICMP message types. Omitting this option specifies all ICMP types. ICMP message types are not supported for use with IPSec. When you use the **access-list** command in conjunction with the **crypto map** command, the *icmp_type* is ignored.
remark	Adds comments to ACLs for easier documentation and tracking. Available with PIX Firewall 6.3 or higher

continues

Table 8-1 access-list *Command Arguments (Continued)*

Argument	Definition
text	Text comments used with remark.
clear access-list	Used to clear hit counts or delete configured ACLs on the PIX Firewall. The **clear access-list** command without an operator removes all configured ACLs. To delete a specific ACL, issue the **clear access-list** command along with the name of the ACL you want to delete.
acl_ID **counters**	Argument used with the **clear access-list** command to reset hit counts for the ACL identified by *acl_ID*.

NOTE   For inbound connections, *destination_addr* is the address after NAT has been performed. For outbound connections, *source_addr* is the address before NAT has been performed.

The **access-group** command binds an ACL to an interface. The ACL is applied to traffic inbound to an interface. (Unlike a router ACL, there is no outbound ACL with the PIX.) You can bind only one ACL to an interface using the **access-group** command.

The **no access-group** command unbinds the *acl_ID* from the interface *interface_name*.

The **show access-group** command displays the current ACL bound to the interfaces.

The **clear access-group** command removes all entries from an ACL indexed by *acl_ID*. If *acl_ID* is not specified, all **access-list** command statements are removed from the configuration.

The syntax for the **access-group** commands is as follows:

```
access-group acl_ID in interface interface_name
no access-group acl_ID in interface interface_name
show access-group acl_ID in interface interface_name
clear access-group
```

Table 8-2 describes the **access-group** command arguments.

Table 8-2 access-group *Command Arguments*

Argument	Definition
acl_ID	The name associated with a given ACL
in interface	Filters inbound packets at the given interface
interface_name	The name of the network interface

Example 8-2 shows the commands required to create an ACL named DMZ1 that denies access from the 192.168.1.0 network to TCP ports less than 1024 on host 192.168.0.1 and is bound to interface dmz.

Example 8-2   *Access List Configuration*

```
pixfirewall(config)# access-list DMZ1 deny tcp 192.168.1.0 255.255.255.0 host
   192.168.0.1 lt 1024
pixfirewall(config)# access-group DMZ1 in interface dmz
```

You can use the **nat** command to enable NAT for a host or network. Policy NAT uses the **nat access-list** command to take this a step further by allowing you to enable NAT for any traffic that is matched by an **access-list** entry. You can also use the **nat 0 access-list** command to exempt the traffic matched by the ACL from address translation.

NOTE   Policy NAT is available only on PIX Firewall Version 6.3(2) or later.

The syntax of the **nat access-list** command is as follows:

```
nat [(if_name)] nat_id access-list acl_name [outside]
```

Table 8-3 describes the **nat access-list** command arguments.

Table 8-3   **nat access-list** *Command Arguments*

Argument	Definition
if_ name	Argument used as the internal network interface name. If the interface is associated with an ACL, the *if_name* is the higher-security-level interface name.
nat_id	An integer between 0 and 65,535. A *nat_id* value of 0 exempts the traffic matching the ACL from translation. A *nat_id* between 1 and 65,535 enables policy NAT.
access-list	Argument that associates an **access-list** command with the **nat 0** command.
acl_name	The name used to identify the **access-list** command statement.
outside	Argument used to specify that the **nat** command apply to the outside interface address.

Example 8-3 shows use of the **nat 0 access-list** command to permit internal host 10.0.0.11 to bypass NAT when connecting to outside host 10.2.1.3.

Example 8-3   **nat-0 access-list** *Command*

```
pixfirewall(config)# access-list NONAT permit ip host 10.0.0.11 host 10.2.1.3
pixfirewall(config)# nat (inside) 0 access-list NONAT
```

Turbo ACLs

An ACL typically consists of multiple ACL entries, organized internally by the PIX Firewall as a linked list. When a packet is subjected to access list control, the PIX Firewall searches this linked list linearly to find a matching element. The matching element is then examined to determine whether the packet is to be transmitted or dropped. With a linear search, the average search time increases proportionally to the size of the ACL.

Turbo ACLs improve the average search time for ACLs containing a large number of entries by causing the PIX Firewall to compile tables for ACLs, as shown in Figure 8-1. You can enable this feature globally and then disable it for specific ACLs, or you can enable it only for specific ACLs. For short ACLs, the Turbo ACL feature does not improve performance. A Turbo ACL search of an ACL of any length requires about the same amount of time as a regular search of an ACL consisting of approximately 12 to 18 entries. For this reason, even when enabled, the Turbo ACL feature is applied only to ACLs with 19 or more entries.

Figure 8-1 *Turbo ACLs*

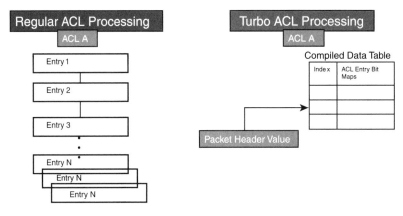

In Figure 8-1, the regular ACL processing shown on the left is characterized as follow:

- ACLs are organized internally as linked lists.
- Linear searches seek a matching entry to deny or permit a packet.
- Search time increases when an ACL contains a large number of elements, which leads to performance degradation.

In Figure 8-1, the Turbo ACL processing shown on the right is characterized as follows:

- ACLs are compiled into sets of lookup data tables.
- Search time is improved for large ACLs.
- The minimum requirement is 2.1 MB of memory.

As outlined in the preceding list, the Turbo ACL feature requires significant amounts of memory. It is most appropriate for high-end PIX Firewall models, such as the PIX Firewall 525 or 535. The minimum memory required for Turbo ACL support is 2.1 MB, and approximately 1 MB of memory is required for every 2000 ACL elements. The actual amount of memory required depends not only on the number of ACL elements but also on the complexity of the entries. Furthermore, when you add or delete an element from a Turbo-enabled ACL, the internal data tables associated with the ACL are regenerated. This produces an appreciable load on the PIX Firewall CPU.

NOTE	Turbo ACLs are not supported in the PIX Firewall 501 model.

You can configure Turbo ACLs globally or on a per-ACL basis. Use the **access-list compiled** command to configure Turbo ACLs on all ACLs with 19 or more entries. This command causes the Turbo ACL process to scan through all existing ACLs. During the scanning, it marks every ACL for Turbo configuration and compiles any ACL that has 19 or more access control entries and has not yet been compiled.

You can enable the Turbo ACL feature for individual ACLs with the **access-list** *acl_ID* **compiled** command. You can also use the **no** form of this command after you globally configure Turbo ACLs to disable the Turbo ACL feature for specific ACLs.

The command **no access-list compiled**, which is the default, causes the PIX Firewall's Turbo ACL process to scan through all compiled ACLs and mark each one as non-Turbo. It also deletes all existing Turbo ACL structures.

To view your Turbo ACL configuration, use the **show access-list** command. When Turbo ACLs are configured, this command displays the memory usage of each individually turbo-compiled ACL and the shared memory usage for all the Turbo-compiled ACLs. If no ACLs are Turbo-compiled, no Turbo statistics are displayed.

Converting Conduits to ACLs

It is recommended to use ACLs rather than conduits in PIX Firewall configurations. This move is for future compatibility and greater ease of use for those familiar with Cisco IOS access control. This section explains how to convert conduits to ACLs.

The **access-list** command in the PIX Firewall uses the same syntax as the Cisco IOS command of the same name with one very important difference. The subnet mask in the PIX Firewall **access-list** command is specified just as it is in all other PIX Firewall commands. This specification is very different from the Cisco IOS version of the command.

Whether you are configuring a PIX Firewall for the first time or converting from conduits to ACLs, it is important to understand the similarities and differences in the two commands. Probably the most important similarity is that you can combine either command with a **static** command to permit or deny connections from outside the PIX Firewall to access TCP/UDP services on hosts inside the network. More specifically, you can use both to permit or deny connections from a lower-security interface to a higher-security interface. Some of the most important differences follow.

As shown in Figure 8-2, a conduit defines the traffic that can flow between two interfaces and creates an exception to the PIX Firewall Adaptive Security Algorithm (ASA) by permitting connections from one interface to access hosts on another. In contrast, the **access-list** command used with the **access-group** command applies only to a single interface and affects all traffic entering that interface regardless of its security level. Also, ACLs have an implicit **deny** at the end. Once you apply an ACL to an interface, packets inbound to that interface must follow the rules of the ACL regardless of the interface security level.

Figure 8-2 *ACLs Compared to Conduits*

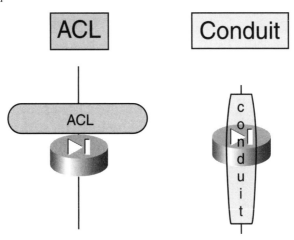

NOTE	In the preceding paragraph, the term *inbound* describing packets means traffic passing through the interface, rather than the more typical PIX Firewall usage of *inbound* meaning traffic passing from a lower-security-level interface to a higher-security-level interface.

The list that follows provides further characteristics of ACLs and conduits:

- The **access-list** command controls access only if used in conjunction with the **access-group** command, which binds it to an interface. Conduits, however, are not bound to an interface at all.

- The **access-list** and **access-group** command statements take precedence over the **conduit** command statements in your configuration.

- ACLs are more flexible than conduits. You can use them to restrict connections from a higher-security interface to a lower-security interface as well as permit or deny connections from a lower-security interface to a higher-security interface.

NOTE   The **conduit** command has been supported to maintain backward compatibility of configurations written for previous PIX Firewall versions. However, Cisco has announced that support for the **conduit** command will be removed from future versions of the PIX Firewall.

You should be careful when combining conduits and ACLs in the same configuration. Consider the example in Figure 8-3.

Figure 8-3   *Differences in the Behaviors of Conduits and ACLs*

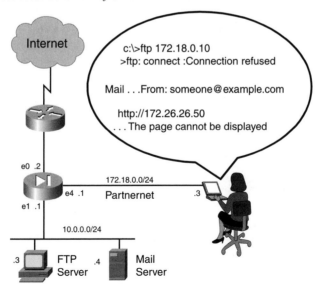

In the Figure 8-3 example, the goals are to

- Allow users on the Partnernet to access the FTP server on the inside.

- Permit access to all HTTP traffic originating from the Partnernet except that which is destined for the inside network.
- Allow users on the Partnernet (extranet) to access the mail server on the inside.
- Deny all other traffic originating from the Partnernet.

In Figure 8-3, the PIX Firewall configuration pertaining to the Partnernet contains:

- A NAT and a global pool for the Partnernet
- Statics for the FTP server and mail server
- A conduit permitting access to the FTP server from the Partnernet
- An ACL on the Partnernet interface permitting access to the mail server

The action specified for both the conduit and the ACL is **permit**, but the configuration is not working as planned. Why?

In the Figure 8-3 scenario, the PIX Firewall already has a conduit statement to allow proper access to FTP resources. A new system engineer decides to implement ACLs to allow access to the mail server, leaving the conduit statement intact for continued access to the FTP server. Configured in this way, an ACL is bound to the Partnernet interface to allow access from the Partnernet clients to the mail server on the internal network, and the users are able to access the mail server. However, the users are now unable to access the Internet or the internal FTP server.

Normally, with correctly configured **nat** and **global** statements in place, connections from a higher-level interface to a lower-level interface should pass through with no problems. It would also seem that the user should be able to access the internal FTP server because the appropriate **static** and **conduit** have been configured. But combining conduits and ACLs can result in undesirable outcomes. Example 8-4 shows the configuration that caused these problems.

Example 8-4   *Incorrect ACL Configuration*

```
pixfirewall(config)# nat (partnernet) 1 0 0
pixfirewall(config)# global (outside) 1 192.168.0.20-192.168.0.254 netmask
  255.255.255.0
pixfirewall(config)# static (inside,partnernet) 172.18.0.10 10.0.0.3 netmask
  255.255.255.255
pixfirewall(config)# static (inside,partnernet) 172.18.0.12 10.0.0.4 netmask
  255.255.255.255
pixfirewall(config)# conduit permit tcp host 172.18.0.10 eq ftp any
pixfirewall(config)# access-list 102 permit tcp 172.18.0.0 255.255.255.0 host
  172.18.0.12 eq smtp
pixfirewall(config)# access-group 102 in interface partnernet
```

The combination of a **conduit** statement and ACL commands failed to provide the desired access for these reasons:

- Because there is an implicit **deny** at the end of any ACL, even an ACL containing the **permit** option and no **deny** options can block traffic. When the ACL was bound to the Partnernet interface, all traffic was denied except that which was explicitly permitted by that ACL.

- Even though a conduit expressly permits access to a host on a higher-level interface, an ACL can override it, rendering it ineffective. This is why Partnernet users were suddenly unable to access the FTP server.

To resolve this issue, appropriate ACL commands should be added to deny HTTP traffic to the inside interface while allowing all other HTTP traffic, and the **conduit** command should be removed and replaced with the following ACL command:

```
pixfirewall(config)# access-list 102 permit tcp 172.18.0.0 255.255.255.0 host
    172.18.0.10 eq ftp
```

Conversion Procedures

Because conduits will not be supported in future versions of the PIX Firewall, you should convert the existing conduits in your configuration to ACLs. A look at the syntax for the **conduit** and **access-list** commands reveals that this is not a difficult task:

```
conduit permit | deny protocol global_ip global_mask operator port [port] foreign_ip
    foreign_mask [operator port[port]]
access-list acl_ID [line line_num] deny | permit protocol source_addr source_mask
    [operator port [port]] destination_addr destination_mask operator port [port]
```

You can create an ACL from a conduit by using the **conduit** command arguments in the **access-list** command. This move works because the *foreign_ip* option of the **conduit** command is the same as the *source_addr* in the **access-list** command, and the *global_ip* option in the **conduit** command is the same as the *destination_addr* in the **access-list** command. The following is an overlay of the **conduit** command on the **access-list** command (and you can use it as a guide in your conversion):

```
access-list acl_ID permit | deny protocol foreign_ip foreign_mask [foreign_operator
    foreign_port [foreign_port]] global_ip global_mask global_operator global_port
    [global_port]
```

Example 8-5 shows a conduit statement followed by the equivalent ACL shown beneath it.

Example 8-5 *Conduit Conversion to ACL*

```
conduit permit tcp host 172.18.0.10 eq ftp 172.18.0.0 255.255.255.0
access-list 102 permit tcp 172.18.0.0 255.255.255.0 host 172.18.0.10 eq ftp
```

The new **access-list** command, like the **conduit** command, permits any host on the Partnernet interface to access global IP address 172.18.0.10 via FTP. Remember, however, that you must associate the ACL with an interface by using the **access-group** command.

Example 8-6 shows the configuration of Example 8-4 with conduits converted to ACLs. In addition, the configuration contains four ACL statements, one for each of the following functions:

- Allow users on the Partnernet to access the FTP server on the inside.
- Allow users on the Partnernet to access the mail server on the inside.
- Prevent users on the Partnernet from accessing hosts on the inside network via HTTP.
- Permit all other HTTP traffic originating from the Partnernet.

Example 8-6 *Correct ACL Configuration*

```
pixfirewall(config)# nat (partnernet) 1 0 0
pixfirewall(config)# global (outside) 1 192.168.0.20-192.168.0.254 netmask
  255.255.255.0
pixfirewall(config)# static (inside,partnernet) 172.18.0.10 10.0.0.3 netmask
  255.255.255.255
pixfirewall(config)# static (inside,partnernet) 172.18.0.12 10.0.0.4 netmask
  255.255.255.255
pixfirewall(config)# access-list 102 permit tcp 172.18.0.0  255.255.255.0 host
  172.18.0.10 eq ftp
pixfirewall(config)# access-list 102 permit tcp 172.18.0.0 255.255.255.0 host
  172.16.0.12 eq smtp
pixfirewall(config)# access-list 102 deny tcp 172.18.0.0 255.255.255.0 10.0.0.0
  255.255.255.0 eq www
pixfirewall(config)# access-list 102 permit tcp 172.18.0.0 255.255.255.0 any eq www
pixfirewall(config)# access-group 102 in interface partnernet
```

NOTE   The implicit **deny** at the end of the ACL blocks all other traffic originating from the Partnernet.

Using ACLs

This section explains how to use ACLs in a variety of scenarios.

On the network shown in Figure 8-4, the ACL *acl_out* is applied to traffic inbound to the inside interface. The ACL *acl_out* denies HTTP connections from an internal network but lets all other IP traffic through. Applying an ACL to the inside interface restricts internal users from establishing outside connections.

NOTE   The internal network addresses (10.0.0.0) are dynamically translated (192.168.0.20 to 254) to allow outbound connections.

Figure 8-4   *Deny Web Access to the Internet*

Example 8-7 shows the ACL configuration for Figure 8-4.

Example 8-7   *Deny Web Access to the Internet*

```
pixfirewall(config)# write terminal
...
nameif ethernet0 outside sec0
nameif ethernet1 inside sec100
access-list acl_out deny tcp any any eq www
access-list acl_out permit ip any any
access-group acl_out in interface inside
nat (inside) 1 10.0.0.0 255.255.255.0
global (outside) 1 192.168.0.20-192.168.0.254 netmask 255.255.255.0
...
```

On the network shown in Figure 8-5, the ACL *acl_in_dmz* is applied to traffic inbound to the outside interface. The ACL *acl_in_dmz* permits web connections on port 80 from the Internet to a public Internet web server. The ACL *acl_in_dmz* denies all other IP traffic access to the demilitarized zone (DMZ) or inside networks.

NOTE   The static mapping of an outside address (192.168.0.11) to the DMZ web server (172.16.0.2) is required to allow the traffic.

Figure 8-5 *Permit Web Access to the DMZ*

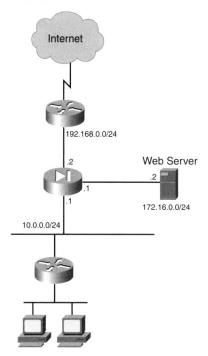

Example 8-8 shows the ACL configuration for this illustration.

Example 8-8 *Permit Web Access to the DMZ*

```
pixfirewall(config)# write terminal
...
nameif ethernet0 outside sec0
nameif ethernet1 inside sec100
nameif ethernet2 dmz sec50
ip address outside 192.168.0.2 255.255.255.0
ip address inside 10.0.0.1 255.255.255.0
ip address dmz 172.16.0.1 255.255.255.0
static (dmz,outside) 192.168.0.11 172.16.0.2
access-list acl_in_dmz permit tcp any host 192.168.0.11 eq www
access-list acl_in_dmz deny ip any any
access-group acl_in_dmz in interface outside
...
```

On the network shown in Figure 8-6, the ACL *acl_partner* is applied to traffic inbound to the Partnernet interface. The ACL *acl_partner* permits web connections from the hosts on network 172.18.0.0/28 to the DMZ web server via its statically mapped address, 172.18.0.17. All other traffic from the Partnernet is denied.

Figure 8-6   *Partner Web Access to DMZ and DMZ Access to Internal Mail*

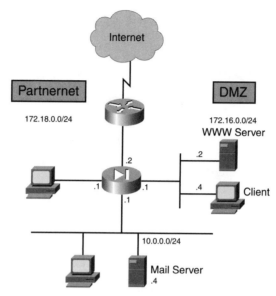

The ACL *acl_dmz_in* is applied to traffic inbound to the DMZ interface. The ACL *acl_dmz_in* permits the host 172.16.0.4 mail access to the internal mail server on the inside interface. All other traffic originating from the DMZ network is denied.

Example 8-9 shows the ACL configuration for this illustration.

Example 8-9   *Partner Web Access to DMZ and DMZ Access to Internal Mail*

```
pixfirewall(config)# write terminal
...
nameif ethernet0 outside sec0
nameif ethernet1 inside sec100
nameif ethernet2 dmz sec50
nameif ethernet3 partnernet sec40
static (dmz,partnernet) 172.18.0.17 172.16.0.2
static (inside,dmz) 172.16.0.11 10.0.0.4
access-list acl_partner permit tcp 172.18.0.0 255.255.255.0 host 172.18.0.17 eq www
access-group acl_partner in interface partnernet
access-list acl_dmz_in permit tcp host 172.16.0.4 host 172.16.0.11 eq smtp
access-group acl_dmz_in in interface dmz
...
```

In the VPN solution shown in Figure 8-7, the PIX Firewall has two dedicated interfaces connected to a Cisco Virtual Private Network (VPN) Concentrator. The dmz interface is connected to the VPN Concentrator's public interface. The dmz2 interface is connected to the VPN Concentrator's private interface. The VPN Concentrator is configured to assign VPN clients an address from the 10.0.21.33–62 pool.

Figure 8-7 *VPN Solution—Dual DMZ and VPN Concentrator*

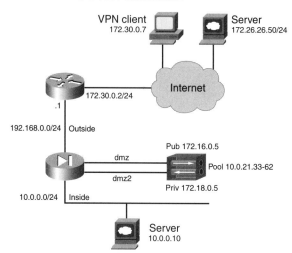

A static route on the PIX Firewall is defined to route outbound traffic to the VPN client. You need a static translation on the PIX Firewall to allow for communication between the VPN client and hosts on the inside network of the PIX Firewall.

You configure the PIX Firewall with the following two ACLs to control traffic inbound from the Internet and outbound from the VPN clients to the PIX Firewall inside network:

- The PIX Firewall ACL IPSEC allows HTTPS traffic from the Internet to the public interface of the VPN Concentrator. The ACL IPSEC permits only IPSec traffic to the VPN Concentrator.

- The PIX Firewall ACL WEB allows HTTP traffic from the VPN clients (10.0.21.33–62) to the inside web server (10.0.0.10).

Example 8-10 shows the ACL configuration for this VPN scenario.

Example 8-10 *VPN Solution—Dual DMZ and VPN Concentrator*

```
pixfirewall(config)# write terminal
...
static (dmz,outside) 192.168.0.12 172.16.0.5 netmask 255.255.255.255 0 0
static (inside,dmz2) 10.0.21.10 10.0.0.10 netmask 255.255.255.255
route dmz2 10.0.21.32 255.255.255.224 172.18.0.5 1
access-list IPSEC permit tcp any host 192.168.0.12 eq 443
access-list IPSEC permit esp any host 192.168.0.12
access-list IPSEC permit udp any host 192.168.0.12 eq isakmp
access-group IPSEC in interface outside
access-list WEB permit tcp 10.0.21.32 255.255.255.224 10.0.21.10 255.255.255.255 eq
  www
access-group WEB in interface dmz2
```

icmp Command

You can enable or disable pinging to a PIX Firewall interface. With pinging disabled, the PIX Firewall cannot be detected on the network. The **icmp** command implements this feature, which is also referred to as *configurable proxy pinging*.

NOTE   By default, pinging through the PIX Firewall to a PIX Firewall interface is not allowed. For example, you cannot ping the outside interface of the PIX from an internal host. But you can ping the inside interface from that same host.

To use the **icmp** command, configure an **icmp** command statement that permits or denies ICMP traffic that terminates at the PIX Firewall. If the first matched entry is a **permit** entry, the ICMP packet continues to be processed. If the first matched entry is a **deny** entry or an entry is not matched, the PIX Firewall discards the ICMP packet and generates the %PIX-3-313001 syslog message. An exception is when an **icmp** command statement is not configured–in which case, **permit** is the default.

NOTE   Cisco recommends that you grant permission for the ICMP unreachable message type (Type 3). Denying ICMP unreachable messages disables ICMP path maximum transmission unit (MTU) discovery, which can halt IP Security (IPSec) and Point-to-Point Tunneling Protocol (PPTP) traffic. See RFC 1195 and RFC 1435 for details about path MTU discovery.

The **clear icmp** command removes **icmp** command statements from the configuration.

The syntax for the **icmp** commands is as follows:

```
icmp permit | deny  src_addr src_mask [icmp-type] if_name
clear icmp
show icmp
```

Table 8-4 describes the **icmp command arguments**.

Table 8-4   **icmp** *Command Arguments*

Argument	Definition
**permit	deny**	Argument that permits or denies the ability to ping a PIX Firewall interface.
src_addr	Address that is either permitted or denied ability to ping an interface. Use the host *src_addr* to specify a single host.

continues

Table 8-4   **icmp** *Command Arguments (Continued)*

Argument	Definition
src_mask	(Optional) Network mask. Specify if a network address is specified.
icmp-type	(Optional) ICMP message type as described in Table 8-5.
if_name	Interface name that can be pinged.

Example 8-11 shows the commands required to deny all ICMP echo-replies at the outside interface while permitting ICMP unreachable messages.

Example 8-11   **icmp** *Configuration*

```
pixfirewall(config)# icmp deny any echo-reply outside
pixfirewall(config)# icmp permit any unreachable outside
```

Table 8-5 lists the ICMP type literals that you can use in the *icmp-type* argument of the **icmp** command to designate which message types are permitted or denied.

Table 8-5   *ICMP Type Literals*

ICMP	Type Literal
0	echo-reply
3	unreachable
4	source-quench
5	redirect
6	alternate-address
8	echo
9	router-advertisement
10	router-solicitation
11	time-exceeded
12	parameter-problem
13	timestamp-reply
14	timestamp-request
15	information-request
16	information-reply
17	mask-request
18	mask-reply
31	conversion-error
32	mobile-redirect

Malicious Active Code Filtering

The PIX Firewall can filter malicious active codes, which can be used in Java and ActiveX applications.

Java Applet Filtering

Java programs can provide a vehicle through which an inside system can be invaded or compromised. To guard against this problem, Java filtering enables you to prevent Java applets from being downloaded by an inside system. Java applets are executable programs that are banned by many site security policies. Java applets might be downloaded when you permit access to port 80 (HTTP), and some Java applets can contain hidden code that can destroy data on the internal network.

The PIX Firewall's Java applet filter can stop Java applications on a per-client or per-IP address basis. When Java filtering is enabled, the PIX Firewall searches for the programmed "cafe babe" string, and if it is found, the firewall drops the Java applet. A sample Java class code snippet looks like the following:

```
00000000: cafe babe 003 002d 0099 0900 8345 0098
```

ActiveX Blocking

ActiveX controls, formerly known as Object Linking and Embedding (OLE) controls (OCX), are applets that can be inserted in web pages and are often used in animations or in other applications. ActiveX controls create a potential security problem because they can provide a way for someone to attack servers. Because of this potential security problem, you can use the PIX Firewall to block all ActiveX controls.

The **filter activex | java** command filters out ActiveX or Java usage from outbound packets.

The syntax for the **filter activex | java** command is as follows:

```
filter activex | java port [-port]  local_ip mask foreign_ip mask
```

Table 8-6 describes the **filter activex | java** command arguments.

Table 8-6   **filter activex | java** *Command Arguments*

Argument	Definition
activex	Argument that blocks outbound ActiveX and other HTML <object> tags from outbound packets
java	Argument that locks Java applets returning from an outbound connection
port	The ports at which Internet traffic is received on the PIX Firewall
local_ip	The IP address of the interface with the highest security level from which access is sought

continues

Table 8-6 **filter activex | java** *Command Arguments (Continued)*

Argument	Definition
mask	Wildcard mask
foreign_ip	The IP address of the interface with the lowest security level to which access is sought

NOTE ActiveX blocking does not occur when users access an IP address referenced by the **alias** command.

The **filter** command enables or disables outbound URL or HTML filtering. Example 8-12 shows the command required to filter ActiveX controls on port 80 from any internal host and for connection to any external host on the network shown in Figure 8-8.

Example 8-12 *ActiveX Filter Command*

```
pixfirewall(config)# filter activex 80 0.0.0.0 0.0.0.0 0.0.0.0 0.0.0.0
```

Figure 8-8 *ActiveX **filter** Command*

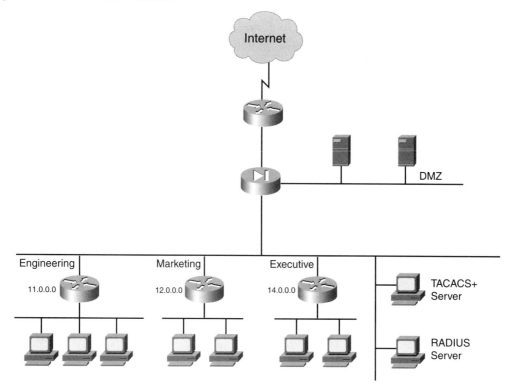

URL Filtering

URL-filtering applications provide URL filtering for the PIX Firewall, enabling network administrators to effectively monitor and control network traffic. URL-filtering applications block specific URLs because the PIX Firewall cannot perform this function. You can enable the PIX Firewall to work with a WebSense or N2H2 URL-filtering application. This step is useful because between the hours of 9 a.m. and 5 p.m.

- 30 to 40 percent of Internet surfing is not business related.

- 70 percent of all Internet porn traffic occurs.

- More than 60 percent of online purchases are made.

When the PIX Firewall receives a request to access a URL from users, it queries the URL-filtering server to determine whether to return the requested URL. The URL-filtering server checks its configurations to determine whether the URL should be blocked. If the URL should be blocked, URL-filtering applications can display blocking messages or direct the user requesting the URL to a specified website.

NOTE   Information about WebSense, N2H2, and other Cisco Partners appears on Cisco.com.

Before you can begin URL filtering, you must designate at least one server on which a WebSense or N2H2 URL-filtering application will run. The limit is 16 URL servers. You can use only one application at a time, either N2H2 or WebSense. Additionally, changing your configuration on the PIX Firewall does not update the configuration on the application server; you must do this step separately, according to the individual vendor's instructions.

Use the **url-server** command to designate the server on which the URL-filtering service runs, and then enable the URL-filtering service with the **filter url** command.

The syntax for the WebSense **url-server** command is as follows:

```
url-server [(if_name)] vendor websense host local_ip [timeout seconds] [protocol TCP
  | UDP version [1 | 4]]
```

Table 8-7 describes the **url-server** command arguments for WebSense.

Table 8-7   *WebSense **url-server** Command Arguments*

Argument	Definition
if_name	The network interface on which the authentication server resides. If not specified, the default is inside.
vendor websense	Indication that the URL-filtering service vendor is WebSense.
host *local_ip*	The server that runs the URL-filtering application.

continues

Table 8-7 *WebSense* **url-server** *Command Arguments (Continued)*

Argument	Definition
timeout *seconds*	The maximum idle time permitted before the PIX Firewall switches to the next server specified. The default is 5 seconds.
protocol	Protocol that can be configured using the **TCP** or **UDP** keywords. The default is TCP protocol, Version 1.
version	Version of the protocol that can be configured using the keywords **1** or **4**. The default is TCP protocol, Version 1. You can configure TCP using Version 1 or Version 4. You can configure UDP using Version 4 only.

The syntax for the N2H2 **url-server** command is as follows:

```
url-server [(if_name)] vendor n2h2 host local_ip [port number] [timeout seconds]
   [protocol TCP | UDP]
```

Table 8-8 describes the **url-server** command arguments for N2H2.

Table 8-8 *N2H2* **url-server** *Command Arguments*

Argument	Definition
if_name	The network interface on which the authentication server resides. If not specified, the default is inside.
vendor n2h2	Argument that indicates the URL-filtering service vendor is N2H2.
host *local_ip*	The server that runs the URL-filtering application.
port *number*	The N2H2 server port. The PIX Firewall also listens for UDP replies on this port. The default port number is 4005.
timeout *seconds*	The maximum idle time permitted before the PIX Firewall switches to the next server specified. The default is 5 seconds.
protocol	The protocol that you can configure using the **TCP** or **UDP** keywords. The default is TCP.

After designating which server runs the URL-filtering application, use the **filter url | ftp | https** command to tell the PIX Firewall to send appropriate requests to that server for filtering. PIX Firewall Version 6.3 adds support for FTP and HTTPS filtering, in addition to the URL-filtering capabilities included in previous versions.

The command in Example 8-13 instructs the PIX Firewall to send all URL requests to the URL-filtering server to be filtered. The **allow** option in the **filter** command is crucial to the use of the PIX Firewall URL-filtering feature. If you use the **allow** option and the URL-filtering server goes offline, the PIX Firewall lets all URL requests continue without filtering. If you do not specify the **allow** option, all port 80 URL requests are stopped until the server is back online.

Example 8-13   **filter** *Command*

```
pixfirewall(config)# filter url http 0 0 0 0 allow
```

The syntax for the **filter url | ftp | https** command is as follows:

```
filter url port [-port] | except local_ip local_mask foreign_ip foreign_mask [allow]
    [proxy-block] [longurl-truncate | longurl-deny] [cgi-truncate]
filter ftp port local_ip local_mask foreign_ip foreign_mask [allow] [interact-block]
filter https port local_ip local_mask foreign_ip foreign_mask [allow]
```

Table 8-9 describes the **filter url | ftp | https** command arguments.

Table 8-9   **filter url | ftp | https** *Command Arguments*

Argument	Definition
url	Filters URLs from data moving through the PIX Firewall.
ftp	Filters FTP addresses from data moving through the PIX Firewall.
https	Filters HTTPS addresses from data moving through the PIX Firewall.
port	Receives Internet traffic on the PIX Firewall. Typically, this is port 80, but other values are accepted. You can use the **http** or **url** literal for port 80.
except	Creates an exception to a previous **filter** condition.
local_ip	Serves as the IP address of the highest-security-level interface from which access is sought.
local_mask	Serves as the network mask of *local_ip*.
foreign_ip	Serves as the IP address of the interface with the lowest security level to which access is sought.
foreign_mask	Serves as the network mask of *foreign_ip*.
allow	Enables outbound connections to pass through the PIX Firewall without filtering when the URL-filtering server is unavailable.
proxy-block	Prevents users from connecting to an HTTP proxy server.
interact-block	Prevents users from connecting to the FTP server through an interactive FTP program.
longurl-truncate	Enables outbound URL traffic whether or not the URL buffer is available.
longurl-deny	Denies the URL request if the URL is over the URL buffer size limit or the URL buffer is not available.
cgi-truncate	Sends a CGI script as a URL.

Long URL Filtering

PIX Firewall Versions 6.1 and earlier do not support the filtering of URLs longer than 1159 bytes. PIX Firewall Version 6.2 and higher support the filtering of URLs up to 4096 bytes for the WebSense filtering server. You can increase the maximum allowable length of a single URL (for WebSense only), by entering the **url-block url-size** command.

When a user issues a request for a long URL, the PIX Firewall breaks the long URL down into multiple IP packets and copies it to buffer memory. The URL is then passed to TCP for sending to the WebSense server. You can use the **url-block url-mempool** command to configure the maximum memory available for buffering long URLs. You can remove both the **url-block url-size** and the **url-block url-mempool** commands by using their **no** forms.

NOTE   The PIX Firewall does not support long URLs for the WebSense UDP server.

If a URL still exceeds the maximum size or URL buffers are not available, new command options in the **filter url** command enable you to control the behavior. These command options appear in the previous paragraphs. The **longurl-truncate** option causes the PIX Firewall to send only the host name or IP address portion of the URL for evaluation to the filtering server when the URL is longer than the maximum length permitted. You can use the **longurl-deny** option to deny outbound URL traffic if the URL is longer than the maximum permitted.

If the long URL request is a CGI request, the **cgi-truncate** option, another new **filter url** command option, speeds up its processing. With the **cgi-truncate** option enabled, the PIX Firewall passes only the CGI script name and location as the URL to the WebSense server. The PIX Firewall omits the parameter list, which can be quite long.

With PIX Firewall Software Version 6.2, you can also use the **url-block block** command to enable the PIX Firewall to buffer the response from the web server until the filtering server responds. This move decreases the time the client must wait for an HTTP response. With PIX Firewall Software Versions 6.1 and earlier, responses from web servers are dropped until the PIX Firewall receives a response from the filtering server, so the client must wait for the web server to resend the response. The response buffering feature works with both the WebSense and N2H2 filtering applications. Use the **no** form of the **url-block block** command to disable response buffering.

NOTE   PIX Firewall Version 6.2 supports a maximum URL length of 1159 bytes for the N2H2 filtering server.

The syntax for the **url-block** commands is as follows:

```
url-block url-mempool memory_pool_size
url-block url-size long_url_size
url-block block block_buffer_limit
```

Table 8-10 describes the **url-block command arguments**.

Table 8-10   **url-block** *Command Arguments*

Argument	Definition
memory_pool_size	A value from 2 to 10,000 for a maximum memory allocation of 2 to 10 MB
long_url_size	A value from 2 to 6 kB for a maximum allowable URL length
block_buffer_limit	The maximum number of blocks allowed in the HTTP response buffer

Example 8-14 shows the configuration required to enable long URL filtering.

Example 8-14   *Long URL Filtering*

```
pixfirewall(config)# url-server (inside) vendor Websense host 10.0.0.30 timeout 5
  protocol TCP version 1
pixfirewall(config)# filter url http 0.0.0.0 0.0.0.0 0.0.0.0 0.0.0.0 longurl-
  truncate cgi-truncate
pixfirewall(config)# url-block url-mempool 1500
pixfirewall(config)# url-block url-size 4
```

Summary

This section summarizes the information you learned in this chapter:

- ACLs enable you to determine which systems can establish connections through your PIX Firewall.

- Cisco recommends migrating from conduits to ACLs.

- You can easily convert existing conduits to ACLs.

- Turbo ACLs improve search time for large ACLs.

- With ICMP ACLs, you can disable pinging to a PIX Firewall interface so that your PIX Firewall cannot be detected on your network.

- PIX Firewall Version 6.3 adds support for ACL editing and comments.

- You can configure the PIX Firewall to filter malicious active codes.

- The PIX Firewall can work with URL-filtering software to control and monitor Internet activity.

Chapter Review Questions

To test what you have learned in this chapter, answer the following questions and then refer to Appendix A, "Answers to Chapter Review Questions," for the answers:

1   What command takes precedence, a conduit or ACLs?

2   Which of the PIX models does not support Turbo ACLs?

3   What command binds an ACL to a specific interface?

4   What is the maximum URL length that can be filtered with PIX Firewall 6.1 or earlier versions?

5   What are the new filter options introduced in PIX Firewall Version 6.3?

6   Which version of the PIX Firewall supports ACL editing (by line number)?

Lab Exercise—Configure ACLs in the PIX Firewall

Complete the following lab exercises to practice ACL configuration procedures. Use the following initial configuration commands and continue with the rest of the lab exercises.

NOTE   Many of the settings shown in this initial configuration are default values and do not need to be entered on your PIX Firewall. Specific commands that must be entered are shown in bold for your convenience.

```
Building configuration...
: Saved
:
PIX Version 6.3(3)
interface ethernet0 100full
interface ethernet1 100full
interface ethernet2 100full
nameif ethernet0 outside security0
nameif ethernet1 inside security100
nameif ethernet2 dmz security50
enable password 8Ry2YjIyt7RRXU24 encrypted
passwd 2KFQnbNIdI.2KYOU encrypted
hostname pixfirewall
domain-name cisco.com
fixup protocol dns maximum-length 512
fixup protocol ftp 21
fixup protocol h323 h225 1720
fixup protocol h323 ras 1718-1719
fixup protocol http 80
fixup protocol rsh 514
fixup protocol rtsp 554
fixup protocol sip 5060
```

```
fixup protocol sip udp 5060
fixup protocol skinny 2000
fixup protocol smtp 25
fixup protocol sqlnet 1521
fixup protocol tftp 69
names
name 10.0.1.11 insidehost
name 172.16.1.2 bastionhost
pager lines 24
mtu outside 1500
mtu inside 1500
mtu dmz 1500
ip address outside 192.168.1.2 255.255.255.0
ip address inside 10.0.1.1 255.255.255.0
ip address dmz 172.16.1.1 255.255.255.0
ip audit info action alarm
ip audit attack action alarm
pdm history enable
arp timeout 14400
static (inside,outside) 192.168.1.10 10.0.1.11 netmask 255.255.255.255 0 0
static (dmz,outside) 192.168.1.11 172.16.1.2 netmask 255.255.255.255 0 0
timeout xlate 3:00:00
timeout conn 1:00:00 half-closed 0:10:00 udp 0:02:00 rpc 0:10:00 h225 1:00:00
timeout h323 0:05:00 mgcp 0:05:00 sip 0:30:00 sip_media 0:02:00
timeout uauth 0:05:00 absolute
aaa-server TACACS+ protocol tacacs+
aaa-server RADIUS protocol radius
aaa-server LOCAL protocol local
http server enable
no snmp-server location
no snmp-server contact
snmp-server community public
no snmp-server enable traps
floodguard enable
telnet timeout 5
ssh timeout 5
console timeout 0
terminal width 80
Cryptochecksum:aa0cc6e47d705ed128e041c2c2a8412b
: end
```

Objectives

In this lab exercise, you perform the following tasks:

- Disable pinging to an interface.

- Configure an inbound ACL.

- Test and verify the inbound ACL.

- Configure an outbound ACL.

- Test and verify the outbound ACL.

Lab Topology

Figure 8-9 displays the topology for the lab exercises in this chapter.

Figure 8-9 *ACL Lab Exercise Visual Objective*

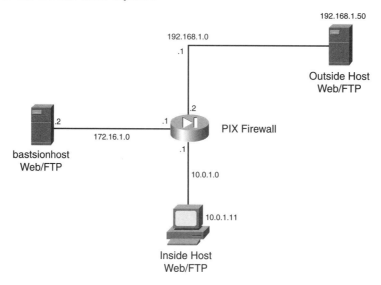

Equipment required to perform the lab includes the following:

- A PIX Firewall with at least three interfaces
- Category 5 patch cables
- PC host for a DMZ running a web server and FTP server
- PC host for the outside subnet running a web server, FTP server, available web browser, and FTP client
- PC host for the inside running a web server, FTP server, available web browser, and FTP client

Task 1—Disable Pinging to an Interface

Perform the following lab steps to configure an ICMP ACL to prevent pinging to your PIX Firewall interfaces:

Step 1 From the inside host, ping the inside interface of the PIX Firewall:

```
C:\>ping 10.0.1.1
```

The ping should be successful.

Step 2   From the inside host, ping the outside interface. By default, pinging through the PIX Firewall to a PIX Firewall interface is not allowed:

```
C:\>ping 192.18.1.2
```

The ping should fail.

Step 3   Use the **icmp** command to prevent pinging the inside interface:

```
pixfirewall(config)# icmp deny any echo inside
```

Step 4   View the ICMP ACL:

```
pixfirewall(config)# show icmp
icmp deny any echo inside
```

Step 5   From your inside host, ping the inside PIX Firewall interface. The ICMP ACL causes the ping to fail:

```
C:\>ping 10.0.1.1
```

The ping should fail.

Step 6   Enable pinging to the PIX Firewall's inside interface:

```
pixfirewall(config)# clear icmp
```

Step 7   Verify that you can again ping the inside interface of the PIX Firewall:

```
C:\>ping 10.0.1.1
```

The ping should be successful again.

Step 8   Configure the PIX Firewall to deny all ping requests and permit all unreachable messages at the outside interface:

```
pixfirewall(config)# icmp deny any echo outside
pixfirewall(config)# icmp permit any unreachable outside
```

Step 9   From the outside host, ping the outside interface of the PIX Firewall. Notice that the ping fails due to the ICMP ACL:

```
C:\>ping 192.168.1.2
```

The ping should fail.

Step 10   Remove the ICMP ACL from your PIX Firewall's outside interface:

```
pixfirewall(config)# clear icmp
```

Step 11   Save the configuration:

```
pixfirewall(config)# write memory
```

Task 2—Configure an Inbound ACL

Perform the following steps to configure ACLs:

- Allow inbound web traffic from outside to the bastion host.
- Allow inbound FTP traffic from an outside host to the bastion host.
- Allow inbound web traffic to the inside host.
- Allow inbound pings to the inside host and the bastion host.
- Allow ICMP echo-replies from hosts on the outside and DMZ interfaces.
- Deny all other inbound traffic.

Step 1   Verify that statics are in place for the bastion host and for the inside host:

```
pixfirewall(config)# show static
static (dmz,outside) 192.168.1.11 bastionhost netmask 255.255.255.255 0 0
static (inside,outside) 192.168.1.10 insidehost netmask 255.255.255.255 0 0
```

Step 2   Test web access to the bastion host from the outside host by completing the following substeps. You should be unable to access the bastion host via its static mapping:

(1) Open a web browser on the outside host.

(2) Use the web browser to access the bastion host by entering **http://192.168.1.11**.

Step 3   Test web access to the inside by completing the following substeps. You should be unable to access the inside host via its static mapping:

(1) Open a web browser on the outside host.

(2) Use the web browser to access the inside host by entering **http://192.168.1.10**.

Test FTP access to the bastion host from the outside host by entering:

```
Start>Run>ftp 192.168.1.11
```

You should be unable to access the bastion host via its static mapping.

Step 4   Create an ACL to permit inbound web and FTP access to the bastion host:

```
pixfirewall(config)# access-list ACLIN permit tcp 192.168.1.0
   255.255.255.0 host 192.168.1.11 eq www
pixfirewall(config)# access-list ACLIN permit tcp 192.168.1.0
   255.255.255.0 host 192.168.1.11 eq ftp
```

Step 5   Add commands to permit inbound web traffic to the inside host, permit inbound pings, permit ICMP echo replies to the inside host, and deny all other traffic from the Internet:

```
pixfirewall(config)# access-list ACLIN permit tcp any host
   192.168.1.10 eq www
pixfirewall(config)# access-list ACLIN permit icmp any any echo
```

```
pixfirewall(config)# access-list ACLIN permit icmp any host
    192.168.1.10 echo-reply
pixfirewall(config)# access-list ACLIN deny ip any any
```

Step 6 Bind the ACL to the outside interface:

```
pixfirewall(config)# access-group ACLIN in interface outside
```

Step 7 Display the access list and observe the hit counts:

```
pixfirewall(config)# show access-list
access-list cached ACL log flows: total 0, denied 0 (deny-flow-max 4096)
            alert-interval 300
access-list ACLIN; 6 elements
access-list ACLIN line 1 permit tcp 192.168.1.0 255.255.255.0 host
    192.168.1.11 eq www (hitcnt=0)
access-list ACLIN line 2 permit tcp 192.168.1.0 255.255.255.0 host
    192.168.1.11 eq ftp (hitcnt=0)
access-list ACLIN line 3 permit tcp any host 192.168.1.10 eq www
    (hitcnt=0)
access-list ACLIN line 4 permit icmp any any echo (hitcnt=0)
access-list ACLIN line 5 permit icmp any host 192.168.1.10 echo-reply
    (hitcnt=0)
access-list ACLIN line 6 deny ip any any (hitcnt=0)
```

Task 3—Test and Verify the Inbound ACL

Perform the following steps to test the inbound ACL:

Step 1 From the outside host ping the inside host:

```
C:\>ping 192.168.1.10
```

The ping should be successful.

Step 2 From the outside host, ping the bastion host:

```
C:\>ping 192.168.1.11
```

The ping should be successful.

Step 3 Test web access to the bastion host by completing the following substeps. You should now be able to access the bastion host via its static mapping:

(1) Open a web browser on your outside host.

(2) Use the web browser to access the bastion host by entering **http://192.168.1.11**.

Step 4 Test web access to the inside hosts by completing the following substeps. You should now be able to access the IP address of the static mapped to the inside host:

> (1) Open a web browser on the outside host.
>
> (2) Use the web browser to access the inside host by entering **http://192.168.1.10**.

Step 5 Test FTP access to the bastion host by completing the following. You should now be able to access the bastion via FTP from the outside:

Step 6 On the FTP client on the outside, attempt to access the bastion host by choosing **Start>Run** and entering **ftp 192.168.1.11**.

Step 7 Display the access lists again and observe the hit counts:

```
pixfirewall(config)# show access-list
```

The hit counts should be increasing, indicating traffic that is matching the configured ACLs.

Task 4—Configure an Outbound ACL

Perform the following lab steps to configure ACLs:

- Deny outbound web traffic.
- Allow outbound FTP traffic from the internal network to 192.168.1.50.

Step 1 Test web access to the Internet by completing the following substeps. You should be able to access 192.168.1.50:

> (1) Open a web browser on the inside host.
>
> (2) Use the web browser to access outside by entering **http://192.168.1.50**.

Step 2 Test FTP access to the outside host at 192.168.1.50. On your FTP client, attempt to access host 172.26.26.50:

```
Start>Run>ftp 192.168.10.50
```

Step 3 Create an ACL that prevents users on the internal network from making outbound HTTP connections:

```
pixfirewall(config)# access-list ACLOUT deny tcp any any eq www
```

Step 4 Enter the **access-group** command to create an access group that will bind the ACL to an interface:

```
pixfirewall(config)# access-group ACLOUT in interface inside
```

Step 5   Display the access list you configured, and observe the hit count:

```
pixfirewall(config)# show access-list ACLOUT
access-list cached ACL log flows: total 0, denied 0 (deny-flow-max 4096)
            alert-interval 300
access-list ACLOUT; 1 elements
access-list ACLOUT line 1 deny tcp any any eq www (hitcnt=0)
```

Step 6   Test web access to the Internet by completing the following substeps. You should be unable to access the Internet host:

   (1)   Open a web browser on the inside host.

   (2)   Use the web browser to access the outside host by entering **http:// 192.168.1.50**.

Test FTP access to the outside host. The FTP connection should fail as well because of the implicit **deny**:

```
Start>Run>ftp 192.168.1.50
```

Step 7   Display the access list ACLOUT again and note that the hit count has incremented:

```
pixfirewall(config)# show access-list ACLOUT
access-list cached ACL log flows: total 0, denied 0 (deny-flow-max 4096)
            alert-interval 300
access-list ACLOUT; 1 elements
access-list ACLOUT line 1 deny tcp any any eq www (hitcnt=1)
```

Step 8   Add a command to the ACL to permit outbound FTP access to host 192.168.1.50:

```
pixfirewall(config)# access-list ACLOUT permit tcp 10.0.1.0
    255.255.255.0 host 192.168.1.50 eq ftp
```

Step 9   Add another **access-list** command statement to deny other outbound IP traffic:

```
pixfirewall(config)# access-list ACLOUT deny ip any any
```

NOTE   You need this access list statement only to enable you to view the hit counts.

View the access list again:

```
pixfirewall(config)# show access-list ACLOUT
access-list cached ACL log flows: total 0, denied 0 (deny-flow-max 4096)
            alert-interval 300
access-list ACLOUT line 1 deny tcp any any eq www (hitcnt=1)
```

```
access-list ACLOUT line 2 permit tcp 10.0.1.0 255.255.255.0 host
192.168.10.50 eq ftp (hitcnt=0)
access-list ACLOUT line 3 deny ip any any (hitcnt=0)
```

Task 5—Test and Verify the Outbound ACL

Perform the following steps to test the outbound ACL:

Step 1 Test web access to the Internet by completing the following substeps. You should be unable to access the Internet host due to the deny ACL:

(1) Open a web browser on the inside host.

(2) Use the web browser to access the outside host by entering **http:// 192.168.1.50**.

Step 2 Test FTP access to an outside host by issuing the following command on the FTP client. At this point, you should be able to connect using FTP:

```
Start>Run>ftp 192.168.1.50
```

Step 3 View the outbound access list again and observe the hit counts:

```
pixfirewall(config)# show access-list ACLOUT
access-list cached ACL log flows: total 0, denied 0 (deny-flow-max 4096)
            alert-interval 300
access-list ACLOUT line 1 deny tcp any any eq www (hitcnt=2)
access-list ACLOUT line 2 permit tcp 10.0.1.0 255.255.255.0 host
192.168.10.50 eq ftp (hitcnt=1)
access-list ACLOUT line 3 deny ip any any (hitcnt=0)
```

Step 4 Remove the outbound ACL:

```
pixfirewall(config)# clear access-list ACLOUT
```

Step 5 Verify that the outbound ACL has been removed:

```
pixfirewall(config)# show access-list
```

ACLOUT should no longer appear in the output of the **show access-list** command.

On completion of this chapter, you will be able to perform the following tasks:

- Describe the PIX Firewall's object grouping feature and its advantages.
- Configure object groups.
- Configure nested object groups.
- Configure efficient access control lists (ACLs) using object groups.

CHAPTER 9

Object Grouping

An ACL can instruct the PIX Firewall to allow a designated client to access a particular server for a specific service. This task is simple and manageable when there is only one client, one host, one service, and one ACL. However, as the number of clients, servers, and services increases, the number of ACLs required increases significantly, and the entire process becomes arduous and unmanageable. PIX Firewall's *object grouping* feature is designed to reduce the complexity and improve the manageability of ACL creation and maintenance.

Getting Started with Object Groups

Object grouping is a feature of PIX Firewalls running software Version 6.2 or higher. This feature allows you to group network objects such as hosts and services to simplify creating and applying ACLs. Object grouping reduces the number of ACLs required to implement complex security policies. For example, a security policy that normally requires 3300 ACLs might require only 40 ACLs after hosts and services are properly grouped.

Applying a PIX Firewall object group to a PIX Firewall command is the equivalent of applying every element of the object group to the command. For example, the group MYCLIENTS contains host 10.0.1.11, host 10.0.2.11, and network 10.0.0.0. Applying the group MYCLIENTS to an ACL (named ACLOUT in this case) is the same as applying both hosts and the network to the ACL. Therefore, the command

```
access-list ACLOUT permit tcp object-group MYCLIENTS any
```

is equivalent to the following:

```
access-list ACLOUT permit tcp host 10.0.1.11 any
access-list ACLOUT permit tcp host 10.0.2.11 any
access-list ACLOUT permit tcp 10.0.0.0 255.255.255.0 any
```

An ACL can apply to the following types of objects:

- **Client host**—A host that makes HTTP, Telnet, FTP, Voice over IP (VoIP), and other service requests

- **Server host**—A host that responds to service requests

- **Subnet**—The network address of internal or external subnetworks where server or client hosts are located

- **Service types**—Services that are assigned to well-known, dynamically assigned, or secondary channel TCP or UDP ports

- **Internet Control Message Protocol (ICMP) types**—ICMP message types, such as ECHO-REPLY

Object grouping provides a way to group objects of a similar type so that a single ACL can apply to all the objects in the group. You can create the following types of object groups:

- **Network**—Client hosts, server hosts, or subnets.

- **Protocol**—Protocols. You can contain one of the keywords **icmp**, **ip**, **tcp**, or **udp** or an integer in the range 1 to 254 representing an IP protocol number. Use the keyword **ip** to match any Internet protocol, including ICMP, TCP, and UDP.

- **Service**—TCP or UDP port numbers assigned to a different service.

- **ICMP type**—ICMP message types to which you permit or deny access.

The best way to understand the functionality of object groups is by studying an example. The following example has three object groups:

- **SERVERS**—A network group that includes the IP addresses of outside hosts to which access is allowed (hosts at 172.26.26.50 and 172.26.26.51)

- **CLIENTS**—A network group that includes the addresses of inside hosts and networks that are allowed to access the servers (hosts at 10.0.1.11 and 10.0.2.11 and network 10.0.0.0 with a subnet mask of 255.255.255.0)

- **MYPROTOCOLS**—A protocol group that includes the protocols the clients are allowed to use (TCP and ICMP)

Using these three object groups dramatically reduces the number of ACL entries you need for enabling all the clients to access both of the servers with both TCP and ICMP. Without object groups, you would need the following ACL entries:

```
access-list ACLOUT permit tcp 10.0.0.0 255.255.255.0 host 172.26.26.50
access-list ACLOUT permit icmp 10.0.0.0 255.255.255.0 host 172.26.26.50
access-list ACLOUT permit tcp 10.0.0.0 255.255.255.0 host 172.26.26.51
access-list ACLOUT permit icmp 10.0.0.0 255.255.255.0 host 172.26.26.51
access-list ACLOUT permit tcp host 10.0.1.11 host 172.26.26.50
access-list ACLOUT permit icmp host 10.0.1.11 host 172.26.26.50
access-list ACLOUT permit tcp host 10.0.1.11  host 172.26.26.51
access-list ACLOUT permit icmp host 10.0.1.11 host 172.26.26.51
access-list ACLOUT permit tcp host 10.0.2.11 host 172.26.26.50
access-list ACLOUT permit icmp host 10.0.2.11 host 172.26.26.50
access-list ACLOUT permit tcp host 10.0.2.11 host 172.26.26.51
access-list ACLOUT permit icmp host 10.0.2.11 host 172.26.26.51
```

Using object groups, the following ACL entry would generate the same results as the previous 12 ACL entries:

```
access-list ACLOUT permit object-group MYPROTOCOLS object-group CLIENTS object-group
  SERVERS
```

As shown in this example, you can enhance the power and flexibility of group objects by applying multiple object groups to a single ACL. Note that you need to include the keyword **object-group** before each group name in the **access-list** command.

Configuring and Using Object Groups

This section presents instructions for using object groups with the **object-group** command and its specific subcommand modes for configuring network, service, protocol, and ICMP-type object groups.

NOTE   Object grouping is available only on PIX Firewall Software Version 6.2 or higher.

---

object-group is the primary command for creating object groups. The keyword after the command specifies the type of object group that is being defined. After you enter this main command, the prompt changes to a subcommand mode appropriate for the type of object. Commands entered in the subcommand mode apply to the object type and group name identified in the **object-group** command. You use subcommand mode to explicitly define the group.

To enter the object group command mode, enter the **object-group** command in the configuration terminal. The syntaxes for the **object-group** commands are as follows:

```
object-group network grp_id
object-group service grp_id {tcp | udp | tcp-udp}
object-group protocol grp_id
object-group icmp-type grp_id
```

Table 9-1 describes the **object-group** command arguments.

Table 9-1   object-group *Command Arguments*

Argument	Definition
network	Group of hosts or subnet IP addresses. After entering the main **object-group network** command, add network objects to the network group with the **network-object** subcommand.
grp_id	Name assigned to the object group (1 to 64 characters). It can be any combination of letters, digits, and the _, -, and . characters.
service	Group of TCP/UDP port specifications such as **eq smtp** and **range 2000 2010**. After entering the main **object-group service** command, add port objects to the service group with the **port-object** subcommand.
tcp	Argument specifying that the service object group contains ports for TCP only.
udp	Argument specifying that the service object group contains ports for UDP only.
tcp-udp	Argument specifying that the service object group contains ports for both TCP and UDP.
protocol	A group of protocols such as TCP and UDP. After entering the main **object-group protocol** command, add protocol objects to the protocol group with the **protocol-object** subcommand.
icmp-type	A group of ICMP types such as **echo** and **echo-reply**. After entering the main **object-group icmp-type** command, add ICMP objects to the ICMP-type group with the **icmp-object** subcommand.

After you enter the **object-group** command, you enter the appropriate subcommand mode. The specific prompt displayed indicates the current subcommand mode, as follows:

```
pixfirewall(config-network)#
pixfirewall(config-service)#
pixfirewall(config-protocol)#
pixfirewall(config-icmp-type)#
```

You can remove the **object-group** command with its **no** form.

NOTE   You cannot remove or empty an object group if it is currently being used in a command.

Now that you are familiar with the **object-group** command, you can configure an object group and use it for configuring ACLs with the following procedure:

Step 1   Use the **object-group** command to enter the appropriate subcommand mode for the type of group to be configured. All subcommands entered from the subcommand prompt apply to the object group identified by the **object-group** command.

Step 2   In subcommand mode, define the members of the object group. In subcommand mode, you can enter object grouping subcommands as well as all other PIX Firewall commands, including **show** commands and **clear** commands. Enter a question mark (**?**) in the subcommand mode to view the permitted subcommands.

Step 3   (Optional) Use the **description** subcommand to describe the object group.

Step 4   Return to configuration mode by entering the **exit** command or the **quit** command. Note that when you enter any valid configuration command other than one designed for object grouping, the subcommand mode is terminated.

Step 5   (Optional) Use the **show object-group** command to verify that you successfully configured the object group. This command displays a list of the currently configured object groups of the specified type. Without a parameter, the command displays all object groups.

Step 6   Apply the **access list** command to the object group. Replace the parameters of the **access list** commands with the corresponding object group, as summarized by the following:

   — Replace the protocol parameter with one protocol object group preceded by the keyword **object-group**.

   — Replace the local IP address and subnet mask with one network object group preceded by the keyword **object-group**.

— Replace the remote IP address and subnet mask with one network object group preceded by the keyword **object-group**.

— Replace the port parameter with one service object group preceded by the keyword **object-group**.

— Replace the **icmp-type** parameter with one ICMP-type object group preceded by the keyword **object-group**.

For example, the following command permits access to the members of the network object group TrustedHosts:

```
access-list EXAMPLE permit tcp any object-group TrustedHosts
```

Step 7 (Optional) Use the **show access-list** command to display the expanded ACL entries.

You are now familiar with the basic steps required for creating object groups and the ACLs using those groups. The following subsections cover the process of creating each specific type of group—network, service, protocol, and ICMP type—in greater detail.

Configuring Network Object Groups

To configure a network object group, first enter the **object-group network** command to name the network object and enable the network object subcommand mode. When inside subcommand mode, you can use the **network-object** command to add a single host or network to the network object group.

The syntax for the **network-object** command is as follows:

```
network-object host host_addr | host_name
network-object net_addr netmask
```

Table 9-2 describes the **network-object** command arguments.

Table 9-2   **network-object** *Command Arguments*

Argument	Definition
host	Keyword used with the **host_addr** parameter to define a host object
host_addr	Host IP address
host_name	Host name (if the host name is already defined using the name command)
net_addr	Network address; used with *netmask* to define a subnet object
netmask	Netmask; used with *net_addr* to define a subnet object

Example 9-1 shows the commands required to create a network object group named CLIENTS, which consists of host 10.0.1.11, host 10.0.2.11, and network 10.0.0.0 with a subnet mask of 255.255.255.0.

Example 9-1   *Creating a Network Object Group*

```
pixfirewall(config)# object-group network CLIENTS
pixfirewall(config-network)# network-object host 10.0.1.11
pixfirewall(config-network)# network-object host 10.0.2.11
pixfirewall(config-network)# network-object 10.0.0.0 255.255.255.0
```

Configuring Service Object Groups

To configure a service object group, first enter the **object-group service** command to name the service object and enable the service object subcommand mode using the following options:

- **tcp** option specifies that the service object group contain ports for TCP only.

- **udp** option specifies that the service object group contain ports for UDP only.

- **tcp-udp** option specifies that the service object group contain ports for both TCP and UDP.

When inside the subcommand mode, you can use the **port-object** command to add a TCP or UDP port number to the service object group. You can also add a range of TCP or UDP port numbers to the service object group.

The syntax for the **port-object** commands is as follows:

```
port-object eq service
port-object range begin_service end_service
```
Table 9-3 describes the **port-object** command arguments.

Table 9-3   **port-object** *Command Arguments*

Argument	Definition
eq	Keyword indicating "equal to"
service	Decimal number or name of a TCP or UDP port for a particular service object
range	Keyword indicating that the range parameters follow
begin_service	Decimal number or name of a TCP or UDP port that is the beginning value for a range of services
end_service	Decimal number or name of a TCP or UDP port that is the ending value for a range of services

Example 9-2 shows the commands required to create a service object group named MYSERVICES, which contains HTTP and FTP.

Table 9-4   *Creating a Service Object Group*

```
pixfirewall(config)# object-group service  MYSERVICES tcp
pixfirewall(config-service)# port-object eq http
pixfirewall(config-service)# port-object eq ftp
```

Configuring Protocol Object Groups

To configure a protocol object group, first enter the **object-group protocol** command to name the protocol object and enable the protocol object subcommand mode. When inside the subcommand mode, you can use the **protocol-object** command to add a protocol to the current protocol object group.

The syntax for the **protocol-object** command is as follows:

protocol-object *protocol*

The keyword *protocol* in the preceding syntax is a numeric identifier of the specific IP protocol (1 to 254) or a literal keyword identifier (**icmp**, **tcp**, or **udp**). If you want to include all IP protocols, use the keyword **ip**.

Example 9-3 shows the commands required to create a protocol object group named MYPROTOCOLS, which contains ICMP and TCP.

Example 9-2   *Creating a Protocol Object Group*

```
pixfirewall(config)# object-group protocol  MYPROTOCOLS
pixfirewall(config-protocol)# protocol-object icmp
pixfirewall(config-protocol)# protocol-object tcp
```

Configuring ICMP-Type Object Groups

To configure an ICMP-type object group, first enter the **object-group icmp-type** command to name the ICMP-type object and enable the ICMP-type subcommand mode. When inside subcommand mode, you can use the **icmp-object** command to add an ICMP type to the object group.

The syntax for the **icmp-object** command is as follows:

icmp-object *icmp-type*

The keyword *icmp-type* in the preceding syntax is a numeric value or name of an ICMP message type. The following are valid ICMP message types:

- **0**—**echo-reply**
- **3**—**unreachable**
- **4**—**source-quench**
- **5**—**redirect**

- **6—alternate-address**
- **8—echo**
- **9—router-advertisement**
- **10—router-solicitation**
- **11—time-exceeded**
- **12—parameter-problem**
- **13—timestamp-request**
- **14—timestamp-reply**
- **15—information-request**
- **16—information-reply**
- **17—address-mask-request**
- **18—address-mask-reply**
- **31—conversion-error**
- **32—mobile-redirect**

Example 9-4 shows the commands required to create an ICMP-type object group named PING, which contains echo and echo-reply message types.

Example 9-3 *Creating an ICMP-Type Object Group*

```
pixfirewall(config)# object-group icmp-type PING
pixfirewall(config-icmp-type)# icmp-object echo
pixfirewall(config-icmp-type)# icmp-object echo-reply
```

Nested Object Groups

An object group can be a member of another object group. Hierarchical object grouping can achieve greater flexibility and modularity for specifying access rules. The **group-object** command enables the construction of hierarchical, or nested, object groups. The command for creating nested groups, **group-object**, and the command for creating object groups, **object-group**, are similar and can be confusing. The difference in object groups and group objects is as follows:

- An object group is a group consisting of objects.
- A group object is an object in a group and is itself a group.

Duplicated objects are allowed only if the duplication is a result of the group objects that were added. For example, if object 1 is in both group A and group B, you can define a group C that includes both A and B. You cannot, however, include a group object, which causes the group hierarchy to become circular. For example, you cannot have group A include group B and also have group B include group A.

The **group-object** command is a subcommand of the **object-group** command, and you use it to nest an object group within another object group. For object groups to be nested, they must be the same type. For example, you can group two or more network object groups together, but you cannot group a protocol group and a network group together.

The syntax for the **group-object** command is as follows:

```
group-object object_group_id
```

In the preceding command, the *object_group_id* is the group name of an existing object group. The type of the object groups, both child and parent, must be the same.

The maximum number of allowed levels of a hierarchical object group is 10. Complete the following steps to configure nested object groups:

Step 1   Assign a group identity to the object group that you want to nest within another object group:

```
pixfirewall(config)# object-group network Group_A
```

Step 2   Add the appropriate type of objects to the object group:

```
pixfirewall(config-network)# network-object host 10.0.0.1
pixfirewall(config-network)# network-object host 10.0.0.2
pixfirewall(config-network)# network-object host 10.0.0.3
```

Step 3   Assign a group identity to the object group within which you want to nest another object group:

```
pixfirewall(config)# object-group network Group_B
```

Step 4   Add the first object group to the group that will contain it:

```
pixfirewall(config-network)# group-object Group_A
```

Step 5   Add any other objects that are required to the group:

```
pixfirewall(config-network)# network-object host 10.0.0.4
```

The resulting configuration of Group_B in this example is equivalent to the following:

```
pixfirewall(config-network)# network-object host 10.0.0.1
pixfirewall(config-network)# network-object host 10.0.0.2
pixfirewall(config-network)# network-object host 10.0.0.3
pixfirewall(config-network)# network-object host 10.0.0.4
```

The commands for nested groups can be confusing, but when mastered, they provide you an extremely powerful tool for managing your ACLs and security policies on a PIX Firewall. Example 9-5 shows how you can use nested groups to simplify configuration. This example creates two network object groups as follows:

- **HOSTGROUP1**—Hosts 10.0.0.11 and 10.0.0.12
- **HOSTGROUP2**—Hosts 10.0.0.13 and 10.0.0.14

Then, these groups are nested inside a new group named ALLHOSTS. Finally, the example creates an ACL named ALL using the new nested group, ALLHOSTS, to allow all hosts in HOSTGROUP1 and HOSTGROUP2 to make outbound FTP sessions.

Example 9-4   *Nested Object Groups*

```
pixfirewall(config)# object-group network HOSTGROUP1
pixfirewall(config-network)# network-object host 10.0.0.11
pixfirewall(config-network)# network-object host 10.0.0.12
pixfirewall(config-network)# exit
pixfirewall(config)# object-group network HOSTGROUP2
pixfirewall(config-network)# network-object host 10.0.0.13
pixfirewall(config-network)# network-object host 10.0.0.14
pixfirewall(config-network)# exit
pixfirewall(config)# object-group network ALLHOSTS
pixfirewall(config-network)# group-object HOSTGROUP1
pixfirewall(config-network)# group-object HOSTGROUP2
pixfirewall(config-network)# exit
pixfirewall(config)# access-list ALL permit tcp object-group ALLHOSTS any eq ftp
pixfirewall(config)# access-group ALL in interface inside
```

After you configure your group objects and nested object groups, you can use the **show object-group** command to display a list of the currently configured object groups. The PIX Firewall displays defined object groups by their *grp_id* when you enter the **show object-group id** *grp_id* command form and by group type when you enter the **show object-group** command with the **protocol**, **service**, **icmp-type**, or **network** option. When you enter **show object-group** without a parameter, all defined object groups are shown.

The syntax for the **show object-group** command is as follows:

```
show object-group [protocol | service | icmp-type | network]
show object-group id grp_id
```

Table 9-4 describes the **object-group** command arguments.

Table 9-5   **show object-group** *Command Arguments*

Argument	Definition
protocol	Instructs the PIX Firewall to display protocol object groups
service	Instructs the PIX Firewall to display service object groups
icmp-type	Instructs the PIX Firewall to display ICMP-type object groups
network	Instructs the PIX Firewall to display network object groups
id	Instructs the PIX Firewall to display the object group specified by *object_grp_id*
grp_id	Is the name of a previously defined object group

NOTE	The **show config** or **write term** commands display ACLs as configured with only the object group names. You can use the **show access-list** command to display the ACL entries expanded into individual statements along with their object groupings.

You can remove any object group command with its **no** form. Use the **no object-group** command to remove a specific object group.

The syntax for the **no object-group** commands is as follows:

```
no object-group service grp_id {tcp | udp | tcp-udp}
no object-group protocol | network | icmp-type grp_id
```

You can use the **clear object-group** command to remove all object groups or all object groups of a specific type. When entered without a parameter, the **clear object-group** command removes all defined object groups that are not being used in a command. Using the **protocol**, **service**, **icmp-type**, or **network** parameter removes all defined object groups that are not being used in a command for that group type only.

The syntax for the **clear object-group** command is as follows:

```
clear object-group [protocol | service | icmp-type | network]
```

Table 9-5 describes the **no object-group** and **clear object-group** command arguments.

Table 9-6   **no object-group** *and* **clear object-group** *Command Arguments*

Argument	Definition
service	Instructs the PIX Firewall to remove service object groups
grp_id	Is the name of a previously defined object group to be removed
tcp	Specifies that the service object group contains ports for TCP only
udp	Specifies that the service object group contains ports for UDP only
tcp-udp	Specifies that the service object group contains ports for both TCP and UDP
protocol	Instructs the PIX Firewall to remove protocol object groups
network	Instructs the PIX Firewall to remove network object groups
icmp-type	Instructs the PIX Firewall to remove ICMP-type object groups

NOTE	You cannot remove or empty an object group if it is currently being used in a command.

Example 9-6 shows the commands required to remove the object group ALLHOSTS and all protocol object groups.

Example 9-5 *Removing an Object Group*

```
pixfirewall(config)# no object-group network ALLHOSTS
pixfirewall(config)# clear object-group protocol
```

Summary

This section summarizes the information you learned in this chapter:

- You can group network objects, services, protocols, and ICMP message types to reduce the number of ACLs required to implement your security policy.

- The main object grouping command, **object-group** command, names an object group and enables a subcommand mode for the type of object specified. There are four types of groups that you can define with the **object-group** command:
    - Network
    - Service
    - Protocol
    - ICMP type

- Members of an object group are defined in the group's subcommand mode.

- Group names are always preceded with the keyword **object-group** when used in an ACL statement.

- Nested object grouping enables greater flexibility and modularity for specifying ACLs.

Chapter Review Questions

To test what you have learned in this chapter, answer the following questions and then refer to Appendix A, "Answers to Chapter Review Questions," for the answers:

1   What is the main benefit of object grouping?

2   What type of objects can you group?

3   What command do you use to start the configuration of object groups?

4   You have created a network object group (MYNETWORK, 10.0.0.0 with subnet mask of 255.255.255.0) and a WEBSERVERS network object group with two hosts, 192.168.100.10 and 192.168.100.11. You now want to configure an ACL called ACLIN to allow inbound HTTP traffic from MYNETWORK to WEBSERVERS. Describe what is wrong with the following command and how it should be restated:

```
Pixfirewall(config)# access-list ACLIN permit tcp MYNETWORK WEBSERVERS eq HTTP
```

5 What is the maximum allowed level of hierarchical object grouping (levels of nesting)?

Lab Exercise—Configure Object Groups

Complete the following lab exercise to practice the object-grouping concepts covered in this chapter. Please note that this lab builds on previous chapter labs. If you have not completed previous lab exercises, you can use the following initial configuration commands and continue with the rest of the lab exercises.

NOTE   Many of the settings shown in this initial configuration are default values and do not need to be entered on the PIX Firewall. Specific commands that you must enter appear in bold for your convenience.

```
:
interface ethernet0 100full
interface ethernet1 100full
interface ethernet2 100full
nameif ethernet0 outside security0
nameif ethernet1 inside security100
nameif ethernet2 dmz security50
enable password 8Ry2YjIyt7RRXU24 encrypted
passwd 2KFQnbNIdI.2KYOU encrypted
hostname pixfirewall
domain-name cisco.com
fixup protocol ftp 21
fixup protocol h323 h225 1720
fixup protocol h323 ras 1718-1719
fixup protocol http 80
fixup protocol ils 389
fixup protocol rsh 514
fixup protocol rtsp 554
fixup protocol sip 5060
fixup protocol sip udp 5060
fixup protocol skinny 2000
fixup protocol smtp 25
fixup protocol sqlnet 1521
pager lines 24
mtu outside 1500
mtu inside 1500
mtu dmz 1500
ip address outside 192.168.1.2 255.255.255.0
ip address inside 10.0.1.1 255.255.255.0
ip address dmz 172.16.1.1 255.255.255.0
ip audit info action alarm
ip audit attack action alarm
pdm location 10.0.1.0 255.255.255.0 inside
pdm location 10.0.1.11 255.255.255.255 inside
pdm location 172.16.1.2 255.255.255.255 dmz
pdm history enable
arp timeout 14400
global (outside) 1 192.168.1.50-192.168.1.200
nat (inside) 1 0.0.0.0 0.0.0.0 0 0
nat (dmz) 1 0.0.0.0 0.0.0.0 0 0
```

```
static (inside,outside) 192.168.1.10 10.0.1.11 netmask 255.255.255.255 0 0
static (dmz,outside) 192.168.1.11 172.16.1.2 netmask 255.255.255.255 0 0
static (inside,dmz) 10.0.1.0 10.0.1.0 netmask 255.255.255.0 0 0
route outside 0.0.0.0 0.0.0.0 192.168.1.1 1
timeout xlate 3:00:00
timeout conn 1:00:00 half-closed 0:10:00 udp 0:02:00 rpc 0:10:00 h225 1:00:00
timeout h323 0:05:00 mgcp 0:05:00 sip 0:30:00 sip_media 0:02:00
timeout uauth 0:05:00 absolute
aaa-server TACACS+ protocol tacacs+
aaa-server RADIUS protocol radius
aaa-server LOCAL protocol local
http server enable
http 10.0.1.0 255.255.255.0 inside
no snmp-server location
no snmp-server contact
snmp-server community public
no snmp-server enable traps
floodguard enable
telnet 10.0.1.0 255.255.255.0 inside
telnet timeout 5
ssh timeout 5
console timeout 0
terminal width 80
Cryptochecksum:aa0cc6e47d705ed128e041c2c2a8412b
: end
```

Objectives

In this lab exercise, you perform the following tasks:

- Configure service and ICMP-type object groups.

- Configure a nested server object group.

- Configure an inbound ACL with object groups.

- Configure web and ICMP access to the inside host.

- Test and verify the inbound ACL.

Lab Topology

Figure 9-1 displays the configuration you need to complete this lab exercise.

Equipment required to perform the lab includes the following:

- PIX 515E with at least three interfaces

- Category 5 patch cables

- PC host running a web server and FTP server

- PC host for outside subnet with a web browser and FTP client

- PC host for the inside subnet running a web server and FTP server

Figure 9-1   *Lab Visual Objective*

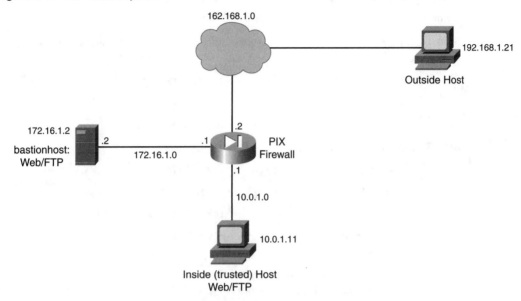

Task 1—Configure a Service Object Group

Complete the following steps to configure a service group containing HTTP and FTP:

Step 1   Create a TCP service group named MYSERVICES. This step assigns a
name to the group and enables the service object subcommand mode:

```
pixfirewall(config)# object-group service MYSERVICES tcp
```

Step 2   Add HTTP and FTP to the service object group:

```
pixfirewall(config-service)# port-object eq http
pixfirewall(config-service)# port-object eq ftp
```

Step 3   Return to configuration mode and verify that the object group has been
configured successfully:

```
pixfirewall(config-network)# exit
pixfirewall(config)# show object-group
object-group service MYSERVICES tcp
    port-object eq www
    port-object eq ftp
```

Task 2—Configure an ICMP-Type Object Group

Complete the following steps to configure an ICMP-type group:

Step 1 Create an ICMP-type object group named PING to assign a name to the group and enable the ICMP-type subcommand mode:

```
pixfirewall(config)# object-group icmp-type PING
```

Step 2 Add ICMP echo to the ICMP-type object group:

```
pixfirewall(config-icmp-type)# icmp-object echo
```

Step 3 Add ICMP echo replies to the ICMP-type object group:

```
pixfirewall(config-icmp-type)# icmp-object echo-reply
```

Step 4 Add ICMP unreachable messages to the ICMP-type object group:

```
pixfirewall(config-icmp-type)# icmp-object unreachable
```

Step 5 Return to configuration mode and verify that the object group has been configured successfully:

```
pixfirewall(config-icmp-type)# exit
pixfirewall(config)# show object-group
object-group service MYSERVICES tcp
    port-object eq www
    port-object eq ftp
object-group icmp-type PING
    icmp-object echo
    icmp-object echo-reply
    icmp-object unreachable
```

Task 3—Configure a Nested Server Object Group

Complete the following steps to nest an object group within another object group:

Step 1 Create a network object group named FTPSERVERS:

```
pixfirewall(config)# object-group network FTPSERVERS
```

Step 2 Add the bastion host to the object group:

```
pixfirewall(config-network)# network-object host 192.168.1.11
```

Step 3 Return to configuration mode:

```
pixfirewall(config-network)# exit
```

Step 4 Create a network object group named ALLSERVERS:

```
pixfirewall(config)# object-group network ALLSERVERS
```

Step 5 Nest the FTPSERVERS group within the ALLSERVERS group:

```
pixfirewall(config-network)# group-object FTPSERVERS
```

Step 6   Add the server 192.168.1.10 to the ALLSERVERS group:

```
pixfirewall(config-network)# network-object host 192.168.1.10
```

Step 7   Verify that the object group has been configured successfully:

```
pixfirewall(config-network)# show object-group
object-group service MYSERVICES tcp
    port-object eq www
    port-object eq ftp
object-group icmp-type PING
    icmp-object echo
    icmp-object echo-reply
    icmp-object unreachable
object-group network FTPSERVERS
    network-object host 192.168.1.11
object-group network ALLSERVERS
    group-object FTPSERVERS
    network-object host 192.168.1.10
```

Task 4—Configure an Inbound ACL with Object Groups

Complete the following steps to configure an inbound ACL to do the following:

- Allow inbound web traffic from the outside host to the bastion host.
- Allow inbound FTP traffic from the outside host to the bastion host.

Step 1   Remove any ACLs currently configured on your firewall. Notice that entering the **clear access-list** command takes you back to configuration mode:

```
pixfirewall(config-network)# clear access-list
```

Step 2   Verify that all ACLs have been removed:

```
pixfirewall(config)# show access-list
```

Step 3   Test web access to the bastion host using a web browser on the outside host (**http://192.168.1.11**). You should be unable to access the bastion host with the current settings.

Step 4   Test web access to the inside host using a web browser on the outside host (**http://192.168.1.10**). You should be unable to access the inside host with the current settings.

Step 5   From the outside host FTP client, test FTP access to the bastion host. You should be unable to access the bastion host via FTP with the current settings:

```
Start>Run>ftp 192.168.1.11
```

Step 6 Now, use the MYSERVICES group to create an ACL permitting inbound web and FTP access to the bastion host and bind it to the outside interface:

```
pixfirewall(config)# access-list ACLIN permit tcp any object-group
FTPSERVERS object-group MYSERVICES
pixfirewall(config)# access-group ACLIN in interface outside
```

Step 7 From the outside, ping the inside host. The ping should fail:

```
C:\> ping 192.168.1.10
Pinging 192.168.1.10 with 32 bytes of data:
Request timed out.
Request timed out.
Request timed out.
Request timed out.
```

Step 8 Now, try to ping the bastion host from the outside. The ping should fail:

```
C:\> ping 192.168.1.11
Pinging 192.168.1.11 with 32 bytes of data:
Request timed out.
Request timed out.
Request timed out.
Request timed out.
```

Step 9 Test web access to the bastion using a web browser on the outside host (**http://192.168.1.11**). You should now be able to access the bastion host from the outside.

Step 10 Test web access to your inside host using a web browser on the outside host (**http://192.168.1.10**). You should still be unable to access the inside web host.

Step 11 Using the FTP client on the outside host, test access to the bastion host. You should now be able to access the bastion host via FTP from the outside:

```
Start>Run>ftp 192.168.1.11
```

Step 12 Using the FTP client on the outside host, test access to the inside host. You should still be unable to access the inside host via FTP:

```
Start>Run>ftp 192.168.1.10
```

Task 5—Configure Web and ICMP Access to the Inside Host

Complete the following steps to configure ACLIN to do the following:

- Permit inbound web and ICMP traffic to all hosts behind the PIX Firewall.

- Deny all other traffic from the Internet.

Step 1   Use a network hosts group to add an ACL entry permitting web traffic to all hosts behind the PIX Firewall:

```
pixfirewall(config)# access-list ACLIN permit tcp any object-group
ALLSERVERS eq www
```

Step 2   Permit ICMP traffic to all hosts behind the PIX Firewall:

```
pixfirewall(config)# access-list ACLIN permit icmp any any object-group
PING
```

Step 3   Deny all other traffic from the Internet:

```
pixfirewall(config)# access-list ACLIN deny ip any any
```

Step 4   Bind the ACL to the outside interface:

```
pixfirewall(config)# access-group ACLIN in interface outside
```

Step 5   Create an ACL to permit echo replies to the inside host from the bastion host:

```
pixfirewall(config)# access-list ACLDMZ permit icmp any any object-
group PING
```

Step 6   Bind the ACL to the demilitarized zone (DMZ) interface:

```
pixfirewall(config)# access-group ACLDMZ in interface dmz
```

Step 7   Display the ACLs and observe the hit counts. PIX Firewall Software 6.2 output shown:

```
pixfirewall(config)# show access-list
access-list ACLIN; 8 elements
access-list ACLIN permit tcp any object-group FTPSERVERS object-group
MYSERVICES
access-list ACLIN permit tcp any host 192.168.1.11 eq www(hitcnt=2)
access-list ACLIN permit tcp any host 192.168.1.11 eq ftp(hitcnt=1)
access-list ACLIN permit tcp any object-group ALLSERVERS eq www
access-list ACLIN permit tcp any host 192.168.1.11 eq www (hitcnt=0)
access-list ACLIN permit tcp any host 192.168.1.10 eq www (hitcnt=0)
access-list ACLIN permit icmp any any object-group PING
access-list ACLIN permit icmp any any echo (hitcnt=0)
access-list ACLIN permit icmp any any echo-reply (hitcnt=0)
access-list ACLIN permit icmp any any unreachable (hitcnt=0)
access-list ACLIN deny ip any any (hitcnt=0)
access-list ACLDMZ; 3 elements
access-list ACLDMZ permit icmp any any object-group PING
access-list ACLDMZ permit icmp any any echo (hitcnt=0)
access-list ACLDMZ permit icmp any any echo-reply (hitcnt=0)
access-list ACLDMZ permit icmp any any unreachable (hitcnt=0)
```

```
access-list ACLDMZ permit icmp any any unreachable (hitcnt=0)
```

Task 6—Test and Verify the Inbound ACL

Complete the following steps to test the inbound ACL:

Step 1 From the outside, ping the inside host:

```
C:\> ping 192.168.1.10
Pinging 192.168.1.10 with 32 bytes of data:
Reply from 192.168.1.10: bytes=32 time<10ms TTL=128
Reply from 192.168.1.10: bytes=32 time<10ms TTL=128
Reply from 192.168.1.10: bytes=32 time<10ms TTL=128
Reply from 192.168.1.10: bytes=32 time<10ms TTL=128
```

Step 2 From the outside, ping the bastion host:

```
C:\> ping 192.168.1.11
Pinging 192.168.1.11 with 32 bytes of data:
Reply from 192.168.1.11: bytes=32 time<10ms TTL=128
Reply from 192.168.1.11: bytes=32 time<10ms TTL=128
Reply from 192.168.1.11: bytes=32 time<10ms TTL=128
Reply from 192.168.1.11: bytes=32 time<10ms TTL=128
```

Step 3 From the inside host, ping the bastion host:

```
C:\> ping 172.16.1.2
Pinging 172.16.1.2 with 32 bytes of data:
Reply from 172.16.1.2: bytes=32 time<10ms TTL=128
Reply from 172.16.1.2: bytes=32 time<10ms TTL=128
Reply from 172.16.1.2: bytes=32 time<10ms TTL=128
Reply from 172.16.1.2: bytes=32 time<10ms TTL=128
```

Step 4 From the inside host, ping the outside host:

```
C:\> ping 192.168.1.21
Pinging 192.168.1.21 with 32 bytes of data:
Reply from 192.168.1.21: bytes=32 time<10ms TTL=128
Reply from 192.168.1.21: bytes=32 time<10ms TTL=128
Reply from 192.168.1.21: bytes=32 time<10ms TTL=128
Reply from 192.168.1.21: bytes=32 time<10ms TTL=128
```

Step 5 Display the ACLs again and observe the hit counts:

```
pixfirewall(config)# show access-list
```

On completion of this chapter, you will be able to perform the following tasks:

- Explain the routing functionality of the PIX Firewall.
- Configure the PIX Firewall to work with Open Shortest Path First (OSPF).
- Configure the PIX Firewall to work with Routing Information Protocol (RIP).
- Configure the PIX Firewall to forward multicast traffic.

CHAPTER 10

Routing

Although the PIX Firewall is not a router, it does have certain routing capabilities and supports two routing protocols. In addition to supporting static routes, previous versions of PIX Firewall have included support for Versions 1 and 2 of the RIP (in passive or listening mode only). PIX Firewall Version 6.3 introduces support for the more robust OSPF routing protocol. This chapter presents an overview of the PIX Firewall routing features and configuration procedures.

Routing Options

As stated previously, the PIX Firewall provides support for static and dynamic routing. *Static* routes are easier to implement and are suitable for smaller, less complex networks. *Dynamic* routing protocols such as RIP or OSPF, however, simplify the configuration and maintenance of the PIX Firewalls implemented in more complex networks. Although the implementation of a routing protocol such as OSPF requires significant planning and preparation, most sites requiring its features have probably already made that investment as part of their overall network design and implementation.

Static Routing

You can use the **route** command to create static routes for accessing networks outside a router on any interface. By creating a static route, you tell the PIX to send packets destined for a specific network to a designated router or other gateway device such as a bridge. To illustrate the function of the **route** command, Figure 10-1 shows a sample layout. In the layout shown in Figure 10-1, the PIX Firewall sends all packets destined to the 10.1.1.0 network to the router at 10.0.0.3. All traffic for which the PIX Firewall has no route is sent to 192.168.0.1, the gateway in the default route. To enter a default route, you set the *ip_address* and *netmask* to 0.0.0.0 or the shortened form of 0. Note that you can use only one default route. Example 10-1 shows the configuration statements required for this configuration.

Figure 10-1 *Static Routes*

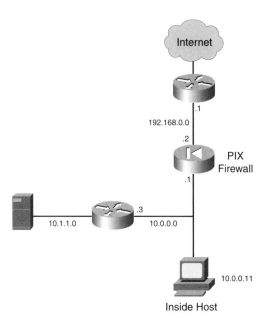

Example 10-1 *Static Route Configuration*

```
pixfirewall(config)# route inside 10.1.1.0 255.255.255.0 10.0.0.3 1
pixfirewall(config)# route outside 0 0 192.168.0.1 1
```

All routes entered using the **route** command are stored in the configuration when it is saved.
You can display them by using the **show route** command, and you can clear most routes by
using the **clear route** command. The only routes not removed with the **clear route**
command are those that show the keyword **CONNECT** when you issue the **show route**
command. The PIX Firewall automatically creates these routes in its routing table when
you enter an IP address for a PIX Firewall interface. A route created in this manner is a route
to the network directly connected to that interface. Figure 10-1 shows examples of these
automatically created routes. Example 10-2 shows the output of the **show route** command
for the layout in Figure 10-1.

Example 10-2 **show route** *Command*

```
pixfirewall(config)# show route
outside 0.0.0.0 0.0.0.0 192.168.0.1 1 OTHER static
inside 10.1.1.0 255.255.255.0 10.0.0.3 1 OTHER static
inside 10.0.0.0 255.255.255.0 10.0.0.1 1 CONNECT static
outside 192.168.0.0 255.255.255.0 192.168.0.2 1 CONNECT static
```

Although the *gateway* argument in the **route** command usually specifies the IP address of the gateway router, the next hop address for this route, you can also specify one of the PIX Firewall's interfaces. When a **route** command statement uses the IP address of one of the PIX Firewall's interfaces as the gateway IP address, the PIX Firewall broadcasts an Address Resolution Protocol (ARP) request for MAC address corresponding to the destination IP address in the packet, instead of broadcasting the ARP request for the MAC address corresponding to the gateway IP address. The following steps show how the PIX Firewall handles routing in this situation:

Step 1   The PIX Firewall receives a packet from the inside interface destined to IP address X.

Step 2   Because a default route is set to itself, the PIX Firewall sends out an ARP for address X.

Step 3   Any Cisco router on the outside interface LAN that has a route to address X replies back to the PIX Firewall with its own MAC address as the next hop. Cisco IOS software has proxy ARP enabled by default.

Step 4   The PIX Firewall sends the packet to the router.

Step 5   The PIX Firewall adds the entry to its ARP cache for IP address X, with the MAC address being that of the router, and retains it for a duration equal to the ARP timeout value in the PIX Firewall configuration (14,400 seconds by default).

NOTE   Do not configure the PIX Firewall with a default route when using the **setroute** argument of the **ip address dhcp** command. To clear a DHCP default route, use the **clear route static** command.

Dynamic Routes

PIX Firewall Version 6.3 adds OSPF support to the PIX Firewall. PIX Firewall versions prior to 6.3 included support for RIP Version 1 and RIP Version 2. The implementation of RIP and OSPF routing protocols on PIX Firewall are discussed in the following subsections.

RIP

You can build the PIX Firewall's routing table by enabling RIP with the **rip** command. You can configure the PIX Firewall to learn routes dynamically from RIP Version 1 or RIP Version 2 broadcasts. Although the PIX Firewall uses the dynamically learned routes itself to forward traffic to the appropriate destinations, it does not propagate learned routes to other devices. The PIX Firewall cannot pass RIP updates between interfaces. It can, however, advertise one of its interfaces as a default route.

When you configure RIP Version 2 in passive mode, the PIX Firewall accepts RIP Version 2 multicast updates with an IP destination of 224.0.0.9. For the RIP Version 2 default mode, the PIX Firewall transmits default route updates using an IP destination of 224.0.0.9. Configuring RIP Version 2 registers the multicast address 224.0.0.9 on the interface specified in the command so that the PIX Firewall can accept multicast RIP Version 2 updates. When you remove the RIP Version 2 commands for an interface, the multicast address is unregistered from the interface card.

If you specify RIP Version 2, you can also encrypt RIP updates using Message Digest 5 (MD5) encryption. Ensure that the *key* and *key_id* values are the same as those in use on any device in your network that makes RIP Version 2 updates.

The IP routing table updates are enabled by default. Use the **no rip** command to disable the PIX Firewall IP routing table updates. The **clear rip** command removes all the **rip** commands from the configuration.

Figure 10-2 shows the PIX Firewall learning routes from a router on its outside interface and the broadcasting of a default route on its inside interface. MD5 authentication is used on the outside interface to enable the PIX Firewall to accept the encrypted RIP updates. Example 10-3 shows the commands necessary to configure RIP for the firewall shown in Figure 10-2. Both the PIX Firewall and Router A are configured with the encryption key **MYKEY** and its *key_id* of 2.

Figure 10-2 *RIP Dynamic Routes*

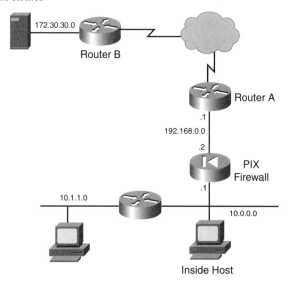

Example 10-3 *RIP Configuration Command*

```
pixfirewall(config)# rip outside passive version 2 authentication md5 MYKEY 2
pixfirewall(config)# rip inside default
```

In Example 10-3, the PIX Firewall accepts encrypted RIP Version 2 multicast updates. For example, it could learn the route to network 172.30.30.0 from Router A. It also broadcasts IP address 10.0.0.1 as the default route for devices on the inside interface.

NOTE   Static routes override dynamic routes.

The syntax for the **rip** command is as follows:

```
rip if_name default | passive [version [1 | 2]] [authentication [text | md5 key
    key_id]]
```

Table 10-1 describes the **rip** command arguments.

Table 10-1   rip *Command Arguments*

Argument	Definition
if_name	The internal or external network interface name.
default	Argument that broadcasts a default route on the interface.
passive	Argument that enables passive RIP on the interface. The PIX Firewall listens for RIP routing broadcasts and uses that information to populate its routing tables.
version	The version of RIP. Use Version 2 for RIP update encryption. Use Version 1 to provide backward compatibility with the older version.
authentication	Argument that enables RIP Version 2 authentication.
text	Argument that sends RIP updates as cleartext.
md5	Argument that ends RIP updates using MD5 authentication.
key	The key to encrypt RIP updates. This value must be the same on the routers and any other device that provides RIP Version 2 updates. The key is a text string of up to 16 characters.
key_id	The key identification value. The *key_id* can be a number from 1 to 255. Use the same *key_id* that is in use on the routers and any other device that provides RIP Version 2 updates.

OSPF

PIX Firewall Version 6.3 introduces support for the OSPF routing protocol to the PIX Firewall 500 series platform. OSPF provides route discovery and propagation and fast route convergence times via an industry standard protocol.

NOTE	Cisco PIX Firewall 501 does not support OSPF.

OSPF support introduced in PIX Firewall 6.3 provides roughly the same feature set and functionality as Cisco IOS Release 12.2(3a). To maintain consistency, the OSPF command-line interface (CLI) commands in PIX Firewall 6.3 are nearly identical to their IOS counterparts. So if you are familiar with OSPF configuration commands on the IOS, you should feel right at home on the PIX.

Coverage of all OSPF design considerations is beyond the scope of this book. Instead, discussions focus on security issues related to the implementation of OSPF on the PIX and present an overview of tasks required to enable and configure OSPF on the PIX Firewall. The next subsection presents a brief overview of OSPF to facilitate more effective discussion of OSPF-related security considerations that follow.

Basic OSPF Concepts

OSPF is a link-state, Interior Gateway Protocol (IGP) routing protocol designed by the Internet Engineering Task Force (IETF) in 1988. It is based on open standards and, as its name implies, uses the Shortest Path First (SPF) algorithm to determine the best (shortest) path to a destination. OSPF supports classless routing (variable-length subnet masks [VLSMs]).

Unlike RIP, a distance-vector routing protocol, OSPF route updates do not include the entire routing table. Instead, OSPF routers periodically send link-state advertisements (LSAs) to other routers with information on the status of interfaces and other metrics. OSPF routers use the SPF algorithm and the information in LSAs to determine the shortest path to a destination.

To reduce the impact of LSAs on network utilization, OSPF operates in a hierarchical design, and the network can be divided into smaller areas. A backbone area is always present. Depending on the size and design of the network, you can also configure additional areas. The collection of all areas under a common administrative authority represents the routing domain, or autonomous system (AS), as it is commonly referred to. Figure 10-3 shows a simple OSPF topology.

LSA traffic is reduced in a hierarchical design because updates can be restricted to routers within an area. However, to enable inter-area routing, routers in different areas must exchange LSAs. Area Border Routers (ABRs) have interfaces in multiple areas within a routing domain and perform this function. Autonomous System Boundary Routers (ASBR) perform a similar function for interdomain routing and redistribute traffic or import external routes between routing domains.

Figure 10-3 *OSPF Network Topology*

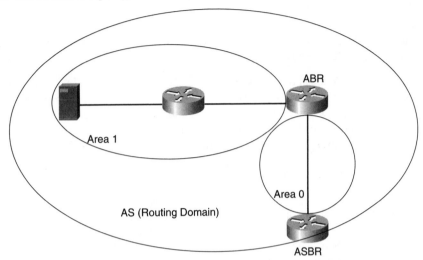

Routers use different types of LSAs depending on their location within an OSPF topology. Type 1 and Type 2 LSAs include intra-area routing information and are only flooded within an area. ABRs use Type 3 LSAs to send summary inter-area routing information to other OSPF routers in all connected areas.

OSPF Security Considerations

Before the introduction of OSPF in PIX Firewall 6.3, there was little concern about potential security issues related to any routing protocols running on the PIX. PIX Firewalls only supported RIP Version 1 and RIP Version 2 in passive mode. In other words, there was no chance of private network routes on the PIX propagating to untrusted networks.

If OSPF is running on your PIX, this may no longer be true. You should therefore pay careful attention to the configuration of OSPF on the PIX to ensure that private routes are not compromised or inadvertently advertised to untrusted networks.

You should use MD5 authentication on all segments to ensure that route redistribution between OSPF and other protocols such as RIP (running on other devices) is not used to subvert routing information.

With OSPF enabled, the physical security of the PIX Firewall is of even greater importance. Physical access to the PIX and configuration information should be kept secure. Also, you should frequently change any shared keys you use.

A PIX Firewall should typically be implemented as an ABR in an OSPF deployment. Because Type 3 LSAs (interarea routes) can be filtered from one area to another, you can use ABR Type 3 LSA filtering and keep routing updates about your private network from the public (untrusted) areas. This setup enables you to use NAT and OSPF together without advertising private networks to public areas.

Alternatively, you can run two separate OSPF processes on the PIX Firewall and isolate private and public networks on each process. PIX Firewalls can run two separate OSPF processes to allow you to do this. Advertising between private and public networks is prevented because different OSPF processes don't exchange LSAs by default. You can then use the **redistribute** command to redistribute external routes into the private network OSPF process.

CAUTION	If the PIX Firewall is implemented as an ASBR on the private network, it will flood the AS with Type 5 LSAs, which include routing information about your private network. Because only Type 3 LSAs can be filtered, you will not be able to keep routing information about your private network from the untrusted areas.

Supported and Unsupported OSPF Features

The following OSPF features are supported on PIX Firewall Version 6.3:

- Intra-area, interarea, and external (Type 1 and Type 2) routes
- Virtual links
- OSPF LSA flooding
- Authentication for OSPF packets (both cleartext and MD5 authentication)
- Configuration of the PIX Firewall as a designated router (DR) or ABR
- Configuration of the PIX Firewall as an ASBR, with route redistribution between OSPF processes, including OSPF, static, and connected routes
- Support for stub areas and not so stubby areas (NSSA)
- ABR Type 3 LSA filtering
- Load balancing among a maximum of three peers on a single interface, using equal-cost multipath routes (ECMP)

NOTE	If using ECMP, note that the default cost for a Fast Ethernet links on the PIX Firewall is consistent with the Firewall Services Module, which is different from a Cisco IOS router.

NOTE	Unlike Cisco IOS, PIX Firewall does not accept spaces within OSPF authentication keys or message digests. This limit might create compatibility issues when a PIX Firewall tries to exchange OSPF messages with an adjacent router using spaces within its authentication key or message digest.

The following OSPF features are not supported in PIX Firewall Version 6.3:

- Point-to-point link/serial interface/nonbroadcast multiaccess (NBMA)
- OSPF on-demand circuit
- Flood reduction
- Redistribution of routes between non-OSPF routing protocols
- Policy routing

Because OSPF does not support overlapping address spaces, you cannot run OSPF on an interface from which it can learn overlapping addresses. To support overlapping address networks, you must use static routes or passive RIP.

NOTE	Running RIP and OSPF together on the same PIX Firewall is not supported.

Configuring OSPF

Configuring OSPF on the PIX Firewall is similar to that on Cisco IOS using the **router ospf** command. The syntax for the global router **ospf command** is as follows:

```
router ospf pid
show router ospf pid
```

The following subcommands are available in **router ospf** command mode:

```
area area_id
area area_id authentication [message-digest]
area area_id default-cost cost
area area_id filter-list prefix {prefix_list_name in | out}
area area_id nssa [no-redistribution] [default-information-originate [metric-type 1
 | 2] [metric metric_value]]
area area_id range ip_address netmask [advertise | not-advertise]
area area_id stub [no-summary]
area area_id virtual-link router_id [authentication [message-digest | null]] [hello-
   interval seconds] [retransmit-interval seconds] [transmit-delay seconds] [dead-
   interval seconds] [authentication-key password] [message-digest-key id md5
   password]
compatible rfc1583
default-information originate [always] [metric metric_value] [metric-type {1 | 2}]
   [route-map map_name]
distance ospf [intra-area d1][inter-area d2][external d3]
ignore lsa mospf
log-adj-changes [detail]
```

```
network prefix ip_address netmask area area_id
redistribute {static | connected} [metric metric_value ] [metric-type metric_type]
    [route-map map_name] [tag tag_value] [subnets]
redistribute ospf pid [match {internal | external [1| 2] | nssa-external [1|2]}]
    [metric metric_value ] [metric-type metric_type] [route-map map_name] [tag
    tag_value] [subnets]
router-id ip_address
summary-address addr netmask [not-advertise] [tag tag_value]
timers {spf spf_delay spf_holdtime | lsa-group-pacing seconds}
```

You can use the **no** form of each command or subcommand to remove the configuration.
Table 10-2 describes the **router ospf** command arguments.

Table 10-2   **router ospf** *Command Arguments*

Argument	Definition
addr	The value of the summary address designated for a range of addresses.
advertise	Argument used with **area range** command to set the address range status to advertise and generates a Type 3 summary LSA. This is the default setting.
always	Argument used with **default-information originate** command to inject a default route into a normal OSPF area even if the ASBR does not have a default route.
area	The **area** command configures a regular OSPF area.
area_id	The ID of the area to be associated with the OSPF address range, specified as either a decimal value or as an IP address.
authentication	(Optional) Argument used with **area** commands to specify the authentication type.
authentication-key *password*	Used with **area virtual-link** command to configure plain text authentication for a virtual link.
compatible rfc1583	Runs OSPF in RFC 1583-compatible mode.
cost	The cost for the default summary route used for a stub or NSSA, from 0 to 65,535. The default value for cost is 1.
d1, *d2*, and *d3*	The distance for different area route types. The default for *d1*, *d2*, and *d3* is 110.
dead-interval *seconds*	Argument used with **area virtual link** command to specify interval in seconds (between 1 and 65,535) during which at least one Hello packet from a neighbor must be received or the neighbor is considered down and removed from the peer list. The value must be the same for all nodes on the network.
default-cost	Argument used with **area** command to specify the cost for the default summary route sent into a stub or NSSA area.
default-information originate	The **default-information originate** command distributes a default route according to the parameters specified.

Table 10-2   **router ospf** *Command Arguments (Continued)*

Argument	Definition
default-information-originate	Argument used with **area nssa** command to generate a Type 7 default in the NSSA area. This keyword takes effect only on an NSSA ABR or NSSA ASBR.
detail	Argument used with **log-adj-changes** command to send a syslog message for every state change.
distance ospf	The **distance ospf** command configures administrative distances for the OSPF process.
external	Argument used with the **distance ospf** command to set the distance for routes from other routing domains, learned by redistribution.
external [1 | 2]	The OSPF metric routes external to a specified AS, either Type 1 or 2. The default is Type 2.
filter-list prefix	Argument used with **area** command to filter prefixes advertised in Type 3 LSAs between OSPF areas of an ABR.
hello-interval *seconds*	Argument used with **area virtual link** command to specify the interval between Hello packets sent on the interface, from 1 to 65,535 seconds. The default is 10 seconds.
ignore lsa mospf	The **ignore lsa mospf** command suppresses syslog for receipt of Type 6 multicast OSPF LSAs.
in	Argument used with **area filter-list prefix** command to apply the configured prefix list to prefixes advertised inbound to the specified area.
inter-area	Argument used with **distance ospf** command to set the distance for all routes from one area to another area.
intra-area	Argument used with **distance ospf** command to set the distance for all routes from one area to another area.
internal	Argument that is internal to a specified autonomous system.
ip_address	The router ID in IP address format.
log-adj-changes	Argument that logs OSPF adjacency changes.
lsa-group-pacing *seconds*	The interval at which OSPF LSAs are collected into a group and refreshed, checksummed, or aged, from 10 to 1,800 sec. The default value is 240 seconds.
map_name	The name of the route map to apply.
match	Argument used with **redistribute ospf** command and **internal**, **external [1 | 2]**, and **nssa-external [1 | 2]** arguments to specify internal, external (Type 1, Type 2, or both), or NSSA-external (Type 1, Type 2, or both) routes for redistribution.

continues

Table 10-2   **router ospf** *Command Arguments (Continued)*

Argument	Definition
message-digest	(Optional) Argument that enables MD5 authentication on the area specified by the *area_id*.
message-digest-key *id* **md5** *password*	Used with **area virtual-link** command to configure MD5 authentication for a virtual link.
metric *metric_value*	Argument that specifies the OSPF default metric value, from 0 to 16777214.
metric-type 1 | 2	(Optional) Argument that specifies the external link type associated with the default route advertised into the OSPF routing domain. Type 1 or Type 2 external routes may be specified. The default is Type 2.
netmask	An IP address mask or IP subnet mask used for a summary route.
network	Adds or removes interfaces to or from the OSPF routing process.
no-redistribution	Argument to use when the OSPF router is an NSSA ABR and you want the **redistribute** command to import routes only into the normal areas and not into the NSSA.
no-summary	Argument that prevents an ABR from sending summary link-state advertisements into the stub area.
not-advertise	Argument that sets the address range status to **DoNotAdvertise**. The Type 3 summary LSA is suppressed, and the component networks remain hidden from other networks.
	In the **summary-address** command, **not-advertise** suppresses routes that match the specified prefix/mask pair.
nssa	Argument used with **area** command to specify an NSSA.
nssa-external [1 | 2]	The OSPF metric type for routes that are external to a NSSA, either Type 1 or 2. The default is Type 2.
null	(Optional) Argument that specifies that no authentication is used. Overrides password or message digest authentication if configured for the OSPF area.
out	Argument used with **area filter-list prefix** command to apply the configured prefix list to prefixes advertised outbound from the specified area.
pid	OSPF routing process ID. A unique value ranging from 1 to 65,535 must be assigned for each OSPF routing process. PIX Firewall Software Version 6.3 supports a maximum of two OSPF processes.
prefix	Indicates that a prefix list is used. (You configure prefix lists with the **prefix-list** command.)
prefix	An IP address.

Table 10-2   **router ospf** *Command Arguments (Continued)*

Argument	Definition
prefix_list_name	Name of a prefix list.
range	Argument used with **area** command to summarize routes at an area boundary.
redistribute ospf	Configures redistribution between OSPF processes according to the parameters specified.
redistribute static | connected	Configures redistribution of static or directly connected routes and OSPF processes according to the parameters specified.
retransmit-interval *seconds*	Argument used with **area virtual link** command to specify the time in seconds between LSA retransmissions. The default value is 5 seconds, with a range from 1 to 65,535.
route-map	Argument used with **redistribute** commands to specify a route map for redistributing routes from one routing protocol to another.
router-id	The **router-id** command configures the router ID for an OSPF process.
router_id	The OSPF router ID.
spf	Argument used with **timers** command to configure SPF delay and holdtime values.
spf_delay	The delay time between when OSPF receives a topology change and when it starts an SPF calculation in seconds, from 0 to 65,535. The default is 5 seconds.
spf_holdtime	The hold time between two consecutive SPF calculations in seconds, from 0 to 65,535. The default is 10 seconds.
stub	Argument used with **area** command to specify an OSPF area that carries a default route and intra-area and interarea routes but does not carry external routes.
subnets	(Optional) For redistributing routes into OSPF.
summary-address	Argument that configures the summary address for OSPF redistribution.
tag_value	The value to match (for controlling redistribution with route maps).
timers	Argument that configures timers for the OSPF process.
transmit-delay *seconds*	Argument used with **area virtual link** command to specify time in seconds that it takes to transmit a link state update. The range is 1 to 65,535 seconds. The default is 1 second.
virtual-link	Argument used with **area** command to configure an OSPF virtual link.

You can configure interface-specific OSPF routing parameters after you globally enable OSPF using the **routing interface** command. The syntax for the **routing interface** command is as follows:

```
routing interface interface_name
```

Subcommands to the **routing interface** command include the following:

```
ospf authentication [message-digest | null]
ospf authentication-key password
ospf cost interface_cost
ospf database-filter all out
ospf dead-interval seconds
ospf hello-interval seconds
ospf message-digest-key key-id md5 key
ospf mtu-ignore
ospf priority number
ospf retransmit-interval seconds
ospf transmit-delay seconds
```

You can use the **no** form of each command or subcommand to remove the configuration. Table 10-3 describes the **routing interface** command and subcommand arguments.

Table 10-3   **routing interface** *Command Arguments*

Argument	Definition
authentication	Specifies the authentication type for the **ospf** process.
authentication-key *password*	Assigns an OSPF authentication password for use by neighboring routing devices. It can be up to 8 bytes of any continuous string of keyboard characters, except for whitespace characters such as tabs or spaces.
database-filter all out	Filters out outgoing LSAs to an OSPF interface.
dead-interval *seconds*	Sets the interval before declaring a neighboring routing device is down if no Hello packets are received, from 1 to 65,535 sec. This value must be the same for all nodes on the network. The default is four times the interval set by the **ospf hello-interval** command.
hello-interval *seconds*	Specifies the interval between hello packets sent on the interface, from 1 to 65,535 sec. The default is 10 sec.
cost *interface_cost*	The cost (a link-state metric) of sending a packet through an interface. It is an unsigned integer value from 0 to 65,535. The higher the interface bandwidth, the lower the associated cost to send packets across that interface. A cost value of 0 represents a network that is directly connected to the interface. The OSPF interface default cost on the PIX Firewall is 10 regardless of interface speed. On a Cisco IOS router, the default cost is 1 for Fast Ethernet and Gigabit Ethernet and 10 for 10BASE-T. This difference in default cost values is important if you are using ECMP in your network.
interface_name	The name of the interface to configure.

Table 10-3   **routing interface** *Command Arguments (Continued)*

Argument	Definition
key_id	A numerical ID number, from 1 to 255, for the authentication key.
md5 *key*	An alphanumeric password of up to 16 bytes. However, whitespace characters such as a tab or space are not supported.
message-digest	Specifies to use OSPF message digest authentication.
message-digest-key	Enables MD5 authentication. (MD5 verifies the integrity of the communication, authenticates the origin, and checks for timeliness.)
mtu-ignore	Disables OSPF MTU mismatch detection on receiving database descriptor (DBD) packets. To reset to default, use the **no** form of this command.
null	Specifies that OSPF authentication should not be used. This overrides password or message digest authentication (if configured) for an OSPF area.
ospf	Keyword for configuring interface-specific OSPF parameters.
priority *number*	A positive integer from 0 to 255 that specifies the priority of the router. The default is 1.
retransmit-interval *seconds*	Specifies the time between LSA retransmissions for adjacent routers belonging to the interface, from 1 to 65,535 sec. The default is 5 sec.
transmit-delay *seconds*	Sets the estimated time required to send a link-state update packet on the interface, from 1 to 65,535 sec. The default is 1 sec.

You can use the **prefix-list** command to filter Type 3 LSA advertisements. The syntax for the **prefix-list** command is as follows:

```
prefix-list list_name [seq seq_number] {permit I deny prefix I len} [ge min_value]
[le max_value]
prefix-list sequence-number
prefix-list list_name description text
```

You can use the appropriate **no** form of each command to remove the configuration. Table 10-4 describes the **prefix-list** command and subcommand arguments.

Table 10-4   **prefix-list** *Command Arguments*

Argument	Definition
/	A required separator between the *prefix* and *len* values.
deny	Denies access for a matching condition.
description *text*	Argument used with **prefix-list** command to add a text description of a prefix list.
ge	Applies the *min_value* to the range specified.
le	Applies the *max_value* to the range specified.

continues

Table 10-4 **prefix-list** *Command Arguments (Continued)*

Argument	Definition
len	The network length (in bits) of the network mask, from 0 to 32.
list_name	The name of the prefix list. The *list_name* and *seq_number* together must be fewer than 64 characters combined.
max_value	Specifies the greater value of a range (the "to" portion of the range description). Values can range from 0 to 32.
min_value	Specifies the lesser value of a range (the "from" portion of the range description). Values can range from 0 to 32.
permit	Permits access for a matching condition.
prefix	The network number.
seq *seq_number*	Specifies the sequence number for the prefix list entry, from 1 to 4,294,967,295. However, the *list_name* and *seq_number* together must be fewer than 64 characters combined.
sequence-number	Enables the generation of sequence numbers for entries in an OSPF prefix list.
text	The text of the description, with a maximum of 80 characters.

Finally, you can use the **route-map** command to configure route redistribution settings. The syntax for the **route-map** command is as follows:

```
route-map map_tag [permit | deny] [seq_num]
show route-map [map_tag]
```

Subcommands to the **route-map** command include the following:

```
match [interface interface_name | metric metric_value | ip address acl_id | route-type
{local | internal | [external [type-1 | type-2]]}| nssa-external [type-1 | type-2] | ip
next-hop acl_id | ip route-source acl_id ]
set metric metric_value
set metric-type {type-1 | type-2 | internal | external}
set ip next-hop ip-address [ip-address]
```

You can use the appropriate **no** form of each command to remove the configuration. Table 10-5 describes the **route-map** command and subcommand arguments.

Table 10-5 **route-map** *Command Arguments*

Argument	Definition
acl_id	The name of an ACL. The **match ip next-hop** and **match ip route-source** commands can accept more than one *acl_id*.
deny	If the match criteria are met for the route map and the **deny** option is specified, the route is not redistributed.

Table 10-5 route-map *Command Arguments (Continued)*

Argument	Definition
external	The OSPF metric routes external to a specified autonomous system.
interface *interface_name*	Used with the **match** command to redistribute routes that have their next hop out of the interface specified.
internal	Routes that are internal to a specified autonomous system.
ip address *acl_id*	Used with the **match** command to redistribute routes based on destination network permitted by a standard or extended access list.
ip next-hop *acl_id*	Used with the match command to redistribute routes that have a next hop router address passed by one of the ACLs specified by *acl_id.*
ip next-hop *ip-address* [*ip-address*]	Indicates where to output packets that pass a match clause of the route map.
ip route-source *acl_id*	Redistributes routes that have been advertised by routers and access servers at the address specified by the *acl_id.*
local	Specifies a preference value for the autonomous system path.
map_tag	Is the text for the route map tag, meant to define a meaningful name for the route map, up to 58 characters in length. Multiple route maps may share the same map tag name.
match	Specifies the criteria used to select routes that are filtered by the route map.
metric *metric_value*	Used with the **set** command to specify the metric value, from 0 to 2,147,483,647.
metric-type	Used with the **set** command and **type-1**, **type-2**, **internal**, and **external** arguments to specify the metric type.
nssa-external [**type-1** | **type-2**]	Used with the **match** command to specify metric type for routes that are external to an NSSA area, either Type 1 or 2. The default is Type 2.
permit	If the match criteria are met for this route map, and the **permit** option is specified, the route is redistributed as controlled by the set actions. If the match criteria are not met, and the **permit** keyword is specified, the next route map with the same *map_tag* is tested. If a route passes none of the match criteria for the set of route maps sharing the same name, it is not redistributed by that set. The **permit** option is the default.
route-type	Used with **match** command and **local**, **internal**, and **external** [**type-1** | **type-2**] arguments to create route maps that filter local, internal, external Type 1, or external Type 2 routes.

continues

Table 10-5   **route-map** *Command Arguments (Continued)*

Argument	Definition
seq_num	If there are any route maps with the same *map_tag*, you must also specify a *seq_num* for the route-maps to differentiate between them. The *seq_num* can be any number from 0 to 65535. Otherwise, no *seq_num* needs to be specified. A default value of 10 is assigned to the first route map if no *seq_num* is specified.
	If given in the **no route-map** *map_tag seq_num* command, *seq_num* is the route map to be deleted.
set	A **route-map** subcommand used to configure metric value, metric type, and next-hop router address settings.
type-1 | type-2	The OSPF metric routes external to a specified autonomous system, either Type 1 or 2. The default is Type 2.

Example 10-4 shows basic configuration commands to enable OSPF on a PIX Firewall with a single process.

Example 10-4   *One-Process OSPF Configuration*

```
pixfirewall(config)# prefix-list secure-ospf seq 1 deny 10.0.1.0/24
pixfirewall(config)# prefix-list secure-ospf seq 2 permit 0.0.0.0/0 le 32

pixfirewall(config)# routing interface outside
pixfirewall(config-routing)# ospf message-digest-key 1 md5 cisco
pixfirewall(config-routing)# ospf authentication message-digest
pixfirewall(config-routing)# routing interface inside
pixfirewall(config-routing)# ospf message-digest-key 1 md5 cisco
pixfirewall(config-routing)# ospf authentication message-digest
pixfirewall(config-routing)# router ospf 1
pixfirewall(config-router)# network 10.0.1.0 255.255.255.0 area 0
pixfirewall(config-router)# network 192.168.0.0 255.255.255.0 area 1
pixfirewall(config-router)# area 0 authentication message-digest
pixfirewall(config-router)# area 1 authentication message-digest
pixfirewall(config-router)# area 1 filter-list prefix secure-ospf in
```

In this example, the **prefix-list** command creates a list named **secure-ospf**. This list is used to filter Type 3 LSAs for the internal network (10.0.1.0). The **routing interface** command configures message-digest authentication for OSPF on each interface. Next, an OSPF process is created using the **router ospf** command. The **network area** command is used to add the 10.0.1.0/24 and the 192.168.0.0/24 network to areas 0 and 1 respectively. The **area authentication** command specifies message-digest authentication for each area. Finally, Type 3 LSAs for network 10.0.1.0/24 are filtered using the **area filter-list prefix** command. Filtering the Type 3 LSAs for the 10.0.1.0/24 network keeps routing information about that network from the untrusted network on the outside.

Example 10-5 shows a two-process OSPF configuration as an alternative to the one-process configuration shown in Example 10-4. (**routing interface** commands are the same as Example 10-4 and are not shown.) Configurations in both examples provide similar functionality and security using one or two OSPF processes.

Example 10-5   *Two-Process OSPF Configuration*

```
pixfirewall(config)# router ospf 1  //Private Process
pixfirewall(config-router)# network 10.0.1.0 255.255.255.0 area 0
pixfirewall(config-router)# area 0 authentication message-digest
pixfirewall(config-router)# redistribute ospf 2
pixfirewall(config-router)# router ospf 2  //Public Process
pixfirewall(config-router)# network 192.168.0.0 255.255.255.0 area 1
pixfirewall(config-router)# area 1 authentication message-digest
```

In Example 10-5, two OSPF processes (IDs 1 and 2) are created using the **router ospf** command. The **network area** command is used to add the 10.0.1.0/24 network to area 0 under process ID 1 and the 192.168.0.0/24 network to area 1 under process ID 2. The **area authentication** command specifies message-digest authentication for each area. With two OSPF processes, there is no need to filter Type 3 LSAs because they are not exchanged between the two processes by default. The **redistribute** command is then used to redistribute the routes from process ID 2 (public) into the private process.

IP Multicast

Most network communications consist of unicasts and broadcasts. (Reducing broadcast traffic is a typical network design goal.) *Unicast* transmissions occur between a single sender and a single receiver. For example, when you use a browser to view a web page on a server, the server unicasts the information to the host used for browsing.

Broadcasts are typically used on LAN segments to find other hosts or services. When a host is broadcasting, the information is sent to all other hosts on the network. For example, a Windows client can use broadcasts to find another Windows client using its NetBIOS name. A properly designed network should keep broadcast traffic to a minimum.

IP multicasting is a bandwidth-conserving technology that reduces traffic by simultaneously delivering a single stream of information to multiple recipients. Applications that take advantage of multicast include video conferencing, corporate communications, distance learning, and distribution of software, stock quotes, and news.

IP multicasting is actually the transmission of an IP datagram to a "host group," a set of hosts identified by a single IP destination address. For multicasting to work, hosts that want to receive multicasts must "tune in" to the multicast by joining a multicast host group, and routers that forward multicast datagrams must know which hosts belong to which group. Routers discover this information by sending Internet Group Management Protocol (IGMP) query messages through their attached local networks. Host members of a multicast group respond to the query by sending IGMP "reports" noting the multicast groups to which they belong. If a host is removed from a multicast group, it sends a "leave" message to the multicast router.

In Software Versions 6.2 and higher, the PIX Firewall supports Stub Multicast Routing (SMR), which enables it to pass multicast traffic. This feature is necessary when hosts that need to receive multicast transmissions are separated from the multicast router by a PIX Firewall. With SMR, the PIX Firewall acts as an IGMP proxy agent. It forwards IGMP messages from hosts to the upstream multicast router, which takes responsibility for forwarding multicast datagrams from one multicast group to all other networks that have members in the group. When using PIX Firewall Version 6.1 or older, which do not support SMR, it is necessary to construct Generic Route Encapsulation (GRE) tunnels to allow multicast traffic to bypass the PIX Firewall.

NOTE	The GRE protocol is used for tunneling data across an IP network.

Allowing Hosts to Receive Multicast Transmissions

When hosts that need to receive a multicast transmission are separated from the multicast router by a PIX Firewall, configure the PIX Firewall to forward IGMP reports from the downstream hosts and to forward multicast transmissions from the upstream router. Complete the following steps to allow hosts to receive multicast transmissions through the PIX Firewall:

NOTE	You can also use PIX Device Manager (PDM) to configure multicast settings on the PIX Firewall. You access multicast settings on the System Properties tab of PDM.

Step 1 Use the **multicast interface** command to enable multicast forwarding on each interface and place the interfaces in multicast promiscuous mode. When you enter this command, the CLI enters multicast subcommand mode, and the prompt changes to (**config-multicast**). From this prompt, you can enter the **igmp** commands for further multicast support. The **clear multicast** command clears all multicast settings.

Step 2 Use the **igmp forward** command to enable IGMP forwarding on each PIX Firewall interface connected to hosts that will receive multicast transmissions. This interface is typically an inside (or more secure) interface. The **igmp forward** command enables forwarding of all IGMP host Report and Leave messages received on the interface specified.

NOTE	All IGMP commands (except **show igmp** and **clear igmp**) are only available as submode commands of the **multicast interface** command.

(Optional) Use the **igmp join-group** command to configure the PIX Firewall to join a multicast group. This command configures the interface to be a statically connected member of the specified group. It allows the PIX Firewall to act for a client that might not be able to respond via IGMP but still requires reception. The **igmp join-group** command is applied to the downstream interface toward the receiving hosts.

A multicast group is defined by a Class D IP address. Although Internet IP multicasting uses the entire range of 224.0.0.0 to 239.255.255.255, any group address you assign must be within the range 224.0.0.2 to 239.255.255.255. Because the address 224.0.0.0 is the base address for Internet IP multicasting, it cannot be assigned to any group. The address 224.0.0.1 is assigned to the permanent group of all IP hosts (including gateways). This address is used to address all multicast hosts on the directly connected network. There is no multicast address (or any other IP address) for all hosts on the total Internet.

Step 3   (Optional) Use the **permit** option of the **access-list** command to configure an ACL that allows traffic to the desired Class D destination addresses. You can also use the **deny** option to deny access to transmissions from specific multicast groups. Within the ACL, the *destination-addr* argument is the Class D address of the multicast group to which you want to permit or deny multicast transmissions. If you use ACLs for this purpose, you must also use the **igmp access-group** command to apply the ACL to the currently selected interface.

NOTE   The **access-list** command is explained in Chapter 8, "Access Control Lists and Content Filtering."

The syntax for the **multicast interface** command is as follows:

```
multicast interface interface_name [max-groups number]
```

Table 10-6 describes the **multicast interface** command arguments.

Table 10-6   **multicast interface** *Command Arguments*

Argument	Definition
interface_name	The name of the interface to pass multicast traffic.
max-groups *number*	The maximum number of IGMP groups you want to allow on the specified interface. The range of groups supported (**max-groups**) is from 1 to 2,000. A value of 0 causes no IGMP groups to be allowed. The default value is 500.

The syntax for the **igmp** subcommands is as follows:

```
igmp forward interface interface_name
igmp join-group group
igmp access-group acl-id
```

Table 10-7 describes the **igmp** subcommand arguments.

Table 10-7 **igmp** *Subcommand Arguments*

Argument	Definition
interface_name	Name of the interface to pass multicast traffic
group	IP address of the multicast group being joined
acl_id	Name of the ACL

Figure 10-4 shows a host behind a PIX Firewall receiving a multicast transmission from a server on the outside DMZ.

Figure 10-4 *Inside Host Receiving Multicast*

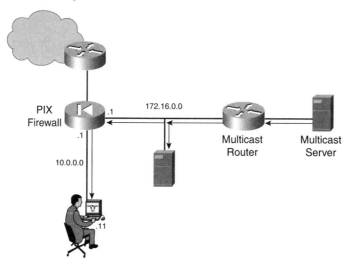

Example 10-6 shows the configuration of the PIX Firewall for the multicast setup shown in Figure 10-4.

Example 10-6 *Multicast Interface Commands for Inside Hosts Receiving Transmission*

```
pixfirewall(config)# multicast interface dmz
pixfirewall(config-multicast)# exit
pixfirewall(config)# multicast interface inside
pixfirewall(config-multicast)# igmp forward interface dmz
```

Example 10-6 shows use of the **multicast** command with corresponding **igmp** subcommands. IGMP query messages are permitted on the **dmz** interface. The **igmp forward** command enables the PIX Firewall to forward IGMP reports from inside hosts to the multicast router on its **dmz** interface. In this example, host 10.0.0.11 joins multicast group 224.1.1.1. The PIX Firewall then permits host 10.0.0.11 to receive multicasts from the multicast server.

Forwarding Multicasts from a Transmission Source

When a multicast transmission source is on a protected (or more secure) interface of a PIX Firewall, you must specifically configure the PIX Firewall to forward multicast transmissions from the source. Enable multicast forwarding on the PIX Firewall interfaces toward each network containing hosts that are registered to receive the multicast transmissions. Complete the following steps to configure the PIX Firewall to forward multicast transmissions from an inside source:

Step 1   Use the **multicast interface** command to enable multicast forwarding on each PIX Firewall interface.

Step 2   Use the **mroute** command to create a static route from the transmission source to the next-hop router interface. Use the **clear mroute** command to clear static multicast routes.

The syntax for the **mroute** commands is as follows:

```
mroute src smask in-if-name dst dmask out-if-name
```

Table 10-8 describes the **mroute** command arguments.

Table 10-8   **mroute** *Command Arguments*

Argument	Definition
src	Multicast source address
smask	Multicast source mask
in-if-name	Input interface to pass multicast traffic
dst	Class D address of the multicast group
dmask	Destination network address mask
out-if-name	Output interface to pass multicast traffic

Figure 10-5 shows an example of a host on the inside interface of the PIX Firewall transmitting multicasts to members of group 230.1.1.2 on the outside of the PIX. There are no internal receivers.

Figure 10-5 *Inside Host Transmitting Multicast*

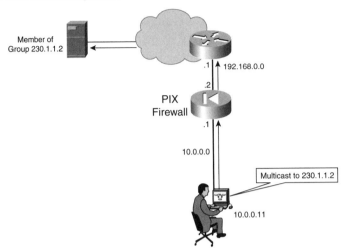

Example 10-7 shows the configuration commands required to enable multicast traffic on the inside and outside interfaces. A static multicast route is configured to enable inside host 10.0.0.11 to transmit multicasts to members of group 230.1.1.2 on the outside interface.

Example 10-7 *Multicast Interface Commands for Source Transmitting from Inside*

```
pixfirewall(config)# multicast interface outside
pixfirewall(config-multicast)# exit
pixfirewall(config)# multicast interface inside
pixfirewall(config-multicast)# mroute 10.0.0.11 255.255.255.255 inside 230.1.1.2
  255.255.255.255 outside
```

Configuring Other IGMP Options

You can choose an IGMP version and configure the IGMP timers with the **igmp version**, **igmp query-interval**, and **igmp query-max-response-time** commands. Specify the version of IGMP you want to use with the **igmp version** command. This command configures which version of IGMP is used on the subnet represented by the specified interface. The default is Version 2.

In addition to the availability of the **igmp query-max-response-time**, Version 2 offers bandwidth-conserving features not available in Version 1. The Leave Group message is one of these features. The advantage of this message is reducing the bandwidth waste between the time the last host in a subnet drops membership and the time the router times out for its queries and decides there are no more members present for that group.

When an IGMP Version 2 router receives a Leave message for a group, it sends group-specific queries to the group being left. IGMP Version 1 has no group-specific queries, so all queries are sent to the all-hosts group. For further information on the differences in Versions 1 and 2, see RFC 2236.

Use the **igmp query-interval** command to configure the frequency at which IGMP query messages are sent by the interface. The default is 60 seconds. The permitted range of values is from 1 to 65,535. Use the command **no igmp query-interval** to set the query interval back to the default.

The **igmp query-max-response-time** command specifies the maximum query response time and is only available with IGMP Version 2. The default is 10 seconds. The permitted range of values is from 1 to 65,535. Use the command **no igmp query-max-response-time** to set the query response time back to the default.

The syntax for these **igmp** commands is as follows:

```
igmp version 1 | 2
igmp query-interval seconds
igmp query-max-response-time seconds
```

Table 10-9 describes the **igmp** command arguments.

Table 10-9   **igmp** *Command Arguments*

Argument	Definition
query-interval	Time interval of the query response
query-max- response-time	Maximum query response time interval
seconds	Number of seconds to wait

Example 10-8 shows a sample IGMP Version 2 configuration with modified query interval and maximum response times.

Example 10-8   *IGMP Configuration*

```
pixfirewall(config)# multicast interface inside
pixfirewall(config-multicast)# igmp version 2
pixfirewall(config-multicast)# igmp query-interval 120
pixfirewall(config-multicast)# igmp query-max-response-time 50
```

Monitoring SMR Configurations

You can use the following commands to view the current multicast and IGMP configuration:

- **show multicast**—Displays all or per-interface multicast settings. This command also displays the IGMP configuration for the interface.

- **show igmp**—Displays multicast-related information about one or more groups.

- **show mroute**—Shows multicast routes.

The syntax for these **show** commands is as follows:

```
show multicast [interface interface_name]
show igmp [group | interface interface-name] [detail]
show mroute [dst [src]]
```

Table 10-10 describes the **show multicast**, **show igmp**, and **show mroute** command arguments.

Table 10-10 **show multicast**, **show igmp**, *and* **show mroute** *Command Arguments*

Argument	Definition
interface_name	Name of the interface for which you want to view configuration settings
group	Address of the multicast group
detail	Argument that displays all information in the IGMP table
dst	Class D address of the multicast group
src	IP address of the multicast source

You can use the following commands for debugging your SMR configuration:

- **debug igmp**—Enables or disables debugging for IGMP events
- **debug mfwd**—Enables or disables debugging for multicast forwarding events

You can remove each of these commands by using its **no** form.

Summary

This section summarizes the information you learned in this chapter:

- You can add static routes to the PIX Firewall to enable access to networks connected outside a router on any interface.
- You can configure the PIX Firewall to listen for RIP Version 1 or RIP Version 2 routing broadcasts.
- The PIX Firewall cannot pass RIP updates between interfaces.
- When RIP Version 2 is configured in passive mode, the PIX Firewall accepts RIP Version 2 multicast updates with the IP destination of 224.0.0.9.
- If configured for the RIP Version 2 default mode, the PIX Firewall transmits default route updates using an IP destination of 224.0.0.9.
- The PIX Firewall Version 6.3 supports the OSPF routing protocol.
- OSPF support on the PIX Firewall is similar to the implementation of OSPF in Cisco IOS Release 12.2(3a).

- The PIX Firewall supports up to two OSPF processes.
- OSPF support is not available on PIX 501.
- OSPF and RIP are not concurrently supported.
- MD5 authentication of route updates (RIP or OSPF) increases the security of a network.
- The PIX Firewall supports SMR, which enables it to pass multicast traffic.
- You can configure the PIX Firewall to forward multicasts from a transmission source on a higher security level interface to receivers on a lower security level interface.
- You can also configure the PIX Firewall to allow hosts on a higher security level interface to receive multicasts from a host on a lower security level interface.

Chapter Review Questions

To test what you have learned in this chapter, answer the following questions and then refer to Appendix A, "Answers to Chapter Review Questions," for the answers:

1 How many default routes can you configure on a PIX Firewall?

2 How many OSPF processes are supported on PIX Firewall Version 6.3?

3 What OSPF LSA type can be filtered? Which type cannot be filtered?

4 What is the required command to configure an OSPF process with ID 5?

5 What should you do to ensure that private network route updates are not sent to public areas in a NAT environment?

6 If you have overlapping network addresses, which dynamic routing protocol can you use on the PIX Firewall?

PART IV

Advanced Configuration Topics

On completion of this chapter, you will be able to perform the following tasks:

- Describe the **fixup protocol** command.
- Describe the need for advanced protocol handling.
- Describe how the Private Internet Exchange (PIX) Firewall handles FTP, remote shell (rsh), and SQL*Net traffic.
- Configure the FTP, rsh, and SQL*Net fixup protocols.
- Describe issues surrounding multimedia applications.
- Describe how the PIX Firewall handles Real-Time Streaming Protocol (RTSP) and H.323 multimedia protocols.
- Configure RTSP and H.323 fixup protocols.
- Describe how the PIX Firewall supports call-handling sessions and Voice over IP (VoIP) call signaling.

CHAPTER 11

Advanced Protocol Handling

Today, many organizations use the Internet for critical transactions, and most implement firewalls on their networks as protection from potential threats on the Internet. Even though these firewalls help protect an organization's internal networks from external threats, firewalls can also create compatibility issues with certain applications and protocols. For example, protocols and applications that negotiate connections through the firewall to dynamically assigned sources or destination ports, or IP addresses, might not function correctly with standard firewalls. For example, sources or destination ports, or IP addresses such as FTP, SQL*Net, or most multimedia protocols might not function correctly.

PIX Firewalls provide support for these types of protocols by utilizing the fixup feature built into the operating system. Cisco continually improves the advanced protocol-handling capabilities of the PIX Firewall by adding additional fixup protocols or improving the functionality of existing fixups with each iteration of the PIX Firewall. This chapter covers advanced protocol-handling capabilities of the PIX Firewall.

Advanced Protocols

The standard behavior of the PIX Firewall can interfere with the operation of certain applications and protocols. These types of applications and protocols, such as FTP or SQL*Net, require special handling for proper operation. Applications and protocols requiring special handling typically do the following:

- Negotiate connections to dynamically assigned source or destination ports or IP addresses.

- Embed source or destination port or IP address information above the network layer.

A good firewall must inspect packets above the network layer and perform the following functions as required by the protocol or application:

- Securely open and close negotiated ports or IP addresses for legitimate client/server connections through the firewall.

- Use relevant instances of network address translation (NAT) of an IP address inside a packet.

- Use relevant instances of port address translation (PAT) of ports inside a packet.

- Inspect packets for signs of malicious application misuse.

The Adaptive Security Algorithm (ASA) provides support for protocols and applications requiring special handling through its application inspection function. You configure application inspection using the **fixup** command.

Typically, when a packet arrives at the PIX Firewall and requires a new connection, the PIX Firewall checks its access control list (ACL) database and creates a new connection entry if a connection is permitted. The ASA process then checks its inspections database to determine whether special handling is required for the connection. The application inspections function performs any required fixups for the packet, and the packet is forwarded to its destination. Subsequent packets belonging to this established session are identified by the PIX Firewall and are also forwarded.

fixup Command

You can configure the Cisco PIX Firewall to allow the required protocols or applications using the **fixup** command. This configuration enables an organization's internal networks to remain secure while still being able to continue day-to-day business over the Internet.

The **fixup** command enables you to change, enable, or disable the use of a service or protocol throughout the PIX Firewall. The ports you specify are those that the PIX Firewall listens at for each respective service. You can change the port value for each service except remote shell rsh. The syntax of the **fixup** command is as follows:

```
[no] fixup protocol protocol_name [port[-port]]
clear fixup
show fixup [protocol {protocol_name}]
```

You enable or modify a fixup protocol using the **fixup** command, the appropriate protocol name, and optional port settings. The **no** form of the command disables the fixup protocol for the specified protocol. The **clear fixup** command restores default fixup configuration on the PIX Firewall. The **show fixup** command lists currently enabled fixup protocols running on the PIX Firewall. You can optionally specify a protocol name with the **show fixup** command to display the settings for a specific protocol. Table 11-1 lists supported protocols and describes the **fixup** command arguments.

Table 11-1   **fixup** *Command Arguments*

Argument	Definition
ctiqbe	Configures the Computer Telephony Interface Quick Buffer Encoding (CTIQBE) fixup on default port TCP 2748. Used with Cisco Telephony Application Programming Interface/Java TAPI (TAPI/JTAPI) applications. Available with PIX Firewall Version 6.3 or higher. Disabled by default.
dns	Configures the Domain Name Service (DNS) fixup on default port User Datagram Protocol (UDP) 53. Enabled by default.
dns maximum-length *length*	Specifies the maximum DNS packet length allowed. Default is 512 bytes.

Table 11-1   **fixup** *Command Arguments (Continued)*

Argument	Definition
esp-ike	Enables PAT for Encapsulating Security Payload (ESP), single tunnel. Available with PIX Firewall version 6.3 or higher.
ftp	Configures FTP fixup protocol on default port TCP 21. Enabled by default.
h323	Configures the H.323 fixup. Available with PIX Firewall Version 6.2 or higher. PIX Firewall Version 6.3 adds support for Version 3 and Version 4. Enabled by default.
h323 h225	Configures H.323 for use with H.225.
h323 ras	Configures H.323 for use with Registration, Admission, and Status (RAS) protocol.
http	Configures HTTP fixup protocol on default port TCP 80. Enabled by default.
icmp error	Configures Internet Control Message Protocol (ICMP) error fixup to enable NAT and PAT of ICMP error messages. Available with PIX Firewall Version 6.3 or higher. Disabled by default.
ils	Configures the Internet Locator Service (ILS) fixup for use with Microsoft NetMeeting, SiteServer, and Active Directory products that use Lightweight Directory Access Protocol (LDAP) to exchange directory information with an ILS server. Available with PIX Firewall Version 6.2 or higher. Disabled by default.
mgcp	Enables the Media Gateway Control Protocol (MGCP) fixup to allow secure transmission of messages between call agents and VoIP media gateways through the PIX Firewall. Available with PIX Firewall Version 6.3 or higher. Disabled by default.
port	Specifies the port on which to enable the fixup (application inspection). The default ports are TCP 21 for **ftp**, TCP LDAP server port 389 for **ils**, TCP 80 for **http**, TCP 1720 for **h323 h225**, UDP 1718-1719 for **h323 ras**, TCP 514 for **rsh**, TCP 554 for **rtsp**, TCP 2000 for **skinny**, TCP 25 for **smtp**, TCP 1521 for **sqlnet**, TCP 5060 for **sip**, UPD 53 for **dns**, and UDP 69 for **tftp**. You cannot change the default port value for **rsh**, but you can add port statements. In addition to port numbers, you can use literal names supported by the PIX Firewall. Check the "ports" section of the "PIX Firewall Commands" documentation on Cisco.com for the most up-to-date list of supported literal port names.
port-port	Specifies a port range.
pptp	Configures Point-to-Point Tunneling Protocol (PPTP) application inspection on port TCP 1723 to enable PPTP use when the PIX Firewall is configured with PAT. Available with PIX Firewall Version 6.3 or higher. Disabled by default.

Table 11-1 *fixup Command Arguments (Continued)*

protocol *protocol_name*	Specifies the protocol to fix up.
Argument	**Definition**
rsh	Configures the rsh fixup on default port TCP 514. Enabled by default.
rtsp	Configures the Real-Time Streaming Protocol (RTSP) fixup on default port TCP 554 to enable use of multimedia applications such as RealAudio, RealPlayer, Cisco IP/TV, or Apple QuickTime. Does not support multicast RTSP. Enabled by default.
sip	Configures the Session Initiation Protocol (SIP) for Voice over TCP connections on default port 5060. UDP SIP is on by default and can be disabled. The port assignment for UDP SIP is fixed at 5060. PIX Firewall Version 6.2 or higher provides PAT support for SIP. Enabled by default.
skinny	Configures Skinny Client Control Protocol (SCCP) application inspection on default port TCP 2000. SCCP protocol supports IP telephony and can coexist in an H.323 environment. Skinny fixup ensures that SCCP signaling and media packets correctly traverse the PIX Firewall and interoperate with H.323 terminals. PIX Firewall Version 6.3 or higher provides PAT support for SCCP. Enabled by default.
smtp	Configures the SMTP fixup on default port TCP 25. Enabled by default.
strict	Used with the FTP fixup protocol, prevents web browsers from sending embedded commands in FTP requests. Each FTP command must be acknowledged before a new command is allowed. Connections sending embedded commands are dropped.
sqlnet	Configures the SQL*Net fixup on default port TCP 1521. Enabled by default.
tftp	Configures Trivial File Transfer Protocol (TFTP) fixup on default port UDP 69. Available with PIX Firewall Version 6.3 or higher. Enabled by default.

Some applications, such as FTP, require that the PIX Firewall understand special properties of the application so that connections that are legitimately part of the application are permitted. During an FTP transfer, the PIX Firewall needs to be aware of the data channel that is opened from the server to the initiating workstation. The PIX Firewall identifies applications by the TCP or UDP port number contained in the IP packets. For example, it recognizes FTP by port number 21, SMTP by port number 25, and HTTP by port number 80.

For the most part, there is no reason to change these port numbers. But in special circumstances, you might have a service listening on a nonstandard port number. For example, you could have an HTTP server listening on port 5000. The PIX Firewall would not recognize that port 5000 is being used for HTTP and would therefore block the returned HTTP data connection from the server. You can resolve this problem by adding port 5000 to the **fixup protocol** command:

```
pixfirewall(config)# fixup protocol http 5000
```

This command enables the PIX Firewall to recognize that connections to port 5000 should be treated in the same manner as connections to port 80. Note that the PIX Firewall supports fixup of the same protocol or application on multiple ports. Therefore, configuring support for HTTP fixup on a nonstandard port such as TCP 5000 does not automatically disable HTTP fixup support on port TCP 80. To specifically disable HTTP fixup on port TCP 80 for the preceding example, you must issue the appropriate **no fixup** command as follows:

```
pixfirewall(config)# no fixup protocol http 80
```

The PIX Firewall security features are based on checking and changing, or "fixing up," information in packets sent over a network. Different network protocols, such as Simple Mail Transfer Protocol (SMTP) for mail transfer, include protocol-specific information in the packets. The fixup protocol for SMTP packets includes changing addresses embedded in the payload of packets, checking for supported commands, replacing bad characters, and so on.

By default, the PIX Firewall is configured to fix up the following protocols: FTP, SMTP, HTTP, rsh, RTSP, SQL*Net, H.323, Skinny, TFTP, DNS, and SIP (TCP and UDP).

NOTE   The SMTP fixup protocol is enabled by default. The SMTP fixup supports only standard SMTP servers. Extended SMTP (ESMTP) servers such as Microsoft Exchange are not supported. If you are running an ESMTP server such as Exchange, you *must* disable the SMTP fixup protocol by using the following command:

```
pixfirewall (config)# no smtp fixup protocol
```

If you do not disable the SMTP fixup protocol while running an ESTMP server, your ESMTP server might function incorrectly or revert to basic SMTP operation mode.

Standard Mode FTP

Standard mode FTP uses two channels for communications, as shown in Figure 11-1. When a client starts an FTP connection, it opens a standard TCP channel from one of its high-order ports to port 21 on the server. This channel is referred to as the *command* channel. When the client requests data from the server, it tells the server to send the data to a specified high-order port. The server acknowledges the request and initiates a connection from its own port 20 to the high-order port that the client requested. This channel is referred to as the *data* channel.

Figure 11-1   *Standard Mode FTP*

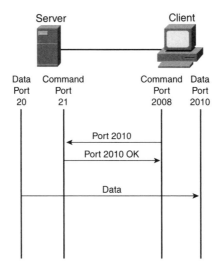

Because the server initiates the connection to the requested port on the client, it was difficult in the past to have firewalls allow this data channel to the client without permanently opening port 20 connections from outside servers to inside clients for outbound FTP connections. This setup created a potential vulnerability by exposing clients on the inside of the firewall. Protocol fixups have resolved this problem.

For FTP traffic, the PIX Firewall behaves in the following manner:

- **Outbound connections**—When the client requests data, the PIX Firewall opens a temporary inbound conduit for the data channel from the server. This conduit is torn down after the data is sent.

- **Inbound connections**:

  — If an ACL exists allowing inbound connections to an FTP server, and if all outbound TCP traffic is implicitly allowed, no special handling is required because the server initiates the data channel from the inside.

  — If an ACL exists allowing inbound connections to an FTP server, and if all outbound TCP traffic is not implicitly allowed, the PIX Firewall opens a temporary conduit for the data channel from the server. This conduit is torn down after the data is sent.

Passive Mode FTP

Passive mode FTP (PFTP) also uses two channels for communications, as shown in Figure 11-2. The command channel works in the same way as in a standard FTP connection, but the data channel setup works differently. When the client requests data from the server, it asks the server whether it accepts PFTP connections. If the server accepts PFTP connections, it sends the client a high-order port number to use for the data channel. The client then initiates the data connection from its own high-order port to the port that the server sent.

Figure 11-2 *PFTP*

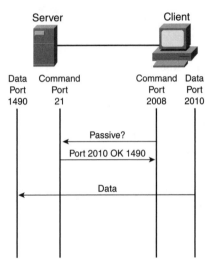

Because the client initiates both the command and data connections, early firewalls could easily support outbound connections without exposing inside clients to attack. Inbound connections, however, proved more of a challenge. The FTP protocol fixup resolved this issue.

For PFTP traffic, the PIX Firewall behaves in the following manner:

- **Outbound connections**:
    - If all outbound TCP traffic is implicitly allowed, no special handling is required because the client initiates both the command and data channels from the inside.
    - If all outbound TCP traffic is not implicitly allowed, the PIX Firewall opens a temporary conduit for the data channel from the client. This conduit is torn down after the data is sent.
- **Inbound connections**—If an ACL exists allowing inbound connections to a PFTP server, when the client requests data, the PIX Firewall opens a temporary inbound conduit for the data channel initiated by client. This conduit is torn down after the data is sent.

FTP Fixup Configuration

By default, the PIX Firewall inspects TCP port 21 connections for FTP traffic. If you have FTP servers using ports other than TCP port 21, you need to use the **fixup protocol ftp** command to have the PIX Firewall inspect these other ports for FTP traffic. Example 11-1 shows the commands required to enable FTP fixup on port 2021.

Example 11-1 *FTP Fixup Protocol*

```
pixfirewall(config)# fixup protocol ftp 2021
pixfirewall(config)# no fixup protocol ftp 21
```

The **fixup protocol ftp** command causes the PIX Firewall to perform the following functions for FTP traffic on the indicated port:

- Perform NAT or PAT in packet payload.
- Dynamically create conduits for FTP data connections.
- Log FTP commands (when syslog is enabled).

The **strict** option to the **fixup protocol ftp** command prevents web browsers from sending embedded commands in FTP requests. Each FTP command must be acknowledged before a new command is allowed. Connections sending embedded commands are dropped.

Use the **no** form of the command to disable the inspection of traffic on the indicated port for FTP connections. If the **fixup protocol ftp** command is not enabled for a given port

- Outbound standard FTP does *not* work properly on that port.
- Outbound PFTP works properly on that port as long as outbound traffic is not explicitly disallowed.
- Inbound standard FTP works properly on that port if a conduit to the inside server exists.
- Inbound PFTP does *not* work properly on that port.

Using the **no fixup protocol ftp** command without any arguments causes the PIX Firewall to clear all previous **fixup protocol ftp** assignments, set port 21 back as the default, and disable the FTP fixup protocol. You can then enable FTP fixup with default settings using the **fixup protocol ftp** command.

The syntax for the **fixup protocol ftp** command is as follows:

```
fixup protocol ftp [strict] port[-port]
no fixup protocol ftp [strict] [port[-port]]
```

Table 11-2 describes the **fixup protocol ftp** command arguments.

Table 11-2   *Fixup Protocol FTP Command Arguments*

Argument	Definition
strict	Prevents web browsers from sending embedded commands in FTP requests
port [*-port*]	Is a single port or port range for which the PIX Firewall inspects FTP connections

Example 11-2 demonstrates the use of the **fixup protocol ftp** command and its **no** form to configure and remove standard and nonstandard ports for FTP:

Example 11-2   *Configuring and Removing Standard and Nonstandard Ports for FTP*

```
pixfirewall#(config) fixup protocol ftp 2121
pixfirewall#(config) fixup protocol ftp 2001
pixfirewall#(config) no fixup protocol ftp 21
pixfirewall#(config) no fixup protocol ftp 2001
```

This example configures nonstandard TCP ports 2121 and 2001 for FTP. Next, it disables the standard TCP port 21 and nonstandard TCP port 2001, leaving FTP fixup enabled on TCP port 2121 only.

rsh

rsh uses two channels for communications, as shown in Figure 11-3. When a client first starts an rsh connection, it opens a standard TCP channel from one of its high-order ports to port 514 on the server. The server opens another channel for standard error output to the client.

Figure 11-3   *rsh*

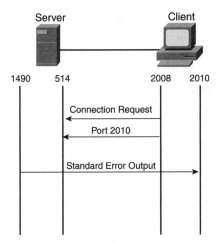

For rsh traffic, the PIX Firewall behaves in the following manner:

- **Outbound connections**—When standard error messages are sent from the server, the PIX Firewall opens a temporary inbound conduit for this channel. This conduit is torn down when no longer needed.

- **Inbound connections**:
  - If an ACL exists allowing inbound connections to an rsh server, and if all outbound TCP traffic is implicitly allowed, no special handling is required because the server initiates the standard error channel from the inside.
  - If an ACL exists allowing inbound connections to an rsh server, and if all outbound TCP traffic is *not* implicitly allowed, the PIX Firewall opens a temporary conduit for the standard error channel from the server. This conduit is torn down after the messages are sent.

By default, the PIX Firewall inspects TCP port 514 connections for rsh traffic. If you have rsh servers using ports other than port TCP 514, you need to use the **fixup protocol rsh** command to have the PIX Firewall inspect these other ports for rsh traffic.

The **fixup protocol rsh** command causes the PIX Firewall to dynamically create conduits for rsh standard error connections for rsh traffic on the indicated port.

Use the **no** form of the command to disable the inspection of traffic on the indicated port for rsh connections. If the **fixup protocol rsh** command is not enabled for a given port

- Outbound rsh does *not* work properly on that port.
- Inbound rsh works properly on that port if an ACL allowing access to the inside server exists and all outbound TCP traffic is implicitly allowed.

Using the **no fixup protocol rsh** command without any arguments causes the PIX Firewall to clear all previous **fixup protocol rsh** assignments, set port 514 back as the default, and disable the rsh fixup protocol. You can then enable rsp fixup with default settings using the **fixup protocol rsh** command.

The syntax for the **fixup protocol rsh** command is as follows:

```
fixup protocol rsh [port[-port]]
no fixup protocol rsh [port[-port]]
```

You can specify a single port or range of ports for which the PIX Firewall inspects rsh connections using the port parameter with the **fixup protocol rsh** command.

Example 11-3 illustrates the use of the **fixup protocol rsh** command to configure rsh support on standard or nonstandard ports.

Example 11-3 *Configuring and Removing Standard and Nonstandard Ports for rsh*

```
pixfirewall#(config) fixup protocol rsh 5141-5143
pixfirewall#(config) no fixup protocol rsh 514
pixfirewall#(config) no fixup protocol rsh 5141-5143
```

In this example, rsh support is enabled on a nonstandard port range (TCP 5141–5143) by the first statement. Next, the standard TCP port 514 and nonstandard TCP port range 5141–5143 are disabled, leaving rsh fixup disabled on the PIX Firewall.

NOTE   When port ranges are configured, you can only use the **no fixup protocol** command to disable support on a matching range enabled by another statement. In other words, you cannot disable a portion of a port range configured with a **fixup protocol** command. For example, you cannot use

```
no fixup protocol rsh 5141-5142
```

to disable a portion of the ports enabled by

```
fixup protocol rsh 5141-5143
```

Instead, you must use the following statement to remove support on the range matching the original statement that enabled the range:

```
no fixup protocol rsh 5141-5143
```

SQL*Net

SQL*Net uses only one channel for communications, but it could be redirected to a different port and even more commonly to a different secondary server altogether. When a client starts an SQL*Net connection, it opens a standard TCP channel from one of its high-order ports to port 1521 on the server, as shown in Figure 11-4. The server then proceeds to redirect the client to a different port or IP address. The client tears down the initial connection and establishes the second connection.

Figure 11-4   *SQL*Net*

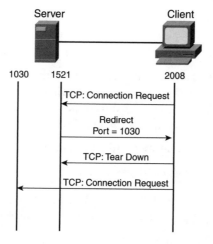

For SQL*Net traffic, the PIX Firewall behaves in the following manner:

- **Outbound connections**:

  — If all outbound TCP traffic is implicitly allowed, no special handling is required because the client initiates all TCP connections from the inside.

  — If all outbound TCP traffic is *not* implicitly allowed, the PIX Firewall opens a conduit for the redirected channel between the server and the client.

- **Inbound connections**—If an ACL exists allowing inbound connections to an SQL*Net server, the PIX Firewall opens an inbound conduit for the redirected channel.

By default, the PIX Firewall inspects TCP port 1521 connections for SQL*Net traffic. If you have SQL*Net servers using ports other than TCP port 1521, you must use the **fixup protocol sqlnet** command to have the PIX Firewall inspect these other ports for SQL*Net traffic.

The **fixup protocol sqlnet** command causes the PIX Firewall to do the following for SQL*Net traffic on the indicated port:

- Perform NAT in packet payload.

- Dynamically create conduits for SQL*Net redirected connections.

Use the **no** form of the command to disable the inspection of traffic on the indicated port for SQL*Net connections. If the **fixup protocol sqlnet** command is not enabled for a given port, the following applies:

- Outbound SQL*Net does work properly on that port as long as outbound traffic is not explicitly disallowed.

- Inbound passive SQL*Net does *not* work properly on that port.

Using the **no fixup protocol sqlnet** command without any arguments causes the PIX Firewall to clear all previous **fixup protocol sqlnet** assignments, set port 1521 back as the default, and disable the SQL*Net fixup protocol. You can then enable SQL*Net fixup with default settings using the **fixup protocol sqlnet** command.

The syntax for the **fixup protocol sqlnet** command is as follows:

```
fixup protocol sqlnet [port[-port]]
no fixup protocol sqlnet [port[-port]]
```

You can specify a single port or port range that the PIX Firewall inspects for SQL*Net connections using the *port* parameter with the **fixup protocol sqlnet** command.

Example 11-4 illustrates the use of the **fixup protocol sqlnet** command.

Example 11-4 *Adding and Removing Standard and Nonstandard Ports for SQL*NET*

```
pixfirewall#(config) fixup protocol sqlnet 1521
pixfirewall#(config) fixup protocol sqlnet 2500-2555
pixfirewall#(config) no fixup protocol sqlnet 1521
```

In this example, SQL*Net support is enabled on TCP ports 1521 and 2500 to 2555. The last statement disables support on standard TCP port 1521.

SIP

SIP enables call-handling sessions, particularly two-party audio conferences, or "calls." SIP works with Session Description Protocol (SDP) for call signaling. SDP specifies the ports for the media stream. Using SIP, the PIX Firewall can support any SIP VoIP gateways and VoIP proxy servers. SIP and SDP are defined in the following RFCs:

- *SIP: Session Initiation Protocol*, RFC 2543
- *SDP: Session Description Protocol*, RFC 2327

To support SIP calls through the PIX Firewall, signaling messages for the media connection addresses, media ports, and embryonic connections for the media must be inspected because although the signaling is sent over a well-known destination port (UDP/TCP 5060), the media streams are dynamically allocated. You can use the **fixup protocol sip** command to enable or disable SIP support. SIP is a text-based protocol and contains IP addresses throughout the text. With the SIP fixup enabled, the PIX Firewall inspects the packets, and both NAT and PAT are supported.

NOTE	PAT support for SIP is only available with PIX Firewall Version 6.2 or higher. Only static and dynamic NAT are supported in earlier versions of the software.

SIP support is enabled by default on port 5060. You can use the **show conn state sip** command to display all active SIP connections.

SCCP

In software versions 6.0 and higher, the PIX Firewall application handling supports the SCCP, used by Cisco IP phones for VoIP call signaling. This capability dynamically opens pinholes for media sessions and NAT-embedded IP addresses. SCCP supports IP telephony and can coexist in an H.323 environment. An application layer ensures that all SCCP signaling and media packets can traverse the PIX Firewall and interoperate with H.323 terminals. Due to SCCP support, you can now place an IP phone and Cisco Call Manager on separate sides of the PIX Firewall. PIX Firewall Software Versions 6.3 or higher add support add NAT and PAT support for SCCP. Using the **no fixup protocol skinny** command without any arguments causes the PIX Firewall to clear all **fixup protocol skinny** assignments.

The syntax for the **fixup protocol skinny** command is as follows:

```
fixup protocol skinny [port[- port]]
no fixup protocol skinny [port[ -port]]
```

You can specify a single port or port range for which the PIX Firewall inspects SCCP connections using the *port* parameter with the **fixup protocol skinny** command. SCCP fixup is enabled by default and operates on port TCP 2000.

Multimedia Support

Multimedia applications present a unique challenge to the PIX Firewall, as shown in Figure 11-5. These applications might transmit requests on TCP, get responses on UDP or TCP, use dynamic ports, use the same port for source and destination, and so on. Every application behaves in a different way. Implementing support for all multimedia applications using a single secure method is very difficult. Two examples of multimedia applications follow:

Figure 11-5   *Why Multimedia Is an Issue*

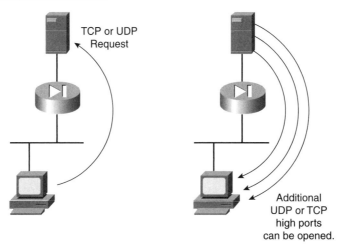

- **RealAudio**—Sends the originating request to TCP port 7070. The RealAudio server replies with multiple UDP streams anywhere from UDP port 6970 through 7170 on the client machine.

- **CUseeMe client**—Sends the originating request from TCP port 7649 to TCP port 7648. The CUseeMe datagram is unique in that it includes the legitimate IP address in the header as well as in the payload and sends responses from UDP port 7648 to UDP port 7648.

The PIX Firewall dynamically opens and closes UDP ports for secure multimedia connections. You do not need to open a large range of ports, which creates a security risk, or reconfigure any application clients.

Also, the PIX Firewall supports multimedia with or without NAT. Many firewalls that cannot support multimedia with NAT limit multimedia usage to only registered users or require exposure of inside IP addresses to the Internet. Lack of support for multimedia with NAT often forces multimedia vendors to join proprietary alliances with firewall vendors to accomplish compatibility for their applications.

The RTSP is a real-time audio and video delivery protocol used by many popular multimedia applications. It uses one TCP channel and sometimes two additional UDP channels. RTSP applications use the well-known port 554, usually TCP, and rarely UDP. RFC 2326 requires only TCP, so the PIX Firewall supports only TCP. This TCP channel is the control channel and is used to negotiate the other two UDP channels depending on the transport mode that is configured on the client.

The first UDP channel is the data connection and can use one of the following transport modes:

- Real-Time Transport Protocol (RTP)
- Real Data Transport Protocol (RDT)

The second UDP channel is another control channel, and it can use one of the following modes:

- Real-Time Control Protocol (RTCP)
- UDP resend

RTSP supports a TCP-only mode. This mode contains only one TCP connection, which is used as the control and data channels. Because this mode contains only one constant standard TCP connection, no special handling by the PIX Firewall is required.

The following are RTSP applications supported by the PIX Firewall:

- Cisco IP/TV
- Apple QuickTime
- RealNetworks
- RealAudio
- RealPlayer
- RealServer

NOTE   RTSP Multicast is not supported.

Standard RTP Mode

In standard RTP mode, RTSP uses the following three channels, as shown in Figure 11-6:

- **TCP control channel**—Standard TCP connection initiated from the client to the server.

- **RTP data channel**—Simplex (unidirectional) UDP session used for media delivery using the RTP packet format from the server to the client. The client's port is always an even-numbered port.

- **RTCP reports**—Duplex (bidirectional) UDP session used to provide synchronization information to the client and packet loss information to the server. The RTCP port is always the next consecutive port from the RTP data port.

Figure 11-6   *Standard RTP Mode*

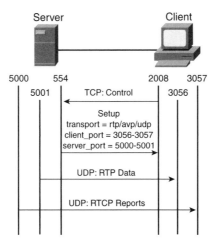

For standard RTP mode RTSP traffic, the PIX Firewall behaves in the following manner:

- **Outbound connections**—After the client and the server negotiate the transport mode and the ports to use for the sessions, the PIX Firewall opens temporary inbound conduits for the RTP data channel and RTCP report channel from the server.

- **Inbound connections**:

  - If an ACL exists allowing inbound connections to an RTSP server, and if all outbound UDP traffic is implicitly allowed, no special handling is required because the server initiates the data and report channel from the inside.

  - If an ACL exists allowing inbound connections to an RTSP server, and if all outbound UDP traffic is *not* implicitly allowed, the PIX Firewall opens temporary conduits for the data and report channels from the server.

RealNetworks RDT Mode

In the RDT mode of RealNetworks, RTSP uses the following three channels, as shown in Figure 11-7:

- **TCP control channel**—Standard TCP connection initiated from the client to the server.

- **UDP data channel**—Simplex (unidirectional) UDP session used for media delivery using the standard UDP packet format from the server to the client.

- **UDP resend**—Simplex (unidirectional) UDP session used for the client to request that the server resend lost data packets.

Figure 11-7 *RDT Mode of RealNetworks*

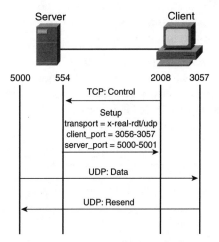

For RTSP traffic in the RDT mode of RealNetworks, the PIX Firewall behaves in the following manner:

- **Outbound connections**:

    - If outbound UDP traffic is implicitly allowed, and after the client and the server negotiate the transport mode and the ports to use for the session, the PIX Firewall opens a temporary inbound conduit for the UDP data channel from the server.

    - If outbound UDP traffic is *not* implicitly allowed, and after the client and the server negotiate the transport mode and the ports to use for the session, the PIX Firewall opens a temporary inbound conduit for the UDP data channel from the server. The PIX Firewall also opens a temporary outbound conduit for the UDP resend channel from the client.

- **Inbound connections**:
  - If an ACL exists allowing inbound connections to an RTSP server, and if all outbound UDP traffic is implicitly allowed, the PIX Firewall opens a temporary inbound conduit for the UDP resend from the client.
  - If an ACL exists allowing inbound connections to an RTSP server, and if all outbound UDP traffic is *not* implicitly allowed, the PIX Firewall opens temporary conduits for the UDP data and UDP resend channels from the server and client, respectively.

RTSP Fixup Configuration

By default, the PIX Firewall does not inspect any ports for RTSP connections. To enable the PIX Firewall to inspect specific ports for RTSP traffic, such as the standard port 554, use the **fixup protocol rtsp** command.

The **fixup protocol rtsp** command causes the PIX Firewall to dynamically create conduits for RTSP UDP channels for RTSP traffic on the indicated port. Use the **no** form of the command to disable the inspection of traffic on the indicated port for RTSP connections. If the **fixup protocol rtsp** command is not enabled for a given port, neither outbound nor inbound RTSP works properly on that port.

Using the **no fixup protocol rtsp** command without any arguments causes the PIX Firewall to clear all previous **fixup protocol rtsp** assignments.

The syntax for the **fixup protocol rtsp** command is as follows:

```
fixup protocol rtsp [port[-port]]
no fixup protocol rtsp [port[-port]]
```

You can use the *port* parameter with the **fixup protocol rtsp** command to specify a single port or port range for which the PIX Firewall inspects RTSP connections.

H.323 Fixup

H.323 is more complicated than other traditional protocols because it uses two TCP connections and several UDP sessions for a single "call." (Only one of the TCP connections goes to a well-known port; all the other ports are negotiated and are temporary.) Furthermore, the content of the streams is far more difficult for firewalls to understand than existing protocols because H.323 encodes packets using Abstract Syntax Notation, or ASN.1.

Microsoft NetMeeting, one of the applications that uses H.323, uses ILS to provide directory services. ILS provides registration and location of endpoints in the ILS/SiteServer Directory and uses LDAP Version 2. The ILS fixup of the PIX Firewall supports NAT for LDAP Version 2 and enables NAT for ILS messages. This setup allows the PIX Firewall to support NAT for H.323 session establishment by NetMeeting. PAT cannot be supported because only IP addresses are stored by an LDAP database.

NOTE	If you are using NAT 0 and not expecting destination NAT interaction, turn off ILS fixup for better performance.

Other protocols and standards supported within H.323 are as follows:

- H.225—RAS
- H.225—Call signaling
- H.245—Control signaling
- TPKT header
- Q.931 messages
- ASN.1 (PIX Firewall 5.2)

Supported H.323 versions are as follows:

- H.323 v1
- H.323 v2 (PIX Firewall Software Versions 5.2 and higher)
- H.323 v3 (PIX Firewall Software Versions 6.3 and higher)
- H.323 v4 (PIX Firewall Software Versions 6.3 and higher)

Supported applications are as follows:

- Cisco Multimedia Conference Manager
- Microsoft NetMeeting
- Intel Video Phone
- Intel InternetPhone
- CUseeMe Networks:
  - MeetingPoint
  - CUseeMe Pro
- VocalTec:
  - Internet Phone
  - Gatekeeper

Configuring H.323 Fixup

By default, the PIX Firewall inspects port 1720 connections for H.323 traffic. If you have H.323 servers using ports other than port 1720, you must use the **fixup protocol h323** command to have the PIX Firewall inspect these other ports for H.323 traffic.

The **fixup protocol h323** command causes the PIX Firewall to carry out the following functions for H.323 traffic on the indicated port:

- Perform NAT in packet payload.
- Dynamically create conduits for TCP or UDP channels.

PIX Firewall Software Versions 5.2 and higher support H.323 Version 2. PIX Firewall Software Version 6.3 or higher add support for H.323 Version 3 and 4 messages. H.323 supports H.323 VoIP gateways and VoIP gatekeepers. H.323 Version 2 adds the following functionality to the PIX Firewall:

- Fast Connect or Fast Start Procedure for faster call setup
- H.245 tunneling for resource conservation, call synchronization, and reduced setup time

Use the **no** form of the command to disable the inspection of traffic on the indicated port for H.323 connections. If the **fixup protocol h323** command is not enabled for a given port, neither outbound nor inbound H.323 works properly on that port.

Using the **no fixup protocol h323** command without any arguments causes the PIX Firewall to clear all previous **fixup protocol h323** assignments and set port 1720 back as the default.

The syntax for the **fixup protocol h323** command is as follows:

```
fixup protocol h323 [h225 | ras] [port[-port]]
no fixup protocol h323 [h225 | ras] [port[-port]]
```

Table 11-3 provides descriptions for the **fixup protocol h323** command arguments.

Table 11-3 **fixup protocol h323** *Command Arguments*

Argument	Definition
h225	Specifies the use of H.225, which is the International Telecommunication Union (ITU) standard that governs H.225.0 session establishment and packetization, with H.323. H.225.0 actually describes several different protocols: RAS, use of Q.931, and use of RTP.
ras	Specifies the use of RAS with H.323 to enable dissimilar communication devices to communicate with each other. H.323 defines a common set of coder-decoders (codecs), call setup and negotiating procedures, and basic data transport methods.
port[-*port*]	Single port or port range that the PIX Firewall inspects for H.323 connections.

Summary

This section summarizes the information you learned in this chapter:

- The PIX Firewall's application inspection function provides support for protocols and applications that
    - Negotiate connections to dynamically assigned source or destination ports, or IP addresses.
    - Embed source or destination port or IP address information above the network layer.
- The **fixup** command enables you to view, change, enable, or disable the use of a service or protocol.
- The PIX Firewall uses special handling for the following advanced protocols: FTP, rsh, and SQL*Net.
- The PIX Firewall handles the following multimedia protocols: RTSP and H.323.
- The PIX Firewall's SIP fixup supports call handling sessions.
- The PIX Firewall's skinny fixup supports VoIP call signaling.

Chapter Review Questions

To test what you have learned in this chapter, answer the following questions and then refer to Appendix A, "Answers to Chapter Review Questions," for the answers:

1   You want to enable HTTP fixup protocol, but the developers at your company are using port 1180 for their development environment. How can you enable the HTTP fixup protocol on port 1180?

2   Which version of PIX Firewall adds support for H.323 v3 and H.323 v4 fixup protocols?

3   What is the difference between the **no fixup protocol** and the **clear fixup** commands?

4   Which version of PIX Firewall adds fixup protocol support for the skinny protocol?

5   What is the function of the **strict** option in FTP fixup protocol?

Lab Exercise—Configure and Test Advanced Protocol Handling on the Cisco PIX Firewall

Complete the following lab exercise to practice the advanced protocol-handling concepts covered in this chapter. Use the following initial configuration commands and continue with the rest of the lab exercises.

NOTE	Many of the settings shown in this initial configuration are default values and do not need to be entered on your PIX Firewall. Specific commands that you must enter are shown in bold for your convenience.

```
:
interface ethernet0 100full
interface ethernet1 100full
nameif ethernet0 outside security0
nameif ethernet1 inside security100
enable password 8Ry2YjIyt7RRXU24 encrypted
passwd 2KFQnbNIdI.2KYOU encrypted
hostname pixfirewall
domain-name cisco.com
fixup protocol dns maximum-length 512
fixup protocol ftp 21
fixup protocol h323 h225 1720
fixup protocol h323 ras 1718-1719
fixup protocol http 80
fixup protocol rsh 514
fixup protocol rtsp 554
fixup protocol sip 5060
fixup protocol sip udp 5060
fixup protocol skinny 2000
fixup protocol smtp 25
fixup protocol sqlnet 1521
fixup protocol tftp 69
access-list allow-ftp permit tcp any any eq ftp
pager lines 24
mtu outside 1500
mtu inside 1500
mtu dmz 1500
ip address outside 192.168.1.2 255.255.255.0
ip address inside 10.0.1.1 255.255.255.0
ip audit info action alarm
ip audit attack action alarm
pdm location 10.0.1.0 255.255.255.0 inside
pdm location 10.0.1.11 255.255.255.255 inside
pdm history enable
arp timeout 14400
global (outside) 1 192.168.1.150-192.168.1.200
nat (inside) 1 0.0.0.0 0.0.0.0 0 0
static (inside,outside) 192.168.1.10 10.0.1.11 netmask 255.255.255.255 0 0
access-group allow-ftp in interface outside
timeout xlate 3:00:00
timeout conn 1:00:00 half-closed 0:10:00 udp 0:02:00 rpc 0:10:00 h225 1:00:00
timeout h323 0:05:00 mgcp 0:05:00 sip 0:30:00 sip_media 0:02:00
timeout uauth 0:05:00 absolute
aaa-server TACACS+ protocol tacacs+
aaa-server RADIUS protocol radius
aaa-server LOCAL protocol local
http server enable
http 10.0.1.0 255.255.255.0 inside
no snmp-server location
no snmp-server contact
snmp-server community public
no snmp-server enable traps
floodguard enable
telnet 10.0.1.0 255.255.255.0 inside
```

```
telnet timeout 5
ssh timeout 5
console timeout 0
terminal width 80
Cryptochecksum:aa0cc6e47d705ed128e041c2c2a8412b
: end
```

Objectives

In this lab exercise, you complete the following tasks:

- Display the fixup protocol configurations.

- Change the fixup protocol configurations.

- Test the outbound FTP fixup protocol.

- Test the inbound FTP fixup protocol.

- Set the fixup protocols to the default settings.

Lab Topology

Figure 11-8 displays the topology you need for the lab exercises in this chapter.

Figure 11-8   *Advanced Protocol-Handling Lab Visual Objective*

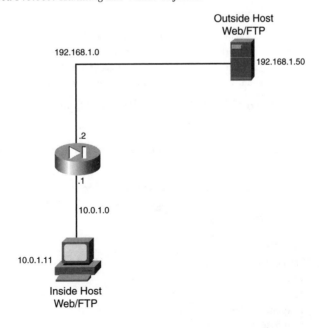

Equipment required to perform the lab includes the following:

- A PIX Firewall with two interfaces
- Category 5 patch cables
- PC host for outside subnet with web browser and FTP server with anonymous access
- PC host for the inside subnet with web browser and FTP server with anonymous access

Task 1—Display the Fixup Protocol Configurations

Complete the following step and enter the command as directed to see the current configurations of your PIX Firewall:

Step 1 List the fixup protocols that are running on your PIX Firewall:

```
pixfirewall(config)# show fixup protocol
```

Task 2—Change the Fixup Protocol Configurations

Complete the following steps and enter the commands as directed to change some of the current configurations of your PIX Firewall:

Step 1 Disable the following fixup protocols:

```
pixfirewall(config)# no fixup protocol http 80
pixfirewall(config)# no fixup protocol smtp 25
pixfirewall(config)# no fixup protocol h323 h225 1720
pixfirewall(config)# no fixup protocol sqlnet 1521
```

Step 2 Define a range of ports for SQL*Net connections:

```
pixfirewall(config)# fixup protocol sqlnet 66-76
```

Step 3 Verify the fixup protocol settings using the **show fixup protocol** command:

```
pixfirewall(config)# show fixup protocol
fixup protocol dns maximum-length 512
fixup protocol ftp 21
no fixup protocol h323 h225 1720
fixup protocol h323 ras 1718-1719
no fixup protocol http 80
fixup protocol rsh 514
fixup protocol rtsp 554
fixup protocol sip 5060
fixup protocol sip udp 5060
fixup protocol skinny 2000
no fixup protocol smtp 25
```

```
no fixup protocol h323 h225 1720
no fixup protocol sqlnet 1521
fixup protocol sqlnet 66-76
fixup protocol tftp 69
```

NOTE   If you are running a different version of the PIX Firewall software, your list of fixup protocols might not match this list exactly. The list displayed here is based on PIX Firewall Software Version 6.3(3).

Task 3—Test the Outbound FTP Fixup Protocol

Complete the following steps and enter the commands as directed to test the outbound FTP fixup protocol:

Step 1   Enable console logging on your PIX Firewall:

```
pixfirewall(config)# logging console debug
```

Step 2   Start an FTP session to the outside host from the inside host using the Windows FTP client:

```
C:\> ftp 192.168.1.50
User (192.168.1.50:(none)): anonymous
Password: user@
```

Step 3   Log in (using anonymous or an account that you have configured on the FTP server) and list the directory at the FTP prompt:

```
ftp> dir
```

Question 1: What logging messages were generated on your PIX Firewall console?

Step 4   Quit your FTP session:

```
ftp> quit
```

Step 5   Turn off the FTP fixup protocol on your PIX Firewall:

```
pixfirewall(config)# no fixup protocol ftp
```

Step 6   Again, connect to the outside host from the inside host using the Windows FTP client:

```
C:\> ftp 192.168.1.50
User (192.168.1.50:(none)): anonymous
Password: user@
```

Question 2: Were you able to log in to the server? Why or why not?

Step 7   Do a directory listing at the FTP prompt:

```
ftp> dir
```

Question 3: Were you able to see a file listing? Why or why not?

Step 8   Quit your FTP session:

```
ftp> quit
```

NOTE   If the FTP client is hung, press **Ctrl-C** until you break back to the C:\ prompt or close the command prompt window.

Step 9   FTP to the outside host from the inside host using your web browser. To do so, enter the following in the URL field:

```
ftp://192.168.1.50
```

Question 4: Were you able to connect? Why or why not?

Question 5: Were you able to see a file listing? Why or why not?

Step 10 Close your web browser.

Task 4—Test the Inbound FTP Fixup Protocol

Complete the following steps and enter the commands as directed to test the inbound FTP fixup protocol:

Step 1   Re-enable the FTP fixup protocol on your PIX Firewall:

```
pixfirewall(config)# fixup protocol ftp 21
```

Step 2   FTP to an inside host from an outside host PC using your web browser. To do so, enter the following in the URL field:

```
ftp://192.168.1.10
```

Question 6: What logging messages were generated on your PIX Firewall console?

Step 3   Close your web browser.

Step 4   Turn off the FTP fixup protocol on your PIX Firewall:

```
pixfirewall(config)# no fixup protocol ftp
```

Step 5   FTP to an inside host from an outside host using your web browser. To do so, enter the following in the URL field:

```
ftp://192.168.1.10
```

Question 7: Were you able to connect to an inside host FTP server? Why or why not?

Task 5—Set the Fixup Protocols to the Default Settings

Complete the following steps and enter the commands as directed to set all fixups to the factory default:

Step 1   Set all fixup protocols to the factory defaults:

```
pixfirewall(config)# clear fixup
```

Step 2   Verify the fixup protocol settings:

```
pixfirewall(config)# show fixup protocol
fixup protocol dns maximum-length 512
fixup protocol ftp 21
fixup protocol h323 h225 1720
fixup protocol h323 ras 1718-1719
fixup protocol http 80
fixup protocol rsh 514
fixup protocol rtsp 554
fixup protocol sip 5060
fixup protocol sip udp 5060
fixup protocol skinny 2000
fixup protocol smtp 25
fixup protocol sqlnet 1521
fixup protocol tftp 69
```

Answers to Task Review Questions

1   What logging messages were generated on your PIX Firewall console?

   a   302013: Built outbound TCP connection 83 for outside:192.168.1.50/21 (192.168.1.50/21) to inside:10.0.1.11/1063 (192.168.1.10/1063).

   b   302013: Built outbound TCP connection 84 for outside:192.168.1.50/20 (192.168.1.50/20) to inside:10.0.1.11/1064 (192.168.1.10/1064).

   c   302014: Teardown TCP connection 84 for outside:192.168.1.50/20 to inside:10.0.1.11/1064 duration 0:00:01 bytes 363 TCP FINs.

2 Were you able to log in to the server? Why or why not?

Yes. Outbound connections are allowed, and only the command channel is set up at this point.

3 Were you able to see a file listing? Why or why not?

No. A **dir** command causes the FTP server to open a data connection back to the client. Without the FTP fixup, the PIX Firewall does not allow this data connection from the outside.

4 Were you able to connect? Why or why not?

Yes. Outbound connections are allowed.

5 Were you able to see a file listing? Why or why not?

Yes. The web browser uses PFTP, so the data channel is initiated from the inside and therefore is allowed by the PIX default policy.

6 What logging messages were generated on your PIX Firewall console?

a `302013: Built inbound TCP connection 85 for outside:192.168.1.50/1473 (192.168.1.50/1473) to inside:10.0.1.11/21 (192.168.1.10/21).`

b `302013: Built outbound TCP connection 86 for outside:192.168.1.50/1474 (192.168.1.50/1474) to inside:10.0.1.11/2525 (192.168.1.10/2525).`

c `302014: Teardown TCP connection 86 for outside:192.168.1.50/1474 to inside:10.0.1.11/2525 duration 0:00:01 bytes 363 TCP FINs.`

7 Were you able to connect to the inside host FTP server? Why or why not?

No. Both the control and data channel are initiated from the outside.

On completion of this chapter, you will be able to perform the following tasks:

- Identify, describe, and configure the attack guards in the PIX Firewall.
- Define intrusion detection.
- Describe signatures.
- Name and identify signature classes supported by the PIX Firewall.
- Configure the PIX Firewall to use intrusion detection system (IDS) signatures.
- Configure the PIX Firewall for shunning.

CHAPTER 12

Attack Guards, Intrusion Detection, and Shunning

The PIX Firewall includes basic intrusion detection system (IDS) capabilities as well as safeguards against known exploits of common services. It also has the ability to shun suspect traffic when certain conditions are met and the device is configured to do so. These capabilities have been expanded with each new version of the PIX Firewall software, thus increasing the value and security provided by the PIX family of firewalls. This chapter provides an overview of the PIX Firewall's attack guards, IDS, and shunning capabilities.

Attack Guards

This section discusses the guards put in place to protect against attacks by e-mail; Domain Name Systems (DNSs); fragmentation; authentication, authorization, and accounting (AAA); and SYN floods. The following guards are covered:

- Mail Guard
- DNS Guard
- FragGuard and Virtual Re-assembly
- AAA Flood Guard
- SYN Flood Guard

Mail Guard

The PIX Firewall's *Mail Guard* feature provides a safe conduit for Simple Mail Transfer Protocol (SMTP) connections from the outside to an inside e-mail server. Mail Guard lets you deploy a mail server within the internal network without exposing it to known security problems that are associated with mail-specific server implementations. Keep in mind, however, that placing mail servers inside your network is not recommended. You should ideally place mail servers on a demilitarized zone (DMZ).

| CAUTION | Mail Guard does not provide total protection for SMTP servers and should not be considered a replacement for proper security configuration, patch management, and appropriate antivirus and host intrusion detection products that can protect mail servers against e-mail–based viruses, worms, and host OS vulnerabilities. |

With Mail Guard enabled, only the SMTP commands specified in RFC 821 section 4.5.1 are allowed to be received by a mail server: HELO, MAIL, RCPT, DATA, RSET, NOOP, and QUIT.

| CAUTION | Mail servers that use the Extended SMTP (ESMTP) protocol such as Microsoft Exchange are not compatible with the PIX Firewall's Mail Guard feature. If you are using an ESMTP server, you should disable Mail Guard on the PIX. When the PIX Firewall receives an unrecognized ESMTP command, such as EHLO, it proxies a "500 command unrecognized" response and packets are dropped before reaching the mail server, resulting in possible loss of mail or reduced functionality. |

By default, the Cisco Secure PIX Firewall inspects port 25 connections for SMTP traffic. If you have SMTP servers using ports other than port 25, you must use the **fixup protocol smtp** command to have the PIX Firewall inspect these other ports for SMTP traffic.

Use the **no** form of the command to disable the inspection of traffic on the indicated port for SMTP connections. If the **fixup protocol smtp** command is not enabled for a given port, potential mail server vulnerabilities are exposed.

Using the **no fixup protocol smtp** command without any arguments causes the PIX Firewall to clear all previous **fixup protocol smtp** assignments, set port 25 back as the default, and disable the Mail Guard function. You can enable Mail Guard again using default settings with a single **fixup protocol smtp** command.

The syntax for the **fixup protocol smtp** command is as follows:

```
fixup protocol smtp [port[-port]]
no fixup protocol smtp[port[-port]]
```

port[-port] is a single port or port range that the PIX Firewall inspects for SMTP connections.

Example 12-1 shows the commands required for adding or removing Mail Guard with standard and nonstandard ports.

Example 12-1 *Mail Guard Commands*

```
pixfirewall(config)# fixup protocol smtp 25
pixfirewall(config)# fixup protocol smtp 2500-2800
pixfirewall(config)# no fixup protocol smtp
```

DNS Guard

Figure 12-1 illustrates DNS operation through a PIX Firewall. *DNS Guard* provides protection against DNS attacks that are common on the Internet. The DNS Guard feature has been enhanced in PIX Firewall Version 6.3(3) and provides protection in several ways:

- It automatically tears down the User Datagram Protocol (UDP) conduit on the PIX Firewall as soon as the first DNS response is received from any given DNS server. It does not wait for the default UDP timer to close the session.

- It prevents UDP session hijacking and denial-of-service (DoS) attacks.

- It drops DNS packets that are larger than a user-configurable size limit.

Figure 12-1 *DNS Guard*

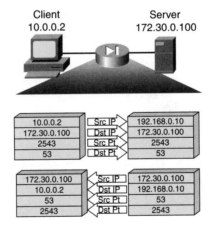

In an attempt to resolve a name to an IP address, a host can query the same DNS server multiple times. The DNS Guard feature of the PIX Firewall recognizes an outbound DNS query and allows only the first answer from the server back through the PIX Firewall. All other replies from the same source are discarded. DNS Guard closes the UDP conduit opened by the DNS request after the first DNS reply and does not wait for the normal UDP timeout (2 minutes by default). Because DNS is frequently attacked, leaving the connection open for the normal UDP timeout creates an unnecessary security risk.

A host can also query several different DNS servers. The connection to each server is handled separately because each request is sent separately. For example, if the DNS resolver sends three identical queries to three different servers, the PIX Firewall creates three different connections. As the PIX Firewall receives a reply through each connection, it shuts down that one connection. It does not tear down all three connections because of the first reply. The DNS responses of all servers queried are allowed through the PIX Firewall.

With PIX Firewall Versions 6.3(3) or higher, DNS Guard checks the size of DNS packets against a configurable allowed maximum length. The PIX Firewall drops DNS packets that exceed the maximum allowed length. The default DNS packet size limit is 512 bytes, but you can change its value using the **fixup protocol dns** command and the **maximum-length** option. The syntax for the **fixup protocol dns** command is as follows:

```
fixup protocol dns [maximum-length <512-65535>]
no fixup protocol dns
```

maximum-length specifies a maximum allowed size for DNS packets between 512 to 65,535 bytes. If you issue the **fixup protocol dns** command without specifying the **maximum-length** option, DNS Guard uses the default **maximum-length** value of 512 bytes. You can disable DNS Guard using the **no fixup protocol dns** command.

NOTE   Enhanced DNS Guard functions, including the ability to disable DNS Guard, are only available with PIX Firewall Software Version 6.3(3) or higher.

Example 12-2 shows the commands required for adding or removing DNS Guard with standard and nonstandard ports.

Example 12-2   *DNS Guard Commands*

```
pixfirewall(config)# fixup protocol dns
pixfirewall(config)# no fixup protocol dns
pixfirewall(config)# fixup protocol dns maximum-length 1024
```

In this example, the first statement configures DNS Guard with default settings. The second statement disables DNS Guard. The last statement enables DNS Guard and sets the maximum allowed length of DNS packets to 1024 bytes.

NOTE   The default maximum length value of 512 bytes for DNS packets provides the most secure configuration and is appropriate for most network settings.

FragGuard and Virtual Re-assembly

FragGuard and Virtual Re-assembly is a PIX Firewall feature that provides protection against IP fragments. Virtual Re-assembly is the process of gathering a set of IP fragments, verifying integrity and completeness, tagging each fragment in the set with the transport header, and refraining from coalescing the fragments into a full IP packet. Virtual Re-assembly, which is enabled by default, provides the benefits of full re-assembly by verifying the integrity of each fragment set and tagging it with the transport header. It also minimizes the buffer space that must be reserved for packet re-assembly. Full re-assembly of packets is expensive in terms of buffer space that must be reserved for collecting and coalescing the fragments. Because coalescing of fragments is not performed with virtual re-assembly, no pre-allocation of the buffer is needed.

FragGuard and Virtual Re-assembly performs full re-assembly of all Internet Control Message Protocol (ICMP) error messages and virtual re-assembly of the remaining IP fragments that are routed through the PIX Firewall. Syslog is used to log any fragment overlapping and small fragment offset anomalies, especially those caused by a Teardrop.c attack.

FragGuard is enabled by default and cannot be selectively enabled or disabled by interface. The **fragment** command enables the management of packet fragmentation used with FragGuard and Virtual Re-assembly and improves the PIX Firewall's compatibility with the Network File System (NFS), a client/server application that enables computer users to view and optionally store and update files on a remote computer as though they were on the user's own computer. In general, you should use the default values of the **fragment** command. However, if a large percentage of the network traffic through the PIX Firewall is NFS, additional tuning might be necessary to avoid database overflow.

NOTE   System log message 209003 provides additional information on IP fragments and is available on the Cisco PIX Firewall documentation site on Cisco.com. (Select Cisco Secure PIX Firewall documentation at http://www.cisco.com/univercd/home/home.htm.)

NOTE   PIX Firewall Software Versions 6.3 or higher no longer support the **sysopt security fragguard** command. FragGuard is now enabled by default, and you use the **fragment** command to configure packet fragmentation settings.

The syntax for the **fragment** commands is as follows:

```
fragment size database-limit [interface]
fragment chain chain-limit [interface]
fragment timeout seconds [interface]
```

Table 12-1 describes the **fragment** command arguments.

Table 12-1   **fragment** *Command Arguments*

Argument	Definition
size *database-limit*	Sets the maximum number of packets in the fragment database. The default is 200. The maximum is 1,000,000 or the total number of blocks.
interface	The PIX Firewall interface. If not specified, the command applies to all interfaces.
chain *chain-limit*	Specifies the maximum number of packets into which a full IP packet can be fragmented. The default is 24. The maximum is 8200.
timeout *seconds*	Specifies the maximum number of seconds that a packet fragment waits to be re-assembled after the first fragment is received before being discarded. The default is 5 seconds. The maximum is 30 seconds.

Example 12-3 illustrates the use of the **fragment** command to configure FragGuard settings on the PIX Firewall.

Example 12-3   *Configuring Fragmentation Settings Using the* **fragment** *Command*

```
pixfirewall(config)# fragment chain 1 inside
pixfirewall(config)# fragment outside size 1000
pixfirewall(config)# fragment chain 40 outside
pixfirewall(config)# fragment outside timeout 10
```

In Example 12-3, the first statement configures FragGuard to prevent all fragmented packets on the inside interface. (The **fragment chain 1** command prevents all fragmentation.) Next, the outside interface is configured with modified **fragment** command settings, including the **size** *database-limit* set at 1000, the *chain-limit* set at 40, and the *timeout* value increased to 10 seconds.

You are now familiar with the **fragment** command syntax, and the remainder of this section describes the use of the **fragment** command and its options to better adapt the behavior of FragGuard to your environment.

In an environment where the maximum transmission unit (MTU) between the NFS server and client is small, such as a WAN interface, the **fragment chain** option might require additional tuning. In this case, NFS over TCP is highly recommended to improve efficiency.

Setting the *database-limit* of the **size** option to a large value can make the PIX Firewall more vulnerable to a DoS attack by fragment flooding. How large a limit you can use also depends on the amount of available memory on the PIX Firewall. You can use the **show blocks** command to display the pre-allocated system buffer utilization on your PIX Firewall and avoid setting the *database-limit* option too high. Ideally, the *database-limit* should be set at less than the total number of blocks in the PIX Firewall's 1550 or 16384 memory pool.

Example 12-4 shows a sample output from the **show blocks** command issued on a PIX Firewall 525 with 256 MB of RAM. In this example, the PIX Firewall has no 16384 size blocks (typical for most configurations) and the 1550 memory pool values will be used. As shown, the PIX Firewall has 1951 blocks of memory available (indicated under the CNT or current column). You should therefore set the *database-limit* to less than 1951. (Again, smaller values provide better security.) The LOW column lists the fewest blocks available since the last reboot, indicating peak memory usage. If this number is 0 or significantly lower than the CNT number, it is an indication that the memory resources of the PIX might already be taxed heavily at times. Changing the *database-limit* from its default value in such circumstances might overtax the resources of the PIX Firewall and is not recommended.

Example 12-4   show blocks *Command Output*

```
pixfirewall# show blocks
  SIZE    MAX    LOW    CNT
     4   1600   1597   1600
    80    400    372    398
   256    500    400    500
  1550   2725   1686   1951
```

CAUTION   You can modify the **fragment** command default settings in these three ways: to allow more fragments in the database; to increase the number of packets into which a full IP packet can be fragmented; or to increase the timeout value. Modifying the **fragment** command default settings in any of these ways elevates the risk of a DoS attack by fragment flooding on the PIX Firewall and is memory and processor intensive. In general, Cisco recommends that packet fragmentation not be permitted on the network if at all possible.

TIP   If you use the PIX Firewall as a tunnel for Fiber Distributed Data Interface (FDDI) packets between routers, you should disable the FragGuard feature.

The **show fragment** command displays the states of the fragment databases. If you specify the interface name, only the database residing at the specified interface is displayed. The following list explains the output of the **show fragment** command:

- **Chain**—Maximum fragments for a single packet set by the **chain** option
- **Timeout**—Maximum seconds set by the **timeout** option
- **Queue**—Number of packets currently awaiting re-assembly
- **Assemble**—Number of packets successfully re-assembled
- **Fail**—Number of packets that failed to be re-assembled
- **Overflow**—Number of packets that overflowed the fragment database

Example 12-5 displays the output of the **show fragment** command on a PIX Firewall showing heavy usage of the fragment database. In this example, the PIX Firewall's standard fragmentation settings have been modified with the *database-limit* set at 2000 packets, the *chain-limit* set at 45 fragments, and the **timeout** value set at 10 seconds. The output shows that 1039 packets are queued for re-assembly and 829 packets have already been fully re-assembled. The output also indicates that no failures or overflows have occurred.

Example 12-5   **show fragment** *Command Output*

```
pixfirewall(config)# show fragment outside
Interface:outside
Size:2000, Chain:45, Timeout:10
Queue:1039, Assemble:829, Fail:0, Overflow:0
```

Use the **clear fragment** command to reset the fragment databases and defaults. This step causes the PIX Firewall to discard all fragments currently waiting for re-assembly and reset the **size**, **chain**, and **timeout** options to their default values.

AAA Flood Guard

The **floodguard** command enables the PIX Firewall to reclaim resources if the user authentication (uauth) subsystem runs out of resources. If an inbound or outbound uauth connection is being attacked or overused, the PIX Firewall actively reclaims TCP resources. When resources are depleted, the PIX Firewall lists messages about it being out of resources or out of TCP users. If the PIX Firewall uauth subsystem is depleted, TCP user resources in different states are reclaimed depending on urgency in the following order:

1 Timewait

2 LastAck

3 FinWait

4 Embryonic

5 Idle

The **floodguard** command is enabled by default.

The syntax for the **floodguard** command is as follows:

```
floodguard enable | disable
```

SYN Flood Guard

SYN flood attacks, also known as TCP flood or half-open connections attacks, are common DoS attacks perpetrated against IP servers. The attacker spoofs a nonexistent source IP address or IP addresses on the network of the target host and floods the target with SYN packets coming ostensibly from the spoofed host. SYN packets to a host are the first step in the three-way handshake of a TCP-type connection; therefore, the target responds as expected with SYN-ACK packets destined to the spoofed host or hosts. Because these SYN-ACK packets are sent to hosts that do not exist, the target sits and waits for the corresponding ACK packets that never show up. This process causes the target to overflow its port buffer with embryonic (half-open) connections and to stop responding to legitimate requests.

Figure 12-2 illustrates a SYN flood attack and the response it evokes:

- The attacker spoofs a nonexistent source IP address and floods the target with SYN packets.

- The target responds to the SYN packets by sending SYN-ACK packets to the spoofed hosts.

- The target overflows its port buffer with embryonic connections and stops responding to legitimate requests.

Figure 12-2 *SYN Flood Attack*

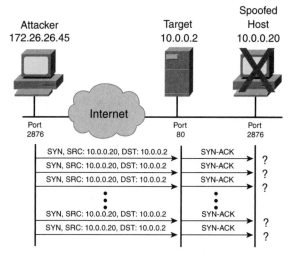

To protect internal hosts against DoS attacks, use the **static** command to limit the number of embryonic connections allowed to the server. Use the *em_limit* argument to limit the number of embryonic or half-open connections that the server or servers to be protected can handle.

The syntax used in the **static** command for enabling the SYN Flood Guard is as follows:

```
static [(prenat_interface, postnat_interface)] mapped_address | interface
    real_address [dns] [netmask mask] [norandomseq] [connection_limit [em_limit]]
```

Table 12-2 provides descriptions for the **static** command arguments used to configure SYN Flood Guard.

Table 12-2   **static** *Command Arguments*

Argument	Definition
prenat_interface	Interface that translation is applied to, usually the inside interface.
postnat_interface	The outside interface when *prenat_interface* is the inside interface.
mapped_address	The address into which *real_address* is translated.
interface	Specifies that the IP address should be taken from the PIX Firewall's interface.
real_address	The address to be mapped.
dns	Specifies that DNS replies that match the translation slot are translated.
mask	The network mask.
norandomseq	Disables the initial TCP/IP packet's sequence number randomization.
connection_limit	The maximum connections permitted to the real address. The default is 0 (unlimited).
em_limit	The maximum number of embryonic connections permitted to the real address. The default is 0 (unlimited).

Setting the *connection_limit* and *em_limit* arguments should not be taken lightly. If you set the limit too high, you risk overloading the IP stack of your statically translated host and falling victim to a DoS attack. If you set the limits too low, there is the risk of denying service to legitimate users. Example 12-6 demonstrates setting the maximum connection and embryonic connection limits on two hosts. The command in Example 12-6 is for illustration purposes only and should not be arbitrarily used. Although no firm guidelines exist for setting these limits, the general rule is to set the *em_limit* and *connection_limit* parameters to a value that won't have a negative impact on the host. Contact the company that wrote the IP stack of your hosts for information on the maximum number of TCP connection slots available, and set the *em_limit* lower than the maximum.

Example 12-6   *Configuring Maximum Connections and Embryonic Connection Limits to Statically Translated Hosts*

```
pixfirewall(config)# static (inside, outside) 200.100.1.10 10.100.1.10 netmask
  255.255.255.255 1000 1500
pixfirewall(config)# static (inside, outside) 200.100.1.15 10.100.1.15
  netmask 255.255.255.255 2000 2500
```

The **show local-host** command assists you in characterizing your "normal" load on a statically translated host, both before and after setting limits.

The **show local-host** command shows you the current number of connections and embryonic connections against any limit you have set using the **static** command.

Example 12-7 shows sample output from the **show local-host** command, indicating that this host has no embryonic connection limit set. (Therefore, it is set to unlimited.)

Example 12-7 *show local-hosts Command Output*

```
pixfirewall# show local-host 10.1.1.15
local host: <10.1.1.15>, conn(s)/limit = 2/0, embryonic(s)/limit = 0/0
   Xlate(s):
         PAT Global 172.16.3.200(1024) Local 10.1.1.15(55812)
         PAT Global 172.16.3.200(1025) Local 10.1.1.15(56836)
         PAT Global 172.16.3.200(1026) Local 10.1.1.15(57092)
         PAT Global 172.16.3.200(1027) Local 10.1.1.15(56324)
         PAT Global 172.16.3.200(1028) Local 10.1.1.15(7104)
   Conn(s):
         TCP out 192.150.49.10:23 in 10.1.1.15:1246 idle 0:00:20 Bytes 449 flags UIO
         TCP out 192.150.49.10:21 in 10.1.1.15:1247 idle 0:00:10 Bytes 359 flags UIO
```

The Xlate(s) field describes the translation slot information and the Conn(s) field provides connection state information.

Use the **nat** command to protect external hosts against DoS attacks and to limit the number of embryonic connections allowed to the server. Use the *em_limit* argument to limit the number of embryonic or half-open connections that the server or servers to be protected can handle.

The syntax of the **nat** command for enabling the SYN Flood Guard is as follows:

```
nat [(if_name)] nat_id {local_ip [mask]} | {access-list acl_id} [dns] [norandomseq]
    [outside] [conn_limit [em_limit]]
```

Table 12-3 describes the **Nat** command arguments.

Table 12-3 **nat** *Command Arguments*

Argument	Definition
if_name	The network interface name.
nat_id	A number used for matching with a corresponding global pool of IP addressees. The matching global pool must use the same ID.
local_ip	The IP address of hosts or networks that are translated to a global pool of IP addresses.
mask	The network mask for the address.
access-list	Specifies policy-based translation or **nat 0** to exempt the host or network from translation.
acl_id	ACL name for use with the **access-list** option.

continues

Table 12-3 **nat** *Command Arguments (Continued)*

Argument	Definition
outside	An argument that specifies that the **nat** command applies to the outside interface address.
dns	An argument that specifies that DNS replies that match the xlate are translated.
norandomseq	An argument that disables the initial TCP/IP packet sequence number randomization.
conn_limit	The maximum number of TCP connections permitted from the interface you specify.
em_limit	The embryonic connection limit. The default is 0, which means unlimited connections. Set it lower for slower systems, higher for faster systems.

Setting the maximum connection and embryonic connection limits on outbound traffic must be considered carefully. If you set the limit too high, you risk giving individuals in your organization the ability to perpetrate a DoS attack. If the limits are set too low, there is the risk of denying service to legitimate internal users. Example 12-8 demonstrates how to set the maximum connection and embryonic connection limits for the inside and DMZ interfaces. The DMZ interface uses much lower limits due to the low number of connections initiated from that interface.

Example 12-8 *Configuring Maximum Connections and Embryonic Connection Limits to Protect Against Initiating DoS Attacks*

```
pixfirewall(config)# nat (inside) 1 0.0.0.0 0.0.0.0 5000 5000
pixfirewall(config)# nat (dmz) 1 0.0.0.0 0.0.0.0 500 500
```

In PIX Firewall Software Versions 5.2 and higher, the **static** command's SYN Flood Guard feature offers an improved mechanism for protecting systems reachable via a static and TCP conduit from TCP SYN attacks. Previously, if an embryonic connection limit was configured in a **static** command statement, the PIX Firewall simply dropped new connection attempts after the embryonic threshold was reached. This process could allow even a modest attack to stop an organization's web traffic. For **static** command statements without an embryonic connection limit, the PIX Firewall passes all traffic. If the target of an attack has no TCP SYN attack protection or insufficient protection (as do most operating systems), its embryonic connection table overloads and all traffic stops.

With the improved TCP intercept feature in PIX Firewall Versions 5.2 and higher, after the optional embryonic connection limit is reached, and until the embryonic connection count falls below this threshold, every SYN bound for the affected server is intercepted. For each SYN, the PIX Firewall responds on behalf of the server with an empty SYN/ACK segment. The PIX Firewall retains pertinent state information, drops the packet, and waits for the client's acknowledgement. If the ACK is received, a copy of the client's SYN segment is sent to the server and the TCP three-way handshake is performed between the PIX Firewall and the server. Only if this three-way handshake completes is the connection allowed to resume as normal.

The TCP intercept feature requires no special configuration. The embryonic connection limits on both the **static** and **nat** commands just have the new behavior.

Antispoofing

Due to inherent weaknesses in the IP protocol, it is relatively simple to modify the IP packet header and forge the source address of the packet. This technique is commonly referred to as *IP spoofing* and is a frequently used form of attack on the Internet. Because most access control lists (ACLs) used by routers and firewalls deny or permit traffic based on source and destination addresses of the packet, IP spoofing can be an effective method for gaining unauthorized access or initiating attacks.

You can configure the PIX Firewall to protect the network against common IP spoofing attacks. With antispoofing configured, the PIX Firewall performs a route lookup based on the source address in addition to its standard lookup based on the destination address. PIX Firewall drops the packet if it cannot find a route for the packet's source address or the route does not match the appropriate interface where the packet arrived (for example, packets with internal source IP addresses arriving on the outside interface of the PIX).

The antispoofing feature is disabled by default, but you can enable it on each interface using the **ip verify reverse-path** command. The syntax of the **ip verify reverse-path** command is as follows:

```
ip verify reverse-path interface if_name
```

if_name specifies the name of the interface on which antispoofing is being configured. For example, to enable antispoofing on the outside interface, issue the following command:

```
pixfirewall(config)# ip verify reverse-path interface outside
```

NOTE   You must configure a default route for the outside interface when you enable antispoofing on the outside interface using the **ip verify reverse-path** command. The **route** command statement must have 0.0.0.0 0.0.0.0 for the IP address and network mask (default gateway).

Use the **no** form of the command to clear IP spoofing protection for an interface, or issue the clear **ip verify** command to disable antispoofing on all interfaces. Use **show ip verify** to view the current configuration.

Intrusion Detection

This section presents an overview of IDSs and outlines the IDS capabilities of the PIX Firewall.

PIX Firewall Software Versions 5.2 and higher have Cisco IDS capabilities. *Intrusion detection* is the ability to detect attacks against a network. Chapter 1, "The Cisco Role in Network Security," defined the three types of network attacks, but the definitions are repeated here to spark your memory:

- **Reconnaissance attack**—An intruder attempts to discover and map systems, services, or vulnerabilities.

- **Access attack**—An intruder attacks networks or systems to retrieve data, gain access, or escalate access privileges.

- **DoS attack**—An intruder attacks a network in such a way that damages or corrupts your computer system or denies you and others access to networks, systems, or services.

The PIX Firewall performs intrusion detection by using intrusion detection signatures. A *signature* is a set of rules pertaining to typical intrusion activity. Highly skilled network engineers research known attacks and vulnerabilities and can develop signatures to detect these attacks and vulnerabilities.

NOTE   Unlike IDS devices that operate passively and rely on other devices and mechanisms to block malicious network activity, a PIX Firewall is an *inline* device that actively controls the flow of traffic across its interfaces. Inline operation allows the PIX Firewall to provide active protection against known network threats, a process commonly referred to as *intrusion protection*.

With intrusion detection enabled, the PIX Firewall can detect signatures and generate a response when this set of rules is matched to network activity. It can monitor packets for more than 55 intrusion detection signatures and can be configured to send an alarm to a syslog server, drop the packet, or reset the TCP connection. The signatures supported by the PIX Firewall are a subset of the signatures supported by the Cisco IDS product family.

NOTE   The number of signatures included in the PIX Firewall depends on the version of PIX Firewall software you are running. Refer to documentation on Cisco.com for the latest information on IDS signatures included in your version of the PIX OS.

The PIX Firewall can detect two different types of signatures: informational signatures and attack signatures. *Information-class* signatures are signatures that are triggered by normal network activity that in itself is not considered to be malicious but can be used to determine the validity of an attack or used for forensics purposes. *Attack-class* signatures are signatures that are triggered by an activity known to be, or that could lead to, unauthorized data retrieval, system access, or privilege escalation.

Table 12-4 lists examples of the IDS signatures supported by the PIX Firewall.

Table 12-4   *PIX Firewall IDS Signature Examples*

Message #	Signature ID	Signature Title	Signature Type
400000	1000	IP options-bad option list	Informational
400001	1001	IP options-record packet route	Informational
400002	1002	IP options-timestamp	Informational
400003	1003	IP options-security	Informational
400007	1100	IP fragment attack	Attack
400010	2000	ICMP echo reply	Informational
400011	2001	ICMP host unreachable	Informational
400013	2003	ICMP redirect	Informational
400014	2004	ICMP echo request	Informational
400023	2150	Fragmented ICMP traffic	Attack
400024	2151	Large ICMP traffic	Attack
400025	2154	Ping-of-death attack	Attack
400032	4051	UDP snork attack	Attack
400035	6051	DNS zone transfer	Attack
400041	6103	Proxied remote-procedure call (RPC) request	Attack

IDS syslog messages all start with %PIX-4-4000*nn* and have the following format: %PIX-4-4000*nn* IDS:*sig_num sig_msg* from *ip_addr* to *ip_addr* on interface *int_name*. Two examples are %PIX-4-400013 IDS:2003 ICMP redirect from 10.4.1.2 to 10.2.1.1 on interface dmz and %PIX-4-400032 IDS:4051 UDP Snork attack from 10.1.1.1 to 192.168.1.1 on interface outside.

Refer to *System Log Messages for the Cisco Secure PIX Firewall Version 6.2* or *System Log Messages for the Cisco Secure PIX Firewall Version 6.3* for a list of all supported messages. You can view documentation online by searching for "Cisco PIX Firewall System Log Messages, Version 6.2 or 6.3" at Cisco.com.

Configuring IDS

You enable intrusion detection, or auditing, on the PIX Firewall with the **ip audit** commands. Using the **ip audit** commands, you can create audit policies to specify the traffic that is audited or to designate actions to be taken when a signature is detected. After you create a policy, you can apply it to any PIX Firewall interface.

Each interface can have two policies: one for informational signatures and one for attack signatures. When a policy for a given signature class is created and applied to an interface, all supported signatures of that class are monitored unless you disable them with the **ip audit signature disable** command.

You perform auditing by looking at the IP packets as they arrive at an input interface. For example, if you apply an attack policy to the outside interface, attack signatures are triggered when attack traffic arrives at the outside interface in an inward direction, whether it's newly initiated inbound traffic or return traffic from an existing outbound connection.

Figure 12-3 shows an attack on a PIX Firewall that has an attack policy that contains the alarm and drop actions applied to its outside interface. Therefore, the following series of events takes place:

Figure 12-3 *Intrusion Detection in the PIX Firewall*

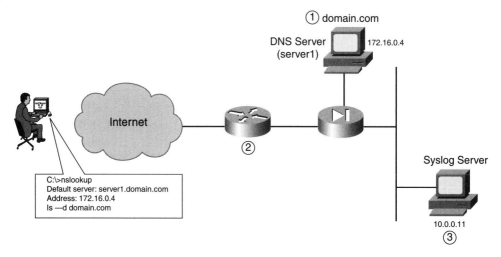

Step 1   The intruder attempts to transfer a DNS zone from the DNS server at 172.16.0.4 on the DMZ.

Step 2   The PIX Firewall detects an attack.

Step 3   The PIX Firewall drops the connection and sends an IDS syslog message to the syslog server at 10.0.0.11.

Use the **ip audit** command to configure IDS signature use. First create a policy with the **ip audit name** command, and then apply the policy to an interface with the **ip audit interface** command.

There are two variations of the **ip audit name** command: **ip audit name info** and **ip audit name attack**. You use the **ip audit name info** command to create policies for signatures classified as informational. All informational signatures, except those disabled or excluded by the **ip audit signature** command, become part of the policy. The **ip audit name attack** command performs the same function for signatures classified as attack signatures.

The **ip audit name** commands also allow you to specify actions to be taken when a signature is triggered. If you define a policy without actions, the default actions take effect. The default action for both attack and information signatures is alarm.

You can use the **no ip audit name** command to remove an audit policy. The **show ip audit name** command displays audit policies. Use the **no ip audit interface** command to remove a policy from an interface. Use the **show ip audit interface** command to display the interface configuration.

The syntax for these **ip audit** commands is as follows:

```
ip audit name audit_name info [action [alarm] [drop] [reset]]
ip audit name audit_name attack [action [alarm] [drop] [reset]]
ip audit interface if_name audit_name
```

Table 12-5 describes the **ip audit name** and **ip audit interface** command arguments.

Table 12-5   **ip audit name** *and* **ip audit interface** *Command Arguments*

Argument	Definition
audit name	Specifies signatures, except those disabled or excluded by the **ip audit signature** command, as part of the policy.
audit_name	Audits the policy name viewed with the **show ip audit name** command.
action *actions*	The **alarm** option that indicates that when a signature match is detected in a packet, the PIX Firewall reports the event to all configured syslog servers. The **drop** option drops the offending packet. The **reset** option drops the offending packet and closes the connection if it is part of an active connection. The default is **alarm**.
audit interface	Applies an audit specification or policy (via the **ip audit name** command) to an interface.
if_name	The interface to which the policy is applied.

Example 12-9 shows the commands required to configure an attack policy named ATTACKPOLICY so that when the PIX Firewall detects an attack signature on its outside interface, it reports an event to all configured syslog servers, drops the offending packet, and closes the connection if it is part of an active connection.

Example 12-9 *Configuring IDS on the PIX Firewall*

```
pixfirewall(config)# ip audit name ATTACKPOLICY attack action alarm reset
pixfirewall(config)# ip audit interface outside ATTACKPOLICY
```

The **ip audit attack** command specifies the default actions to be taken for attack signatures. The **no ip audit attack** command resets the action to be taken for attack signatures to the default action. The **show ip audit attack** command displays the default attack actions. The **ip audit info**, **no ip audit info**, and **show ip audit info** commands perform the same functions for signatures classified as informational. Specify the **ip audit info** command without an action option to cancel event reactions.

The syntax for these **ip audit** commands is as follows:

```
ip audit attack [action [alarm] [drop] [reset]]
ip audit info [action [alarm] [drop] [reset]]
```

Table 12-6 provides descriptions for the **ip audit attack** and **ip audit info** command arguments.

Table 12-6 **ip audit attack** *and* **ip audit info** *Command Arguments*

Argument	Definition
audit attack	Specifies the default actions to be taken for attack signatures.
audit info	Specifies the default actions to be taken for informational signatures.
action *actions*	The **alarm** option that indicates that when a signature match is detected in a packet, the PIX Firewall reports the event to all configured syslog servers. The **drop** option drops the offending packet. The **reset** option drops the offending packet and closes the connection if it is part of an active connection. The default is **alarm**.

Example 12-10 shows the command required to configure the PIX Firewall so that when it detects an information signature, it reports an event to all configured syslog servers and drops the offending packet.

Example 12-10 *Specifying the Default Action for Signatures*

```
pixfirewall(config)# ip audit info action alarm drop
```

If you want to exclude a signature from auditing, use the **ip audit signature disable** command. You use the **no ip audit signature** command to re-enable a signature, and the **show ip audit signature** command displays disabled signatures. Settings configured with these commands apply to all interfaces.

The syntax for the **ip audit signature** command is as follows:

```
ip audit signature signature_number disable
```

Table 12-7 provides descriptions for the **ip audit signature disable** command arguments.

Table 12-7   **ip audit signature disable** *Command Arguments*

Argument	Definition
audit signature	Specifies what messages to display, attaches a global policy to a signature, and disables or excludes a signature from auditing
signature_number	The intrusion detection signature number

Example 12-11 shows the command required to disable signature 6102.

Example 12-11   *Disabling a Specific IDS Signature*

```
pixfirewall(config)# ip audit signature 6102 disable
```

Shunning

When combined with a Cisco IDS sensor, the PIX Firewall's *shun* feature allows a PIX Firewall to dynamically respond to an attacking host by preventing new connections and disallowing packets from any existing connection. A Cisco IDS device instructs the PIX Firewall to shun sources of traffic when those sources of traffic are determined to be malicious.

The **shun** command, intended for use primarily by a Cisco IDS device, applies a blocking function to an interface receiving an attack. Packets containing the IP source address of the attacking host are dropped and logged until the blocking function is removed manually or by the Cisco IDS master unit. No traffic from the IP source address is allowed to traverse the PIX Firewall, and any remaining connections time out as part of the normal processing. The blocking function of the **shun** command is applied whether or not a connection with the specified host address is currently active.

The offending host can be inside or outside the PIX Firewall. If you use the **shun** command only with the source IP address of the host, no further traffic from the offending host is allowed.

The **show shun** command displays all shuns currently enabled in the exact format specified. The **no** form of the **shun** command disables a shun based on the *src_ip*.

NOTE   PIX Firewall shunning is only supported with Cisco Secure IDS devices with IDS Software Version 3.0 or higher.

The syntax for the **shun** command is as follows:

```
shun src_ip [dst_ip sport dport [protocol]]
show shun src_ip
clear shun [statistics]
```

Table 12-8 describes the **shun** command arguments.

Table 12-8   **shun** *Command Arguments*

Argument	Definition
clear	Argument that disables all shuns currently enabled and clears shun statistics. Specifying **statistics** only clears the counters for that interface.
dport	The destination port of the connection causing the shun.
dst_ip	The address of the target host.
protocol	The optional IP protocol, such as UDP or TCP.
sport	The source port of the connection causing the shun.
src_ip	The address of the attacking host.
statistics	Argument that clears only interface counters.

Figure 12-4 illustrates the shunning functionality in PIX Firewall. In this figure, host 172.26.26.45 has been attempting a DNS zone transfer from host 192.168.0.10 using a source port other than the well-known DNS port of TCP 53. The offending host (172.26.26.45) has made a connection with the victim (192.168.0.10) with TCP.

Figure 12-4   *Shunning an Attacker*

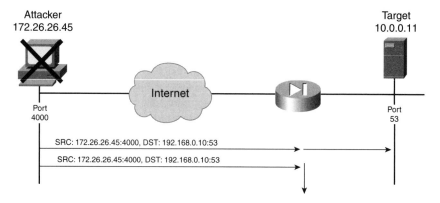

The connection in the PIX Firewall connection table reads as follows:

```
172.26.26.45, 4000 -> 10.0.0.11 PROT TCP
```

The following **shun** command is applied:

```
pixfirewall(config)# shun 172.26.26.45 192.168.0.10 4000 53
```

The PIX Firewall deletes the connection from its connection table and prevents packets from 172.26.26.45 from reaching the inside host.

NOTE   On Figure 12-4, the PIX Firewall configuration contains a static mapping of host 10.0.0.11 to global address 192.168.0.10.

Summary

This section summarizes the information you learned in this chapter:

- The PIX Firewall has the following attack guards to help protect systems from malicious attacks:
    - Mail Guard
    - DNS Guard
    - FragGuard and Virtual Re-assembly
    - AAA Flood Guard
    - SYN Flood Defender
- PIX Firewall Software Versions 5.2 and higher support intrusion detection.
- Intrusion detection is the ability to detect attacks against a network, including the following:
    - Reconnaissance attacks
    - Access attacks
    - DoS attacks
- The PIX Firewall supports signature-based intrusion detection.
- Each signature can generate a unique alarm and response.
- Informational signatures collect information to help determine the validity of an attack or are used for forensics.
- Attack signatures trigger on an activity known to be, or that could lead to, unauthorized data retrieval, system access, or privilege escalation.
- You can configure the PIX Firewall to shun the source addresses of attacking hosts.
- The PIX Firewall provides automatic shunning capability when you use it with Cisco Secure IDS devices with Software Version 3.0 and higher.

Chapter Review Questions

To test what you have learned in this chapter, answer the following questions and then refer to Appendix A, "Answers to Chapter Review Questions," for the answers:

1 You are running Microsoft Exchange as your mail server. What should you do regarding the Mail Guard feature of the PIX Firewall?

2 What type of attack is mitigated by the SYN Flood Guard feature of the PIX Firewall?

3 What two types of signatures are available on the Cisco PIX Firewall?

4 What command do you use to enable the IDS functionality of PIX Firewall?

5 Which version of the Cisco Secure IDS software is required for shunning on the PIX Firewall?

6 How is DNS Guard enabled, and what is its major security benefit?

Lab Exercise—Configure Intrusion Detection

Complete the following lab exercise to practice the intrusion detection concepts covered in this chapter. Use the following initial configuration commands and continue with the rest of the lab exercises.

NOTE   Many of the settings shown in this initial configuration are default values, and you do not need to enter them on your PIX Firewall. Specific commands that you must enter appear in bold for your convenience.

```
:
interface ethernet0 100full
interface ethernet1 100full
interface ethernet2 100full
nameif ethernet0 outside security0
nameif ethernet1 inside security100
nameif ethernet2 dmz security50
enable password 8Ry2YjIyt7RRXU24 encrypted
passwd 2KFQnbNIdI.2KYOU encrypted
hostname pixfirewall
domain-name cisco.com
fixup protocol dns maximum-length 512
fixup protocol ftp 21
fixup protocol h323 h225 1720
fixup protocol h323 ras 1718-1719
fixup protocol http 80
fixup protocol rsh 514
fixup protocol rtsp 554
fixup protocol sip 5060
fixup protocol sip udp 5060
fixup protocol skinny 2000
```

```
fixup protocol smtp 25
fixup protocol sqlnet 1521
fixup protocol tftp 69
access-list allow_icmp permit icmp any any
pager lines 24
logging on
logging timestamp
logging trap debugging
logging host inside 10.0.1.11
mtu outside 1500
mtu inside 1500
mtu dmz 1500
ip address outside 192.168.1.2 255.255.255.0
ip address inside 10.0.1.1 255.255.255.0
ip address dmz 172.16.1.1 255.255.255.0
ip audit info action alarm
ip audit attack action alarm
pdm location 10.0.1.0 255.255.255.0 inside
pdm location 10.0.1.11 255.255.255.255 inside
pdm location 172.16.1.2 255.255.255.255 dmz
pdm history enable
arp timeout 14400
global (outside) 1 192.168.1.150-192.168.1.200
nat (inside) 1 0.0.0.0 0.0.0.0 0 0
nat (dmz) 1 0.0.0.0 0.0.0.0 0 0
static (inside,outside) 192.168.1.10 10.0.1.11 netmask 255.255.255.255 0 0
static (dmz,outside) 192.168.1.11 172.16.1.2 netmask 255.255.255.255 0 0
static (inside,dmz) 10.0.1.0 10.0.1.0 netmask 255.255.255.0 0 0
access-group allow_icmp in interface outside
timeout xlate 3:00:00
timeout conn 1:00:00 half-closed 0:10:00 udp 0:02:00 rpc 0:10:00 h225 1:00:00
timeout h323 0:05:00 mgcp 0:05:00 sip 0:30:00 sip_media 0:02:00
timeout uauth 0:05:00 absolute
aaa-server TACACS+ protocol tacacs+
aaa-server RADIUS protocol radius
aaa-server LOCAL protocol local
http server enable
http 10.0.1.0 255.255.255.0 inside
no snmp-server location
no snmp-server contact
snmp-server community public
no snmp-server enable traps
floodguard enable
telnet 10.0.1.0 255.255.255.0 inside
telnet timeout 5
ssh timeout 5
console timeout 0
terminal width 80
Cryptochecksum:aa0cc6e47d705ed128e041c2c2a8412b
: end
```

Objectives

In this lab exercise, you perform the following tasks:

- Configure the use of Cisco IDS information signatures and send Cisco IDS syslog output to a syslog server.

- Configure the use of IDS attack signatures and send Cisco IDS syslog output to a syslog server.

Lab Topology

Figure 12-5 displays the topology you need for the lab exercises in this chapter.

Table 21-5 *IDS Lab Exercise Visual Objective*

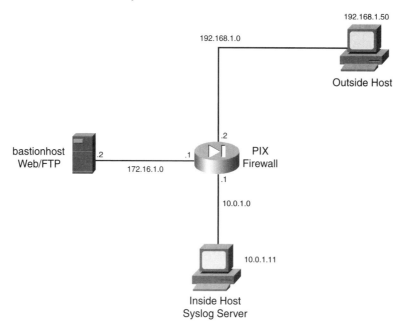

Equipment required to perform the lab includes the following:

- A PIX Firewall with at least three interfaces
- Category 5 patch cables
- PC host running a web server and FTP server
- PC host for the outside subnet with a web browser and FTP client
- PC host for the inside subnet running the Kiwi syslog server (available at http://www.kiwisyslog.com)

Task 1—Configure the Use of IDS Information Signatures and Send Cisco IDS Syslog Output to a Syslog Server

Complete the following steps to configure the use of Cisco IDS signatures and to send Cisco IDS syslog output to a syslog server:

Step 1 Verify that you can ping your internal host from your outside host. The ping should succeed:

```
C:\> ping 192.168.1.10
```

Step 2   Specify an information signature policy on your PIX Firewall:

```
pixfirewall(config)# ip audit name INFOPOLICY info action alarm reset
```

Step 3   Apply the information signature policy to the outside interface:

```
pixfirewall(config)# ip audit interface outside INFOPOLICY
```

Step 4   Open and minimize the Kiwi syslog daemon on your desktop.

Step 5   Return to your outside host command line and attempt to ping your internal host. The ping should fail:

```
C:\> ping 192.168.1.10
```

Step 6   Observe the messages that appear on the Kiwi syslog daemon display. The log should be similar to the following:

```
%PIX-4-400014: IDS:2004 ICMP echo request from 192.168.1.50 to
192.168.1.10 on interface outside
%PIX-4-400014: IDS:2004 ICMP echo request from 192.168.1.50 to
192.168.1.10 on interface outside
%PIX-4-400014: IDS:2004 ICMP echo request from 192.168.1.50 to
192.168.1.10 on interface outside
%PIX-4-400014: IDS:2004 ICMP echo request from 192.168.1.50 to
192.168.1.10 on interface outside
```

Step 7   Remove the information signature policy from the outside interface:

```
pixfirewall(config)# no ip audit interface outside INFOPOLICY
```

Step 8   Remove the audit policy:

```
pixfirewall(config)# no ip audit name INFOPOLICY
```

Step 9   Verify that the information signature policy has been removed from the outside interface, the default informational actions have been restored, and the IP audit name has been removed:

```
pixfirewall(config)# show ip audit interface
pixfirewall(config)# show ip audit info
ip audit info action alarm
pixfirewall(config)# show ip audit name
```

Task 2—Configure the Use of IDS Attack Signatures and Send Cisco IDS Syslog Output to a Syslog Server

Complete the following steps to configure the use of IDS attack signatures and send IDS syslog output to a syslog server:

Step 1   From your internal host command line, ping your bastion host with an ICMP packet size of 10,000. The ping should succeed:

```
C:\> ping -l 10000 172.16.1.2
```

Step 2   Specify an attack policy:

```
pixfirewall(config)# ip audit name ATTACKPOLICY attack action alarm
reset
```

Step 3   Apply the attack policy to the inside interface:

```
pixfirewall(config)# ip audit interface inside ATTACKPOLICY
```

Step 4   From your internal host command line, ping your bastion host with an
ICMP packet size of 10,000. The ping should fail:

```
C:\> ping -l 10000 172.16.1.2
```

Step 5   Observe the messages that appear on the Kiwi syslog daemon display.
The log should be similar to the following:

```
%PIX-4-400025: IDS:2154 ICMP ping of death from 10.0.1.11 to 172.16.1.2
on interface inside
%PIX-4-400023: IDS:2150 ICMP fragment from 10.0.1.11 to 172.16.1.2 on
interface inside
%PIX-4-400023: IDS:2150 ICMP fragment from 10.0.1.11 to 172.16.1.2 on
interface inside
%PIX-4-400023: IDS:2150 ICMP fragment from 10.0.1.11 to 172.16.1.2 on
interface inside
%PIX-4-400023: IDS:2150 ICMP fragment from 10.0.1.11 to 172.16.1.2 on
interface inside
%PIX-4-400023: IDS:2150 ICMP fragment from 10.0.1.11 to 172.16.1.2 on
interface inside
%PIX-4-400023: IDS:2150 ICMP fragment from 10.0.1.11 to 172.16.1.2 on
interface inside
%PIX-4-400025: IDS:2154 ICMP ping of death from 10.0.1.11 to 172.16.1.2
on interface inside
%PIX-4-400023: IDS:2150 ICMP fragment from 10.0.1.11 to 172.16.1.2 on
interface inside
%PIX-4-400023: IDS:2150 ICMP fragment from 10.0.1.11 to 172.16.1.2 on
interface inside
%PIX-4-400023: IDS:2150 ICMP fragment from 10.0.1.11 to 172.16.1.2 on
interface inside
%PIX-4-400023: IDS:2150 ICMP fragment from 10.0.1.11 to 172.16.1.2 on
interface inside
%PIX-4-400023: IDS:2150 ICMP fragment from 10.0.1.11 to 172.16.1.2 on
interface inside
%PIX-4-400023: IDS:2150 ICMP fragment from 10.0.1.11 to 172.16.1.2 on
interface inside
```

Step 6   From your internal host command line, ping your bastion host with an
increased ICMP packet size. The ping should fail:

```
C:\> ping -l 20000 172.16.1.2
```

Step 7   Observe the messages that appear on the Kiwi syslog daemon display.
The log should be similar to the following:

```
%PIX-4-400025: IDS:2154 ICMP ping of death from 10.0.1.11 to 172.16.1.2
on interface inside
%PIX-4-400025: IDS:2154 ICMP ping of death from 10.0.1.11 to 172.16.1.2
on interface inside
%PIX-4-400025: IDS:2154 ICMP ping of death from 10.0.1.11 to 172.16.1.2
on interface inside
%PIX-4-400025: IDS:2154 ICMP ping of death from 10.0.1.11 to 172.16.1.2
on interface inside

%PIX-4-400023: IDS:2150 ICMP fragment from 10.0.1.11 to 172.16.1.2 on
interface inside
%PIX-4-400023: IDS:2150 ICMP fragment from 10.0.1.11 to 172.16.1.2 on
interface inside
%PIX-4-400023: IDS:2150 ICMP fragment from 10.0.1.11 to 172.16.1.2 on
interface inside
%PIX-4-400023: IDS:2150 ICMP fragment from 10.0.1.11 to 172.16.1.2 on
interface inside
%PIX-4-400023: IDS:2150 ICMP fragment from 10.0.1.11 to 172.16.1.2 on
interface inside
```

On completion of this chapter, you will be able to perform the following tasks:

- Define authentication, authorization, and accounting (AAA).
- Describe the differences between authentication, authorization, and accounting.
- Describe how users authenticate to the PIX Firewall.
- Describe how cut-through proxy technology works.
- Name the AAA protocols supported by the PIX Firewall.
- Install and configure Cisco Secure Access Control Server (CSACS) for Windows NT.
- Define and configure downloadable access control lists (ACLs).
- Configure AAA on the PIX Firewall.

Authentication, Authorization, and Accounting

AAA is a set of services that the PIX Firewall and other networking devices use to provide secure access to the device itself or various other network resources. In addition to user access control, authentication and authorization can also control access between network devices and networks. AAA provides the following functionality:

Authentication—This service validates the identity of the user (who you are).

Authorization—This service grants access to specific resources based on the identity of the user validated by authentication (what can you do).

Accounting—This service tracks and records the activity performed by users (what you did).

This chapter introduces the AAA concepts and how the Cisco PIX Firewall supports them.

AAA Basics

Authentication determines a user's identity and verifies the information. Traditional authentication uses a name (or some unique identifier) and a fixed password. Accessing a device or network with a user ID defines who the user is. The authentication server can be configured to allow specific *authorization*, based on the user ID and password, once a user has authenticated. *Authorization* defines what the user can do. When a user has logged in and is accessing a service, host, or network, you can keep a record of what that user is doing. *Accounting* is tracking user actions. Having an accounting record of what is being accessed in a network can be very helpful. If problems arise in the network, having historical records can help to identify and eventually rectify those problems. You can also use accounting records for billing, forensics, and planning.

The PIX Firewall uses AAA to identify who the user is, what the user can do, and what the user did. The basic access controls for the PIX itself are based on IP addresses and ports. These access controls do not provide a mechanism to identify individual users and then control traffic flow based on that user. Authentication is valid without authorization. Authorization is never valid without authentication.

When used with the PIX, AAA is generally processed in the following manner:

1 The client requests access to a service. The PIX, as a gateway between the client and the device the service is on, requires the client to forward a user ID and password (based on the request and the configuration on the PIX).

2 The PIX receives that information and forwards it to an AAA server, where the request is confirmed to be permitted or is denied. A *server* is defined as a logical entity that provides any of the three AAA functions. The AAA server can hold the user ID/ password database for confirmation that a client can access the requested service.

Using AAA, it is possible to give certain authenticated users or devices access to the network while restricting access to others. Consider the example in which you have 100 users inside the network and you want only 6 of these users to perform FTP, Telnet, or HTTP outside the network. You can tell the PIX Firewall to authenticate outbound traffic and give all six users identifications on the TACACS+ or RADIUS AAA server. With simple authentication, these six users are authenticated with usernames and passwords and then permitted outside the network. The remaining users cannot access the resources outside the network. The PIX Firewall prompts users for their usernames and passwords and then passes their usernames and passwords to the TACACS+ or RADIUS AAA server. Depending on the response, the PIX Firewall opens or denies the connection.

NOTE	Having a separate AAA server reduces the CPU load on the firewall and simplifies configuration and management of the firewall. It also allows you to maintain one set of accounts, authorization policies, and accounting to share among multiple PIX Firewalls, thus increasing scalability.

Suppose you want one of these users to perform FTP, but not HTTP or Telnet, to the outside network. You must add authorization—that is, authorize what users can do in addition to authenticating who they are. This process is only valid with TACACS+. When you add authorization to the PIX Firewall, it first prompts the user for a username and password to pass on to the AAA server. It then sends an authorization request telling the AAA server what command the user is trying to perform. With the server set up properly, the user is allowed to perform FTP but is not allowed to perform HTTP or Telnet.

NOTE	Due to a limitation of the RADIUS protocol, PIX Firewall command authorization is not supported in RADIUS. You can use the TACACS+ service to enable command authorization.

You can authenticate with the PIX Firewall in one of three ways:

Telnet—You get a prompt generated by the PIX Firewall, as shown on the example in Figure 13-1. You have up to four chances to log in. If the username or password fails after the fourth attempt, the PIX Firewall drops the connection. If authentication and authorization are successful, the destination server prompts you for a username and password.

Figure 13-1 *What the User Sees*

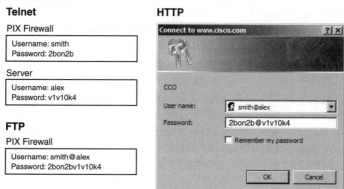

FTP—You get a prompt from the FTP program. If you enter an incorrect password, the connection is dropped immediately. If the username or password on the authentication database differs from the username or password on the remote host which you are accessing via FTP, enter the username and password in the following formats:

aaa_username@remote_username

aaa_password@remote_password

The PIX Firewall sends the *aaa_username* and *aaa_password* to the AAA server, and if authentication and authorization are successful, the *remote_username* and *remote_password* are passed to the destination FTP server.

NOTE   Some FTP GUIs do not display challenge values.

HTTP—You see a window generated by the web browser. If you enter an incorrect password, you are prompted again. If the username or password on the authentication database differs from the username or password on the remote host to which you are using HTTP to access, enter the username and password in the following formats:

aaa_username@remote_username

aaa_password@remote_password

The PIX Firewall sends the *aaa_username* and *aaa_password* to the AAA server, and if authentication and authorization are successful, the *remote_username* and *remote_password* are passed to the destination HTTP server.

NOTE   Remember that browsers cache usernames and passwords. If you believe that the PIX Firewall should be timing out an HTTP connection but it is not, re-authentication might actually be taking place with the web browser sending the cached username and password back to the PIX Firewall. The syslog service shows this phenomenon. If Telnet and FTP seem to work normally but HTTP connections do not, this reauthentication is usually the reason.

NOTE   The PIX Firewall supports authentication usernames of up to 127 characters and passwords of up to 63 characters. A password or username may not contain an "at" (@) character as part of the password or username string.

If PIX Firewalls are in tandem, Telnet authentication works in the same way as a single PIX Firewall, but FTP and HTTP authentication have additional complexity because you have to enter each password and username with an additional "at" (@) character and password or username for each in-tandem PIX Firewall.

Cut-Through Proxy Operation

Although the addition of AAA provides flexibility and granularity in access control, it also negatively impacts the performance of most firewalls because of additional overhead. The PIX Firewall, however, gains dramatic performance advantages because of the *cut-through proxy*, a method of transparently verifying the identity of users at the firewall and permitting or denying access to any TCP- or User Datagram Protocol (UDP)-based application. This method eliminates the price and performance impact that UNIX system-based firewalls impose in similar configurations and leverages the authentication and authorization services of the CSACS.

The PIX Firewall's cut-through proxy challenges a user initially at the application layer and then authenticates against standard TACACS+ or RADIUS databases. After the policy is checked, the PIX Firewall shifts the session flow, and all traffic flows directly and quickly between the server and the client while maintaining session state information.

A typical design for this technology is a user on the Internet accessing an HTTP server on a company demilitarized zone (DMZ). The sequence of events shown in Figure 13-2 is as follows:

1 A user on the Internet enters the appropriate URL to get to the XYZ web server.

2 The AAA requirement on the PIX prompts the user to input a username and password.

3 The user inputs the information, which is passed to the PIX in cleartext, and the PIX forwards the information to the AAA server, in this case running CSACS software.

4 If authenticated, the user is permitted to interact with the destination. If the destination web server also requires authentication, the remote username and password are passed on.

Figure 13-2 *Cut-Through Proxy Operation*

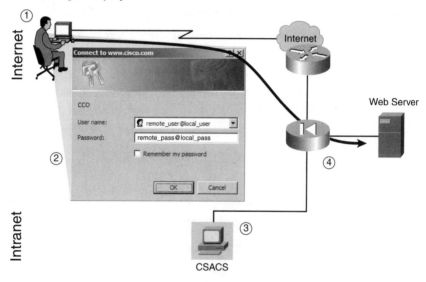

Supported AAA Servers

The PIX Firewall supports the following AAA protocols and servers:

TACACS+

— CSACS for Windows NT (CSACS-NT)

— CSACS for UNIX (CSACS-UNIX)

— TACACS+ Freeware

RADIUS

— CSACS-NT

— CSACS-UNIX

— Livingston

— Merit

Installation of CSACS for Windows NT

CSACS provides standard AAA services. This service can be utilized by PIX Firewalls as well as other network devices such as Cisco IOS-based routers and switches. CSACS provides a web-based administration interface for configuring accounts and policies to control user access through the PIX Firewall.

NOTE Close all Windows programs before you run the CSACS setup program.

Perform the following steps to install CSACS for Windows 2000:

Step 1 Log in to the Windows 2000 Server as system administrator.

Step 2 Insert the CSACS CD-ROM into your CD-ROM drive. The Installation window shown in Figure 13-3 opens if Autorun is enabled. Otherwise, start the installation manually by running the setup program. Click **Install** to proceed.

Figure 13-3 *CSACS Installation Window*

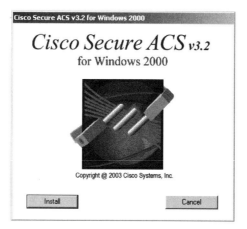

Step 3 The Software License Agreement window shown in Figure 13-4 opens. Read the Software License Agreement. Click **Accept** to agree to the licensing terms and conditions.

Figure 13-4 *Software License Agreement Window*

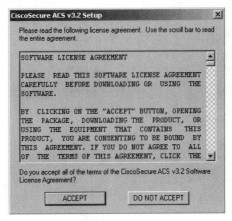

Step 4 The Welcome window shown in Figure 13-5 opens. Click **Next**.

Figure 13-5 *CSACS Welcome Window*

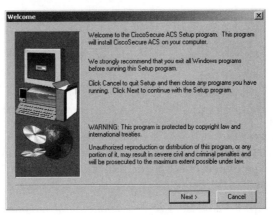

Step 5 The Before You Begin window shown in Figure 13-6 opens. This screen lists a number of requirements for installation of CSACS. Click **Explain** for more information about the listed items. If any condition is not met, click **Cancel** to exit setup.

Figure 13-6 *Before You Begin Window*

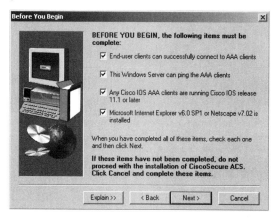

Step 6 After you verify that each condition is met, select the check box for each item and click **Next** to proceed.

NOTE If this is a new installation, skip to Step 9.

Step 7 (Optional) If CSACS is already installed, the Previous Installation window opens. You are prompted to remove the previous version and save the existing database information. Click **Yes, keep existing database** and click **Next** to keep the existing data. To use a new database, deselect the check box and click **Next**. If you selected the check box, the setup program backs up the existing database information and removes the old files. When the files are removed, click **OK**.

Step 8 If setup finds an existing configuration, you are prompted on whether you want to import the configuration. Click **Yes, import configuration** and click **Next** to keep the existing configuration. Deselect the check box and click **Next** to use a new configuration.

Step 9 The Choose Destination Location window shown in Figure 13-7 opens. Click **Next** to install the software in the default directory, or click **Browse** and enter a different directory. If the directory you specified does not exist, you are prompted to create it. Click **Yes**.

Figure 13-7   *Choose Destination Location Window*

Step 10 The Authentication Database Configuration window shown in Figure 13-8 opens. Click the radio button for the authentication databases to be used by CSACS. You can select **Check the CSACS Database only** option (the default), or if you'd like to use existing accounts from your Windows environment, select the **Also check the Windows 2000/NT User Database** option. If you select the first option, CSACS uses only the CSACS database for authentication; if you select the second option, CSACS checks both databases. You can click **Explain** to see an explanation of various options on this screen.

Figure 13-8   *Authentication Database Configuration Window*

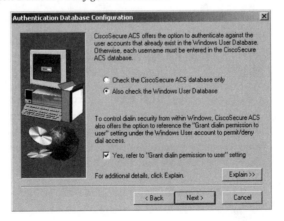

Step 11 (Optional) Click the **Yes, refer to "Grant dialin permission to user"** setting to limit dial-in access to only those users you specified in the Windows NT User Manager. Click **Next**.

Figure 13-9 *CSACS Network Access Server Details Window*

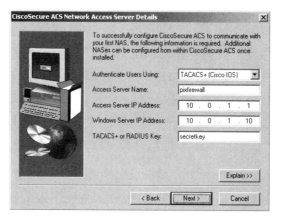

Step 12 On the Network Access Server Details window shown in Figure 13-9, complete the following information:

— **Authenticate Users Using**—Type of security protocol to be used. TACACS+ (Cisco IOS) is the default.

— **Access Server Name**—Name of the network access server (NAS) that will be using the CSACS services.

— **Access Server IP Address**—IP address of the NAS that will be using the CSACS services.

— **Windows 2000 Server IP Address**—IP address of this Windows 2000 server.

— **TACACS+ or RADIUS Key**—Shared secret of the NAS and CSACS. These passwords must be identical to ensure proper function and communication between the NAS and CSACS. Shared secrets are case sensitive. Click **Next**. Setup installs the CSACS files and updates the Registry, as shown in Figure 13-10.

Figure 13-10 *CSACS Installation Window*

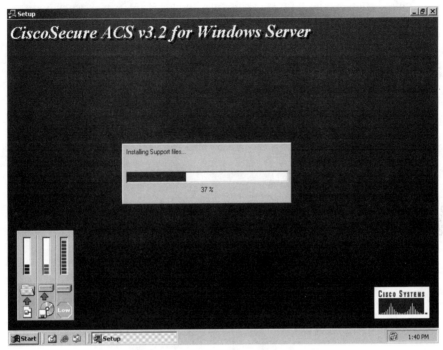

Step 13 After the files are copied, the Advanced Options window shown in Figure 13-11 opens. These options are disabled by default. Select the check box to enable any or all of the options listed. (You can click **Explain** to see an explanation of each option.) Click **Next**.

Figure 13-11 *Advanced Options Window*

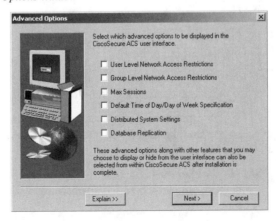

NOTE   Configuration options for these items appear in the CSACS interface only if they are enabled. You can also disable or enable any or all of these and additional options after installation in the Interface Configuration: Advanced Options window.

Step 14   The Active Service Monitoring window shown in Figure 13-12 opens. To enable the CSACS monitoring service, CSMon, select the **Enable Log-in Monitoring** check box.

Figure 13-12   *Active Service Monitoring Window*

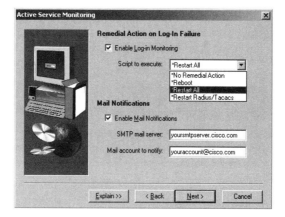

Then select a script to execute when the login process fails the test:

— **No Remedial Action**—Leave CSACS operating as is.

— **Reboot**—Reboot the system on which CSACS is running.

— **Restart All**—(Default) Restart all CSACS services.

— **Restart RADIUS/TACACS+**—Restart only RADIUS, TACACS+, or both protocols.

You can also develop your own scripts to be executed if there is a system failure. See the online documentation for more information.

Step 15   To have CSACS generate an e-mail message when administrator events occur, select the **Enable Mail Notifications** check box, and then enter the following information:

— **SMTP Mail Server**—The name and domain of the sending mail server (for example, server1.company.com).

— **Mail account to notify**—The complete e-mail address of the intended recipient (for example, msmith@company.com).

Step 16 Click **Next**. The CSACS Network Access Server Configuration window shown in Figure 13-13 opens. If you do not want to configure a NAS from setup, click **Next**. To configure a single NAS now, click **Yes, I want to configure Cisco IOS** now, and then click **Next**.

Figure 13-13 *Network Access Server Configuration*

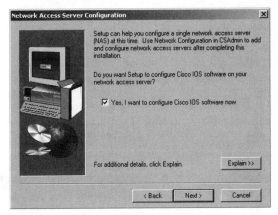

Step 17 The CSACS Service Initiation window shown in Figure 13-14 opens. Select the appropriate options to start the CSACS service, launch the administrative interface on your browser, or view the readme file with the latest information on CSACS.

Figure 13-14 *CSACS Service Initiation Window*

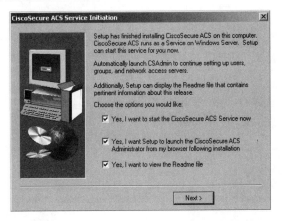

Adding Users to CSACS

After you successfully install CSACS, you can add users to the system. Keep in mind that here the term "user" applies to actual users and network devices alike. You can create users in a local CSACS database, or their accounts can reside in an external database such as Windows NT/2000 user database. Typically, an external database such as Active Directory is used for individuals, whereas accounts for network devices such the PIX Firewall are created in the local database.

Complete the following steps to add users to the CSACS:

Step 1 Click **User Setup** from the navigation bar. The Select window opens.

Step 2 Enter a name in the User field.

NOTE The username can contain up to 32 characters. Names cannot contain the following special characters: #, ?, ", *, >, and <. Leading and trailing spaces are not allowed.

Step 3 Click **Add/Edit**. The User Setup window shown in Figure 13-15 opens. The username being added or edited appears at the top of the window.

Figure 13-15 *CSACS User Setup Window*

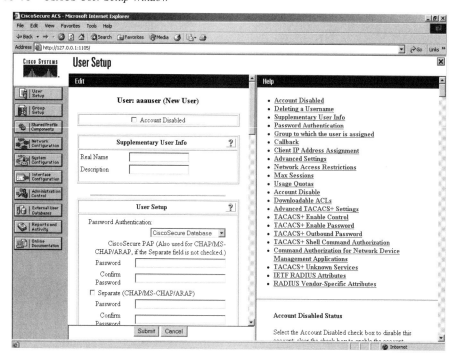

The User Setup windows includes the following sections (additional sections such as Advanced Settings or Downloadable ACLs may also be included if they have been previously enabled):

— Account Disabled

— Supplementary User Info

— User Setup

— Account Disable

Using these sections, you can edit the following options when creating a new account or modifying an existing account.

Account Disabled

If you need to disable an account, select the **Account Disabled** check box in the Account Disabled section to deny access for this user.

NOTE   You must click **Submit** to have this action take effect.

Supplementary User Info

In this section, you can enter supplemental information to appear in each user profile. The fields in the list that follows are available by default; however, you can insert additional fields by clicking Interface Configuration in the navigation bar and then clicking User Data Configuration (configuring supplemental information is optional):

Real Name—If the username is not the user's real name, enter the real name here.

Description—Enter a detailed description of the user.

User Setup

In the User Setup group box, you can edit or enter the following information for the user as applicable:

Password authentication—From the drop-down menu, choose a database to use for username and password authentication. You can select the Windows NT/2000 user database or the CSACS database. The Windows NT option authenticates a user with an existing account in the Windows NT user database located on the same machine as the CSACS. The Cisco Secure Database option authenticates a user from the local CSACS database. If you select this database, enter and confirm the Password Authentication Protocol (PAP) password to be used. The Separate CHAP/MS-CHAP/ARAP option is not used with the PIX Firewall.

NOTE	The Password and Confirm Password fields are required for all authentication methods except for all third-party user databases.

Group to which the user is assigned—From the group to which the user is assigned drop-down menu, choose the group to which to assign the user. The user inherits the attributes and operations assigned to the group. By default, users are assigned to the Default Group. Users who authenticate via the Unknown User method and are not found in an existing group are also assigned to the Default Group.

- **Callback**—This option is not used with the PIX Firewall.
- **Client IP address assignment**—This option is not used with the PIX Firewall.

Account Disable

You can use the Account Disable group box (not to be confused with the Account Disabled section discussed earlier) to define the circumstances under which the user's account becomes disabled.

NOTE	You should also avoid confusing the Account Disable group with account expiration due to password aging. Password aging is defined for groups only, not for individual users.

Options available in the Account Disable group box are as follows:

Never (radio button)—Select to keep the user's account always enabled. This option is the default.

Disable account if (radio button)—Select to disable the account under the circumstances you specify in the following fields:

- **Date exceeds**—From the drop-down menu, choose the month, date, and year on which to disable the account. The default is 30 days after the user is added.
- **Failed attempts exceed**—Select the check box and enter the number of consecutive unsuccessful login attempts to allow before disabling the account. The default is 5.
- **Failed attempts since last successful login**—This counter shows the number of unsuccessful login attempts since the last time this user logged in successfully.

Reset current failed attempts count on submit—If an account is disabled because the failed attempts count has been exceeded, select this check box and click **Submit** to reset the failed attempts counter to 0 and reinstate the account.

If you use the Windows NT/2000 user database, this expiration information is in addition to the information in the Windows user account. Changes here do not alter settings configured in Windows NT/2000.

When you finish configuring all user information, click **Submit**.

Authentication Configuration

After you finish the installation of CSACS and create user accounts, you must add appropriate AAA configuration statements to the PIX Firewall configuration. An administrator can configure many different options for AAA and the PIX. First, you must create an AAA group and specify an authentication protocol. Next, you create the AAA server and assign it to be a part of the AAA group. You can define multiple AAA servers to be a part of the same AAA group. This step allows for server access failure. If the first AAA server is not reachable (there is a configurable timer, which is described later in the chapter), the request is made to the next defined AAA server.

Use the **aaa-server** command to specify AAA server groups. The PIX Firewall enables you to define separate groups of TACACS+ or RADIUS servers for specifying different types of traffic, such as a TACACS+ server for inbound traffic and another for outbound traffic. The **aaa** command references the group tag to direct authentication, authorization, or accounting traffic to the appropriate AAA server.

You can have up to 14 tag groups, and each group can have up to 14 AAA servers for a total of up to 196 TACACS+ or RADIUS servers. When a user logs in, the servers are accessed one at a time, starting with the first server you specify in the tag group, until a server responds.

The default configuration provides the following two AAA server groups for TACACS+ and RADIUS protocols:

```
aaa-server TACACS protocol tacacs+
aaa-server RADIUS protocol radius
```

NOTE	If you are upgrading from a previous version of the PIX Firewall (which did not require creating a AAA group) and you have **aaa** command statements in your configuration, using the default server groups enables you to maintain backward compatibility with the **aaa** command statements in your configuration.

NOTE   The previous server type option at the end of the **aaa authentication** and **aaa accounting** commands has been replaced with the **aaa-server group** tag. Backward compatibility with previous versions is maintained by the inclusion of two default protocols for TACACS+ and RADIUS.

NOTE   The PIX Firewall listens for RADIUS on ports 1645 and 1646. If your RADIUS server uses ports 1812 and 1813, you need to reconfigure it to listen on ports 1645 and 1646.

The syntax for the **aaa-server** commands is as follows:

```
aaa-server group_tag (if_name) host server_ip key timeout seconds
no aaa-server group_tag (if_name) host server_ip key timeout seconds
aaa-server group_tag protocol auth_protocol
clear aaa-server [group_tag]
```

Table 13-1 describes the **aaa-server** command arguments.

Table 13-1   aaa-server *Command Arguments*

Argument	Definition
group_tag	An alphanumeric string that is the name of the server group. Use the *group_tag* in the **aaa** command to associate **aaa authentication**, **aaa authorization**, and **aaa accounting** command statements with an AAA server.
if_name	The interface name on the side on which the AAA server resides.
host *server_ip*	The IP address of the TACACS+ or RADIUS server.
key	A case-sensitive, alphanumeric keyword of up to 127 characters that is the same value as the key on the TACACS+ server. Any characters entered past 127 are ignored. The client and server use the key to encrypt data between them. The key must be the same on both the client and server systems. Spaces are not permitted in the key, but other special characters are. If you do not specify a key, encryption does not occur.
timeout *seconds*	A retransmit timer that specifies the duration that the PIX Firewall retries access. Access to the AAA server is retried 4 times before choosing the next AAA server. The default is 5 seconds. The maximum time is 30 seconds. For example, if the timeout value is 10 seconds, the PIX Firewall retransmits for 10 seconds and, if no acknowledgment is received, tries 3 times more, for a total of 40 seconds to retransmit data before the next AAA server is selected.
protocol *auth_protocol*	The type of AAA server, either TACACS+ or RADIUS.

Example 13-1 demonstrates the **aaa-server** command. The first statement in the example creates an AAA group named MYTACACS and assigns the authentication protocol TACACS+ to the group. The second statement assigns the server to the group MYTACACS, specifies that the inside interface of the PIX Firewall will be used to communicate with the AAA server, defines the IP address of the AAA server (10.0.0.2), assigns a key (secretkey), and defines a timeout period of 10 seconds.

Example 13-1   *Specifying AAA Server Groups*

```
pixfirewall(config)# aaa-server MYTACACS protocol tacacs+
pixfirewall(config)# aaa-server MYTACACS (inside) host 10.0.0.2 secretkey timeout 10
```

After the **aaa-server** command is configured, it is now time for the administrator to configure **authentication**. The **aaa authentication** command enables or disables user authentication services. When you start a connection via Telnet, FTP, or HTTP, you are prompted for a username and password. An AAA server, designated previously with the **aaa-server** command, verifies whether the username and password are correct. If they are correct, the PIX Firewall's cut-through proxy permits further traffic between the initiating host and the target host.

The **aaa authentication** command is not intended to mandate your security policy. The AAA servers determine whether a user can or cannot access the system, what services can be accessed, and what IP addresses the user can access. The PIX Firewall interacts with Telnet, FTP, and HTTP to display the prompts for logging. You can specify that only a single service be authenticated, but this specification must agree with the AAA server to ensure that both the firewall and server agree.

For each IP address, you can have one **aaa authentication** command for inbound connections and one for outbound connections. The PIX Firewall permits only one authentication type per network. For example, if one network connects through the PIX Firewall using TACACS+ for authentication, another network connecting through the PIX Firewall can authenticate with RADIUS, but one network cannot authenticate with both TACACS+ and RADIUS.

NOTE   The new **include** and **exclude** options are not backward compatible with PIX Firewall Versions 5.0 and earlier. If you downgrade to an earlier version, the **aaa authentication** command statements are removed from your configuration.

The syntax for the **aaa authentication** commands is as follows:

```
aaa authentication include | exclude authen_service inbound | outbound | if_name
   local_ip local_mask foreign_ip foreign_mask group_tag
no aaa authentication [include | exclude authen_service inbound | outbound | if_name
   local_ip local_mask foreign_ip foreign_mask group_tag]
clear aaa [authentication include | exclude authen_service inbound | outbound | if_name
   local_ip local_mask foreign_ip foreign_mask group_tag]
```

Table 13-2 describes the **aaa authentication** command arguments.

Table 13-2   **aaa authentication** *Command Arguments*

Argument	Definition
include	Creates a new rule with the specified service to include.
exclude	Creates an exception to a previously stated rule by excluding the specified service from authentication to the specified host. The **exclude** parameter improves the former **except** option by enabling the user to specify a port to exclude to a specific host or hosts.
authen_service	The services that require user authentication before they are let through the firewall. Use **any**, **FTP**, **HTTP**, or **Telnet** service. The **any** value enables authentication for all TCP services.
inbound	Authenticates inbound connections. **inbound** means the connection originates on the outside interface and is being directed to the inside or any other perimeter interface.
outbound	Authenticates outbound connections. **outbound** means the connection originates on the inside and is being directed to the outside or any other perimeter interface.
if_name	Interface name from which users require authentication. Use *if_name* in combination with the *local_ip* address and the *foreign_ip* address to determine where access is sought and from whom. The *local_ip* address is always on the interface with the highest security level and *foreign_ip* is always on the lowest.
local_ip	The IP address of the host or network of hosts that you want to be authenticated. Setting this address to 0 indicates all hosts and allows the authentication server to decide which hosts are authenticated.
local_mask	Network mask of *local_ip*. Always specify a specific mask value. Use 0 if the IP address is 0. Use 255.255.255.255 for a host.
foreign_ip	The IP address of the hosts you want to access the *local_ip* address. Use 0 to mean all hosts.
foreign_mask	Network mask of *foreign_ip*. Always specify a specific mask value. Use 0 if the IP address is 0. Use 255.255.255.255 for a host.
group_tag	The group tag set with the **aaa-server** command. To use the local PIX Firewall user authentication database, enter **LOCAL** for this parameter.

In the example shown in Figure 13-16, workstations on the 10.0.0.0 network can originate outbound connections, but users must be authenticated. Host 10.0.0.42, however, is allowed to start outbound connections without being authenticated.

Figure 13-16 *AAA Authentication Example*

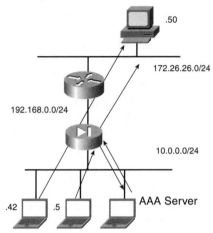

Example 13-2 shows the configuration for this example. This example uses a previously defined AAA group named MYTACACS. The first statement in Example 13-2 defines the NAT settings for hosts inside the PIX Firewall, allowing hosts on the 10.0.0.0 network to make outbound connections. The next statement specifies that all such connections require user authentication with the MYTACACS AAA group. The last statement, however, specifies that host 10.0.0.42 is exempt from the user authentication requirement and is allowed to start outbound connections without authentication.

Example 13-2 *AAA Authentication Example*

```
pixfirewall(config)# nat  (inside) 1 10.0.0.0 255.255.255.0
pixfirewall(config)# aaa authentication include any outbound 0 0 MYTACACS
pixfirewall(config)# aaa authentication exclude any outbound 10.0.0.42
  255.255.255.255 0.0.0.0 0.0.0.0 MYTACACS
```

Authentication of Other Services

The PIX Firewall authenticates users via Telnet, FTP, or HTTP. But what if users need to access a Microsoft file server on port 139 or a Cisco IP/TV server, for instance? How are they authenticated? Whenever users are required to authenticate to access services other than Telnet, FTP, or HTTP, they need to do one of the following:

Option 1—Authenticate first by accessing a Telnet, FTP, or HTTP server before accessing other services.

Option 2—Authenticate to the PIX Firewall Virtual Telnet service before accessing other services. When there are no Telnet, FTP, or HTTP servers with which to authenticate, or just to simplify authentication for the user, the PIX Firewall provides a Virtual Telnet authentication option. This option permits the user to authenticate directly with the PIX Firewall using the Virtual Telnet IP address.

Virtual Telnet

The Virtual Telnet option provides pre-authentication of users who require connections through the PIX Firewall using services or protocols that do not support authentication. The Virtual Telnet IP address is used both to authenticate in and authenticate out of the PIX Firewall.

When an unauthenticated user Telnets to the virtual IP address, the user is challenged for the username and password and then authenticated with the TACACS+ or RADIUS server. Once authenticated, the user sees the message "Authentication Successful," and the authentication credentials are cached in the PIX Firewall for the duration of the user authentication (uauth) timeout.

If a user wants to log out and clear the entry in the PIX Firewall uauth cache, the user can again Telnet to the virtual address. The user is prompted for a username and password, the PIX Firewall removes the associated credentials from the uauth cache, and the user receives a "Logout Successful" message.

The syntax for the **virtual telnet** command is as follows:

```
virtual telnet ip_address
```

When you use Virtual Telnet to authenticate inbound clients, the IP address must be an unused global address. When using Virtual Telnet to authenticate outbound clients, the IP address must be an unused global address routed directly to the PIX Firewall.

In the example shown in Figure 13-17, the user wants to establish a NetBIOS session on port 139 to access the file server named superserver. The sequence of events is as follows:

1 The user Telnets to the Virtual Telnet address at 192.168.0.5 and is immediately challenged for a username and password before being authenticated with the TACACS+ AAA server.

2 The PIX Firewall passes the username and password to the AAA server at 10.0.0.11 for authentication.

3 If the AAA server verifies that the username and password are correct, the PIX Firewall caches the user's authentication credentials for the duration of the uauth timeout.

4 The user is able to connect to superserver on port 139 using the **run** command without being required to re-authenticate.

Figure 13-17 *Virtual Telnet Example*

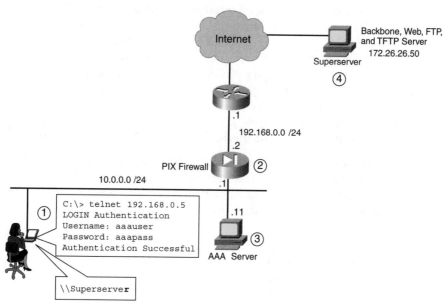

Example 13-3 shows the configuration for this outbound Virtual Telnet example.

Example 13-3 *Virtual Telnet Configuration*

```
pixfirewall(config)# virtual telnet 192.168.0.5
pixfirewall(config)# aaa-server MYTACACS protocol tacacs+
pixfirewall(config)# aaa-server MYTACACS (inside) host 10.0.0.11 secretkey
pixfirewall(config)# aaa authentication include any outbound 0.0.0.0 0.0.0.0 0.0.0.0
   0.0.0.0 MYTACACS
```

Virtual HTTP

Virtual HTTP solves the problem of HTTP requests failing when web servers require credentials that differ from those required by the PIX Firewall's AAA server. The PIX Firewall assumes that the AAA server database is shared with a web server and automatically provides the AAA server and web server with the same information. The virtual HTTP option works with the PIX Firewall to authenticate the user, separate the AAA server information from the web client's URL request, and direct the web client to the web server. The virtual HTTP option works by redirecting the web browser's initial connection to an IP address, which resides in the PIX Firewall; authenticating the user; and then redirecting the browser back to the URL that the user originally requested. This option is so named because it accesses a virtual HTTP server on the PIX Firewall.

This option is especially useful for PIX Firewall interoperability with Microsoft Internet Information Server (IIS) but is useful for other authentication servers. When you use HTTP authentication to a site running Microsoft IIS that has "Basic text authentication" or "NT Challenge" enabled, users might be denied access from the Microsoft IIS server because the browser appends the string "Authorization: Basic=Uuhjksdkfhk==" to the HTTP GET commands. This string contains the PIX Firewall authentication credentials. Windows NT Microsoft IIS servers respond to the credentials and assume that a Windows NT user is trying to access privileged pages on the server. Unless the PIX Firewall username and password combination is exactly the same as a valid Windows NT username and password combination on the Microsoft IIS server, the HTTP GET command is denied.

To solve this problem, the PIX Firewall redirects the browser's initial connection to its virtual HTTP IP address, authenticates the user, and then redirects the browser back to the URL that the user originally requested. Virtual HTTP is transparent to the user; therefore, users enter actual destination URLs in their browsers as they normally would.

NOTE   Do not set the timeout uauth duration to 0 seconds when using the virtual HTTP option. Doing so prevents HTTP connections to the real web server.

The virtual address identifies the IP address of the virtual HTTP server on the PIX Firewall. For inbound use, *ip_address* can be any unused global address. An **access-list** and **static** command pair must provide access to this address. For outbound use, *ip_address* must be an address routed directly to the PIX Firewall.

The syntax for the **virtual http** command is as follows:

```
virtual http ip_address [warn]
no virtual http ip_address
```

Table 13-3 describes the **virtual http** command arguments.

Table 13-3   **virtual http** *Command Arguments*

Argument	Definition
ip_address	The PIX Firewall's network interface IP address.
warn	Informs **virtual http** command users that the command was redirected. This option is only applicable for text-based browsers for which the redirect cannot happen automatically.

For outbound use, *ip_address* must be an address routed to the PIX Firewall. Use an RFC 1918 address that is not in use on any interface.

For inbound use, *ip_address* must be an unused global address. An **access-list** or **conduit** and **static** command pair must provide access to *ip_address*, as well as an **aaa authentication** command statement.

For example, for outbound use, if an inside client at 192.168.0.100 has a default gateway set to the inside interface of the PIX Firewall at 192.168.0.1, the IP address set with the **virtual http** command can be any IP address not in use on that segment, such as 192.168.0.120.

Authentication of Console Access

You use the **aaa authentication console** command to require authentication verification for access to the PIX Firewall's console. Authenticated access to the PIX Firewall console has different types of prompts, depending on the option you choose. The **telnet**, **ssh**, and **enable** options allow three unsuccessful tries before stopping with an access denied message. The **serial** option causes you to be prompted continually until you successfully log in.

The **serial** option requests a username and password before the first command-line interface (CLI) prompt on the serial console connection. The **telnet** option forces you to specify a username and password before the first CLI prompt of a Telnet console connection. The **ssh** option requests a username and password before the first CLI prompt on the Secure Shell (SSH) console connection. The **enable** option requests a username and password before accessing privileged mode for serial, Telnet, or SSH connections.

Telnet access to the PIX Firewall console is available from any internal interface (and from the outside interface with IP Security [IPSec] configured) and requires previous use of the **telnet** command. SSH access to the PIX Firewall console is available from any interface without IPSec configured and requires previous use of the **ssh** command.

NOTE	Before Version 5.0, Telnet access was restricted to the inside interface of the PIX Firewall. The option of enabling Telnet to the outside interface is available with PIX Firewall Version 5.0 or higher. However, Telnet traffic to the outside interface must be encrypted. To enable Telnet on the outside interface, configure IPSec on the outside interface of the PIX Firewall.

Authentication of the serial console creates a potential deadlock situation if the authentication server requests are not answered and you need access to the console to attempt diagnosis. If the console login request times out, you can gain access to the PIX Firewall from the serial console by entering the PIX Firewall username and the enable password. The maximum password length for accessing the console is 16 characters.

The **aaa authentication** command also supports PIX Device Manager (PDM) authentication. By using the **aaa authentication http console** command, you can configure the PIX Firewall to require authentication before allowing PDM to access it. If an **aaa authentication http console** command statement is not defined, you can gain access to the PIX Firewall (via PDM) with no username and the PIX Firewall enable password (set with the **password** command). If the **aaa** command is defined but the HTTP authentication request times out, which implies that the AAA server might be down or unavailable, you can gain access to the PIX Firewall using the username pix and the enable password.

NOTE   The serial console option also logs to a syslog server the changes made to the configuration from the serial console.

The syntax for the **aaa authentication console** commands is as follows:

```
aaa authentication [serial | enable | telnet | ssh | http] console group_tag
no aaa authentication [serial | enable | telnet | ssh | http] console group_tag
```

Table 13-4 describes the **aaa authentication console** command arguments.

Table 13-4   **aaa authentication console** *Command Arguments*

Argument	Definition
serial	Access verification for the PIX Firewall's serial console.
enable	Access verification for the PIX Firewall's privilege mode.
telnet	Access verification for Telnet access to the PIX Firewall console.
ssh	Access verification for SSH access to the PIX Firewall console.
http	Access verification for HTTP access to the PIX Firewall (via PDM).
console	Specifies that access to the PIX Firewall console requires authentication.
group_tag	The group tag set with the **aaa-server** command. To use the local PIX Firewall user authentication database, enter **LOCAL** for this parameter.

Example 13-4 shows the configuration statements required to enable AAA authentication of console access through serial, Telnet, SSH, and HTTP (PDM or PIX Management Center [MC]). Privileged access (enable) is also configured for authentication with an AAA server in this example.

Example 13-4   *Authentication of Console Access*

```
pixfirewall(config)# aaa authentication serial console MYTACACS
pixfirewall(config)# aaa authentication enable console MYTACACS
pixfirewall(config)# aaa authentication telnet console MYTACACS
pixfirewall(config)# aaa authentication ssh console MYTACACS
pixfirewall(config)# aaa authentication http console MYTACACS
```

Changing Authentication Timeouts

Use the **timeout uauth** command to specify how long the cache should be kept after the user connections become idle. The timeout command value must be at least 2 minutes. Using the **clear uauth** command to delete all authorization caches for all users causes them to reauthenticate the next time they create a connection.

The inactivity and absolute qualifiers cause users to re-authenticate after either a period of inactivity or an absolute duration. The inactivity timer starts after a connection becomes idle. If a user establishes a new connection before the duration of the inactivity timer, the user is not required to re-authenticate. If a user establishes a new connection after the inactivity timer expires, the user must re-authenticate.

The absolute timer runs continuously but waits to reprompt the user when the user starts a new connection, such as by clicking a link after the absolute timer has elapsed. The user is then prompted to re-authenticate. The absolute timer must be shorter than the xlate timer; otherwise, a user could be reprompted after his session already ended.

The inactivity timer gives users the best Internet access because they are not prompted to regularly reauthenticate. Absolute timers provide security and manage the PIX Firewall connections better. By being prompted to reauthenticate regularly, users manage their resources more efficiently. Also by reprompting, you minimize the risk that someone will attempt to use another person's access after he leaves his workstation, such as in a college computer lab. You might want to set an absolute timer during peak hours and an inactivity timer during other times.

Both an inactivity timer and an absolute timer can operate at the same time, but you should set the absolute timer duration for a longer time than the inactivity timer. If the absolute timer is set to less than the inactivity timer, the inactivity timer never occurs. For example, if you set the absolute timer to 10 minutes and the inactivity timer to an hour, the absolute timer reprompts the user every 10 minutes, and the inactivity timer never starts.

If you set the inactivity timer to some duration but the absolute timer to 0, users are only re-authenticated after the inactivity timer elapses. If you set both timers to 0, users have to re-authenticate on every new connection.

NOTE   Do not set the **timeout uauth** duration to 0 seconds when using the virtual HTTP option or passive FTP.

The syntax for the **timeout uauth** commands is as follows:

```
timeout uauth hh:mm:ss [absolute | inactivity]
show timeout
clear uauth
```

Table 13-5 describes the **timeout uauth** command arguments.

Table 13-5   **timeout uauth** *Command Arguments*

Argument	Definition
uauth *hh:mm:ss*	Duration before the authentication and authorization cache times out and the user has to re-authenticate the next connection. This duration must be shorter than the xlate values. Set to 0 to disable caching.
absolute	Runs the uauth timer continuously, but after timer elapses, waits to reprompt the user until the user starts a new connection (for example, clicking a link in a web browser). To disable absolute, set it to 0. The default is 5 minutes.
inactivity	Starts the uauth timer after a connection becomes idle. The default is 0.

Example 13-5 demonstrates the configuration of the absolute and inactivity timeout periods.

Example 13-5   *Configuring Authentication Timeouts*

```
pixfirewall(config)# timeout uauth 3:00:00 absolute
pixfirewall(config)# timeout uauth 0:30:00 inactivity
```

Changing Authentication Prompts

Use the **auth-prompt** command to change the AAA challenge text for HTTP, FTP, and Telnet access. This text appears above the username and password prompts that you view when logging in.

NOTE   Microsoft Internet Explorer displays only up to 37 characters in an authentication prompt, Netscape Navigator displays up to 120 characters, and Telnet and FTP display up to 235 characters in an authentication prompt.

The syntax for the **auth-prompt** commands is as follows:

```
auth-prompt [accept | reject | prompt] string
no auth-prompt [accept | reject | prompt] string
show auth-prompt
clear auth-prompt
```

Table 13-6 describes the **auth-prompt** command arguments.

Table 13-6   **auth-prompt** *Command Arguments*

Argument	Definition
accept	If a user authentication via Telnet is accepted, the accept message is displayed.
reject	If a user authentication via Telnet is rejected, the reject message is displayed.
prompt	The AAA challenge prompt string follows this keyword. This keyword is optional for backward compatibility.
string	A string of up to 235 alphanumeric characters. You cannot use special characters; however, spaces and punctuation characters are permitted. Entering a question mark or pressing the Enter key ends the string. (The question mark appears in the string.)

Example 13-6 demonstrates the configuration of alternatives prompts for all three authentication prompts.

Example 13-6   *Configuring Authentication Prompts*

```
pixfirewall(config)# auth-prompt prompt Please Authenticate to the Firewall
pixfirewall(config)# auth-prompt reject Authentication Failed, Try Again
pixfirewall(config)# auth-prompt accept You've been Authenticated
```

Authorization Configuration

The PIX Firewall uses authorization services with TACACS+ AAA servers that determine which services an authenticated user can access.

NOTE   Due to a limitation of the RADIUS protocol, the PIX Firewall does not support RADIUS authorization.

The syntax for the **aaa authorization** commands is as follows:

```
aaa authorization include | exclude author_service inbound | outbound | if_name
    local_ip local_mask foreign_ip foreign_mask group_tag
no aaa authorization include | exclude author_service inbound | outbound | if_name
    local_ip local_mask foreign_ip foreign_mask group_tag
clear aaa authorization [include | exclude author_service inbound | outbound | if_name
    local_ip local_mask foreign_ip foreign_mask group_tag]
```

Table 13-7 describes the **aaa authorization** command arguments.

Table 13-7   **aaa authorization** *Command Arguments*

Arguments	Definition
include *author_service*	The services that require authorization. Use any, FTP, HTTP, or Telnet. Services not specified are authorized implicitly. Services specified in the **aaa authentication** command do not affect the services, which require authorization.
exclude *author_service*	Creates an exception to a previously stated rule by excluding the specified service from authorization to the specified host. The **exclude** parameter improves the former **except** option by allowing the user to specify a port to exclude for a specific host or hosts.
inbound	Authenticates or authorizes inbound connections. Inbound means the connection originates on the outside interface and is being directed to the inside or any other perimeter interface.
outbound	Authenticates or authorizes outbound connections. Outbound means the connection originates on the inside and is being directed to the outside or any other perimeter interface.
if_name	Interface name from which users require authentication. Use *if_name* in combination with the *local_ip* address and the *foreign_ip* address to determine where access is sought and from whom.
local_ip	The IP address of the host or network of hosts that you want to be authenticated or authorized. You can set this address to 0 to mean all hosts and to let the authentication server decide which hosts are authenticated.
local_mask	Network mask of *local_ip*. Always specify a specific mask value. Use 0 if the IP address is 0. Use 255.255.255.255 for a host.
foreign_ip	The IP address of the hosts you want to access the *local_ip* address. Use 0 to mean all hosts.
foreign_mask	Network mask of *foreign_ip*. Always specify a specific mask value. Use 0 if the IP address is 0. Use 255.255.255.255 for a host.
group_tag	The group tag set with the **aaa-server** command. Enter the **LOCAL** value for local AAA services such as local command authorization using privilege levels, or use the AAA server group tag as defined by the **aaa-server** command.

Example 13-7 shows sample **include** and **exclude** authorization commands.

Example 13-7   *Enable Authorization*

```
pixfirewall(config)# aaa authorization include ftp outbound 0.0.0.0 0.0.0.0 0.0.0.0
   0.0.0.0 MYTACACS
pixfirewall(config)# aaa authorization exclude ftp outbound 10.0.0.33
   255.255.255.255 0.0.0.0 0.0.0.0 MYTACACS
```

Adding Authorization Rules

Using authorization rules within CSACS, it is possible to allow access to a specific service such as FTP for a group of users while restricting access to other services. For example, you can complete the following steps to add authorization rules for FTP only in CSACS:

Step 1   Click **Group Setup** from the navigation bar of the CSACS and select a group from the drop-down list. The Group Setup window shown in Figure 13-18 opens.

Figure 13-18   *Authorization Rules Allowing Specific Services*

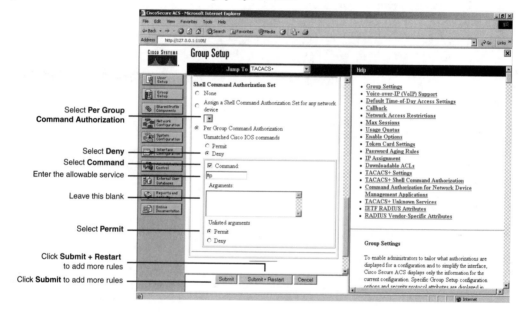

Step 2   Scroll down in the Group Setup window until you find Shell Command Authorization Set.

Step 3   Select **Per Group Command Authorization**.

Step 4   Select **Deny**, which appears under Unmatched Cisco IOS commands.

Step 5   Select the **Command** check box.

Step 6   In the Command field, enter one of the following allowable services: **ftp**.

Step 7   Leave the Arguments field blank.

Step 8   Select **Permit**, which appears under Unlisted arguments.

Step 9   Click **Submit** to add more rules, or click **Submit + Restart** when finished.

You can also configure authorization rules for services to specific hosts in CSACS by completing the following steps:

Step 1   Click **Group Setup** from the navigation bar and select a group. The Group Setup window shown in Figure 13-19 opens.

Figure 13-19   *Authorization Rules Allowing Specific Hosts*

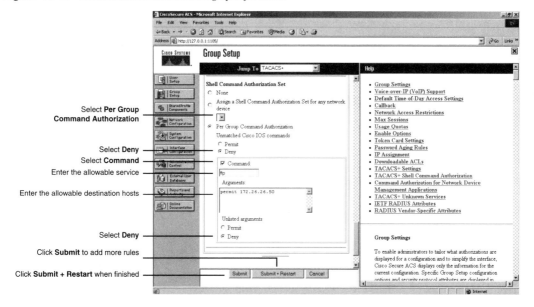

Step 2   Scroll down in the Group Setup window until you find Shell Command Authorization Set.

Step 3   Select **Per Group Command Authorization**.

Step 4   Select **Deny**, which appears under Unmatched Cisco IOS commands.

Step 5   Select the **Command** check box.

Step 6   In the Command field, enter one of the following allowable services: **ftp**, **telnet**, or **http**.

Step 7   In the Arguments field, enter the IP addresses of the host that users are authorized to access. Use the following format:

```
permit ip_addr
```
(*ip_addr* is the IP address of the host.)

Step 8   Select **Deny**, which appears under Unlisted arguments.

Step 9   Click **Submit** to add more rules, or click **Submit + Restart** when finished.

Downloadable ACLs

This section describes the advantages of downloadable ACLs and explains how to configure them. The PIX Firewall supports per-user ACL authorization, by which a user is authorized to do only what is permitted in the user's individual ACL entries. Using the PIX Firewall's downloadable ACL feature, you can download per-user ACLs on an AAA server to the PIX Firewall during user authentication.

Downloadable ACLs enable you to enter an ACL once, in CSACS, and then load that ACL to any number of PIX Firewalls. Downloadable ACLs work in conjunction with ACLs that are configured directly on the PIX Firewall and applied to its interfaces. Neither type of ACL takes precedence over the other. To pass through the PIX Firewall, traffic must be permitted by both the interface ACL and the dynamic ACL if both are applicable. If either ACL denies the traffic, the traffic is blocked.

Downloadable ACLs are applied to the interface from which the user is prompted to authenticate. They expire when the uauth timer expires, and you can remove them by entering the **clear uauth** command.

NOTE   Downloadable ACLs are supported with RADIUS only. They are not supported with TACACS+.

As shown in Figure 13-20, the following sequence of events takes place when named downloadable ACLs are configured and a user attempts to establish a connection through the PIX Firewall:

Figure 13-20 *Downloadable ACLs*

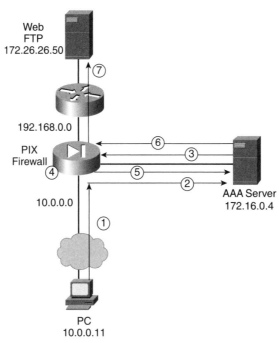

1 The user initiates a connection to the web server at 172.26.26.50. The application connection request is intercepted by the PIX Firewall, which then interacts with the user to obtain the username and password.

2 The PIX Firewall builds a RADIUS request containing the user identification and password and sends it to the AAA server.

3 The AAA server authenticates the user and retrieves from its configuration database the ACL name associated with the user. The AAA server then builds a RADIUS response packet containing the ACL name and sends it to the PIX Firewall.

4 The PIX Firewall checks to see whether it already has the named ACL. A downloadable ACL is not downloaded again as long as it exists on the PIX Firewall. Furthermore, to keep ACLs synchronized between a PIX Firewall and an AAA server, the AAA server downloads a version identification to the PIX Firewall along with the ACL name. This step enables the PIX Firewall to determine whether it needs to request an updated ACL.

5 If the named ACL is not present, the PIX Firewall uses the name as a user identification and a null password to build a RADIUS access request. The PIX Firewall then sends the RADIUS access request to the AAA server.

6 The AAA server retrieves from its configuration database the ACL associated with the ACL name. The AAA server then builds a RADIUS response packet containing the ACL and sends it to the PIX Firewall.

7 The PIX Firewall extracts the ACL, adds it to its configuration, and forwards the connection request to the application server. The user then connects and interacts with the application server.

8 The downloaded ACL appears on the PIX Firewall as shown in the code segment that follows. The **acs_ten_acl** is the name for the ACL as defined in the Shared Profile Component (SPC), and **3b5385f7** is a unique version identification:

```
access-list #ACSACL#-PIX-acs_ten_acl-3b5385f7 permit tcp any host
   172.26.26.50
access-list #ACSACL#-PIX-acs_ten_acl-3b5385f7 permit udp any host
   172.26.26.50
access-list #ACSACL#-PIX-acs_ten_acl-3b5385f7 permit icmp any host
   172.26.26.50
access-list #ACSACL#-PIX-acs_ten_acl-3b5385f7 permit tcp any host
   172.26.26.51
access-list #ACSACL#-PIX-acs_ten_acl-3b5385f7 permit udp any host
   172.26.26.51
access-list #ACSACL#-PIX-acs_ten_acl-3b5385f7 permit icmp any host
   172.26.26.51
access-list #ACSACL#-PIX-acs_ten_acl-3b5385f7 permit tcp any host
   172.26.26.52
access-list #ACSACL#-PIX-acs_ten_acl-3b5385f7 permit udp any host
   172.26.26.52
access-list #ACSACL#-PIX-acs_ten_acl-3b5385f7 permit icmp any host
   172.26.26.52
access-list #ACSACL#-PIX-acs_ten_acl-3b5385f7 deny ip any any
```

Configuring Downloadable ACLs in CSACS

There are two methods of configuring downloadable ACLs on the AAA server. The first method, downloading named ACLs, is to configure a user authentication profile to include an SPC and then configure the SPC to include both the ACL name and the actual ACL. If you configure a downloadable ACL as a named SPC, you can apply that ACL to any number of CSACS user, or user group, profiles. You should use this method when there are frequent requests for downloading a large ACL.

The second method is to configure on an AAA server a user authentication profile that includes the actual PIX Firewall ACL. In this case, the ACL is not identified by a name. You must define each ACL entry in the user profile. You should use this method when requests are not frequent for the same ACL. For instructions on downloading ACLs without names, refer to the documentation on Cisco.com.

Complete the following steps on the AAA server to configure named downloadable ACLs:

Step 1   Select **Interface Configuration > Advanced Options** from the main CSACS window to enable the Downloadable ACLs option. Within the Advanced Options group box shown in Figure 13-21, select the following:

— **User-Level Downloadable ACLs**

— **Group-Level Downloadable ACLs**

Figure 13-21   *Interface Configuration Windows*

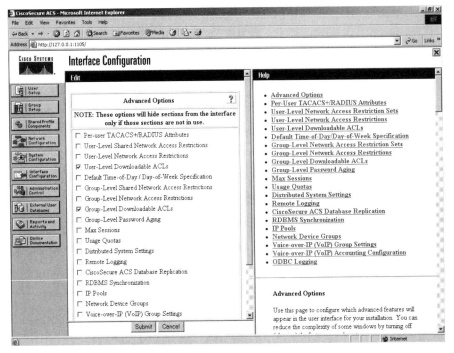

Step 2   Select **Downloadable PIX ACLs** from the SPC menu item.

Step 3   Click **Add** to add an ACL definition. Enter the name, description, and the actual definitions for the ACL, as shown in Figure 13-22.

Figure 13-22 *Shared Profile Components Window*

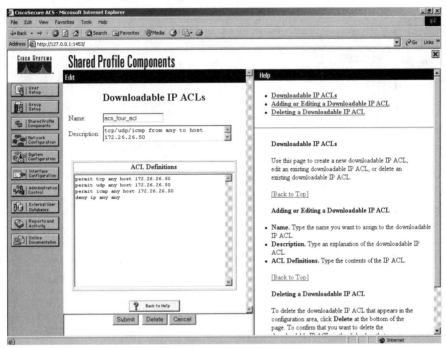

The ACL definition consists of one or more PIX Firewall **access-list** command statements with each statement on a separate line. You must enter each statement without the **access-list** keyword and the *acl_ID* for the ACL. The rest of the command line must conform to the syntax and semantics rules of the PIX Firewall **access-list** command. A PIX Firewall syslog message is logged if there is an error in a downloaded **access-list** command. When you finish specifying the ACL, click **Submit**.

Assigning the ACL to the User

After you configure the downloadable ACL, configure a CSACS user through User Setup to include the defined ACL in the user settings. Enter the username you want to configure downloadable ACLs for and click **Add/Edit**. in the User Setup screen shown in Figure 13-23, click the **Assign IP ACL** check box and select a previously configured ACL from the drop-down list. Click **Submit** to apply the configuration. You can follow the same procedure to assign downloadable ACLs to a group using the Group Setup screen..

Figure 13-23 *Assigning the ACL to the User*

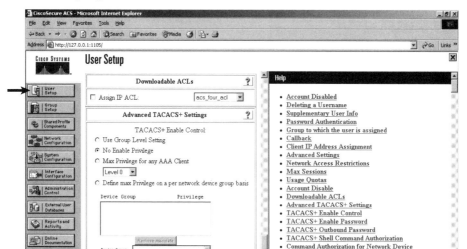

Accounting Configuration

This section demonstrates how to enable and configure accounting. Accounting information tracks who is accessing specific hosts or services on the network. It can also track the amount of time that a user is logged in or the amount of traffic that the user is generating. You can use the accounting information to satisfy organizational policy requirements or even for billing purposes.

The syntax for the **aaa accounting** commands is as follows:

```
aaa accounting include | exclude acctg_service inbound | outbound | if_name local_ip
  local_mask foreign_ip foreign_mask group_tag
no aaa accounting include | exclude authen_service inbound | outbound | if_name
  group_tag
clear aaa [accounting [include | exclude authen_service inbound | outbound | if_name
  group_tag]]
```

Table 13-8 describes the **aaa accounting** command arguments.

Table 13-1   **aaa accounting** *Command Arguments*

Argument	Definition
include *acctg_service*	The accounting service. Accounting is provided for all services, or you can limit it to one or more services. Possible values are any, FTP, HTTP, Telnet, or protocol/port. Use any to provide accounting for all TCP services. To provide accounting for UDP services, use the protocol/port form.
exclude *acctg_service*	Create an exception to a previously stated rule by excluding the specified service from authentication, authorization, or accounting to the specified host. The **exclude** parameter improves the former **except** option by allowing the user to specify a port to exclude to a specific host or hosts.
inbound	Authenticates or authorizes inbound connections. Inbound means the connection originates on the outside interface and is being directed to the inside or any other perimeter interface.
outbound	Authenticates or authorizes outbound connections. Outbound means the connection originates on the inside and is being directed to the outside or any other perimeter interface.
if_name	Interface name from which users require authentication. Use *if_name* in combination with the *local_ip* address and the *foreign_ip* address to determine where access is sought and from whom.
local_ip	The IP address of the host or network of hosts that you want to be authenticated or authorized. You can set this address to 0 to mean all hosts and to let the authentication server decide which hosts are authenticated.
local_mask	Network mask of *local_ip*. Always specify a specific mask value. Use 0 if the IP address is 0. Use 255.255.255.255 for a host.
foreign_ip	The IP address of the hosts that you want to access the *local_ip* address. Use 0 to mean all hosts.
foreign_mask	Network mask of *foreign_ip*. Always specify a specific mask value. Use 0 if the IP address is 0. Use 255.255.255.255 for a host.
group_tag	The group tag set with the **aaa-server** command.

You specify the value of the *acctg_service* argument using the protocol/port form, and enter the protocol as a number (6 for TCP and 17 for UDP). The port is the TCP or UDP destination port. A port value of 0 means all ports. Example 13-8 demonstrates **aaa accounting** commands using the protocol/port form.

Example 13-8 *Accounting Configuration*

```
pixfirewall(config)# aaa accounting include 17/53 inbound 0 0 0 0 MYTACACS
pixfirewall(config)# aaa accounting include 6/25 inbound 0 0 0 0 MYTACACS
```

In Example 13-8, the first statement enables accounting for DNS lookups from the outside interface. The second statement enables accounting of SMTP packets from the outside interface.

match *acl_name* Option

In PIX Firewall Software Versions 5.2 and higher, the **match** *acl_name* option is available in the **aaa** command. With the **match** *acl_name* option, the **aaa** command can take part of its input from an ACL.

The syntax for the **aaa authentication | authorization | accounting** command with the **match** *acl_name* option is as follows:

```
aaa authentication | authorization | accounting match acl_name inbound | outbound |
if_name group_tag
```

Table 13-9 describes the **aaa** command arguments.

Table 13-2   **aaa** *Command Arguments*

Argument	Definition
match *acl_name*	Specifies an access-list command statement name.
inbound	Authenticates or authorizes inbound connections. Inbound means the connection originates on the outside interface and is being directed to the inside interface.
outbound	Authenticates or authorizes outbound connections. Outbound means the connection originates on the inside and is being directed to the outside interface.
if_name	Interface name from which users require authentication. Use *if_name* in combination with the *local_ip* address and the *foreign_ip* address to determine where access is sought and from whom.
group_tag	The group tag set with the **aaa-server** command. To use the local PIX Firewall user authentication database, enter **LOCAL** for this parameter.

Example 13-9 demonstrates how you use this option to configure authentication. In this example, the ACL **mylist** permits all TCP traffic from network 10.0.0.0 to network 172.26.26.0. The **match** *acl_name* option in the **aaa** command instructs the PIX Firewall to require authentication when the action the user is trying to perform matches the actions specified in **mylist**. Therefore, any time a user on the 10.0.0.0 internal network uses any TCP application to access network 172.26.26.0, he is required to authenticate. In other words, the command **aaa authentication match mylist outbound MYTACACS** is equal to **aaa authentication include any outbound 10.0.0.0 255.255.255.0 172.26.26.0 255.255.255.0 MYTACACS**.

Example 13-9   **aaa match** *acl_name Option*

```
pixfirewall(config)# access-list mylist permit tcp 10.0.0.0 255.255.255.0
   172.26.26.0 255.255.255.0
pixfirewall(config)# aaa authentication match mylist outbound MYTACACS
```

Traditional **aaa** command configuration and functionality continue to work as in previous versions and are not converted to the ACL format. Hybrid configurations, which are traditional configurations combined with the new ACL configurations, are not recommended.

Viewing Accounting Information in CSACS

Complete the following steps to view accounting records within CSACS:

Step 1   In the navigation bar, select **Reports and Activity**. The Reports and Activity window shown in Figure 13-24 opens.

Figure 13-24   *Viewing Accounting Records*

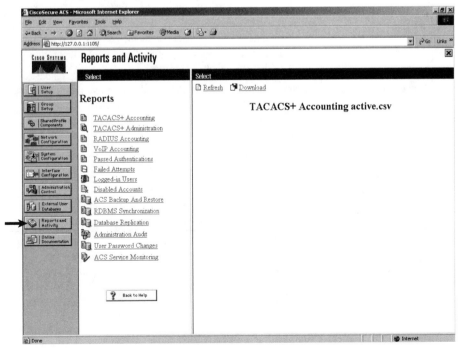

Step 2   Click **TACACS+ Accounting from the Reports** to display the accounting records.

Troubleshooting AAA Configurations

You can use the **show aaa** and **show aaa-server** commands to confirm the configuration of the various **aaa** commands. The output from the **show aaa** command reviews the configured **aaa authentication, aaa authorization,** and **aaa accounting** commands that have been input. The syntax for the **show aaa-server** and **show aaa** commands is as follows:

```
show aaa-server
clear aaa-server [group_tag]
no aaa-server group_tag (if_name) host server_ip key timeout seconds
show aaa [authentication | authorization | accounting]
```

Table 13-10 describes the **show aaa-server** and **show aaa** command arguments.

Table 13-10   **show aaa-server** *and* **show aaa** *Command Arguments*

Argument	Definition
group_tag	An alphanumeric string that is the name of the server group.
if_name	The interface name on which the server resides.
host *server_ip*	The IP address of the TACACS+ or RADIUS server.
key	A case-sensitive, alphanumeric keyword of up to 127 characters that is the same value as the key on the TACACS+ server. Any characters entered past 127 are ignored. The key is used between the client and server for encrypting data between them. The key must be the same on both the client and server systems. Spaces are not permitted in the key, but other special characters are.
timeout *seconds*	A retransmit timer that specifies the duration that the PIX Firewall retries access. Access to the AAA server is retried 4 times before choosing the next AAA server. The default is 5 seconds. The maximum time is 30 seconds.
authentication	Displays user authentication, prompts user for username and password, and verifies information with the authentication server.
authorization	Displays TACACS+ user authorization for services. (The PIX Firewall does not support RADIUS authorization.) The authentication server determines what services the user is authorized to access.
accounting	Displays accounting services with the authentication server. Use of this command requires that you previously used the **aaa-server** command to designate an authentication server.

You can also use the **show auth-prompt**, **show timeout uauth**, and the **show virtual** commands to view the configuration settings for those commands. The syntax for the **show auth-prompt**, **show timeout uauth**, and the **show virtual** commands is as follows:

```
show auth-prompt [prompt | accept | reject]
show timeout uauth
show virtual [http | telnet]
```

Table 13-11 describes the **show auth-prompt**, **show timeout uauth**, and the **show virtual** command arguments.

Table 13-11 **show auth-prompt**, **show timeout uauth**, *and* **show virtual** *Command Arguments*

Argument	Definition
prompt	Displays the prompt users get when authenticating
accept	Displays the message users get when successfully authenticating
reject	Displays the message users get when unsuccessfully authenticating
timeout uauth	Displays the current uauth timer values for all authenticated users
http	Displays the virtual HTTP configuration
telnet	Displays the virtual Telnet configuration

Example 13-10 shows sample outputs for the **show aaa-server**, **show aaa**, **show auth-prompt**, **show timeout uauth**, and the **show virtual** commands.

Example 13-10 **show** *Command Outputs*

```
pixfirewall(config)# show aaa-server
aaa-server TACACS+ protocol tacacs+
aaa-server RADIUS protocol radius
aaa-server LOCAL protocol local
aaa-server MYTACACS protocol tacacs+
aaa-server MYTACACS (inside) host 10.0.0.11 secretkey timeout 5

pixfirewall(config)# show aaa
aaa authentication any outbound 0.0.0.0 0.0.0.0 0.0.0.0 0.0.0.0 MYTACACS
aaa authentication telnet console MYTACACS
aaa authorization telnet outbound 0.0.0.0 0.0.0.0 0.0.0.0 0.0.0.0 MYTACACS
aaa accounting any outbound 0.0.0.0 0.0.0.0 0.0.0.0 0.0.0.0 MYTACACS

pixfirewall(config)# show auth-prompt
auth-prompt prompt prompt Authenticate to the Firewall
auth-prompt prompt accept You've been Authenticated
auth-prompt prompt reject Authentication Failed

pixfirewall(config)# show timeout uauth
timeout uauth 3:00:00 absolute uauth 0:30:00 inactivity

pixfirewall(config)# show virtual
virtual http 192.168.0.2
virtual telnet 192.168.0.2
```

Summary

This section summarizes the information you learned in this chapter:

- Authentication is who you are, authorization is what you can do, and accounting is what you did.

- Authentication is valid without authorization, but authorization is never valid without authentication.

- The PIX Firewall supports the following AAA protocols: TACACS+ and RADIUS.

- Users are authenticated with Telnet, FTP, or HTTP by the PIX Firewall.

- Cut-through proxy technology allows users through the PIX Firewall after authenticating.

- Two steps must be taken to enable AAA:

  — Configure AAA on the PIX Firewall.

  — Install and configure CSACS on a server.

- Downloadable ACLs enable you to enter an ACL once, in CSACS, and then load that ACL to any number of PIX Firewalls during user authentication.

Chapter Review Questions

To test what you have learned in this chapter, answer the following questions and then refer to Appendix A, "Answers to Chapter Review Questions," for the answers:

1 What is the function of Virtual Telnet?

2 What is authentication?

3 What is authorization?

4 How does the cut-through proxy operation improve the performance of the PIX Firewall?

5 What are downloadable ACLs?

Lab Exercise—Configure the PIX Firewall with AAA

Complete the following lab exercise to practice what you learned in this chapter. Use the following initial configuration commands and continue with the rest of the lab exercises.

NOTE   Many of the settings shown in this initial configuration are default values and do not need to be entered on your PIX Firewall. Specific commands that must be entered are shown in bold for your convenience.

```
: Saved
:
PIX Version 6.3(3)
interface ethernet0 100full
interface ethernet1 100full
interface ethernet2 100full
nameif ethernet0 outside security0
nameif ethernet1 inside security100
nameif ethernet2 dmz security50
enable password 8Ry2YjIyt7RRXU24 encrypted
passwd 2KFQnbNIdI.2KYOU encrypted
hostname pixfirewall
domain-name cisco.com
fixup protocol dns maximum-length 512
fixup protocol ftp 21
fixup protocol h323 h225 1720
fixup protocol h323 ras 1718-1719
fixup protocol http 80
fixup protocol rsh 514
fixup protocol rtsp 554
fixup protocol sip 5060
fixup protocol sip udp 5060
fixup protocol skinny 2000
fixup protocol smtp 25
fixup protocol sqlnet 1521
fixup protocol tftp 69
names
access-list ACLIN permit tcp any host 192.168.1.11 eq www
access-list ACLIN permit tcp any host 192.168.1.10 eq www
access-list ACLIN permit tcp any host 192.168.1.11 eq ftp
access-list ACLIN permit tcp any host 192.168.1.10 eq ftp
pager lines 24
mtu outside 1500
mtu inside 1500
mtu dmz 1500
ip address outside 192.168.1.2 255.255.255.0
ip address inside 10.0.1.1 255.255.255.0
ip address dmz 172.16.1.1 255.255.255.0
ip audit info action alarm
ip audit attack action alarm
pdm history enable
arp timeout 14400
static (inside,outside) 192.168.1.10 10.0.1.11 netmask 255.255.255.255 0 0
static (dmz,outside) 192.168.1.11 172.16.1.2 netmask 255.255.255.255 0 0
access-group ACLIN in interface outside
timeout xlate 3:00:00
timeout conn 1:00:00 half-closed 0:10:00 udp 0:02:00 rpc 0:10:00 h225 1:00:00
timeout h323 0:05:00 mgcp 0:05:00 sip 0:30:00 sip_media 0:02:00
timeout uauth 0:05:00 absolute
aaa-server TACACS+ protocol tacacs+
aaa-server RADIUS protocol radius
aaa-server LOCAL protocol local
http server enable
no snmp-server location
no snmp-server contact
snmp-server community public
no snmp-server enable traps
floodguard enable
telnet timeout 5
ssh timeout 5
console timeout 0
terminal width 80
Cryptochecksum:aa0cc6e47d705ed128e041c2c2a8412b
: end
```

Objectives

In this lab exercise, you complete the following tasks:

- Install the CSACS for a Windows 2000 server.
- Add a user to the CSACS database.
- Identify the AAA server and protocol.
- Configure and test inbound authentication.
- Configure and test outbound authentication.
- Configure and test console access authentication.
- Configure and test Virtual Telnet authentication.
- Change and test authentication timeouts and prompts.
- Configure CSACS to write downloadable ACLs during authentication.
- Test downloadable ACLs with inbound authentication.
- Configure and test accounting.

Lab Topology

Figure 13-25 displays the topology you need for the lab exercises in this chapter.

Figure 13-25 *AAA Lab Exercise Visual Objective*

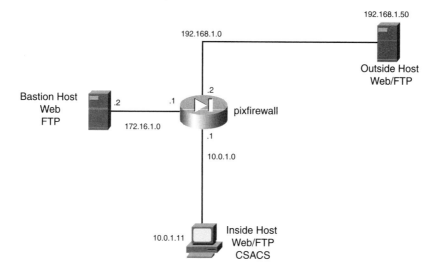

Equipment required to perform the lab includes the following:

- A PIX Firewall with three interfaces
- Category 5 patch cables
- PC host running for DMZ with a web server and FTP server
- PC host for the outside subnet with a web server and FTP server
- PC host for the inside subnet for CSACS installation

Task 1—Install the CSACS for a Windows 2000 Server

Complete the following steps to install CSACS on your inside host running Windows 2000 Server:

Step 1   To install CSACS on Host 1, run its **setup.exe** program.

Step 2   Click **Accept** to accept the Software License Agreement. The Welcome window opens.

Step 3   Read the Welcome window. Click **Next** to continue. The Before You Begin window opens.

Step 4   Read and then select all four check boxes for the items in the Before You Begin frame. This list is a reminder of things you should do before installation. Click **Next** to continue. The Choose Destination Location window opens.

Step 5   Use the default installation folder indicated in the Choose Destination Location windows by clicking **Next** to continue. The Authentication Database Configuration windows open.

Step 6   Verify that **Check the Cisco Secure ACS database only** is already selected in the Authentication Database Configuration frame. Click **Next** to continue.

Step 7   Enter the following information in the CSACS Network Access Server Details frame:

— Authenticate users: **RADIUS (Cisco IOS/PIX)**

— Access server name: **pixfirewall**

— Access server IP address: **10.0.1.1**

— Windows 2000 Server IP address: **10.0.1.11**

— TACACS+ or RADIUS key: **secretkey**

Step 8   Click **Next** to start the file installation process.

Step 9 Select all six items displayed in the Advanced Options frame. Click **Next** to continue.

Step 10 Verify that **Enable Log-in Monitoring** is already selected in the Active Service Monitoring frame. Click **Next** to continue.

Step 11 Deselect **Yes, I want to configure IOS software now**.

Step 12 Click **Next** to continue.

Step 13 Verify that the following are already selected in the CSACS Service Initiation window:

— Yes, I want to start the Cisco Secure ACS Service now.

— Yes, I want Setup to launch the Cisco Secure ACS Administrator from my browser following installation.

Step 14 Deselect **Yes, I want to review the Readme file**.

Step 15 Click **Next** to start the CSACS service.

Step 16 Read the Setup Complete window and then click **Finish** to end the installation wizard and start your web browser with CSACS.

Task 2—Add a User to the CSACS Database

Complete the following steps to add a user to the CSACS database in your Windows 2000 server:

Step 1 The CSACS interface should now appear in your web browser. Click **User Setup** to open the User Setup interface.

Step 2 Add a user by entering **aaauser** in the User field.

Step 3 Click **Add/Edit** to go into the User Information edit window.

Step 4 Within the User Setup group box, locate the Password and Confirm Password fields directly beneath the following text:

```
Cisco Secure PAP (Also used for CHAP/MS-CHAP/ARAP, if the Separate
field is not checked.)
```

Step 5 Give the user a password by entering **aaapass** in both the Password and Confirm Password fields.

Step 6 Click **Submit** to add the new user to the CSACS database. Wait for the interface to return to the User Setup main window.

Task 3—Identify the AAA Server and Protocol

Complete the following steps to identify the AAA server and the AAA protocol on the PIX Firewall:

Step 1   Create a group tag called **MYRADIUS** and assign the TACACS+ protocol to it:

```
pixfirewall(config)# aaa-server MYRADIUS protocol radius
```

Step 2   Assign the CSACS IP address and the encryption key **secretkey**:

```
pixfirewall(config)# aaa-server MYRADIUS (inside) host insidehost
secretkey
```

Step 3   Verify your configuration:

```
pixfirewall(config)# show aaa-server
aaa-server TACACS+ protocol tacacs+
aaa-server RADIUS protocol radius
aaa-server LOCAL protocol local
aaa-server MYRADIUS protocol radius
aaa-server MYRADIUS (inside) host insidehost secretkey timeout 10
```

Task 4—Configure and Test Inbound Authentication

Complete the following steps to enable the use of inbound authentication on the PIX Firewall:

Step 1   Configure the PIX Firewall to require authentication for all inbound traffic:

```
pixfirewall(config)# aaa authentication include any inbound
0 0 0 0 MYRADIUS
```

Step 2   Verify your configuration:

```
pixfirewall(config)# show aaa authentication
aaa authentication include tcp/0 outside 0.0.0.0 0.0.0.0 0.0.0.0 0.0.0.0
MYRADIUS
```

Step 3   Enable console logging of all messages:

```
pixfirewall(config)# logging console debug
```

Step 4   You must now test inbound web authentication. Open a web browser on the outside host and access the DMZweb server:

```
http://192.168.1.11
```

When the web browser prompts you, enter **aaauser** for the username and **aaapass** for the password. On the PIX Firewall console, you should see log entries indicating successful authentication.

Step 5   Display the PIX Firewall authentication statistics:

```
pixfirewall(config)# show uauth
                        Current     Most Seen
Authenticated Users     1           1
Authen In Progress      0           1
user 'aaauser' at 192.168.1.50, authenticated
    absolute   timeout: 0:05:00
    inactivity timeout: 0:00:00
```

Task 5—Configure and Test Outbound Authentication

Complete the following steps to enable the use of outbound authentication on the PIX Firewall:

Step 1   Configure the PIX Firewall to require authentication for all outbound connections to the 192.168.1.0 network:

```
pixfirewall(config)# aaa authentication include any outbound 0 0
    192.168.1.0 255.255.255.0 MYRADIUS
```

Step 2   Test FTP outbound authentication from the inside host:

```
C:\> ftp 192.168.1.50
```

When connected, log in using username **aaauser** and password **aaapass@ftppass**.

On the PIX Firewall console, you should see the following:

```
109001: Auth start for user '???' from 10.0.1.11/3142 to 192.168.1.50/21
109011: Authen Session Start: user 'aaauser', sid 13
109005: Authentication succeeded for user 'aaauser' from 10.0.1.11/3142
to 192.168.1.50 on interface inside
302013: Built outbound TCP connection 218 for outside:192.168.1.50/21
(192.168.1.50/21) to inside:10.0.1.11/3142 (192.168.1.10/3142)
(aaauser)
```

Step 3   Display authentication statistics on the PIX Firewall:

```
pixfirewall(config)# show uauth
                        Current     Most Seen
Authenticated Users     1           1
Authen In Progress      0           1
user 'aaauser' at 10.0.1.11, authenticated
    absolute   timeout: 0:05:00
    inactivity timeout: 0:00:00
```

Step 4   Clear the uauth timer:

```
pixfirewall(config)# clear uauth
pixfirewall(config)# show uauth
                            Current    Most Seen
Authenticated Users           0            2
Authen In Progress            0            2
```

Step 5   If the inside host web browser is open, close it. Choose **File > Exit** from the web browser's menu.

Step 6   Test outbound web authentication. Open the browser on the inside host and go to the following URL:

```
http://192.168.1.50
```

Step 7   When you are prompted for a username and password, enter **aaauser** as the username and **aaapass** as the password:

```
User Name: aaauser
Password: aaapass
```

On the PIX Firewall console, you should see log entries indicating successful authentication.

Step 8   Display authentication statistics on the PIX Firewall:

```
pixfirewall(config)# show uauth
                            Current    Most Seen
Authenticated Users           1            1
Authen In Progress            0            1
user 'aaauser' at 10.0.1.11, authenticated
    absolute   timeout: 0:05:00
    inactivity timeout: 0:00:00
```

Step 9   Close the browser.

Task 6—Configure and Test Console Access Authentication

Complete the following steps to enable console Telnet authentication at the PIX Firewall:

Step 1   Configure the PIX Firewall to require authentication for Telnet console connections:

```
pixfirewall(config)# aaa authentication telnet console MYRADIUS
```

Step 2   Configure the PIX Firewall to allow console Telnet logins:

```
pixfirewall(config)# telnet 10.0.1.11 255.255.255.255 inside
```

Step 3   From the inside host, Telnet to the PIX Firewall console:

```
C:\> telnet 10.0.1.1
Username: aaauser
Password: aaapass
Type help or '?' for a list of available commands.
pixfirewall>
```

On the PIX Firewall console, you should see the following:

```
307002: Permitted Telnet login session from 10.0.1.11
111006: Console Login from aaauser at console
```

Task 7—Configure and Test Virtual Telnet Authentication

Complete the following steps to enable the use of authentication with virtual Telnet on the PIX Firewall:

Step 1   Configure the PIX Firewall to accept authentication to a Virtual Telnet service:

```
pixfirewall(config)# virtual telnet 192.168.1.5
```

Step 2   Clear the uauth timer:

```
pixfirewall(config)# clear uauth
```

Step 3   Telnet to the virtual Telnet IP address to authenticate from the inside host:

```
C:\> telnet 192.168.1.5
LOGIN Authentication
Username: aaauser
Password: aaapass
Authentication Successful
```

Step 4   Test that you are authenticated. Open your web browser and enter the following in the URL field:

```
http://192.168.1.50
```

You should not be prompted to authenticate.

Step 5   Close the browser and clear the uauth timer:

```
pixfirewall(config)# clear uauth
```

Step 6   Test that you are not authenticated and need to re-authenticate. Open the browser on the inside host and enter the following in the URL field:

```
http://192.168.1.50
```

Step 7   When prompted, enter **aaauser** for the username and **aaapass** for the password.

Step 8   Close your browser.

Task 8—Change and Test Authentication Timeouts and Prompts

Complete the following steps to change the authentication timeouts and prompts:

Step 1   View the current uauth timeout settings:

```
pixfirewall(config)# show timeout uauth
timeout uauth 0:05:00 absolute
```

Step 2   Set the uauth absolute timeout to 3 hours:

```
pixfirewall(config)# timeout uauth 3 absolute
```

Step 3   Set the uauth inactivity timeout to 30 minutes:

```
pixfirewall(config)# timeout uauth 0:30 inactivity
```

Step 4   Verify the new uauth timeout settings:

```
pixfirewall(config)# show timeout uauth
timeout uauth 3:00:00 absolute uauth 0:30:00 inactivity
```

Step 5   View the current authentication prompt settings:

```
pixfirewall(config)# show auth-prompt
```

Nothing should be displayed.

Step 6   Set the prompt that users get when authenticating:

```
pixfirewall(config)# auth-prompt prompt Please Authenticate
```

Step 7   Set the message that users get when successfully authenticating:

```
pixfirewall(config)# auth-prompt accept You've been Authenticated
```

Step 8   Set the message that users get when their authentication is rejected:

```
pixfirewall(config)# auth-prompt reject Authentication Failed, Try
Again
```

Step 9   Verify the new prompt settings:

```
pixfirewall(config)# show auth-prompt
auth-prompt prompt Please Authenticate
auth-prompt accept You've been Authenticated
auth-prompt reject Authentication Failed, Try Again
```

Step 10   Clear the uauth timer:

```
pixfirewall(config)# clear uauth
```

Step 11 Telnet to the Virtual Telnet IP address to test your new authentication prompts. From your Windows 2000 server, enter the following:

```
C:\> telnet 192.168.1.5
LOGIN Authentication
Please Authenticate
Username: aaauser
Password: badpass
Authentication Failed, Try Again
LOGIN Authentication
Please Authenticate
Username: aaauser
Password: aaapass
You've been Authenticated
Authentication Successful
Connection to host lost.
```

Task 9—Configure ACS to Write Downloadable ACLs During Authentication

Complete the following steps to configure ACS to write downloadable ACLs to the PIX Firewall:

Step 1 If the ACS Admin is not already open, launch it by double-clicking the **ACS Admin** icon on the inside host.

Step 2 From the ACS Admin window, click the **Interface Configuration** button. The Interface Configuration window opens.

Step 3 Click **Advanced Options**. The Edit>Advanced Options window opens.

Step 4 Select the check boxes for the following and then click **Submit**. Do not change the other defaults:

— **User-Level Downloadable ACLs**

— **Group-Level Downloadable ACLs**

Step 5 Click the **Shared Profile Components** button. The Shared Profile Components window opens.

Step 6 Click **Downloadable IP ACLs**. The Select>Downloadable IP ACLs window opens.

Step 7 Click the **Add** button. The Edit>Downloadable IP ACLs window opens.

Step 8 Enter **RADIUSAUTH** in the Name field.

Step 9   Add the access-list statements that follow in the ACL Definitions field:

— **permit tcp any host 192.168.1.10**

— **permit tcp any host 192.168.1.11 eq ftp**

— **permit icmp any host 192.168.1.10**

— **deny ip any any**

Step 10   Click **Submit**. The Select>Downloadable IP ACLs page appears with the downloadable ACL highlighted in blue.

Step 11   In ACS Admin, click the **User Setup** button. The User Setup page opens.

Step 12   Click **Find**. The User List appears.

Step 13   Click **aaauser**. The Edit>User: aaauser page opens.

Step 14   Scroll down to Downloadable ACLs, and select the check box for **Assign IP ACL**.

Step 15   Verify that the name of the downloadable ACL you created is displayed in the drop-down box to the right of your checkmark.

Step 16   Click **Submit**.

Task 10—Test Downloadable ACLs with Inbound Authentication

Complete the following steps to test downloadable ACLs with inbound authentication.

Step 1   From the PIX console, clear the uauth cache:

```
pixfirewall(config)# clear uauth
```

Step 2   View existing ACLs before testing authorization. Notice that the outside host is permitted FTP and HTTP access to the bastion host:

```
pixfirewall(config)# show access-list
access-list cached ACL log flows: total 0, denied 0 (deny-flow-max 4096)
            alert-interval 300
access-list ACLIN; 4 elements
access-list ACLIN line 1 permit tcp any host 192.168.1.11 eq www
(hitcnt=0)
access-list ACLIN line 2 permit tcp any host 192.168.1.10 eq www
(hitcnt=0)
access-list ACLIN line 3 permit tcp any host 192.168.1.11 eq ftp
(hitcnt=0)
access-list ACLIN line 4 permit tcp any host 192.168.1.10 eq ftp
(hitcnt=0)
```

Step 3   Test inbound web authentication and authorization by opening a browser on the outside host and accessing the DMZ web server. When prompted to authenticate, enter **aaauser** as the username and **aaapass** as the password. You should be denied access and receive an error:

```
http://192.168.1.11
```

Step 4   View the ACLs again. Notice that the authorization ACL was downloaded to the PIX Firewall. Although the ACL ACLIN does permit HTTP access to the bastion host, the downloaded ACL is blocking access:

```
pixfirewall(config)# show access-list
access-list ACLIN; 4 elements
access-list ACLIN line 1 permit tcp any host 192.168.1.11 eq www
(hitcnt=0)
access-list ACLIN line 2 permit tcp any host 192.168.1.10 eq www
(hitcnt=0)
access-list ACLIN line 3 permit tcp any host 192.168.1.11 eq ftp
(hitcnt=0)
access-list ACLIN line 4 permit tcp any host 192.168.1.10 eq ftp
(hitcnt=0)
access-list #ACSACL#-PIX-RADIUSAUTH-3ddb8ab6; 4 elements
access-list #ACSACL#-PIX-RADIUSAUTH-3ddb8ab6 line 1 permit tcp any host
192.168.1.10 (hitcnt=0)
access-list #ACSACL#-PIX-RADIUSAUTH-3ddb8ab6 line 2 permit tcp any host
192.168.1.11 eq ftp (hitcnt=0)

access-list #ACSACL#-PIX-RADIUSAUTH-3ddb8ab6 line 3 permit icmp any
host 192.168.1.10 (hitcnt=0)

access-list #ACSACL#-PIX-RADIUSAUTH-3ddb8ab6 line 4 deny ip any any
(hitcnt=1)
```

Step 5   Clear the uauth cache:

```
pixfirewall(config)# clear uauth
```

Step 6   View your ACL again:

```
pixfirewall(config)# show access-list
```

The downloadable ACL should no longer be listed.

Task 11—Configure and Test Accounting

Complete the following steps to enable the use of accounting on the PIX Firewall:

Step 1 Configure the PIX Firewall to perform accounting for all outbound traffic:

```
pixfirewall(config)# aaa accounting include any inbound 0 0 0 0 MYRADIUS
```

Step 2 Clear the uauth timer:

```
pixfirewall(config)# clear uauth
```

Step 3 Test FTP inbound accounting by accessing the bastion host via FTP from the outside host:

```
C:\> ftp 192.168.1.11
```

Step 4 View the accounting records. On CSACS, click **Reports and Activity** to open the Reports and Activity interface.

Step 5 Click the **RADIUS Accounting** link.

Step 6 Click the **RADIUS Accounting active.csv** link to open the accounting records.

You should see a record related to the FTP access in Step 3.

Upon completion of this chapter, you will be able to perform the following tasks:

- Describe how failover works.
- Define the primary, secondary, active, and standby PIX Firewalls.
- Identify the four failover interface tests.
- Define failover, LAN-based failover, and stateful failover.
- Configure failover.
- Configure stateful failover.
- Configure LAN-based stateful failover.

CHAPTER 14

Failover

The failover function for the Cisco Secure PIX Firewall provides a safeguard if a PIX Firewall fails. Specifically, when one PIX Firewall fails, another unit takes its place. For failover to work, both firewalls must be exactly the same model and have the same number and types of interfaces, software version, activation key type, Flash memory, and RAM.

Two PIX Firewalls function during the failover process: the primary PIX Firewall and the secondary PIX Firewall. Initially, the primary PIX Firewall functions as the active PIX Firewall and performs normal network functions. The secondary PIX Firewall functions as the standby PIX Firewall, ready to take control should the active PIX Firewall fail to perform. When the primary PIX Firewall fails, the secondary PIX Firewall becomes active while the primary PIX Firewall goes on standby. This entire process is called *failover*.

Understanding Failover

There are two types of failover, *standard* failover and *LAN-based* failover. The two types of failover work the same way. The difference lies in the means by which the primary firewall connects to the secondary firewall. For standard failover, the primary PIX Firewall connects to the secondary PIX Firewall through a special failover cable. The failover cable has one end labeled *primary*, which plugs into the primary PIX Firewall, and the other end labeled *secondary*, which plugs into the secondary PIX Firewall.

In LAN-based failover, the primary and standby firewalls use a dedicated Ethernet connection in place of the serial failover cable. A failover occurs when one of the following situations takes place:

- A power-off or a power-down condition occurs on the active PIX Firewall.
- The active PIX Firewall is rebooted.
- A link goes down on the active PIX Firewall for more than two failover poll intervals (30 seconds total by default).
- The active firewall is forced to failover by the **no failover active** command on the active unit or by the **failover active** command on the standby unit.
- Block memory exhaustion occurs for 15 consecutive seconds or more on the active PIX Firewall.

IP Addresses for Failover

When actively functioning, the primary PIX Firewall uses system IP addresses and MAC addresses. When on standby, the secondary PIX Firewall uses failover IP addresses and MAC addresses.

When the primary PIX Firewall fails and the secondary PIX Firewall becomes active, the secondary PIX Firewall assumes the system IP addresses and MAC addresses of the primary PIX Firewall. The primary PIX Firewall, functioning in standby, then assumes the failover IP addresses and MAC addresses of the secondary PIX Firewall.

You can configure the PIX Firewall to use a virtual MAC address instead of assuming the MAC address of its failover peer. This setup enables the PIX Firewall failover pair to maintain the correct MAC addresses after failover. If you do not specify a virtual MAC address, the PIX Firewall failover pair uses the burned-in network interface card (NIC) address as the MAC address.

NOTE   The virtual MAC address feature is available only in PIX Firewall Software Version 6.2 and higher.

Configuration Replication

Configuration replication is the configuration of the primary PIX Firewall being replicated to the secondary PIX Firewall. To perform configuration replication, both the primary and secondary PIX Firewalls must be configured exactly the same and run the same software release. Configuration replication from the active PIX Firewall to the standby PIX Firewall occurs in three ways:

- When the standby PIX Firewall completes its initial bootup, the active PIX Firewall replicates its entire configuration to the standby PIX Firewall.

- As commands are entered on the active PIX Firewall, they are sent across the failover cable to the standby PIX Firewall.

- Entering the **write standby** command on the active PIX Firewall forces the entire configuration in memory to be sent to the standby PIX Firewall.

Configuration replication occurs only from memory to memory. Because it is not a permanent place to store configurations, you must use the **write memory** command to write the configuration into Flash memory. If a failover occurs during the replication, the new active PIX Firewall has only a partial configuration. The newly active PIX Firewall then reboots itself to recover the configuration from the Flash memory or resynchronize with the new standby PIX Firewall.

When replication starts, the PIX Firewall console displays the message "Sync Started," and when replication finishes, it displays the message "Sync Completed." During replication, you cannot enter information on the PIX Firewall console. Replication can take a long time to complete with standard failover for a large configuration because configuration replication occurs over the failover cable.

Stateful Failover

As stated earlier in the chapter, failover enables the standby PIX Firewall to take over the duties of the active PIX Firewall when the active PIX Firewall fails. There are two types of failover:

- **Failover**—When the active PIX Firewall fails and the standby PIX Firewall becomes active, all connections are lost, and client applications must make a new connection to restart communication through the PIX Firewall. The disconnection happens because the active PIX Firewall does not pass the stateful connection information to the standby PIX Firewall.

- **Stateful failover**—Beginning with PIX Firewall Software Version 5.0, the PIX Firewall provides stateful failover capability. When the active PIX Firewall fails and the standby PIX Firewall becomes active, the same connection information is available at the new active PIX Firewall, and end-user applications are not required to reconnect to keep the same communication session. The connections remain because in stateful failover, stateful information for each connection is passed onto the standby PIX Firewall.

Stateful failover requires a 100 Mbps Ethernet interface to be used exclusively for passing state information between the two PIX Firewalls. This interface can be connected to any of the following:

- Category 5 crossover cable directly connecting the primary PIX Firewall to the secondary PIX Firewall
- 100BASE-TX half-duplex hub using straight Category 5 cables
- 100BASE-TX full duplex on a dedicated switch or the dedicated VLAN of a switch

If you have any Gigabit interfaces on the PIX Firewall, a Gigabit interface is also required for the failover link. The Gigabit interfaces used for failover should be connected to 1000BASE-TX full-duplex ports on a dedicated switch or the dedicated VLAN of a switch.

| NOTE | The PIX Firewall does not support the use of either Token Ring or Fiber Distributed Data Interface (FDDI) for the stateful failover dedicated interface. Data is passed over the dedicated interface using IP protocol 105. No hosts or routers should be on this interface. |

Stateful failover provides a more advanced high-availability solution and does not impact most applications that require uninterrupted sessions.

NOTE   Stateful failover is not currently extended to IP Security (IPSec) and virtual private network (VPN) protocols. Check Cisco.com for the latest information on protocols and services supported with stateful failover.

Failover Interface Test

Both the primary and secondary PIX Firewalls send special failover hello packets to each other over all network interfaces and the failover cable every 15 sec to make sure that everything is working. When a failure occurs in the active PIX Firewall and it is not because of a loss of power in the standby PIX Firewall, failover begins a series of tests to determine which PIX Firewall has failed. The purpose of these tests is to generate network traffic to determine which, if either, PIX Firewall has failed.

At the start of each test, each PIX Firewall clears its received packet count for its interfaces. At the conclusion of each test, each PIX Firewall looks to see whether it has received any traffic. If it has, the interface is considered operational. If one PIX Firewall receives traffic for a test and the other PIX Firewall does not, the PIX Firewall that did not receive traffic is considered to have failed. If neither PIX Firewall has received traffic, the tests then continue.

The following are the four different tests used to assess failover status:

- **Link Up/Down**—This test is a test of the NIC itself. If an interface card is not plugged into an operational network, it is considered failed. For example, the hub or switch has failed, the hub or switch has a failed port, or a cable is unplugged. If this test does not find anything, the network activity test begins.

- **Network activity**—This test is a received network activity test. The PIX Firewall counts all received packets for up to 5 sec. If packets are received at any time during this interval, the interface is considered operational and testing stops. If no traffic is received, the Address Resolution Protocol (ARP) test begins.

- **ARP**—The ARP test consists of reading the PIX Firewall's ARP cache for the 10 most-recently acquired entries. The PIX Firewall sends ARP requests one at a time to these machines, attempting to stimulate network traffic. After each request, the PIX Firewall counts all received traffic for up to 5 sec. If traffic is received, the interface is considered operational. If no traffic is received, an ARP request is sent to the next machine. If at the end of the list no traffic has been received, the ping test begins.

- **Broadcast ping**—The ping test consists of sending out a broadcast ping request. The PIX Firewall then counts all received packets for up to 5 sec. If packets are received at any time during this interval, the interface is considered operational and testing stops. If no traffic is received, the testing starts over again with the ARP test.

Hardware Requirements

Failover is supported on the following PIX Firewall 500-series devices:

- PIX Firewall 515E
- PIX Firewall 525
- PIX Firewall 535

In addition, legacy models 515 and 520 support failover functionality. However, current PIX Firewall models 501 and 506E do not support failover. These models are designed for specific applications and market segments that traditionally do not need or cannot afford redundant hardware configurations.

If your PIX Firewall is one of the models that does support failover, you should note the following requirements before enabling failover:

- Failover can function only on two identical models. For example, you can configure two PIX Firewall 515E models for failover. You cannot use a PIX Firewall 515 and 515E as a failover combination even if the other requirements mentioned here are met.
- The PIX Firewall units in a failover pair should have the same hardware specifications, such as RAM, Flash memory, the number of interfaces, the types of interfaces, and any other hardware component, such as a VPN acceleration card (VAC).
- The PIX Firewall units in a failover pair should have exactly the same version of the PIX Firewall software installed.
- The PIX Firewall units in a failover pair should have the same type of activation key installed. For example, both units should have the Triple Data Encryption Standard/ Advanced Encryption Standard (3DES/AES) activation key, or they should both have the DES activation key.
- If you intend to use stateful failover, you need a 100BASE-TX or 1000BASE-TX interface for that purpose, depending on the configuration of your PIX Firewall.
- If you intend to use LAN-based failover, you need a 100BASE-TX interface for that purpose.

NOTE   You might be able to use the same interface for the stateful and LAN-based failover options, depending on the amount of traffic and the capacity of the interface.

Licensing Requirements

In addition to hardware, failover involves software and licensing considerations. Certain licenses disable failover, even on hardware that supports that feature. For example, a PIX

Firewall 515E with restricted software does not support failover, even though the hardware platform is failover-capable. In that case, you need to upgrade the software license on the PIX Firewall to a version supporting failover. Refer to Cisco.com for the latest licensing and feature set information because this type of information changes frequently.

Cisco provides incentives to deploy failover configurations by providing failover units at substantial discounts compared to standard PIX Firewall prices. You can also purchase failover bundles, which include all the hardware, software, and licensing necessary to implement a PIX Firewall failover solution. These bundles are significantly cheaper than purchasing two separate units with unrestricted and failover licenses and are not that much more expensive than even a single comparably configured PIX Firewall with an unrestricted license.

Cable-Based Failover Configuration

This section explains how to configure both stateful and nonstateful serial failover. Complete the following steps to configure failover with a failover cable. Important details for these steps are explained in the pages that follow. You should power-off the standby firewall and leave it off until instructed to power it on for this procedure:

Step 1   After verifying that the secondary PIX Firewall is powered off, attach a network cable between the primary and secondary firewalls for each network interface you plan to use. If you plan to implement stateful failover, one of the interfaces must be dedicated to this function.

Step 2   Connect the failover cable to the primary PIX Firewall, ensuring that the end of the cable marked primary attaches to the primary firewall and that the end marked secondary connects to the secondary firewall. Do not power on the secondary firewall.

CAUTION   If you install the primary end of the cable in the secondary PIX Firewall, the secondary PIX Firewall will (by virtue of the orientation of the failover cable) synchronize its potentially blank configuration to the primary PIX Firewall.

TIP   If you have made the mistake of incorrectly orienting the failover cable, and have overwritten the configuration of the primary PIX Firewall, remove the failover cable from both firewalls and power cycle the primary PIX Firewall. Unless you issue a **write memory** on the secondary PIX Firewall, the change does not overwrite the startup configuration.

Step 3   Configure the primary PIX Firewall as follows:

(1)   If you have not done so already, use the **nameif** command to assign names and security levels to each interface you plan to use. If you plan to implement stateful failover, one interface must be dedicated to this function.

(2)   For each interface you plan to use, specify a speed such as **10baset** for 10 Mbps or **100basetx** for 100 Mbps. Do not use the **auto** or the **1000auto** option in any interface command in your configuration. For stateful failover, set the interface you will use as the dedicated stateful failover interface to **100full** or **1000sxfull**. If you make changes by using the **interface** command, use the **clear xlate** command after doing so.

(3)   Use the **ip address** command to assign an IP address to each interface you plan to use.

(4)   Specify the **clock set** command on the active PIX Firewall to synchronize the time on both PIX Firewalls.

(5)   For stateful failover, ensure that the maximum transmission unit (MTU) size is 1500 or larger on the stateful failover link.

(6)   Use the **failover** command to enable failover on the primary firewall. You can use the **active** option to make a PIX Firewall the active firewall. Use the **failover active** command to initiate a failover switch from the standby firewall, or use the **no failover active** command from the active firewall to initiate a failover switch. Use this feature to return a failed firewall to service or to force an active firewall offline for maintenance.

(7)   Use the **failover ip address** command to enter a failover IP address for each interface. These IP addresses for the standby firewall differ from the active firewall's addresses, but they should be in the same subnet for each interface.

(8)   If you are configuring stateful failover, use the **failover link** command to specify the name of a dedicated stateful failover interface.

(9)   If you want failover to occur faster, use the **failover poll** command to set a time shorter than 15 sec for the firewalls to exchange hello packets. Set the poll time to a lower value for stateful failover. With a faster poll time,

the PIX Firewall can detect failure and trigger failover faster; however, faster detection might cause unnecessary switchovers when the network is temporarily congested or a network card starts slowly. The default failover poll time is 15 sec. The minimum value is 3 sec, and the maximum is 15 sec.

(10) Use the **write memory** command to save the configuration to Flash memory.

Step 4 Power on the secondary firewall. As soon as the secondary firewall starts, the primary firewall recognizes it and starts synchronizing the configurations. As the configurations synchronize, the messages "Sync Started" and "Sync Completed" appear.

The syntax for the **failover** configuration commands is as follows:

```
failover [active]
failover ip address if_name ip_address
failover link [stateful_if_name]
failover poll seconds
```

Table 14-1 describes the **failover** command arguments.

Table 14-1   **failover** *Command Arguments*

Argument	Definition
active	Makes a PIX Firewall the active PIX Firewall. Use this command when you need to force control of the connection back to the unit you are accessing, such as when you want to switch control back from a PIX Firewall after you fix a problem and want to restore service to the primary PIX Firewall.
if_name	Specifies the interface name for the failover IP address.
ip_address	Specifies the IP address used by the standby firewall to communicate with the active firewall. Use this IP address with the **ping** command to check the status of the standby firewall. This address must be on the same network as the system IP address. For example, if the system IP address is 192.159.1.3, you could set the failover IP address to 192.159.1.4.
link	Specifies the interface where a fast LAN link is available for stateful failover.
stateful_if_name	Specifies a dedicated fast LAN link for stateful failover.
poll *seconds*	Specifies how long failover waits before sending special failover hello packets between the primary and standby firewalls over all network interfaces and the failover cable. The default is 15 sec. The minimum value is 3 sec, and the maximum is 15 sec.

The **failover replicate http** command enables the stateful replication of HTTP sessions in a stateful failover environment. The **no** form of this command disables HTTP replication in a stateful failover configuration. When HTTP replication is enabled, the **show failover** command displays the **failover replicate http** configuration.

The syntax for the **failover replicate http** command is as follows:

```
failover replicate http
```

The **write standby** command writes the configuration stored in RAM on the active failover firewall to the RAM on the standby firewall. When the secondary firewall boots, the primary firewall automatically writes the configuration to the secondary. Use the **write standby** command if the primary and secondary firewall configurations have different information.

The syntax for the **write standby** command is as follows:

```
write standby
```

The **failover reset** command forces both firewalls back to an unfailed state. You can enter this command from either firewall, but it is best to always enter commands at the active firewall. Entering the **failover reset** command at the active firewall places the standby firewall back to an unfailed state.

The syntax for the **failover reset** command is as follows:

```
failover reset
```

The **failover mac address** command enables you to configure a virtual MAC address for a PIX Firewall failover pair. You can remove it with the **no failover mac address** command.

The **failover mac address** command sets the PIX Firewall to use the virtual MAC address stored in the PIX Firewall configuration after failover, instead of assuming the MAC address of its failover peer. This setup enables the PIX Firewall failover pair to maintain the correct MAC addresses after failover. If a virtual MAC address is not specified, the PIX Firewall failover pair uses the burned-in NIC address as the MAC address.

When adding the **failover mac address** command to your configuration, it is best to configure the virtual MAC address, save the configuration to Flash memory, and then reload the PIX Firewall pair. You must also write the complete PIX Firewall configuration, including the **failover mac address** command, into the Flash memory of the secondary PIX Firewall for the virtual MAC addressing to take effect.

The syntax of the **failover mac address** command is as follows:

```
failover mac address mif_name act_mac stn_mac
```

Table 14-2 describes the **failover mac address** command arguments.

Table 14-2 **failover mac address** *Command Arguments*

Argument	Definition
mif_name	Specifies the name of the interface to set the MAC address
act_mac	Specifies the interface MAC address for the active PIX Firewall
stn_mac	Specifies the interface MAC address for the standby PIX Firewall

NOTE   If the virtual MAC address is added when there are active connections, those connections are dropped.

Example 14-1 shows the commands required to configure a virtual MAC address for a PIX Firewall failover pair.

Example 14-1   *Configuring a Virtual MAC Address on a PIX Firewall Failover Pair*

```
pixfirewall(config)# failover ip address outside 192.168.0.7
pixfirewall(config)# failover ip address inside 10.0.0.7
pixfirewall(config)# failover ip address dmz 172.16.0.7
pixfirewall(config)# failover ip address MYFAILOVER 172.17.0.7
pixfirewall(config)# failover mac address outside 00a0.c989.e481 00a0.c969.c7f1
pixfirewall(config)# failover mac address inside 00a0.c976.cde5 00a0.c922.9176
pixfirewall(config)# failover mac address dmz 00a0.c969.87c8 00a0.c918.95d8
pixfirewall(config)# failover mac address MYFAILOVER 00a0.c959.e341 00a0.c696.c7g2
```

You can use the **show failover** command to check the status of the failover pair, as shown in Examples 14-2 and 14-3. These examples show the result of the **show failover** command both before and after failure on the primary PIX Firewall. These examples show the primary PIX Firewall going from active mode to standby mode and the secondary PIX Firewall going from standby mode to active mode during a failover. During this process, the primary PIX Firewall swaps its system IP addresses with the secondary PIX Firewall's failover IP addresses.

Example 14-2   *Showing Failover Output Before Failover on the Primary PIX*

```
pixfirewall(config)# show failover
Failover On
Serial Failover Cable status: Normal
Reconnect timeout 0:00:00
Poll frequency 15 seconds
Last Failover at: 16:08:18 UTC Wed Sep 3 2003
        This host: Primary - Active
                Active time: 360 (sec)
                Interface outside (192.168.0.2): Normal
                Interface inside (10.0.0.1): Normal
                Interface dmz (172.16.0.1): Normal
                Interface intf3 (0.0.0.0): Link Down (Shutdown)
                Interface intf4 (0.0.0.0): Link Down (Shutdown)
                Interface intf5 (0.0.0.0): Link Down (Shutdown)
        Other host: Secondary - Standby
                Active time: 0 (sec)
                Interface outside (192.168.0.7): Normal
                Interface inside (10.0.0.7): Normal
                Interface dmz (172.16.0.7): Normal
                Interface intf3 (0.0.0.0): Link Down (Shutdown)
                Interface intf4 (0.0.0.0): Link Down (Shutdown)
                Interface intf5 (0.0.0.0): Link Down (Shutdown)

Stateful Failover Logical Update Statistics
        Link : Unconfigured
```

Example 14-3 *Showing Failover Output After Failover on the Primary PIX*

```
pixfirewall(config)# show failover
Failover On
Cable status: Normal
Reconnect timeout 0:00:00
Poll frequency 15 seconds
Last Failover at: 16:16:23 UTC Wed Sep 3 2003
        This host: Primary - Standby (Failed)
                Active time: 485 (sec)
                Interface outside (192.168.0.7): Normal (Waiting)
                Interface inside (10.0.0.7): Failed (Waiting)
                Interface dmz (172.16.0.7): Normal (Waiting)
                Interface intf3 (0.0.0.0): Link Down (Shutdown)
                Interface intf4 (0.0.0.0): Link Down (Shutdown)
                Interface intf5 (0.0.0.0): Link Down (Shutdown)
        Other host: Secondary - Active
                Active time: 12 (sec)
                Interface outside (192.168.0.2): Normal (Waiting)
                Interface inside (10.0.0.1): Normal (Waiting)
                Interface dmz (172.16.0.1): Normal (Waiting)
                Interface intf3 (0.0.0.0): Link Down (Shutdown)
                Interface intf4 (0.0.0.0): Link Down (Shutdown)
                Interface intf5 (0.0.0.0): Link Down (Shutdown)

Stateful Failover Logical Update Statistics
        Link : Unconfigured
```

In this example, the primary firewall has detected a failure of its inside interface and has
changed its state to standby. Both units are in waiting mode because of the failure. The
failed unit has removed itself from the network and is no longer sending hello packets on
the network. The new active unit remains in a waiting state until the problem is resolved
and failover communications start again. The **show failover** command output with stateful
failover enabled is shown in Example 14-4.

Example 14-4 *Showing Failover Output for Stateful Failover*

```
pixfirewall# show fail
Failover On
Serial Failover Cable status: Normal
Reconnect timeout 0:00:00
Poll frequency 5 seconds
failover replication http
Last Failover at: 14:12:17 UTC Wed Sep 4 2003
        This host: Primary - Active
                Active time: 7957584 (sec)
                Interface outside (192.168.0.2): Normal
                Interface inside (10.0.0.1): Normal
                Interface DMZ (172.16.0.1): Normal
                Interface MYFAILOVER (172.17.0.1): Normal
                Interface intf4 (0.0.0.0): Link Down (Shutdown)
                Interface intf5 (0.0.0.0): Link Down (Shutdown)
        Other host: Secondary - Standby
```

The failover interface flags shown in Example 14-4 appear to the right of each interface's IP address in the **show failover** command display. The failover flags indicate the following:

- **Failed**—The interface has failed.
- **Link Down**—The interface line protocol is down.
- **Normal**—The interface is working correctly.
- **Shutdown**—The interface has been administratively shut down.
- **Waiting**—A failover event has occurred and the PIX Firewall is not yet monitoring the other unit's interface.

NOTE   After a failover event occurs, the active PIX Firewall enters a waiting state. The active PIX Firewall remains in a waiting state until it receives two hello packets from the standby unit (30 sec by default). While in a waiting state, the active PIX Firewall passes traffic, but it does not monitor and test the interfaces. The waiting period prevents needless testing of interfaces in a switched environment, in which ports might take 30 sec or longer to transition to forwarding mode and thus interfere with failover operation.

In Example 14-4, the items in the top row of the Stateful Failover Logical Update Statistics section of the **show failover** command are as follows:

- **Stateful Obj**—PIX Firewall stateful object
- **xmit**—Number of transmitted packets to the other firewall
- **xerr**—Number of errors that occurred while transmitting packets to the other firewall
- **rcv**—Number of received packets
- **rerr**—Number of errors that occurred while receiving packets from the other firewall

The items in the first column of the following list provide an object static count for each statistic:

- **General**—Sum of all stateful objects
- **sys cmd**—Logical update system commands; for example, **LOGIN** and **Stay Alive**
- **up time**—Up time, which the active firewall passes to the standby firewall
- **xlate**—Translation information
- **tcp conn**—TCP connection information
- **udp conn**—Dynamic User Datagram Protocol (UDP) connection information
- **ARP tbl**—Dynamic ARP table information
- **RIF Tbl**—Dynamic router table information

In Example 14-4, the items in Logical Update Queue Information list the current, maximum, and total number of packets in the receive (rcv) and transmit (xmit) queues.

LAN-Based Failover Configuration

LAN-based failover overcomes the distance limitations imposed by the 6-foot length of the failover cable. With LAN-based failover, you can use an Ethernet cable to replicate configuration from the primary PIX Firewall to the secondary PIX Firewall; the special failover cable is not required. Instead, LAN-based failover requires a dedicated LAN interface and a dedicated switch, hub, or VLAN. You cannot use a crossover Ethernet cable to connect the two PIX Firewalls.

The same LAN interface used for LAN-based failover can also be used for stateful failover. However, the interface needs enough capacity to handle both the LAN-based failover and stateful failover traffic. If the interface does not have the necessary capacity, use two separate, dedicated interfaces.

LAN-based failover allows traffic to be transmitted over Ethernet connections that are relatively less secure than the special failover cable; therefore, to secure failover transmissions, LAN-based failover provides message encryption and authentication using a manual preshared key.

Complete the following steps to configure LAN-based failover:

Step 1 Perform the following steps on any Cisco switch that connects to the PIX Firewall:

   (1)   Enable portfast.

   (2)   Turn off trunking.

   (3)   Turn off channeling.

   (4)   If using a Catalyst 6000 or 6500 series switch, ensure that the Multilayer Switch Feature Card (MSFC) is not running a deferred Cisco IOS Software version.

Step 2 Attach a network cable between the primary and secondary firewalls for each network interface, except the interface to be used for LAN-based failover. If the failover cable is connected to the PIX Firewall, disconnect it.

Step 3 Complete the following substeps to configure the primary PIX Firewall before connecting the failover LAN interface:

   (1)   Use the **clock set** command on the active PIX Firewall to synchronize the time on the primary and secondary PIX Firewalls.

(2)   Ensure that you have not used the **auto** or the **1000auto** option in any interface command in your configuration. If you have used one of these options, change it by re-entering the command with the correct information. Always specify the speed for the interface, such as **10baset** for 10 Mbps or **100basetx** for 100 Mbps. Ensure that the speeds and duplexes are the same for any devices on the subnets, including switches and routers. For stateful failover, set the stateful failover dedicated interface speed to **100full** or **1000sxfull**. This step is extremely important and should be performed even if you are using a crossover connector to connect the PIX Firewalls directly to each other. If you make changes by using the **interface** command, use the **clear xlate** command after doing so.

CAUTION   You must specify the speed and duplex setting for all interfaces when using LAN-based or stateful failover. You should also configure the settings on other devices, such as switches and routers that are directly connected to the PIX Firewall interfaces. Using the **auto** or **1000auto** command interferes with LAN-based and stateful failover operations.

---

(3)   Use the **interface** command to shut down any interfaces you are not using. Leave them unconnected.

(4)   Configure a dedicated LAN-based failover interface as follows:

— Use the **nameif** command to set its name and security level.

— Use the **interface** command to enable it and set its hardware speed.

— Use the **ip address** command to assign an IP address for it.

(5)   Use the **failover** command to enable failover.

(6)   (Optional) For stateful failover, set the failover poll time lower than the default of 15 sec.

NOTE   Setting the failover poll time to a value lower than the default of 15 sec speeds up the failover process, which is important for stateful failover. (If the failover process takes too long, sessions might time out and become useless, even if they are maintained by the new active unit.) However, setting this value too low can cause needless switchovers between the failover pair if hello packets are delayed as a result of normal temporary network congestion or the interfaces starting slowly.

(7)   Set a failover IP address using the **failover ip address** command for each standby firewall interface. It is not necessary for the two firewalls to be configured for this command to work correctly. If you have not entered a failover IP address, **show failover** displays 0.0.0.0 for the IP address, and the monitoring of the interfaces remains in the waiting state. You must set a failover IP address for failover to work. The IP addresses on the standby firewall are different from the active firewall's addresses but should be in the same subnet for each interface.

(8)   If you are configuring stateful failover, use the **failover link** command to specify the name of the dedicated interface you are using.

(9)   Use the **write memory** command to save the primary PIX Firewall's configuration.

(10)   Connect the primary PIX Firewall's failover interface to the network.

(11)   Use the **no failover** command to disable failover.

(12)   Use the **failover lan unit** command to designate this firewall as the primary firewall.

(13)   Use the **failover lan interface** command to specify the name of the failover interface.

(14)   Use the **failover lan key** command to create a shared secret key for failover security.

(15)   Use the **failover lan enable** command to enable LAN-based failover.

(16)   Use the **failover** command to enable failover.

Step 4 Save the primary PIX Firewall's configuration to Flash memory.

You can disable the **failover lan** commands by using the **no** forms of the commands. The syntax of the **failover lan** commands is as follows:

```
failover lan unit primary | secondary
failover lan interface if_name
failover lan key key_secret
failover lan enable
```

Table 14-3 describes the **failover lan** command arguments.

Table 14-3 **failover lan** *Command Arguments*

Argument	Definition
if_name	Specifies the interface name for LAN-based failover
interface *if_name*	Enables encryption and authentication of LAN-based failover messages between PIX Firewalls
unit primary | **secondary**	Command to designate the unit as the primary or secondary firewall.
key_secret	Specifies the shared secret key

NOTE On an interface configured for LAN-based failover, the **failover mac address** command is unnecessary and, therefore, cannot be used because the **failover lan interface** command does not change the IP and MAC addresses when failover occurs.

Step 5 Power on the secondary PIX Firewall.

Step 6 Without the LAN-based failover interface connected, complete the following substeps on the secondary firewall (the secondary unit requires these commands to initially communicate with the primary unit):

(1) Use the **nameif** command to specify a name and security level for the failover interface.

(2) Use the **interface** command to enable the failover interface and set its connection speed.

(3) Use the **ip address** command to specify a name and security level for the failover interface.

(4) Use the **failover ip address** command to assign a failover IP address to the failover interface.

(5) Use the **failover lan unit** command to designate this firewall as the secondary firewall.

(6)   Use the **failover lan interface** command to specify the name of the failover interface.

(7)   Use the **failover lan key** command to enter the secret key shared with the primary firewall.

(8)   Use the **failover lan enable** command to enable LAN-based failover.

(9)   Use the **failover** command to enable failover.

Example 14-5 shows the commands entered as part of Step 6 for a secondary PIX Firewall using **ethernet3** as the failover interface with the following parameters:

— Interface name: MYFAILOVER

— Security level: 55

— Speed and duplex: 100full

— IP address: 172.17.0.1

— Netmask: 255.255.255.0

— Failover IP address: 172.17.0.7

— Failover LAN key: 1234567

Example 14-5   *Configuring a Secondary PIX Firewall for LAN-Based Failover*

```
pixfirewall(config)# nameif ethernet3 MYFAILOVER security55
pixfirewall(config)# interface ethernet3 100full
pixfirewall(config)# ip address MYFAILOVER 172.17.0.1 255.255.255.0
pixfirewall(config)# failover ip address MYFAILOVER 172.17.0.7
pixfirewall(config)# failover lan unit secondary
pixfirewall(config)# failover lan interface MYFAILOVER
pixfirewall(config)# failover lan key 1234567
pixfirewall(config)# failover lan enable
```

The commands in Example 14-5 are the same commands that were used in Step 3 for the primary PIX Firewall. The only difference is the argument for the **failover lan unit** command. On the primary firewall, you should use the **failover lan unit** command with a value of **primary**.

Step 7   Use the **write memory** command to save your configuration to Flash memory.

Step 8   Connect the secondary firewall's failover interface to the network.

Step 9   Use the **reload** command to reboot the secondary PIX Firewall.

After the firewalls are configured, you can use the **show failover** command to view the status of the failover pair. Example 14-6 shows the output of the **show failover** when LAN-based failover is configured. It includes a section for LAN-based failover, which displays the name and IP address of the interface used for LAN-based failover. Notice that this interface does not appear in the interface list that displays the status of the interfaces.

Example 14-6   *Showing Failover Command Output for LAN-Based Failover*

```
pixfirewall# show fail
Failover On
Serial Failover Cable status: My side not connected
Reconnect timeout 0:00:00
Poll frequency 15 seconds
Last Failover at: 14:12:17 UTC Wed Sep 4 2003
        This host: Primary - Active
                Active time: 256305 (sec)
                Interface outside (192.168.0.2): Normal
                Interface inside (10.0.0.1): Normal
                Interface DMZ (172.16.0.1): Normal
                Interface intf4 (0.0.0.0): Link Down (Shutdown)
                Interface intf5 (0.0.0.0): Link Down (Shutdown)
        Other host: Secondary - Standby
                Active time: 54 (sec)
                Interface outside (192.168.0.7): Normal
```

Summary

This section summarizes the information you learned in this chapter:

* PIX Firewall models 515E, 525, 535, and legacy models 515, and 520 support failover. PIX Firewall 501 and 506E do not support failover.

* For failover to work, both firewalls must be identical models and have the same types and numbers of interfaces, software version, activation key type, Flash memory, and RAM.

* The primary and secondary PIX Firewalls are the two firewalls used for failover. The primary PIX Firewall is typically the active unit, whereas the secondary PIX Firewall is usually in standby mode. During a failover, the primary PIX Firewall goes on standby while the secondary becomes active.

* The configuration of the primary PIX Firewall is replicated to the secondary PIX Firewall during configuration replication.

- During failover, connections are dropped, whereas during stateful failover, connections remain active.
- Four interface tests ensure that the PIX Firewalls are running:
  — Link Up and Down test
  — Network activity test
  — ARP test
  — Broadcast ping test
- LAN-based failover enables you to use Ethernet cabling with a dedicated hub, switch, or VLAN for long-distance failover.

Chapter Review Questions

To test what you have learned in this chapter, answer the following questions and then refer to Appendix A, "Answers to Chapter Review Questions," for the answers:

1 What version of PIX Firewall software is required to enable LAN-based failover?

2 What version of the PIX Firewall software is required to enable stateful failover?

3 Which models of the PIX Firewall 500 series support failover?

4 What type of interface is required for stateful failover?

5 Which version of the PIX Firewall software supports virtual MAC addresses for the failover pair?

6 What are the four failover interface tests initiated when a failover occurs?

7 When is the configuration of the primary PIX Firewall replicated to the secondary unit?

Lab Exercise—Configure LAN-Based Failover

Complete the following lab exercise to practice the configuration of LAN-based failover.

Objectives

In this lab exercise, you complete the following tasks:

- Configure the primary PIX Firewall for LAN-based stateful failover to the secondary PIX Firewall.
- Configure the secondary PIX Firewall for LAN-based failover.
- Test LAN-based stateful failover.
- Make the primary PIX Firewall active.

Lab Topology

Figure 14-1 illustrates the configuration you use in this lab exercise.

Figure 14-1 *Failover Lab Topology*

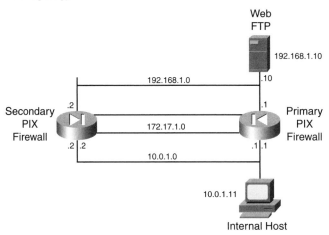

Equipment required to perform the lab includes the following:

- Two identical failover-capable PIX Firewalls with appropriate licensing and at least three interfaces.
- Category 5 patch cables
- 100BASE-T hubs or Catalyst switch with 100 MB ports
- PC host running a web server and FTP server
- PC host for the inside subnet with a web browser and FTP client

Task 1—Configure the Primary PIX Firewall for LAN-Based Stateful Failover to the Secondary PIX Firewall

Complete the following steps to configure the primary PIX Firewall for failover to the secondary PIX Firewall:

Step 1   Assign IP addresses to each interface of the PIX Firewall:

```
pix(config)# ip address outside 192.168.1.1 255.255.255.0
pix(config)# ip address inside 10.0.1.1 255.255.255.0
```

Step 2   Use the **clock set** command on the active PIX Firewall to synchronize the time on both PIX Firewalls:

```
pix(config)# clock set hh:mm:ss month day year
```

Step 3   Disable the unused interfaces (if more than three interfaces are present):

```
pix(config)# interface e3 shutdown
```

Step 4   Assign the PIX Firewall interface name (MYFAILOVER) and security level (55):

```
pix(config)# nameif e2 MYFAILOVER security55
```

Step 5   Enable the interface for 100-Mbps speed and full duplex:

```
pix(config)# interface e2 100full
```

Step 6   Assign an IP address to the interface:

```
pix(config)# ip address MYFAILOVER 172.17.1.1 255.255.255.0
```

Step 7   Use the **failover** command to enable failover on the primary unit:

```
pix(config)# failover
```

Step 8   Change the failover poll time to 8 sec so the PIX Firewall triggers failover faster.

```
pix(config)# failover poll 8
```

Step 9   Use the **show failover** command to verify that the primary PIX Firewall is active:

```
pix(config)# show failover
Failover On
Cable status: My side not connected
Reconnect timeout 0:00:00
Poll frequency 8 seconds
Last Failover at: 14:12:17 UTC Wed Sep 4 2003
        This host: Secondary - Active
                Active time: 255 (sec)
                Interface outside (192.168.1.1): Normal (Waiting)
                Interface inside (10.0.1.1): Normal (Waiting)
                Interface MYFAILOVER (172.17.1.1): Link Down (Waiting)
        Other host: Secondary - Standby
                Active time: 0 (sec)
                Interface outside (0.0.0.0): Unknown (Waiting)
                Interface inside (0.0.0.0): Unknown (Waiting)
                Interface intf2 (0.0.0.0): Unknown (Waiting)

    Stateful Failover Logical Update Statistics
    Link : Unconfigured
```

Step 10   Assign a failover IP address for each interface to specify the standby unit's interface addresses:

```
pix(config)# failover ip address inside 10.0.1.2
pix(config)# failover ip address outside 192.168.1.2
pix(config)# failover ip address MYFAILOVER 172.17.1.2
```

Step 11 Enter the **show failover** command to verify that the secondary unit now has IP addresses for each interface:

```
pix(config)# show failover
Failover On
Cable status: My side not connected
Reconnect timeout 0:00:00
Poll frequency 8 seconds
Last Failover at: 14:12:17 UTC Wed Sep 4 2003
        This host: Secondary - Active
                Active time: 523 (sec)
                Interface outside (192.168.1.1): Normal (Waiting)
                Interface inside (10.0.1.1): Normal (Waiting)
                Interface MYFAILOVER (172.17.1.1): Link Down (Waiting)
        Other host: Secondary - Standby
                Active time: 0 (sec)
                Interface outside (192.168.1.2): Unknown (Waiting)
                Interface inside (10.0.1.2): Unknown (Waiting)
                Interface MYFAILOVER (172.17.1.2): Unknown (Waiting)


Stateful Failover Logical Update Statistics
        Link : Unconfigured
```

Step 12 Use the **failover link** command to specify the name of the dedicated interface you are using:

```
pix(config)# failover link MYFAILOVER
```

Step 13 Save all changes to Flash memory:

```
pix(config)# write memory
```

Step 14 Configure LAN-based failover on the primary unit. Connect the LAN failover interface to the network, and complete the following substeps:

    (1)   Disable failover:

```
pix(config)# no failover
```

    (2)   Specify the primary PIX Firewall to use for LAN-based failover:

```
pix(config)# failover lan unit primary
```

    (3)   Specify the interface name for LAN-based failover:

```
pix(config)# failover lan interface MYFAILOVER
```

    (4)   Enable encryption and authentication of LAN-based failover messages between PIX Firewalls:

```
pix(config)# failover lan key 1234567
```

(5)   Enable LAN-based failover:

```
pix(config)# failover lan enable
```

(6)   Enable failover:

```
pix(config)# failover
```

Step 15 Save all changes to Flash memory:

```
pix(config)# write memory
```

Step 16 Make sure that the primary PIX Firewall is enabled for stateful failover by using the **show failover** command:

```
pix(config)# show failover
Failover On
Cable status: My side not connected
Reconnect timeout 0:00:00
Poll frequency 8 seconds
Last Failover at: 14:12:17 UTC Wed Sep 4 2003
        This host: Primary - Active
                Active time: 698 (sec)
                Interface outside (192.168.1.1): Normal (Waiting)
                Interface inside (10.0.1.1): Normal (Waiting)
                Interface MYFAILOVER (172.17.1.1): Link Down (Waiting)
        Other host: Secondary - Standby
                Active time: 0 (sec)
                Interface outside (192.168.1.2): Unknown (Waiting)
                Interface inside (10.0.1.2): Unknown (Waiting)
                Interface MYFAILOVER (172.17.1.2): Unknown (Waiting)

    Stateful Failover Logical Update Statistics
        Link : MYFAILOVER
        Stateful Obj    xmit        xerr        rcv         rerr
        General         0           0           0           0
        sys cmd         0           0           0           0
        up time         0           0           0           0
        xlate           0           0           0           0
        tcp conn        0           0           0           0
        udp conn        0           0           0           0
        ARP tbl         0           0           0           0
        RIP Tbl         0           0           0           0

        Logical Update Queue Information
                        Cur         Max         Total
        Recv Q:         0           0           0
        Xmit Q:         0           0           0
```

```
LAN-based Failover is Active
        interface MYFAILOVER (172.17.1.1): Normal, peer (172.17.1.2):
Down
```

Step 17 Wait for the failover initialization process to complete. You see the following messages on your PIX Firewall console:

```
LAN-based Failover startup ping test failed!!
Wait for pix LAN-based failover init process to complete...
LAN-based Failover: Send hello msg and start failover monitoring
```

Step 18 Verify that you can ping the web and FTP server:

```
C:\> ping 192.168.1.10
```

Task 2—Configure the Secondary PIX Firewall for LAN-Based Failover

Complete the following steps to prepare the secondary PIX Firewall for failover:

Step 1 Without the LAN-based failover interface connected, complete the following substeps on the secondary PIX Firewall:

(1) When prompted to configure the PIX Firewall through interactive prompts, press **Ctrl-Z** to escape.

(2) Enter configuration mode.

(3) Assign a name and security level to the failover interface:

```
pix(config)# nameif e2 MYFAILOVER security55
```

(4) Enable the interface for 100 Mbps speed and full duplex:

```
pix(config)# interface e2 100full
```

(5) Assign an IP address to the interface:

```
pix(config)# ip address MYFAILOVER 172.17.1.1 255.255.255.0
```

(6) Assign a failover IP address to the interface:

```
pix(config)# failover ip address MYFAILOVER 172.17.1.2
   255.255.255.0
```

(7) Designate this firewall as the secondary firewall:

```
pix(config)# failover lan unit secondary
```

(8) Specify the name of the interface to be used for LAN-based failover:

```
pix(config)# failover lan interface MYFAILOVER
```

      (9)   Enter the secret key shared with the primary PIX
             Firewall:

```
pix(config)# failover lan key 1234567
```

      (10)   Enable LAN-based failover:

```
pix(config)# failover lan enable
```

      (11)   Enable failover:

```
pix(config)# failover
```

      (12)   Save the configuration to Flash memory:

```
pix(config)# write mem
```

Step 2   Connect the secondary PIX Firewall to the network.

Step 3   Reload the secondary PIX Firewall:

```
pix(config)# reload
```

Task 3—Test LAN-Based Stateful Failover

Complete the following steps to test LAN-based stateful failover:

Step 1   After you see the message "Sync Completed" on your primary PIX
Firewall console, start a FTP session on your internal host and verify
connection to the FTP server at 192.168.1.10.

Step 2   Now, reload the primary PIX Firewall:

```
pix(config)# reload
```

Step 3   When asked to confirm the reload, press **Enter**.

Step 4   Return to your FTP connection to the outside host. Verify that it is still
active by entering the **dir** command.

Step 5   Check the failover status by entering the **show failover** command on the
primary:

```
pix(config)# show failover
Failover On
Cable status: My side not connected
Reconnect timeout 0:00:00
Poll frequency 8 seconds
Last Failover at: 14:27:29 UTC Wed Sep 4 2003
        This host: Primary - Standby
                Active time: 912 (sec)
                Interface outside (192.168.1.2): Normal
                Interface inside (10.0.1.2): Normal
```

```
                    Other host: Secondary - Active
                          Active time: 33 (sec)
                          Interface outside (192.168.1.1): Normal
                          Interface inside (10.0.1.1): Normal

        Stateful Failover Logical Update Statistics
              Link : MYFAILOVER
              Stateful Obj    xmit        xerr        rcv         rerr
              General         93          0           3           0
              sys cmd         3           0           3           0
              up time         0           0           0           0
              xlate           1           0           0           0
              tcp conn        90          0           0           0
              udp conn        0           0           0           0
              ARP tbl         0           0           0           0
              RIP Tbl         0           0           0           0


              Logical Update Queue Information
                              Cur     Max     Total
              Recv Q:         0       1       3
              Xmit Q:         0       1       58


        LAN-based Failover is Active
              interface MYFAILOVER (172.17.1.1): Normal, peer (172.17.1.2):
        Normal
```

Task 4—Make the Primary PIX Firewall Active

Complete the following steps to make the primary PIX Firewall the active PIX Firewall:

Step 1   Make the primary PIX Firewall the active PIX Firewall by using the **failover active** command. Make sure that you are connected to the primary PIX Firewall's console port:

```
pix(config)# failover active
```

Step 2   Verify that the **failover active** command worked by using the **show failover** command. The primary PIX Firewall should show that it is in active mode and the secondary PIX Firewall should show that it is in the standby mode:

```
pix(config)# show failover

Failover On

Cable status: My side not connected

Reconnect timeout 0:00:00

Poll frequency 8 seconds
```

```
Last Failover at: 14:28:29 UTC Wed Sep 4 2003
        This host: Primary - Active
                Active time: 927 (sec)
                Interface outside (192.168.1.1): Normal
                Interface inside (10.0.1.1): Normal
        Other host: Secondary - Standby
                Active time: 93 (sec)
                Interface outside (192.168.1.2): Normal
                Interface inside (10.0.1.2): Normal


Stateful Failover Logical Update Statistics
        Link : MYFAILOVER
        Stateful Obj    xmit      xerr      rcv       rerr
        General         112       0         3         0
        sys cmd         3         0         3         0
        up time         0         0         0         0
        xlate           1         0         0         0
        tcp conn        108       0         0         0
        udp conn        0         0         0         0
        ARP tbl         0         0         0         0
        RIP Tbl         0         0         0         0


        Logical Update Queue Information
                        Cur       Max       Total
        Recv Q:         0         1         22
        Xmit Q:         0         1         87


LAN-based Failover is Active
        interface MYFAILOVER (172.17.1.1): Normal, peer (172.17.1.2):
Normal
```

VPN Configuration

On completion of this chapter, you will be able to perform the following tasks:

- Define virtual private networks (VPNs).
- Identify how the PIX Firewall enables a secure VPN.
- Describe basic Internet Key Exchange (IKE) operation.
- Describe the difference between IP Security (IPSec) tunnel and transport modes.
- Identify IPSec standards supported by the PIX Firewall.

CHAPTER 15

Virtual Private Networks

A VPN is a service offering secure, encrypted connectivity over a shared, public network infrastructure such as the Internet. Because the infrastructure is shared, connectivity can be provided at a lower cost than by existing dedicated private networks.

The Cisco PIX Firewall is a powerful enabler of VPN services. The PIX Firewall's high performance, conformance to open standards, and ease of configuration make it a versatile VPN gateway.

PIX Firewall Enabling a Secure VPN

The PIX Firewall enables VPNs in several topologies, as illustrated in Figure 15-1:

- **PIX Firewall to PIX Firewall secure VPN gateway**—Two or more PIX Firewalls can enable a VPN that secures traffic from devices behind the PIX Firewalls. The secure VPN gateway topology eliminates the need for the user to implement VPN devices or software inside the network and thereby makes the secure gateway transparent to users.

- **PIX Firewall to Cisco 3000 VPN Concentrator gateway**—The PIX Firewall and Cisco 3000 VPN Concentrator can interoperate to create a secure VPN gateway between networks.

- **PIX Firewall to Cisco IOS router secure VPN gateway**—The PIX Firewall and Cisco router, running Cisco VPN software, can interoperate to create a secure VPN gateway between networks.

- **Cisco VPN Client to PIX Firewall through dialup**—The PIX Firewall can become a VPN endpoint for the VPN client over a dialup network. The dialup network can consist of ISDN, Public Switched Telephone Network (PSTN) (analog modem), or digital subscriber line (DSL) communication channels.

- **Cisco VPN client to PIX Firewall through network**—The PIX Firewall can become a VPN endpoint for the VPN client over an IP network.

- **Other vendor products to PIX Firewall**—Products from other vendors can connect to the PIX Firewall if they conform to open VPN standards.

Figure 15-1 *PIX Firewall VPN Topologies*

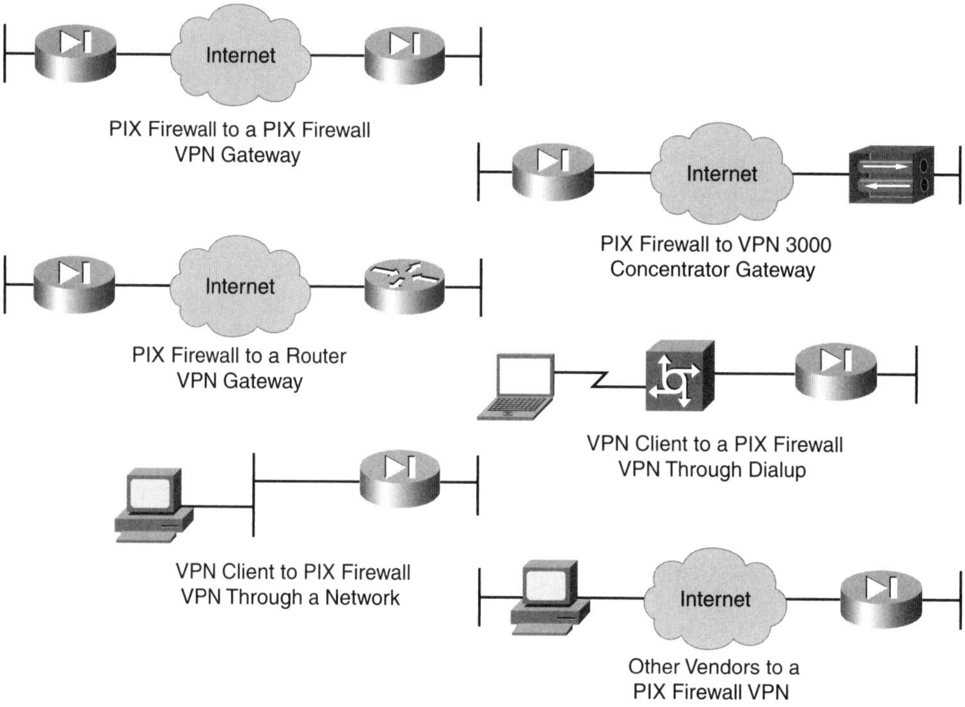

A VPN itself can be constructed in a number of scenarios. The most common are as follows:

- **Internet VPN**—A private, encrypted communications channel over the public access Internet. This type of VPN can be divided into the following:

  — Connecting remote offices across the Internet—Chapter 16, "Site-to-Site VPNs," presents detailed descriptions of PIX Firewall features, commands, and configuration procedures for this type of VPN.

  — Connecting remote dialup users to their home gateways through an Internet service provider (ISP) (sometimes called a virtual private dial network or VPDN)—Detailed descriptions of PIX Firewall features, commands, and configuration procedures for remote access VPNs are presented in Chapter 17, "Client Remote Access VPNs."

- **Intranet VPN**—A private, encrypted communication channel within an enterprise or organization that might or might not involve traffic traversing a WAN.

- **Extranet VPN**—A private, encrypted communication channel between two or more separate entities that can involve data traversing the Internet or some other WAN.

In all cases, the VPN or tunnel consists of two endpoints that can be represented by PIX Firewalls, Cisco VPN Concentrators, Cisco routers, individual client workstations running the VPN client, or other vendors' VPN products that conform to open standards.

IPSec Overview

PIX Firewall Versions 5.0 and higher use the industry-standard IPSec protocol suite to enable advanced VPN features. The PIX Firewall IPSec implementation is based on Cisco IOS IPSec that runs in Cisco routers.

IPSec is a framework of open standards that provides a mechanism for secure data transmission over IP networks, ensuring confidentiality, integrity, and authenticity of data communications over unprotected networks such as the Internet. IPSec acts at the network layer, protecting and authenticating IP packets between a PIX Firewall and other participating IPSec devices (peers), such as PIX Firewalls, Cisco routers, the Cisco VPN client, and other IPSec-compliant products.

The PIX Firewall uses the IPSec protocol to enable secure VPNs. IPSec enables the following PIX Firewall VPN features:

- **Data confidentiality**—The IPSec sender can encrypt packets before transmitting them across a network.

- **Data integrity**—The IPSec receiver can authenticate IPSec peers and packets sent by the IPSec sender to ensure that the data has not been altered during transmission.

- **Data origin authentication**—The IPSec receiver can authenticate the source of the IPSec packets sent. This service depends on the data integrity service.

- **Antireplay**—The IPSec receiver can detect and reject replayed packets, helping prevent spoofing and man-in-the-middle attacks.

IPSec and related security protocols conform to open standards promulgated by the Internet Engineering Task Force (IETF) and documented RFCs and IETF-draft papers. Internet RFCs documenting IPSec are available at http://www.ietf.org/rfc.html. The overall IPSec implementation is guided by *Security Architecture for the Internet Protocol*, RFC 2401. IPSec consists of the following two main protocols:

- **Authentication Header (AH)**—A security protocol that provides authentication and optional replay-detection services. AH acts as a "digital signature" to ensure that tampering has not occurred with the data in the IP packet. With the exception of fields that change in transit, such as checksum and Time-To-Live, AH provides authentication for the entire packet, not just for the data payload. AH was assigned IP protocol number 51 by IANA (Internet Assigned Numbers Authority). AH does not provide data encryption and decryption services. AH can be used either by itself or with ESP.

- **Encapsulating Security Payload (ESP)**—A security protocol that provides data confidentiality and protection with optional authentication and replay-detection services. The PIX Firewall uses ESP to encrypt the data payload of IP packets. ESP can be used either by itself or in conjunction with AH. ESP was assigned IP protocol number 50.

You can configure IPSec to work in two different modes:

- **Tunnel mode**—IPSec between two PIX Firewalls is typically implemented using tunnel mode. In this mode, the entire IP packet, including the original header, is encrypted in ESP. A new unencrypted IP header is used for routing. In this mode, the PIX Firewall is acting as the IPSec proxy and performs all the encryption. This mode does not require the host to perform any encryption.

- **Transport mode**—In this mode, only the IP payload is encrypted. The original IP header is left intact and the ESP header is inserted after the IP header. Because a new IP header is not added, there is less overhead with transport mode.

NOTE   Transport mode is typically used with Layer 2 Tunneling Protocol (L2TP) to allow authentication of native Windows 2000 VPN clients.

To enable IPSec encryption, both parties must share a secret key. IPSec operates in two phases to allow the confidential exchange of a shared secret:

- **Phase 1**—This phase is responsible for securing the initial conversation between IPSec peers, as they begin negotiating the IKE security association (SA). Phase 1 establishes a secure channel between IPSec peers, which is used for exchange of security information in Phase 2.

NOTE   IKE is synonymous with Internet Security Association and Key Management Protocol (ISAKMP/Oakley) in PIX Firewall configuration.

- **Phase 2**—IPSec peers use the secure channel created in Phase 1 to negotiate the IPSec SAs that are used for encryption and transmission of actual user data.

An IPSec SA describes the security settings and services that two IPSec peers use to establish a secure connection. The types of information specified by the SA include transform sets (such as Data Encryption Standard [DES] encryption and a Message Digest 5 [MD5] hash) and the secret keys used by the peers.

NOTE	SAs are unidirectional. A successful bidirectional VPN connection between two IPSec peers requires two SAs.

IPSec Standards Supported

The PIX Firewall supports the following IPSec and related standards:

- IPSec
- IKE
- DES
- Triple DES (3DES)
- Advanced Encryption Standard (AES)
- Diffie-Hellman (D-H)
- MD5
- Secure Hash Algorithm-1 (SHA-1)
- Rivest, Shamir, and Adleman (RSA) signatures
- Certificate authority (CA)
- Network address translation (NAT) Traversal (NAT-T)

Each standard is defined further in the following subsections.

IKE

IKE is a hybrid protocol that provides utility services for IPSec: authentication of the IPSec peers, negotiation of IKE and IPSec SAs, and establishment of keys for encryption algorithms used by IPSec. IKE is synonymous with ISAKMP in PIX Firewall configuration.

DES

Used to encrypt and decrypt packet data, *DES* has a 56-bit key and thereby ensures high-performance encryption. DES is used by both IPSec and IKE.

CAUTION   With the advent of fast desktop computers, DES is no longer considered strong encryption. In 1998, the Electronic Frontier Foundation, using a specially developed computer called the DES Cracker, managed to break DES in less than three days; it performed this task for less than $250,000. The encryption chip that powered the DES Cracker was capable of processing 88 billion keys per second. To protect your production data, Cisco recommends using 3DES or AES encryption.

3DES

3DES is a variant of DES, which iterates three times with three separate keys, effectively tripling the strength of DES. IPSec uses 3DES to encrypt and decrypt data traffic. 3DES uses a 168-bit key, ensuring strong encryption.

AES

AES is a new standard for encrypting and decrypting packet data. Both IPSec and IKE can use AES, which was designed to provide stronger encryption than DES and 3DES, while reducing the encryption overhead relative to DES and 3DES standards. AES can use 128-bit, 192-bit, or 256-bit keys, providing strong encryption and high performance.

D-H

D-H is a public-key cryptography protocol. It enables two parties to establish a shared secret key over an insecure communications channel. D-H is used within IKE to establish session keys. In the PIX Firewall, 768-bit (group 1), 1024-bit (group 2), and 1536-bit (group 5) D-H groups are supported. The 1536-bit group is more secure.

MD5

MD5 is a hash algorithm used to authenticate packet data. The PIX Firewall uses the MD5 hashed message authentication code (HMAC) variant, which provides an additional level of hashing. A hash is a one-way encryption algorithm that takes an input message of arbitrary length and produces a fixed-length output message. IKE, AH, and ESP use MD5 for authentication.

SHA-1

SHA-1 is a hash algorithm used to authenticate packet data. The PIX Firewall uses the SHA-1 HMAC variant, which provides an additional level of hashing. IKE, AH, and ESP use SHA-1 for authentication.

RSA Signatures

RSA is a public-key cryptographic system used for authentication. IKE on the PIX Firewall uses a D-H exchange to determine secret keys on each IPSec peer used by encryption algorithms. The D-H exchange can be authenticated with RSA (or preshared keys).

CA

The *CA* support of the PIX Firewall enables the IPSec-protected network to scale by providing the equivalent of a digital identification card to each device. When two IPSec peers want to communicate, they exchange digital certificates to prove their identities (thus removing the need to manually exchange public keys with each peer or to manually specify a shared key at each peer). The digital certificates are obtained from a CA. The support on the PIX Firewall uses RSA signatures to authenticate the CA exchange.

NAT-T

NAT-T enables transparent IPSec tunnels through NAT devices. NAT-T accomplishes this task by encapsulating the IPSec packet inside a User Datagram Protocol (UDP) wrapper, thus NAT-T autodetects NAT devices and encapsulates IPSec packets only when necessary. NAT-T operates on UDP port 4500.

NOTE   Support for AES encryption, 1536-bit D-H group 5, and NAT-T was introduced in PIX Firewall Version 6.3.

SA

The concept of an SA is fundamental to IPSec. An *SA* is a connection between IPSec peers that determines the IPSec services available between the peers and is thereby similar to a TCP or UDP port. Each IPSec peer maintains in memory an SA database containing SA parameters. SAs are uniquely identified by the IPSec peer address, security protocol, and security parameter index (SPI). You need to configure SA parameters and monitor SAs on the PIX Firewall.

IKE Overview

Before IPSec peers negotiate IPSec SAs and establish security settings for encryption and transmission of user data in Phase 2, they must establish a secure channel in Phase 1. This channel secures negotiations between peers as they establish Phase 2 IPSec SAs. You can configure the settings manually or use IKE with preshared keys or digital certificates for this purpose. IKE operates on UDP port 500 and provides the following benefits:

- Eliminates manual configuration of IPSec parameters

- Lets you specify a lifetime for the IKE SAs

- Provides additional security by allowing encryption keys to change during IPSec sessions

- Provides antireplay capabilities

- Can be used with digital certificates and a CA to provide a scalable solution

- Enables dynamic authentication of peers

There are five parameters to define in each IKE policy. These parameters apply to the IKE negotiations when the IKE SA is established:

- **Encryption algorithm**—Specifies the symmetric encryption algorithm used between IPSec peers. The default encryption is 56-bit DES, but you can also specify 168-bit 3DES. With PIX Firewall Version 6.3 or higher, you can also specify AES with 128-bit, 192-bit, or 256-bit key lengths.

- **Hash algorithm**—Specifies hash algorithm used to ensure data integrity. You can select MD5 or SHA-1. Both algorithms use the HMAC variant, which provides additional security.

- **Authentication**—Specifies the authentication method for IKE negotiations. You can choose digital certificates or preshared keys.

- **D-H group**—Specifies the D-H group used for securing shared key transmission during IKE negotiation. You can select group 1 (768-bit), group 2 (1024-bit), or group 5 (1536-bit). Group 5 is available only with PIX Firewall Version 6.3.

- **SA lifetime**—Specifies the life of the SA in seconds and defaults to 86,400. Shorter SA lifetime values provide more security. However, with longer lifetimes, fewer SA negotiations are required.

You can create multiple IKE policies with different combinations of security settings and assign a priority to each policy. During negotiations, the first peer sends its list of IKE policies to the other peer. The second peer then matches one of its configured IKE policies with the list it receives from the first peer. If multiple matches exist, the highest priority policy is selected, and the IKE SA is established. If no match exists, the SA is not established.

CA Overview

The use of preshared keys for IKE authentication works only when you have a few IPSec peers. CAs enable scaling to a large number of IPSec peers. Although there are a number of methods, using a CA server is the most scalable solution. Other IKE authentication methods require manual intervention to generate and distribute the keys on a per-peer basis. The CA server enrollment process can be largely automated so that it scales well to large deployments. Each IPSec peer individually enrolls with the CA server and obtains public and private encryption keys compatible with other peers enrolled with the server, as shown in Figure 15-2.

Figure 15-2 *CA Server Fulfilling Requests from IPSec Peers*

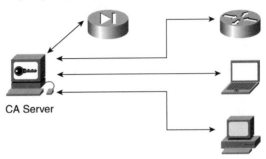

CA Server

PIX Firewalls support the following CA servers:

- VeriSign Private Certificate Services (PCS) and the OnSite service

- Entrust, Entrust VPN Connector, Version 4.1 (build 4.1.0.337) or higher (an in-house CA server solution)

- Baltimore Technologies, UniCERT Certificate Management System, Version 3.1.2 or higher (an in-house CA server solution)

- Windows 2000 Advanced Server, Version 5.00.2195 or higher (an in-house CA server solution)

NOTE   The Windows 2000 Advanced Server CA must be a standalone root CA, not subordinated; otherwise, it is rejected.

Peers enroll with a CA server in a series of steps in which specific keys are generated and then exchanged by the PIX Firewall and the CA server to ultimately form a signed certificate. CA support is configured using the **ca** command, and the enrollment steps can be summarized as follows:

Step 1   Configure a host name:

```
Pixfirewall(config)# hostname pixfirewall
```

Step 2   Configure the domain name:

```
Pixfirewall(config)# domain-name cisco.com
```

Step 3   Generate an RSA key pair:

```
Pixfirewall(config)# ca generate rsa key 1024
```

A general-purpose RSA key pair is generated with a key modulus size of 1024.

Step 4   Declare the CA that will be used by the PIX Firewall:

```
Pixfirewall(config)# ca identity ca.cisco.com 10.0.1.10
```

The CA is identified by its nickname (ca.cisco.com in this example) and its IP address.

Step 5   Configure communication between the PIX and the CA:

```
Pixfirewall(config)# ca configure ca.cisco.com ca 1 100
```

In this example, the PIX is configured for a retry period of 1 minute (min) and retry count of 100.

Step 6   Authenticate the CA:

```
Pixfirewall(config)# ca authenticate ca.cisco.com
```

This command configures the PIX Firewall to authenticate the CA by obtaining its public key and certificate. When configured with an optional fingerprint, the PIX discards certificates that do not contain a matching fingerprint.

Step 7   Request certificates from the CA:

```
Pixfirewall(config)# ca enroll ca.cisco.com capassword123 serial
ipaddress
```

This command submits a request for certificates from the CA. The optional keywords **serial** and **ipaddress** include the PIX Firewall's serial number and IP address in the signed certificate. The challenge password (**capassword123** in this example) is required if you need to revoke this certificate in the future.

Step 8   Verify successful configuration and enrollment:

```
Pixfirewall(config)# show ca certificate
```

Step 9   Save your certificates and configuration:

```
Pixfirewall(config)# ca save all
Pixfirewall(config)# write memory
```

The syntax of the **ca** command is as follows:

```
ca authenticate ca_nickname [fingerprint]
[no] ca configure ca_nickname ca ¦ ra retry_period retry_count [crloptional]
[no] ca crl request ca_nickname
[no] ca enroll ca_nickname challenge_password [serial] [ipaddress]
```

```
ca generate rsa {key | specialkey} key_modulus_size
[no] ca identity ca_nickname [ca_ipaddress| hostname [:ca_script_location]
[ldap_ipaddress| hostname]]
[no] ca save all
[no] ca subject-name ca_nickname X.500_string
[no] ca verifycertdn X.500_string
ca zeroize rsa [keypair_name]
show ca certificate
show ca crl
show ca configure
show ca identity
show ca mypubkey rsa
show ca subject-name
show ca verifycertdn
```

Table 15-1 describes the **ca** command options and parameters.

Table 15-1   **ca** *Command Options and Parameters*

Parameter	Definition
authenticate	The **ca authenticate** command configures the PIX Firewall to authenticate the CA by obtaining the CA's self-signed certificate, which contains the CA's public key.
ca_ipaddress	The CA's IP address that is used with the **ca identity** command.
ca_nickname	The name of the CA used with the **ca identity** command. Currently, the PIX Firewall supports only one CA at a time.
ca	**ra**	Indicates whether to contact the CA or registration authority (RA) when using the **ca configure** command. If the CA you use provides an RA, select the **ra** option.
:ca_script_location	Used to identify the location of the Common Gateway Interface (CGI) scripts on the CA server with the **ca identity** command. Default location and script on the CA server is /cgi-bin/pkiclient.exe. A PIX Firewall uses a subset of the HTTP protocol to contact the CA, so it must identify a particular cgi-bin script to handle CA requests.
challenge_password	A required password (up to 80 characters) used with the **ca enroll** command. Allows the administrator to authenticate certificate revocation requests.
configure	The **ca configure** command specifies communication parameters between the PIX Firewall and the CA.
crloptional	Allows the PIX Firewall to accept other peers' certificates even if the appropriate certificate revocation list (CRL) is not accessible. The default does not include the **crloptional** option.
crl request	The **ca crl request** is used to obtain an updated CRL from the CA at any time. The **no ca crl** command deletes the CRL within the PIX Firewall.
enroll	The **ca enroll** command is used to send an enrollment request to the CA requesting a certificate for all of the PIX Firewall's key pairs.

continues

Table 15-1   ca *Command Options and Parameters (Continued)*

Parameter	Definition
generate rsa	The **ca generate rsa** command generates RSA key pairs (public and private) for the PIX Firewall. If the PIX Firewall has existing RSA keys, you will be warned and prompted to replace the existing keys with new keys.
	The PIX Firewall must be configured with a host name and a domain name before you can successfully issue this command.
hostname	The host name.
identity	The **ca identity** command specifies the CA that is used by the PIX Firewall. Only one CA at a time is supported. The **no ca identity** command removes the **ca identity** command from the configuration and deletes all certificates issued by the specified CA and CRLs.
ipaddress	Returns the PIX Firewall IP address in the certificate.
key	Used with the **ca generate rsa** command to generate a general-purpose RSA key pair.
key_modulus_size	The size of the key modulus, which is between 512 and 2048 bits. Choosing a size greater than 1024 bits might cause key generation to take a few minutes.
ldap_ipaddress	The IP address of the Lightweight Directory Access Protocol (LDAP) server. By default, querying of a certificate or a CRL is done via the Cisco PKI protocol. If the CA supports LDAP, query functions may also use LDAP.
retry_count	Specifies the number of times (between 1 and 100) that the PIX Firewall resends a certificate request when it has not received a certificate from the CA from the previous request.
	The default value of 0 indicates that there is no limit to retries.
retry_period	Specifies the number of minutes the PIX Firewall waits before resending a certificate request to the CA. Configurable from 1 to 60 min. Default value is 1 min.
save all	The **ca save all** command saves the PIX Firewall's RSA key pairs, the CA, RA and PIX Firewall's certificates, and the CA's CRLs in Flash memory. The **no ca save** command removes the saved data from Flash memory.
serial	Returns the PIX Firewall's serial number in the certificate.
show ca certificate	The **show ca certificate** command displays the CA Server's subject name, CRL distribution point (where the PIX Firewall will obtain the CRL), and lifetime of both the CA server's root certificate and the PIX Firewall's certificates.

Table 15-1   ca *Command Options and Parameters (Continued)*

Parameter	Definition
show ca crl	The **show ca crl** command is used to determine if there is a CRL in RAM, and where and when the CRL is downloaded.
show ca identity	The **show ca identity** command displays the current CA configuration parameters on the PIX Firewall.
show ca mypubkey rsa	The **show ca mypubkey rsa** command displays current PIX Firewall public keys.
specialkey	Used with the **ca generate rsa** command to generate two special-purpose RSA key pairs.
subject-name	Configures the device certificate request with the specified subject name.
verifycertdn	Verifies the certificate's distinguished name (DN) and acts as a subject name filter, based on the *X.500_string*. If the subject name of the peer certificate matches the *X.500_string*, it is filtered out and ISAKMP negotiation fails.
X.500_string	Specify per RFC 1779. The entered string will be the DN sent.
zeroize rsa	The **ca zeroize rsa** command deletes all RSA keys previously generated by the PIX Firewall. You can specify *keypair_name* to delete specific RSA key pairs.

NOTE   For more details on how CA servers work and how to configure the PIX Firewall for CA support, refer to the "Configuring IPSec and Certification Authorities" section of the PIX Firewall documentation available on Cisco.com.

Summary

This section summarizes the information you learned in this chapter:

- PIX Firewall enables secure VPNs.
- IPSec configuration tasks include configuring IKE and IPSec parameters.
- CAs enable scaling to a large number of IPSec peers.
- CA support is configured using the **ca** command.
- PIX Firewalls support IKE with preshared keys and digital certificates.
- PIX Firewall Version 6.3 adds support for AES encryption, D-H group 5, and NAT-T.

Chapter Review Questions

To test what you have learned in this chapter, answer the following questions and then refer to Appendix A, "Answers to Chapter Review Questions," for the answers:

1 Which port is used for IKE negotiations?

2 What is the benefit of using digital certificates and a CA for IKE?

3 What happens to the IP header when IPSec is configured in the tunnel mode?

4 What are the advantages and disadvantages of IPSec tunnel mode?

5 What version of the PIX Firewall supports AES?

6 What is the function of IKE Phase 1?

On completion of this chapter, you will be able to perform the following tasks:

- Identify the tasks to configure PIX Firewall IP Security (IPSec) support.
- Configure site-to-site VPN connections.
- Configure VPN connections using the PIX Device Manager (PDM).
- Configure Easy VPN Remote and Server devices.

CHAPTER 16

Site-to-Site VPNs

With the maturation of VPN technologies and products, an increasing number of organizations, businesses, government agencies, and academic institutions are considering using the public network to connect their geographically dispersed locations. Traditionally, private leased lines or Frame Relay circuits have been used to connect remote locations. Although these technologies work and have proven records, they tend to be expensive. The result is that most companies use slower connections to keep costs low or, worse yet, exclude smaller and remote locations.

There are many benefits to using site-to-site encrypted connections over the public network to replace more traditional options such as leased lines and Frame Relay. The primary benefits are lower costs and increased flexibility. Typically, organizations can reduce their costs or increase speed while maintaining costs. Also, they have the flexibility of using a greater variety of Internet connections, such as T1/T3 or faster speed links, cable, or digital subscriber line (DSL) connectivity to suit the specific needs of each location.

PIX Firewalls provide extensive VPN functionality and are well suited for building site-to-site VPNs (sometimes referred to as LAN-to-LAN). The addition of network address translation (NAT) traversal (NAT-T) and Advanced Encryption Standard (AES) support in PIX Firewall Version 6.3 provides even greater flexibility and compatibility for organizations expanding their use of VPN technologies. This chapter presents an overview of the VPN features of the PIX Firewall and configuration procedures for building site-to-site VPNs.

NOTE PIX Firewall Version 6.3 adds support for AES and the new VPN Acceleration Card Plus (VAC+) hardware acceleration card.

IPSec Configuration Tasks

This section demonstrates how to configure an IPSec-based VPN between two PIX Firewalls operating as secure gateways, using preshared keys for authentication. The IPSec configuration process can be summed up as comprising two major tasks: configuring an IPSec encryption policy and applying the policy to an interface.

The four major tasks used to configure IPSec encryption on the PIX Firewall follow:

- **Task 1—Prepare to configure VPN support**. This task consists of several steps to determine IPSec policies, ensure that the network works, and ensure that the PIX Firewall can support IPSec.

- **Task 2—Configure IKE parameters**. This task consists of several configuration steps that ensure that Internet Key Exchange (IKE) can set up secure channels to desired IPSec peers. IKE can set up IPSec security associations (SAs), enabling IPSec sessions. IKE negotiates IKE parameters and sets up IKE SAs during an IKE Phase 1 exchange called main mode.

- **Task 3—Configure IPSec parameters**. This task consists of several configuration steps that specify IPSec SA parameters between peers and set global IPSec values. IKE negotiates SA parameters and sets up IPSec SAs during an IKE Phase 2 exchange called quick mode.

- **Task 4—Test and verify VPN configuration**. After you configure IPSec, you need to verify that you have configured it correctly and ensure that it works.

Each configuration task in discussed in greater detail in the following subsections.

Task 1—Prepare to Configure VPN Support

Successful implementation of an IPSec network requires advanced preparation before beginning the configuration of individual PIX Firewalls. This section outlines how to determine network design details.

Configuring IPSec encryption can be complicated. You must plan in advance if you want to configure IPSec encryption correctly the first time and minimize misconfiguration. You should begin this task by defining the strategy and overall security needs based on the overall company security policy. Some planning steps include the following:

Step 1 Determine the IKE (IKE Phase 1, or main mode) policy. Determine the IKE policies between peers based on the number and location of IPSec peers.

Step 2 Determine the IPSec (IKE Phase 2, or quick mode) policy. You need to identify IPSec peer details such as IP addresses and IPSec modes. You then configure crypto maps to gather all IPSec policy details together.

Step 3 Ensure that the network works without encryption. Ensure that basic connectivity has been achieved between IPSec peers using the desired IP services before configuring PIX Firewall IPSec.

Step 4 Implicitly permit IPSec packets to bypass PIX Firewall access control lists (ACLs), access groups, and conduits. In this step, you enter the **sysopt connection permit-ipsec** command.

Plan for IKE (Phase 1)

An IKE policy defines a combination of security parameters to be used during the IKE negotiation. You should determine the IKE policy and then configure it. By implementing the following advanced planning steps, you can minimize misconfiguration errors later. These steps include the following:

- **Determine IKE Phase 1 (ISAKMP) policies for peers**—An IKE policy defines a combination of security parameters to be used during the IKE negotiation. Each IKE negotiation begins by each peer agreeing on a common (shared) IKE policy. The IKE policy suites must be determined in advance of configuration.

- **Determine key distribution methods based on the numbers and locations of IPSec peers**—You might want to use a certification authority (CA) server to support the scalability of IPSec peers. You must then configure IKE to support the selected key distribution method.

- **Identify IPSec peer router IP addresses or host names**—You need to determine the details of all the IPSec peers that will use IKE for establishing SAs.

IKE negotiations must be protected, so each IKE negotiation begins by each peer agreeing on a common (shared) IKE policy. This policy states which security parameters will be used to protect subsequent IKE negotiations.

After the two peers agree on a policy, an SA established at each peer identifies the security parameters of the policy. These SAs apply to all subsequent IKE traffic during the negotiation.

You can create multiple, prioritized policies at each peer to ensure that at least one policy will match the policy of a remote peer.

You can select specific values for each IKE parameter, per the IKE standard. You choose one value over another based on the security level you desire and the type of IPSec peer to which you will connect.

There are five parameters to define in each IKE policy, as listed in Table 16-1. Default values for each parameter are also listed in Table 16-1.

Table 16-1 *IKE Policy Parameters*

Parameter	Accepted Values	Keyword	Default
Message encryption algorithm	56-bit Data Encryption Standard (DES) 168-bit Triple DES (3DES) 128-bit AES 192-bit AES 256-bit AES	DES 3DES AES AES-192 AES-256	DES

continues

Table 16-1   *IKE Policy Parameters (Continued)*

Parameter	Accepted Values	Keyword	Default
Message integrity (hash) algorithm	Secure Hash Algorithm-1 (SHA-1) (hashed message authentication code [HMAC] variant) Message Digest 5 (MD5) (HMAC variant)	SHA-1 MD5	SHA-1
Peer authentication method	Preshared keys Rivest, Shamir, and Adleman (RSA) signatures	pre-share rsa-sig	RSA signatures
Key exchange parameters (Diffie-Hellman [D-H] group identifier)	768-bit D-H 1024-bit D-H 1536-bit D-H	1 2 5	1 (768-bit D-H)
Internet Security Association and Key Management Protocol (ISAKMP)–established SA's lifetime	Can specify any number of seconds		86,400 seconds (1 day)

NOTE   AES encryption algorithm and 1536-bit D-H (Group 5) are supported only on PIX Firewall Version 6.3 or higher.

Table 16-2 shows the relative strength of each of the IKE policy parameter values.

Table 16-2   *IKE Policy Parameter Relative Strength*

Parameter	Strong Security	Stronger Security
Message encryption algorithm	56-bit DES	168-bit DES 128-AES, 192-AES, 256-AES
Message integrity (hash) algorithm	MD5 (HMAC variant)	SHA-1 (HMAC variant)
Authentication method	Preshared keys	RSA signatures
Key exchange parameters (D-H group identifier)	768-bit D-H (Group 1)	1536-bit D-H (Group 5)
ISAKMP-established SA's lifetime	86,400 seconds	< 86,400 seconds

NOTE   Stronger encryption is provided by 3DES than by DES. Some tradeoffs of 3DES are that it takes more processing power, and it might be restricted for export or import into some countries. AES provides even stronger encryption with a lower processing hit than 3DES. AES is supported only on PIX Firewall Version 6.3 or higher.

NOTE   RSA signatures are used with CA support and require enrollment to a CA server. They are more secure but require more planning and their implementation is complex.

After you determine the proper parameters to use, you can configure an appropriate IKE policy on each of the IPSec peers. Figure 16-1 shows an example of a PIX-to-PIX VPN scenario with matching IKE policies on each side. As shown in this figure, it is important that parameters are identical on both peers.

Figure 16-1   *IKE Phase 1 Policy*

Parameter	Site 1	Site 2
Encryption Algorithm	3DES	3DES
Hash Algorithm	SHA	SHA
Authentication Method	Pre-share	Pre-share
Key Exchange	1024-bit D-H	1024-bit D-H
IKE SA Lifetime	86,400 Seconds	86,400 Seconds

Plan for IPSec (Phase 2)

Planning for IPSec (IKE Phase 2) is another important step you should complete before actually configuring the PIX Firewall. Again, advanced planning helps minimize misconfiguration errors later. Decisions to be made at this stage include the following:

- Select IPSec algorithms and parameters for optimal security and performance. You should determine what type of IPSec security will be used to secure interesting traffic. Some IPSec parameters require you to make tradeoffs between high performance and stronger security.

- Identify IPSec peer details. You must identify the IP addresses and host names of all IPSec peers you will connect to.

- Determine IP addresses and applications of hosts to be protected at the local peer and remote peer.

- Decide whether SAs are manually established or are established via IKE.

Determining network design details includes defining a more detailed security policy for protecting traffic. You can then use the detailed policy to help select IPSec transform sets and modes of operation. Your security policy should answer the following questions:

- What protections are required or are acceptable for the protected traffic?

- What traffic should or should not be protected?

- Which PIX Firewall interfaces are involved in protecting internal networks, external networks, or both?

- What are the peer IPSec endpoints for the traffic?

- How should SAs be established?

Table 16-3 lists a summary of IKE policy details that are configured in the examples later in this chapter for the PIX Firewall peers shown in Figure 16-1.

Table 16-3   *IKE Policy Details for PIX Firewall Peers*

Parameter	PIX1 Value	PIX2 Value
Message encryption algorithm	3DES	3DES
Message integrity (hash) algorithm	SHA-1	SHA-1
Peer authentication method	Preshared key	Preshared key
Key exchange parameters (D-H group identifier)	1024-bit D-H Group 2	1024-bit D-H Group 2
IKE-established security association's lifetime	86,400 (default)	86,400 (default)
Encryption hosts	10.0.1.11	10.0.6.11
IP address of IPSec peer	192.168.6.2	192.168.1.2

Task 2—Configure IKE Parameters

The next major task in configuring PIX Firewall IPSec is to configure IKE parameters gathered in the previous task. This section presents the steps used to configure IKE parameters for IKE preshared keys.

You use the **isakmp policy** command to define an IKE policy. IKE policies define a set of parameters to be used during the IKE negotiation. Use the **no** form of this command to delete an IKE policy. The command syntax is as follows:

```
isakmp policy priority authentication pre-share | rsa-sig
isakmp policy priority encryption aes | aes-192 | aes-256 | des | 3des
isakmp policy priority group 1 | 2 | 5
isakmp policy priority hash md5 | sha
isakmp policy priority lifetime seconds
```

Table 16-4 describes the command parameters for the **isakmp policy** command.

Table 16-4   **isakmp policy Command Parameters**

Command Parameter	Description
policy *priority*	Uniquely identifies the IKE policy and assigns it a priority. Use an integer from 1 to 65,534, with 1 being the highest priority and 65,534 the lowest.
authentication pre-share	Specifies preshared keys as the authentication method.
authentication rsa-sig	Specifies RSA signatures as the authentication method. This is the default value.
encryption des	Specifies 56-bit DES–cipher block chaining (CBC) as the encryption algorithm to be used in the IKE policy. This value is the default.
encryption 3des	Specifies the 3DES encryption algorithm for the IKE policy.
encryption aes	Specifies the 128-bit AES encryption algorithm for the IKE policy.
encryption aes-192	Specifies the 192-bit AES encryption algorithm for the IKE policy.
encryption aes-256	Specifies the 256-bit AES encryption algorithm for the IKE policy.
group 1	Specifies the 768-bit D-H group for the IKE policy. This value is the default.
group 2	Specifies the 1024-bit D-H group for the IKE policy.
group 5	Specifies the 1536-bit D-H group for the IKE policy.
hash md5	Specifies MD5 (HMAC variant) as the hash algorithm for the IKE policy.
hash sha	Specifies SHA-1 (HMAC variant) as the hash algorithm for the IKE policy. This hash algorithm is the default.
lifetime *seconds*	Specifies how many seconds each SA should exist before expiring. Use an integer from 60 to 86,400 seconds (1 day). You can usually leave this value at the default of 86,400.

NOTE   AES encryption and D-H Group 5 support is available only with PIX Firewall 6.3 or later.

The specific steps for configuring IKE are as follows:

Step 1   Enable or disable IKE (ISAKMP) negotiation:

```
pixfirewall(config)# isakmp enable interface-name
```

Specify the PIX Firewall interface on which the IPSec peer will communicate. IKE is enabled by default and for individual PIX Firewall interfaces. Use the **no isakmp enable** *interface-name* command to disable IKE.

Step 2   Configure an IKE Phase 1 policy with the **isakmp policy** command to match expected IPSec peers by completing the following substeps:

(1) Specify the encryption algorithm (the default is **des**):

```
pixfirewall(config)# isakmp policy priority encryption des
    | 3des | aes | aes-192 | aes-256
```

(2) Specify the hash algorithm (the default is **sha**):

```
pixfirewall(config)# isakmp policy priority hash md5 | sha
```

(3) Specify the authentication method (the default is **rsa-sig**):

```
pixfirewall(config)# isakmp policy priority authentication
    pre-share | rsa-sig
```

NOTE   If you specify the authentication method of preshared keys, you must manually configure these keys, as outlined in Step 3.

---

(4) Specify the D-H group identifier (the default is **group 1**):

```
pixfirewall(config)# isakmp policy priority group 1 | 2 | 5
```

(5) Specify the IKE SA's lifetime in seconds (the default is **86400**):

```
pixfirewall(config)# isakmp policy priority lifetime
    seconds
```

NOTE   PIX Firewall software has preset default values. If you enter a default value for a given policy parameter, it will not be written in the configuration. If you do not specify a value for a given policy parameter, the default value is assigned. You can observe configured and default values with the **show isakmp policy** command.

Step 3   Configure the IKE preshared key:

```
pixfirewall(config)# isakmp key keystring address peer-address [netmask
peer-netmask]
```

The *keystring* is any combination of alphanumeric characters up to 128 bytes. This preshared key must be identical at both peers.

The *peer-address* and *peer-netmask* should point to the IP address of the IPSec peer. You can configure a wildcard peer address and netmask of 0.0.0.0 0.0.0.0 to share the preshared key among many peers. However, it is strongly recommended that you use a unique key for each peer.

You can also use the peer's host name for the preshared key.

Step 4   (Optional) Configure NAT-T support:

```
pixfirewall(config)# isakmp nat-traversal [natkeepalive]
```

NAT-T supports site-to-site IPSec VPNs across networks implementing NAT. If one of the peers is behind a network device translating the address of that peer, you must enable NAT-T support. Once enabled, the peers determine if one or both devices are behind a NAT device and enable IPSec over User Datagram Protocol (UDP) port 4500. This feature is available only on PIX Firewall Version 6.3 or higher.

Step 5   Verify IKE Phase 1 policies.

The **show isakmp policy** command displays configured and default policies. The **show isakmp** command displays configured policies much as they would appear with the **write terminal** command.

Example 16-1 shows the commands required to enable IKE, configure a Phase 1 policy, and configure a preshared key for peer PIX1 in Figure 16-1.

Example 16-1 *IKE Configuration*

```
pixfirewall(config)# isakmp enable outside
pixfirewall(config)# isakmp policy 10 encryption 3des
pixfirewall(config)# isakmp policy 10 hash sha
pixfirewall(config)# isakmp policy 10 authentication pre-share
pixfirewall(config)# isakmp policy 10 group 2
pixfirewall(config)# isakmp policy 10 lifetime 86400
pixfirewall(config)# isakmp key cisco123 address 192.168.6.2
```

In Example 16-1, IKE is enabled on the outside interface, and a policy with priority number 10 is created. 3DES encryption is configured along with SHA-1, D-H Group 2 key exchange, and an SA lifetime of 84,600 seconds. Authentication is set for preshared key and a key value of cisco123 is specified. Finally, the remote peer's IP address is specified (192.168.6.2).

Example 16-2 shows the output of the **show isakmp** and **show isakmp policy** commands for the configuration shown in Example 16-1.

Example 16-2   **show isakmp policy** *Command Output*

```
pixfirewall(config)# show isakmp
isakmp enable outside
isakmp key ******** address 192.168.6.2 netmask 255.255.255.255
isakmp policy 10 authentication pre-share
isakmp policy 10 encryption 3des
isakmp policy 10 hash sha
isakmp policy 10 group 2
isakmp policy 10 lifetime 86400
pixfirewall(config)# sh isakmp policy
Protection suite of priority 10
        encryption algorithm:    Three key triple DES
        hash algorithm:          Secure Hash Standard
        authentication method:   Pre-Shared Key
        Diffie-Hellman group:    #2 (1024 bit)
        lifetime:                86400 seconds, no volume limit
Default protection suite
        encryption algorithm:    DES - Data Encryption Standard (56 bit keys).
        hash algorithm:          Secure Hash Standard
        authentication method:   Rivest-Shamir-Adleman Signature
        Diffie-Hellman group:    #1 (768 bit)
        lifetime:                86400 seconds, no volume limit
```

The actual value of the preshared key is not shown on the output shown in Example 16-2. Preshared keys are masked to increase security.

Task 3—Configure IPSec Parameters

The next major task in configuring PIX Firewall IPSec is to configure the previously gathered IPSec parameters. This section presents the steps used to configure IPSec parameters for IKE preshared keys:

Step 1   Configure crypto access lists with the **access-list** command.

Step 2   Configure transform set suites with the **crypto ipsec transform-set** command.

Step 3   (Optional) Configure global IPSec SA lifetimes with the **crypto ipsec security-association lifetime** command.

Step 4   Configure crypto maps with the **crypto map** command and apply crypto maps to the terminating/originating interface with the **crypto map map-name interface** command.

Step 5   Verify IPSec configuration with the variety of available **show** commands.

Table 16-5 summarizes IPSec encryption policy details that are configured in examples in this chapter for the PIX Firewall peers shown in Figure 16-1.

Table 16-5   *IPSec Policy Details for PIX Firewall Peers*

Parameter	PIX1 Value	PIX2 Value
Transform set	Authentication Header (AH)-MD5, Encapsulating Security Payload (ESP)-3DES	AH-MD5, ESP-3DES
IPSec mode	Tunnel	Tunnel
Hash algorithm	MD5	MD5
Peer host name	PIX2	PIX1
Peer interface	Ethernet0 (outside)	Ethernet0 (outside)
Peer IP address	192.168.6.2	192.168.1.2
IP address of hosts to be protected	10.0.1.0/24	10.0.6.0/24
Traffic (packet) type to be encrypted	TCP	TCP
SA establishment	ipsec-isakmp	ipsec-isakmp

The following sections discuss each of these configuration steps in more detail.

Step 1—Configure Crypto ACLs

Crypto ACLs are traffic selection ACLs. You use them to define which IP traffic is interesting and will be protected by IPSec and which traffic will not be protected by IPSec. Crypto ACLs perform the following functions:

- Indicate the data flow to be protected by IPSec
- Select outbound traffic to be protected by IPSec
- Process inbound traffic to filter out and discard traffic that should be protected by IPSec
- Determine whether to accept requests for IPSec SAs for the requested data flows when processing IKE negotiations

Although the crypto access list syntax is the same as that for regular access lists, the meanings are slightly different for crypto access lists: **permit** specifies that matching packets must be encrypted, and **deny** specifies that matching packets will not be encrypted. Crypto access lists behave similarly to access lists applied to outbound traffic on a PIX Firewall interface.

To configure a crypto access list, use the **access-list** configuration command. To delete a single line of an access list, use the **no** form of the command. To delete the entire **access-list** and its associated **access-group** command, use the **clear access-list** command. The command syntax is as follows:

```
access-list acl_ID [line line_num] deny | permit protocol source_addr source_mask
[operator port [port]] destination_addr destination_mask operator port [port]
```

Table 16-6 provides descriptions for the **access-list** command arguments.

Table 16-6   access-list *Command Arguments*

Argument	Definition
acl_ID	Name of an ACL.
line	Optional keyword to specify the line number of the ACL entry. Only supported in PIX Firewall Version 6.3 or higher.
line_num	Line number starting at 1.
deny	Does not select a packet for IPSec protection. Prevents traffic from being protected by IPSec in the context of that particular crypto map entry.
permit	Selects a packet for IPSec protection. Causes all IP traffic that matches the specified conditions to be protected by IPSec, using the policy described by the corresponding crypto map entry.
protocol	Specifies the name or number of an IP protocol. It can be one of the keywords **icmp**, **ip**, **tcp**, or **udp** or an integer in the range 1 to 254 representing an IP protocol number. To match any Internet protocol, use the keyword **ip**.
source_addr destination_addr	Specifies the address of the network or host from which the packet is being sent or from where the packet was received. There are three other ways to specify the source or destination: • Use a 32-bit quantity in four-part, dotted-decimal format. • Use the keyword **any** as an abbreviation for a source and source netmask or destination and destination netmask of 0.0.0.0 0.0.0.0. This keyword is normally not recommended for use with IPSec. • Use the host source or host destination as an abbreviation for a source and source netmask of 255.255.255.255 or a destination and destination netmask of destination 255.255.255.255.

Table 16-6   **access-list** *Command Arguments (Continued)*

Argument	Definition
source_mask *destination_mask*	Specifies the netmask bits (mask) to be applied to source or destination. There are three other ways to specify the source or destination netmask: • Use a 32-bit quantity in four-part dotted-decimal format. Place 0s in the bit positions you want to ignore. • Use the keyword **any** as an abbreviation for a source and source netmask or destination and destination netmask of 0.0.0.0 0.0.0.0. This keyword is not recommended. • Use the host source or host destination as an abbreviation for a source and source netmask of source 255.255.255.255 or a destination and destination netmask of destination 255.255.255.255.
operator	(Optional) Specifies a port or a port range to compare source or destination ports. Possible operands include **lt** (less than), **gt** (greater than), **eq** (equal), **neq** (not equal), and **range** (inclusive range). The **range** operator requires two port numbers. Each of the other operators requires one port number.
port	IP services you permit based on the TCP or UDP protocol. Specify ports by either a literal name or a number in the range of 0 to 65,535. You can specify all ports by not specifying a port value.

Any unprotected inbound traffic (non-IPSec) that matches a permit entry in the ACL for a crypto map entry will be dropped because this traffic was expected to be protected by IPSec.

If you want certain traffic to receive one combination of IPSec protection (for example, authentication only) and other traffic to receive a different combination of IPSec protection (for example, both authentication and encryption), you must create two different crypto ACLs to define the two different types of traffic. You then use these different ACLs in different crypto map entries, which specify different IPSec policies.

In a later configuration step, you associate the crypto ACLs to particular interfaces when you configure and apply crypto map sets to the interfaces.

WARNING   Cisco recommends that you avoid using the **any** keyword to specify source or destination addresses. The **permit any any** statement is strongly discouraged because it causes all outbound traffic to be protected (and all protected traffic sent to the peer, specified in the corresponding crypto map entry) and requires protection for all inbound traffic. All inbound packets that lack IPSec protection will then be silently dropped, including packets for routing protocols, Network Time Protocol (NTP), echo, echo response, and so on.

WARNING   Exercise caution when modifying crypto ACLs on a remote PIX with crypto map applied. You might lose connectivity to the outside interface of the PIX Firewall because of ACL changes. You should remove the crypto map first, modify the crypto ACLs, and then reapply the crypto map as necessary.

Try to be as restrictive as possible when defining which packets to protect in a crypto ACL. If you must use the **any** keyword in a **permit** statement, you must preface that statement with a series of **deny** statements to filter out any traffic (that would otherwise fall within that **permit** statement) which you do not want protected.

CAUTION   It's imperative that you configure mirror-image crypto access lists for use by IPSec. The crypto access lists on each peer should be symmetrical. Failure to create symmetrical access lists on both crypto peers will result in the inability to form an SA.

Example 16-3 shows the appropriate crypto ACLs for the network diagram shown in Figure 16-1.

Example 16-3   *Crypto ACLs*

```
PIX1
pix1(config)# show access-list
access-list cached ACL log flows: total 0, denied 0 (deny-flow-max 1024)
            alert-interval 300
access-list crypto_acl_6; 1 elements
access-list crypto_acl_6 line 1 permit ip 10.0.1.0 255.255.255.0 10.0.6.0
  255.255.255.0 (hitcnt=0)
pix1(config)# show nat
nat (inside) 0 access-list crypto_acl_6
PIX2
pix2(config)# show access-list
access-list cached ACL log flows: total 0, denied 0 (deny-flow-max 1024)
            alert-interval 300
access-list crypto_acl_1; 1 elements
access-list crypto_acl_1 line 1 permit ip 10.0.6.0 255.255.255.0 10.0.1.0
  255.255.255.0 (hitcnt=0)
pix1(config)# show nat
nat (inside) 0 access-list crypto_acl_1
```

Example 16-3 uses the **show access-list** command to display currently configured ACLs. Each PIX Firewall in this example has an ACL that defines the traffic to be encrypted. A **nat 0** command exempts this traffic from address translation before encryption.

Step 2—Configure an IPSec Transform Set

The next major step in configuring the PIX Firewall IPSec is to use the IPSec security policy to define a transform set. A *transform set* is a combination of individual IPSec transforms that enact a security policy for traffic. Transform sets combine the following IPSec factors:

- A mechanism for packet authentication—the AH transform
- A mechanism for payload encryption and optional authentication—the ESP transform
- The IPSec mode, either transport or tunnel

You define a transform set with the **crypto ipsec transform-set** command. To delete a transform set, you use the **no** form of the command. The command syntax is as follows:

```
pixfirewall(config)# crypto ipsec transform-set transform-set-name transform1
    [transform2 [transform3]]
```

Table 16-7 provides descriptions for the **crypto ipsec transform-set** command arguments.

Table 16-7   **crypto ipsec transform-set** *Command Arguments*

Argument	Definition
transform-set-name	The name of the transform set to create or modify
transform1 *transform2* *transform3*	Specify up to three transforms

You can specify multiple transform sets and then specify one or more of these transform sets in a crypto map entry. The transform set defined in the crypto map entry will be used in the IPSec SA negotiation to protect the data flows specified by the ACL of that crypto map entry.

During the IPSec SA negotiation, the peers agree to use a particular transform set for protecting a particular data flow.

A transform set equals an AH transform and an ESP transform plus the mode (transport or tunnel). Transform sets are limited to one AH and two ESP transforms. The default mode is tunnel. Be sure to configure matching transform sets between IPSec peers.

NOTE   In PIX Firewall Versions 6.0 and higher, Layer 2 Tunneling Protocol (L2TP) is the only protocol that can use the IPSec transport mode. The PIX Firewall discards all other types of packets using IPSec transport mode.

Table 16-8 shows the IPSec transforms supported by the PIX Firewall.

Table 16-8 *PIX-Supported IPSec Transforms*

Transform	Description
ah-md5-hmac	AH-MD5-HMAC transform used for authentication
ah-sha-hmac	AH-SHA-HMAC transform used for authentication
esp-null	ESP transform without cipher
esp-des	ESP transform using DES cipher (56 bits)
esp-3des	ESP transform using 3DES cipher (168 bits)
esp-aes	ESP transform using AES cipher (128 bits)
esp-aes-192	ESP transform using AES cipher (192 bits)
esp-aes-256	ESP transform using AES cipher (256 bits)
esp-md5-hmac	ESP transform with HMAC-MD5 authentication used with an **esp-des**, **esp-3des**, **esp-aes**, **esp-aes-192**, or **esp-aes-256** transform to provide additional integrity of ESP packets
esp-sha-hmac	ESP transform with HMAC-SHA authentication used with an **esp-des**, **esp-3des**, **esp-aes**, **esp-aes-192**, or **esp-aes-256** transform to provide additional integrity for ESP packets

Choosing IPSec transform combinations can be complex. The following tips might help you select transforms that are appropriate for your situation:

- If you want to provide data confidentiality, include an ESP encryption transform.
- Also consider including an ESP authentication transform or an AH transform to provide authentication services for the transform set:
  - To ensure data authentication for the outer IP header as well as the data, include an AH transform.
  - To ensure data authentication, use either ESP or AH. You can choose from the MD5 or SHA (HMAC keyed hash variants) authentication algorithms.
- The SHA algorithm is generally considered stronger than MD5, but it is slower.

Examples of acceptable transform combinations are as follows:

- **esp-des** for high-performance encryption
- **ah-md5-hmac** for authenticating packet contents with no encryption
- **esp-3des** and **esp-md5-hmac** for strong encryption and authentication
- **esp-aes-256** and **esp-sha-hmac** for strongest encryption and authentication

NOTE As with Cisco routers, AH is seldom used with ESP because authentication is available with the **esp-sha-hmac** and **esp-md5-hmac** transforms. AH is also incompatible with NAT and port address translation (PAT) because they change the IP address in the TCP/IP packet header, breaking the authentication established by AH. You can use AH for data authentication alone, but it does not protect the confidentiality of the packet contents because it does not provide encryption.

Transform Set Negotiation

Transform sets are negotiated during quick mode in IKE Phase 2 using previously configured transform sets. You can configure multiple transform sets and then specify one or more of the transform sets in a crypto map entry. You should configure the transforms from most secure to least secure per your security policy. The transform set defined in the crypto map entry is used in the IPSec SA negotiation to protect the data flows specified by that crypto map entry's access list.

During the negotiation, the peers search for a transform set that is the same at both peers. When such a transform set is found, it is selected and applied to the protected traffic as part of both peers' IPSec SAs. IPSec peers agree on one transform proposal per SA (unidirectional).

Step 3—Configure Global IPSec Security Association Lifetimes

The IPSec SA lifetime determines how long IPSec SAs remain valid before they are renegotiated. The PIX Firewall supports a global lifetime value that applies to all crypto maps. You can override the global lifetime value within a crypto map entry. The lifetimes apply only to SAs established via IKE. Manually established SAs do not expire. When an SA expires, a new one is negotiated without interrupting the data flow.

Transform Set Negotiated Between IPSec Peers

You can change global IPSec SA lifetime values by using the **crypto ipsec security-association lifetime** configuration command. To reset a lifetime to the default value, use the **no** form of the command. The command syntax is as follows:

```
crypto ipsec security-association lifetime {seconds seconds | kilobytes kilobytes}
```

The **seconds** *seconds* parameter specifies the number of seconds an SA lives before it expires. The default is 28,800 seconds (8 hours). The **kilobytes** *kilobytes* parameter specifies the volume of traffic that can pass between IPSec peers using a given SA before that SA expires. The default is 4,608,000 KB (10 MBps for 1 hour).

Cisco recommends that you use the default lifetime values. The SAs are configured using crypto maps discussed later.

NOTE   The lifetime you set for ISAKMP is separate from the IPSec lifetime just discussed. They can be set to different values.

Global IPSec SA Lifetime Examples

A general principle in cryptanalysis is that, given enough time or enough traffic protected under a single key, an attacker can break that key. Over time, a key's effective lifetime is reduced by advances made in cryptanalysis. The PIX Firewall allows you to fine-tune the key lifetime with the **crypto ipsec security-association lifetime** command. Consider the sample global IPSec SA lifetime shown in Example 16-4.

Example 16-4 *Sample Global IPSec SA Lifetime*

```
crypto ipsec security-association lifetime kilobytes 1382400
```

This lifetime is about 3 Mbps for 1 hour, adequate for a PIX Firewall behind a perimeter router with an E1 WAN interface to an Internet service provider (ISP) at 2.048 MBps. Example 16-5 shows a lifetime of 15 minutes, which is rather short but provides less time for breaking a key.

Example 16-5 *Sample Lifetime of 15 Minutes*

```
crypto ipsec security-association lifetime seconds 900
```

Before a key expires, IKE negotiates another one based on the IPSec SA lifetime value to allow for a smooth transition from key to key without the need to tear down connections.

Step 4—Configure Crypto Maps

You must create crypto map entries for IPSec to set up SAs for traffic flows that must be encrypted. Crypto map entries created for IPSec set up SA parameters, tying together the various parts configured for IPSec, including the following:

- Which traffic should be protected by IPSec (crypto access list)
- The granularity of the traffic to be protected by a set of SAs
- Where IPSec-protected traffic should be sent (who the remote IPSec peer is)
- The local interface to be used for the IPSec traffic
- What IPSec security protocol should be applied to this traffic (transform sets)

- Whether SAs are established manually or via IKE
- IPSec SA lifetime
- Other parameters that might be necessary to define an IPSec SA

The following sections discuss crypto map parameters, examine the **crypto map** command, show how to configure crypto maps, and present examples of crypto maps.

Crypto Map Parameters

You can apply only one crypto map set to a single interface. The crypto map set can include a combination of IPSec using IKE and IPSec with manually configured SA entries. Multiple interfaces can share the same crypto map set if you want to apply the same policy to multiple interfaces.

If you create more than one crypto map entry for a given interface, use the sequence number (seq-num) of each map entry to rank the map entries: the lower the seq-num, the higher the priority. At the interface that has the crypto map set, traffic is evaluated against higher-priority map entries first. You must create multiple crypto map entries for a given interface if you have any of the following conditions:

- Different data flows are to be handled by separate IPSec peers.
- You want to apply different IPSec security to different types of traffic (to the same or separate IPSec peers)—for example, if you want traffic between one set of subnets to be authenticated and traffic between another set of subnets to be both authenticated and encrypted. In this case, you should have defined the different types of traffic in two separate access lists, and you must create a separate crypto map entry for each crypto access list.
- You are not using IKE to establish a particular set of SAs, and you want to specify multiple access list entries. You must create separate access lists (one per permit entry) and specify a separate crypto map entry for each access list.

Backup Gateways

You can define multiple remote peers by using crypto maps to allow for gateway redundancy. If one peer fails, there is still a protected path. The peer that packets are actually sent to is determined by the last peer that the PIX Firewall heard from (received either traffic or a negotiation request from) for a given data flow. If the attempt fails with the first peer, IKE tries the next peer on the crypto map list.

Configuring Crypto Maps

You use the **crypto map** configuration command to create or modify a crypto map entry. You set the crypto map entries referencing dynamic maps to be the lowest-priority entries in a crypto map set (that is, to have the highest sequence numbers). Use the **no** form of this command to delete a crypto map entry or set. The command syntax is as follows:

```
crypto map map-name seq-num {ipsec-isakmp | ipsec-manual} [dynamic dynamic-map-name]
crypto map map-name seq-num match address acl_name
crypto map map-name seq-num set peer {hostname | ip-address}
crypto map map-name seq-num set pfs [group1 | group2 | group5]
crypto map map-name seq-num set security-association lifetime {seconds seconds |
  kilobytes kilobytes}
crypto map map-name seq-num set transform-set transform-set-name1
  [transform-set-name6]
crypto map map-name client authentication aaa-server-name
crypto map map-name client configuration address {initiate | respond}
```

Table 16-9 shows the arguments and options for the **crypto map** command sequence.

Table 16-9   **crypto map** *Command Arguments/Options*

Argument	Description
map-name	Assigns a name to the crypto map set.
seq-num	Assigns a number to the crypto map entry.
ipsec-manual	Indicates that IKE will not be used to establish the IPSec SAs for protecting the traffic specified by this crypto map entry.
ipsec-isakmp	Indicates that IKE will be used to establish the IPSec SAs for protecting the traffic specified by this crypto map entry.
acl_name	Identifies the named encryption access list. This name should match the name argument of the named encryption access list being matched.
match address	Specifies an access list for a crypto map entry.
set peer	Specifies an IPSec peer in a crypto map entry. Specify multiple peers by repeating this command. The peer is the terminating interface of the IPSec peer.
hostname	Specifies a peer by its host name. This is the peer's host name concatenated with its domain name, such as myhost.example.com.
ip-address	Specifies a peer by its IP address.
set pfs	Specifies that IPSec should ask for perfect forward secrecy (PFS). With PFS, every time a new SA is negotiated, a new D-H exchange occurs. PFS provides additional security for secret key generation at a cost of additional processing.
group1	Specifies that IPSec should use the 768-bit D-H prime modulus group when performing the new D-H exchange. Used with the **esp-des**, **esp-3des**, **esp-aes**, **esp-aes-192**, or **esp-aes-256** transforms.
group2	Specifies that IPSec should use the 1024-bit D-H prime modulus group when performing the new D-H exchange. Used with the **esp-des**, **esp-3des**, **esp-aes**, **esp-aes-192**, or **esp-aes-256** transforms.

Table 16-9   **crypto map** *Command Arguments/Options (Continued)*

Argument	Description
group5	Specifies that IPSec should use the 1536-bit D-H prime modulus group when performing the new D-H exchange. Used with the **esp-des**, **esp-3des**, **esp-aes**, **esp-aes-192**, or **esp-aes-256** transforms.
set transform-set	Specifies which transform sets can be used with the crypto map entry. List multiple transform sets in order of priority, with the highest-priority (most secure) transform set first.
transform-set-name	Specifies the name of the transform set. For an ipsec-manual crypto map entry, you can specify only one transform set. For an ipsec-isakmp or dynamic crypto map entry, you can specify up to 6 transform sets.
kilobytes *kilobytes*	Specifies the volume of traffic (in kilobytes) that can pass between peers using a given SA before that SA expires. The default is 4,608,000 KB. The SA lifetime in a crypto map entry overrides the global SA lifetime value.
seconds *seconds*	Specifies the number of seconds a SA lives before it expires. The default is 3600 seconds (1 hour).
dynamic	(Optional) Specifies that this crypto map entry references a pre-existing static crypto map. If you use this keyword, none of the crypto map configuration commands are available.
dynamic-map-name	(Optional) Specifies the name of the dynamic crypto map set that should be used as the policy template.
aaa-server-name	Specifies the name of the AAA server that authenticates the user during IKE authentication. The two available AAA server options are TACACS+ and RADIUS.
initiate	Indicates that the PIX Firewall attempts to set IP addresses for each peer.
respond	Indicates that the PIX Firewall accepts requests for IP addresses from any requesting peer.

To create a crypto map, follow these steps:

Step 1   Create a crypto map entry in IPSec ISAKMP mode:

```
pixfirewall(config)# crypto map map-name seq-num ipsec-isakmp
```

This identifies the crypto map with a unique crypto map name and sequence number.

Step 2   Assign an ACL to the crypto map entry:

```
pixfirewall(config)# crypto map map-name seq-num match address
    access-list-name
```

Step 3   Specify the peer to which the IPSec protected traffic can be forwarded:

```
pixfirewall(config)# crypto map map-name seq-num set peer
    hostname | ip-address
```

This specifies the peer host name or IP address. You can specify multiple peers by repeating this command.

Step 4   Specify which transform sets are allowed for this crypto map entry.

```
pixfirewall(config)# crypto map map-name seq-num set transform-set
    transform-set-name1 [transform-set-name2, transform-set-name9]
```

If you use multiple transform sets, list them in order of priority (highest priority first). You can specify up to nine transform sets.

Step 5   (Optional) Specify whether IPSec should ask for PFS when requesting new SAs for this crypto map entry or should require PFS in requests received from the peer:

```
pixfirewall(config)# crypto map map-name seq-num set pfs [group1 |
    group2 | group5]
```

NOTE   PFS provides additional security for D-H key exchanges at a cost of additional processing.

Step 6   (Optional) Specify the SA lifetime for the crypto map entry if you want the SAs for this entry to be negotiated using different IPSec SA lifetimes other than the global lifetimes:

```
pixfirewall(config)# crypto map map-name seq-num set security-
    association
lifetime seconds seconds | kilobytes kilobytes
```

Step 7   (Optional) Specify dynamic crypto maps with the **crypto dynamic-map** *dynamic-map-name dynamic-seq-num* command. A dynamic crypto map entry is essentially a crypto map entry without all the parameters configured. It acts as a policy template where the missing parameters are later dynamically configured (as the result of an IPSec negotiation) to match a peer's requirements. This process allows peers to exchange IPSec traffic with the PIX Firewall even if the PIX Firewall does not have a crypto map entry specifically configured to meet all the peer's requirements.

Step 8   Apply the crypto map to an interface:

```
pixfirewall(config)# crypto map map-name interface interface-name
```

This command applies the crypto map to an interface and the command activates the IPSec policy. If IKE is enabled and you are using a CA to obtain certificates, the interface specified in Step 8 should be the one with the address specified in the CA certificates.

IPSec tunnels can be terminated on any PIX Firewall interface. This does not mean you terminate traffic coming from the outside on the inside interface. Traffic terminated on the inside interface is traffic from the inside network. Traffic terminated on the outside is traffic from the outside. Traffic terminated on a demilitarized zone (DMZ) is traffic from the DMZ.

As soon as you apply the crypto map, the SA database should initialize in system memory. The SAs are available for setup when traffic defined by the crypto access list is transmitted or received.

Only one crypto map set can be assigned to an interface. If multiple crypto map entries have the same map name but a different seq-num, they are considered part of the same set and are all applied to the interface. The crypto map entry with the lowest seq-num is considered the highest priority and is evaluated first.

Example 16-6 shows the commands required to configure the crypto map and apply it to the outside interface of peer PIX1 in Figure 16-1. A second peer (not shown on Figure 16-1) is also specified. You can optionally specify additional peers for redundancy.

Example 16-6   *Crypto Map Configuration*

```
crypto map MYMAP 10 ipsec-isakmp
crypto map MYMAP 10 match address crypto_acl_6
crypto map MYMAP 10 set peer 192.168.6.2
crypto map MYMAP 10 set peer 192.168.6.3
crypto map MYMAP 10 set transform-set pix6
crypto map MYMAP 10 set pfs group2
crypto map MYMAP 10 set security-association lifetime seconds 28800
crypto map MYMAP interface outside
```

Setting Manual Keys

You can configure IPSec SAs manually and not use IKE to set up the SA. Cisco recommends that you use IKE to set up the SAs because it is very difficult to ensure that the SA values match between peers, and D-H is a more secure method to generate secret keys between peers. If you must, you can use **crypto map** commands to manually specify the IPSec session keys and other SA parameters within a crypto map entry.

SAs established via the **crypto map** command do not expire (unlike SAs established via IKE). Session keys at one peer must match the session keys at the remote peer. If you change a session key, the SA using the key is deleted and reinitialized.

Step 5—Verify IPSec Configuration

You can use the **show crypto map** command to verify the crypto map configuration, as shown in Example 16-7. (Refer to Figure 16-1 for the network diagram related to this example.) You can also use **show access-list** to view the crypto ACL configuration, as previously shown in Example 16-3.

Example 16-7   show crypto map

```
pix1(config)# show crypto map

Crypto Map "MYMAP" 10 ipsec-isakmp
    Peer = 192.168.6.2
    Peer = 192.168.6.3
    access-list crypto_acl_6; 1 elements
    access-list crypto_acl_6 line 1 permit ip 10.0.1.0 255.255.255.0 10.0.6.0
    255.255.255.0 (hitcnt=0)
    Current peer: 192.168.6.2
    Security association lifetime: 4608000 kilobytes/28800 seconds
    PFS (Y/N): N
    Transform sets={ pix6, }
```

You can view the currently defined transform sets with the **show crypto ipsec transform-set** command. This command has the following syntax:

```
show crypto ipsec transform-set [tag transform-set-name]
```

The optional **tag** *transform-set-name* parameter shows only the transform sets with the specified *transform-set-name.*

If you use no keyword, all transform sets configured at the PIX Firewall are displayed. Example 16-8 shows the transform set pix6.

Example 16-8   show crypto ipsec transform-set *Command*

```
pix1# show crypto ipsec transform-set
Transform set pix6: { esp-3des  }
will negotiate = { Tunnel,  },
```

You can use the **show crypto ipsec security-association lifetime** command to view the current global IPSec SA lifetime.

Management Access

The PIX Firewall does not normally allow access to its inside interface through a VPN tunnel. Using the **management-access** command introduced in PIX Firewall Version 6.3, it is now possible to have management access to the inside interface of a PIX through a VPN tunnel, providing a necessary remote management option. Example 16-9 shows the command required to provide access to PIX1 from Site 2 at 10.0.1.1 (PIX1's inside interface IP address) over an encrypted tunnel. Refer to Figure 16-1 for this example:

Example 16-9   **management-access** *Command Configuration*

```
pix1(config)# management-access inside
```

Task 4—Test and Verify VPN Configuration

The last major task in configuring PIX Firewall IPSec is to test and verify the IKE and IPSec configurations accomplished in the previous tasks. You can perform the following actions to test and verify that you have correctly configured the VPN on the PIX Firewall:

- Verify ACLs and select interesting traffic with the **show access-list** command.
- Verify correct IKE configuration with the **show isakmp** and **show isakmp policy** commands.
- Verify correct IPSec configuration of transform sets with the **show crypto ipsec transform-set** command.
- Verify the correct crypto map configuration with the **show crypto map** command.
- Clear IPSec SAs for testing of SA establishment with the **clear crypto ipsec sa** command.
- Clear IKE SAs for testing of IKE SA establishment with the **clear crypto isakmp sa** command.
- Debug IKE and IPSec traffic through the PIX Firewall with the **debug crypto ipsec** and **debug crypto isakmp** commands.

The **show isakmp sa** command is useful for viewing all current IKE SAs at a peer, as shown in Example 16-10.

Example 16-10   The **show isakmp sa** *Command for Viewing All Current IKE SAs at a Peer*

```
pix1(config)# sh isakmp sa
Total    : 1
Embryonic : 0
        dst              src         state     pending    created
    192.168.1.2      192.168.6.2     QM_IDLE        0         1
```

The **clear isakmp** command clears active IKE connections, as shown in Example 16-11.

Example 16-11   *The* **clear isakmp** *Command for Clearing Active IKE Connections*

```
pix1(config)# show  isakmp sa
Total    : 1
Embryonic : 0
        dst              src         state     pending    created
   66.162.245.243    38.223.230.3     QM_IDLE        0         1
pix1(config)# clear isakmp sa
pix1(config)# show isakmp sa
Total    : 1
Embryonic : 0
        dst              src         state     pending    created
```

Easy VPN Operation

Technically, Easy VPN is not considered a true site-to-site VPN solution. However, when configured in the Network Extension mode (defined later in this section), Easy VPN can provide similar functionality to site-to-site connections and can be used in typical hub-and-spoke site-to-site VPN implementations. This option provides simple configuration and is particularly useful for small office/home office (SOHO) implementations where the remote device typically has an IP address dynamically assigned to its outside interface by the ISP.

Easy VPN consists of an Easy VPN Server and an Easy VPN Remote device. PIX Firewalls can function in both roles in an Easy VPN implementation. In addition to the PIX Firewall, Cisco VPN 3000 Concentrators and Cisco IOS Routers Version 12.2(8)T can also function as Easy VPN Servers. Easy VPN Remote devices include PIX Firewalls; Cisco VPN 3002 Hardware Clients; and Cisco 800, UBR900, and 1700 series routers with supported Cisco IOS versions or software clients.

NOTE   Other devices and versions of the Cisco IOS might also support Easy VPN functionality. Check Cisco.com for an updated list of devices supporting Easy VPN.

Easy VPN supports split tunneling to let you send Internet-bound traffic directly to the Internet without encryption. This functionality minimizes the encryption overhead and allows more efficient use of resources at the Easy VPN Server site.

When configured with backup Easy VPN servers, the remote device can automatically failover to a backup Easy VPN Server in the event of a network or service failure. The PIX Firewall Easy VPN Remote client can also participate in cluster-based load balancing when used with a VPN 3000 Concentrator Server, automatically connecting to the least-utilized concentrator.

You can configure the Easy VPN Remote client in one of two modes:

- **Client mode**—With this mode, the clients behind the Easy VPN Remote device are not directly accessible from the server side. Instead, the clients are port-address translated by the Easy VPN Remote device for tunneled traffic. This mode requires that a single private IP address be allocated to the remote device. Client mode causes VPN connections to be initiated by traffic from the Easy VPN Remote device, so resources are only used on demand.

- **Network Extension mode**—With this mode, the clients behind the Easy VPN Remote device are directly accessible from the server side. The IP addresses of the clients are not translated in this mode. Consequently, an appropriate number of IP addresses must be allocated when you use Easy VPN Network Extension mode. Network Extension mode keeps VPN connections open even when not required for transmission of traffic. This mode provides functionality that is similar to standard IPSec site-to-site VPN connections.

Configuring Easy VPN

As the name implies, Easy VPN is rather easy to configure. You use the **vpnclient** and **vpngroup** commands to configure Easy VPN on the PIX Firewall. The **vpnclient** command configures a PIX Firewall for Easy VPN Remote operation. You use the **vpngroup** command to set up the PIX Firewall as an Easy VPN Server. The syntax of the **vpnclient** command is as follows:

```
vpnclient vpngroup group_name password preshared_key
vpnclient username xauth_username password xauth_password
vpnclient server ip_primary [ip_secondary_1 ip_secondary_2 ... ip_secondary_10]
vpnclient mac-exempt mac_addr_1 mac_mask_1 [mac_addr_2 mac_mask_2]
vpnclient mode client-mode | network-extension-mode
vpnclient management {[tunnel {ip_addr_1 ip_mask_1} [{ip_addr_2 ip_mask_1}...
   ]] | [clear]}
no vpnclient management
[no] vpnclient connect
vpnclient disconnect
vpnclient enable
no vpnclient {server | mode | vpngroup | username | mac-exempt | management | enable}
clear vpnclient
show vpnclient [detail]
```

Table 16-10 shows the arguments and options for the **vpnclient** command sequence.

Table 16-10 **vpnclient** *Command Arguments*

Argument	Definition
clear	The **clear vpnclient** command is used to clear the Easy VPN Remote configuration and security policy stored in Flash memory.
connect	The **vpnclient connect** command is used to initiate configured tunnel connections to an Easy VPN Server.
disconnect	The **vpnclient disconnect** command is used to disconnect active tunnel connections to an Easy VPN Server. You can also use the **no vpnclient connect** command to disconnect all active tunnels to the Easy VPN Server.
enable	The **vpnclient enable** command enables Easy VPN Remote device functionality on the PIX Firewall. Easy VPN Remote settings must be configured on the PIX Firewall before you can issue the **vpnclient enable** command.
group_name	The name of the VPN group configured on the VPN head end. The maximum length is 63 characters and no spaces are permitted.
ip_addr_1, ip_addr_2, ...	The IP address of the remote network managing the client through the VPN tunnel.
ip_mask_1, ip_mask_2, ...	The IP mask of the remote network managing the client through the VPN tunnel.
ip_primary	The IP address of the primary Cisco Easy VPN Server.
ip_secondary_1... , ip_secondary_10	The IP address of a secondary Cisco Easy VPN Server. There can be from 1 to 10 secondary Cisco Easy VPN Servers (backup VPN head ends) configured. However, check your platform-specific documentation for applicable peer limits on your PIX Firewall platform.

continues

Table 16-10 vpnclient *Command Arguments (Continued)*

Argument	Definition
mac-exempt	Command used to specify user authentication exemption based on client MAC address.
mac_addr_n	The MAC address for user authentication exemption.
mac_mask_n	The MAC mask for user authentication exemption.
management clear	Specifies to use clear network traffic for management access to an Easy VPN Remote device.
management tunnel {*ip_addr_1 ip_mask_1*} [{*ip_addr_2 ip_mask_1*}...]	Specifies to use a VPN tunnel for management access to an Easy VPN Remote device.
mode client-mode | network-extension-mode	The **mode** command is used to specify the mode of operation for the Easy VPN Remote Device. Valid operand keywords are **client-mode** and **network-extension-mode**.
	Use **client-mode** to configure the Easy VPN Remote device in the client mode. Client mode requires a single IP address for the device and all hosts behind the device, and VPN connections are initiated by traffic from the Easy VPN Remote device, so resources are used only on demand.
	Use **network-extension-mode** to configure the Easy VPN Remote device in the Network Extension mode. Network extension mode requires an IP address for each host and keeps VPN connections open even when not required for transmission of traffic.
password	Command used to specify the password.
preshared_key	The IKE preshared key used for authentication by the Easy VPN Server. The maximum length is 127 characters.
server	The **vpnclient server** command is used to specify the Easy VPN Server. You can specify more than one server device for redundancy.
username	Command used to specify the username.
vpngroup	Command used to specify the group name.
xauth_password	The user password to be used for XAUTH. The maximum length is 127 characters.
xauth_username	The username to be used for XAUTH. The maximum length is 127 characters.

The syntax of the **vpngroup** command is as follows:

```
vpngroup group_name address-pool pool_name
vpngroup group_name authentication-server server_tag
vpngroup group_name backup-server {{ip1 [ip2 ... ip10]} | clear-client-cfg}
vpngroup group_name default-domain domain_name
vpngroup group_name device-pass-through
vpngroup group_name dns-server dns_ip_prim [dns_ip_sec]
vpngroup group_name idle-time idle_seconds
vpngroup group_name max-time max_seconds
vpngroup group_name password preshared_key
vpngroup group_name pfs
vpngroup group_name secure-unit-authentication
vpngroup group_name split-dns domain_name1 [domain_name2 ... domain_name8]
vpngroup group_name split-tunnel access_list
vpngroup group_name user-authentication
vpngroup group_name user-idle-timeout user_idle_seconds
vpngroup group_name wins-server wins_ip_prim [wins_ip_sec]
show vpngroup [group_name]
```

Table 16-11 shows the arguments and options for the **vpngroup** command sequence.

Table 16-11 vpngroup *Command Arguments*

Argument	Definition
access_list	The name of the access list for the split-tunnel configuration.
authentication-server	Specifies the individual user authentication (IUA) AAA server on the firewall headend.
backup-server	Configures a backup server list to be used for access by VPN clients if the primary server is not available.
clear-client-cfg	Clears backup servers from the client configuration.
default-domain	Command used to specify the default domain.
device-pass-through	Command used to exempt devices based on their MAC address from authentication. This option is used with devices such as Cisco IP phones that cannot use IUA for authentication. Use with the **vpnclient mac-exempt** command.
dns-server	Command used to specify the DNS servers.
dns_ip_prim	The IP address of the primary DNS server.
dns_ip_sec	The IP address of the secondary DNS server.
domain_name	The default domain name, up to 127 characters.
domain_name1 [domain_name2, domain_name3, ... , domain_name8]	The domains to configure for split DNS. The maximum length for a domain name is 127 characters.
group_name	Specifies the VPN policy group name and is an ASCII string with a maximum length of 63 characters. (You choose the name.)
idle-time	Command used to specify the idle timeout value.

continues

Table 16-11 vpngroup *Command Arguments (Continued)*

Argument	Definition
idle_seconds	The idle timeout in seconds, from 60 to 86,400. The default is 1800 seconds (30 minutes).
max-time	Command used to specify the maximum connection time value.
max_seconds	The maximum connection time in seconds that the VPN group is allowed, from 60 to 31,536,000. The default maximum connection time is set to unlimited.
password	Command used to specify the password.
pfs	Specifies the requirement that the VPN client or Easy VPN Remote device is to perform PFS.
pool_name	The IP address pool name, up to 63 characters.
preshared_key	The VPN group preshared key. The maximum is 127 characters.
server_tag	AAA server tag to authenticate remote users of a hardware client.
split-dns	Command used to specify split DNS.
split-tunnel	The **vpngroup split-tunnel** command is used to enable split tunneling on the PIX Firewall. Split tunneling provides access to the corporate network over an encrypted tunnel, while providing clear access to the Internet.
user-authentication	Enables user authentication on the Easy VPN Server.
user-idle-timeout	Command used to specify the user idle timeout value.
user_idle_seconds	Idle timeout for user authentication, in seconds.
wins-server	Command used to specify the WINS servers used.
wins_ip_prim	The IP address of the primary WINS server.
wins_ip_sec	The IP address of the secondary WINS server.

Example 16-12 shows the **vpnclient** commands required to configure a PIX Firewall as an Easy VPN Remote device in client mode with a primary and a secondary server.

Example 16-12 *Easy VPN Remote Client Mode Configuration*

```
Pixfirewall(config)# vpnclient mode client-mode
Pixfirewall(config)# vpnclient vpngroup MYGROUP password cisco123
Pixfirewall(config)# vpnclient username MYUSER password cisco123
Pixfirewall(config)# vpnclient server 192.168.6.2 192.168.6.3
Pixfirewall(config)# vpnclient enable
```

In this example, Easy VPN servers 192.168.6.2 and 192.168.6.3 provide redundancy for the connection.

Example 16-13 demonstrates usage of the **vpngroup** command to configure a PIX Firewall as an Easy VPN Server with split tunneling.

NOTE   Configuration of Easy VPN Servers and VPN groups for remote access clients are similar and use the same **vpngroup** command.

Example 16-13   *Easy VPN Server Configuration*

```
pixfirewall(config)# access-list nonat permit ip 10.0.1.0 255.255.255.0 10.0.6.0
  255.255.255.0
pixfirewall(config)# access-list easy_acl permit ip 10.0.1.0 255.255.255.0 10.0.6.0
  255.255.255.0
pixfirewall(config)# nat (inside) 0 access-list nonat
pixfirewall(config)# ip local pool easypool 10.0.6.50-10.0.6.100
!
pixfirewall(config)# crypto ipsec transform-set esp-3des-md5 esp-3des esp-md5-hmac
pixfirewall(config)# crypto dynamic-map dyna 20 set transform-set esp-3des-md5
pixfirewall(config)# crypto map easy 50 ipsec-isakmp dynamic dyna
pixfirewall(config)# crypto map easy client configuration address initiate
pixfirewall(config)# crypto map easy interface outside
!
pixfirewall(config)# isakmp enable outside
pixfirewall(config)# isakmp identity hostname
pixfirewall(config)# isakmp nat-traversal 60
pixfirewall(config)# isakmp policy 20 authentication pre-share
pixfirewall(config)# isakmp policy 20 encryption 3des
pixfirewall(config)# isakmp policy 20 hash md5
pixfirewall(config)# isakmp policy 20 group 2
pixfirewall(config)# isakmp policy 20 lifetime 86400
!
pixfirewall(config)# vpngroup MYGROUP address-pool easypool
pixfirewall(config)# vpngroup MYGROUP backup-server 192.168.6.3
pixfirewall(config)# vpngroup MYGROUP dns-server 10.0.6.10
pixfirewall(config)# vpngroup MYGROUP wins-server 10.0.6.11
pixfirewall(config)# vpngroup MYGROUP default-domain cisco.com
pixfirewall(config)# vpngroup MYGROUP split-tunnel easy_acl
pixfirewall(config)# vpngroup MYGROUP idle-time 1800
pixfirewall(config)# vpngroup MYGROUP password cisco123
```

This example shows the commands required for Easy VPN Server configuration. In addition to the **vpngroup** commands, appropriate IKE and IPSec statements and a dynamic crypto map are also required. In this example, traffic between the 10.0.1.0/24 and 10.0.6.0/24 networks is encrypted and exempted from address translation. The Easy VPN Remote device directly routes other traffic to the Internet. The configuration defines a pool of addresses for use by MYGROUP, assigns default DNS and WINS servers to the group, and specifies a backup server.

Notice that the configuration of remote device settings is completed on the server once and pushed to the clients when they connect. This functionality greatly simplifies the management of Easy VPN devices.

VPN Configuration Using PDM

PDM provides an alternative method for creating and maintaining VPN configurations on the PIX Firewall. PDM 3.0 fully supports configuration of site-to-site and remote access VPNs and Easy VPN Remote devices. PDM also provides a VPN Wizard that further simplifies the configuration of site-to-site and remote access VPNs. Using a few simple screens, the VPN Wizard creates the proper IKE policy, IPSec transform sets, crypto ACLs, and crypto map statements to configure site-to-site or remote access VPN connections for you.

NOTE	Easy VPN Remote device configuration is included in the Startup Wizard but not in the VPN Wizard. However, configuration of Easy VPN remote devices is accessible within PDM and the process is simple even without a wizard.

NOTE	PDM is an excellent tool for learning VPN configuration requirements and techniques on the PIX Firewall. You will better understand VPN configuration requirements by viewing the command-line interface (CLI) commands generated by PDM.

The following subsections explain how to use PDM to create site-to-site VPNs.

System Options

To begin creating your VPN, implicitly permit IPSec packets to bypass PIX Firewall ACLs and conduits by selecting **VPN System Options** from the Categories tree and selecting the **Bypass access check for IPSec and L2TP traffic** check box, as shown in Figure 16-2. When you use the VPN Wizard, this option is automatically enabled.

Figure 16-2   *VPN System Options*

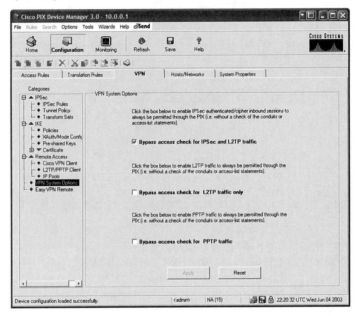

IKE-related screens are grouped under the IKE branch of the Categories tree shown in Figure 16-3. You can view your IKE policies by selecting **Policies** from the IKE branch. Add, edit, or delete policies by clicking the buttons on the right side of the screen. You can also set general IKE setting on this screen. For example, you can enable NAT-T by selecting its option on this screen.

Figure 16-3 *IKE Configuration Screen*

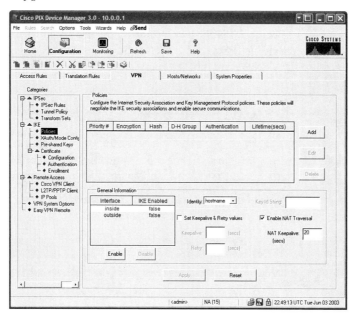

Clicking **Add** opens a window shown on Figure 16-4 where you can configure an IKE policy by using encryption algorithm, hash algorithm, D-H group, SA lifetime, and authentication methods. There is a separate section for preshared keys. If you select preshare as the authentication type, you need to specify the key and identify the peer that will be sharing this key with your PIX Firewall.

Figure 16-4 *Add IKE Policy Screen*

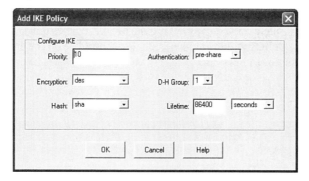

Digital Certificates

PDM supports the configuration of the interoperability of CAs with IPSec. This enables the PIX Firewall and the CA to communicate so that the PIX Firewall can obtain and use digital certificates from the CA.

The PIX Firewall currently supports CA servers from VeriSign, Entrust, Baltimore Technologies, and Microsoft. You must ensure that the PIX Firewall clock is set to GMT, month, day, and year before configuring the CA. If the clock is set incorrectly, the CA might reject certificates based on the incorrect timestamps. Also, the lifetime of the certificate and the certificate revocation list (CRL) is checked in GMT time.

The PDM window for configuring a CA is accessible from the IKE branch of the Categories tree and is shown in Figure 16-5. You can configure the following parameters in this window:

- **Nickname**—Name given to the CA.

- **CA IP**—The IP address of the CA server.

- **LDAP IP**—The IP address of the Lightweight Directory Access Protocol (LDAP) server.

- **CA Script Location**—The location of the CA script. The default location and script on the CA server is /cgi-bin/pkiclient.exe. If the CA administrator has not put the CGI script in this location, provide the location and the name of the script in the **ca identity** command. A PIX Firewall uses a subset of the HTTP protocol to contact the CA, so it must identify a particular cgi-bin script to handle CA requests.

- **Retry Interval**—The number of minutes the PIX Firewall waits before resending a certificate request to the CA when it does not receive a response from the previous request. Specify 1 to 60 minutes. By default, the PIX Firewall retries every minute.

- **Retry Count**—Number of times the PIX Firewall resends a certificate request when it does not receive a certificate from the CA from the previous request. Specify 1 to 100. The default is 0, which indicates it will keep retrying.

- **Key Modulus**—The size of the key modulus, which is between 512 and 2048 bits.

- **Certificate Authority**—Indicates whether to contact the CA or registration authority (RA). Some CA systems provide an RA, which the PIX Firewall contacts instead of the CA.

Figure 16-5 *Certificate Configuration Screen*

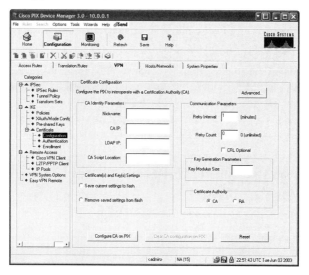

Creating Transform Sets

To create transform sets, select **Transform Sets** from the IPSec branch of the Categories tree. The screen shown in Figure 16-6 enables you to view, add, edit, and delete transform sets.

Figure 16-6 *Transform Sets Configuration Screen*

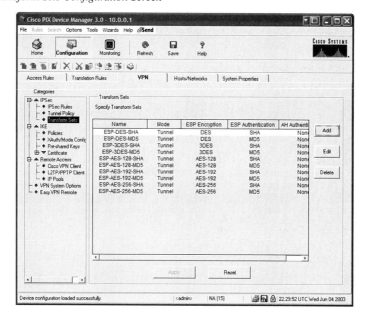

The available transform sets are listed on the left side of the screen. On selection, PDM populates the right border panel with the properties of the selected transform set. You can then can change any attribute and click **Add** to modify it. You can also enter a new name. ESP-DES-SHA, ESP-DES-MD5, ESP-3DES-SHA, ESP-3DES-MD5, ESP-AES-128-SHA, ESP-AES-128-MD5, ESP-AES-192-SHA, ESP-AES-192-MD5, ESP-AES-256-SHA, and ESP-AES-256-MD5 are predefined by PDM.

Creating a Crypto Map

Use the Tunnel Policy window to create crypto maps. *Tunnel policies* are the equivalent of crypto maps in the PIX Firewall CLI. When you select **Tunnel Policy** from the IPSec branch of the Categories tree, the Tunnel Policies table appears, displaying your currently configured tunnels. You can add, edit, or delete policies by clicking the buttons on the right side of the screen.

Figure 16-7 shows the window that appears when you click **Add** in the Tunnel Policy window. This window is where which you define or modify tunnel policies. As you create a tunnel policy, you must bind it to an interface. The PIX Firewall CLI enables you to configure a crypto map and then apply it to an interface. PDM hides the concept of the crypto map. It does not support crypto maps that are not applied to any interface. If such a map exists in the configuration, PDM parses and ignores it. PDM also does not support crypto maps that are applied to more than one interface. This includes dynamic crypto maps.

Figure 16-7 *Add Tunnel Screen*

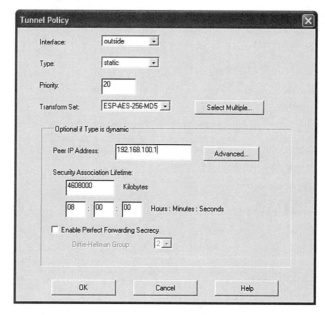

A tunnel policy can have more than one transform set and more than one peer. This is the purpose of the Select Multiple button beside the Transform Set field and the Advanced button beside the Peer IP Address field. Each opens a window where you can configure multiple values per field.

Creating an IPSec Rule

IPSec-related screens are grouped under the IPSec branch of the Categories tree. To select traffic to be protected by IPSec, select **IPSec Rules** from the IPSec branch. Right-click within the IPSec Rules table and choose **Add** from the drop-down menu. The Add Rule panel shown on Figure 16-8 appears. This panel consists of a table similar to the Access Rule panel. This is where you select the traffic to be protected. When applied to the PIX Firewall, the rule you create is implemented by attaching an ACL to a crypto map.

Figure 16-8 *IPSec Rule Configuration Screen*

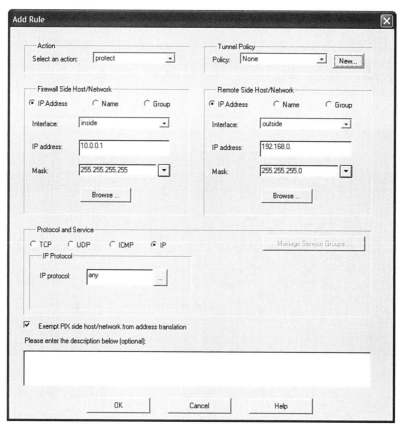

In the Add Rule panel, the action choices are protect and do not protect, rather than permit or deny. Use the PIX Side Host/Network and Remote Side Host/Network group boxes to select the traffic to be protected. Like the Access Rule table, PDM displays the real IP addresses of the hosts and networks. The ACL, however, might show translated addresses depending on your current NAT configuration and where the crypto map is applied.

At the bottom of the panel is the Exempt from address translation check box. If you select it, PDM generates **nat 0 match acl** commands to allow IPSec traffic to bypass the NAT engine. This check box is selected by default.

Use the Tunnel Policy group box in the top-right corner to attach your traffic selection rule to a tunnel policy. This is the equivalent of attaching an ACL to a crypto map. The New button provides a shortcut for defining a new tunnel policy without leaving the Add Rule panel.

You can add, edit, and delete traffic selector rules by using the main Rules menu or the buttons in the toolbar or by right-clicking within the table. You can also cut, copy, and paste rules between the access rule tables, NAT exemption rule table, and IPSec rule table.

VPN Wizard

You can also use the VPN Wizard, accessed through the Wizards menu item of the PDM, to create site-to-site VPNs. To do so, follow these steps:

Step 1   Start the VPN Wizard from the Wizard menu.

Step 2   On the initial wizard screen shown on Figure 16-9, select site-to-site as the type of VPN and the interface you want to enable VPN on (typically the outside interface). Click **Next**.

Figure 16-9   *VPN Wizard Welcome Screen*

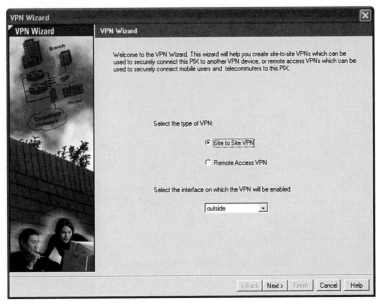

Step 3   On the next screen, which is shown in Figure 16-10, specify the IP
address of the peer and preshared key you want to use. You can also
specify certificate-based authentication settings on this screen. Click
Next and you see the screen shown on Figure 16-11.

Figure 16-10   *VPN Wizard: Remote Site Peer*

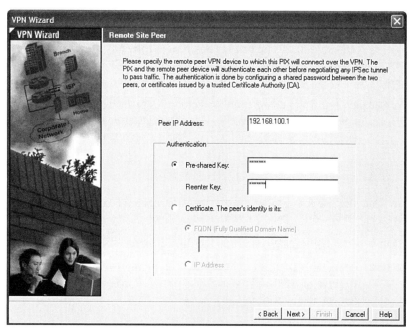

Step 4   On the next screen, shown in Figure 16-11, select the IKE policy setting
for Encryption, Authentication, and D-H Group. Click **Next**.

Figure 16-11   *VPN Wizard: IKE Policy*

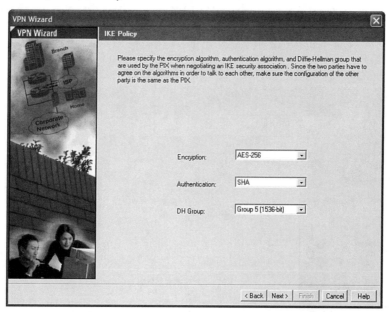

Step 5   On the next screen, shown in Figure 16-12, select the transform set
settings for Encryption and Authentication. Click **Next**.

Figure 16-12   *VPN Wizard: Transform Set*

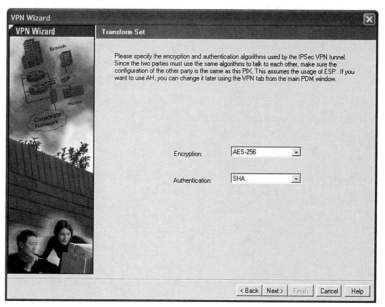

Step 6   On the next screen, shown in Figure 16-13, select the local host or
network whose traffic will be protected by this VPN. You can use the
Browse button to view any predefined hosts or network on your PIX
Firewall. Click **Next**.

Figure 16-13   *VPN Wizard: IPSec Traffic Selector*

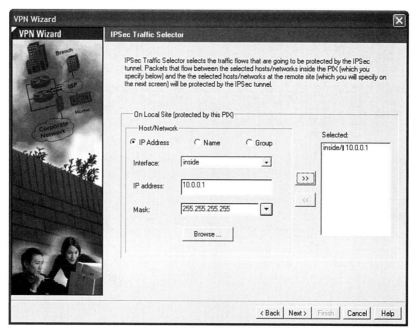

Step 7   On the next screen, shown in Figure 16-14, select the remote host or
network whose traffic will be protected by this VPN. You can use the
Browse button to view any predefined hosts or network on your PIX
Firewall. Click **Finish**.

Figure 16-14   *VPN Wizard: IPSec Traffic Selector (Continued)*

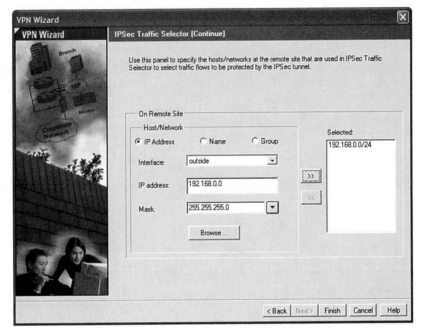

PDM now configures all the required settings for the site-to-site VPN.

NOTE   You can view the CLI commands generated by PDM VPN Wizard by looking at the running configuration. From the File menu of PDM, select **Show Running Configuration in New Window**.

Easy VPN

To configure Easy VPN using the PDM, follow these steps:

Step 1   Click **VPN > Easy VPN Remote**. The Easy VPN Remote configuration page shown in Figure 16-15 appears.

Figure 16-15   *Easy VPN Remote Configuration Page*

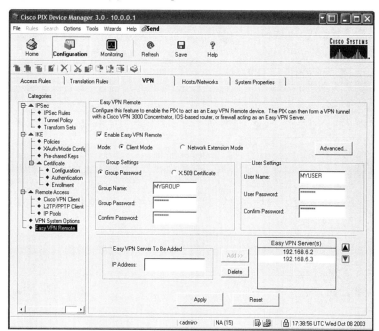

Step 2   Click the **Enable Easy VPN Remote** check box to enable Easy VPN Remote on the PIX.

Step 3   Select **Client Mode** or **Network Extension Mode** by clicking the appropriate radio button.

Step 4   Configure group settings by completing the following substeps:

> (1) Select **X.509** if you are using certificates, or select the **Group Password** radio button.
>
> (2) Enter the group name in the Group Name field.
>
> (3) Enter the group password in the Group Password field.
>
> (4) Re-enter the group password in the Group Password field to confirm.

Step 5   Configure User settings by completing the following substeps:

> (1) Enter the username in the User Name field.
>
> (2) Enter the user password in the User Password field.
>
> (3) Re-enter the user password in the User Password field to confirm.

Step 6 Enter the IP address of the Easy VPN Server in the Easy VPN Server To Be Added field. Click **Add** to add the server to the Easy VPN Server list. You can add additional backup servers and reorder the server as needed.

Step 7 Click **Apply** to send the configuration to the PIX Firewall.

Step 8 Click **Save** to write the configuration to memory on the PIX Firewall.

Case Study: Three-Site Full-Mesh IPSec Tunnels Using Preshared Keys

In this case study, the XYZ Company has three sites connected to the Internet. Its goal is to save money for site-to-site communication by using the Internet for secure communications between offices. This step will allow it to eliminate the costly point-to-point T1s that they currently have in place. In this case study, all traffic from internal users bound for the Internet is sent unencrypted. Traffic bound for another office's internal network will be protected by IPSec.

Figure 16-16 shows the proposed topology that is possible using IPSec.

Figure 16-16 *IPSec Topology for XYZ Company*

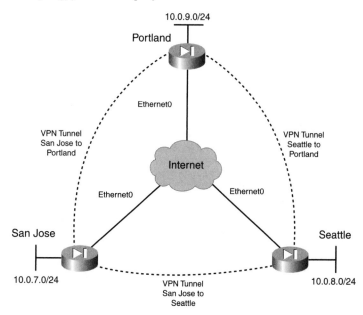

Network Security Policy

The network security policy that XYZ Company wants to implement is as follows:

- Use the Internet to securely connect its two branch offices to the corporate network in Portland.

- Authenticate data traffic between the corporate network and branch offices over the Internet to ensure that no one is inserting or changing packets in transit.

- Use IKE preshared keys and SHA for authentication.

- Ensure the data integrity of traffic between the corporate network and branch offices over the Internet using 168-bit 3DES encryption.

Sample Configuration for Portland, Seattle, and San Jose PIX Firewalls

Examine the configuration examples shown in Examples 16-14, 16-15, and 16-16 for the Portland, Seattle, and San Jose PIX Firewalls of the XYZ Company. These examples implement the network security policy statements related to IPSec network security. Unused interfaces and other unrelated commands have been deleted for brevity.

Example 16-14 *PIX Configuration for Portland*

```
hostname Portland
! access-list 101 specifies that any ip traffic from Portland to Seattle will be
  encrypted
access-list 101 permit ip 10.0.9.0 255.255.255.0 10.0.8.0 255.255.255.0
! access-list 102 specifies that any ip traffic from Portland to San Jose will be
  encrypted
access-list 102 permit ip 10.0.9.0 255.255.255.0 10.0.7.0 255.255.255.0
! access-list 103 is used by nat 0 below
access-list 103 permit ip 10.0.9.0 255.255.255.0 10.0.8.0 255.255.255.0
access-list 103 permit ip 10.0.9.0 255.255.255.0 10.0.7.0 255.255.255.0
ip address outside 192.168.9.2 255.255.255.0
ip address inside 10.0.9.1 255.255.255.0
global (outside) 1 192.168.9.20-192.168.9.254 netmask 255.255.255.0
! nat 0 is used here with access-list 103. The effect of the access-list bound to
  nat 0 is that traffic going to and coming from the inside networks specified in
  the access-list will not be translated. This is necessary because translation
  occurs before encryption. Failure to add the nat 0 and the access-list will result
  in failure to communicate to crypto peers.
nat (inside) 0 access-list 103
nat (inside) 1 10.0.9.0 255.255.255.0 0 0
route outside 0.0.0.0 0.0.0.0 192.168.9.1 1
! Allow IPSec protected traffic to bypass the regular conduit/access-list
  processing.
sysopt connection permit-ipsec
! Use 168-bit 3DES to encrypt traffic between the protected networks.
  crypto ipsec transform-set Portland esp-3des
! Use ISAKMP to establish the phase 1 SA to the first peer.
  crypto map VPN 10 ipsec-isakmp
```

Example 16-14 *PIX Configuration for Portland (Continued)*

```
! Apply protection to any traffic specified in this access-list
crypto map VPN 10 match address 101
! Define the first crypto peer.
crypto map VPN 10 set peer 192.168.8.2
! Use transform-set Portland for the first peer.
crypto map VPN 10 set transform-set Portland
! Use ISAKMP to establish the phase 1 SA to the second peer.
crypto map VPN 20 ipsec-isakmp
! Apply protection to any traffic specified in this access-list
crypto map VPN 20 match address 102
! Define the second crypto peer.
crypto map VPN 20 set peer 192.168.7.2
! Use transform-set Portland for the first peer.
crypto map VPN 20 set transform-set Portland
! Bind the crypto map to operate on the Outside interface.
crypto map VPN interface outside
! Bind IKE to operate on the Outside interface.
isakmp enable outside.
! Define the pre-shared keys to use for both peers.
isakmp key cisco123 address 192.168.8.2 netmask 255.255.255.255
isakmp key cisco456 address 192.168.7.2 netmask 255.255.255.255
! IKE will use IP addresses to define crypto peers.
isakmp identity address
! IKE will use pre-shared keys to authenticate crypto peers.
isakmp policy 10 authentication pre-share
! IKE will protect the phase 1 SA with 3DES.
isakmp policy 10 encryption 3DES
! IKE will send the pre-shared key to its crypto peers as a sha hash.
isakmp policy 10 hash sha
! IKE will use a 1024-bit prime number to generate the Symmetric encryption key.
isakmp policy 10 group 2
! IKE will require re-authentication of its crypto peer once a day.
isakmp policy 10 lifetime 86400
```

Example 16-15 *PIX Configuration for Seattle*

```
hostname Seattle
access-list 101 permit ip 10.0.8.0 255.255.255.0 10.0.7.0 255.255.255.0
access-list 102 permit ip 10.0.8.0 255.255.255.0 10.0.9.0 255.255.255.0
access-list 103 permit ip 10.0.8.0 255.255.255.0 10.0.7.0 255.255.255.0
access-list 103 permit ip 10.0.8.0 255.255.255.0 10.0.9.0 255.255.255.0
ip address outside 192.168.8.2 255.255.255.0
ip address inside 10.0.8.1 255.255.255.0
global (outside) 1 192.168.8.20-192.168.8.254 netmask 255.255.255.0
nat (inside) 0 access-list 103
nat (inside) 1 10.0.8.0 255.255.255.0 0 0
route outside 0.0.0.0 0.0.0.0 192.168.8.1 1
sysopt connection permit-ipsec
crypto ipsec transform-set Seattle esp-3des
crypto map VPN 10 ipsec-isakmp
crypto map VPN 10 match address 101
```

continues

Example 16-15 *PIX Configuration for Seattle (Continued)*

```
crypto map VPN 10 set peer 192.168.7.2
crypto map VPN 10 set transform-set Seattle
crypto map VPN 20 ipsec-isakmp
crypto map VPN 20 match address 102
crypto map VPN 20 set peer 192.168.9.2
crypto map VPN 20 set transform-set Seattle
crypto map VPN 103 ipsec-isakmp
crypto map VPN interface outside
isakmp enable outside
isakmp key cisco123 address 192.168.9.2 netmask 255.255.255.255
isakmp key cisco123 address 192.168.7.2 netmask 255.255.255.255
isakmp identity address
isakmp policy 10 authentication pre-share
isakmp policy 10 encryption 3des
isakmp policy 10 hash sha
isakmp policy 10 group 2
isakmp policy 10 lifetime 86400
```

Example 16-16 *PIX Configuration for San Jose*

```
hostname San_Jose
access-list 101 permit ip 10.0.7.0 255.255.255.0 10.0.8.0 255.255.255.0
access-list 102 permit ip 10.0.7.0 255.255.255.0 10.0.9.0 255.255.255.0
access-list 103 permit ip 10.0.7.0 255.255.255.0 10.0.8.0 255.255.255.0
access-list 103 permit ip 10.0.7.0 255.255.255.0 10.0.9.0 255.255.255.0
ip address outside 192.168.7.2 255.255.255.0
ip address inside 10.0.7.1 255.255.255.0
global (outside) 1 192.168.7.20-192.168.7.254 netmask 255.255.255.0
nat (inside) 0 access-list 103
nat (inside) 1 10.0.7.0 255.255.255.0 0 0
route outside 0.0.0.0 0.0.0.0 192.168.7.1 1
sysopt connection permit-ipsec
crypto ipsec transform-set San_Jose esp-3des
crypto map VPN 10 ipsec-isakmp
crypto map VPN 10 match address 101
crypto map VPN 10 set peer 192.168.8.2
crypto map VPN 10 set transform-set San_Jose
crypto map VPN 20 ipsec-isakmp
crypto map VPN 20 match address 102
crypto map VPN 20 set peer 192.168.9.2
crypto map VPN 20 set transform-set San_Jose
crypto map VPN interface outside
isakmp enable outside
isakmp key cisco456 address 192.168.9.2 netmask 255.255.255.255
isakmp key cisco123 address 192.168.8.2 netmask 255.255.255.255
isakmp identity address
isakmp policy 10 authentication pre-share
isakmp policy 10 encryption 3des
isakmp policy 10 hash sha
isakmp policy 10 group 2
isakmp policy 10 lifetime 86400
```

Summary

This section summarizes the information you learned in this chapter:

- To properly plan for IPSec configuration, you must determine the types of traffic that will be encrypted and the hosts or networks that will be protected and specify the IPSec gateways that will terminate the tunnels.

- You use the **isakmp policy** command to specify preshared keys for authentication and to configure IKE policy parameters.

- Some IPSec transforms require you to make trade-offs between high performance and stronger security.

- IPSec transforms are grouped into sets, and the sets can be grouped into supersets in crypto maps, where you place the strongest security transform sets first.

- Crypto access lists act like outgoing access lists, in which permit means encrypt. Crypto access lists also check to see whether incoming traffic *should* have been encrypted but wasn't.

- Crypto access lists should mirror each other between peers.

- Crypto maps pull together all IPSec details and are applied to interfaces and, in this way, they enable IPSec SA setup.

- The PIX Firewall can terminate IPSec tunnels on any interface from traffic coming in on that interface.

- PIX Firewalls Version 6.3 or later support NAT-T, 1536-bit D-H protocol (Group 5), and AES (128 bit, 192 bit, and 256 bit).

- The **show crypto map** command shows a summary of all IPSec parameters used to set up IPSec SAs.

- PDM provides simplified configuration of site-to-site VPNs.

- The VPN Wizard is the easiest way to create site-to-site VPNs on the PIX Firewall.

Chapter Review Questions

To test what you have learned in this chapter, answer the following questions and then refer to Appendix A, "Answers to Chapter Review Questions," for the answers:

1 What version of PIX Firewall supports the NAT-T standard?

2 List the four IPSec configuration tasks.

3 You would like to use AES. What version of the PIX Firewall do you need?

4 What is the command syntax for configuring IKE on an interface?

5 What is the benefit of using the SHA algorithm versus MD5? What is the drawback?

6   What is the most secure encryption standard supported on the PIX Firewall Version 6.2?

7   You are creating a dynamic crypto map. What consideration must be given to the sequence number you choose for this map entry?

Lab Exercise—Configure Site-to-Site VPNs

Complete the following lab exercises to practice VPN configuration procedures. Use the following initial configuration commands and continue with the rest of the lab exercises. Only the relevant commands are included for each device. You should do a **write erase** on each device to reset the configuration and apply the commands listed to prepare for this lab.

Following is the configuration for pix1:

```
interface ethernet0 100full
interface ethernet1 100full
hostname pix1
ip address outside 192.168.1.1 255.255.255.0
ip address inside 10.0.1.1 255.255.255.0
pdm location 10.0.1.11 255.255.255.255 inside
http server enable
http 10.0.1.0 255.255.255.0 inside
```

Following is the configuration for pix2:

```
interface ethernet0 100full
interface ethernet1 100full
hostname pix2
ip address outside 192.168.1.2 255.255.255.0
ip address inside 10.0.2.1 255.255.255.0
pdm location 10.0.2.11 255.255.255.255 inside
http server enable
http 10.0.1.0 255.255.255.0 inside
```

Objectives

In this lab exercise, you complete the following tasks:

- Prepare to configure VPN support.
- Configure IKE parameters.
- Configure IPSec parameters.
- Test and verify the IPSec configuration.

Lab Topology

Figure 16-17 displays the topology you will need for the lab exercises in this chapter.

Figure 16-17   *Site-to-Site VPN Lab Exercise Visual Objective*

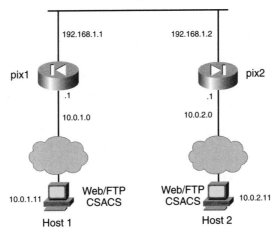

Equipment required to perform the lab includes the following:

- Two PIX Firewalls with at least two interfaces
- Category 5 patch cables
- Two PC hosts running a web server and FTP server

Task 1—Configure IKE Parameters

Complete the following steps to configure IKE on pix1 and pix2 (commands for one
device are shown):

Step 1   Ensure that IKE is enabled on the outside interface:

```
pix1(config)# isakmp enable outside
```

Step 2   Configure a basic IKE policy using preshared keys for authentication:

```
pix1(config)# isakmp policy 10 authentication pre-share
```

Step 3   Set the IKE identity:

```
pix1(config)# isakmp identity address
```

Step 4   Configure the ISAKMP preshared key to point to the outside IP address
of the peer PIX Firewall:

```
pix1(config)# isakmp key cisco123 address 192.168.1.2 netmask
255.255.255.255
```

Task 2—Configure IPSec Parameters

Complete the following steps to configure IPSec (IKE Phase 2) parameters on pix1 and pix2. You must modify the configurations appropriately for pix2:

Step 1 Create an ACL to select traffic to protect. The ACL should protect IP traffic between the networks:

```
pix1(config)# access-list 101 permit ip 10.0.1.0 255.255.255.0 10.0.2.0
255.255.255.0
```

Step 2 Create an ACL to exempt the selected traffic from address translation:

```
pix1(config)# access-list nonat permit ip 10.0.1.0 255.255.255.0
10.0.2.0 255.255.255.0
```

Step 3 View your ACL:

```
pix1(config)# show access-list
access-list cached ACL log flows: total 0, denied 0 (deny-flow-max 1024)
            alert-interval 300
access-list 101; 1 elements
access-list 101 line 1 permit ip 10.0.1.0 255.255.255.0 10.0.2.0
255.255.255.0 (hitcnt=0)
access-list nonat; 1 elements
access-list nonat line 1 permit ip 10.0.1.0 255.255.255.0 10.0.2.0
255.255.255.0 (hitcnt=0)
```

Step 4 Configure an IPSec transform set (IKE Phase 2 parameters) to use ESP and 3DES. Use a *transform-set-name* of pix2:

```
pix1(config)# crypto ipsec transform-set pix2 esp-3des
```

Step 5 Create a crypto map by completing the following substeps:

(1) Create a crypto map entry. Use a *map-name* of peer2:

```
pix1(config)# crypto map peer2 10 ipsec-isakmp
```

(2) Look at the crypto map and observe the defaults:

```
pix1(config)# show crypto map
Crypto Map "peer2" 10 ipsec-isakmp
No matching address list set.
Current peer: 0.0.0.0
Security association lifetime: 4608000 kilobytes/
  28800 seconds
PFS (Y/N): N
Transform sets={ }
```

(3) Assign the ACL to the crypto map:

```
pixfirewall1(config)# crypto map peer2 10 match address 101
```

(4) Define the peer. The peer IP address should be set to the peer's outside interface IP address:

```
pixfirewall1(config)# crypto map peer2 10 set peer
    192.168.1.2
```

(5) Specify the transform set used to reach the peer.

```
pixfirewall(config)# crypto map peer2 10 set transform-set
    pix2
```

(6) Apply the crypto map set to the outside interface:

```
pixfirewall(config)# crypto map peer2 interface outside
```

Task 3—Test and Verify the IPSec Configuration

Complete the following steps to test and verify the IPSec configuration:

Step 1 Verify the IKE policy you just created. Note the default values:

```
pix1(config)# show isakmp
isakmp enable outside
isakmp key ******** address 192.168.1.2 netmask 255.255.255.255
isakmp policy 10 authentication pre-share
isakmp policy 10 encryption 3des
isakmp policy 10 hash sha
isakmp policy 10 group 1
isakmp policy 10 lifetime 86400
```

Step 2 Examine the IKE policies in your PIX Firewall:

```
pix1(config)# show isakmp policy
Protection suite of priority 10
        encryption algorithm:   Three key triple DES
        hash algorithm:         Secure Hash Standard
        authentication method:  Pre-Shared Key
        Diffie-Hellman group:   #1 (768 bit)
        lifetime:               86400 seconds, no volume limit
Default protection suite
        encryption algorithm:   DES - Data Encryption Standard (56 bit
keys).
        hash algorithm:         Secure Hash Standard
        authentication method:  Rivest-Shamir-Adleman Signature
        Diffie-Hellman group:   #1 (768 bit)
        lifetime:               86400 seconds, no volume limit
```

Step 3 Verify the crypto ACL:

```
pix1(config)# show access-list 101
access-list 101; 1 elements
```

```
access-list 101 line 1 permit ip 10.0.1.0 255.255.255.0 10.0.2.0
255.255.255.0 (hitcnt=0)
```

Step 4   Verify that the IPSec parameters (IKE Phase 2) are correct:

```
pix1(config)# show crypto ipsec transform-set
Transform set pix2: { esp-3des  }
   will negotiate = { Tunnel,  },
```

Step 5   Verify that the crypto map configuration is correct:

```
pix1(config)# show crypto map
Crypto Map: "peer2" interfaces: { outside }
Crypto Map "peer2" 10 ipsec-isakmp
  Peer = 192.168.1.2
  access-list 101; 1 elements

  access-list 101 line 1 permit ip 10.0.1.0 255.255.255.0 10.0.2.0
255.255.255.0 (hitcnt=0)

  Current peer: 192.168.1.2
  Security association lifetime: 4608000 kilobytes/28800 seconds
  PFS (Y/N): N
  Transform sets={ pix2, }
```

Step 6   Turn on debugging for IPSec and ISAKMP:

```
pix1(config)# debug crypto ipsec
pix1(config)# debug crypto isakmp
```

Step 7   Clear the IPSec SA by using the following command:

```
pix1(config)# clear crypto ipsec sa
```

Step 8   Initiate a web session from Host 1 to Host 2 using its private address:

```
http://10.0.2.11
```

Step 9   Observe the debug output and verify that the web session was
established. The debug should state the following status indicating that
IPSec was successful:

```
return status is IKMP_NO_ERROR
```

Step 10 Examine the IPSec SAs. Note the number of packets encrypted and
decrypted.

```
pix1(config)# show crypto ipsec sa
```

Task 4—Using PDM (Optional)

Perform the first four tasks again, this time using the PDM to configure various VPN settings.

Compare the CLI commands generated to the configuration you created using CLI commands.

Task 5—Using PDM VPN Wizard (Optional)

Use the PDM VPN Wizard to configure a site-to-site VPN between your two PIX Firewalls.

Compare the CLI commands generated to the configuration you created using CLI commands.

On completion of this chapter, you will be able to perform the following tasks:

- Describe the Cisco VPN Client.
- Configure remote access virtual private networks (VPNs) using the **vpngroup** command.
- Configure remote access VPNs using the PIX Device Manager (PDM).
- Configure Point-to-Point Tunneling Protocol (PPTP) remote access VPNs.

CHAPTER 17

Client Remote Access VPNs

In the previous chapter, you became familiar with site-to-site VPNs, designed for securely connecting remote sites to each other or to a central site over the public network. Remote access VPNs are another type of VPN service designed for connecting remote access users, typically on dialup or broadband (digital subscriber line [DSL] or cable modem) connections, to corporate resources over the public network in a secure and efficient manner.

Cisco VPN Client

PIX Firewall supports the VPN client, a software program that runs on all current Windows operating systems, including Windows 98, Millennium Edition (Me), NT 4.0, 2000, and XP. The VPN client enables you to establish secure, end-to-end encrypted tunnels to Cisco remote access VPN devices supporting the unified client framework.

The VPN client is intended for use by low- or high-speed remote users who need to securely access their corporate networks across the Internet. Users can load the client on their PCs and launch tunnels as needed to establish connections to a VPN device that supports the VPN client. The software VPN client supports only the device on which it is loaded.

As a remote user, you probably first connect to the Internet before establishing your VPN tunnel. The VPN client enables you to use plain old telephone service (POTS), ISDN, DSL, or cable modem connection technologies for this connection. It is compatible with Point-to-Point Protocol (PPP) over Ethernet-based DSL and has been tested with Efficient Networks EnterNet, Fine Point Technologies WinPOET, and Point-to-Point Protocol over Ethernet (PPPoE) for Windows 95, 98, Me, NT, 2000, and XP.

You can also configure the VPN client for mass deployments, and initial logins require very little user intervention. Policies and configurations for VPN access are downloaded from the central gateway and pushed to the VPN client when a connection is established, allowing simple deployment and management as well as high scalability. Items pushed to the VPN client from the central site concentrator include the following:

- Domain Name System (DNS)
- Windows Internet Naming System (WINS)

- Split tunneling networks
- Default domain name
- IP address
- Ability to save a password for the VPN connection

NOTE The VPN client works with any Cisco VPN-enabled products that support the unified client framework. The Cisco Unified Client Framework is an initiative that enables consistent VPN client operation between service providers and enterprises and compatibility across various Cisco VPN platforms. The unified client framework currently includes the Cisco VPN 3000 Concentrator Series, the Cisco PIX 500 Firewall Series, and Cisco IOS routers.

The network topology in Figure 17-1 shows that the remote user with the VPN client installed sets up an IP Security (IPSec) tunnel to the PIX Firewall via remote access. The PIX Firewall is configured for preshared keys, XAUTH, and IKE mode configuration and has VPN groups configured with the **vpngroup** command to enable the PIX Firewall to push IPSec policy to the VPN client.

Figure 17-1 *Typical Network for Remote Access*

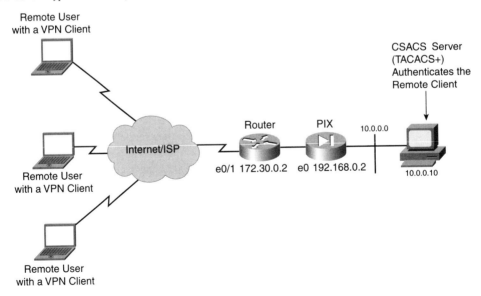

Preshared keys are used for authentication, although the PIX Firewall and VPN client also support digital certificates. Cisco Secure Access Control Server (CSACS) TACACS+ is used for user authentication via XAUTH.

Cisco VPN Client Features

Cisco VPN Client 4.0 features the following:

- IPSec tunneling protocol.
- Internet Key Exchange (IKE) key management protocol.
- IKE keepalives, which monitor the continued presence of a peer and report the VPN client's continued presence to the peer. This enables the VPN client to notify you when the peer is no longer present. Another type of keepalive keeps network address translation (NAT) ports alive.
- Data compression for modem users, which speeds transmission.
- (LZS) data compression, which also benefits modem users.
- Split tunneling, which provides the ability to simultaneously direct packets over the Internet in cleartext and in encrypted form through an IPSec tunnel.
- Local LAN access, the ability to access resources on a local subnet while connected through a secure gateway to a central-site VPN device (if the central site grants permission).
- Stateful personal firewall functionality.
- User authentication by way of a VPN central-site device:
  - Internal through the VPN device's database
  - RADIUS
  - Windows NT/2000 domain
  - RSA (formerly SDI) SecurID or SoftID

NOTE PIX Firewall does not directly support Windows NT/2000 domain authentication. To use Windows NT/2000 domain authentication with the PIX, use a RADIUS server such as CSACS, and configure the RADIUS server to authenticate against the NT/2000 directory.

- Automatic connection by way of Microsoft Dial-Up Networking or any other third-party remote access dialer.
- Automatic VPN client configuration option, which provides the ability to import a configuration file.
- Log Viewer, which is an application that collects events for viewing and analysis.
- Set maximum transmission unit (MTU) size feature, which enables the VPN client to automatically set a size that is optimal for your environment. However, you can set the MTU size manually as well.

- Certificate Manager, which is an application that enables you to manage your identity certificates.

- Complete browser-based, context-sensitive HTML help.

- Support for PIX Firewall platforms that run Release 6.0 and above.

- Command-line interface (CLI) to the VPN Dialer.

- Start Before Logon feature, which provides the ability to establish a VPN connection before logging on to a Windows NT platform. This includes Windows NT 4.0, Windows 2000, and Windows XP systems.

- The ability to disable automatic disconnect when logging off of a Windows NT platform. This allows for roaming profile synchronization.

- Application Launcher, with the ability to launch an application or a third-party dialer from the VPN client.

- Software update notifications from the VPN device upon connection.

- Ability to use Entrust Intelligence certificates.

NOTE   VPN Client Version 3.6 provides most of the same features as Version 4.0. The main difference between the two versions is the use of a virtual adapter in Version 4.0. The virtual adapter in Version 4.0 results in fewer incompatibilities with PPPoE stacks or shims that might be running on the host system.

The VPN client also supports the following IPSec attributes:

- Main mode for negotiating Phase 1 of establishing Internet Security Association and Key Management Protocol (ISAKMP) security associations (SAs)

- Aggressive mode for negotiating Phase 1 of establishing ISAKMP SAs

- Authentication algorithm, which has the hashed message authentication code (HMAC) with Message Digest 5 (MD5) hash function

- HMAC with Secure Hash Algorithm 1 (SHA-1) hash function

- Authentication mode with preshared keys

- X.509 digital certificates

- Diffie-Hellman (D-H) Groups 1, 2, and 5

- Encryption algorithms

- 56-bit Data Encryption Standard (DES)

- 168-bit Triple DES (3DES)

- 128-bit and 256-bit Advanced Encryption Standard (AES)

- XAUTH
- Mode Configuration (also known as ISAKMP configuration method)
- Tunnel encapsulation mode
- IP compression (IPCOMP) using LZS
- Transparent tunneling over User Datagram Protocol (UDP) port 4500 (NAT-Traversal [NAT-T])
- Transparent tunneling over TCP

NOTE   PIX Firewall Software Version 6.3 or later provides support for NAT-T. Cisco VPN 3000 Concentrator provides proprietary IPSec over TCP and UDP (as well as industry standard NAT-T).

Configuring Remote Access VPNs

To enable remote access VPNs on the PIX Firewall, you must configure the following on the PIX Firewall:

- Create an access list to identify interesting traffic (traffic that is encrypted).
- Create a pool of addresses to be assigned to the remote access VPN clients.
- Disable NAT for traffic inside the tunnel.
- Configure an authentication, authorization, and accounting (AAA) server group (if you are using external user databases).
- Permit IPSec traffic through the PIX Firewall.
- Configure the transform set to use with the remote access VPN clients.
- Create appropriate crypto map statements.
- Configure ISAKMP and enable it on the outside interface. Your ISAKMP policy can use preshared keys or digital certificates for authentication.
- Create a VPN group. This is the same group name used on the VPN client's connection profile settings.

When creating your IKE Phase 1 policy, you can choose either preshared keys or digital certificates for ISAKMP authentication. Which is the better choice depends largely on your security requirements, as well as existing resources within your organization. Preshared keys are easier to configure and use, but they are scalable. Digital certificates, however, are more difficult to implement and require more upfront planning and preparation, but they provide a more scalable solution than preshared keys. If your organization already has a public key infrastructure (PKI) in place, you should consider using digital certificates for ISAKMP for better scalability and greater security.

You configure groups for remote access VPNs using the **vpngroup** command. The syntax of the **vpngroup** command is as follows:

```
vpngroup group_name address-pool pool_name
vpngroup group_name authentication-server server_tag
vpngroup group_name backup-server {{ip1 [ip2 ... ip10]} | clear-client-cfg}
vpngroup group_name default-domain domain_name
vpngroup group_name device-pass-through
vpngroup group_name dns-server dns_ip_prim [dns_ip_sec]
vpngroup group_name idle-time idle_seconds
vpngroup group_name max-time max_seconds
vpngroup group_name password preshared_key
vpngroup group_name pfs
vpngroup group_name secure-unit-authentication
vpngroup group_name split-dns domain_name1 [domain_name2 ... domain_name8]
vpngroup group_name split-tunnel access_list
vpngroup group_name user-authentication
vpngroup group_name user-idle-timeout user_idle_seconds
vpngroup group_name wins-server wins_ip_prim [wins_ip_sec]
show vpngroup [group_name]
```

Table 17-1 shows the arguments and options for the **vpngroup** command.

Table 17-1 **vpngroup** *Command Arguments*

Argument	Definition
access_list	The name of the access list for the split-tunnel configuration.
authentication-server	Specifies the individual user authentication (IUA) AAA server on the firewall headend.
backup-server	Configures a backup server list to be used for access by VPN clients if the primary server is not available.
clear-client-cfg	Clears backup servers from the client configuration.
default-domain	Command used to specify the default domain.
device-pass-through	Command used to exempt devices based on their MAC address from authentication. This option is used with devices such as Cisco IP phones that cannot use IUA for authentication. Use with the **vpnclient mac-exempt** command.
dns-server	Command used to specify the DNS servers.
dns_ip_prim	The IP address of the primary DNS server.
dns_ip_sec	The IP address of the secondary DNS server.
domain_name	The default domain name, up to 127 characters.
domain_name1 [domain_name2, domain_name3, ... , domain_name8]	The domains to configure for split DNS. The maximum length for a domain name is 127 characters.
group_name	Specifies the VPN policy group name and is an ASCII string with a maximum length of 63 characters. (You choose the name.)
idle-time	Command used to specify the idle timeout value.

Table 17-1   **vpngroup** *Command Arguments (Continued)*

Argument	Definition
idle_seconds	The idle timeout in seconds, from 60 to 86,400. The default is 1800 seconds (30 minutes).
max-time	Command used to specify the maximum connection time value.
max_seconds	The maximum connection time in seconds that the VPN group is allowed, from 60 to 31,536,000. The default maximum connection time is set to unlimited.
password	Command used to specify the password.
pfs	Specifies the requirement that the VPN client or Easy VPN Remote device is to perform perfect forward secrecy.
pool_name	The IP address pool name, up to 63 characters.
preshared_key	The VPN group preshared key. The maximum is 127 characters.
server_tag	AAA server tag to authenticate remote users of a hardware client.
split-dns	Command used to specify split DNS. Split DNS is used with split tunneling to forward private doman queries to internal DNS servers through the encrypted tunnel, while queries for other domains are sent in cleartext to external DNS servers.
split-tunnel	The **vpngroup split-tunnel** command is used to enable split tunneling on the PIX Firewall. Split tunneling provides access to the corporate network over an encrypted tunnel, while providing clear access to the Internet.
user-authentication	Enables user authentication on the Easy VPN Server.
user-idle-timeout	Command used to specify the user idle timeout value.
user_idle_seconds	Idle timeout for user authentication, in seconds.
wins-server	Command used to specify the WINS servers used.
wins_ip_prim	The IP address of the primary WINS server.
wins_ip_sec	The IP address of the secondary WINS server.

NOTE   If you choose preshared keys for ISAKMP authentication and need greater security, you might want to consider using a two-factor authentication option such as RSA SecurID.

NOTE   The command syntax for **isakmp** and **crypto** commands shown in this chapter is provided in Chapter 16, "Site-to-Site VPNs."

To configure remote access VPN support using the CSACS and preshared keys for ISAKMP authentication for the network diagram shown in Figure 17-1, complete the following 14 steps on the PIX Firewall:

Step 1   Configure an ACL to designate traffic between the inside network and the IP local pool as interesting traffic. The source is the inside network, and the destination is the network address of the IP local pool, a range of addresses that is dynamically assigned to the VPN clients:

```
pixfirewall(config)# access-list 80 permit ip 10.0.0.0 255.255.255.0
   10.0.20.0 255.255.255.0
```

Step 2   Use the **nat 0 access list** command to specify that no NAT takes place inside the tunnel:

```
pixfirewall(config)# nat (inside) 0 access-list 80
```

Step 3   Specify the pool of IP addresses that will be dynamically assigned to VPN clients:

```
pixfirewall(config)# ip local pool MYPOOL 10.0.20.1-10.0.20.254
```

Step 4   Configure CSACS for XAUTH user authentication. CSACS (or a remote database it uses such as Microsoft Windows 2000/NT) must be configured with usernames and passwords and must point to the PIX Firewall as the network access server (NAS). Configure the PIX Firewall to require all inbound connections to be authenticated by the 10.0.0.10 CSACS server. The TACACS+ key (**tacacskey**, in this example) should match the key configured on CSACS:

```
pixfirewall(config)# aaa-server MYTACACS protocol tacacs+
pixfirewall(config)# aaa-server MYTACACS (inside) host 10.0.0.10
tacacskey timeout 5
pixfirewall(config)# aaa authentication include any inbound 0 0 0 0
   MYTACACS
```

Step 5   Enable the PIX Firewall to permit any packet from an IPSec tunnel and bypass checking with an associated **conduit** or **access-group** command for IPSec connections:

```
pixfirewall(config)# sysopt connection permit-ipsec
```

Step 6   Create a transform set to be used for the VPN clients:

```
pixfirewall(config)# crypto ipsec transform-set AAADES esp-des
   esp-md5-hmac
```

NOTE	This example shows AES or DES encryption with an MD5 hash. You can choose 3DES and an SHA-1 hash for greater security.

Step 7   Create a dynamic crypto map to enable the VPN clients to connect to the PIX Firewall. You must set a transform set in the dynamic map as a minimum. You might also want to set up an ACL for additional security:

```
pixfirewall(config)# crypto dynamic-map DYNOMAP 10 set transform-set
    AAADES
```

Step 8   Create a crypto map and assign the dynamic crypto map to it:

```
pixfirewall(config)# crypto map VPNPEER 20 ipsec-isakmp dynamic DYNOMAP
```

Step 9   Configure XAUTH and point to the TACACS+ server:

```
pixfirewall(config)# crypto map VPNPEER client authentication MYTACACS
```

Step 10   Apply the crypto map to the PIX Firewall interface:

```
pixfirewall(config)# crypto map VPNPEER interface outside
```

Step 11   Enable ISAKMP on the outside interface and define the ISAKMP identity as IP address of the interface:

```
pixfirewall(config)# isakmp enable outside
pixfirewall(config)# isakmp identity address
```

Step 12   (Optional) Enable NAT-T if you have clients who will connect to the PIX Firewall from behind a NAT or PAT device (such as another PIX Firewall). Set NAT keepalive interval, from 10 to 3600 seconds (default is 20 if not defined in the **isakmp nat-traversal** command):

```
pixfirewall(config)# isakmp nat-traversal 60
```

NOTE	NAT-T extends support for site-to-site and remote access IPSec VPNs to environments implementing NAT or PAT, such as most broadband connections and wireless hotspots. NAT-T encapsulates IPSec packets inside UDP packets and operates on UDP port 4500.

NOTE	NAT-T support is available only with PIX Firewall Version 6.3 or higher. The addition of this feature greatly expands the capabilities of the PIX Firewall platform for use in remote access VPN implementations.

Step 13 Configure the actual ISAKMP policy you want to use:

```
pixfirewall(config)# isakmp policy 10 authentication pre-share
pixfirewall(config)# isakmp policy 10 encryption des
pixfirewall(config)# isakmp policy 10 hash md5
pixfirewall(config)# isakmp policy 10 group 2
pixfirewall(config)# isakmp policy 10 lifetime 86400
```

Step 14 Create a VPN group to push configuration parameters to the VPN client. The VPN group name used here must match the group name used in the VPN client. Also, the VPN group password (which is really the preshared key) must match the password in the VPN client. You can also configure the VPN group to push DNS, WINS, domain name, and split tunneling information to the VPN client:

```
pixfirewall(config)# vpngroup TRAINING address-pool MYPOOL
pixfirewall(config)# vpngroup TRAINING idle-time 1800
pixfirewall(config)# vpngroup TRAINING password MYPASSWORD
```

NOTE   Cisco VPN Client Versions 3.0 and higher use D-H Group 2, and Cisco VPN Client 3000 Version 2.5 uses D-H Group 1 or 5. If you are using the VPN Client Version 3.0 or higher, configure D-H Group 2 or 5 by using the **isakmp policy** command.

The PIX Firewall is now ready for remote access VPN connectivity. Steps 15 through 23 should then be completed to make a connection to the PIX Firewall configured in Steps 1 through 14 using the Cisco VPN Client:

Step 15 Start the Cisco VPN Client. Initially, there are no connection entries listed, as shown in Figure 17-2.

Figure 17-2   *Cisco VPN Client*

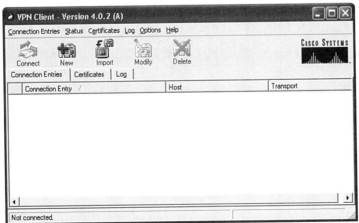

Step 16 Click **New** to open the Create New VPN Connection Entry window shown in Figure 17-3.

Figure 17-3 *Create New VPN Connection Entry, Authentication Tab*

Step 17 Create a new connection entry using the following values:

— Enter **vpnpeer0** in the Connection Entry field.

— (Optional) Enter a description for this connection entry.

— Enter **192.168.0.2** (the host name or IP address of the PIX Firewall's outside interface) in the Host field.

— Enter the Group Authentication settings in the same window.

— Enter **TRAINING** in the Name field.

NOTE   All the fields in the Group Authentication form, including Name, are case sensitive:

— Enter **MYPASSWORD** in the Password field.

— Enter **MYPASSWORD** in the Confirm Password field.

NOTE   If you are using digital certificates, you must select Certificate Authentication as your authentication method and specify the name of the certificate.

Step 18 (Optional) Click the **Transport** tab to enable transparent tunneling, as shown in Figure 17-4. You can specify IPSec over UDP or TCP. PIX Firewalls support only the NAT-T standard, which provides IPSec over UDP 4500 transparent tunneling.

Figure 17-4 *Create New VPN Connection Entry, Transport Tab*

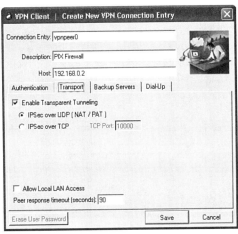

Step 19 (Optional) Click the **Backup Servers** tab to specify backup servers, as shown in Figure 17-5, in case the primary server is unavailable.

Figure 17-5 *Create New VPN Connection Entry, Backup Servers Tab*

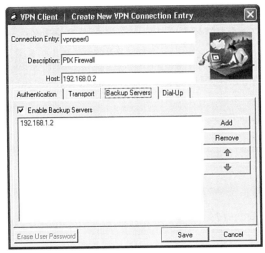

Step 20 (Optional) Click the **Dial-Up** tab to configure dialup networking
features, as shown in Figure 17-6. Select **Connect to Internet via dialup** and specify the Phonebook Entry for the Cisco VPN Client to use.
With this configuration, the Cisco VPN Client automatically initiates a
dial up connection when you try to make a VPN connection.

Figure 17-6   *Create New VPN Connection Entry, Dial-Up Tab*

Step 21 Click **Save** to save the new connection entry. The new entry is listed
in the Connection Entries tab, as shown in Figure 17-7.

Figure 17-7   *Cisco VPN Client Connection Entries*

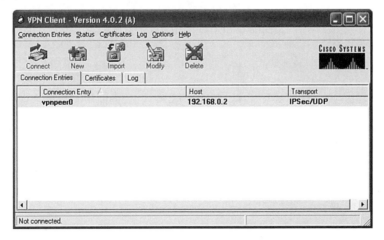

Step 22 Click **Connect** to activate the entry and connect to the PIX Firewall.

Step 23 If XAUTH is required by the PIX, a username and password window will open. Enter the correct credentials to complete the VPN connection to the PIX Firewall.

When the VPN client initiates ISAKMP with the PIX Firewall, the VPN group name and preshared key are sent to the PIX Firewall. The PIX Firewall then uses the group name to look up the configured VPN client policy attributes for the given VPN client and downloads the matching policy attributes to the VPN client during the IKE negotiation.

As shown in Figure 17-8, the PIX Firewall uses IKE mode configuration to push IPSec policy defined with the **vpngroup** command to the VPN client. You set the VPN client IP address (10.0.20.1, in this example) with the PIX Firewall **ip local pool** and **vpngroup** commands.

Figure 17-8　*PIX Firewall Assigns IP Address to VPN Client*

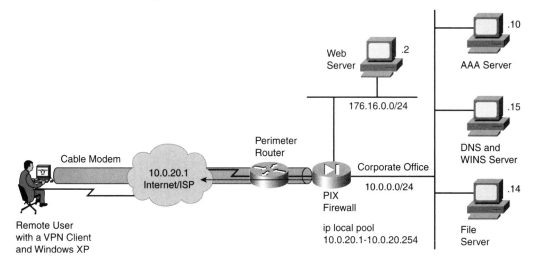

Once you are connected, select **Statistics** from the Status menu on the VPN client to view the current connection statistics. Figure 17-9 shows a typical statistics screen indicating assigned client IP address, server IP address, encryption and authentication settings, transparent tunneling status, LAN status, and various network activity statistics. The Route Details tab shows the secured routes for the connection.

Figure 17-9 *VPN Client Statistics*

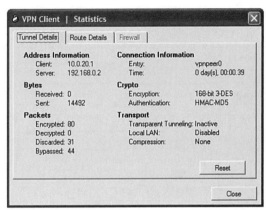

PPTP Client Configuration

PIX Firewall provides support for PPTP remote access VPNs. Although PPTP is not as secure as IPSec, it is a commonly used VPN protocol because a PPTP client is included in most versions of Microsoft Windows operating systems. This eliminates the hassles of installing another VPN client and the potential incompatibilities that might result from such installations.

You use the **vpdn** command to configure PPTP on the PIX Firewall. The syntax of the **vpdn** command is as follows:

```
vpdn group group_name [accept dialin pptp | l2tp] | [ ppp authentication pap | chap |
    mschap] | [ppp encryption mppe 40 | 128 | auto [required]] | [ client configuration
    address local address_pool_name ] | [client configuration dns dns_ip1 [dns_ip2]]
    | [ client configuration wins wins_ip1 [wins_ip2]] | [client authentication local
    | aaa auth_aaa_group] | [ client accounting acct_aaa_group] | [pptp echo echo_time]
    | [ l2tp tunnel hello hello_time]
vpdn username name password passwd [store-local]
vpdn enable if_name
show vpdn tunnel [l2tp | pptp | pppoe] [id tnl_id | packets | state | summary | transport]
show vpdn session [l2tp | pptp | pppoe] [id sess_id | packets | state| window]
show vpdn pppinterface [id dev_id]
show vpdn group [group_name]
show vpdn username [name]
clear vpdn [group | interface | tunnel tnl_id | username]
```

Table 17-2 describes the **vpdn** command parameters.

Table 17-2 **vpdn** *Command Parameters*

Argument	Definition
**accept dialin pptp	lt2p**	Accept a dial-in request using PPTP or Layer 2 Tunneling Protocol (L2TP).
client accounting *acct_aaa_group*	Specifies the AAA server group for accounting.
client authentication aaa *auth_aaa_group*	Specifies the AAA server group for user authentication.
client authentication local	Authenticate using the local username and password entries specified on the PIX Firewall.
client configuration address local *address_pool_name*	Specifies the local address pool used to allocate an IP address to a client. Use the **ip local pool** command to specify the IP addresses for use by the clients.
client configuration dns *dns_ip1* [*dns_ip2*]	Specifies up to two DNS server IP addresses. PIX Firewall sends this information to the Windows client during the IP Control Protocol (IPCP) phase of PPP negotiation.
client configuration wins *wins_ip1* [*wins_ip2*]	Specifies up to two WINS server IP addresses.
enable *if_name*	Enable the virtual private dialup network (VPDN) function on a PIX Firewall interface specified. Only inbound connections are supported.
group	Used with the **clear** command to remove all **vpdn group** commands from the configuration.
group *group_name*	Specifies the VPDN group name. The maximum length is 63 ASCII characters.
id sess_id	Unique session identifier.
id *tnl_id*	Unique tunnel identifier.
**l2tp	pptp	pppoe**	Select either **l2tp**, **pptp**, or **pppoe** to display information for only that tunnel type.
l2tp tunnel hello *hello_time*	Specifies L2TP tunnel keepalive hello timeout value in seconds. Default is 60 seconds if not specified. The value can be between 10 and 300 seconds.
packets	Packet and byte count.
passwd	Specifies the password for the local group used for PPPoE.

Table 17-2   **vpdn** *Command Parameters (Continued)*

Argument	Definition
password	Specifies local user password.
ppp authentication PAP | CHAP | MSCHAP	Specifies the PPP authentication protocol. Settings on client and the PIX must match. PAP passes the host name or username in cleartext (not recommended). Challenge Handshake Authentication Protocol (CHAP) and MS-CHAP (a Microsoft derivation) are more secure. PIX Firewall supports MS-CHAP Version 1 only (not Version 2.0).
ppp encryption mppe 40 | 128 | auto [required]	Specifies the number of session key bits used for MPPE (Microsoft Point-to-Point Encryption) negotiation. The domestic version of the Windows client can support 40- and 128-bit session keys, but international version of the Windows client supports only 40-bit session keys. On the PIX Firewall, use **auto** to accommodate both. Use **required** to indicate that MPPE must be negotiated or the connection will be terminated.
pppinterface id *intf_id*	A PPP virtual interface is created for each PPTP or PPPoE tunnel.
pptp echo *echo_time*	Specifies the PPTP keepalive echo timeout value in seconds. PIX Firewall terminates a tunnel if an echo reply is not received within the timeout period you specify.
state	Session state.
store-local	Store user account in local Flash memory instead of using external configuration.
summary	Tunnel summary information.
transport	Tunnel transport information.
tunnel *tnl_id*	Use with **clear** command to remove PPTP tunnels matching *tnl_id* from the configuration.
username *name*	Enter or display local username. However, when used as a clear command option, **username** removes all VPDN username commands from the configuration.
window	Window information.

NOTE   You also use the **vpdn** command to configure PPPoE and L2TP. Options related to PPPoE and L2TP are included in Table 17-2 for completeness but are not used with PPTP.

Example 17-1 shows the commands required to enable PPTP remote access VPN support on the PIX Firewall.

Example 17-1 *PPTP Remote Access Configuration*

```
pixfirewall(config)# sysopt connection permit-pptp
pixfirewall(config)# ip local pool MYPOOL 10.0.20.1-10.0.20.254
pixfirewall(config)# vpdn group PPTPGROUP accept dialin pptp
pixfirewall(config)# vpdn group PPTPGROUP ppp authentication chap
pixfirewall(config)# vpdn group PPTPGROUP ppp authentication mschap
pixfirewall(config)# vpdn group PPTPGROUP ppp encryption mppe 128
pixfirewall(config)# vpdn group PPTPGROUP client configuration address local MYPOOL
pixfirewall(config)# vpdn group PPTPGROUP client configuration dns 10.0.1.10
pixfirewall(config)# vpdn group PPTPGROUP client configuration wins 10.0.1.10
pixfirewall(config)# vpdn group PPTPGROUP pptp echo 60
pixfirewall(config)# vpdn group PPTPGROUP client authentication local
pixfirewall(config)# vpdn username MYUSER password cisco123
pixfirewall(config)# vpdn enable outside
```

This configuration enables PPTP access on the outside interface of the PIX and uses local user authentication. CHAP and MS-CHAP authentication protocols are enabled and 128-bit MPPE is specified (but not required). The address pool named MYPOOL is used to allocate IP addresses to clients, and they will receive DNS and WINS settings upon connection.

You can use **debug vpdn event** and **debug vpdn error** commands to troubleshoot PPTP connectivity issues.

Remote Access VPN Configuration with PDM

You can also use the PDM to configure remote access VPNs on the PIX Firewall. The VPN Wizard built in to the PDM is an easy-to-use interface for creating VPN connections on the PIX Firewall for both remote access and site-to-site VPNs.

The PDM is also a valuable tool for learning the CLI commands required for configuring VPNs on the PIX Firewall. Use the Preview Commands Before Sending to the Firewall option in PDM to view the CLI commands that PDM generates before sending the configuration to the firewall. You can then use the VPN Wizard to create the VPN connection definitions and view the actual CLI commands generated by PDM to create the VPN connection.

Complete the following steps to create the same VPN configuration you created in Steps 1 through 14 in the last section using the CLI environment:

Step 1   Start the PDM and select **VPN Wizard** from the Wizards menu.

Step 2   Select **Remote Access VPN** as the type of VPN, as shown in Figure 17-10. Select **outside** as the interface on which the VPN will be enabled. Click **Next**.

Figure 17-10   *VPN Wizard*

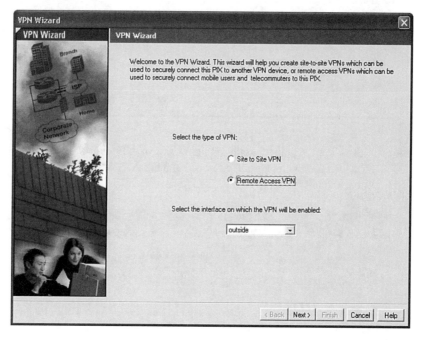

Step 3   Select **Cisco VPN Client, Release 3.x or higher** as the Remote Access Client, as shown in Figure 17-11. Click **Next**.

Figure 17-11 *Remote Access Client*

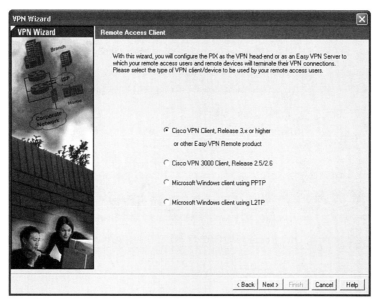

Step 4 Enter the VPN client group settings as shown in Figure 17-12 (group name of **TRAINING** and group password of **MYPASSWORD**). Click **Next**.

Figure 17-12 *VPN Client Group*

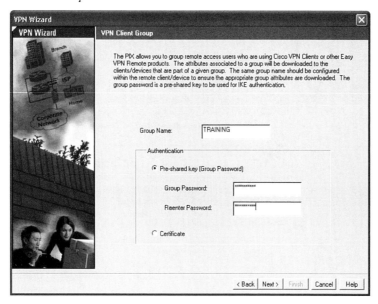

Step 5   On the Extended Client Authentication page shown in Figure 17-13, click **New** to configure the AAA group. Notice that default groups of TACACS+, RADIUS, and LOCAL are also available.

Figure 17-13   *Extended Client Authentication*

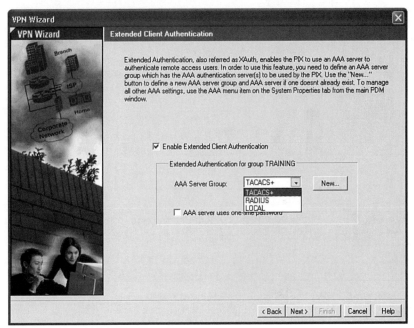

Step 6   On the Add AAA Server page, shown in Figure 17-14, configure the AAA group with **TACACS+** protocol, a server group name of **MYTACACS**, IP address of **10.0.0.10**, the inside interface, and a key of **tacacskey**. Click **OK** to create the group and return to the Extended Client Authentication page in Figure 17-13.

Figure 17-14 *Adding a AAA Server*

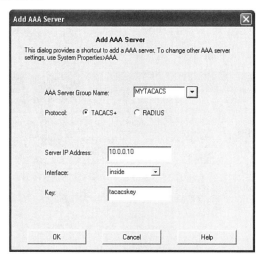

Step 7 On the Extended Client Authentication page, select the newly created AAA group and click **Next**.

Step 8 Create a client address pool named **MYPOOL** with a range start address of **10.0.20.1** and a range end address of **10.0.20.254**, as shown on Figure 17-15. Click **Next**.

Figure 17-15 *Address Pool*

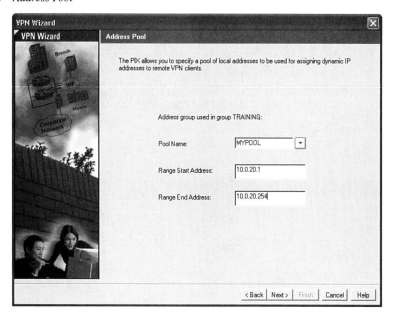

Step 9   (Optional) Specify attributes for the group TRAINING on the Attributes
Pushed to Client page shown in Figure 17-16, or leave the fields blank for
no options. Click **Next**.

Figure 17-16   *Attributes Pushed to Client*

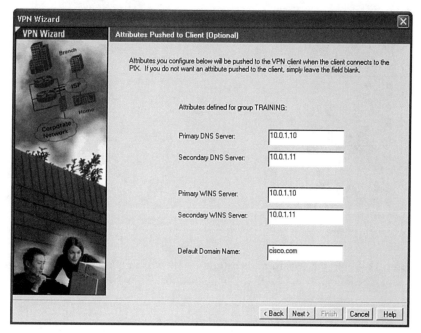

Step 10   Configure IKE Policy Setting (Phase 1) as shown in Figure 17-17. Select
DES for encryption, **MD5** for authentication, and **Group 2** (1024-bit) for
D-H group. Click **Next**.

Figure 17-17 *IKE Policy*

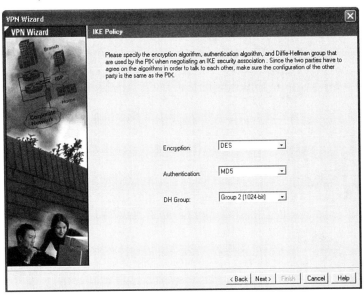

Step 11 Configure transform set settings as shown in Figure 17-18. Use **DES** for encryption and **MD5** for authentication. Click **Next**.

Figure 17-18 *Transform Set*

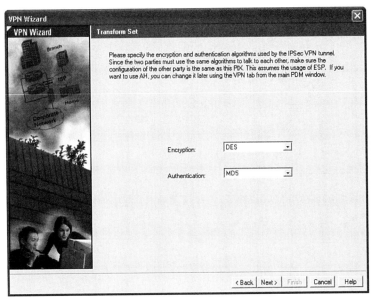

Step 12 Specify the address translation exemption as shown in Figure 17-19.
Select the inside interface, an IP address of **10.0.0.0**, and a subnet mask
of **255.255.255.0**. Click **Finish**.

Figure 17-19 *Address Translation Exemption*

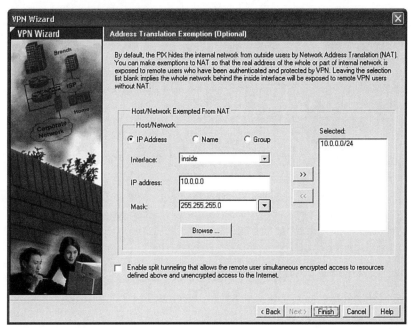

NOTE   You can optionally enable split tunneling on this page.

Step 13 (Optional) If you set the PDM option to display the CLI commands
before sending to the PIX Firewall, you see the Preview CLI Commands
window shown in Figure 17-20. Click **Send** to send the CLI commands
to the PIX Firewall.

Figure 17-20 *Preview CLI Commands*

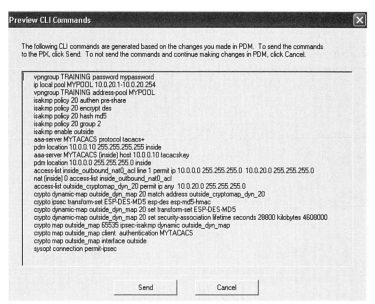

The VPN configuration is now complete.

Summary

This section summarizes the information you learned in this chapter:

- The PIX Firewall enables a secure VPN.

- IPSec configuration tasks include configuring IKE and IPSec parameters.

- PIX Firewall Version 6.3 adds support for NAT-T, enabling much broader remote access VPN deployments using the **vpngroup** command. PPTP remote access VPNs are configured using the **vpdn** command.

- CAs enable scaling to a large number of IPSec peers.

- Remote users can establish secure VPN tunnels between PCs running Cisco VPN Client software and any Cisco VPN-enabled product, such as the PIX Firewall, that supports the unified client framework.

Chapter Review Questions

To test what you have learned in this chapter, answer the following questions and then refer to Appendix A, "Answers to Chapter Review Questions," for the answers:

1 What is the function of NAT-T?

2 How do you enable NAT-T support on the PIX Firewall?

3 Which version of PIX Firewall software supports NAT-T?

4 What does split tunneling mean?

5 How do you enable NAT-T support on the Cisco VPN Client?

Lab Exercise—Remote Access VPNs

Complete the following lab exercise to practice what you learned in this chapter. Use the following initial configuration commands and continue with the rest of the lab exercises.

NOTE   Many of the settings shown in this initial configuration are default values and do not need to be entered on your PIX Firewall. Specific commands that must be entered are shown in bold for your convenience.

```
: : Saved
:
PIX Version 6.3(3)
interface ethernet0 100full
interface ethernet1 100full
nameif ethernet0 outside security0
nameif ethernet1 inside security100
enable password 8Ry2YjIyt7RRXU24 encrypted
passwd 2KFQnbNIdI.2KYOU encrypted
hostname pixfirewall
domain-name cisco.com
fixup protocol dns maximum-length 512
fixup protocol ftp 21
fixup protocol h323 h225 1720
fixup protocol h323 ras 1718-1719
fixup protocol http 80
fixup protocol rsh 514
fixup protocol rtsp 554
fixup protocol sip 5060
fixup protocol sip udp 5060
fixup protocol skinny 2000
fixup protocol smtp 25
fixup protocol sqlnet 1521
fixup protocol tftp 69
pager lines 24
mtu outside 1500
mtu inside 1500
mtu dmz 1500
```

```
ip address outside 192.168.1.2 255.255.255.0
ip address inside 10.0.1.1 255.255.255.0
ip audit info action alarm
ip audit attack action alarm
pdm history enable
arp timeout 14400
timeout xlate 3:00:00
timeout conn 1:00:00 half-closed 0:10:00 udp 0:02:00 rpc 0:10:00 h225 1:00:00
timeout h323 0:05:00 mgcp 0:05:00 sip 0:30:00 sip_media 0:02:00
timeout uauth 0:05:00 absolute
aaa-server TACACS+ protocol tacacs+
aaa-server RADIUS protocol radius
aaa-server LOCAL protocol local
http server enable
http 10.0.1.0 255.255.255.0 inside
no snmp-server location
no snmp-server contact
snmp-server community public
no snmp-server enable traps
floodguard enable
telnet timeout 5
ssh timeout 5
console timeout 0
terminal width 80
Cryptochecksum:aa0cc6e47d705ed128e041c2c2a8412b
: end
```

Objectives

In this lab exercise, you complete the following tasks:

- Configure the PIX Firewall.

- Install the Cisco VPN Client.

- Configure the Cisco VPN Client.

- Verify the Cisco VPN Client properties.

- Launch the Cisco VPN Client.

- Verify the VPN connection.

Lab Topology

Figure 17-21 displays the topology you will need for the lab exercises in this chapter.

Equipment required to perform the lab includes the following:

- A PIX Firewall 6.3 with two interfaces

- Category 5 patch cables

- PC host running Cisco VPN Client 4.0 or later

- PC host for an inside subnet with a web server and CSACS

Figure 17-21   *Remote Access VPN Visual Objective*

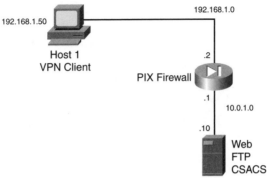

192.168.1.50

192.168.1.0

Host 1
VPN Client

.2

PIX Firewall

.1

10.0.1.0

.10

Web
FTP
CSACS

Task 1—Configure the PIX Firewall

Use a console connection to the PIX and complete the following tasks:

Step 1   Create an access list that permits traffic from the inside network to hosts using addresses from mode-config pool:

```
pixfirewall(config)# access-list 101 permit ip 10.0.1.0 255.255.255.0
    10.0.20.0 255.255.255.0
```

Step 2   Instruct the PIX Firewall to bypass NAT for VPN traffic:

```
pixfirewall(config)# nat (inside) 0 access-list 101
```

Step 3   Set up a pool of IP addresses that are dynamically assigned to the VPN clients via IKE mode configuration:

```
pixfirewall(config)# ip local pool MYPOOL 10.0.20.1-10.0.20.10
```

Step 4   Configure the PIX Firewall for TACACS+ by completing the following substeps:

(1)   Create a group tag called **MYTACACS** and assign the TACACS+ protocol to it:

```
pixfirewall(config)# aaa-server MYTACACS protocol tacacs+
```

(2)   Assign the CSACS IP address and the encryption key **secretkey**:

```
pixfirewall(config)# aaa-server MYTACACS (inside) host
    10.0.1.10 secretkey timeout 5
```

(3)   Configure the PIX Firewall to require authentication for all inbound traffic:

```
pixfirewall(config)# aaa authentication include any inbound
    0 0 0 0 MYTACACS
```

Step 5 Enable the PIX Firewall to implicitly permit any packet from an IPSec tunnel, and bypass checking with an associated conduit or an **access-group** command for IPSec connections:

```
pixfirewall(config)# sysopt connection permit-ipsec
```

Step 6 Set up a transform set that will be used for the VPN clients:

```
pixfirewall(config)# crypto ipsec transform-set AAADES esp-des
    esp-md5-hmac
```

Step 7 Set up a dynamic crypto map to enable the VPN clients to connect to the PIX Firewall:

```
pixfirewall(config)# crypto dynamic-map DYNOMAP 10 set transform-set
    AAADES
```

Step 8 Create a crypto map, and assign the dynamic crypto map to it:

```
pixfirewall(config)# crypto map VPNPEER 20 ipsec-isakmp dynamic DYNOMAP
```

Step 9 Configure XAUTH to point to the RADIUS server:

```
pixfirewall(config)# crypto map VPNPEER client authentication MYTACACS
```

Step 10 Apply the crypto map to the PIX Firewall interface:

```
pixfirewall(config)# crypto map VPNPEER interface outside
```

Step 11 Enable IKE on the outside interface:

```
pixfirewall(config)# isakmp enable outside
```

Step 12 Set the IKE identity:

```
pixfirewall(config)# isakmp identity address
```

Step 13 Configure the ISAKMP policy by completing the following substeps:

(1) Configure a basic IKE policy using preshared keys for authentication:

```
pixfirewall(config)# isakmp policy 10 authentication
    pre-share
```

(2) Specify the encryption algorithm:

```
pixfirewall(config)# isakmp policy 10 encryption des
```

(3) Specify the hash algorithm:

```
pixfirewall(config)# isakmp policy 10 hash md5
```

(4) Specify the D-H by group identifier:

```
pixfirewall(config)# isakmp policy 10 group 2
```

(5) Specify the IKE SA's lifetime:

```
pixfirewall(config)# isakmp policy 10 lifetime 86400
```

Step 14 Configure the VPN group to support pushing mode configuration parameters to the VPN client. The VPN group name of **training** must match the group name in the VPN client. The VPN group password must match the password in the VPN client. Complete the following substeps:

> (1) Configure the IP address pool name:
>
> ```
> pixfirewall(config)# vpngroup training address-pool MYPOOL
> ```
>
> (2) Configure the inactivity timeout in seconds:
>
> ```
> pixfirewall(config)# vpngroup training idle-time 1800
> ```
>
> (3) Configure the domain name:
>
> ```
> pixfirewall(config)# vpngroup training default-domain
>     cisco.com
> ```
>
> (4) Configure the VPN group password:
>
> ```
> pixfirewall(config)# vpngroup training password training
> ```

Task 2—Create a User in CSACS

On the CSACS server, complete the following tasks:

Step 1 Create a user named **user1**.

Step 2 Set the password for user1 to **cisco123**.

Task 3—Verify Your Configuration

Complete the following steps to verify your PIX Firewall's configuration:

Step 1 Verify your IP local pool:

```
pixfirewall(config)# sh ip local pool
Pool            Begin        End           Free      In use
MYPOOL          10.0.20.1    10.0.20.254   10        0
Available Addresses:
10.0.20.1
10.0.20.2
10.0.20.3
10.0.20.4
10.0.20.5
10.0.20.6
10.0.20.7
10.0.20.8
10.0.20.9
10.0.20.10
```

Step 2 Verify your NAT configuration:

```
pixfirewall(config)# sh nat
nat (inside) 1 10.1.1.0 255.255.255.0 0 0
nat (inside) 0 access-list 101
```

Step 3 Verify your AAA server configuration:

```
pixfirewall(config)# show aaa-server
aaa-server TACACS+ protocol tacacs+
aaa-server RADIUS protocol radius
aaa-server LOCAL protocol local
aaa-server MYTACACS protocol tacacs+
aaa-server MYTACACS (inside) host 10.0.1.10 secretkey timeout 5
```

Step 4 Verify your crypto map:

```
pixfirewall(config)# show crypto map
Crypto Map: "VPNPEER" interfaces: { outside }
        client authentication MYTACACS

Crypto Map "VPNPEER" 20 ipsec-isakmp
        Dynamic map template tag: DYNOMAP
```

Step 5 Verify your transform set:

```
pixfirewall(config)# show crypto ipsec transform-set
Transform set AAADES: { esp-des esp-md5-hmac  }
   will negotiate = { Tunnel,  },
```

Step 6 Verify your IKE policy:

```
pixfirewall(config)# show isakmp policy
Protection suite of priority 10
        encryption algorithm:   DES - Data Encryption Standard
                                (56 bit keys).
        hash algorithm:         Message Digest 5
        authentication method:  Pre-Shared Key
        Diffie-Hellman group:   #2 (1024 bit)
        lifetime:               86400 seconds, no volume limit
Default protection suite
        encryption algorithm:   DES - Data Encryption Standard
                                (56 bit keys).
        hash algorithm:         Secure Hash Standard
        authentication method:  Rivest-Shamir-Adleman Signature
        Diffie-Hellman group:   #1 (768 bit)
        lifetime:               86400 seconds, no volume limit
```

Step 7 Verify your VPN group configuration:

```
pixfirewall(config)# show vpngroup
vpngroup training address-pool MYPOOL
vpngroup training idle-time 1800
vpngroup training default-domain cisco.com
vpngroup training password ********
```

Task 4—Install the Cisco VPN Client on Host 1

Step 1 Download the latest version of the Cisco VPN Client software from Cisco.com.

Step 2 Initiate setup by running the appropriate .exe or .msi file. The Cisco Systems VPN Client Setup window opens.

Step 3 Click **Next**. The License Agreement window opens.

Step 4 Read the License Agreement and click **Yes**. You are prompted to choose a destination location.

Step 5 Accept the default destination folder by clicking **Next**. You are prompted to choose a program folder.

Step 6 Accept the defaults by clicking **Next**. The Start Copying Files window opens.

Step 7 The files are copied to the hard disk drive, and the InstallShield Wizard Complete window opens.

Step 8 Select **Yes, I want to restart my computer now** and click **Finish**.

Step 9 After restart, log in to Host 1 again.

Task 5—Configure the Cisco VPN Client

Use the following procedure to configure the networking parameters of the VPN client. (This procedure assumes you are using Windows 2000 or XP.)

Step 1 Choose **Start > Programs > Cisco Systems VPN Client > VPN Dialer**. The Cisco Systems VPN Client window opens.

Step 2 Click **New**. The New Connection Entry Wizard opens.

Step 3 Enter **vpnpeer1** as the name for the new connection entry in the Name of the new connection entry field.

Step 4 Click **Next**.

Step 5   Enter the PIX Firewall's public interface IP address, **192.168.1.2**, as the IP address of the server.

Step 6   Click **Next**.

Step 7   Select **Group Access Information** and complete the following substeps. The following entries are always case sensitive. Use lowercase characters for this lab exercise:

   (1)   Enter a group name: **training**.

   (2)   Enter a group password: **training**.

   (3)   Confirm the password: **training**.

Step 8   Click **Next**.

Step 9   Click **Finish** and leave the Cisco Systems VPN Client window open.

Task 6—Verify the Cisco VPN Client Properties

Complete the following steps to verify the VPN client parameters you just configured:

Step 1   Ensure that the Cisco Systems VPN Client window is open. If the Cisco Systems VPN Client window is not open, choose **Start > Programs > Cisco Systems VPN Client > VPN Dialer**.

Step 2   Select **vpnpeer1** within the Connection Entry group box.

Step 3   Verify that the IP address of the remote server is set to the PIX Firewall's public interface IP address, 192.168.1.2.

Step 4   Click **Options**. A popup menu opens.

Step 5   Choose **Properties**. The Properties for vpnpeer1 window opens.

Step 6   Select the **General** tab and view the available options. Do not change any of the default settings.

Step 7   Select the **Authentication** tab and verify the spelling of the group name. If you needed to, you could edit the group name and password here.

Step 8   Select the **Connections** tab and view the available options. Do not change any of the default settings.

Step 9   Click **OK**.

Step 10 Close the Cisco Systems VPN Client window.

Task 7—Launch the Cisco VPN Client

Complete the following steps to launch the VPN client on Host 1:

Step 1 Choose **Start > Programs > Cisco Systems VPN Client > VPN Dialer**.

Step 2 Verify that the connection entry is vpnpeer1.

Step 3 Verify that the IP address of the remote server is set to the PIX Firewall's public interface IP address, 192.168.1.2.

Step 4 Click **Connect**. The Connection History window opens, and several messages flash by quickly.

When prompted for a username, enter **user1**.
When prompted to enter a password, enter **cisco123**.

Step 5 Click **OK**. The following messages flash by quickly:

(1) Initializing the connection

(2) Contacting the security gateway at 192.168.1.2.

(3) Authenticating user

The window closes and a Cisco VPN Dialer (lock) icon appears in the system tray.

Task 8—Verify the VPN Connection

Complete the following steps to verify the IPSec connection:

Step 1 Test access to the inside web server from the remote client by completing the following substeps:

(1) Open a web browser on Host 1.

(2) Use the web browser to access the inside web server by entering **http://10.0.1.10**.

(3) The web server's home page should appear.

Step 2 Double-click the **Cisco VPN Dialer icon** in the system tray and observe the IP address that was assigned to Host 1.

Step 3 Click the **Statistics** tab and view the information provided. Notice the number of packets encrypted and decrypted.

Step 4 Refresh your browser.

Step 5   Return to the Cisco Systems VPN Client Connection Status window and notice that the number of packets encrypted and decrypted has incremented.

Task 9—Reconfigure Remote Access VPN Connection Using PDM (Optional)

PIX System Management

On completion of this chapter, you will be able to perform the following tasks:

- Configure Telnet access to the PIX Firewall console.
- Configure Secure Shell (SSH) access to the PIX Firewall console.
- Configure command authorization.
- Recover PIX Firewall passwords using general password recovery procedures.
- Use Trivial File Transfer Protocol (TFTP) to install and upgrade the software image on the PIX Firewall.

CHAPTER 18

System Maintenance

If you work with PIX Firewalls long enough, chances are you will at some time have to recover or replace a forgotten system password. You are also likely to use other system maintenance functions such as PIX Firewall and PIX Device Manager (PDM) software images, Telnet and SSH access, Simple Network Management Protocol (SNMP), and command authorization. PIX Firewall system maintenance features and associated procedures are the focus of this chapter of the book.

Remote Access

The serial console permits a single user to configure the PIX Firewall, but often this setup is not convenient for a site with more than one administrator. By configuring remote access via Telnet or SSH, you can enable up to five hosts or networks to access the PIX Firewall command-line interface (CLI) simultaneously.

Telnet

You can enable Telnet to the PIX Firewall on all interfaces. However, the PIX Firewall requires that all Telnet traffic to the outside interface be IPSec protected. To enable a Telnet session to the outside interface, configure IPSec on the outside interface to include IP traffic generated by the PIX Firewall and enable Telnet on the outside interface.

NOTE	With PIX Firewall Version 6.3 or higher, you can access the inside interface of the PIX Firewall through a virtual private network (VPN) tunnel by using the **management-access** command and specifying the inside interface as your management interface. Access to the inside interface of the PIX through a VPN tunnel is not possible with earlier versions of the PIX Firewall. Use of the **management-access** command is discussed in more detail in Chapters 16, "Site-to-Site VPNs," and 22, "PIX Firewall in SOHO Networks."

The following are the Telnet configuration commands:

- **telnet**—Specifies which hosts can access the PIX Firewall console via Telnet. You can specify up to 16 hosts or networks.

- **telnet timeout**—Sets the maximum time a console Telnet session can be idle before being logged off by the PIX Firewall. The default is 5 minutes.

- **passwd**—Sets the password for Telnet access to the PIX Firewall. The default value is cisco. The **show passwd** command displays the Telnet password, and the **clear passwd** command removes it.

The syntax for the Telnet configuration commands is as follows:

```
telnet ip_address [netmask [if_name]]
telnet timeout minutes
passwd password [encrypted]
```

Table 18-1 describes the **telnet** command arguments.

Table 18-1   **telnet** *Command Arguments*

Argument	Definition
ip_address	An IP address of a host or network that can access the PIX Firewall Telnet console. If an interface name is not specified, the address is assumed to be on an internal interface. The PIX Firewall automatically verifies the IP address against the IP addresses specified by the **ip address** commands to ensure that the address you specify is on an internal interface. If an interface name is specified, the PIX Firewall only checks the host against the interface you specify.
netmask	The bit mask of *ip_address*. To limit access to a single IP address, use 255 in each octet (for example, 255.255.255.255). If you do not specify the netmask, it defaults to 255.255.255.255 regardless of the class of *local_ip*. Do not use the subnetwork mask of the internal network. The netmask is only a bit mask for the IP address in *ip_address*.
if_name	If IP Security (IPSec) is operating, the PIX Firewall enables you to specify an unsecure interface name, typically, the outside interface. At a minimum, you must configure the **crypto map** command to specify an interface name with the **telnet** command.
minutes	The number of minutes that a Telnet session can be idle before being closed by the PIX Firewall. The default is 5 minutes. The range is 1 to 60 minutes.
password	A case-sensitive password of up to 16 alphanumeric and special characters. You can use any character in the password except a question mark and a space.
encrypted	Specifies that the password you entered is already encrypted. The password you specify with the encrypted option must be 16 characters in length.

Example 18-1 shows the commands required to allow a host with an IP address of 10.0.0.11 on the internal interface access the PIX Firewall console via Telnet using the password telnetpass. If the Telnet session is idle more than 15 minutes, the PIX Firewall closes it.

Example 18-1 *Telnet Configuration*

```
pixfirewall(config)# telnet 10.0.0.11 255.255.255.255 inside
pixfirewall(config)# telnet timeout 15
pixfirewall(config)# passwd telnetpass
```

The following commands enable you to view and clear Telnet configuration and Telnet sessions:

- **show telnet**—Displays the current list of IP addresses authorized to access the PIX Firewall via Telnet.

- **clear telnet** and **no telnet**—Removes Telnet access from a previously authorized IP address.

- **who**—Enables you to view which IP addresses are currently accessing the PIX Firewall console via Telnet.

- **kill**—Terminates a Telnet session. When you kill a Telnet session, the PIX Firewall lets any active commands terminate and then drops the connection without warning the user.

The syntax for these commands is as follows:

```
show telnet
clear telnet [ip_address [netmask [if_name]]]
no telnet [ip_address [netmask [if_name]]]
who [local_ip]
kill telnet_id
```

Table 18-2 describes these Telnet monitoring command arguments.

Table 18-2 *Telnet Monitoring Command Arguments*

Argument	Definition
ip_address	An IP address of a host or network that can access the PIX Firewall Telnet console. If an interface name is not specified, the address is assumed to be on an internal interface. The PIX Firewall automatically verifies the IP address against the IP addresses specified by the *ip_address* command to ensure that the address you specify is on an internal interface. If an interface name is specified, the PIX Firewall checks the host only against the interface you specify.
netmask	The bit mask of *ip_address*. To limit access to a single IP address, use 255 in each octet (for example, 255.255.255.255). If you do not specify the netmask, it defaults to 255.255.255.255 regardless of the class of *local_ip*. Do not use the subnetwork mask of the internal network. The netmask is only a bit mask for the IP address in *ip_address*.

continues

Table 18-2 *Telnet Monitoring Command Arguments (Continued)*

Argument	Definition
if_name	If IPSec is operating, the PIX Firewall enables you to specify an unsecure interface name—typically, the outside interface. At a minimum, you must configure the **crypto map** command to specify an interface name with the **telnet** command.
local_ip	An optional internal IP address to limit the listing to one IP address or to a network IP address.
telnet_id	The Telnet session identification.

NOTE   If you are running PIX Firewall Version 6.3 or later, you can use the **banner** command to add session, login, or message-of-the-day banners to Telnet and SSH sessions.

SSH

SSH provides another option for the remote management of the PIX Firewall. SSH provides a higher degree of security than Telnet, which provides lower-layer encryption and application security. The PIX Firewall supports the SSH remote functionality, as provided in SSH Version 1, which provides strong authentication and encryption capabilities. SSH, an application running on top of a reliable transport layer such as TCP, supports logging on to another computer over a network, executing commands remotely, and moving files from one host to another.

Both ends of an SSH connection are authenticated, and passwords are protected by encryption. Because SSH uses Rivest, Shamir, and Adleman (RSA) public key cryptography, an Internet encryption and authentication system, you must generate an RSA key pair for the PIX Firewall before clients can connect to the PIX Firewall console. Your PIX Firewall must also have a Data Encryption Standard (DES) or Triple DES/Advanced Encryption Standard (3DES/AES) activation key.

The PIX Firewall allows up to five SSH clients to simultaneously access its console. You can define specific hosts or networks that are authorized to initiate an SSH connection to the PIX Firewall, as well as the length of time the session can remain idle before being disconnected.

NOTE   The PIX Firewall SSH implementation provides a secure remote shell session without IPSec and only functions as a server, which means that the PIX Firewall cannot initiate SSH connections.

Now that you understand how SSH works, complete the following steps to configure an SSH connection to your PIX Firewall:

Step 1 Obtain an SSH client and install it on the system from which you want to establish the SSH connection.

SSH v1.x and v2 are entirely different protocols and are not compatible. Make sure that you download a client such as PuTTY that supports SSH v1.x.

Step 2 Use the **ca zeroize rsa** command to delete any previously created RSA keys.

Step 3 Use the **ca save all** command to save the certificate authority (CA) state and complete the erasure of the old RSA key pair.

Step 4 Use the **domain-name** command to configure the domain name.

Step 5 Use the **ca generate rsa key** command to generate an RSA key pair to use to encrypt SSH sessions.

Step 6 Use the **ca save all** command to save the keys to Flash memory.

Step 7 Use the **ssh** *ip_address* command to specify the host or network authorized to initiate an SSH connection to the PIX Firewall. Use the **no** keyword to remove this command from the configuration.

Step 8 Use the **ssh timeout** command to specify the duration in minutes that a session can be idle before being disconnected. The default duration is 5 minutes.

NOTE   The password used to perform local authentication is the same as that used for Telnet access. The default for this password is cisco. To change it, use the **passwd** command. SSH authentication using an authentication, authorization, and accounting (AAA) server is explained in Chapter 13, "Authentication, Authorization, and Accounting."

The syntax for the **ca** commands is as follows:

```
ca zeroize rsa
ca save all
ca generate rsa {key | specialkey} key_modulus_size
```

Table 18-3 describes the **ca** command arguments.

Table 18-3 ca *Command Arguments*

Argument	Definition
key	Specifies that one general-purpose RSA key pair will be generated.
specialkey	Specifies that two special-purpose RSA key pairs will be generated instead of one general-purpose key.
key_modulus_size	Indicates the size of the key modulus, which is between 512 and 2048 bits. Choosing a size greater than 1024 bits might cause key generation to take a few minutes.

The syntax for the **domain-name** command is as follows:

```
domain-name name
```

name is the domain that the PIX Firewall belongs to.

The syntax for the **ssh** configuration commands is as follows:

```
ssh ip_address [netmask [interface_name]]
ssh timeout minutes
```

Table 18-4 describes the **ssh** command arguments.

Table 18-4 ssh *Command Arguments*

Argument	Definition
ip_address	IP address of the host or network authorized to initiate an SSH connection to the PIX Firewall.
netmask	Network mask for *ip_address*. If you do not specify a netmask, the default is 255.255.255.255 regardless of the class of *ip_address*.
interface_name	PIX Firewall interface name on which the host or network initiating the SSH connection resides.
minutes	The duration that a session can be idle before being disconnected. The default duration is 5 minutes. The allowable range is from 1 to 60 minutes.

To establish an SSH connection to your PIX Firewall console, enter the username **pix** and the Telnet password at the SSH client. When starting an SSH session, the PIX Firewall displays a dot (**.**) on the console before the SSH user authentication prompt appears, as follows:

```
pixfirewall(config)# .
```

The display of the dot does not affect the functionality of SSH. The dot appears at the console when the PIX Firewall is generating a server key or decrypting a message using private keys during SSH key exchange before user authentication occurs. These tasks can take up to 2 minutes or longer. The dot is a progress indicator that verifies that the PIX Firewall is busy and has not hung.

The example shown in Figure 18-1 generates an RSA key pair for the PIX Firewall using a key modulus size of 768. Host 172.26.26.50 is authorized to initiate an SSH connection to the PIX Firewall.

Figure 18-1 *Connecting to a PIX Firewall with SSH*

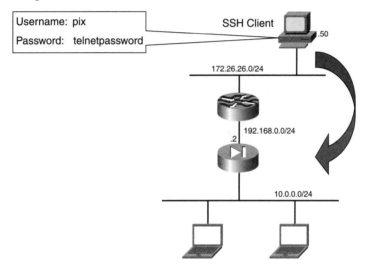

Example 18-2 shows the commands required for the configuration shown in Figure 18-1.

Example 18-2 *SSH Configuration*

```
pixfirewall(config)# ca zeroize rsa
pixfirewall(config)# ca save all
pixfirewall(config)# domain-name cisco.com
pixfirewall(config)# ca generate rsa key 768
pixfirewall(config)# ca save all
pixfirewall(config)# ssh 172.26.26.50 255.255.255.255 outside
pixfirewall(config)# ssh timeout 30
```

You can use the **show ssh sessions** command to list all active SSH sessions on the PIX Firewall. The **ssh disconnect** command enables you to disconnect a specific session.

Example 18-3 shows a typical output of the **show ssh sessions**.

Example 18-3 **show ssh sessions** *Output*

```
pixfirewall# show ssh sessions
Session ID    Client IP      Version Encryption    State    Username
    0        172.16.25.15    1.5     3DES          4        -
    1        172.26.26.50    1.5     DES           6        pix
    2        172.16.25.11    1.5     3DES          4        -
```

The following are the different parts of the **show ssh sessions** command display:

- **Session ID column**—A unique number that identifies an SSH session.
- **Client IP column**—The IP address of the system running an SSH client.
- **Version column**—List of protocol version numbers that the SSH client supports.
- **Encryption column**—The type of encryption the SSH client is using.
- **State column**—A number between 0 and 10 corresponding to the SSH state of the client. Table 18-5 lists the SSH states.
- **Username column**—List of the login username that has been authenticated for the session. The pix username appears when non-AAA authentication is used.

Table 18-5   *SSH States Displayed with the* **show ssh sessions** *Command*

Number	SSH State
0	SSH_CLOSED
1	SSH_OPEN
2	SSH_VERSION_OK
3	SSH_SESSION_KEY_RECEIVED
4	SSH_KEYS_EXCHANGED
5	SSH_AUTHENTICATED
6	SSH_SESSION_OPEN
7	SSH_TERMINATE
8	SSH_SESSION_DISCONNECTING
9	SSH_SESSION_DISCONNECTED
10	SSH_SESSION_CLOSED

You can use the **clear ssh** command to remove all **ssh** command statements from the configuration and the **no ssh** command to remove selected **ssh** command statements. The **debug ssh** command displays information and error messages associated with the **ssh** command.

The syntax for these SSH commands is as follows:

```
show ssh sessions [ip_address]
ssh disconnect session_id
clear ssh
ssh debug
```

Table 18-6 describes the **ssh** monitoring command arguments.

Table 18-6   **ssh** *Monitoring Command Arguments*

Argument	Definition
ip_address	The IP address of a system running an SSH client
session_id	Identifier for the specific session that you want to disconnect

Command Authorization

This section explains how to configure and use local user authentication and command authorization.

Command authorization is a way of facilitating and controlling administration of the PIX Firewall. You can use three types of command authorizations to control which users execute certain commands:

- Enable-level command authorization with passwords
- Command authorization using the local user database
- Command authorization using Cisco Secure Access Control Server (CSACS)

Command Authorization with Enable-Level Passwords

The first type of command authorization, enable level with passwords, allows you to use the **enable** command with the *priv_level* option to access a PIX Firewall privilege level and then use any command assigned to that privilege level or to a lower privilege level.

The basic tasks for configuring and using enable-level command authorization are as follows:

- Use the **enable** command to create privilege levels and assign passwords to them.
- Use the **privilege** command to assign specific commands to privilege levels.
- Use the **aaa authorization** command to enable the command authorization feature.
- Use the **enable** command to access the desired privilege level.

The PIX Firewall supports up to 16 privilege levels: levels 0 through 15. You can create privilege levels and secure them by using the **enable password** command. You can then gain access to a particular privilege level from the > prompt by entering the **enable** command with a privilege level designation and entering the password for that level when prompted.

After you are inside a privilege level, you can execute the commands assigned to that level as well as commands assigned to lower privilege levels. For example, from privilege level 15, you can execute every command because it is the highest privilege level. If you do not specify a privilege level when entering enable mode, the default of 15 is used. Therefore, creating a strong password for level 15 is important.

The syntax for the **enable** commands when used with command authorization is as follows:

```
enable [priv_level]
enable password pw [level priv_level] [encrypted]
```

Table 18-7 describes the **enable** command arguments.

Table 18-7   **enable** *Command Arguments*

Argument	Definition
priv_level	Enables a privilege level, from 0 to 15
pw	The privilege-level password string
encrypted	Specifies that the provided password is already encrypted

Example 18-4 shows the command for creating an enable password for level 10 access and the steps for logging in to the PIX Firewall using the created level 10 enable password from the console.

Example 18-4   *Creating a Password-Protected Privilege Level*

```
pixfirewall (config)# enable password Passw0rD level 10
pixfirewall> enable 10
Password: Passw0rD
pixfirewall#
```

To assign commands to privilege levels, use the **privilege** command. Replace the level argument with the privilege level, and replace the command argument with the command you want to assign to the specified level. You can use the **show**, **clear**, or **configure** parameters to optionally set the privilege level for the **show**, **clear**, or **configure** command modifiers of the specified command. You can remove the **privilege** command by using the **no** keyword.

In the configuration shown in Example 18-5, privilege levels are set for the different command modifiers of the **access-list** command. The first **privilege** command entry sets the privilege level of **show access-list** (the show modifier of command **access-list**) to 8. The second **privilege** command entry sets the privilege level of the configure modifier to 10. The **aaa authorization command LOCAL** command is then used to enable command authorization. The user knows the highest privilege level to which the **access-list** command is assigned and also knows the level's password. A user in this example is therefore able to view and create access control lists (ACLs) by entering level 10.

Example 18-5   *Configuring User-Defined Privilege Levels for PIX Firewall Commands*

```
pixfirewall(config)# enable password Passw0rD level 10
pixfirewall(config)# privilege show level 8 command access-list
pixfirewall(config)# privilege configure level 10 command access-list
pixfirewall(config)# aaa authorization command LOCAL
```

Use the **privilege** command without a **show**, **clear**, or **configure** parameter to set the privilege level for all the modifiers of the command. For example, to set the privilege level of all modifiers of the **access-list** command to a single privilege level of 10, enter the following command:

```
privilege level 10  command access-list
```

For commands that are available in multiple modes, use the **mode** parameter to specify the mode in which the privilege level applies. Do not use the **mode** parameter for commands that are not mode-specific.

The syntax of the **privilege** command is as follows:

```
privilege [show | clear | configure] level level [mode enable | configure] command
command
```

Table 18-8 describes the **privilege** command arguments.

Table 18-8   privilege *Command Arguments*

Argument	Definition
show	Sets the privilege level for the **show** command corresponding to the command specified.
clear	Sets the privilege level for the **clear** command corresponding to the command specified.
configure	Sets the privilege level for the **configure** command corresponding to the command specified.
level	Specifies the privilege level, from 0 to 15. (Lower numbers are lower privilege levels.)
mode	Specifies the mode in which the privilege level applies.
enable	For commands with both enable and configure modes, indicates that the level is for the enable mode of the command.
configure	Sets the privilege level for the **configure** command corresponding to the command specified.
command	The command on which to set the privilege level.

The syntax for the **aaa authorization** command for use with command authorization is as follows:

```
aaa authorization command LOCAL | tacacs_server_tag
```

Table 18-9 describes the **aaa authorization** command arguments.

Table 18-9   **aaa authorization** *Command Arguments*

Argument	Definition
command	Specifies command authorization
LOCAL	Specifies that the PIX Firewall local user database is used for local command authorization (using privilege levels)
tacacs_server_tag	Specifies that a TACACS user authentication server is used

For command authorization with passwords, you should specify **LOCAL** in the **aaa authorization** statement.

Command Authorization with Local User Database

A second way of controlling which commands users can execute is to configure command authorization using the local user database. After assigning commands to privilege levels with the **privilege** command, use the **username** command to define user accounts and their privilege levels in the local PIX Firewall user database. You can define as many user accounts as you need. After defining the user accounts, enable command authorization with the **aaa authorization** command. To enable a direct username and password prompt, enable authentication via the local user database by entering the **aaa authentication enable console LOCAL** command.

NOTE   With PIX Firewall Version 6.2, you can only use the LOCAL database for controlling access *to* the PIX Firewall, not for controlling access *through* the PIX Firewall. PIX Firewall Version 6.3 adds support for local user authentication for network and VPN access, as well as the PIX Firewall itself.

Use the **username** command to create user accounts in the local user database. You can create a password for the user or you can use the **nopassword** keyword to create a user account with no password. Use the **encrypted** keyword if the password you are supplying is already encrypted, and use the **privilege** keyword to assign a privilege level to the user.

To delete an existing user account, use the **no username** command. To remove all the entries from the user database, enter the **clear username** command.

In Example 18-6, the **username** command assigns a privilege level of 15 to the user account admin and a privilege level of 14 to the user account kenny.

Example 18-6   *Creating User Accounts in the Local Database*

```
pixfirewall(config)# username admin password passw0rd privilege 15
pixfirewall(config)# username kenny password cisco privilege 14
```

The syntax for the **username** commands is as follows:

```
username username nopassword | password password [encrypted] [privilege level]
no username username
clear username
```

Table 18-10 describes the **username** command arguments.

Table 18-10   **username** *Command Arguments*

Argument	Definition
username	The username assigned to the user account
nopassword	Used to create a user account with no password
password	The password assigned to the user account
encrypted	Specifies that the password you are supplying is already encrypted
level	Specifies the privilege level for the user account

After you enter the **aaa authentication enable console LOCAL** command, the console prompts for a username and password when you execute the **enable** or **login** command. You can log in to the PIX Firewall using the LOCAL internal user database. After you enter the **aaa authentication enable console LOCAL** command, you are no longer able to access the PIX Firewall using the **enable** command with the **priv_level** option.

When users log in to the PIX Firewall, they can enter any command assigned to their privilege level or to lower privilege levels. For example, a user account with a privilege level of 15 can access every command because it is the highest privilege level. A user account with a privilege level of 0 can access only the commands assigned to level 0.

The syntax for the **aaa authentication** command is as follows:

```
aaa authentication [serial | enable | telnet | ssh | http] console group_tag
```

Table 18-11 describes the **aaa authentication** command arguments.

Table 18-11   **aaa authentication** *Command Arguments for Command Authorization*

Argument	Definition
serial	Verifies access for the PIX Firewall's serial console
enable	Verifies access for the PIX Firewall's privilege mode
telnet	Verifies Telnet access to the PIX Firewall console
ssh	Verifies SSH access for the PIX Firewall console

continues

Table 18-11 **aaa authentication** *Command Arguments for Command Authorization (Continued)*

Argument	Definition
http	Verifies HTTP access to the PIX Firewall (via the PDM)
console	Specifies that access to the PIX Firewall console requires authentication
group_tag	Enables entry of LOCAL to specify use of the local user authentication database

NOTE   The **logout** command logs you out of the currently logged-in user account.

Example 18-7 shows a sample configuration for enabling command authorization with local user database authentication. In this example, access to the command **access-list** is assigned to accounts with privilege levels of 10 or higher, a local user account is created with a username of kenny and a password of cisco, the account is assigned a privilege level of 10, command authorization is enabled with local user accounts, and it is specified that console access to the PIX Firewall requires local user database authentication.

Example 18-7 *Command Authorization with Local Database*

```
pixfirewall(config)# privilege configure level 10 command access-list
pixfirewall(config)# username kenny password cisco privilege 10
pixfirewall(config)# aaa authorization command LOCAL
pixfirewall(config)# aaa authentication enable console LOCAL
```

Command Authorization with CSACS

If you are absolutely sure that you have fulfilled the following requirements, you can use a third method of command authorization, authorization with CSACS:

- You have created entries for enable_1, enable_15, and any other levels to which you have assigned commands.

- If you are enabling authentication with usernames

  — You have a user profile on the TACACS+ server with all the commands that the user is permitted to execute.

  — You have tested authentication with the TACACS+ server.

- You are logged in as a user with the necessary privileges.

- Your TACACS+ system is completely stable and reliable. The necessary level of reliability typically requires that you have a fully redundant TACACS+ server system and fully redundant connectivity to the PIX Firewall.

When configuring the command authorization feature, do not save your configuration until you are sure it works the way you want. If you get locked out of your PIX Firewall, you can usually recover access by simply reloading it. If you have already saved your configuration and you find that you configured authentication using the LOCAL database but did not configure any usernames, you have created a lockout problem. You can also encounter a lockout problem by configuring command authorization using a TACACS+ server if the TACACS+ server is unavailable, down, or misconfigured.

If you cannot recover access to the PIX Firewall by restarting your PIX Firewall, you can check the latest password recovery documentation on Cisco.com. This website provides a downloadable password recovery tool specific to the PIX Firewall version you are using. It also contains instructions for using the password recovery tool to remove the lines in the PIX Firewall configuration that enable authentication and cause the lockout problem. Password recovery procedures are presented in more detail later in this chapter.

NOTE	The web page titled "Password Recovery Procedure for the PIX" is currently available at http://www.cisco.com/warp/public/110/34.shtml. If the page is not available at this URL, try searching Cisco.com for "PIX Firewall password recovery."

You can encounter a different type of lockout problem if you use the **aaa authorization** command and *tacacs_server_tag* argument and you are not logged in as the correct user. For every command you enter, the PIX Firewall displays the following message:

```
Command Authorization failed
```

This occurs because the TACACS+ server does not have a user profile for the user account that you used for logging in. To prevent this problem, make sure that the TACACS+ server has all the users configured with the commands that they can execute. Also make sure that you are logged in as a user with the required profile on the TACACS+ server.

Use the **aaa authorization** command to enable command authorization with a TACACS+ server. You must also use the **aaa-server** command to create the *tacacs_server_tag*.

The syntax for the **aaa authorization** command, when used to configure command authorization using CSACS, is as follows:

```
aaa authorization command LOCAL | tacacs_server_tag
```

Table 18-12 describes the **aaa authorization** command arguments.

Table 18-12 aaa authorization *Command Arguments*

Argument	Definition
command	Specifies command authorization.
LOCAL	Instructs the PIX Firewall to use its own local user database for command authorization. Should not be used for CSACS authentication and authorization.
tacacs_server_tag	Instructs the PIX Firewall to use the specified TACACS+ server for command authorization.

Example 18-8 shows a sample configuration, which enables command authorization with CSACS.

Example 18-8 *Command Authorization and User Authentication with CSACS*

```
pixfirewall(config)# aaa-server MYTACACS protocol tacacs+
pixfirewall(config)# aaa-server MYTACACS (inside) host 10.0.0.11 thekey timeout 20
pixfirewall(config)# aaa authorization command MYTACACS
pixfirewall(config)# aaa authentication enable console MYTACACS
```

In this example, a TACACS+ server group named MYTACACS is created, server 10.0.0.11 is added to MYTACACS and provides authentication on the inside interface, an encryption key value of the key is established, command authorization with TACACS server group MYTACACS is enabled, and the console access to the PIX Firewall requires authentication with MYTACACS.

Viewing Command Authorization Configuration

To view the command assignments for each privilege level, use the **show privilege all** command. The system displays the current assignment of each CLI command to a privilege level. Example 18-9 illustrates the first part of the display.

Example 18-9 **show privilege all** *Output*

```
pix(config)# show privilege all
privilege show level 15 command aaa
privilege clear level 15 command aaa
privilege configure level 15 command aaa
privilege show level 15 command aaa-server
privilege clear level 15 command aaa-server
privilege configure level 15 command aaa-server
privilege show level 15 command access-group
privilege clear level 15 command access-group
privilege configure level 15 command access-group
privilege show level 15 command access-list
privilege clear level 15 command access-list
privilege configure level 15 command access-list
privilege show level 15 command activation-key
privilege configure level 15 command activation-key
```

Use the **show privilege level** command with the **level** option to display the command assignments for a specific privilege level. Use the **show privilege** command to display the privilege level assignment of a specific command.

To view the user account that is currently logged in, enter the **show curpriv** command. The system displays the current user name and privilege level, as shown in Example 18-10.

Example 18-10 **show curpriv** *Output*

```
pix(config)# show curpriv
Username:admin
Current privilege level: 15
Current Mode/s:P_PRIV.
```

The syntax for the **show** commands is as follows:

```
show privilege [all | command command | level level]
show curpriv
```

Table 18-13 describes the **show privilege** and **show curpriv** command arguments.

Table 18-13 **show privilege** *and* **show curpriv** *Command Arguments*

Argument	Definition
level	The privilege level for which you want to display the command assignments
command	The command for which you want to display the assigned privilege level

SNMP

This section explains how to use SNMP to monitor your PIX Firewall and how to permit SNMP through the PIX Firewall for the management and monitoring of other network devices.

SNMP is an application layer protocol designed to facilitate the exchange of management information between network devices. By using SNMP-transported data, such as packets per second and network error rates, network administrators can remotely manage and monitor network devices. As shown in the Figure 18-2, devices managed by SNMP send information to a management server from which an administrator manages and monitors the device.

Figure 18-2 *SNMP Overview*

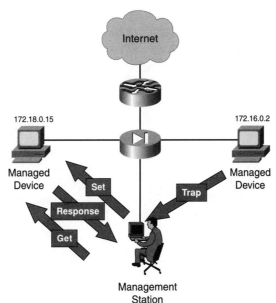

You can use SNMP to monitor system events on the PIX Firewall. SNMP events can be read (RO or read-only), but information on the PIX Firewall cannot be changed (RW or read-write) with SNMP. You can also enable SMTP through the PIX Firewall so that any device can be managed and monitored by a management server on a PIX Firewall interface other than that on which it resides.

To understand SNMP support in the PIX Firewall, it is important to understand the following SNMP-related terminology:

- **Managed devices**—Hardware devices such as computers, routers, and terminal servers that are connected to networks.

- **Agents**—Software modules that reside in managed devices. Agents collect and store management information such as the number of error packets received by a network element.

- **Managed object**—A manageable component of a managed device. A managed object might be the hardware, configuration parameters, or performance statistics of a device. For example, a list of currently active TCP circuits in a particular host computer is a managed object. Managed objects differ from variables, which are particular object instances. Whereas a managed object might be a list of currently active TCP circuits in a particular host, an object instance is a single active TCP circuit in a particular host. Managed objects have object identifiers (OIDs).

- **Management information base (MIB)**—A collection of managed objects. A MIB can be depicted as an abstract tree with an unnamed root. Individual data items make up the leaves of the tree. These leaves have OIDs that uniquely identify or name them. OIDs are like telephone numbers; they are organized hierarchically with specific digits assigned by different organizations. An OID is written as a sequence of subidentifiers, starting with the tree root in dotted decimal notation.

- **Network management stations (NMSs)**—A device that executes management applications that monitor and control network elements. The NMS is the console through which the network administrator performs network management functions. It is usually a computer with a fast CPU, megapixel color display, substantial memory, and abundant disk space.

- **Trap**—An event notification sent from an agent to the NMS. A trap is one of four types of interaction between an NMS and a managed device. Traps are unsolicited comments from the managed device to the NMS for certain events, such as link up, link down, and syslog event generated. Traps are defined in MIB files.

- **Community**—A string value that provides a simple kind of password protection for communications between an SNMP agent and the SNMP NMS. The common default string for RO (read-only) is "public."

SNMP is a request and response protocol. It uses the following operations:

- **Get**—Enables the NMS to retrieve an object instance from an agent.

- **GetNext**—Enables the NMS to retrieve the next object instance from a table or list within an agent.

- **GetBulk**—Used in place of the GetNext operation to simplify acquiring large amounts of related information.
- **Set**—Enables the NMS to set values for object instances within an agent.
- **Trap**—Used by the agent to asynchronously inform the NMS of an event.
- **Inform**—Enables one NMS to send trap information to another.

NOTE Cisco SNMP agents communicate successfully with all SNMP-compliant NMSs, including those of Sun Microsystems (SunNet Manager), IBM (NetView/6000), and Hewlett-Packard (OpenView).

In the example shown in Figure 18-2, the NMS uses a Get operation through the PIX to request management information contained in an agent on host 172.18.0.15. Within the Get request, the NMS includes a complete OID so that the agent knows exactly what is being sought. The response from the agent contains a variable binding containing the same OID and the data associated with it. The NMS then uses a Set request to tell the agent to change a piece of information. In an unrelated communication, host 172.16.0.2 sends a trap to the NMS because some urgent condition has occurred.

MIB Support

An MIB is a collection of information that is organized hierarchically. MIBs are accessed using a network-management protocol such as SNMP. They comprise managed objects and are identified by OIDs.

A managed object is one of any number of specific characteristics of a managed device. An example of a managed object is cpmCPUTotal5sec, which is the Overall CPU busy percentage in the last 5 second period. An object identifier uniquely identifies a managed object in the MIB hierarchy. The MIB hierarchy can be depicted as a tree with a nameless root, the levels of which are assigned by different organizations.

The top-level MIB object identifiers belong to different standards organizations, whereas lower-level object identifiers are allocated by associated organizations. Vendors can define private branches that include managed objects for their own products. Cisco appears in the MIB tree as the number 9. The PIX Firewall's managed object cpmCPUTotal5sec can be uniquely identified by its OID, 1.3.6.1.4.1.9.9.109.1.1.1.3. If you start at the top of the tree and move downward through the branches as directed by the digits in the OID, the first nine you encounter constitute the Cisco branch. It shows that cpmCPUTotal5sec is a Cisco-managed object.

NOTE	See the document titled "Configuring Simple Network Management Protocol (SNMP)," which provides further information on MIB tree and SNMP and is available at http://www.cisco.com/univercd/cc/td/doc/product/webscale/css/advcfggd/snmp.htm.

The PIX Firewall supports the following MIBs:

- **PIX Firewall Software Versions 4.0 through 5.1**—System and interface groups of MIB-II (see RFC 1213) but not the Address Translation (AT), Internet Control Message Protocol (ICMP), TCP, UDP, Exterior Gateway Protocol (EGP), transmission, IP, or SNMP groups CISCO-SYSLOG-MIB-V1SMI.my.

- **PIX Firewall Software Versions 5.1.x and later**—Previous MIBs and CISCO-MEMORY-POOL-MIB.my and the cfwSystem branch of the CISCO-FIREWALL-MIB.my.

- **PIX Firewall Software Versions 5.2.x and later**—Previous MIBs and the ipAddrTable of the IP group.

- **PIX Firewall Software Versions 6.0.x and later**—Previous MIBs and modification of the MIB-II OID to identify PIX by model (and enable CiscoView 5.2 support). The new OIDs are found in the CISCO-PRODUCTS-MIB; for example, the PIX 515 has the OID 1.3.6.1.4.1.9.1.390.

- **PIX Firewall Software Versions 6.2.x and later**—Previous MIBs and CISCO-PROCESS-MIB-V1SMI.my.

The Cisco Firewall MIB, Cisco Memory Pool MIB, and Cisco Process MIB provide the following PIX Firewall information through SNMP:

- Buffer usage from the **show block** command
- Connection count from the **show conn** command
- CPU usage through the show **cpu usage** command
- Failover status
- Memory usage from the **show memory** command

The supported section of the PROCESS MIB is the cpmCPUTotalTable branch of the cpmCPU branch of the ciscoProcessMIBObjects branch.

There is no support for the following branches:

- ciscoProcessMIBNotifications
- ciscoProcessMIBconformance
- Two tables: cpmProcessTable and cpmProcessExtTable, in the cpmProcess branch of the ciscoProcessMIBObjects branch of the MIB

NOTE	An SNMP OID for the PIX Firewall displays in SNMP event traps sent from the PIX Firewall. The model-specific OIDs are found in the CISCO-PRODUCTS-MIB.

Configuring SNMP

The PIX Firewall can generate the following traps and send them to an NMS. Each trap is listed with its respective MIB file:

- **authenticationFailure**—CISCO-GENERAL-TRAPS.my
- **clogNotificationsSent**—CISCO-SYSLOG-MIB-V1SMI.my
- **coldStart**—CISCO-GENERAL-TRAPS.my
- **linkDown**—CISCO-GENERAL-TRAPS.my
- **linkUp**—CISCO-GENERAL-TRAPS.my
- **warmStart**—CISCO-GENERAL-TRAPS.my

To enable the PIX Firewall to receive SNMP requests from an NMS and send traps to an NMS, complete the following steps:

Step 1 Identify the IP address of the SNMP management station with the **snmp-server host** command. If you use the **trap** option of the **snmp-server host** command, the PIX Firewall sends traps to the NMS, but the NMS cannot query the PIX Firewall. If the poll option is used, the NMS is allowed to poll but the PIX Firewall does not send traps to it.

Step 2 Set the **snmp-server** options for location, contact, and the community password as required. If you want to receive only SNMP requests sent the cold start, link up, and link down generic traps, no further configuration is required. The **snmp-server community** command is required. It specifies a secret password to be shared among the NMS and the network nodes being managed. The PIX Firewall uses the community key to determine whether an incoming SNMP request is valid and responds only to requests that contain a valid community string.

Step 3 Add an **snmp-server enable traps** command statement to start sending traps to the SNMP management station. You can remove this and all **snmp-server** commands by using their **no** forms. The **show snmp-server** command displays the entire SNMP configuration.

Step 4 Set the logging level with the **logging history** command. This sets the severity level for SNMP syslog messages:

```
logging history debugging
```

NOTE   It is recommended that you use the debugging level during initial setup and during testing. Thereafter, set the level from debugging to a lower value for production use.

NOTE   You set the severity level for SNMP logs using the **logging history** command. You use the **logging trap level** command to set the logging level for syslog messages; it does not impact the configuration of SNMP severity levels.

Step 5   Start sending syslog traps to the management station with the **logging on** command.

In Example 18-11, the PIX Firewall receives SNMP requests and sends traps to host 10.0.0.11. The PIX Firewall and host 10.0.0.11 are members of the community MYCOMMUNITY.

Example 18-11   *SNMP Configuration*

```
pixfirewall(config)# logging on
pixfirewall(config)# logging history debugging
pixfirewall(config)# snmp-server host inside 10.0.0.11
pixfirewall(config)# snmp-server community MYCOMMUNITY
pixfirewall(config)# snmp-server enable traps
```

The syntax for the **snmp-server** commands is as follows:

```
snmp-server host [if_name] ip_addr [trap | poll]
snmp-server community key
snmp-server enable traps
```

Table 18-14 describes the **snmp-server** commands arguments.

Table 18-14   **snmp-server** *Commands Arguments*

Argument	Definition
if_name	The name of the interface where the SNMP management station resides.
ip_addr	THE IP address of a host to which SNMP traps should be sent and from which the SNMP requests come.
trap	Specifies that this host is not allowed to poll. Only traps are sent.
poll	Specifies that this host is allowed to poll, but traps are not sent. The default allows both traps and polls to be acted upon.
key	The password key value in use at the SNMP management station. The key is a case-sensitive value up to 32 characters in length. Spaces are not permitted. The default is public if a key is not set. Consequently for security reasons, it is important to specify a new key value.

To enable SNMP through the PIX Firewall so that network devices other than the PIX Firewall can be managed and monitored, you must use the appropriate **static** and **access-list** commands. For example, consider the two scenarios depicted in Figure 18-3.

Figure 18-3 *SNMP Through the PIX Firewall*

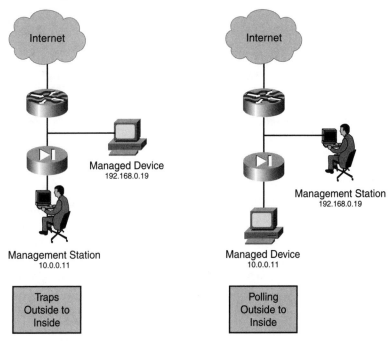

SNMP can be enabled as follows:

- **Traps outside to inside**—To allow traps from outside host 192.168.0.19 to inside management system 10.0.0.11, use the following commands:

  ```
  static (inside,outside) 192.168.0.10 10.0.0.11 netmask 255.255.255.255
  access-list TRAPSIN permit udp host 192.168.0.19 host 192.168.0.10 eq snmptrap
  access-group TRAPSIN in interface outside
  ```

- **Traps inside to outside**—In the absence of outbound ACLs, outbound traffic is allowed by default.

- **Polling outside to inside**—To allow polling from the NMS, outside host 192.168.0.19, to inside host 10.0.0.11, use the following configuration:

  ```
  static (inside,outside) 192.168.0.10 10.0.0.11 netmask 255.255.255.255
  access-list POLLIN permit udp host 192.168.0.19 host 192.168.0.10 eq snmp
  access-group POLLIN in interface outside
  ```

- **Polling inside to outside**—In the absence of outbound ACLs, outbound traffic is allowed by default.

Management Tools

This section outlines several tools available for managing PIX Firewalls, including the PDM, Cisco Secure Policy Manager (CSPM), and Management Center for Firewalls (Firewall MC).

PDM is the primary graphical user interface (GUI) for management of a single PIX Firewall and is covered in greater detail in Chapter 6, "Cisco PIX Device Manager."

CSPM and Firewall MC are GUI-based tools for managing multiple PIX Firewalls in enterprise and service provider networks. CSPM, however, is being phased out and the user base is being migrated to the Firewall MC. CSPM is covered in this chapter for informational purposes only. Cisco recommends the Firewall MC for managing multiple PIX Firewalls in large enterprise networks. Firewall MC is covered in greater detail in Chapter 20, "PIX Firewall Maintenance in Enterprise Networks."

PDM

PDM is a browser-based configuration tool designed to help you graphically set up, configure, and monitor a PIX Firewall, without requiring an extensive knowledge of the PIX Firewall CLI.

PDM monitors and configures a single PIX Firewall. You can use PDM to create a new configuration, or you can use PDM in addition to a configuration you create or maintain from the PIX Firewall console or the Firewall MC. You can point your browser to more than one PIX Firewall and administer several PIX Firewall from a single workstation.

Cisco Secure Policy Manager

CSPM is a scalable and powerful security policy management system for Cisco firewalls and VPN gateways. With it, Cisco customers can define, distribute, enforce, and audit network-wide security policies from a central location. CSPM streamlines the tasks of managing complicated network security elements, such as perimeter access control, network address translation (NAT), and IPSec-based VPNs.

NOTE CSPM has reached end-of-sale status, and the user base is being migrated to the Firewall MC. CSPM is covered in this chapter for informational purposes only. Cisco recommends Firewall MC for management of multiple PIX Firewalls in large enterprise networks. Firewall MC is covered in greater detail in Chapter 19, "PIX Firewall Management in Enterprise Networks."

With the CSPM's GUI shown in Figure 18-4, administrators can visually define high-level security policies for multiple PIX Firewalls and VPN gateways. When created, these policies can be distributed from a central location eliminating the costly, time-consuming practice of implementing security commands on a device-by-device basis via the CLI. In addition, the product provides system-auditing functions, including event notification and a web-based reporting system. As the management cornerstone of the Cisco end-to-end security product line, CSPM simplifies the deployment of security products and services within Cisco networks.

Figure 18-4 *CSPM Management Console*

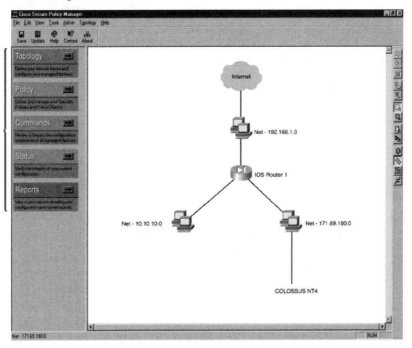

CSPM replaces the PIX Firewall configuration completely. It provides the following firewall management capabilities:

- Defines the interface settings by specifying the perimeter name and number; interface type, name, IP address, and number; and the network name and IP address.

- Defines device characteristics by specifying timeouts, and enables Flood Guard and logging.

- Defines access rules by managing information flow on Context-Based Access Control (CBAC)–enabled routers by adding commands generated from policy statements.

- Converts policy into firewall configuration by converting policy statements into commands that are inserted into an existing configuration for a router-based firewall. It completely replaces the configuration of a PIX Firewall.

- Manages local and remote devices over the network.

Management Center for Firewalls

Whereas PDM addresses single device management, the Firewall MC addresses the enterprise multidevice management. Firewall MC uses terminology and concepts consistent with PDM and has a look and feel consistent with PDM as well.

Activation Keys

You can upgrade the license for your PIX by purchasing a new license, registering the new license by phone or on Cisco.com to obtain a new activation key, and installing the new activation key. You can use the CLI command **activation-key** to install the new activation key on PIX Firewall Version 6.2 or higher.

NOTE   Versions of the PIX Firewall earlier than 6.2 require you to install the new activation key by installing a new PIX Firewall image. You must first enter the monitor mode and initiate the download of a new PIX Firewall image from a TFTP server. After the new image downloads, you must write the image to the Flash memory. At this point, you are provided with an opportunity to enter a new activation key to upgrade the license on your firewall.

Before entering the activation key, ensure that the image in Flash and the running image are the same. You can do this by performing a **write memory** and rebooting the PIX Firewall before entering the new activation key. For the change to take effect, you also need to reboot the PIX Firewall after entering the new activation key.

The syntax for the **activation-key** command is as follows:

```
activation-key activation-key-four-tuple
```

Use the **activation-key** command to enter a new activation key, replacing *activation-key-four-tuple* with the activation key you obtained with your new license. The leading 0x hexadecimal indicator in *activation-key-four-tuple* is optional. If it is omitted, the parameter is assumed to be a hexadecimal number.

Example 18-12 shows the output generated after you enter a new activation key and the activation key has been successfully changed.

Example 18-12 *Activation Key Change Output*

```
pixfirewall(config)# activation-key 0x01234567 0x89abcdef01 0x23456789 0xabcdef01
Serial Number: 12345678 (0xbc614e)

Flash activation key:  0x01234567 0x89abcdef01 0x23456789 0xabcdef01
Licensed Features:
Failover:       Enabled
VPN-DES:        Enabled
VPN-3DES:       Enabled
Maximum Interfaces: 10
Cut-through Proxy:  Enabled
Guards:         Enabled
URL-filtering:  Enabled
Inside Hosts:   Unlimited
Throughput:     Unlimited
IKE peers:      Unlimited

The flash activation key has been modified.
The flash activation key is now DIFFERENT than the running key.
The flash activation key will be used when the unit is reloaded.
pixfirewall(config)#
```

If you are upgrading the image to a newer version and the activation key is also being changed, reboot the system twice, as shown in the following procedure:

Step 1 Install the new image.

Step 2 Reboot the system.

Step 3 Update the activation key.

Step 4 Reboot the system.

After the key update is complete, the system is reloaded a second time so the updated licensing scheme can take effect.

If you are downgrading an image, you need only reboot once, after installing the new image. In this situation, the old key is both verified and changed with the current image.

Troubleshooting the Activation Key Upgrade

To view your current activation key, enter the **show activation-key** command. Example 18-13 shows the output from this command under normal circumstances.

Example 18-13   **show activation-key** *Output*

```
pixfirewall(config)# show activation-key

Serial Number: 12345678 (0xbc614e)

Running activation key: 0xe02888da 0x4ba7bed6 0xf1c123ae 0xffd8624e
Licensed Features:
Failover:        Enabled
VPN-DES:         Enabled
VPN-3DES:        Enabled
Maximum Interfaces: 6
Cut-through Proxy:  Enabled
Guards:          Enabled
Websense:        Enabled
Throughput:      Unlimited
ISAKMP peers:    Unlimited

The flash activation key is the SAME as the running key.
```

Example 18-14 shows the output of the **show activation-key** command on a firewall with an upgraded activation key, before a reboot. (Running and Flash activation keys are different.)

Example 18-14   **show activation-key** *Output for Upgraded Activation Key, No Reboot*

```
pixfirewall(config)# show activation-key

Serial Number: 12345678 (0xbc614e)

Running activation key: 0xe02888da 0x4ba7bed6 0xf1c123ae 0xffd8624e
Licensed Features:
Failover:        Enabled
VPN-DES:         Enabled
VPN-3DES:        Enabled
Maximum Interfaces:  8
Cut-through Proxy:  Enabled
Guards:          Enabled
URL-filtering:   Enabled
Throughput:      Unlimited
ISAKMP peers:    Unlimited

Flash activation key: 0xe02388da 0x5ca7bed2 0xf1c123ae 0xffd8624t
Licensed Features:
Failover:        Enabled
VPN-DES:         Enabled
VPN-3DES:        Disabled
Maximum Interfaces:  8
Cut-through Proxy:   Enabled
Guards:          Enabled
```

Example 18-14 **show activation-key** *Output for Upgraded Activation Key, No Reboot (Continued)*

```
URL-filtering:   Enabled
Throughput:      Unlimited
ISAKMP peers:    Unlimited

The flash activation key is DIFFERENT than the running key.
The flash activation key takes effect after the next reload.
```

Example 18-15 shows the output of the **show activation-key** command on a firewall with an upgraded image, before a reboot. (Running and Flash images are different.)

Example 18-15 **show activation-key** *Output for Upgraded Image, No Reboot*

```
pixfirewall(config)# show activation-key

Serial Number: 12345678 (0xbc614e)

Running activation key: 0xe02888da 0x4ba7bed6 0xf1c123ae 0xffd8624e
Licensed Features:
Failover:        Enabled
VPN-DES:         Enabled
VPN-3DES:        Enabled
Maximum Interfaces:  6
Cut-through Proxy:   Enabled
Guards:          Enabled
Websense:        Enabled
Throughput:      Unlimited
ISAKMP peers:    Unlimited

The flash image is DIFFERENT than the running image.
The two images must be the same in order to examine the flash activation key.
pixfirewall(config)#
```

Password Recovery and Image Upgrade

This section explains how to perform password recovery and upgrade the PIX Firewall image.

Password Recovery Procedures

The password recovery for PIX Firewall models 501, 506/506E, 515/515E, 525, and 535 requires a TFTP server. To perform a password recovery using TFTP, complete the following steps:

Step 1 Download the PIX Password Lock utility for the PIX Firewall software version you are running from Cisco.com. Each version requires a different file. For example, if you are running PIX Firewall Version 6.3, you must download the file named np63.bin. You need a Cisco Connection Online (CCO) login to download this data.

Step 2   Move the binary file you just downloaded to the TFTP home folder on your TFTP server.

Step 3   Reboot your PIX Firewall and interrupt the boot process to enter monitor mode. To do this, you must press the **Escape** key or send a break character.

Step 4   Specify which PIX Firewall interface is to be used for TFTP:

```
monitor> interface [num]
```

Step 5   Specify the PIX Firewall interface's IP address:

```
monitor> address [IP_address]
```

Step 6   Specify the default gateway (if needed):

```
monitor> gateway [IP_address]
```

Step 7   Verify connectivity to the TFTP server:

```
monitor> ping [server_address]
```

Step 8   Name the server:

```
monitor> server [IP_address]
```

Step 9   Name the image filename:

```
monitor> file [name]
```

Step 10   Start the TFTP process:

```
monitor> tftp
```

Step 11   When prompted, enter **y** to erase the password:

```
Do you wish to erase the passwords? [yn] y
Passwords have been erased
```

The system automatically erases the password and starts rebooting.

NOTE   To obtain the files needed for password recovery, go to http://www.cisco.com/warp/public/ 110/34.shtml#files. You must select the appropriate tool for the PIX Firewall version you are running.

Image Upgrade

The **copy tftp flash** command enables you to change software images without accessing the TFTP monitor mode. You can use this command to download a software image via TFTP with any PIX Firewall model running Version 5.1 or later. The image you download is made available to the PIX Firewall on the next reload.

Be sure to configure your TFTP server to point to the image you want to download. For example, to download the pix633.bin file from the D: partition on a Windows system whose IP address is 172.26.26.50, you would access the Cisco TFTP server **View > Options** menu and enter the filename path in the TFTP server root directory edit box (for example, **D:\pix_images**). Then, to copy the file to the PIX Firewall, use the following command:

```
copy tftp://172.26.26.50/pix633.bin flash
```

The TFTP server receives the command and determines the actual file location from its root directory information. The server then downloads the TFTP image to the PIX Firewall.

NOTE   Your TFTP server must be open when you enter the **copy tftp** command on the PIX Firewall.

The syntax for the **copy tftp flash** command is as follows:

```
copy tftp[:[[//location] [/pathname]]] flash[:[image | pdm]]
```

Table 18-15 describes the **copy tftp flash** command arguments.

Table 18-15   **copy tftp flash** *Command Arguments*

Argument	Definition
copy tftp flash	Enables you to download Flash memory software images via TFTP without using monitor mode.
location	Specifies the IP address or name of the server on which the TFTP server resides.
pathname	Specifies any directory names in the path to the file as well as the actual file name. The PIX Firewall must know how to reach this location via its routing table information, which is determined by the **ip address** command, the **route** command, or Routing Information Protocol (RIP), depending on your configuration.
image	Enables you to download the selected PIX Firewall image to Flash memory. An image you download is made available to the PIX Firewall on the next reboot.
pdm	Enables you to download the selected PDM image files to Flash memory. These files are available to the PIX Firewall immediately, without a reboot.

Summary

This section summarizes the information you learned in this chapter:

- SSH provides secure remote management of the PIX Firewall.

- You use TFTP to upgrade the software image on PIX Firewalls.

- You can configure three different types of command authorization: enable-level with password, local command authorization, and CSACS command authorization.

- You can configure the PIX Firewall to permit multiple users to access its console simultaneously via Telnet.

- You can enable Telnet to the PIX Firewall on all interfaces.

- Password recovery for the PIX Firewall requires a TFTP server and a server-specific password recovery file available on Cisco.com.

Chapter Review Questions

To test what you have learned in this chapter, answer the following questions and then refer to Appendix A, "Answers to Chapter Review Questions," for the answers:

1 You want to upgrade the PDM image on your PIX Firewall to Version 3.01 using a TFTP server with an address of 10.0.0.1 and a PDM image file named pdm301.bin. What command do you use to download this image to the PIX Firewall?

2 You are currently running PIX Firewall Version 6.0 and want to enable 3DES functionality by upgrading the activation key. What should you do to upgrade the activation key?

3 What is the maximum number of Telnet commands allowed on the PIX Firewall?

4 What are the three different types of authentication databases that you can use with command authorization?

5 List the valid RSA key modulus sizes that you can specify in the **ca generate rsa key** command.

6 What are the basic tasks required to configure command authorization with enable-level passwords?

Lab Exercise—System Maintenance

Complete the following lab exercise to practice the system maintenance concepts you learned in this chapter. Use the following initial configuration and continue with the rest of the lab exercises.

NOTE	Many of the settings shown in this initial configuration are default values and do not need to be entered on your PIX Firewall. Specific commands that must be entered are shown in bold for your convenience.

```
: Saved
: Written by enable_15 at 13:06:45.740 UTC Sun Oct 5 2003
PIX Version 6.3(3)
!--- If the PIX Firewall you are using does not support 100full,
!--- use the appropriate setting here instead
interface ethernet0 100full
interface ethernet1 100full
nameif ethernet0 outside security0
nameif ethernet1 inside security100
enable password 8Ry2YjIyt7RRXU24 encrypted
passwd 2KFQnbNIdI.2KYOU encrypted
hostname pixfirewall
domain-name cisco.com
fixup protocol dns maximum-length 512
fixup protocol ftp 21
fixup protocol h323 h225 1720
fixup protocol h323 ras 1718-1719
fixup protocol http 80
fixup protocol rsh 514
fixup protocol rtsp 554
fixup protocol sip 5060
fixup protocol sip udp 5060
fixup protocol skinny 2000
fixup protocol smtp 25
fixup protocol sqlnet 1521
fixup protocol tftp 69
pager lines 24
mtu outside 1500
mtu inside 1500
mtu dmz 1500
ip address outside 192.168.1.2 255.255.255.0
ip address inside 10.0.1.1 255.255.255.0
arp timeout 14400
timeout xlate 3:00:00
timeout conn 1:00:00 half-closed 0:10:00 udp 0:02:00 rpc 0:10:00 h225 1:00:00
timeout h323 0:05:00 mgcp 0:05:00 sip 0:30:00 sip_media 0:02:00
timeout uauth 0:05:00 absolute
aaa-server TACACS+ protocol tacacs+
aaa-server RADIUS protocol radius
aaa-server LOCAL protocol local
http server enable
no snmp-server location
no snmp-server contact
snmp-server community public
no snmp-server enable traps
floodguard enable
telnet timeout 5
ssh timeout 5
console timeout 0
terminal width 80
Cryptochecksum:aa0cc6e47d705ed128e041c2c2a8412b
: end
```

Objectives

In this lab exercise, you complete the following tasks:

- Configure enable-level command authorization with passwords.
- Test enable-level command authorization.
- Generate an RSA key pair for encrypted SSH sessions.
- Establish an SSH connection to your PIX Firewall.
- Configure command authorization using the local user database.
- Test command authorization using the local user database.
- Perform a password recovery.
- Upgrade the PIX Firewall software image.

Lab Topology

Figure 18-5 displays the topology you need for the lab exercises in this chapter.

Figure 18-5 *System Maintenance Visual Objective*

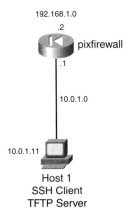

192.168.1.0

.2

pixfirewall

.1

10.0.1.0

10.0.1.11

Host 1
SSH Client
TFTP Server

Equipment required to perform the lab includes the following:

- A PIX Firewall with two interfaces
- Category 5 patch cables
- PC host for the inside subnet running a TFTP server, Telnet, and an SSH client
- PIX Firewall software image available from Cisco.com (with a CCO account)
- PIX Password Recovery utility available from Cisco.com
- PC host for the inside subnet running TFTP Server, Telnet, and SSH client such as PuTTY or Tetra Term Pro SSH (TTSSH)

Task 1—Configure Enable-Level Command Authorization with Passwords

To enable command authorization with privileged mode passwords, complete the following steps:

Step 1 Set privilege level 10 for the enable mode's **configure** command:

```
pixfirewall(config)# privilege configure level 10 mode enable
command configure
```

Step 2 Set privilege level 10 for the **nameif** command:

```
pixfirewall(config)# privilege level 10 command nameif
```

Step 3 Set privilege level 12 for the **interface** command:

```
pixfirewall(config)# privilege level 12 command interface
```

Step 4 Assign an enable password for privilege level 15:

```
pixfirewall(config)# enable password prmode15
```

Step 5 Assign an enable password for privilege level 5:

```
pixfirewall(config)# enable password prmode5 level 5
```

Step 6 Assign an enable password to privilege level 10:

```
pixfirewall(config)# enable password prmode10 level 10
```

Step 7 Assign an enable password to privilege level 12:

```
pixfirewall(config)# enable password prmode12 level 12
```

Step 8 Enable command authorization by entering the following command:

```
pixfirewall(config)# aaa authorization command LOCAL
```

Step 9 Exit configuration mode:

```
pixfirewall(config)# exit
pixfirewall#
```

Step 10 Exit privileged mode:

```
pixfirewall# exit

Logoff

Type help or '?' for a list of available commands.
pixfirewall>
```

Task 2—Test Enable-Level Command Authorization

To test the command authorization you configured in Task 1, complete the following steps:

Step 1   Enter privileged mode level 12. When prompted for a password, enter **prmode12**:

```
pixfirewall> enable 12
Password: prmode12
pixfirewall#
```

Step 2   Enter configuration mode:

```
pixfirewall# config t
```

Step 3   Verify that you can use the **nameif** command:

```
pixfirewall(config)# nameif e1 test sec90
```

Step 4   View your configuration:

```
pixfirewall(config)# show nameif
nameif ethernet0 outside security0
nameif ethernet1 test security90
```

Step 5   Verify that you can use the **interface** command:

```
pix1(config)# interface e1 10full
```

Step 6   Reconfigure the inside interface to its original settings:

```
pixfirewall(config)# nameif e1 inside sec100
pixfirewall(config)# interface e1 100full
```

Step 7   View your configuration:

```
pixfirewall(config)# show interface
interface ethernet0 "outside" is up, line protocol is up
   Hardware is i82559 ethernet, address is 0003.e300.483a
   IP address 192.168.1.2, subnet mask 255.255.255.0
   MTU 1500 bytes, BW 100000 Kbit full duplex
        10640 packets input, 1374788 bytes, 0 no buffer
        Received 7179 broadcasts, 0 runts, 0 giants
        0 input errors, 0 CRC, 0 frame, 0 overrun, 0 ignored, 0 abort
        3458 packets output, 348972 bytes, 0 underruns
        0 output errors, 0 collisions, 0 interface resets
        0 babbles, 0 late collisions, 0 deferred
        0 lost carrier, 0 no carrier
          input queue (curr/max blocks): hardware (128/128) software (0/6)
          output queue (curr/max blocks): hardware (0/9) software (0/2)
interface ethernet1 "inside" is up, line protocol is up
   Hardware is i82559 ethernet, address is 0003.e300.483b
   IP address 10.0.1.1, subnet mask 255.255.255.0
```

```
MTU 1500 bytes, BW 100000 Kbit full duplex
        11119 packets input, 1438842 bytes, 0 no buffer
        Received 7554 broadcasts, 0 runts, 0 giants
        0 input errors, 0 CRC, 0 frame, 0 overrun, 0 ignored, 0 abort
        4153 packets output, 390555 bytes, 0 underruns
        0 output errors, 0 collisions, 0 interface resets
        0 babbles, 0 late collisions, 0 deferred
        0 lost carrier, 0 no carrier
    input queue (curr/max blocks): hardware (128/128) software (0/4)
    output queue (curr/max blocks): hardware (0/15) software (0/14)
```

Step 8 Exit configuration mode:

```
pixfirewall(config)# exit
pixfirewall#
```

Step 9 Exit privileged mode:

```
pixfirewall# exit

Logoff
Type help or '?' for a list of available commands.
pixfirewall>
```

Step 10 Enter privilege mode level 10. When prompted for a password, enter
prmode10:

```
pixfirewall> enable 10
Password: prmode10
pixfirewall#
```

Step 11 Enter configuration mode:

```
pixfirewall# config t
pixfirewall(config)#
```

Step 12 Verify that you can use the **nameif** command:

```
pixfirewall(config)# nameif e1 test sec90
```

Step 13 View your configuration:

```
pixfirewall(config)# show nameif
nameif ethernet0 outside security0
nameif ethernet1 test security90
```

Step 14 Reconfigure the inside interface to its original settings:

```
pixfirewall(config)# nameif e1 inside sec100
```

Step 15 Try to use the **interface** command:

```
pixfirewall(config)# interface e0 10full
Command authorization failed.
```

Step 16 Exit configuration mode:

```
pixfirewall(config)# exit
pixfirewall#
```

Step 17 Exit privileged mode:

```
pixfirewall# exit

Logoff
Type help or '?' for a list of available commands.
pixfirewall>
```

Step 18 Enter privilege mode level 5. When prompted for a password, enter **prmode5**:

```
pixfirewall> enable 5
Password: prmode5
pixfirewall#
```

Step 19 Try to enter configuration mode:

```
pixfirewall# config t
Command authorization failed.
```

Step 20 Exit privileged mode:

```
pixfirewall# exit

Logoff
Type help or '?' for a list of available commands.
pixfirewall>
```

Step 21 Enter privileged mode. When prompted for a password, enter **prmode15**:

```
pixfirewall> enable
Password: prmode15
pixfirewall#
```

Step 22 Enter configuration mode:

```
pixfirewall# config t
pixfirewall(config)#
```

Task 3—Generate an RSA Key Pair for Encrypted SSH Sessions

To generate an RSA key pair to encrypt the SSH terminal session, complete the following steps:

Step 1   Delete any previously created RSA keys:

```
pixfirewall(config)# ca zeroize rsa
```

Step 2   Save the CA state to complete the erasure of the old RSA key pair:

```
pixfirewall(config)# ca save all
```

Step 3   Configure the domain name:

```
pixfirewall(config)# domain-name cisco.com
```

Step 4   Generate an RSA key pair to use to encrypt SSH sessions:

```
pixfirewall(config)# ca generate rsa key 1024
For <key_modulus_size> >= 1024, key generation could
   take up to several minutes. Please wait.
```

Step 5   Save the keys to Flash memory:

```
pixfirewall(config)# ca save all
```

Step 6   View your public key:

```
pixfirewall(config)# sh ca mypubkey rsa
% Key pair was generated at: 18:34:29 UTC Apr 17 2002
Key name: pixfirewall.cisco.com
 Usage: General Purpose Key
 Key Data:
  30819f30 0d06092a 864886f7 0d010101 05000381 8d003081 89028181
00bc43bf
  33d9c65d e508b6df ecf71e37 5574a21d 56185faf cbb9fe14 5a345222
42cd2927
  604fd719 a58d4f82 dc382fc4 ae037d15 f4f11ca8 06020c8d 5cd350d1
9bf19457
  a6dc1a86 f1e101ae 842b0281 f42f38c5 c8e5c095 711ac751 f28d693f
ffdcb40f
  2892169e 90be60dd 15c2fdc9 b8bda690 e55b29bf 670ed794 30e9c012
5f020301 0001
```

Task 4—Establish an SSH Connection to the PIX Firewall

To securely connect to your PIX Firewall via SSH, complete the following steps:

Step 1   Enable SSH debugging:

```
pixfirewall(config)# debug ssh
SSH debugging on
```

Step 2   Grant SSH access to your inside subnet:

```
pixfirewall(config)# ssh 10.0.1.0 255.255.255.0 inside
```

Step 3   Set the SSH inactivity timeout to 30 minutes:

```
pixfirewall(config)# ssh timeout 30
```

Step 4   Minimize but do not close your Telnet session window. Start **ttssh.exe** or **PuTTY** on Host 1.

Step 5   Specify **10.0.1.1**, the IP address of the PIX Firewall's inside interface.

Step 6   Select the **SSH** radio button.

Step 7   Click **OK**. The Security Warning window opens.

Step 8   Select **Add** this new key to the known hosts lists.

Step 9   Click **Continue**. The SSH Authentication window opens.

NOTE   If you get a message saying the known hosts file does not exist, click **OK** and continue with Step 10.

Step 10 Enter **pix** as the username and **cisco** as the password. Click **OK**.

Step 11 Enter privileged mode. When prompted for a password, enter **prmode15**:

```
pixfirewall>enable
Password: prmode15
pixfirewall#
```

Step 12 Enter configuration mode:

```
pixfirewall# config t
pixfirewall(config)#
```

Step 13 To view the status of your SSH session, enter the following command:

```
pixfirewall(config)# show ssh sessions
Session ID     Client IP     Version Encryption     State   Username
    0          insidehost      1.5      3DES           6       pix
```

Step 14 Disconnect your SSH session:

```
pixfirewall(config)# ssh disconnect 0
```

Step 15 Click **OK** in the (TTSSH) window.

Step 16 Return to your Telnet session window, and change the PIX Firewall's Telnet password from cisco to **sshpass**:

```
pixfirewall(config)# passwd sshpass
```

Step 17 Exit configuration mode:

```
pixfirewall(config)# exit
pixfirewall#
```

Step 18 Exit privileged mode:

```
pixfirewall# exit

Logoff
Type help or '?' for a list of available commands.
pixfirewall>
```

Step 19 Minimize your Telnet window. Do not close it.

Step 20 Establish another SSH session to the PIX Firewall. When prompted to authenticate, enter **pix** as the username and **sshpass** as the password.

Task 5—Configure Command Authorization Using the Local User Database

To configure local user authentication via a secure SSH session, complete the following steps:

Step 1 Enter privileged mode. When prompted for a password, enter **prmode15**:

```
pixfirewall>enable
Password: prmode15
pixfirewall#
```

Step 2 Enter configuration mode:

```
pixfirewall# config t
pixfirewall(config)#
```

Step 3 Create three user accounts in the local database:

```
pixfirewall(config)# username user10 password user10pass privilege 10
pixfirewall(config)# username user12 password user12pass privilege 12
pixfirewall(config)# username admin password adminpass privilege 15
```

Step 4 Enable authentication using the LOCAL database:

```
pixfirewall(config)# aaa authentication enable console LOCAL
```

Step 5 Disconnect your SSH session.

Task 6—Test Command Authorization Using the Local User Database

To test command authorization with local user authentication, complete the following steps:

Step 1   Return to your Telnet session.

Step 2   Enter privileged mode. When prompted for a username, enter **user12**.
When prompted for a password, enter **user12pass**:

```
pixfirewall> enable
Username: user12
Password: user12pass
pixfirewall#
```

Step 3   Enter configuration mode:

```
pixfirewall# config t
pixfirewall(config)#
```

Step 4   View the user account that is currently logged in:

```
pixfirewall(config)# show curpriv
Username : user12
Current privilege level : 12
Current Mode/s : P_PRIV P_CONF
```

Step 5   Verify that you can use the **nameif** command by attempting to change the name and security level of Ethernet 2:

```
pixfirewall(config)# nameif e1 test sec90
```

Step 6   View your configuration:

```
pixfirewall(config)# show nameif
nameif ethernet0 outside security0
nameif ethernet1 test security90
```

Step 7   Verify that you can user the **interface** command:

```
pixfirewall(config)# interface e1 10full
```

Step 8   Reconfigure the inside interface to its original settings:

```
pixfirewall(config)# nameif e1 inside sec100
pixfirewall(config)# interface e1 100full
```

Step 9   View your configuration:

```
pixfirewall(config)# show int
interface ethernet0 "outside" is up, line protocol is up
  Hardware is i82559 ethernet, address is 0003.e300.486a
  IP address 192.168.1.2, subnet mask 255.255.255.0
```

```
       MTU 1500 bytes, BW 100000 Kbit full duplex
            0 packets input, 0 bytes, 0 no buffer
            Received 0 broadcasts, 0 runts, 0 giants
            0 input errors, 0 CRC, 0 frame, 0 overrun, 0 ignored, 0 abort
            0 packets output, 0 bytes, 0 underruns
            0 output errors, 0 collisions, 0 interface resets
            0 babbles, 0 late collisions, 0 deferred
            0 lost carrier, 0 no carrier
          input queue (curr/max blocks): hardware (128/128) software (0/0)
          output queue (curr/max blocks): hardware (0/0) software (0/0)
    interface ethernet1 "inside" is up, line protocol is up
      Hardware is i82559 ethernet, address is 0003.e300.486b
      IP address 10.0.1.1, subnet mask 255.255.255.0
      MTU 1500 bytes, BW 100000 Kbit full duplex
            6197 packets input, 597517 bytes, 0 no buffer
            Received 2231 broadcasts, 0 runts, 0 giants
            0 input errors, 0 CRC, 0 frame, 0 overrun, 0 ignored, 0 abort
            4698 packets output, 356441 bytes, 0 underruns
            0 output errors, 0 collisions, 0 interface resets
            0 babbles, 0 late collisions, 0 deferred
            0 lost carrier, 0 no carrier
          input queue (curr/max blocks): hardware (128/128) software (0/5)
          output queue (curr/max blocks): hardware (1/3) software (0/2)
```

Step 10 Try to create a static mapping for inside host 10.0.1.11:

```
pixfirewall(config)# static (inside,outside) 192.168.1.11 10.0.1.11
netmask 255.255.255.255
Command authorization failed
```

Step 11 Log out of the user12 account:

```
pixfirewall(config)# logout


Logoff
Type help or '?' for a list of available commands.
pixfirewall>
```

Step 12 Log in to user 10's account. When prompted for a username, enter
user10. When prompted for a password, enter **user10pass**:

```
pixfirewall>login
Username: user10
Password: user10pass
pixfirewall#
```

Step 13 Enter configuration mode:

```
pixfirewall# config t
pixfirewall(config)#
```

Step 14 Verify that you can use the **nameif** command by creating a name and
security level for Ethernet 1:

```
pixfirewall(config)# nameif e1 test sec90
```

Step 15 View your configuration:

```
pixfirewall(config)# show nameif
nameif ethernet0 outside security0
nameif ethernet1 test security90
```

Step 16 Try to use the interface command to enable Ethernet 1 for 10-Mbps
Ethernet full-duplex communication:

```
pixfirewall(config)# interface e1 10full
Command authorization failed
```

Step 17 Reconfigure the inside interface to its original settings:

```
pixfirewall(config)# nameif e1 inside sec100
```

Step 18 Log out of the user10 account:

```
pixfirewall(config)# logout


Logoff
Type help or '?' for a list of available commands.
pixfirewall>
```

Step 19 Log in to user admin's account. When prompted for a username, enter
admin. When prompted for a password, enter **adminpass**:

```
pixfirewall>login
Username: admin
Password: adminpass
pixfirewall#
```

Step 20 Enter configuration mode:

```
pixfirewall# config t
pixfirewall(config)#
```

Step 21 Clear your AAA configuration:

```
pixfirewall(config)# clear aaa
```

Step 22 Save your configuration:

```
pixfirewall(config)# write mem
Building configuration...
Cryptochecksum: a2d046eb daa27d65 f4a7a65f cdb3b13d
[OK]
```

Task 7—Perform a Password Recovery

To perform a password recovery for the PIX Firewall, complete the following steps:

Step 1 Open and minimize the TFTP server on Host 1.

Step 2 Clear the translation table:

```
pixfirewall(config)# clear xlate
```

Step 3 Create an enable password for entering into privileged mode:

```
pixfirewall(config)# enable password badpassword
```

Step 4 Save your configuration:

```
pixfirewall(config)# write memory
Building configuration...
Cryptochecksum: e18c684e d86c9171 9f63acf0 f64a8b43
[OK]
```

Step 5 Log out of the admin account:

```
pixfirewall(config)# logout


Logoff
Type help or '?' for a list of available commands.
pixfirewall>
```

Step 6 Attempt to enter privileged mode with the old password, **prmode15**:

```
pixfirewall> enable
Password: prmode15
Invalid password:
```

Step 7 Enter privileged mode with the new password, **badpassword**:

```
Password: badpassword
pixfirewall#
```

Step 8 Reboot your PIX Firewall and interrupt the boot process to enter monitor mode. To do so, press the **Escape** key or send a break character:

```
pixfirewall# reload
```

Step 9 Specify the PIX Firewall interface to be used for TFTP:

```
monitor> int 1
```

Step 10 Specify the PIX Firewall interface's IP address:

```
monitor> address 10.0.1.1
```

Step 11 Verify connectivity to the TFTP server:

```
monitor> ping 10.0.1.11
```

Step 12 Name the server:

```
monitor> server 10.0.1.11
```

Step 13 Name the image filename:

```
monitor> file np63.bin
```

Step 14 Start the TFTP process:

```
monitor> tftp
tftp
np63.bin@10.0.1.11....................................................
.....
...............................................................
..........
........
Received 92160 bytes

Cisco Secure PIX Firewall password tool (3.0) #0: Thu Jul 17 08:01:09
PDT 2003
System Flash=E28F128J3 @ 0xfff00000
BIOS Flash=am29f400b @ 0xd8000
```

Step 15 When prompted, press **y** to erase the password:

```
Do you wish to erase the passwords? [yn] y
The following lines will be removed from the configuration:
        enable password GlFe5rCOwv2JUi5H level 5 encrypted
        enable password .7P6WvOReYzHKnus level 10 encrypted
        enable password tgGMO76/Nf26X5Lv encrypted
        passwd w.UT.4mPsVA418Ij encrypted

Do you want to remove the commands listed above from the configuration?
[yn]
Please enter a y or n.
```

Step 16 When prompted to remove the commands listed from the configuration,
press **y**:

```
Do you want to remove the commands listed above from the configuration?
[yn] y
Passwords and aaa commands have been erased.
```

The system automatically erases the passwords and starts rebooting.

Step 17 Verify that the password **badpassword** has been erased by entering
privileged mode on your PIX Firewall:

```
pix> enable
password: <Enter>
pixfirewall#
```

Task 8—Upgrade the PIX Firewall Software Image

To load the PIX Firewall 515 image using TFTP, complete the following steps:

Step 1   Use the **copy tftp flash** command to load the image file pix633.bin:

```
pixfirewall# copy tftp://10.0.1.11/pix633.bin flash:image
```

Step 2   After the PIX Firewall has received the image from the TFTP server and you see the message "Image installed," reload the PIX Firewall. When prompted to confirm, press **Enter**:

```
pixfirewall# reload
Proceed with reload? [confirm] <Enter>
```

Step 3   Enter the **show version** command to verify that you have loaded PIX Firewall Software Version 6.3(3):

```
pixfirewall> show version
Cisco PIX Firewall Version 6.3(3)
Cisco PIX Device Manager Version 3.0(1)

Compiled on Wed 13-Aug-03 13:55 by morlee
Pixfirewall up 4 mins 12 secs

Hardware:   PIX-515, 64 MB RAM, CPU Pentium 200 MHz
Flash E28F128J3 @ 0x300, 16MB
BIOS Flash E28F400B5T @ 0xfffd8000, 32KB

0: ethernet0: address is 0003.e300.486a, irq 10
1: ethernet1: address is 0003.e300.486b, irq 7

Licensed Features:
Failover:          Disabled
VPN-DES:           Enabled
VPN-3DES-AES:      Enabled
Maximum Interfaces: 6
Cut-through Proxy: Enabled
Guards:            Enabled
URL-filtering:     Enabled
Inside Hosts:      Unlimited
Throughput:        Unlimited
IKE peers:         Unlimited

This PIX has an Unrestricted (UR) license.

Serial Number: 480430946 (0x1ca2cb62)
Running Activation Key: 0xf4e352a3 0xef857686 0x468be692 0xbd984b0b
Configuration last modified by enable_15 at 20:41:52.372 UTC Sun Oct 5
2003
```

On completion of this chapter, you will be able to perform the following tasks:

- Define key features and concepts of the Management Center for Firewalls (Firewall MC).
- Install Firewall MC.
- Import devices for management.
- Manage devices and groups.
- Configure PIX Firewall settings using Firewall MC.
- Manage activities and jobs.
- Administer the Firewall MC server.
- Manage multiple PIX Firewalls with Firewall MC.

CHAPTER 19

PIX Firewall Management in Enterprise Networks

As discussed in earlier chapters, the availability of PIX Firewalls in several different models addresses the unique requirements of various customers and market segments. The models range from telecommuter and small office/home office (SOHO) installations all the way up to the largest enterprise and service provider networks. Although you can use the PIX Firewall to secure small and large networks alike, how you manage them in these environments can differ significantly.

This chapter provides an overview of the Firewall MC. Firewall MC is the Cisco solution for managing PIX Firewalls in enterprise and service provider implementations. Firewall MC provides unique features that are designed to make the task of configuring and managing a large number of PIX Firewalls in enterprise networks easier.

Introduction to Firewall MC

The Firewall MC provides a web-based interface for configuring and managing multiple PIX Firewalls. It provides a similar look and feel to the PIX Device Manager (PDM) but supplies the additional features and capabilities necessary to manage multiple devices instead of a single firewall.

Firewall MC centralizes and accelerates the deployment and management of multiple PIX Firewalls. It enables you to configure new PIX Firewalls or import existing firewalls to be managed by the Firewall MC and provides the following features:

- Support for up to 1000 PIX Firewalls
- Web-based interface for configuring and managing multiple PIX Firewalls
- Configuration hierarchy and user interface to facilitate the configuration of settings, rules, and building blocks applied to groups, subgroups, and devices
- Support for PIX Firewall Operating Systems 6.0 and above
- Ability to import configurations from existing PIX Firewalls
- Ability to support dynamically addressed PIX Firewalls
- Secure Sockets Layer (SSL) protocol support to ensure secure, remote connectivity between communicating browsers and servers and between communicating servers and devices
- Workflow and audit trail

NOTE   This chapter introduces you to the Firewall MC and provides a broad overview of its features, basic configuration, and reporting tasks. However, you should refer to documentation for Firewall MC available on Cisco.com for comprehensive instructions and more up-to-date information.

Key Features and Concepts

Understanding these key concepts helps you maximize Firewall MC functionality:

- **Configuration hierarchy**—The Firewall MC provides a way to group PIX Firewalls that have similar attributes, such as common rules and settings:

  - The Global group contains all groups, subgroups, and devices.

  - Groups contain one or more subgroups or devices.

  - Devices are individual device units that can be listed only once in the configuration hierarchy.

  - A device cannot be a member of more than one group.

- **Configuration elements**—The Firewall MC allows you to configure four types of elements:

  - **Settings**—Configuration elements that control individual features of a PIX Firewall, such as interface configuration.

NOTE   When you configure a PIX Firewall with settings that differ from the group's settings, you need to deselect the **Inherit settings** check box on the configuration page for each property that you want to change. If you want to enforce all PIX Firewalls within a group to inherit settings from the parent group, select the **Enforce/Mandate settings for children** check box.

  - **Access Rules**—Recognized in the form of an ordered list, which is represented in the Firewall MC as a table:

    - **Mandatory**—Rules that apply to an enclosing group and are ordered down to a device. Mandatory rules cannot be overridden.

    - **Default**—Rules that apply to all devices in a group but can be overridden.

  - **Translation rules**—Allow you to view the address translation rules applied to the network.

  - **Building blocks**—Allow you to associate a name with one or more values— for example, to name a subnet in the network. You can use building block names in place of corresponding data values in settings and rules.

- **Workflow process**—The Firewall MC allows you to separate responsibilities for defining, implementing, and deploying firewall configurations:
  - **Defining an activity**—A collection of policy changes typically made for a single purpose.
  - **Defining a job**—A set of configuration files to be deployed to devices, configuration files, or an Auto Update Server (AUS). After you define a job, you can submit it for approval.
  - **Deploying a job**—After a job is approved, the final stage is to deploy the job. This step downloads configuration files to specified devices on your network, saves them as files, or sends them to an AUS.

Supported Devices

Firewall MC 1.2.1 supports PIX Firewalls with operating systems running Version 6.0 and higher and the Firewall Services Module (FWSM) with Software Version 1.1.1 or higher.

The Firewall MC supports only the following Firewall models:

- PIX Firewall 501
- PIX Firewall 506
- PIX Firewall 506E
- PIX Firewall 515
- PIX Firewall 515E
- PIX Firewall 525
- PIX Firewall 535
- FWSM

NOTE   Firewall MC 1.2.1 fully supports most but not all commands in the PIX Firewall Software Versions 6.1, 6.2, and 6.3. Refer to Cisco.com for information on the latest version of Firewall MC, supported devices, supported software versions, and a complete list of supported commands.

Installation

Firewall MC is one of the components of the Cisco VPN Security Management Solution (VMS). Just as for all other VMS components, CiscoWorks Common Services is required for the Firewall MC. CiscoWorks Common Services provides the CiscoWorks server-based components, software libraries, and software packages developed for the Firewall MC.

NOTE   For more information on VMS, see the *Quick Start Guide for VPN Security Management Solution* or *Installing VMS Common Services on Windows 2000* on Cisco.com.

Installation Requirements

Before you begin, verify that the server on which you plan to install the Firewall MC 1.2.1 meets the CiscoWorks Common Services 2.2 requirements listed in Table 19-1.

NOTE   Firewall MC versions up to and including 1.1.2 require CiscoWorks Common Services 1.0. Firewall MC 1.1.3, 1.2, and 1.2.1 require CiscoWorks Common Services 2.2 to operate.

Table 19-1   *Installation Requirements for Firewall MC 1.2.1/CiscoWorks Common Services 2.2 Server*

Component	Minimum Requirements
Hardware	IBM PC-compatible computer with a CD-ROM drive 10BASE-T or faster network connection Color monitor with video card capable of 256 color or more
Processor	1 GHz or faster Pentium processor
Memory	1 GB of RAM
Disk drive space	9 GB of free hard disk space New Technology File System (NTFS) 2 GB of virtual memory
Software	Windows 2000 Server or Professional with Service Pack (SP) 2, 3, or 4 Open Database Connectivity (ODBC) Driver Manager 3.510 or later

---

NOTE   You should not install Firewall MC on domain controllers or servers used for Terminal Services in Application mode.

Table 19-2 lists the client system requirements for accessing the Firewall MC.

Table 19-2   *System Requirements for Firewall MC Client Access*

Component	Minimum Requirements
Hardware	IBM PC-compatible computer with 300 MHz or faster Pentium processor
Software	One of the following: • Windows 98 • Windows 2000 Professional or Server with SP2 or later • Windows XP Professional
Memory	256 MB of RAM
Disk drive space	400 MB virtual memory (Windows)
Browser	Microsoft Internet Explorer 6.0 (Version 6.0.2600.0000) or 6.0 with SP1 (Version 6.0.2800.1106) and Java Virtual Machine (JVM) 5.00.3186 or later

NOTE   Several JVM-related security vulnerabilities have been identified and corrected in subsequent versions. You should check for the latest available version of the JVM that includes fixes for known security vulnerabilities.

NOTE   Firewall MC 1.2.1 provides support for Netscape Navigator 7.0.2 and 7.1 for Windows and Netscape Navigator 7.0.2 for Solaris. However, Netscape Navigator operation requires support for Java Plug-In Version 1.4.1_02 or higher in CiscoWorks Common Services 2.2, which was added in SP2 for Common Services. Check Cisco.com for availability of the patch and installation instructions.

Installation Process

Assuming the CiscoWorks Common Services has been installed, complete the following steps to install the Firewall MC:

Step 1   Launch the installation of the Firewall MC. The Extracting Files window displays, and then the Welcome Window displays.

Step 2   Click **Next** to view the Software License Agreement window.

Step 3   If you agree to the Software License Agreement, click **Yes** to process. The System Requirements window shown in Figure 19-1 displays. If you click **No**, the installation process stops.

Figure 19-1 *Firewall MC System Requirements Window*

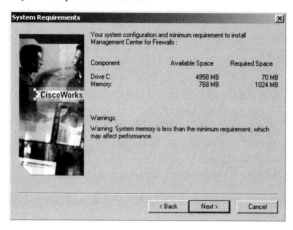

> **Step 4** Click **Next**. The Port Configuration window shown in Figure 19-2 displays.

Figure 19-2 *Firewall MC Port Configuration Window*

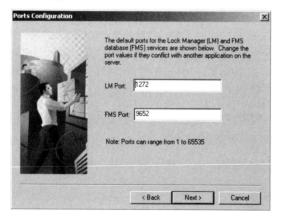

> **Step 5** If necessary, configure new port values for Lock Manager (LM) and the Firewall Management System (FMS) database. Otherwise, use default port numbers 1272 for LM and 9652 for FMS and click **Next**. The Verification window shown in Figure 19-3 displays.

Figure 19-3 *Firewall MC Installation Verification Window*

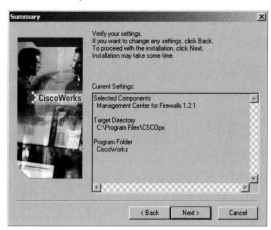

Step 6 Click **Next** to start the installation of the Firewall MC. When setup is complete, the Setup Complete window displays.

Step 7 Click **Finish** to complete the installation.

Getting Started

Before you can manage a PIX Firewall with the Firewall MC, you must configure the PIX Firewall with a minimum configuration. If the PIX Firewall is already operating, you must configure the firewall to allow configuration with a browser and specify what host or network is allowed to initiate an HTTP connection to the PIX Firewall.

If the PIX Firewall is not configured, it must be bootstrapped to use the Firewall MC. Complete the following steps to bootstrap a PIX Firewall:

Step 1 Console into the PIX Firewall and enter the privileged mode.

Step 2 Enter the configuration mode:

```
pixfirewall# configure terminal
```

Step 3 Configure the PIX Firewall's enable password:

```
pixfirewall(config)# enable password password
```

Step 4 Specify the interface network settings:

```
pixfirewall(config)# interface hardware_id hw_speed
```

Step 5 Name the interface where the Firewall MC will connect to the PIX Firewall:

```
pixfirewall(config)# nameif hardware_id if_name security_level
```

Step 6 Assign an IP address to the network interface:

```
pixfirewall(config)# ip address if_name ip_address [netmask]
```

Step 7 Specify a static or default route for the interface:

```
pixfirewall(config)# route if_name ip_address netmask gateway_ip
    [metric]
```

Step 8 Enable the PIX Firewall to have its configuration modified from a browser:

```
pixfirewall(config)# http server enable
```

Step 9 Specify the host or network authorized to initiate an HTTP connection to the PIX Firewall:

```
pixfirewall(config)# http ip_address [netmask] [if_name]
```

Step 10 Store the current configuration in Flash memory:

```
pixfirewall(config)# write memory
```

Step 11 Exit the configuration mode:

```
pixfirewall(config)# exit
```

NOTE   You can also use the initial interactive prompts to prepare a PIX Firewall for management with Firewall MC. Interactive prompts are available when accessing a new PIX Firewall for the first time, or you can issue the **write erase** command and reboot the PIX. The **write erase** command erases the entire configuration on the PIX Firewall: Do not use it if you want to maintain current configuration settings.

Example 19-1 shows the commands required to configure a PIX Firewall to use Firewall MC. In this example, the PIX Firewall is configured with an enable password of Cisco123 and configured for management by Firewall MC on its inside interface; its inside interface is assigned an address of 10.0.1.2 and subnet mask of 255.255.255.0. A Firewall MC server on the 10.10.10.0 network can now access and manage the PIX Firewall in Example 19-1.

Example 19-1 *Firewall MC Bootstrap Commands*

```
pixfirewall(config)# enable password Cisco123
pixfirewall(config)# interface ethernet1 100full
pixfirewall(config)# nameif ethernet1 inside security100
pixfirewall(config)# ip address inside 10.0.1.2 255.255.255.0
pixfirewall(config)# route inside 10.0.0.0 255.0.0.0 10.0.1.1
pixfirewall(config)# http server enable
pixfirewall(config)# http 10.10.10.0 255.255.255.0
pixfirewall(config)# write memory
pixfirewall(config)# exit
```

If the PIX Firewall is already configured and in production, you simply need to enable Firewall MC access by using the **http server enable** and **http** commands as specified in Steps 8 and 9.

When you are importing an existing PIX Firewall, you must be aware that the Firewall MC does not support the use of conduits or outbound lists to define network security policies. A conversion tool is provided with Firewall MC for the purpose of converting conduits and outbound lists to access control list (ACL) commands that are accepted by the Firewall MC. This conversion tool uses a command-line interface (CLI) to read the configuration file named on the command line and writes the converted configuration to the standard output accepted by Firewall MC.

NOTE   You can also find the latest version of the conduit and outbound list conversion tool on Cisco.com.

Complete the following steps to convert a PIX Firewall configuration:

Step 1   Capture the PIX Firewall configuration to a text file with an extension of .cfg. For example, pixconfig.cfg is an acceptable form.

NOTE   You can use the **write net** command to capture a copy of your current configuration file to a Trivial File Transfer Protocol (TFTP) server.

Step 2   Place the text file into the directory C:\Program Files\CSCOpx\MDC\ bin\pix\ (where C:\Program Files\CSCOpx is the default installation directory for CiscoWorks).

Step 3   Open a command prompt window and change directories to C:\Program Files\CSCOpx\MDC\bin\pix\:

```
C:\>cd Program Files\CSCOpx\MDC\bin\pix\
```

Step 4   Enter the following command, substituting the filenames shown with actual filenames:

```
C:\Program Files\CSCOpx\MDC\bin\pix>conv pixconfig.cfg >
pixconfignew.cfg
```

Step 5   Wait for the conversion process to finish. Now you can import or use the converted text file to reconfigure the PIX Firewall for a successful importation into the Firewall MC. The converted text file will reside within the same directory with the conversion tool.

You can use this new configuration file to prepare your PIX Firewall for Firewall MC management. You should review this file before applying it to a production firewall.

NOTE   The conduit and outbound list conversion tool is useful for converting basic PIX Firewall configurations. However, it is not compatible with all PIX Firewall commands and might be unable to properly convert complex configurations.

CiscoWorks

To access the Firewall MC, you must first log in to CiscoWorks as follows:

Step 1   Open a browser and point your browser to the IP address of the CiscoWorks machine with a port number of 1741. If the CiscoWorks server is local, you can type the following address into the browser:

```
http://127.0.0.1:1741 <enter>
```

Step 2   On the login screen shown in Figure 19-4, use the default username and password of **admin** and **admin** to log in to CiscoWorks for the first time.

Figure 19-4   *CiscoWorks Login Screen*

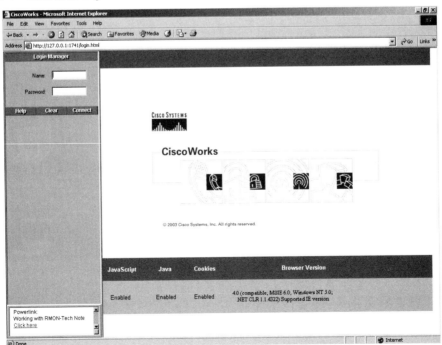

After your username and password pair is authenticated, your authorization is based on the privileges that you have. Your role is a collection of privileges that dictate the type of system access you have.

You can use authorization roles to delegate responsibilities to users who log in to the Firewall MC. For example, you can specify who can generate configurations or who can approve configurations. The following types of user authorization roles are available if you use CiscoWorks as your AAA provider:

- **Help Desk**—Read-only for the entire system
- **Approver**—Can review policy change and accept or reject changes
- **Network Operator**—Can create and submit jobs
- **Network Administrator**—Can perform administrative tasks on the Firewall MC
- **System Administrator**—Can perform all tasks on the Firewall MC

Users can be assigned multiple authorization roles.

CiscoWorks User Management

Before logging in to the Firewall MC, you might want to add some users based on how your organization's security policy is set up. Complete the following steps to add users based on how CiscoWorks user authorization roles work:

Step 1 Log in to the CiscoWorks 2000 Server Desktop. The CiscoWorks 2000 Server Desktop displays.

Step 2 Select **Server Configuration > Setup > Security > Add Users**. The Add User page shown in Figure 19-5 displays.

Step 3 Complete the following substeps to add a user to the CiscoWorks database:

   (1) Enter the user's name in the User Name field.

   (2) Enter the password for the user in the Local Password field.

   (3) Re-enter the password in the Confirm Password field.

   (4) (Optional) Enter the user's e-mail address in the E-mail field.

   (5) (Optional) Enter the user's CCO login name in the Cisco Connection Online (CCO) Login field, if the user has one.

   (6) (Optional) Enter the password that is associated with the CCO login in the CCO Password field. Confirm this password by entering it in the Confirm Password field.

(7) (Optional) Enter the username for the proxy server login in the Proxy Login field, if a proxy server exists on the network.

(8) (Optional) Enter the password associated with the proxy server login in the Proxy Password field. Confirm this password by entering it in the Confirm Password field.

(9) (Optional) Locate the Roles section on the lower-left side of the Add User page. Use the check boxes to select the appropriate roles the user will fulfill.

Step 4 Click **Add** to complete the addition of the user to the CiscoWorks database. The Add User page refreshes to indicate that the change was received.

With the appropriate users created, you are now ready to launch Firewall MC.

Figure 19-5 *CiscoWorks Add User Screen*

Navigating the Firewall MC

To launch Firewall MC, you must first log into the CiscoWorks server. The following steps walk you through the process of logging into CiscoWorks and accessing the Firewall MC console:

Step 1 Log in to the CiscoWorks server where the Firewall MC has been installed.

Step 2 Select **VPN/Security Management Solution > Management Center**. After the Management Center folder has expanded, you see the icon for the Firewalls.

Step 3 Click the **Firewalls** icon to launch the Firewall MC. A Security Alert window displays, as shown in Figure 19-6.

Figure 19-6 *Firewall MC Security Alert Window*

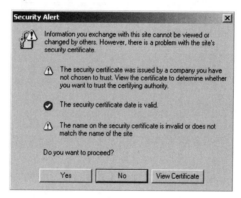

Step 4 Click **Yes** to accept the security certificate. The Firewall MC opens in another window.

Step 5 Minimize CiscoWorks in the background to avoid confusion when working with the Firewall MC.

Figure 19-7 shows the Firewall MC graphical user interface (GUI) and highlights the major elements on this page. By learning the elements contained in the Firewall MC interface, you will be able to carry out the basic user task flow and navigate the Firewall MC with ease.

Figure 19-7 *Firewall MC Interface*

The elements of the Firewall MC are as follow:

- **Path bar**—Provides a context for the displayed page. Shows tab, option, and then current page.

- **TOC**—Table of contents. Displays available suboptions.

- **Options bar**—Displays the options available for the tab.

- **Tabs**—Provides access to product functionality. By clicking a tab, you can access its options:

  - **Devices**. Set up the Firewall MC for operation; import devices and arrange them into groups.

  - **Configuration**. Enter PIX Firewall configuration information by identifying settings, rules, and building blocks.

  - **Workflow**. Manage activities and jobs.

  - **Reports**. Display a report listing activity information.

  - **Admin**. Perform administrative tasks.

- **Activity bar**—Displays activity action icons that change, depending on what state the activity is in. Viewed from Devices and Configuration tabs only. Options are:

  - **Add New Activity**. Creates a new activity.

  - **Open**. Opens an existing activity.

- **Submit Activity**. Submits an activity for approval.

- **Approve Activity**. Approves the activity shown on the activity bar. Only visible when the activity has been submitted for approval.

- **Reject Activity**. Rejects the activity shown on the activity bar. Only visible when the activity has been submitted for approval.

- **Discard Activity**. Discards the activity shown by the activity bar. Only visible when the activity is being edited before its submittal.

- **View Activity Detail**. Displays detailed information about the activity shown by the activity bar.

- **Close**. Closes the activity shown by the activity bar.

- **Tools**—Contains the following buttons:

  - **Logout**. Logs you out of CiscoWorks 2000.

  - **Help**. Opens a new window that displays context-sensitive help for the displayed page. The window also contains buttons that you use to go to the overall help contents, index, and search tool.

  - **About**. Displays the version of the application.

- **Instructions**—Provides a brief overview of how to use the page.

- **Page**—Displays the area in which you perform application tasks.

- **Object bar**—Displays the object selected in the object selector.

- **Object selector**—Enables you to select groups and devices.

Now that you are familiar with the basic elements of the Firewall MC interface, you can begin management tasks within Firewall MC. Various configuration processes and the task flow are covered in detail in the following section.

Firewall MC Task Flow

The Firewall MC enables you to navigate to various areas of the application as appropriate to your needs and the task at hand. For first-time users, it is useful to understand the basic flow for performing a common task from beginning to end. The basic user task flow is as follows:

- **Create new activity**—Creating an activity prepares a proposal to create or change PIX Firewall configurations. This proposal must be approved before configurations can be deployed to devices.

- **Manage devices and groups**

  - **Create device groups**. This task is an optional task that allows you to define groups for grouping PIX Firewalls during the importation process or after the importation process.

— **Import devices**. In the Firewall MC, the expression "importing a device" can be defined as either creating a device or importing the PIX Firewall configuration.

- **Configure settings, rules, and building blocks**

  — **Configure building blocks**. With this task, you can optimize your configuration through the logical grouping of hosts, protocols, or services.

  — **Configure settings**. You can configure various options for PIX Firewalls, such as routing and advanced security.

  — **Configure access and translation rules**. With this task, you configure rules for access control and the translation of addresses.

- **Manage activities and jobs**

  — **Generate and view the configuration**. When you generate and view the configuration before submission, you can check for errors in the configuration. If errors are encountered, you can go back and correct them on an as-needed basis.

  — **Submit the activity for approval**. This task is an optional task that places an extra safeguard in the approval process of an activity.

  — **Create a job**—With this task, you define a job that represents a set of configuration files to be deployed.

  — **Submit the job for approval**. This task is an optional task that places an extra safeguard in the approval process of an activity.

  — **Deploy the job**. With this task, you deploy configuration files to devices.

NOTE   If the approval process is enabled, all activities must be approved before you can propose configuration changes for deployment. If the approval process is *disabled*, the submit and approve process is a single step and the activity is approved automatically when it is submitted. The approval process for activities and jobs is disabled by default. Select **Admin > Workflow Setup** to enable the approval process.

- **Generate reports**—Reporting tools in Firewall MC allow you to display information about specific activities in Firewall MC and maintain a history of configuration activities and changes.

Each of the tasks in the previous list is covered in detail in the following subsections.

Task 1—Create a New Activity

The first step in the basic user task flow is to create an activity. By creating an activity, you are able to make changes to devices or groups. Without creating an activity, you are not able to make changes to devices or groups. Complete the following steps to create a new activity:

Step 1   Select the **Devices** tab. The Devices management page shown in Figure 19-8 displays.

Figure 19-8   *Firewall MC Devices Management Page*

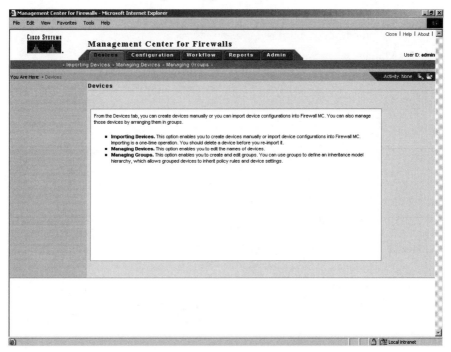

Step 2   Select the **Add New Activity** icon. A Creating New Activity window displays, as shown in Figure 19-9.

NOTE   If the approval process is *disabled*, you do not see the Add New Activity button referred to in Step 2. The approval process for activities and jobs is disabled by default.

Figure 19-9 *Creating New Activity Screen*

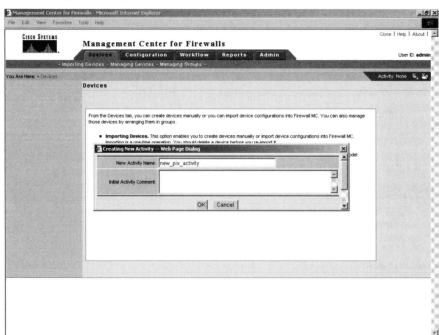

Step 3 Enter an activity name in the New Activity Name field. Enter an optional comment in the Initial Activity Comment field.

Step 4 Click **OK**. The Creating New Activity window disappears and the Devices page refreshes to indicate that a new activity has been created. This new activity is listed on the activity bar, located on the upper-right side of the page.

NOTE Job management is covered later within this chapter. The management of jobs and activities is associated with the workflow that takes place within the Firewall MC.

When you create a new activity, you are preparing a proposal to create or change PIX Firewall configurations. An *activity* is a task that is accomplished by one or more people in succession. For example, a network administrator sets configuration parameters for a PIX Firewall, and a system administrator approves the configuration settings. This separation of responsibilities helps maintain the integrity of deployed device configurations.

When you open or create an activity, the system must acquire a lock, which can happen only if no other activity holds a lock on the same groups or devices. Other users are locked out until the activity is approved and committed or undone. This process guarantees that when you change elements associated with a global group, no other user can read or write changes to the group that you are editing.

You can access the Activity Management Interface shown in Figure 19-10 by choosing **Workflow > Activity Management**.

Figure 19-10 *Activity Management Interface Elements*

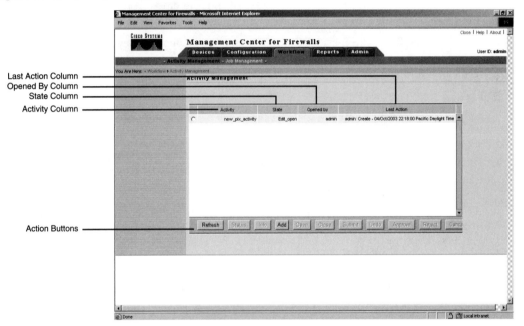

The Activity Management Interface is comprised of the following elements:

- **Activity column**—Lists the user-defined activity name.
- **State column**—Lists the state of the activity:
    - **Edit**. The activity is unlocked, but it cannot be configured within the context of another activity.
    - **Edit_Open**. The activity is opened from the Edit state, or a new activity has been created that automatically results in an Edit_Open state. You can make configuration changes to the devices and groups selected.
    - **Submitted**. The activity is submitted for review from the Edit_Open state.

- **Submitted_Open**. The activity is opened for review from the Submitted state. The devices and groups selected for the activity are still locked to other activities. You can approve or reject the activity while it is in the Submitted_Open state.

- **Approved**. The activity was approved by a person with approval authority from the Submitted_Open state.

- **Rejected**. The activity was rejected by a person with approval authority from the Submitted_Open state.

- **Generate_Open**. The activity is being submitted. You can cancel the activity from the Generate_Open state.

- **ReverseGenerate_Open**. The activity is importing new devices. You can cancel the activity from the ReverseGenerate_Open state.

- **Discarded**. The activity is discarded and further changes to the activity are disallowed.

- **Opened By column**—Lists the username of the person who opened last opened the activity.

- **Last Action column**—Lists the last action, date, and timestamp that occurred for the activity.

- **Activity action buttons**

  - **Refresh**. Manually refreshes the table. The table refreshes automatically every 60 seconds.

  - **Status**. Opens a popup window showing the detailed status of a selected activity.

  - **Add**. Adds a new activity to the Activity Management table.

  - **Open**. When activity is in Edit or Rejected state, opens the activity. Changes the activity state to Edit_Open. When the activity is in Submitted state, opens the activity. Changes the activity state to Submitted_Open.

  - **Close**. Closes the activity. Changes the activity state to Edit.

  - **Submit**. Visible when the formal approval process is enabled. Notifies a person with approval authority that an activity is ready for review. Changes the activity state to Submitted.

  - **Undo**. Discards the activity. Changes the activity state to Discarded.

  - **Approve**. When the formal approval process is *disabled*, the person who created the activity uses this button. When the formal approval process is *enabled*, the person with approval authority uses this button to approve an activity. Changes the activity state to Approved.

— **Reject**. Visible when the formal approval process is enabled. Used by the person with approval authority to reject the activity. Changes the activity state to Rejected.

— **Cancel**. Cancels the active import/generate operations associated with a selected table row.

NOTE   Choose **Admin > Workflow Setup** to enable the formal approval process for activities and jobs. After the Workflow Setup page displays, you can select the **Require Activity Approval** check box or the **Require Job Approval** check box.

If the approval process is *disabled*, the submit and approval process is a single step and the activity is approved automatically when it is submitted. If the approval process is *enabled*, you must submit an activity to someone in your organization for review and approval. When you submit an activity for review, it must be in the Edit or Edit_Open state. After you submit an activity for approval, a person with approval authority reviews the changes.

If the changes are approved, they are *committed*. The activity is completed, and no further changes can be made. Groups and devices affected by the activity are unlocked. If the changes are rejected, you can

- Re-enter the activity and fix any problems identified by a person with approval authority.

- Discard all changes by performing an *undo*. In this instance, the undo feature undoes all changes made for an activity, not just the last change in a sequence.

There are two ways to submit an activity:

- Using the activity bar located on the Device or Configure tabs

- Using the Workflow > Activity Management page

Complete the following steps to submit an activity:

Step 1   Choose **Workflow > Activity Management**. The Activity Management page shown in Figure 19-10 displays.

Step 2   Choose an activity to submit by selecting the radio button that corresponds to the activity.

Step 3   Click **Submit**. The Submitting Activity window shown in Figure 19-11 displays.

Figure 19-11 *Submitting Activity Screen*

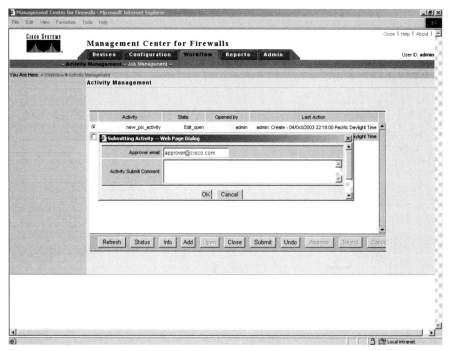

Step 4 Enter an e-mail for the person who is in charge of activity approval in the Approver e-mail field.

Step 5 Enter a comment in the Activity Submit Comment field.

Step 6 Click **OK**. The Review Device Generation List(new) page displays.

Step 7 Review the devices for which configurations will be generated.

Step 8 Click **Next**. The Summary page displays.

Step 9 Verify that the information listed is correct and click **Finish**. A window displays showing the progress of generating the device configuration.

Step 10 Close the window after the status is completed. The Activity State should now read Submitted.

After you submit the activity, it is ready to be turned into a job and deployed.

Task 2—Create Device Groups

The Managing Groups feature is an optional task that allows you to add new groups to the system, modify existing groups, or delete existing groups. You access this feature by selecting **Devices > Managing Groups**.

When you set up a new group, Cisco recommends that you use a name and description that can easily be identified. For example, you can define and identify groups by department and region within your company or any other grouping based on a commonality. A subgroup cannot have the same name as the enclosing group, and no two subgroups within an enclosing group can have the same name.

Complete the following steps to add a group:

Step 1   Select or create an activity.

Step 2   Select **Devices > Managing Groups**. The Managing Groups page displays.

Step 3   Select the Global group and then click **Add**. The Define Group Information page displays, as illustrated by Figure 19-12.

Figure 19-12   *Define Group Information Page*

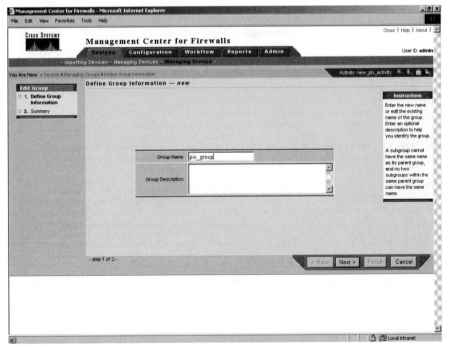

<table>
<tr><td>**NOTE**</td><td>The Global group is the default group that is installed with the Firewall MC. If other groups have been defined before, you receive the option to create a subgroup within each container.</td></tr>
</table>

Step 4   Enter a group name in the Group Name field and an optional description in the Group Description field.

Step 5   Click **Next**. The Summary page displays.

Step 6   Verify that the information listed is correct and click **Finish**. The Managing Groups page displays with the new group.

Complete the following steps to edit a group:

Step 1   Select or create an activity.

Step 2   Select **Devices > Managing Groups**. The Managing Groups page displays.

Step 3   Select a group from the list of available groups and click **Edit**.

Step 4   Enter a group name in the Group Name field and an optional description in the Group Description field.

Step 5   Click **Next**. The Summary page displays.

Step 6   Verify that the information listed is correct and click **Finish**. The Managing Groups page displays with the edited group.

Complete the following steps to delete a group:

Step 1   Select or create an activity.

Step 2   Select **Devices > Managing Groups**. The Managing Groups page displays.

Step 3   Select a group from the list of available groups and click **Delete**. A window appears requesting confirmation that you want to delete the target group.

Step 4   Click **Yes**. The Managing Groups page refreshes to remove the deleted group.

With the groups defined, you are now ready to add or import devices into Firewall MC for management.

Task 3—Import and Manage Devices

After creating an activity (and optionally defining groups), you are ready to import a device. The first step for importing a device is to select the group in which you want the device to reside. To select a group, go to **Devices > Importing Devices > Select Target Group**. If you have not specifically defined any groups, you can use only the default global group that Firewall MC provides.

In the Firewall MC, importing a device can be defined as any of the following:

- **Create device**—Allows you to add a single device manually.

- **Import configuration from a device**—Allows you to manually provide device credentials that enable the Firewall MC server to "talk" directly to a device to retrieve configuration information. This option specifies that you want the Firewall MC to connect to and discover current settings on a PIX Firewall.

- **Import configuration file for a device**—Allows you to import configuration information for a single device from a configuration file.

- **Import multiple firewall configurations from a comma-separate values (CSV) file**—Allows the Firewall MC server to "talk" directly to multiple PIX Firewalls specified in a CSV file to retrieve configuration information.

- **Import configuration files for multiple devices**—Allows you to import multiple configuration files from a single directory. Each file contains configuration information for a single device.

Complete the following steps to perform any type of import:

Step 1 Either select an existing activity or create a new one.

Step 2 Choose **Devices > Importing Devices**. The Importing Devices page displays.

Step 3 Click **Import**. The Select Target Group(new) page shown in Figure 19-13 displays.

Step 4 Select a target group and click **Next**. The Select Import Type(new) page displays, as shown in Figure 19-14.

Figure 19-13 *Select Target Group(new) Page*

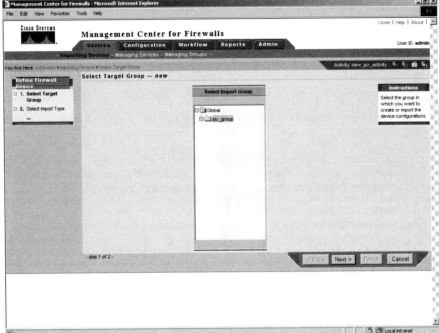

Step 5 Select an import type and click **Next**. From this point forward, each import type requires the definition of different information. The following subsections explain how to complete each import type.

Step 6 Define the PIX Firewall information, based on the type of import chosen.

Step 7 Verify the summary information.

Step 8 Verify the status of the import task. The Import Status window refreshes automatically every 60 seconds; however, you can click **Refresh** to update the import status manually. If the import is successful, the message "COMPLETED" displays in the Status column. If the import is unsuccessful, an error message displays.

NOTE You can import from a device only once. If you need to re-import a PIX Firewall's configuration information, you must delete and then re-import it.

Figure 19-14 *Select Import Type(new) Page*

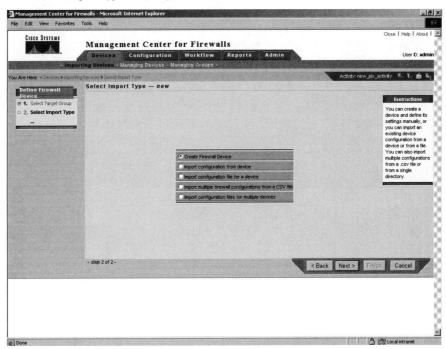

Creating a Device

If you select **Create Firewall Device** from the Select Import Type(new) page and click **Next**, the Define Firewall Device Basic Info(new) page shown in Figure 19-15 displays. Enter the following information into this page:

- **PIX Firewall Name**—The name of the PIX Firewall

- **Contact User Name**—The authentication, authorization, and accounting (AAA) username, if the PIX Firewall uses AAA

- **Contact IP Address**—The IP address that the Firewall MC uses to contact the PIX Firewall

- **Enable Password**—The enable password

Figure 19-15 *Define Firewall Device Basic Info(new) Page*

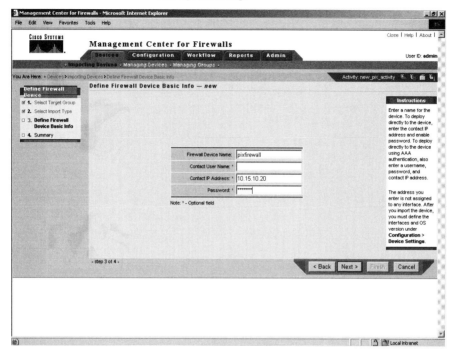

After you supply the required information, click **Next**, verify the information on the Summary page, and click **Finish**. The Importing Devices page displays with the newly created PIX Firewall with a status of STATUS_COMPLETED.

Importing Configuration from a Device

When you create a device, you must define its settings manually after the device is created. If you want to create a device and import the existing device configuration, you must import the device. To import a device, select **Import configuration from device** from the Select Import Type(new) page and click **Next**. The Define Firewall Device Contact Info(new) page shown in Figure 19-16 displays. Enter the following information into this page:

- **Contact User Name**—Optional AAA user name, if the PIX Firewall uses AAA
- **Contact IP Address**—The IP address that the Firewall MC uses to contact the PIX Firewall
- **Enable Password**—The enable password

Figure 19-16 *Define Firewall Device Contact Info(new) Page*

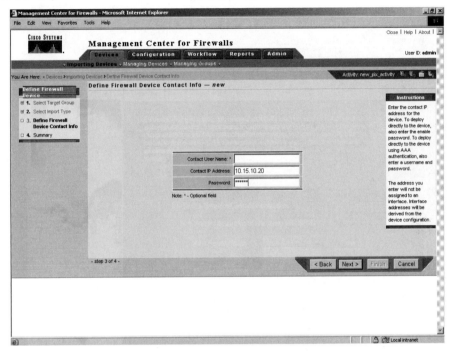

When you supply the required information, click **Next**, verify that the information displayed on the Summary page is correct, and click **Finish**. The Import Status window opens.

After the import status displays in the Status column, you can select a device in the table and click **View Config**. A new window opens with the configuration file displayed.

Close the window after you view the contents, and then close the import status popup window. You are returned to the Importing Devices page, which shows the imported device information.

Importing Configuration File for a Device

If you select **Import configuration file for a device** from the Select Import Type(new) page and click **Next**, the Enter Config File(new) page shown in Figure 19-17 displays. In the Config File Name field, enter the location of the configuration file either manually or by using the Browse button. You can optionally specify Contact User Name (if using AAA), Contact IP Address, and Password to allow direct deployment of the imported configuration file to a PIX Firewall. After you click **Next**, verify the information displayed on the Summary page, and click **Finish.** The Import Status window displays.

Figure 19-17 *Enter Config File(new) Page*

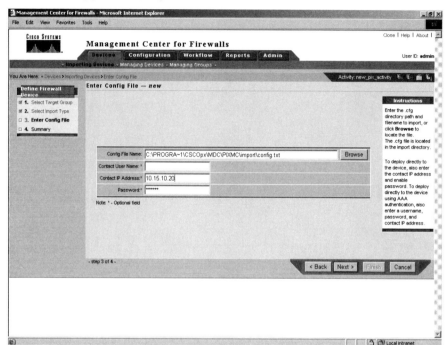

NOTE	When you import configuration files for devices, make sure the imported file references a software version at the beginning of the file. If version information is not included, the import will fail. The version syntax information can be represented as either of the following: `:! PIX Version 6.n(n)` (a comment immediately following an exclamation point) or `PIX Version 6.n(n)`

Importing Multiple Configurations from a CSV File

If you select **Import multiple firewall configurations from a CSV file** from the Select Import Type(new) page and click **Next**, the Enter CSV File(new) page shown in Figure 19-18 displays. In the CSV Filename field, enter the location of the CSV file either manually or by using the Browse button. After you click **Next**, verify the information displayed on the Summary page, and click **Finish**. The Import Status window displays.

Figure 19-18 *Enter CSV File(new) Page*

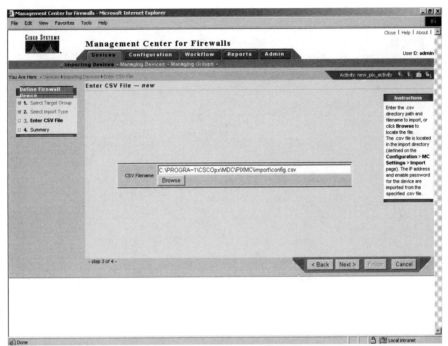

Importing Configuration Files for Multiple Devices

If you select **Import configuration files for multiple devices** from the Select Import Type(new) page and click **Next**, the Enter Config File Directory(new) page shown in Figure 19-19 displays. In the Config Directory field, enter the location of the configuration files either manually or using the Browse button. After you click **Next**, verify the information displayed on the Summary page, and click **Finish**. The Importing Devices page displays with the newly created PIX Firewalls with a status of STATUS_COMPLETED.

Figure 19-19 *Enter Config File Directory(new) Page*

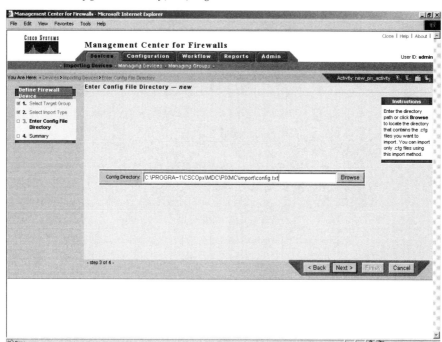

Managing Devices

After you import or create a device as outlined in the previous sections, you might want to rename or delete it later. The Firewall MC allows you to edit the target group and name of a PIX Firewall or delete it from the device inventory.

Complete the following steps to edit a PIX Firewall's name:

Step 1 Choose **Devices > Managing Devices**. The Managing Devices page shown in Figure 19-20 displays.

Figure 19-20 *Managing Devices Page*

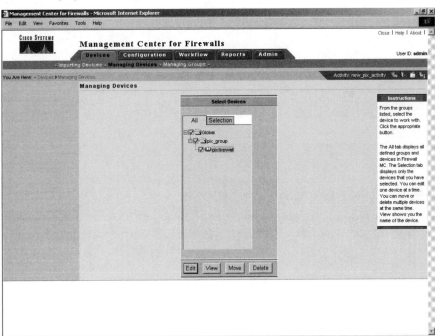

Step 2 Select a PIX Firewall to edit by using the check box located next to the PIX Firewall.

Step 3 Click **Edit**. The Select Target Group page displays.

Step 4 Select the target group and click **Next**. The Edit PIX Firewall Identity page displays.

Step 5 Enter a new name in the PIX Firewall Name field and Click **Next**. The Summary page displays.

Step 6 Verify that the information displayed on the Summary page is correct and click **Finish**. The Managing Devices page displays with the edited PIX Firewall.

Complete the following steps to delete a PIX Firewall from the Firewall MC's device inventory:

Step 1 Choose **Devices > Managing Devices**. Once again, the Managing Devices page shown in Figure 19-20 displays.

Step 2 Select a PIX Firewall to edit by using the check box located next to the PIX Firewall.

Step 3 Click **Delete**. A window displays asking whether you want to delete the selected targets.

Step 4 Click **OK**. The Managing Devices page displays with the selected PIX Firewall removed.

Once you create your activity, create the appropriate groups (optional), and import or create the devices you want to configure and manage, you can move on to the configuration tasks discussed in the next several subsections.

Task 4—Configure Building Blocks

Building blocks allow you to optimize your configuration. You can group objects such as hosts, protocols, or services, allowing you to issue a single command to every item in the group by using the name of the group. You use the Building Blocks feature to associate names that can be used in place of corresponding data values in settings and rules. This facilitates ease of maintenance.

Building blocks consist of the following items:

- Network Objects feature
- Service definitions
- Service groups
- AAA server groups
- Address translation pools

Using building blocks, you identify objects that will be used on your network, which you configure separately. For example, you can identify the servers used for AAA authentication. The protocols used to connect to those servers, however, are configured in Settings. This design facilitates network updates because building blocks are defined only once and in one location.

Network Objects

The Network Objects feature allows you to group a set of network addresses represented by IP addresses. This information provides the basic identification information for that network. The Firewall MC uses the name and IP address–netmask pair to resolve references to the network in the source and destination conditions of access rules and in translation rules. The Firewall MC uses the interface value to apply access and translation rules that refer the network to the correct interface.

Complete the following steps to configure a network object:

Step 1   Choose **Configuration > Device Settings**. The Device Settings page displays.

Step 2   Use the activity bar to select an existing activity or create a new activity.

Step 3   Use the Object Selector to select a group or device.

Step 4   Choose **Building Blocks > Network Objects** from the TOC. The Network Objects page displays.

Step 5   Click **Add**. The Enter Definition (new) page shown in Figure 19-21 displays.

Figure 19-21   *Enter Definition (new) Page*

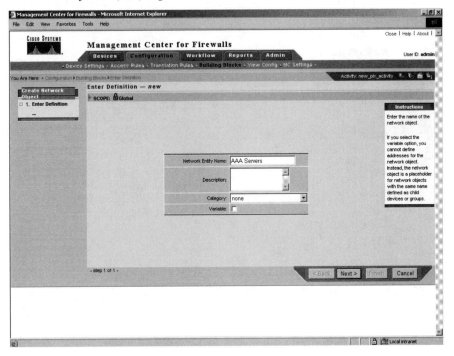

Step 6   Complete the following substeps to enter the settings of a definition:

    (1)   Enter a descriptive name in the Network Entity Name field.

    (2)   Enter a description of the network object in the Description field.

(3) Optionally define a category using the Category field. Each category is assigned a unique background and foreground color that is displayed in the access rules table. The different colors improve the visibility of rules assigned to each network object when you view the rule tables. You can also filter the rule tables based on the category you define in this field.

(4) Select the **Variable** option to create a network object that serves as a placeholder for network objects with the same name defined as child devices or groups. Deselect the **Variable** check box to define addresses for the network object at this level.

Step 7   Click **Next**. The Enter IP(s)(new) page shown in Figure 19-22 displays.

Figure 19-22   *Enter IP(s)(new) Page*

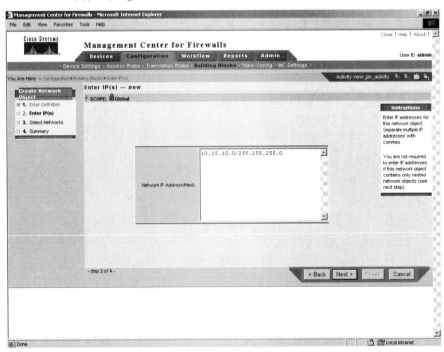

Step 8   Enter the IP address and mask for a host or network in the Network IP Address/Mask field.

Step 9   Click **Next**. The Select Networks(new) page shown in Figure 19-23 displays.

Figure 19-23 *Select Networks(new) Page*

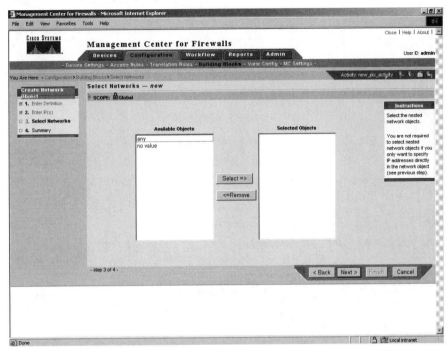

Step 10 To include previously defined network objects in the network object you are creating (nesting network objects), choose an object from the list of Available Objects and click **Select** to move it to Selected Objects.

Step 11 Click **Next**. The Summary page displays.

Step 12 Verify that the information listed is correct and click **Finish**. The Network Objects page displays with the new fragment settings for the interface specified.

To edit an existing network object, select the network object to edit and click the **Edit action** button instead of clicking **Add** in Step 5 and continue with the remaining steps.

To delete a network object, complete the following steps:

Step 1 Select the network object.

Step 2 Click the **Delete action** button.

Step 3 You are asked whether you want to delete the Network Object. Click **OK**.

Service Definitions

The Service Definition feature allows you to create a single access rule that controls access to multiple protocols. Complete the following steps to create a TCP-based service definition:

Step 1 Choose **Configuration > Device Settings**. The Settings page displays.

Step 2 Use the activity bar to select an existing activity or create a new activity.

Step 3 Use the object selector to select a group or device.

Step 4 Choose **Building Blocks > Service Definitions** from the TOC. The Service Definitions page displays, showing existing service definitions.

Step 5 Click **Add**. The Specify Name and Select Transport(new) page shown in Figure 19-24 displays.

Figure 19-24 *Specify Name and Select Transport(new) Page*

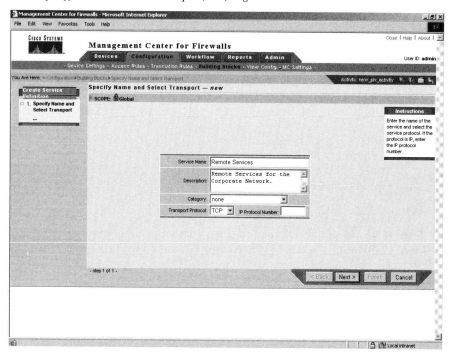

Step 6 Complete the following substeps to specify the name and the mode of transportation settings:

(1) Enter a descriptive name in the Service Name field.

(2) Enter a description in the Description field.

(3) Select a category for this service definition in the Category field.

(4) Choose **ICMP** (Internet Control Message Protocol), **TCP**, **IP**, or **UDP** (User Datagram Protocol) from the Transport Protocol drop-down menu. If you choose IP in the Transport Protocol field, also specify the IP protocol number in the IP Protocol Number field.

Step 7   Skip to Step 11 if you selected IP in the Transport Protocol field in Step 6; otherwise, click **Next**. If you selected TCP or UDP in the Transport Protocol field in Step 6, the Select TCP/UDP Values(new) page shown in Figure 19-25 displays.

Figure 19-25   *Select TCP/UDP Values(new) Page*

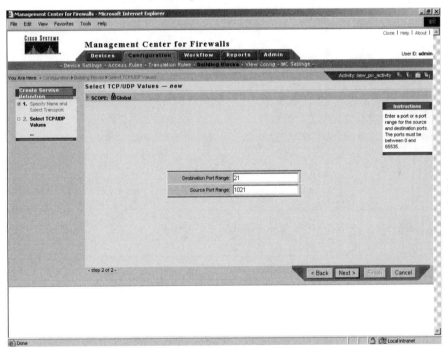

Step 8   For either TCP or UDP, enter the destination port or port range in the Destination Port Range field and the source port or port range in the Source Port Range and go to Step 11.

Step 9   If you selected ICMP in the Transport Protocol field in Step 6, the Select ICMP Values(new) page shown in Figure 19-26 displays.

Figure 19-26 *Select ICMP Values(new) Page*

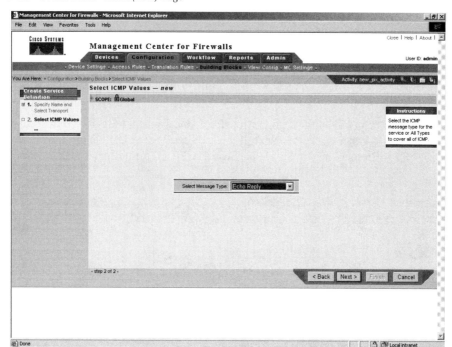

Step 10 Select the appropriate ICMP message type from the Select Message Type drop-down menu.

Step 11 Click **Next**. The Summary page displays.

Step 12 Verify that the information listed is correct and click **Finish**. The Service Definitions page displays the new service definition.

Service Groups

The Service Groups feature allows you to create a single access rule that controls access to multiple services. Complete the following steps to add a Service Group:

Step 1 Choose **Configuration > Device Settings**. The Device Settings page displays.

Step 2 Use the activity bar to select an existing activity or create a new activity.

Step 3 Use the object selector to select a group or device.

Step 4   Choose **Building Blocks > Service Groups** from the TOC. The Service
Groups page displays listing previously defined service groups.

Step 5   Click **Add**. The Add Name and Description(new) page shown in Figure
19-27 displays.

Figure 19-27   *Add Name and Description(new) Page*

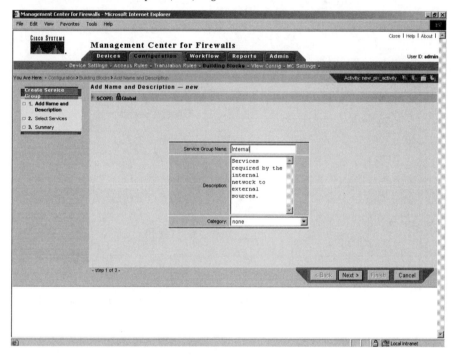

Step 6   Enter a name in the Service Group Name field.

Step 7   Enter a description in the Description field.

Step 8   Optionally select a category.

Step 9   Click **Next**. The Select Services(new) page shown in Figure 19-28
displays.

Figure 19-28 *Select Services(new) Page*

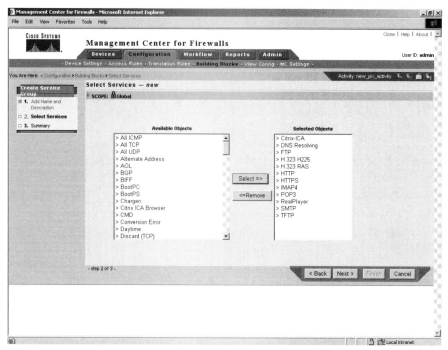

Step 10 Choose the services you want to include in this service group from the list of available objects and click **Select**.

Step 11 Click **Next**. The Summary page displays.

Step 12 Verify that the information listed is correct and click **Finish**. The Service Groups page displays the new Service Group.

To edit an existing service group, select the service group to edit and click the **Edit** button instead of clicking **Add** in Step 5.

To delete a service group, complete the following steps:

Step 1 Select the service group.

Step 2 Click the **Delete action** button.

Step 3 You are asked whether you want to delete the service group. Click **OK**.

AAA Server Group

The Firewall MC lets you define separate groups of TACACS+ or RADIUS servers for specifying different types of traffic, up to 14 tag groups with 14 servers each. Complete the following steps to create an AAA server group along with AAA servers within the group:

Step 1 Choose **Configuration > Device Settings**. The Settings page displays.

Step 2 Use the activity bar to select an existing activity or create a new activity.

Step 3 Use the object selector to select a group or device.

Step 4 Choose **Building Blocks > AAA Server Groups** from the TOC. The AAA Server Groups page displays.

Step 5 Click **Create**. The Select Group Name(new) page shown in Figure 19-29 displays.

Figure 19-29 *Select Group Name(new) Page*

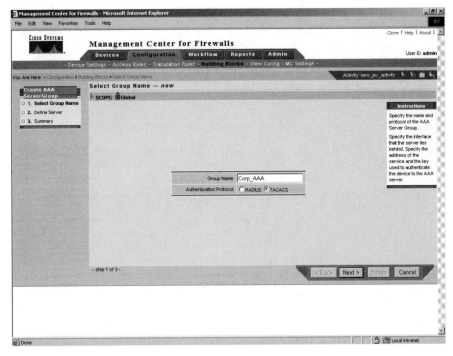

Step 6 Complete the following substeps to configure AAA server group name settings:

(1) Enter a group name in the Group Name field.

(2) Select either the **TACACS** or the **RADIUS** radio button for the Authentication Protocol radio buttons.

Step 7   Click **Next**. The Define Server(new) page shown in Figure 19-30 displays.

Figure 19-30   *Define Server(new) Page*

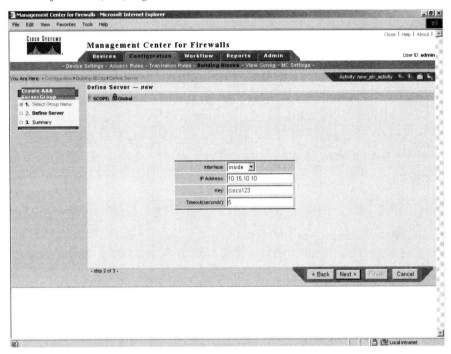

Step 8   Complete the following substeps to configure AAA server settings:

(1) Choose the interface from the Interface drop-down menu.

(2) Enter the IP address of the AAA server in the IP Address field.

(3) Enter the key that is defined on the TACACS+ or RADIUS server in the Key field.

(4) Enter the timeout value in the Timeout(seconds) field; the default is 5 seconds.

Step 9   Click **Next**. The Summary page displays.

Step 10 Verify that the information listed is correct and click **Finish**. The AAA Server Group page displays with the new AAA Server Group.

NOTE	Firewall MC includes a default AAA server group named LOCAL, which cannot be modified or disabled. This group is used for administrative authentication and relies on the local user database available with PIX Firewall Version 6.2 or later.

Address Translation Pool

The Address Translation Pool feature allows you to create global address pools used in dynamic network address translation (NAT) rules. Complete the following steps to create an address translation pool:

Step 1 Choose **Configuration > Device Settings**. The Settings page displays.

Step 2 Use the activity bar to select an existing activity or create a new activity.

Step 3 Use the object selector to select a group or device.

Step 4 Choose **Building Blocks > Address Translation Pools** from the TOC. The Address Translation Pool page displays.

Step 5 Click **Create**. The Enter Pool Name(new) page displays.

Step 6 Enter a name for the pool in the Pool Name field and click **Next**. The Enter Pool Element(new) page shown in Figure 19-31 displays.

Figure 19-31 *Enter Pool Element(new) Page*

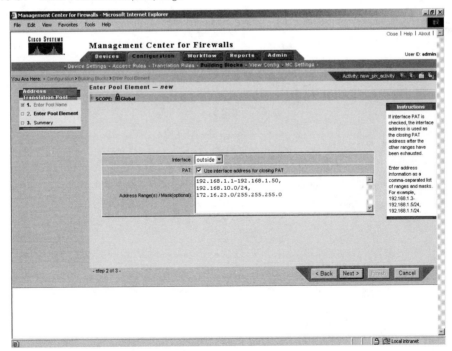

Step 7 Complete the following substeps to configure address translation pool elements:

> (1) Choose an interface from the Interface drop-down menu.
>
> (2) If you want to use the interface address as the final address for port address translation (PAT), select the **PAT** check box.
>
> (3) Enter the IP address of a host or network or enter a range of IP addresses in the Address Range(s)/Mask (optional) field. Click **Next**. The Summary page displays.

Step 8 Verify that the information listed is correct and click **Finish**. The Address Translation Pool page displays with the new address translation pool.

Task 5—Configure Settings

Settings are configuration elements that control individual features of a PIX Firewall. Settings applied to a group are inherited by enclosed subgroups and devices contained in that group. These settings are as follow:

- **PIX Firewall Software Version**
- **Interfaces**—Allows you to configure interface settings.
- **Failover**—Allows you to configure the PIX Firewall for failover.
- **Routing**—Allows you to configure the following routing settings:
  - Static route
  - Routing Information Protocol (RIP)
  - Proxy Address Resolution Protocol (ARP)
- **PIX Firewall Administration**—Allows you to configure the following PIX Firewall administration settings:
  - Passwords
  - Unique identity
  - HTTPS (SSL)
  - Telnet
  - Secure Shell (SSH)
  - SNMP
  - ICMP interface rules
  - AAA admin authentication

- **Logging**—Allows you to configure the following logging settings:
    - Logging setup
    - Syslog
    - Logging level
- **Servers and Services**—Allows you to change the following server and service settings:
    - Authentication prompts
    - URL filter server
    - Dynamic Host Configuration Protocol (DHCP) server
    - TFTP server
    - Easy VPN Remote
    - AUS
- **Advanced Security**—Allows you to change the following advanced security settings:
    - Intrusion detection system (IDS) policy
    - IDS signatures
    - Antispoofing
    - Fragment
    - TCP options
    - Timeouts
    - Fixups
    - Flood Guard
- **Firewall MC Controls**—Defines how the Firewall MC operates with the following options:
    - Management
    - Deployment
    - Import
    - PIX Device Contact Information
    - AUS Contact
- **Configuration Additions**—Allows you to use commands that are not supported in the Firewall MC to configure PIX Firewalls.

PIX Firewall Version

The PIX Firewall Version feature allows you to identify the version of the PIX operating system from which to generate a configuration file. By manually specifying the PIX software version, you enable the Firewall MC to generate the proper command syntax to allow for PIX Firewalls to come online at a later date. Complete the following steps to identify the version from which to create a configuration file:

Step 1 Choose **Configuration > Device Settings**. The Settings page displays.

Step 2 Use the activity bar to select an existing activity or create a new activity.

Step 3 Use the object selector to select a group or device.

NOTE When configuring device settings, you must choose the devices to configure with the object selector. The object selector is an expandable display. When clicked, it opens to reveal a hierarchical list of device groups from which you make your device selections.

Step 4 Click **Firewall OS Version** in the TOC. The Firewall OS Version page shown in Figure 19-32 displays.

Figure 19-32 *Firewall OS Version Page*

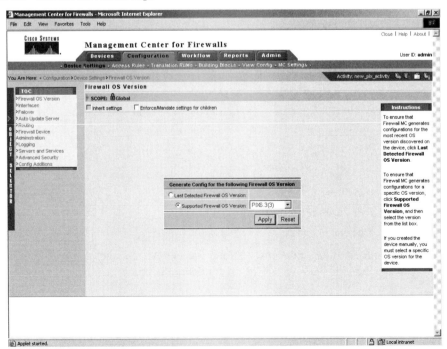

Step 5   Use the radio buttons **Last Detected Firewall OS Version** or **Supported Firewall OS Version** to select the version of software with which the PIX Firewall will be configured.

NOTE   The Last Detected Firewall OS Version option instructs the Firewall MC to automatically generate a configuration file for the last detected PIX Firewall software version as it is discovered on the target device. The Supported Firewall OS Version option instructs the Firewall MC to generate a configuration file for a specific OS version from a list of available OS versions by way of a drop-down menu.

Step 6   Click **Apply**. The Firewall OS Version page refreshes to indicate that the Firewall MC received the changes.

Interface Settings

The Interfaces feature allows you to enable, disable, and edit network interface configurations. Each PIX Firewall must be configured, and each active interface must be enabled. Inactive interfaces can be disabled. When disabled, the interface does not transmit or receive data, but the configuration information is retained.

Complete the following steps to add an interface with a static address:

Step 1   Choose **Configuration > Device Settings**. The Settings page displays.

Step 2   Use the activity bar to select an existing activity or create a new activity.

Step 3   Use the object selector to select a group or device.

Step 4   Click **Interfaces** in the TOC. The Interfaces page shown in Figure 19-33 displays.

NOTE   Because PIX Firewalls inherit their settings from the group to which they belong, it might be necessary to uncheck the Inherit Settings check box. When this box is unchecked, a window appears asking whether you want to continue.

Step 5   Click **Add**. The Add Interface Name(new) page shown in Figure 19-34 displays.

Figure 19-33 *Interfaces Page*

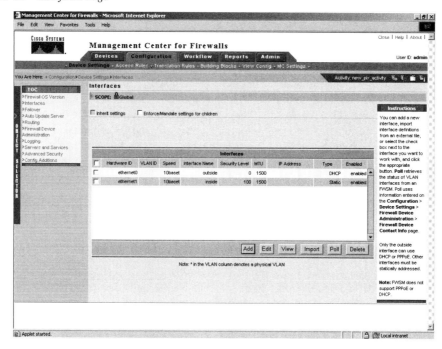

Figure 19-34 *Add Interface Name(new) Page*

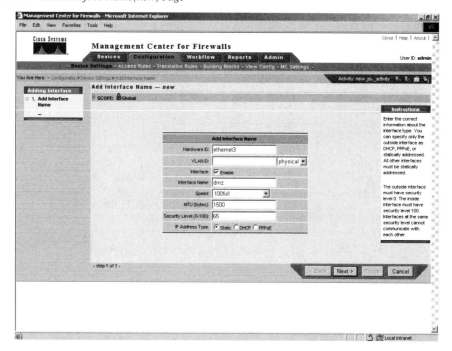

Step 6 Enter the network interface's hardware ID in the Hardware ID field. Possible values are ethernet0, ethernet1–ethernet$n$, and gb-ethernet$n$, where n is the number of firewall interfaces in the PIX Firewall.

Step 7 If you are defining a VLAN interface, enter its VLAN ID and select **Physical** or **Logical** from the drop-down menu to specify the type of VLAN interface.

NOTE VLAN interfaces (802.1Q protocol) are available on the FWSM and PIX Firewall appliances with PIX Firewall Software Version 6.3(1) or later. PIX Firewall 501 and 506/506E models do not support VLAN interfaces.

Step 8 Select the **Enable** check box in the Interface field.

Step 9 Enter a name for the interface in the Interface Name field.

Step 10 Select the interface speed from the Speed drop-down menu.

Step 11 Enter the maximum transmission unit (MTU) size of the interface in the MTU (bytes) field.

Step 12 Enter the security level of the interface in the Security Level (0–100) field.

Step 13 Select the **Static** radio button to assign a static IP address, the **DHCP** radio button to configure the interface to obtain an IP address dynamically, or the **PPPoE** button to enable Point-to-Point Protocol over Ethernet (PPPoE) support on the interface.

NOTE You can enable DHCP and PPPoE options only on the outside interface of the PIX Firewall.

Step 14 Click **Next**. If you selected **Static** in the previous step, the Add Static Address Information(new) page displays, enabling you to enter the IP address and network mask. If you selected **DHCP**, the Add DHCP Information page opens, enabling you to configure DHCP parameters such as the number of times the interface attempts to obtain an address from a DHCP server. If you selected **PPPoE**, the Add PPPoE Information page opens, enabling you to configure PPPoE parameters including username and password, authentication protocol, static IP address if required, and the option to create a default route using the PPPoE Set Route option.

Step 15   Click **Next**. The Summary page displays.

Step 16   Verify that the information displayed on the Summary page is correct and click **Finish**. The Interfaces page displays with the newly created interface.

Static Routes

Complete the following steps to configure a static route:

Step 1   Choose **Configuration > Device Settings**. The Settings page displays.

Step 2   Use the activity bar to select an existing activity or create a new activity.

Step 3   Use the object selector to select a group or device.

Step 4   Click **Routing > Static Route** in the TOC. The Static Route page displays.

Step 5   Click the **Add** action button. The Enter Static Route Information(new) page shown in Figure 19-35 displays.

Figure 19-35   *Enter Static Route Information(new) Page*

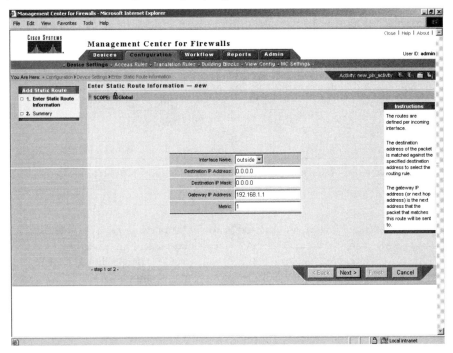

Step 6 Complete the following substeps to configure static route settings:

    (1) Choose the interface to define a static route from the Interface Name drop-down menu.

    (2) Enter the IP address that is the destination in the Destination IP Address field.

    (3) Enter the network mask of the destination IP address in the Destination IP Mask field.

    (4) Enter the gateway address in the Gateway IP Address field.

    (5) Enter the weight of the route in the Metric field.

Step 7 Click **Next**. The Summary page displays.

Step 8 Verify that the information listed is correct and click **Finish**. The Interfaces page displays with the newly created interface.

Administration: Passwords

The Firewall MC allows you to change the enable and Telnet passwords on the PIX Firewall. Complete the following steps to change the enable and Telnet passwords on the PIX Firewall:

Step 1 Choose **Configuration > Device Settings**. The Settings page displays.

Step 2 Use the activity bar to select an existing activity or create a new activity.

Step 3 Use the object selector to select a group or device.

Step 4 Click **Firewall Device Administration > Password** in the TOC. The Password page shown in Figure 19-36 displays.

Step 5 Complete the following substeps to change the administration passwords of the PIX Firewall:

    (1) Enter the enable password and re-enter the password in the New Password. Confirm the New Password fields.

    (2) Enter the Telnet password and re-enter the password in the New Password. Confirm the New Password fields.

Step 6 Click **Apply**. The Password page refreshes to indicate that the Firewall MC received the change.

Figure 19-36 *Password Page*

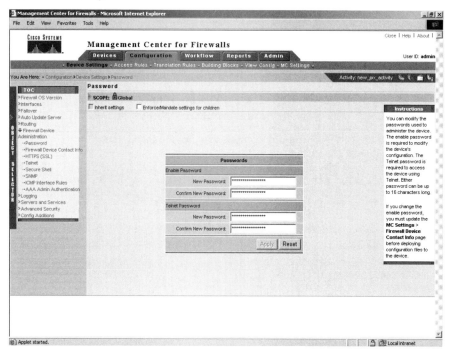

Administration: HTTPS (SSL)

The HTTPS (SSL) feature allows you to configure rules that permit only specific hosts or networks to connect to the PIX Firewall using HTTPS. You need a secure connection to allow a PC or workstation client running a network browser or Firewall MC to communicate with the PIX Firewall. The rules restrict HTTPS access through a PIX Firewall interface to a specific IP address and netmask. Any HTTPS connection attempts that comply with the rules must be authenticated using a preconfigured AAA server or the enable password. Once established, SSL protocol is used to encrypt the data.

Complete the following steps to enable HTTPS to the PIX Firewall:

Step 1 Choose **Configuration > Device Settings**. The Settings page displays.

Step 2 Use the activity bar to select an existing activity or create a new activity.

Step 3 Use the object selector to select a group or device.

Step 4 Choose **Firewall Device Administration > HTTPS(SSL)** from the TOC. The HTTPS (SSL) page displays.

Step 5 Click **Add**. The Enter HTTPS Client(new) page shown in Figure 19-37 displays.

Figure 19-37 *Enter HTTPS Client(new) Page*

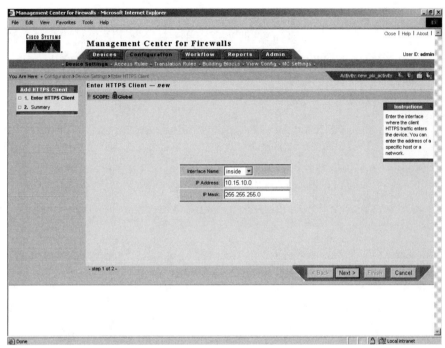

Step 6 Complete the following substeps to configure HTTPS client settings:

(1) Choose an interface to define the HTTPS client from the Interface Name drop-down menu.

(2) Enter the IP address of the host or network in the IP Address field.

(3) Enter the network mask in the IP Mask field.

Step 7 Click **Next**. The Summary page displays.

Step 8 Verify that the information listed is correct and click **Finish**. The HTTPS page displays with the newly created interface.

Administration: SSH

The SSH feature lets you configure rules that permit only specific hosts or networks to connect to the PIX Firewall for administrative access using the SSH protocol. The rules restrict SSH access through a PIX Firewall interface to a specific IP address and netmask.

SSH connection attempts that comply with the rules must be authenticated by a preconfigured AAA Server or the Telnet password.

Complete the following steps to enable SSH access to the PIX Firewall:

Step 1   Choose **Configuration > Device Settings**. The Settings page displays.

Step 2   Use the activity bar to select an existing activity or create a new activity.

Step 3   Use the object selector to select a group or device.

Step 4   Choose **Firewall Device Administration > Secure Shell** from the TOC. The Secure Shell page displays.

Step 5   Enter the SSH timeout in minutes (the default is 5 minutes) in the Timeout (minute) field.

Step 6   Click **Add**. The Enter SSH Client(new) page shown in Figure 19-38 displays.

Figure 19-38   *Enter SSH Client(new) Page*

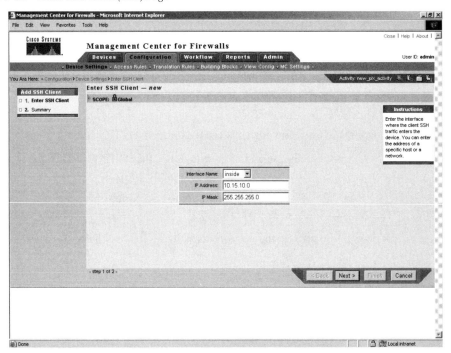

Step 7   Complete the following substeps to configure SSH client settings:

>   (1)   Choose an interface to define the Telnet options from the Interface Name drop-down menu.
>
>   (2)   Enter the IP address of the host or network that is going to connect using SSH in the IP Address field.
>
>   (3)   Enter the network mask in the IP Mask field.

Step 8   Click **Next**. The Summary page displays.

Step 9   Verify that the information listed is correct and click **Finish**. The SSH page displays with the newly created interface.

Administration: Log Setup

The Logging features allow you to configure logging for the PIX Firewall. You can enable logging, identify a syslog server, identify a server used for debugging, and include syslog message types to log.

Complete the following steps to set up logging:

Step 1   Choose **Configuration > Device Settings**. The Settings page displays.

Step 2   Use the activity bar to select an existing activity or create a new activity.

Step 3   Use the object selector to select a group or device.

Step 4   Choose **Logging > Logging Setup** from the TOC. The Logging Setup page shown in Figure 19-39 displays.

Step 5   Select the **Enable Logging Setup** check box to enable logging.

Step 6   Select the **Enable Logging Failover** check box to enable logging messages to be sent to a syslog server when failover occurs.

Step 7   Click **Apply**. The Logging Setup page refreshes to indicate that the Firewall MC received the changes.

Figure 19-39 *Logging Setup Page*

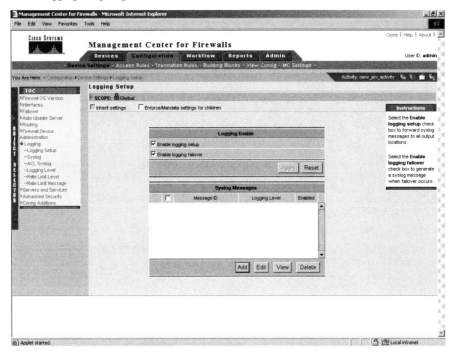

Step 8 Optionally modify the logging level for a PIX Firewall message ID by completing the following substeps:

(1) Click **Add** in the Syslog Messages section of the Logging Setup page shown in Figure 19-39. The Enter Syslog Message(new) page displays.

(2) Enter the six-digit integer value as the message ID for which you want to modify logging levels in the Message ID field.

(3) Select the desired logging level from the drop-down list.

(4) Select the **Enable** radio button.

(5) Click **Next**. The Summary page displays.

(6) Verify that the information listed is correct and click **Finish**. The Logging Setup page displays the newly created entries.

NOTE	Message IDs depend on the PIX Firewall software version that is running on the firewall device. Check the product documentation for the applicable PIX Firewall software version on Cisco.com.

Syslog Configuration

The Syslog feature enables you to specify the syslog servers to which the PIX Firewall will send syslog messages.

NOTE	You can send syslogs to the Security Monitor tool, in addition to third-party products.

Complete the following steps to configure syslog logging settings:

Step 1   Choose **Configuration > Device Settings**. The Device Settings page displays.

Step 2   Use the activity bar to select an existing activity or create a new activity.

Step 3   Use the object selector to select a group or device.

Step 4   Choose **Logging > Syslog** from the TOC. The Syslog page shown in Figure 19-40 displays.

Figure 19-40   *Syslog Page*

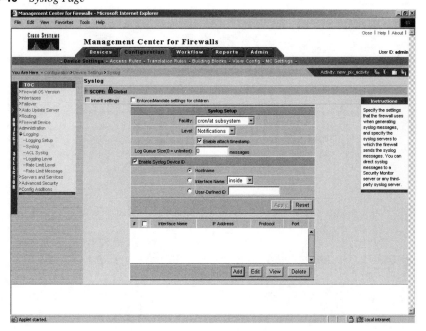

Step 5 Complete the following substeps to configure syslog settings:

    (1) Select the syslog facility that will be used by the PIX Firewall in the Facility drop-down menu.

    (2) Select the level of logging from the Level drop-down menu.

    (3) Select the **Enable attach timestamp** check box to turn on timestamps for syslog messages.

    (4) Enter the log queue size in the Log Queue Size (0 means unlimited) field.

Step 6 Click **Apply**. The Syslog page refreshes to indicate that the Firewall MC received the changes.

Step 7 Click **Add**. The Enter Syslog Server(new) page shown in Figure 19-41 displays.

Figure 19-41 *Enter Syslog Server(new) Page*

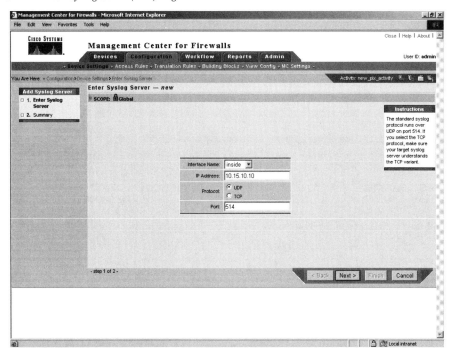

Step 8 Complete the following substeps to configure syslog server settings:

    (1) Select the interface to source syslog traffic from the Interface Name drop-down menu.

(2) Enter the IP address of a host or network to which to send syslog traffic in the IP address field.

(3) Select the protocol to be used to send syslog traffic with the Protocol radio buttons, **TCP** or **UDP**.

(4) In the Port field, enter the port number to be used for sending syslog traffic.

Step 9   Click **Next**. The Summary page displays.

Step 10   Verify that the information listed is correct and click **Finish**. The Syslog page displays with the new syslog server.

Logging Level

The Firewall MC allows you to change the message logging level on the PIX Firewall. Complete the following steps to configure logging levels:

Step 1   Choose **Configuration > Device Settings**. The Device Settings page displays.

Step 2   Use the activity bar to select an existing activity or create a new activity.

Step 3   Use the object selector to select a group or device.

Step 4   Choose **Logging > Logging Level** in the TOC. The Logging Level page shown in Figure 19-42 displays.

Figure 19-42   *Logging Level Page*

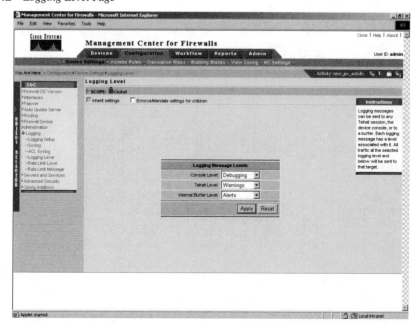

Step 5   Complete the following substeps to configure the logging level settings:

    (1) Choose the logging level for the console using the Console Level drop-down menu.

    (2) Choose the logging level for Telnet using the Telnet Level drop-down menu.

    (3) Choose the logging level for the internal buffer using the Internal Buffer Level drop-down menu.

Step 6   Click **Apply**. The Logging Level page refreshes to indicate that the Firewall MC received the changes.

Servers and Services: Easy VPN Remote

Easy VPN settings are another type of setting that you can configure within Firewall MC. The Easy VPN Remote feature allows you to configure a PIX Firewall to operate as a Cisco Secure VPN client. Complete the following steps to configure the PIX Firewall to operate as a Cisco Secure VPN client:

Step 1   Choose **Configuration > Device Settings**. The Device Settings page displays.

Step 2   Use the activity bar to select an existing activity or create a new activity.

Step 3   Use the object selector to select a group or device.

Step 4   Choose **Servers and Services > Easy VPN Remote** from the TOC. The Easy VPN Remote page shown in Figure 19-43 displays.

Figure 19-43   *Easy VPN Remote Page*

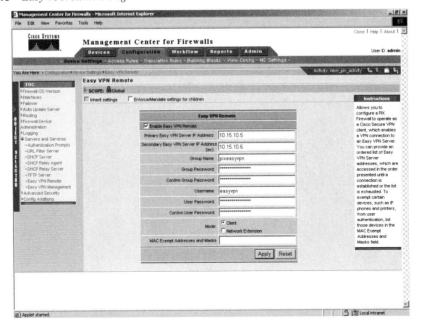

Step 5 Complete the following substeps to configure Easy VPN Remote settings:

(1) Select the **Enable Easy VPN Remote** check box to turn on the Easy VPN Remote feature.

(2) Enter the primary VPN server IP address in the Primary Easy VPN Remote Server IP Address field.

(3) Enter the secondary VPN server IP address in the Secondary Easy VPN Remote Server IP Address field.

(4) Enter the group name in the Group Name field.

(5) Enter the password that is associated with the group in the Group Password field.

(6) Enter the confirmation of the group password in the Confirm Group Password field.

(7) Enter an optional username to configure extended user authentication in the Username field.

(8) Enter the password that is associated with the username in the User Password field.

(9) Enter the confirmation of the group password in the Confirm User Password field.

(10) Select the mode of operation for the Easy VPN Remote by selecting either the **Client** or **Network Extension** radio buttons.

NOTE   If the Easy VPN Remote has been configured for Client Mode operation, to make this feature work you must also enable its DHCP on the inside interface. Additionally, Client Mode operates by NATing the address on the inside interface, but Network Extension does not offer NAT.

(11) Enter the MAC address and mask for devices that should be exempt from user authentication (such as IP phones or printer) in the MAC Exempt Addresses and Masks field.

Step 6 Click **Apply**. The Easy VPN Remote page refreshes to indicate that the Firewall MC received the changes.

NOTE   The AUS section of "Servers and Services" is designed to enable the PIX Firewall to use the AUS. This feature is covered in more depth in Chapter 20, "PIX Firewall Maintenance in Enterprise Networks."

MC Settings: Management

The Management feature allows you to control how the Firewall MC operates. When you modify a PIX Firewall configuration outside of the Firewall MC, the changes are temporary unless you save them in the device's nonvolatile storage. Each time the device is rebooted, it reads its configuration from nonvolatile storage. As a result, temporary changes are lost if they are not saved.

The Firewall MC detects any permanent changes made to the PIX Firewall by a method other than the Firewall MC. You can request that the Firewall MC fail the deployment when other methods are detected. If you request that the Firewall MC deploy a configuration to a device to which permanent changes have been made, a warning is generated in the deploy status window.

NOTE   To retain changes made to a PIX Firewall configuration by a means other than the Firewall MC, you can delete the device and then re-import it; however, doing so results in the need to redefine device name, group, and hierarchy information.

Complete the following steps to configure the management features of the Firewall MC:

Step 1   Choose **Configuration > MC Settings**. The MC Settings page displays.

Step 2   Choose **Management** from the TOC. The Management page shown in Figure 19-44 displays.

Step 3   Complete the following substeps to configure the Management Controls settings:

(1) Select the **On**, **Off**, or **Only** radio button in the Identity Address Translation Rules section to configure auto-identity NAT. A setting of Only is typical; it generates identity address translation rules when no user-defined rules exist. Select the **Error** or **Warning** radio button in the Action on Unknown Commands section to issue an error or warning when unknown commands are encountered during an import.

Figure 19-44 *Management Page*

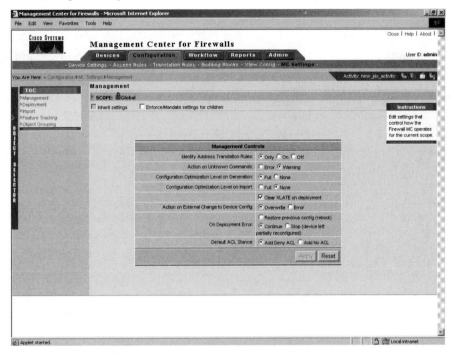

NOTE   If an unknown command is treated as a warning, it becomes an ending command for that device.

---

(2) Select the **None** or **Full** radio button in the Configuration Optimization Level on Generation section to control the amount of optimization on enabled ACLs during generation. The goal of optimization is to reduce the number of commands and simplify the ACLs. The default setting for Configuration Optimization Level on Generation is Full, which enables optimization.

(3) Select the **None** or **Full** radio button in the Configuration Optimization Level on Import section to control the amount of optimization on enabled ACLs. The default setting for Configuration Optimization Level on Import is None, which disables optimization.

(4) Select the **Clear xlate** check box to clear the translation tables in the On Deployment section.

(5) Select the **Error** or **Overwrite** radio button in the Action on External Change to Device Config section. When Error is selected, if the Firewall MC detects that the configuration file has been changed by any means other than the Firewall MC, the Firewall MC errors out and the configuration file is not deployed. When Overwrite is selected, if the Firewall MC detects that the configuration file has been changed by any means other than the Firewall MC, the Firewall MC overwrites the existing configuration file on deployment.

(6) Select the **Continue**, **Restore previous config (reboot)**, or **Stop (device left partially refigured)** radio button in the On Deployment Error section. This setting determines how the Firewall MC proceeds if errors occur during deployment. The Continue setting ignores errors and continues deployment. Restore previous config (reboot) setting reverts to the existing configuration by rebooting the device, and the Stop (device left partially refigured) setting stops deployment without reverting to previous configuration (no reboot).

(7) Select the **Add Deny ACL** or the **Add No ACL** radio button in the Default ACL Stance section. The Add Deny ACL setting prevents traffic flows on any interface for which an ACL has not been defined.

Step 4   Click **Apply**. The Management page refreshes to indicate that the Firewall MC received the changes.

NOTE   The deployment section of "Firewall MC Controls" is meant to change the way the Firewall MC deploys configuration files. This feature is covered in more depth in Chapter 20.

MC Settings: Import Devices

The Importing Devices feature allows you to set the import directory default setting. This directory is used to select configuration files when you import devices from a file or directory.

Complete the following steps to configure the import directory:

Step 1   Choose **Configuration > MC Settings**. The MC Settings page displays.

Step 2   Choose **Import** from the TOC. The Import page shown in Figure 19-45 displays.

Figure 19-45   *Import Page*

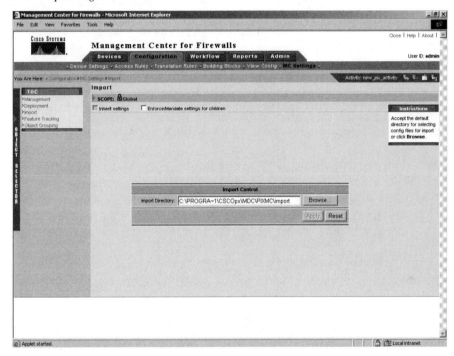

Step 3   Manually enter or use the **Browse** button to enter the path from which the configuration files will be imported. The default directory is C:\Program Files\CSCOpx\MDC\PIXMC\deploy (which assumes that the Program Files directory resides on drive C).

Step 4   Click **Apply**. The Import page refreshes to indicate that the Firewall MC received the changes.

MC Settings: Firewall Device Contact Information

The Firewall Device Contact Info feature allows you to authenticate a PIX Firewall using the current username, password, and IP address. Either the Firewall MC or the AUS uses the username and password credentials to authenticate to a PIX Firewall. You can use the enable password with an empty username or an AAA username with an associated password, depending on the target PIX Firewall setting. You can also enter a future username, password, and IP address, which are recognized after the configuration files and activity reports are deployed to devices.

You use the PIX Device Contact Info feature if you are deploying configuration files to an AUS or directly to devices:

- **AUS**—The AUS supports a feature that allows you to manually initiate an immediate auto-update request on the AUS. The credentials defined in the GUI are passed to the AUS. This process enables the AUS to authenticate with the device during the immediate auto update.

- **Firewall MC direct deployment to devices**—The credentials defined in the GUI are used to authenticate the Firewall MC to the PIX Firewalls.

Complete the following steps to configure the PIX Device Contact Info feature:

Step 1   Choose **Configuration > Device Settings**. The Settings page displays.

Step 2   Use the activity bar to select an existing activity or create a new activity.

Step 3   Use the object selector to select a device.

Step 4   Choose **Firewall Device Administration > Firewall Device Contact Info** from the TOC. The Firewall Device Contact Info page shown in Figure 19-46 displays.

Figure 19-46   *Firewall Device Contact Info Page*

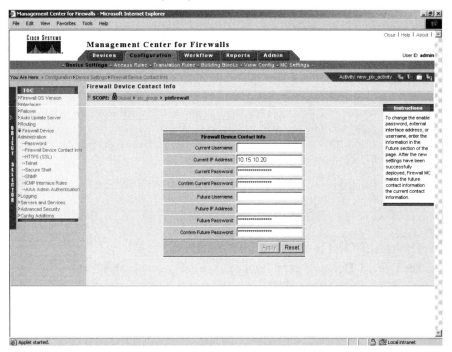

Step 5   Complete the following substeps to configure the Firewall Devices Contact Info settings:

(1)   Enter a username for the PIX Firewall to authenticate by means of the AAA in the Current Username field. Leave it blank if the PIX Firewall does not have AAA configured.

(2)   Optionally enter an IP address for the Firewall MC to use to contact the PIX Firewall in the Current IP Address field. Typically, you use the address of the PIX Firewall interface, but you might need to specify a different address if you use address translation between the PIX Firewall and the Firewall MC.

(3)   Enter a password that is either an AAA password associated with the username specified in Step A or the local enable password in the Current Password field.

(4)   Enter the same password again to confirm the original entry in the Confirm Current Password field.

NOTE   If you are using the immediate auto-update feature, completing the GUI elements labeled "future" is optional. If you are deploying directly to devices, completing the GUI elements labeled "future" is required.

---

(5)   Enter in the Future Username field a username that is to be changed once the configuration file has been deployed to the PIX Firewall.

(6)   (Optional) Enter an IP address for the Firewall MC to use to contact the PIX Firewall in the Future IP Address field.

(7)   Enter a password for the Future Username in the Future Password field.

(8)   Enter the same password again to confirm the original entry in the Confirm Future Password field.

Step 6   Click **Apply**. The Firewall Device Contact Info page refreshes to indicate that the Firewall MC received the changes.

Firewall MC Controls: Configuration Additions

As mentioned previously in this chapter, Firewall MC supports PIX Firewall Versions 6.0 or higher. However, all CLI commands might not be fully supported. The Beginning Commands and Ending Commands provide the means to configure unsupported CLI commands if necessary.

NOTE	Always check Cisco.com for information on the latest version of PIX Firewall Version CLI commands and the level of support provided by the latest release of the Firewall MC.

You can configure configuration additions by choosing **Configuration > Device Settings > Config Additions** and then choosing **Beginning Commands** or **Ending Commands**. Figure 19-47 shows the Beginning Commands page, where you can add specific CLI commands to the configuration. Ending commands appear after all other commands and before the command **write mem**. Both beginning and ending commands are always replaced when the configuration files are deployed.

Figure 19-47 *Beginning Commands Page*

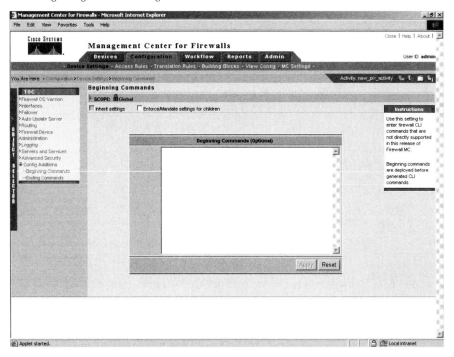

Task 6—Configure Access and Translation Rules

This section introduces and explains configuring access rules using the Firewall MC along with generating configurations for viewing before activity approval or job deployment.

The Firewall MC is based on a hierarchical list of device groups containing PIX Firewalls. Each group has two sets of access rules: *mandatory* and *default*. Each device has one set of access rules. These rules comprise the ACLs for each interface on the device. Within each group, access rules are evaluated in the same order as you configure them. This method is the default method used to permit or block traffic for a specific service, protocol, or both. You can also define rules for AAA and web filtering.

Each access rule defined in the Firewall MC eventually corresponds to a single entry in the ACL for an interface on a particular PIX Firewall. Access rules are grouped by the interface on which they are configured and enforced. The Firewall MC sorts the rules by interface and uses the remaining information in the rule to create the access control entry (ACE) that will be included in the ACL for that interface.

Rules are recognized as either mandatory or default and can be applied at the global level, a group level, or to an individual device:

- **Mandatory**—Rules that apply at an enclosing group and are ordered down to a device. Mandatory rules cannot be overridden.
- **Default**—Rules that are ordered from the device up to enclosing groups. Default rules can be overridden.

The mandatory and default access rule sets generate a block of ACEs. These blocks are linked together in a series to form the ACL for an interface on the PIX Firewall. The order to link together in a series is as follows:

1 Mandatory access rules

2 Device access rules

3 Default access rules

Mandatory rules are listed first, so they take precedence over any rules that come later. Device rules take effect only if no relevant mandatory rules apply. Finally, default rules take effect if no mandatory or device-specific rules apply.

The blocks from the mandatory rules are ordered from the highest group (global) down to the group that directly contains the device, whereas the blocks from the default rules are ordered in the opposite direction.

It is likely that the resulting ACL will have ACEs that are either redundant or conflicting. Because a PIX Firewall uses the first-match method to evaluate ACLs, these extraneous entries do not cause a problem.

Rules are recognized in the form of an ordered list, which is represented in the Firewall MC as a table. Rules are recognized and processed by a PIX Firewall from first to last. When a rule matches the network traffic that a PIX Firewall is processing, the PIX Firewall uses that rule to decide whether traffic is permitted.

The Firewall MC is designed with a GUI that displays separate rules tables for mandatory and default rules at each scope. To determine the rules that apply to a device, you identify the mandatory rules for each enclosing group *before* rules set at the device level; then, identify the default rules for each enclosing group *after* rules set at the device level.

Access Rules

Firewall MC 1.2.1 allows you to create access rules at the global, group, or device level. When creating rules at the global or group levels, you can specify default or mandatory rules. At the device level, the mandatory setting is not available and you can create or view only default rules for the device. However, mandatory access rules from a parent group would still apply to the device.

Firewall MC provides three types of access rules. The access rules types and their functions are as follows:

- **Firewall rules**—Permit or deny traffic based on source and destination host or network addresses and the specific service, protocol, or both.

- **AAA rules**—Adds AAA control of traffic.

- **Web-filtering rules**—Adds URL filtering to permit or deny traffic based on destination URLs.

Procedures for configuring each access rule type are presented in the following subsections.

Firewall Rules

Before configuring firewall rules with the Firewall MC, you can define network objects for hosts, groups of hosts, or subnets that the firewall rule will impact. This step is optional, but network objects simplify the creation of firewall rules and their use is recommended. To create network objects, select **Configuration > Building Blocks > Network Object**.

Complete the following steps to configure a mandatory global firewall rule:

Step 1   Choose **Configuration > Access Rules**. The Firewall Rules page displays.

Step 2   Use the object selector to select a group.

Step 3   Use the activity bar to select an existing activity or create a new activity.

Step 4   Choose **Firewall Rules > Mandatory** from the TOC. The Firewall Rules page refreshes to reveal that you are configuring the mandatory global firewall rules by displaying Mandatory Global Firewall Rules on the page.

Step 5   Click **Insert**. The Firewall Rule page shown in Figure 19-48 displays.

Figure 19-48 *Firewall Rule Page*

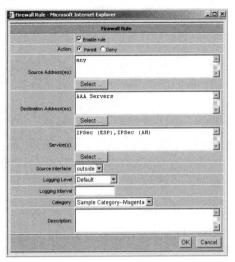

Step 6 Complete the following substeps to configure the Firewall Rule Data settings:

(1) Select the **Enable rule** check box to enable the rule.

(2) Select **Permit** or **Deny** as the action for the Control Traffic radio buttons.

(3) Click the **Select** button below the Source Address(es) field. A Selecting Network Objects window appears.

(4) Select a network object from the list of Available Objects and click **Select**. The Available Object moves to the Selected Objects list.

(5) Click **OK**. The Firewall Rule page refreshes to display the selected network object in the Source Address(es) field.

(6) Click the **Select** button below the Destination Address(es) field. A Selecting Network Objects window appears.

(7) Select a network object from the list of Available Objects and click **Select**. The Available Object moves to the Selected Objects list.

(8) Click **OK**. The Firewall Rule page refreshes to display the selected network object in the Destination Address(es) field.

(9) Click the **Select** button below the Services field. A Selecting Services window appears.

(10) Select a service from the list of Available Objects and click **Select**. The Available Object moves to the Selected Objects list.

(11) Click **OK**. The Firewall Rule page refreshes to display the selected service in the Services field.

(12) Choose an interface that will be the source of the traffic from the Source Interface drop-down menu. Select a logging level from the Logging Level drop-down list.

(13) Specify the logging interval time in seconds in the Logging Interval field. The default value is 300 seconds.

(14) (Optional) Specify a category for this rule.

(15) Enter an optional description in the Description field.

Step 7   Click **OK**. The Mandatory Global Firewall Rules page refreshes to display the newly created firewall rule.

Firewall MC 1.2.1 adds support for categories that are useful for viewing and filtering purposes. Using the Category field, you can assign a different color to firewall rules or groups or rules that are related. For example, you can categorize a set of firewall rules related to a business partner with the color red. You can then find all the rules related to this business partner by filtering the rule table to show only red firewall rules. You can also visually distinguish these rules much more easily in the rules table without any filtering.

AAA Rules

Before configuring AAA rules with the Firewall MC, you must identify a AAA server group by selecting **Configuration > Building Blocks > AAA Server Group**. As mentioned with firewall rules, you should also create network objects for hosts, groups of hosts, or subnets that the AAA rule will impact. This step is optional, but recommended. To create network objects, select **Configuration > Building Blocks > Network Object**.

Complete the following steps to configure a mandatory global AAA rule:

Step 1   Choose **Configuration > Access Rules**. The Firewall Rules page displays.

Step 2   Use the object selector to select a group.

Step 3   Use the activity bar to select an existing activity or create a new activity.

Step 4   Choose **AAA Rules > Mandatory** from the TOC. The Firewall Rules page refreshes to reveal that you are configuring the mandatory global AAA rules by displaying Mandatory Global AAA Rules on the page.

Step 5   Click **Insert**. The AAA Rule page shown in Figure 19-49 displays.

Figure 19-49 *AAA Rule Page*

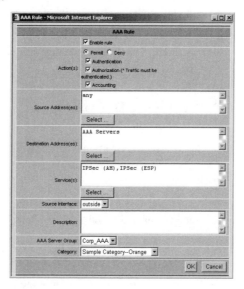

Step 6 Complete the following substeps to configure the AAA Rule Data settings:

(1) Select the **Enable rule** check box to enable the rule.

(2) Select **Permit** or **Deny** as the action for the Control Traffic radio buttons.

(3) Select **Authentication**, **Authorization**, or **Accounting** check boxes to enable any or all AAA actions. Keep in mind that you cannot use authorization without authentication.

(4) Click the **Select** button below the Source Address(es) field. A Selecting Network Objects window appears.

(5) Select a network object from the list of Available Objects and click **Select**. The Available Object moves to the Selected Objects list.

(6) Click **OK**. The AAA Rule page refreshes to display the selected network object in the Source Address(es) field.

(7) Click the **Select** button below the Destination Address(es) field. A Selecting Network Objects window appears.

    (8) Select a network object from the list of Available Objects and click **Select**. The Available Object moves to the Selected Objects list.

    (9) Click **OK**. The AAA Rule page refreshes to display the selected network object in the Destination Address(es) field.

    (10) Click the **Select** button below the Services field. A Selecting Services window appears.

    (11) Select a service from the list of Available Objects and click **Select**. The Available Object moves to the Selected Objects list.

    (12) Click **OK**. The AAA Rule page refreshes to display the selected service in the Services field.

    (13) Choose an interface that will be the source of the traffic from the Source Interface drop-down menu.

    (14) Enter an optional description in the Description field.

    (15) Select a predefined AAA server group from the AAA Server Group drop-down menu.

    (16) (Optional) Specify a category for this rule.

Step 7 Click **OK**. The Mandatory Global AAA Rules page refreshes to display the newly created AAA rule.

Web Filter Rules

Before configuring web filter rules with the Firewall MC, you must identify the URL filter server by selecting **Configuration > Device Settings > Servers and Services > URL Filter Server**. You should also create network objects for hosts, groups of hosts, or subnets that the web-filter rule will impact. This step is optional, but recommended. To create network objects, select **Configuration > Building Blocks > Network Object**.

Complete the following steps to configure a mandatory global web filter rule:

Step 1 Choose **Configuration > Access Rules**. The Firewall Rules page displays.

Step 2 Use the object selector to select a group.

Step 3 Use the activity bar to select an existing activity or create a new activity.

Step 4 Choose **Web Filter Rules > Mandatory** from the TOC. The Firewall Rules page refreshes to reveal that you are configuring the mandatory global web filter rules by displaying Mandatory Global Web Filter Rules on the page.

Step 5 Click **Insert**. The Web Filter Rule page shown in Figure 19-50 displays.

Figure 19-50 *Web Filter Rule Page*

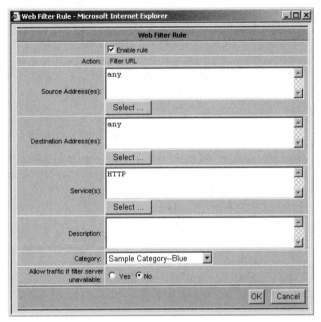

Step 6 Complete the following substeps to configure the Web Filter Rule Data settings:

(1) Select the **Enable rule** check box to enable the rule.

(2) Click the **Select** button below the Source Address(es) field. A Selecting Network Objects window appears.

(3) Select a network object from the list of Available Objects and click **Select**. The Available Object moves to the Selected Objects list.

(4) Click **OK**. The Web Filter Rule page refreshes to display the selected network object in the Source Address(es) field.

(5) Click the **Select** button below the Destination Address(es) field. A Selecting Network Objects window appears.

(6) Select a network object from the list of Available Objects and click **Select**. The Available Object moves to the Selected Objects list.

(7) Click **OK**. The Web Filter Rule page refreshes to display the selected network object in the Destination Address(es) field.

(8) Click the **Select** button below the Services field. A Selecting Services window appears.

(9) Select a service from the list of Available Objects and click **Select**. The Available Object moves to the Selected Objects list.

(10) Click **OK**. The Web Filter Rule page refreshes to display the selected service in the Services field.

(11) Enter an optional description in the Description field.

(12) (Optional) Specify a category for this rule.

(13) Select the **Yes** or **No** radio button in the Allow traffic if filter server unavailable field. If you select No, all traffic defined by the web-filter rule is blocked if the PIX Firewall cannot contact the URL filter server.

Step 7 Click **OK**. The Mandatory Global Web Filter Rules page refreshes to display the newly created web filter rule.

Static Translation Rule

Translation rules allow you to view all address translation rules applied to your network. Both PAT and NAT are supported by the Firewall MC.

Static translation rules have internal IP addresses that are assigned permanently to a global IP address. These rules assign a host address on a lower security-level interface to a global address on a higher-security-level interface. For example, use a static rule to assign the local address of a web server (on a perimeter network) to a global address that hosts (on the outside interface) use to access the web server.

Complete the following steps to create a static translation rule:

Step 1 Choose **Configuration > Translation Rules**. The Translation Rules page displays.

Step 2 Use the activity bar to select an existing activity or create a new activity.

Step 3 Use the object selector to select a group or device.

Step 4 Choose **Static Translation Rules** in the TOC. The Static Translation Rules page displays.

Step 5   Click **Add**. The Enter Static Translation Rule page shown in Figure 19-51 displays.

Figure 19-51   *Enter Static Translation Rule Page*

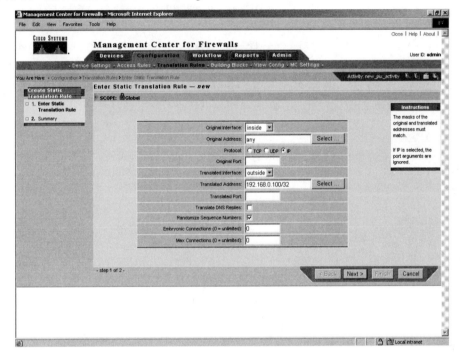

Step 6   Complete the following substeps to configure the Static Translation Rules settings:

   (1)   Choose an interface from the Original Interface drop-down menu.

   (2)   Either click the **Select** button or manually enter an IP address for a host or network in the Original IP Address field.

   (3)   Select the **TCP**, **UDP**, or **IP** radio button for the Protocol.

   (4)   If TCP or UDP is selected for the protocol, enter a protocol port in the Original Port field.

   (5)   Choose an interface from the Translated Interface drop-down menu.

> (6) Either click the **Select** button or manually enter an IP address for a host or network in the Translated IP Address field.
>
> (7) If TCP or UDP is selected for the Protocol, enter a protocol port in the Original Port field.
>
> (8) Select the **Translate DNS Replies** check box if you want the PIX Firewall to translate DNS queries.
>
> (9) Select the **Randomize Sequence Numbers** check box to have the PIX Firewall randomize sequence numbers.

NOTE   Disable the Randomize Sequence Numbers feature only if another inline firewall is also randomizing sequence numbers and the result is scrambling the data.

> (10) Enter the number of embryonic connections that are allowed before PIX Firewall denies connections in the Embryonic Connections field. (The default value is 0 with a range of 0 to 65,535, and 0 is unlimited.)
>
> (11) Enter the number of maximum connections that are allowed to be statically translated. (The default value is 0 with a range of 0 to 65,535, and 0 is unlimited.)

Step 7   Click **Next**. The Summary page displays.

Step 8   Verify that the information listed is correct and click **Finish**. The Static Translation Rule page displays with the new Static Translation Rule.

Dynamic Translation Rule

Dynamic translation rules use internal IP addresses that are dynamically translated using IP addresses from a pool of global addresses or, in the case for PAT, a single address. These rules translate host addresses on a higher-security-level interface to addresses selected from a pool of addresses for traffic sent to a lower-security-level interface. Dynamic translations are often used to assign local, RFC 1918 IP addresses to addresses that can be routed through the Internet.

Before configuring a dynamic translation rule, you need to configure an address translation pool by selecting **Configuration > Building Blocks > Address Translation Pool**. Complete the following steps to configure a dynamic translation rule:

Step 1   Choose **Configuration > Translation Rules**. The Translation Rules page displays.

Step 2   Use the activity bar to select an existing activity or create a new activity.

Step 3   Use the object selector to select a group or device.

Step 4   Choose **Dynamic Translation Rules** from the TOC. The Dynamic Translation Rules page displays.

Step 5   Click **Add**. The Enter Dynamic Translation Rule(new) page shown in Figure 19-52 displays.

Figure 19-52   *Enter Dynamic Translation Rule Page*

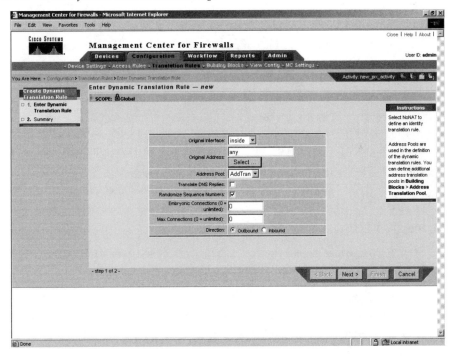

Step 6   Complete the following substeps to configure the Dynamic Translation Rule settings:

(1)   Choose an interface from the Original Interface drop-down menu.

(2) Either click the **Select** button or manually enter an IP address for a host or network in the Original IP Address field.

(3) Choose an address pool from the Address Pool drop-down menu.

(4) Select the **Translate DNS Replies** check box if you want the PIX Firewall to translate DNS queries.

(5) Select the **Randomize Sequence Numbers** check box to have the PIX Firewall randomize sequence numbers.

NOTE   Disable the Randomize Sequence Numbers feature only if another inline firewall is also randomizing sequence numbers and the result is scrambling the data.

---

(6) Enter the number of embryonic connections that are allowed before PIX Firewall denies connections in the Embryonic Connections field. (The default value is 0 with a range of 0 to 65,535, and 0 is unlimited.)

(7) Enter the number of maximum connections that are allowed to be statically translated. (The default value is 0 with a range of 0 to 65,535, and 0 is unlimited.)

(8) Select the **Outbound** or **Inbound** radio button in the Direction field to specify the traffic that will result in address translation.

Step 7   Click **Next**. The Summary page displays.

Step 8   Verify that the information listed is correct and click **Finish**. The Dynamic Translation Rules page displays with the new Dynamic Translation Rule.

Tasks 7 and 8—Generate and View the Configuration and Submit Activity for Approval

After you import and configure PIX Firewalls, you can view the configurations before activity approval and job deployment. If you have approval authority, you can generate a configuration file for each device associated with an activity before approving the activity. If there are caveats, the generated file includes them at the beginning of the file and inline and shows caveat summaries at the end of the file.

Complete the following steps to generate a PIX Firewall configuration:

Step 1   Choose **Configuration > View Config**. The view Config page shown in
Figure 19-53 displays.

Figure 19-53   *View Config Page*

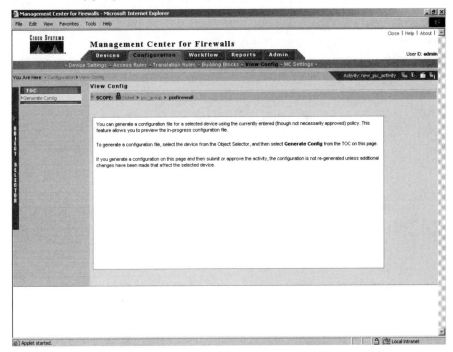

Step 2   Use the activity bar to select an existing activity or create a new activity.

Step 3   Use the object selector to select the PIX Firewall you want to generate a
configuration file for.

Step 4   Choose **Generate Config** from the TOC. The Generate Config page
refreshes to display a message indicating that the config is being
generated.

NOTE   The generation of a config file can take several minutes.

If the configuration file is generated successfully, you can submit the activity along with all
the configurations made in Tasks 1 through 7 for approval. This task is optional and is

required only if you have enabled the approval process. If the approval process is not enabled (the default setting), you can move on to the job management tasks.

If Firewall MC finds errors in the configuration file, it displays the configuration file along with a list of errors that it detected. You can click each of the listed errors to display the section of the configuration file with commands that resulted in the error. A typical Generate Config page listing configuration errors is shown in Figure 19-54.

Figure 19-54 *Generate Config Page Showing List of Errors*

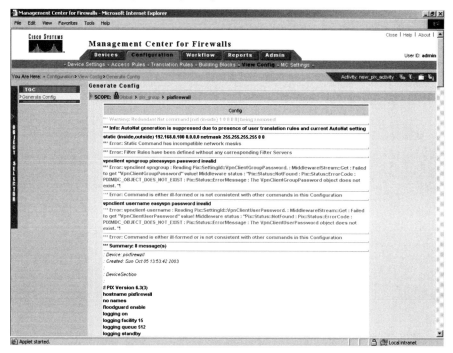

Tasks 9 and 10—Create a Job and Submit the Job for Approval

The Job Management interface is similar to that of the Activity Management interface. After an activity is submitted and approved (optional), it is ready to be defined in a job. A *job* identifies a set of devices, and new configuration files for downloading and defines a method for deployment. After a job is defined, it is submitted for approval. On approval, it is ready for deployment.

Complete the following steps to define and approve a job:

Step 1   Choose **Workflow > Job Management**. The Job Management page displays.

Step 2   Click **Add**. The Job Name(new) page shown in Figure 19-55 displays.

Figure 19-55   *Job Name(new) Page*

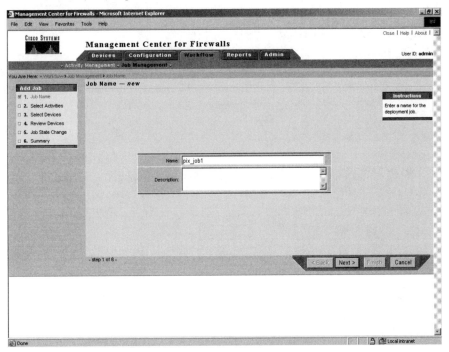

Step 3   Enter a job name in the Name field.

Step 4   Enter a description in the Description field.

Step 5   Click **Next**. The Select Activities(new) page shown in Figure 19-56 displays.

Figure 19-56 *Select Activities(new) Page*

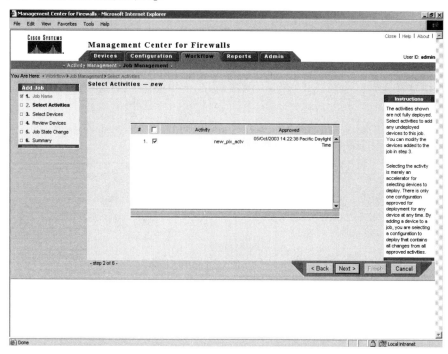

Step 6 Select the activities that you want to have completed upon deployment by using the check box located next to each activity.

Step 7 Click **Next**. The Select Devices(new) page shown in Figure 19-57 displays.

Step 8 Select the PIX Firewalls to which you want to have configuration files deployed by selecting the check box located next to the PIX Firewall.

Step 9 Click **Next**. The Review Devices(new) page shown in Figure 19-58 displays.

Figure 19-57 *Select Devices(new) Page*

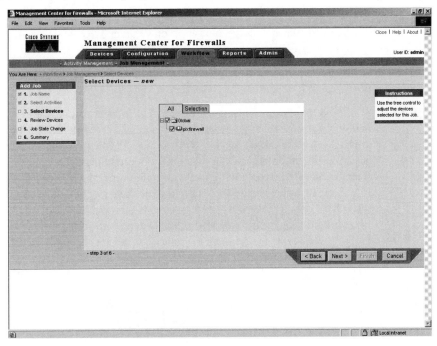

Figure 19-58 *Review Devices(new) Page*

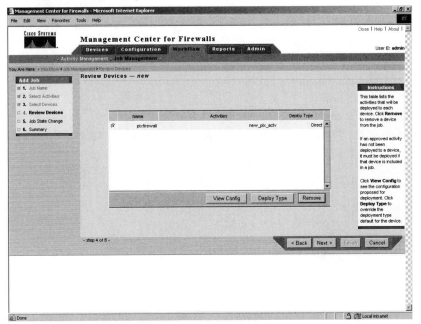

Step 10 Select the PIX Firewall to which you are going to deploy a configuration file by using the radio button located next to it. Click **View Config**.

Step 11 A window displays with the configuration generated. Review the configuration and close the window.

Step 12 Select the PIX Firewall to which you are going to deploy a configuration file by using the radio button located next to it. Click **Deploy Type**.

Step 13 A window displays indicating the current deployment type as well as options to change the deployment type. You can select **File**, **Direct to device**, or **Auto Update Server** on this screen. If you are using AUS to deploy configurations, you can select that option. Otherwise, you can select **Direct to device** to write the new configuration file directly to the PIX Firewall. You use the **File** option to write the new configuration to a file, which you can review and deploy later. If you want to remove a PIX Firewall from a configuration file that is deployed to it, select the PIX Firewall to remove by using the radio button located next to the PIX Firewall. Click **Remove**.

NOTE   You are allowed to remove any number of devices as long as there is one left. If you try to remove the last device, a window displays indicating that it is not possible to remove the last device.

Step 14 Click **Next**. The Job State Change(new) page shown in Figure 19-59 displays.

Step 15 Select the **Submit on Finish** check box to have the device automatically submitted upon finishing.

NOTE   If the Submit on Finish check box is not marked, a separate job approval process is necessary.

Step 16 Enter the e-mail addresses of people responsible for approving the job in the approver's e-mail field.

Step 17 Enter a descriptive comment in the Comment field.

Step 18 Click **Next**. The Summary page displays.

Step 19 Verify that the information listed is correct and click **Finish**. The Job
Management page displays.

Figure 19-59 *Job State Change(new) Page*

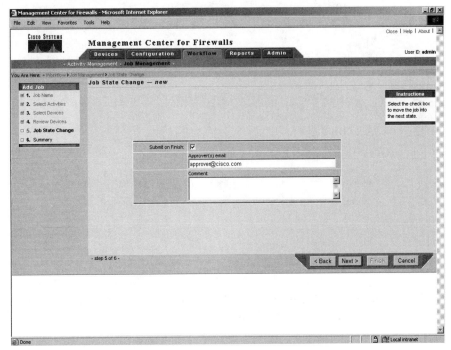

Once you create a new job, you might have to submit the job for approval (Task 10—
Submit Job for Approval). This task is optional, and it is only required if you have enabled
the approval process on Firewall MC.

Task 11—Deploy a Job

After a job is defined, submitted, and approved (optional), it is ready for deployment.
Complete the following steps to deploy an approved job:

Step 1 Choose **Workflow > Job Management**. The Job Management page
shown in Figure 19-60 displays.

Figure 19-60 *Job Management Page*

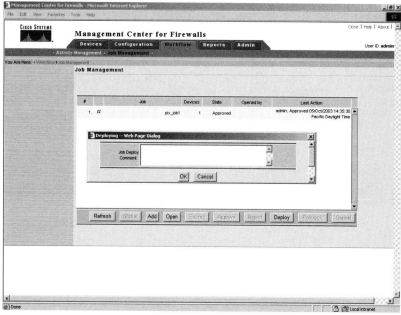

Step 2 Select the job that you are working with by using the radio button located next to it. The state will read Approved.

NOTE If the state of the job reads Submitted, you must approve the job before you can deploy it. In this case, the Deploy button on the Job Management page is grayed out and the Approve button is available. You must click **Approve**, enter a comment in the Job Approve Comment field, and click **OK** to approve the job.

Step 3 Click the **Deploy** Action button. The Deploying–Web Page Dialog window displays.

Step 4 Enter a comment in the Job Deploy Comment field.

Step 5 Click **OK**. The Job Management page refreshes to change the state of the job to read Deploying.

Before the job state reads Deployed, you can use the **Cancel Action** button to stop the deployment. If errors are encountered during the deployment, the Job Management page displays them and you can go back to the original configuration by clicking the Rollback Action button.

Reporting, Tools, and Administration

This section introduces and explains the report, tools, and administration tabs of the Firewall MC.

Reporting

The Report feature allows you to display information about the activities in the Firewall MC. The Activity report provides two types of information about an activity. The first type identifies actions performed on an activity by a user and the time the action occurred. For example, one user created an activity on Monday, and another user submitted the activity for approval on Wednesday. The second type of information shows policy changes that were made as part of the activity; for example, an access rule was added when an activity was created.

The Activity report is useful when you want to review

- Changes that were made to an activity before submitting the activity for approval.
- Changes that were made before submitting the activity for job deployment.

Activity reports can be generated as follows:

Step 1 Choose **Reports > Activity**. The Activity page displays.

Step 2 Select the activity for which you want to generate a report by using the radio button located next to the activity.

Step 3 Click **View**. A window displays with the report generated as shown in Figure 19-61. The report displays the date and timestamp, who performed the action, the action performed, and comments.

Figure 19-61 *Firewall MC Report*

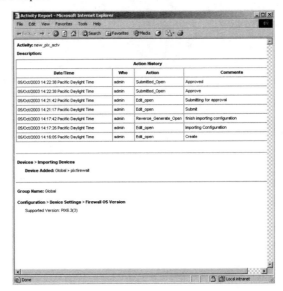

Support

The Support page on the Firewall MC allows you to produce a file that captures the state of your entire system, which can help you troubleshoot any problems that might occur. The file is a snapshot of all PIX Firewall settings on your network. It includes configuration settings, defined policies, and administrative accounts.

This feature is useful should you ever need to call Cisco Systems Technical Assistance Center (TAC) for assistance with Firewall MC issues. You can attach the file generated by the Support tool to an e-mail and send it directly to TAC. Upon receipt, TAC personnel can make any needed corrections and return the file to you.

Complete the following steps to create a support file:

Step 1   Choose **Admin > Support**. The Support page displays.

Step 2   Manually enter or use the Browse button to locate a directory in which to place the support file once it is generated.

The default path is \Program Files\CSCOpx\MDC\PIXMC\support\

Step 3   Click **Execute**. The Support page refreshes to display a message indicating that the Support Tool is running, as shown in Figure 19-62. The Support page refreshes a second time to display a message indicating that the Support Tool has finished.

Figure 19-62   *Firewall MC Support Tool*

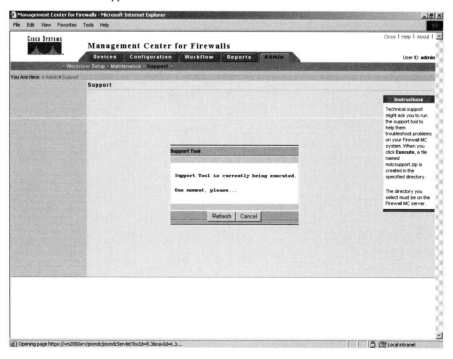

Step 4   Locate MDCSupportInformation.zip in the directory specified in Step 2 and send it to TAC as requested. Figure 19-63 shows the contents of a typical zip file generated by the Support tool.

Figure 19-63   *Support Tool MDCSupportInformation.zip File*

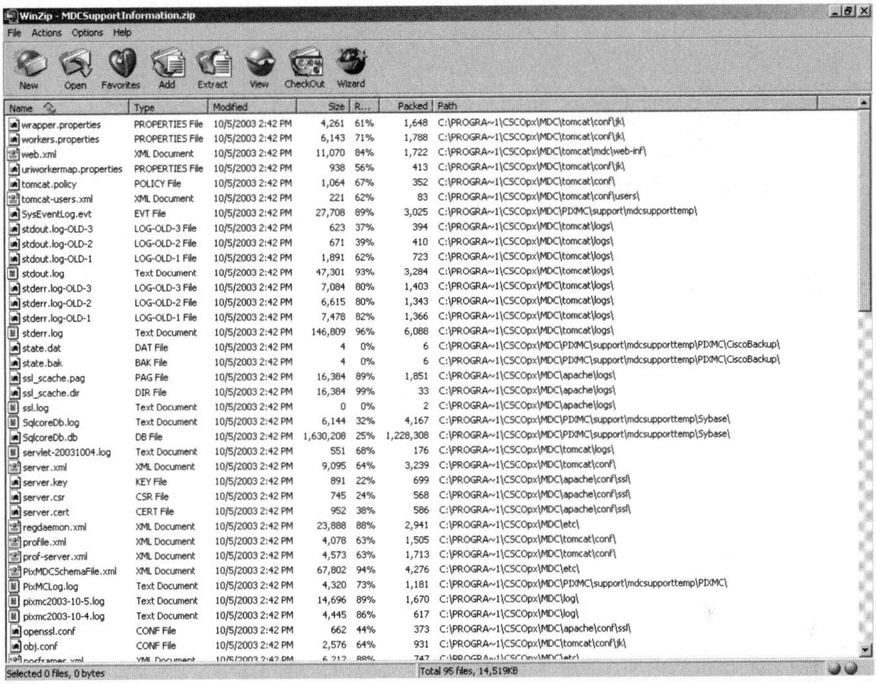

NOTE   The Support tool takes several minutes to complete its task.

Administration: Workflow Setup

Many organizations benefit from separating responsibility for defining, implementing, and deploying corporate firewall policies. For example, a security administrator might be responsible for defining a device configuration file, another administrator for approving the configuration file, and a network operator for deploying the resulting configuration to a device. This separation of responsibility helps maintain the integrity of deployed device configurations.

The Firewall MC supports this separation of responsibility by using activities and jobs, which define tasks that are accomplished by one or more people in succession.

The approval feature is disabled by default, but you can enable the feature if your organization requires a formal approval process. Complete the following steps to enable the activity and job approval processes:

Step 1   Choose **Admin > Workflow Setup**. The Workflow Setup page displays as shown in Figure 19-64.

Figure 19-64   *Workflow Setup Page*

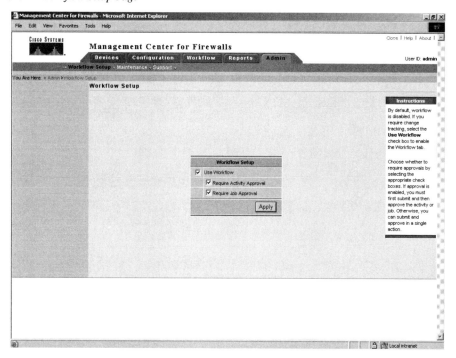

Step 2   Select the **Use Workflow** check box to enable workflow operation.

Step 3   Select the **Require Activity Approval** check box to enable approval process for activities.

Step 4   Select the **Require Job Approval** check box to enable approval process for jobs.

Step 5   Click **Apply**. The Workflow Setup page refreshes to indicate that the Firewall MC received the changes. Click **Reset** if you want to reverse the changes to this screen.

Administration: Maintenance

The Maintenance feature allows you to remove older files after a user-defined time frame to maintain the database and prevent it from growing indefinitely. You can purge only discarded activities and deployed jobs after the expiration date.

Complete the following steps to change the activity and job expiration dates:

Step 1   Choose **Admin > Maintenance**. The Maintenance page displays as shown in Figure 19-65.

Figure 19-65   *Maintenance Page*

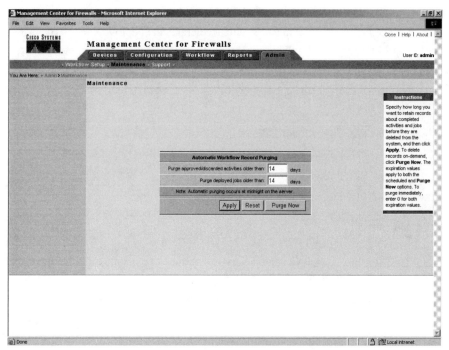

Step 2   Enter the number of days that will transpire before discarded activities are removed from the database in the Activity Expiration (days) field. The default value is 30 days.

Step 3   Enter the number of days that will transpire before deployed jobs are removed from the database in the Job Expiration (days) field. The default value is 30 days.

Step 4 Click **Apply**. The Maintenance page refreshes to indicate that the Firewall MC received the changes. Click **Reset** if you want to reverse the changes you have made. Or click **Purge Now** to purge all activities and jobs that are subject to deletion based on settings in Steps 2 and 3.

Summary

This section summarizes the information you learned in this chapter:

- The Firewall MC provides a web-based interface for configuring and managing multiple PIX Firewalls without requiring CLI knowledge.

- The Firewall MC centralizes and accelerates the deployment and management of multiple PIX Firewalls.

- Firewall MC 1.2.1 supports PIX Firewall Version 6.0 or higher.

- Firewall MC 1.2.1 supports the following hardware models:
  - PIX Firewall 501
  - PIX Firewall 506/506E
  - PIX Firewall 515/515E
  - PIX Firewall 525
  - PIX Firewall 535
  - FWSM

- Firewall MC supports up to 1000 PIX Firewalls.

- CiscoWorks 2000 Common Services 2.2 must be installed on the server before you install Firewall MC 1.1.3 or later.

- The Firewall MC enables the grouping of PIX Firewalls for ease of management and configuration.

- The Firewall MC allows you to generate activity reports based on configuration changes to the PIX Firewall and the Firewall MC.

Chapter Review Questions

To test what you have learned in this chapter, answer the following questions and then refer to Appendix A, "Answers to Chapter Review Questions," for the answers:

1 What version of the PIX Firewall is supported on Firewall MC?

2 What Cisco software package must be installed before installation of Firewall MC?

3 Which protocol does Firewall MC use to securely communicate with the PIX Firewalls it manages?

4 Which models of the PIX Firewall can be managed by Firewall MC?

5 List the basic user task flow for managing PIX Firewalls in Firewall MC:

6 What command do you use to enable configuration access for Firewall MC on a PIX Firewall?

7 How many PIX Firewalls can you manage with Firewall MC?

8 You are importing a PIX Firewall into Firewall MC for management. The PIX Firewall is currently configured with several **conduit** commands. What must you do to successfully import and manage this firewall with Firewall MC?

Lab Exercise—Enterprise PIX Firewall Management

Complete the following lab exercise to practice what you learned in this chapter.

Objectives

In this lab exercise, you complete the following tasks:

- Install Firewall MC.
- Bootstrap the PIX Firewalls.
- Launch the Firewall MC.
- Open an activity and create a group.
- Import PIX Firewalls.
- Configure building blocks.
- Enable the inside and outside interfaces.
- Configure service definitions, service groups, and address translation pool building blocks.
- Create translation rules.
- Configure the PIX Firewall to allow HTTP and CiscoWorks traffic to your inside host.
- Configure a global security policy.
- Approve an activity, create a job, and deploy a job.
- Test the PIX Firewall configuration.

Lab Topology

Figure 19-66 displays the topology you need for the lab exercises in this chapter.

Figure 19-66 *Firewall MC Lab Exercise Visual Objective*

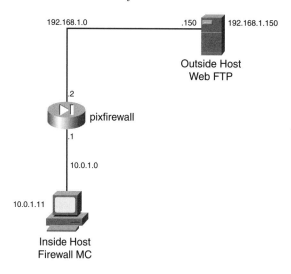

Equipment required to perform the lab includes the following:

- PIX Firewall MC with two interfaces
- Category 5 patch cables
- PC host for an outside subnet with a web server and FTP server
- PC host for the inside subnet running Kiwi Syslog and CiscoWorks Common Services 2.2 and meeting the installation requirements for Firewall MC 1.1.2 server.

NOTE   CiscoWorks Common Services 2.2 is required for installation of Firewall MC. If you do not have CiscoWorks Common Services installed, you must install it before installing Firewall MC in this lab.

Task 1—Install the Firewall MC

This task involves installing the Firewall MC on the inside host. Complete the following steps to install the Firewall MC:

Step 1   Log in to the inside host as the local administrator.

Step 2   Run the Firewall MC 1.2.1 installation files.

Step 3   Once the installation process starts, the Welcome Window displays.

Step 4   Click **Next**. The Software License Agreement window displays.

Step 5   Click **Yes** to agree to the Software License Agreement. The System Requirements window displays.

Step 6   Click **Next**. The Verification window displays.

Step 7   Click **Next**. The Ports Configuration window displays. Use default ports.

Step 8   Click **Next** to start the installation of the Firewall MC. Once setup is finished, the Setup Complete window displays.

Step 9   Click **Finish** to complete the installation.

Task 2—Bootstrap the PIX Firewall

A PIX Firewall must allow SSH connections before a Firewall MC can use it. Complete the following steps to bootstrap the PIX Firewalls:

Step 1   Access the PIX Firewall console.

Step 2   Erase your current PIX Firewall configuration. When prompted to confirm, press **Enter**.

```
pixfirewall(config)# write erase
Erase PIX configuration in flash memory? [confirm]
```

Step 3   Reload the PIX Firewall. When prompted to confirm, press **Enter**:

```
pixfirewall(config)# reload
Proceed with reload? [confirm]
```

Step 4   When prompted to preconfigure the PIX Firewall through interactive prompts, press **Enter**.

Step 5   Enter **cisco** as the enable password:

```
Enable password [<use current password>]: cisco
```

Step 6   Accept the default year by pressing **Enter**:

```
Clock (UTC):
  Year [2003]: <Enter>
```

Step 7   Accept the default month by pressing **Enter**:

    Month [Nov]: **<Enter>**

Step 8   Accept the default day by pressing **Enter**:

    Day [14]: **<Enter>**

Step 9   Accept the default time stored in the host computer by pressing **Enter**:

    Time [11:21:25]: **<Enter>**

Step 10   Enter the IP address of your PIX Firewall's inside interface:

    Inside IP address: **10.0.1.1**

Step 11   Enter the network mask that applies to inside IP address:

    Inside network mask: **255.255.255.0**

Step 12   Enter the host name you want to display at the PIX Firewall command-line prompt:

    Host name: **pixfirewall**

Step 13   Enter the DNS domain name of the network on which the PIX Firewall runs:

    Domain name: **cisco.com**

Step 14   Enter the IP address of the host running PDM:

    IP address of host running PIX Device Manager: **10.0.1.11**

NOTE   Although the PIX Firewall is configured to use PIX Device Manager with this setup dialog, we will be using the Firewall MC. The PIX Firewall needs to enable the HTTP server and HTTP access from the inside interface, the same commands that the Firewall MC and PIX Device Manager require to control the PIX Firewall.

Step 15   Enter **y** at the prompt to save the information to the PIX Firewall's Flash memory.

Task 3—Launch the Firewall MC

Complete the following tasks to launch the Firewall MC:

Step 1   Access the CiscoWorks Server from your web browser by entering the following in the URL field:

`http://127.0.0.1:1741`

Step 2   Click **Yes** in the Security Warning window.

NOTE   Be patient when connecting to the CiscoWorks server. The server might require additional software to be installed during the initial access. Subsequent attempts should not require you to install additional software. Select **Grant Always** when you see the Java Plug-In security window.

Step 3   Log in by entering the default username and password of **admin** and **admin**, respectively.

Step 4   Click **Connect**. You are now logged into the CiscoWorks Desktop.

Step 5   Select the **VPN/Security Management Solution** drawer located in the left panel.

Step 6   Select the **Management Center** folder located in the VPN/Security Management Solution drawer.

Step 7   Select **Firewalls** from the Management Center folder. The Security Alert window opens prompting you to accept a digital certificate.

Step 8   Click **Yes**. You are now logged in to the Firewall MC.

Task 4—Open an Activity and Create a Group

Complete the following steps to open an activity and create a group:

Step 1   Locate the activity bar on the right-hand side of the Firewall MC, toward the top.

Step 2   Click the **Add New Activity Icon**. The Creating New Activity window opens.

Step 3   Enter **activity1** in the New Activity Name field. Enter **Import pixfirewall** in the Initial Activity Comment field.

Step 4 Click **OK**. The Firewall MC page refreshes to display the newly created activity on the activity bar.

Step 5 Select **Devices > Managing Groups**. The Managing Groups page displays.

Step 6 Select the **Global** group and click **Add**. The Define Group Information(new) page displays.

Step 7 Enter **group1** in the Group Name field. Enter a description in the Group Description field.

Step 8 Click **Next**. The Summary page displays.

Step 9 Verify that information displayed in the Summary page is correct and click **Finish**. The Managing Groups page displays with the newly created group, group1.

Task 5—Import the PIX Firewall

Complete the following steps to open an activity and import the PIX Firewall:

Step 1 Select **Devices > Importing Devices**. The Importing Devices page displays.

Step 2 Click **Import**. The Select Target Group(new) page displays.

Step 3 Select the **group1** group and click **Next**. The Select Import Type(new) page displays.

Step 4 Select the **Import configuration from device** radio button and click **Next**. The Define PIX Firewall Contact Info(new) page displays.

Step 5 Enter **10.0.1.1** in the Contact IP address field. Enter **cisco** in the Enable Password field.

Step 6 Click **Next**. The Summary page displays.

Step 7 Verify that the information displayed is correct and click **Finish**. The Import Status page displays. Wait until the status reads COMPLETED before proceeding.

Step 8 Click **Close** to close the Import Status window.

Task 6—Configure the Inside and Outside Interfaces

Complete the following steps to enable the inside and outside interfaces for the PIX Firewalls:

Step 1   Complete the following substeps to configure the inside interface of pixfirewall:

    (1) Select **Configuration > Device Settings**.

    (2) Use the object selector to select **pixfirewall**. The object bar refreshes to indicate that pixfirewall is being configured.

    (3) Select **Interfaces** from the TOC. The Interfaces page displays.

    (4) Select **ethernet1** using the check box located next to the interface and click **Edit**. The Add Interface Name page displays.

    (5) Verify that the **Enable** check box for the interface is selected.

    (6) Select **100full** from the Speed drop-down menu.

    (7) Select **Static** for the IP Address Type radio button.

    (8) Click **Next**. The Add Static Address Information page displays.

    (9) Verify that **10.0.1.1** appears in the IP Address field.

    (10) Verify that **255.255.255.0** appears in the Mask field.

    (11) Click **Next**. The Summary page displays. Verify that the settings displayed on the Summary page are correct.

    (12) Click **Finish**. The Interfaces page displays with the changes to the interface, ethernet1.

Step 2   Complete the following substeps to configure the outside interface:

    (1) Select **Configuration > Device Settings**. The Settings page displays.

    (2) Select **Interfaces** from the TOC. The Interfaces page displays.

    (3) Select **ethernet0** using the check box located next to the interface and click **Edit**. The Add Interface Name page displays.

(4) Select the **Enable** check box for the interface.

(5) Select **100full** from the Speed drop-down menu.

(6) Select **Static** for the IP Address Type radio button.

(7) Click **Next**. The Add Static Address Information page displays.

(8) Enter **192.168.1.2** in the IP Address field. Enter **255.255.255.0** in the Mask field.

(9) Click **Next**. The Summary page displays. Verify that the settings displayed on the Summary page are correct.

(10) Click **Finish**. The Interfaces page displays with the changes to the interface, ethernet0.

Task 7—Configure Service Definitions, Service Groups, and Address Translation Pool Building Blocks

Complete the following steps to configure the building blocks that are used later to enable traffic to the inside host:

Step 1   Select **Configuration > Building Blocks**. The Building Blocks page displays.

Step 2   Use the object selector to select **group1**. The object bar refreshes to indicate that group1 is being configured.

Step 3   Complete the following substeps to add your host as a network object:

(1) Select **Network Objects** from the TOC. The Network Objects page displays.

(2) Click **Add**. The Enter Definition(new) page displays.

(3) Enter **insidehost** in the Network Entity Name. Enter **group1 inside host** in the Description field.

(4) Click **Next**. The Enter IP(s)(new) page displays.

(5) Enter the **10.0.1.11/32** as the IP address and the netmask of your PC in the Network IP Address/Mask field.

(6) Click **Next**. The Select Networks(new) page displays.

(7) Highlight **any** in the Available Objects column and click **Select** to move any to the Selected Objects column.

(8) Click **Next**. The Summary page displays. Verify that the settings listed are correct.

(9) Click **Finish**. The Network Objects page displays with the newly created network object.

Step 4   Complete the following substeps to configure a service definition that defines a service with a range of ports:

(1) Select **Service Definitions** from the TOC. The Service Definitions page displays.

(2) Click **Add**. The Specify Name and Select Transport(new) page displays.

(3) Enter **CiscoWorks** in the Service Name field.

(4) Select **TCP** from the Transport Protocol drop-down menu.

(5) Click **Next**. The Select TCP/UDP Values(new) page displays.

(6) Enter **1741** in the Destination Port Range field.

(7) Enter **0–65535** in the Source Port Range field.

(8) Click **Next**. The Summary page displays. Verify that the settings listed are correct.

(9) Click **Finish**. The Service Definitions page displays with the newly created service definition. To locate the new service definition, use the scroll bar to find the definition among the list.

Step 5   Complete the following substeps to configure a service group that defines traffic to be referenced in ACLs:

(1) Select **Service Groups** from the TOC. The Service Groups page displays.

(2) Click **Add**. The Add Name and Description(new) page displays.

(3) Enter **group1 service group** in the Service Group Name field.

(4) Click **Next**. The Select Services(new) page displays.

(5) Scroll to the bottom of the list of Available Services and highlight **CiscoWorks**.

(6) Click the **Select** button to move CiscoWorks to the list of Selected Services.

(7) Scroll through the list of Available Services and highlight **HTTP**.

(8) Click the **Select** button to move HTTP to the list of Selected Services.

(9) Click **Next**. The Summary page displays.

(10) Verify that the information listed is correct and click **Finish**. The page of the Service Group displays with the newly created Service Group.

Step 6 Complete the following substeps to create an IP address pool for NAT:

(1) Use the object selector to select **pixfirewall**. The object bar refreshes to indicate that pixfirewall is being configured.

(2) Select **Address Translation Pool** from the TOC. The Address Translation Pool window opens.

(3) Click **Create**. The Enter Pool Name(new) page displays.

(4) Enter **OutsidePool** in the Pool Name field.

(5) Click **Next**. The Enter Pool Elements(new) page displays.

(6) Select **outside** from the Interface drop-down menu.

(7) Enter **192.168.1.20-192.168.1.100** in the Address Ranges/Mask (optional) field.

(8) Click **Next**. The Summary page displays.

(9) Verify that the information list is correct and click **Finish**. The Address Translation Pool page displays with the new address translation pool.

Task 8—Create Translation Rules

Complete the following steps to create the following translation rules:

- A static translation for the inside host
- A dynamic translation rule for the inside network

Step 1 Select **Configuration > Translation Rules**. The Translation Rules page displays.

Step 2 Select **Static Translation Rules** from the TOC. The Static Translation Rules page displays.

Step 3   Click **Add**. The Enter Static Translation Rule(new) page displays.

Step 4   Select **inside** from the Original Interface drop-down menu.

Step 5   Enter **10.0.1.11** as the address of the host1 in the Original Address field.

Step 6   Select **outside** from the Translated Interface drop-down menu.

Step 7   Enter **192.168.1.10** in the Translated Address field.

Step 8   Click **Next**. The Summary page displays.

Step 9   Verify that the information displayed is correct and click **Finish**. The Static Translation Rules page displays with the new translated address.

Step 10   Select **Dynamic Translation Rules** from the TOC. The Dynamic Translation Rules page displays.

Step 11   Click **Add**. The Enter Dynamic Translation Rule(new) page displays.

Step 12   Select **inside** from the Original Interface drop-down menu.

Step 13   Enter **10.0.1.0/24** as the address of the network to be translated in the Original Address field.

Step 14   Verify that **OutsidePool** appears in the Address Pool drop-down menu.

Step 15   Click **Next**. The Summary page displays.

Step 16   Verify that the information displayed is correct and click **Finish**. The Dynamic Translation Rules page displays with the new address translation.

Task 9—Configure the PIX Firewall to Allow HTTP and CiscoWorks Traffic to the Inside Host

Complete the following steps to configure the PIX Firewall to allow HTTP and CiscoWorks traffic to the inside host:

Step 1   Select **Configuration > Access Rules**. The Firewall Rules page displays.

Step 2   Use the object selector to select **pixfirewall**. The Firewall Rules page refreshes to indicate that you are configuring access rules at the pixfirewall level.

Step 3   Click **Insert**. The Enter Rule Data(new) page displays.

Step 4   Select the **Permit** radio button.

Step 5   Click the **Select** button below the Source Addresses field. The Selecting Network Objects page displays.

Step 6 Select **Any** from the list of Available Objects and click **Select** to move it to the list of Selected Objects.

Step 7 Click **OK**. The Enter Rule Data(new) page is refreshed with the Source Addresses field containing a new address.

Step 8 Click the **Select** button below the Destination Addresses field. The Selecting Network Objects page displays.

Step 9 Select **group1 > insidehost** from the list of Available Objects and click **Select** to move it to the list of Selected Objects.

Step 10 Click **OK**. The Enter Rule Data(new) page is refreshed with the Destination Addresses field containing a new address.

Step 11 Click the **Select** button below the Services field. The Selecting Services page displays.

Step 12 Select **group1 service group** from the list of Available Objects and click **Select** to move it to the list of Selected Objects.

Step 13 Click **OK**. The Enter Rule Data(new) page is refreshed with the Services field containing the new service.

Step 14 Select **outside** from the Source Interface drop-down menu.

Step 15 Click **OK**. The Firewall Rules page is refreshed with the newly created Firewall Rule.

Task 10—Configure a Global Security Policy

Complete the following steps to configure a security policy for the global group:

Step 1 Complete the following substeps to enable syslog generation for the global group and all children objects:

(1) Select **Configuration > Device Settings**. The Settings page displays.

(2) Click the object selector to select the **Global** group. The object bar refreshes to indicate that global group is being configured.

(3) Click **Logging > Logging Setup** from the TOC. The Logging Setup page displays.

(4) Select the **Enforce/Mandate settings for children** check box. A window displays, which reads, "The members of the current group will lose their values. Are you sure you want to mandate these group values?"

(5) Click **OK**.

(6) Select the **Enable Logging Setup** check box to enable Syslog generation on all output interfaces.

(7) Click **Apply**. The Logging Setup page refreshes to indicate that the Firewall MC received the changes.

Step 2   Complete the following substeps to configure syslog settings for the global group and all children objects:

(1) Click **Logging > Syslog** from the TOC. The Syslog page displays.

(2) Select the **Enforce/Mandate settings for children** check box. A window displays, which reads, "The members of the current group will lose their values. Are you sure you want to mandate these group values?"

(3) Click **OK**.

(4) The Syslog page refreshes to indicate that the Firewall MC received the changes.

(5) Select **local7** from the Facility drop-down menu.

(6) Select **Debugging** from the Level drop-down menu.

(7) Select the **Enable attach timestamp** check box.

(8) Enter **0** in the Log Queue Size field.

(9) Click **Apply**. The Syslog page refreshes to indicate that the Firewall MC received the changes.

(10) Click **Add**. The Enter Syslog Server(new) page displays.

(11) Select **Inside** from the Interface drop-down menu.

(12) Enter **10.0.1.11** in the IP Address field.

(13) Verify that the **UDP** radio button is selected for Protocol.

(14) Enter **1111** in the Port field.

(15) Click **Next**. The Summary page displays.

(16) Verify that the information listed is correct and click **Finish**. The Syslog page refreshes to display the newly created interface.

Step 3   Use the object selector to select **pixfirewall**. The object bar refreshes to indicate that pixfirewall is being configured.

Step 4   Select **Logging > Logging Setup** from the TOC. The Logging Setup page displays.

Step 5   Try to change the Logging Setup settings. Notice that the options to configure are grayed out. We enforced the settings for children objects at the global group level.

Step 6   Select **Logging > Syslog** from the TOC. The Syslog page displays.

Step 7   Try to change the syslog settings. Notice that the options to configure are grayed out. We enforced the settings for children objects on the global group level.

Task 11—Approve an Activity, Create a Job, and Deploy a Job

You have been configuring the PIX Firewall within the context of an activity. Now it is time to deploy the configuration to the PIX Firewall. Complete the following tasks to first approve the activity and then deploy the configuration to the PIX Firewall by creating and deploying a job:

Step 1   Complete the following substeps to approve an activity:

(1) Click the **Submit Activity** icon on the activity bar. A Submitting Activity window displays.

(2) Enter a comment and click **OK**. The Review Device Generation page displays.

(3) Click **Next**. The Summary page displays.

(4) Verify that the information listed on the page is correct and click **Finish**. Wait until the status column shows COMPLETE.

(5) Select the radio button to the left of the pixfirewall icon.

(6) Click **View Configuration** to verify that the operation was successful.

(7) Close the status window. The Activity Management page displays with the pixfirewall activity showing a state of Generate_Open.

(8) Select the radio button to the left of group1.

(9) Click **Refresh**. The status changes to Approved.

Step 2 Complete the following substeps to create a job for deployment:

  (1) Click **Workflow > Job Management**. The Job Management page displays.

  (2) Click **Add**. The Job Name(new) page displays.

  (3) Enter **group1 Deployment Job** in the Job Name field.

  (4) Click **Next**. The Select Activities(new) page displays.

  (5) Verify that the check box next to group1 is selected, and click **Next**. The Select Devices(new) page displays.

  (6) Verify that the check box next to group1 is selected.

  (7) Click **Next**. The Review Devices(new) page displays.

  (8) Click **Next**. The Job State Change(new) page displays.

  (9) Select the **Submit on Finish** check box and click **Next**. The Summary page displays.

  (10) Verify that the information displayed is correct and click **Finish**. The Job Management page displays.

Step 3 Complete the following substeps to deploy the configuration to the PIX Firewall by means of deploying a job:

  (1) Click **Workflow > Job Management**. The Job Management page displays.

  (2) Select the radio button **pixfirewall Deployment Job** and click **Deploy**. The Deploying page displays.

  (3) Enter a Job Comment and click **OK**. The Job Management page refreshes to change the state of the group1 Deployment Job from Approved to Deploying.

Task 12—Test the PIX Firewall Configuration

Complete the following steps to test the configuration:

Step 1 Test logging by completing the following substeps:

  (1) Launch the Kiwi Syslog Daemon.

  (2) Change the syslog port to **1111**.

  (3) Access **pixfirewall**.

    (4) Execute the **show interface** command to generate syslog messages.

    (5) Verify that the Kiwi Syslog Server has received syslog messages from the firewall in reference to the commands that were issued.

Step 2 Test web access to the inside host by completing the following substeps. You should be able to access the inside host from the outside host:

    (1) Open a web browser on the outside host.

    (2) Use the web browser to access the inside host by entering the following:

    `http://192.168.1.10`

Step 3 Test web access to the Firewall MC running on the inside host by completing the following substeps. You should be able to access Firewall MC from the outside host:

    (1) Open a web browser on your outside host.

    (2) Use the web browser to access Firewall MC on Inside Host by entering the following:

    `http://192.168.1.10:1741`

On completion of this chapter, you will be able to perform the following tasks:

- Define key features and concepts of the Auto Update Server (AUS).

- Install AUS.

- Configure the AUS to update Private Internet Exchange (PIX) Firewall configuration files and upgrade images.

- Configure the AUS to remotely manage dynamically addressed PIX Firewalls.

CHAPTER 20

PIX Firewall Maintenance in Enterprise Networks

This chapter introduces the PIX Firewall maintenance for enterprise networks using the AUS. AUS allows you to manage PIX operating system (OS) images running on a large number of PIX Firewalls (up to 1000) and is designed to work with PIX Firewall Version 6.2 and higher.

Introduction to the AUS

AUS facilitates management of up to 1000 firewalls. Firewalls operating in auto-update mode periodically contact AUS to upgrade software images, configurations, and versions of PIX Device Manager (PDM) and to pass device information and status to AUS. Using AUS also facilitates management of devices that obtain their addresses through Dynamic Host Configuration Protocol (DHCP) or that sit behind network access translation (NAT) boundaries.

If you want to deploy AUS behind a NAT boundary in either the enterprise network or the enterprise demilitarized zone (DMZ), the PIX Firewalls being managed by AUS must all be on the same side of the NAT boundary. For example, you can deploy AUS in the DMZ behind a NAT boundary and manage devices that were deployed only on the Internet; however, you cannot deploy AUS in the DMZ behind a NAT boundary with some devices using private addresses on the inside of the boundary and some outside on the Internet.

AUS 1.1 provides the following features:

- Web-based interface for maintaining multiple PIX Firewalls
- Support for PIX Firewall OSs 6.2 or later
- Ability to support dynamically addressed PIX Firewalls
- Support for up to 1000 PIX Firewalls

AUS 1.1 supports the following hardware:

- PIX Firewall 501
- PIX Firewall 506/506E
- PIX Firewall 515/515E
- PIX Firewall 525
- PIX Firewall 535

NOTE	AUS 1.1 also provides support for Management Center for VPN Routers (Router MC) and several Cisco 830 series and 1700 series routers.

Installation Overview

You can install AUS 1.1 on Windows 2000 or Solaris systems. CiscoWorks Common Services 2.2 is required for installation of AUS 1.1. Common Services provides the base components, software libraries, and software packages developed for the AUS. You must first install CiscoWorks Common Services 2.2 and then install AUS 1.1.

NOTE	Support for Solaris systems was introduced in version 1.1 of AUS. AUS 1.0 supports only Windows 2000 systems.

Installation Requirements

Before you begin, verify that the server on which you plan to install the AUS meets the requirements listed in Table 20-1

Table 20-1 *Windows 2000 and Solaris Server Requirements*

Item	Windows 2000	Solaris
Platform	IBM PC-compatible computer with 1 GHz or faster Pentium processor	Sun UltraSPARC 60 MB with 440 MHz or faster processor or Sun UltraSPARCIII (Sun Blade 2000 Workstation or Sun Fire 280R Workgroup Server)
Additional hardware	CD-ROM drive 100BASE-T or faster connection Color monitor with 16-bit video card	
Memory	1 GB minimum	
Available disk space	9 GB minimum on the install drive 2 GB virtual memory NT File System (NTFS) recommended	9 GB on the installation partition (default is /opt) Swap space equal to double the amount of memory (RAM) (for example, 1 GB swap space if your system has 512 MB of RAM)
Operating system	Windows 2000 Server, Professional, or Advanced Server[1] with Service Pack 3 (SP3) or 4	Solaris 2.8

[1]Terminal Services are not supported on Windows 2000 Advanced Server.

Client Access Requirements

Before you log in to the AUS 1.1, verify that the client machine used to log in to the AUS meets the requirements listed in Table 20-2.

Table 20-2 *Windows 2000 and Solaris Client Requirements*

Item	Windows 2000	Solaris
Platform	IBM PC-compatible computer with 300 MHz or faster Pentium processor	Sun SPARCstation or Sun Ultra 10
Additional hardware	Color monitor with 24-bit video card	
Operating system	Windows 2000 Server, Windows 2000 Professional, or Windows XP with SP1[1]	Solaris 2.8[2]
Memory	256 MB minimum	
Available disk space	400 MB virtual memory	
Java	Sun Java plug-in 1.3.1-b24	
Browser	Internet Explorer 6.0 with SP1 or Netscape Navigator 4.79	Netscape Navigator 4.76

[1] Windows XP Service Pack 1a is not supported because it does not include Java Virtual Machine (JVM) support.

[2] If Java Console is not listed in View, you must enable it.

Installation Process

Complete the following steps to install the AUS 1.1, assuming that the CiscoWorks Common Services 2.2 has been installed before beginning:

Step 1 Insert the Cisco AUS CD into the CD-ROM drive. If autorun is enabled, the CD-ROM should start the installation process automatically. If not, locate the **setup.exe** file on the CD-ROM and execute it. Once the installation process starts, the Welcome Window appears.

Step 2 Click **Next**. The Software License Agreement window opens.

Step 3 If you agree to the Software License Agreement, click **Yes** to proceed. If not, click **No** and the installation process stops. The System Requirements window opens.

Step 4 Click **Next**. The Verification window opens.

Step 5 Click **Next**. A Question window appears.

Step 6 If you want to change the AUS database password, click **Yes**. If you do not want to change the AUS database password, click **No**. After making your selection, the AUS installation process begins. On completion, the Setup Complete window opens.

Step 7 Click **Finish**. The AUS installation is now complete.

AUS Initial Configuration Settings

This section introduces and explains the Firewall MC and AUS communication interactions along with using the Firewall MC to prepare the PIX Firewall to use the AUS.

Firewall MC and AUS Communications

Before configuring the Firewall MC to operate with the AUS, you need to understand the interaction between the two components.

Figure 20-1 *Firewall MC and AUS Communication*

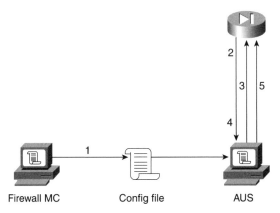

Firewall MC   Config file   AUS

The following steps, shown in Figure 20-1, describe the interaction between the PIX Firewall, Firewall MC, and AUS:

Step 1 The Firewall MC deploys the configuration file to the AUS.

Step 2 At the preset polling interval, the PIX Firewall contacts the AUS for updates.

Step 3 The AUS sends a list of the files that the PIX Firewall should be running. The list can include image files and configuration files.

Step 4 The PIX Firewall verifies whether it is running the correct file. If not, it requests the file from the AUS.

Step 5 The file is downloaded to the PIX Firewall.

AUS Activation

To activate the AUS, complete the following steps:

NOTE   These steps assume that the PIX Firewall is already configured with a minimal configuration that allows it to communicate with the Firewall MC and that the Firewall MC is installed and operational.

Step 1 From the PIX Firewall console, use the **http** commands to enable the PIX Firewall to accept HTTP connections from the AUS:

```
pixfirewall(config)# http server enable
pixfirewall(config)# http ip_address [netmask] [if_name]
```

Step 2 In the Firewall MC, complete the following substeps:

   (1) Enable the AUS and configure the settings that the PIX Firewall will use to communicate with the AUS.

   (2) Configure the method of identification that will be used in these communications.

   (3) Configure settings to enable the Firewall MC to communicate with the AUS.

   (4) Configure the deployment of configuration files to the AUS.

Step 3 Configure the PIX Firewall to use the AUS by copying and pasting the auto-update configuration from the Firewall MC to the PIX Firewall.

AUS and PIX Firewall Communications

After you configure the PIX Firewall to accept HTTP connections from the AUS, you are ready to configure the AUS settings in the Firewall MC. Complete the following steps to enable the AUS and PIX Firewall communication settings:

Step 1   Launch and log in to the Firewall MC.

Step 2   Choose **Configuration > Device Settings > Auto Update Server > Server and Contact Information**. The Server and Contact Information page shown in Figure 20-2 appears.

Figure 20-2   *AUS Server and Contact Information Page*

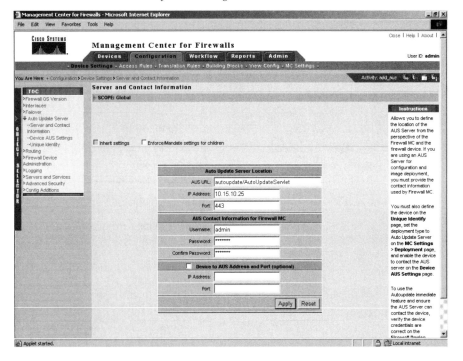

Step 3   Use the Activity Bar to select an existing activity or create a new activity.

Step 4   Enter the IP address of the AUS in the IP Address field.

Step 5   Enter the port number on which AUS is listing in the Port field, typically port 443.

Step 6   Enter the directory path where the update is stored on the AUS. The default path is /autoupdate/AutoUpdateServelet in the Path field.

Step 7   Enter the unique ID that Firewall MC will use to contact the AUS in the Username field.

Step 8   Enter a password that corresponds to the username in the Password field.

Step 9   Confirm the password by entering it into the Confirm Password field.

Step 10   Click **Apply**. The Server and Contact Information refreshes to indicate that Firewall MC received the changes.

Step 11   Choose **Configuration > Device Settings > Auto Update Server > Device AUS Settings**. The Device AUS Settings page shown in Figure 20-3 appears.

Figure 20-3   *Device AUS Settings Page*

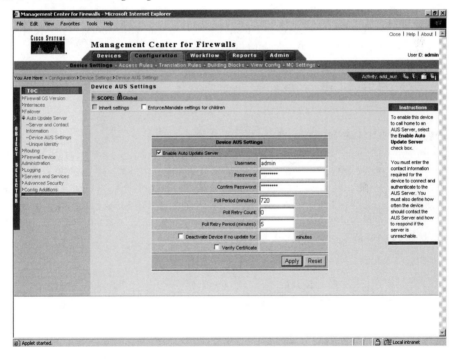

Step 12   Select the **Enable Auto Update Server** check box.

Step 13   Enter the unique ID that the PIX Firewall will use to contact the AUS in the Username field.

Step 14   Enter a password that corresponds to the username in the Password field.

Step 15   Confirm the password by entering it into the Confirm Password field.

Step 16   Enter the number of minutes that elapse between tries for the PIX
Firewall to check the AUS for updates in the Poll Period (minutes) field.
The default is 720 minutes.

Step 17   Enter the number of times the PIX Firewall will try to contact the AUS,
if the initial contact fails, in the Poll Retry Count field. The default is 0.

Step 18   Enter the number of minutes between poll retries in the Poll Retry Period
(minutes) field; the default is 5 minutes.

Step 19   Select the check box to enable **Deactivate Device if no Update for**
option. You use this setting if you want the PIX to operate only with
a specific configuration or update and would rather have the device
deactivated if the update is not completed.

Step 20   If you enabled **Deactivate Device if no Update for** option in Step 19,
enter the number of minutes the PIX Firewall will count down until it
deactivates itself; the default is 0.

Step 21   Click **Apply**. The Device AUS Settings page refreshes to indicate that the
Firewall MC received the changes.

PIX Firewall Unique Identity

The *unique identity* feature enables you to assign an identifier to each PIX Firewall. When
the PIX Firewall "calls home" to check for updates, it uses the unique identifier to identify
itself to the AUS. The AUS then uses the unique identifier to match the current version of
software or configuration of the PIX Firewall to its database of current assignments.
Complete the following steps to configure the method of identification for communications
between the PIX Firewall and the AUS:

Step 1   Launch and log in to the Firewall MC.

Step 2   Choose **Configuration > Device Settings > Auto Update Server >
Unique Identity**. The Unique Identity page shown in Figure 20-4
appears.

Step 3   Use the activity bar to select an existing activity or create a new activity.

Step 4   Use the object selector to select a group or device.

Figure 20-4   *PIX Firewall Unique Identity*

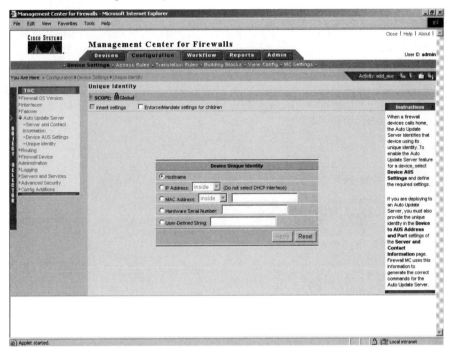

Step 5   Set the unique identifier by selecting the radio button next to one of the following:

— **Hostname**—When you choose this option, the host name configured on the PIX Firewall is used as the unique identifier.

— **IP Address**—When you choose this option, you must use the corresponding drop-down menu to choose from a list of interfaces.

— **MAC Address**—When you choose this option, you must use the corresponding drop-down menu to choose from a list of interfaces.

— **Hardware Serial Number**—When you choose this option, you must enter the hardware serial number of the PIX Firewall.

— **User-Defined String**—When you choose this option, you must manually enter a unique identification string.

Step 6   Click **Apply**. The Unique Identity page refreshes to indicate that the Firewall MC received the change.

PIX Firewall Configuration Deployment

The *deployment* feature allows you to specify the method by which configuration information is deployed by the Firewall MC. Deployment options include saving the information to a file, downloading directly to devices, or using the AUS to act as a repository. Complete the following steps to configure the deployment of configuration files to the AUS:

Step 1   In Firewall MC, Choose **MC Settings > Deployment**. The Deployment page shown in Figure 20-5 opens.

Figure 20-5   *PIX Firewall Deployment Page*

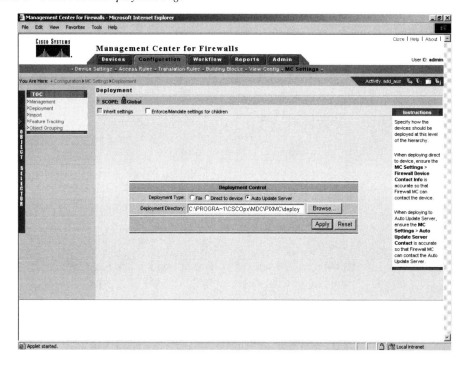

Step 2   Select the **Auto Update Server** radio button to change the deployment type.

Step 3   Click **Apply**. The deployment page refreshes to indicate that the Firewall MC received the changes.

Follow the procedures outlined in Chapter 19, "PIX Firewall Management in Enterprise Networks," to deploy the configuration you created in Firewall MC. If workflow is enabled on Firewall MC, users must follow proper procedures for submittal, approval, and deployment of activities and jobs. You can also manually generate a configuration file within Firewall MC and apply it to the PIX Firewall to enable AUS communications on the device.

Getting Started

You access AUS through the CiscoWorks console. This section introduces launching the AUS and explains the AUS interface.

CiscoWorks Login

Complete the following steps to launch the AUS:

Step 1   Open a browser and point your browser to the IP address of the CiscoWorks machine with a port number of 1741. If the CiscoWorks server is local, you type the following address in the browser:

```
http://127.0.0.1:1741 <enter>
```

Step 2   Use the default username and password of **admin** and **admin** to log in to CiscoWorks for the first time. If you changed the default admin password during installation, use that password instead.

Step 3   Select the **VPN/Security Management Solution** drawer located on the lower-left side of the CiscoWorks page. The VPN/Security Management Solution drawer displays to reveal a set of folders and the AUS icon.

Step 4   Click the **Auto Update Server** icon to launch the AUS. A security alert window appears.

Step 5   Click **Yes** to accept the security certificate. The AUS opens in another window.

Step 6   Minimize CiscoWorks in the background to avoid confusion when working with the AUS.

AUS Interface

By learning the elements of the AUS interface, you can carry out the basic user task flow and navigate the AUS with ease. Figure 20-6 illustrates the AUS graphical user interface (GUI).

Figure 20-6 *AUS Interface*

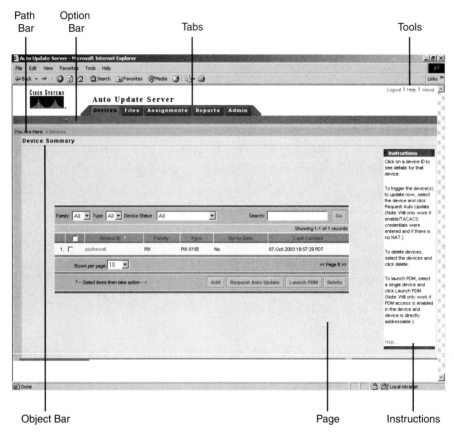

The elements of the AUS are as follow:

- **Path bar**—Provides a context for the displayed page. Shows the tab, option, and the current page.

- **Options bar**—Displays the options available for the tab.

- **Tabs**—Provide access to product functionality. By clicking a tab, you are able to access its options:.

  — **Devices**—Displays summary information about devices.

  — **Images**—Provides information about PIX Firewall software images, PDM images, and configuration files. Images also allow you to add and delete PIX Firewall software images and PDM images.

    — **Assignments**—Provides assignment information and allows you to change device-to-image assignments and image-to-device assignments.

    — **Reports**—Displays reports.

    — **Admin**—Allows you to perform administrative tasks.

- **Tools**—Contains the following buttons:

    — **Logout**—Logs you out of CiscoWorks 2000.

    — **Help**—Opens a new window that displays context-sensitive help for the displayed page. The window also contains buttons for accessing overall help contents, index listings, and search tools.

    — **About**—Displays the version of the application.

- **Instructions**—Provides a brief overview of how to use the page.

- **Page**—Displays the area in which you perform application tasks.

NOTE   If you are having issues with devices, images, or reports appearing or not appearing as normally expected, it might be necessary to clear your browser cache.

Devices, Images, and Assignments

This section explains the devices, images, and assignment tabs of the AUS management screen.

AUS Devices

Clicking the Device tab displays the Device Summary table shown in Figure 20-7. The table shows all managed PIX Firewalls, PIX Firewalls that have not yet contacted AUS, or PIX Firewalls whose image files are not current. The table contains information about the PIX Firewalls in AUS, such as the device ID, platform family, platform type, and the last time that the PIX Firewall device contacted AUS.

You can click a column name to sort the table by column information, or you can filter and search the table. Use the drop-down menus for Family, Type, or Device Status to filter the Device Summary table. Use the Search field to enter a search string and then the Go button to execute the search.

Figure 20-7 *AUS Devices Tab*

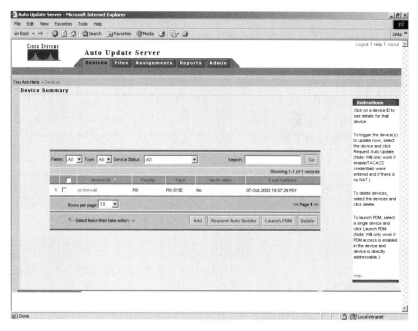

The Device Summary table columns are as follow, from left to right:

- **Device ID**—Displays the name the PIX Firewall device uses when identifying itself to AUS. It is typically the unique ID that is displayed, which can be a host name or serial number, among others. Click an entry in the Device ID column to display a table that shows details and associated files for that particular Device ID. The table appears in a new window.

- **Family**—The series to which the PIX Firewall belongs. Select the family from the list to filter the table according to family.

- **Type**—Select the type from the list to filter the table according to type. The options that are available in the Type list correspond to the family specified in the Family list.

- **Up to Date**—Indicates whether the device is running the newest files.

- **Last Contact**—Displays the last time that the PIX Firewall contacted the AUS.

You use the Request Auto Update button to make the PIX Firewall contact the AUS immediately. Such a step ensures that the PIX Firewall is running the newest files instead of waiting for the device to contact AUS at the specified interval. For example, you might want to request that a device contact AUS if the security of your network has been affected.

Complete the following steps to force the PIX Firewall to contact the AUS:

Step 1   Choose **Devices**. The Devices page appears.

Step 2   Select the check box next to the PIX Firewall that you want to contact the AUS immediately.

Step 3   Click the **Request Auto Update** button below the Device Summary table. The Request Auto Update Confirmation page appears. The Request Auto Update Confirmation page displays a message that reads, "Requests are successfully queued. Please check Event Report for details."

Step 4   Click **Event Report** to see whether the AUS was contacted. The Event Report page appears with the event report for the PIX Firewall.

AUS Images

The AUS allows you to manage PIX Firewall software images, PDM images, and PIX Firewall configuration files. From the Files tab shown in Figure 20-8, you can add or delete PIX Firewall software images or PDM images and delete PIX Firewall configuration files. You can add PIX Firewall configuration files to the AUS only by using the Firewall MC deployment feature.

Figure 20-8   *AUS Files Tab*

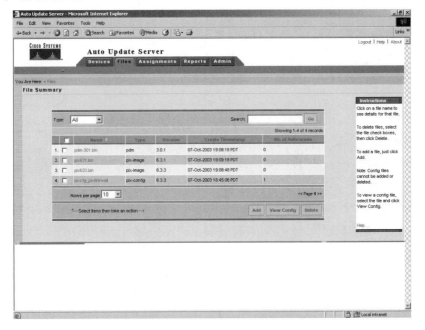

The Software Images table columns are as follow, from left to right:

- **Name**—Name of the image or configuration file that is stored on the AUS. You can click an entry in the Name column to display a table of information about the file.

- **Type**—Type of image, such as PDM, PIX Firewall software image, or configuration file.

- **Version**—Version of the image.

- **Create Timestamp**—Time that the image was added to the AUS.

- **No. of References**—Number of devices that have been assigned to the file.

To add an image to the AUS, complete the following steps:

Step 1 Choose **Files**. The Files page appears.

Step 2 Click the **Add**. The Add File page appears.

Step 3 Manually enter the location and name of the image file or use the **Browse** button to locate the software image.

Step 4 Select either **PDM** or **pix-image** from the Image Type drop-down menu.

Step 5 Click **OK**. The Software Images page refreshes to display the newly added PDM or PIX Firewall image file.

Complete the following steps to delete an image from the AUS:

Step 1 Select the **Images** tab. The Images page appears.

Step 2 Select the check box next to the image that you want to delete.

Step 3 Click **Delete**. The Delete Image page appears.

Step 4 Click **OK**. The Images page appears with the image removed from the list of images.

NOTE Deleting an image file that is assigned to multiple devices deletes all references between the image file and the devices. To delete a PIX configuration file, you must use the Firewall MC.

AUS Assignments

When a new image file is released, you can download the file, add it to AUS, and assign the image to a device. This process is beneficial, for example, when a new file release fixes a security problem that an older version of the file did not address or when you want to upgrade the configuration files after deployment using the AUS.

Figure 20-9   *AUS Assignments Tab*

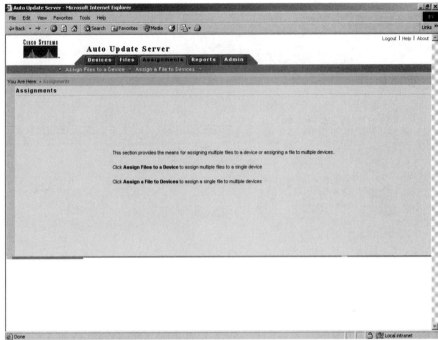

From the Assignments tab shown in Figure 20-9, you can do the following:

- Assign one or more images to one device
- Assign one or more images to multiple devices

Multiple Images to a Single Device

Complete the following steps to assign one or more images to a single PIX Firewall:

Step 1   Choose **Assignments**. The Assignments page appears as shown in Figure 20-10.

Step 2   Select **Assign Files to a Device**. The Device Assignment Summary page appears as shown in Figure 20-10.

Figure 20-10   *AUS Assignment—Multiple Files to a Single Device*

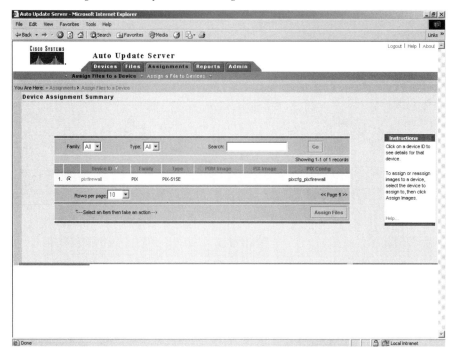

Step 3   Select the radio button next to the PIX Firewall to which you want to assign images and click **Assign Images**. The Assign Files to Devices page shown in Figure 20-11 appears.

Step 4   Select the PIX Firewall software image you want to assign from the PIX Image drop-down menu.

Step 5   Select the PDM image you want to assign from the PDM drop-down menu.

Step 6   Click **OK**. The Device Assignment Summary page appears with the appropriate image files updated in the respective columns.

Figure 20-11   *AUS Assignment—Multiple Images to a Single Device*

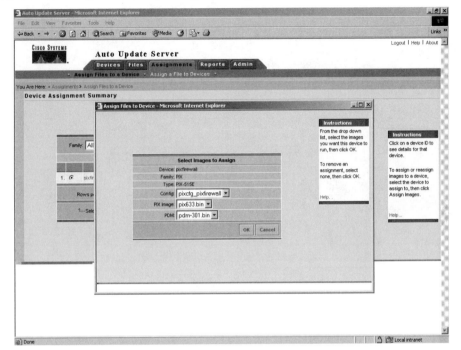

Single Image to Multiple Devices

Complete the following steps to assign one or more images to multiple PIX Firewalls:

Step 1   Choose **Assignments**. The Assignments page shown in Figure 20-12 appears.

Step 2   Select **Assign a File to Devices**. The File Assignment Summary page appears as shown in Figure 20-12.

Step 3   Select the radio button by the image that you want to assign to Devices and click **Assign Devices**. The Assign File to Devices page appears.

Step 4   Select the check box next to the PIX Firewall to which you want to have the image assigned.

Step 5   Click **OK**. The File Assignment Summary page appears with the No. of Devices column incremented with the number of PIX Firewalls chosen earlier.

Figure 20-12 *AUS Assignment—Single Image to Multiple Devices*

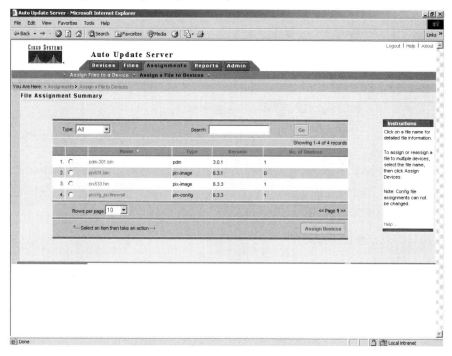

Step 6 Click the filename to see what PIX Firewalls are assigned to certain images. In addition to PIX Firewall software images and PDM images, you can also assign PIX Firewall configuration files.

NOTE Depending on the speed of your network and the sizes of the images that you are deploying, the amount of time varies greatly. Be patient.

Reports and Administration

This section introduces the reporting and administration feature of the AUS.

Reports—System Information

The System Info Report table shown in Figure 20-13 shows general information about AUS and also shows how busy the server is. The report contains information such as how many devices have contacted AUS and how many configuration files have been downloaded within the last 24 hours. Choose **Reports > System Info** to view the System Info Report.

Figure 20-13 *System Information Report*

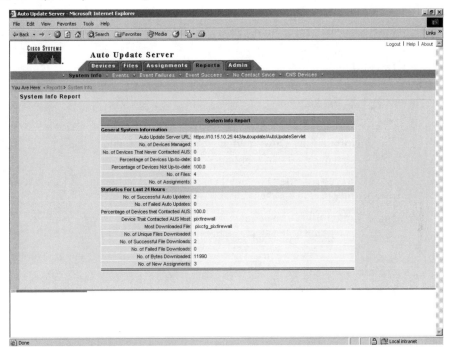

The System Info Report table contains the following information:

- **Auto Update Server URL**—URL that the PIX Firewalls use to contact the AUS.

- **No. of Devices Managed**—The number of PIX Firewalls that are being managed by the AUS.

- **No. of Devices That Never Contacted AUS**—The number of PIX Firewalls that are configured on the AUS but have never contacted the AUS.

- **Percentage of Devices Up-to-Date**—The percentage of devices that have contacted AUS and are up-to-date.

- **Percentage of Devices Not Up-to-Date**— The percentage of devices that have contacted AUS previously but are not up-to-date.

- **No. of Files**—The number of files that the AUS contains. These files include PIX Firewall images, PDM images, and PIX Configuration files.

- **No. of Assignments**—The number of image-to-device and device-to-image assignments.

- **No. of Successful Auto Updates**—The number of times that devices successfully contacted AUS during the last 24 hours.

- **No. of Failed Auto Updates**—The number of times that devices did not contact AUS during the last 24 hours.

- **Percentage of Devices that Contacted AUS**—Percentage of devices that contacted AUS during the last 24 hours.

- **Device That Contacted AUS Most**—The device that contacted AUS most often during the last 24 hours.

- **Most Downloaded File**—The file that has been downloaded most often in a 24-hour period.

- **No. of Unique Files Downloaded**—The number of unique files that the AUS downloaded during the last 24 hours.

- **No. of Successful File Downloads**—The number of file downloads that completed successfully during last 24 hours.

- **No. of Failed File Downloads**—The number of times an error occurred while a device was performing an auto update during the last 24 hours.

- **No of Bytes Downloaded**—The number of bytes that have been downloaded during the last 24 hours.

- **No. of New Assignments**—The number of new image-to-device and device-to-image assignments during the last 24 hours.

Reports—Event Report

The event report, shown in Figure 20-14, describes information such as the event type and the result of the event. It also shows information about notifications sent from PIX Firewall devices to AUS. For example, if a PIX Firewall device downloads a configuration file and discovers errors, it sends an alert to the AUS, which the table displays. Entries are added each time a device contacts the AUS or a file is downloaded.

Click a column name to sort the table by column information. When you click the Device ID column, the table is sorted first by device ID, then by timestamp. You can also filter the table and search the table for a specified device ID. Another way to filter the event report data is to use the drop-down menus located at the top of the event report.

Figure 20-14 *Event Report*

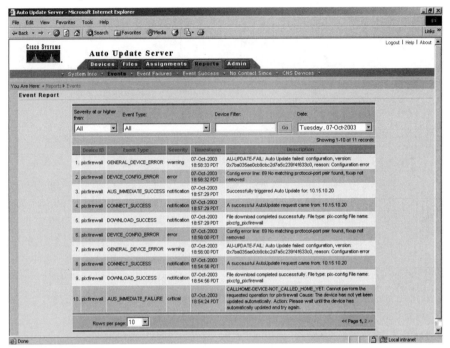

The possible event types are as follow:

- **CONNECT_SUCCESS**—The PIX Firewall contacted the AUS successfully and reported its inventory details.

- **CONNECT_FAILURE**—A problem occurred during an auto-update attempt. Possible causes are

    — Error while parsing Extensible Markup Language (XML).

    — Invalid credentials.

    — Device has not been added to AUS.

    — Connectivity problems.

    — Database down while trying to add record.

- **DEVICE_CONFIG_ERROR**—The PIX Firewall reported errors to the AUS, or errors occurred while loading the configuration file assigned to the device.

- **GENERAL_DEVICE_ERROR**—The PIX Firewall reported a nonconfiguration file error to AUS. Possible causes are

    — Problems connecting to the Auto Update servlet.

    — Problems with the downloaded image (invalid checksum).

- **DOWNLOAD SUCCESS**—The file was successfully sent to the remote device without error. This does not mean that the device is running the image successfully; this message could be followed by either DEVICE_CONFIG_ERROR or GENERAL_DEVICE_ERROR.

- **DOWNLOAD_FAILURE**—An error occurred while an image or configuration file was being downloaded. Possible causes are

  — Invalid credentials.

  — Communication problems.

  — Database problem.

- **AUS_IMMEDIATE_SUCCESS**—The AUS successfully contacted and updated the device.

- **AUS_IMMEDIATE_FAILURE**—An error occurred while the device was being updated. Possible causes are

  — The server does not have direct connectivity to the device. (For example, it is behind a NAT boundary.)

  — The enable or TACACS+ username and password that the device uses to authenticate AUS are incorrect.

  — An internal error occurred.

- **SYSTEM_ERROR**—An internal error occurred.

Admin—NAT Settings

The Admin screen shown in Figure 20-15 allows you to change NAT settings. NAT settings allow you to specify the correct address for devices to use when they try to download images or report errors. If AUS is behind a NAT boundary, the address that the device uses to contact AUS is most likely different from the actual IP address. Therefore, you must specify the IP address that devices on the public side of the NAT boundary must use to access AUS.

Complete the following steps to configure NAT settings:

Step 1   Choose **Admin > NAT Settings**. The NAT Settings page appears.

Step 2   Select the **NAT Address** radio button.

Step 3   Enter the IP address that corresponds to the public IP address.

Step 4   Click **Update**. The NAT Settings page refreshes to indicate that the AUS received the changes.

Figure 20-15 *NAT Settings Screen*

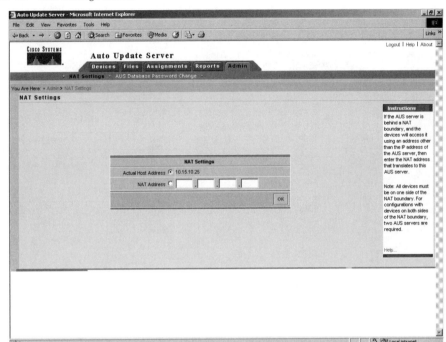

Admin—AUS Database Password Change

The AUS Database Password Change page shown in Figure 20-16 allows you to change the password of the AUS database. It is recommended that you change this password for security purposes.

Figure 20-16 *AUS Database Password Change Screen*

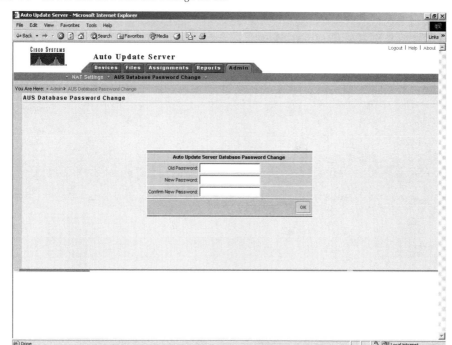

Complete the following steps to change the AUS database password:

Step 1 Choose **Admin > AUS Database Password Change**. The AUS Database Password Change page appears.

Step 2 Enter the current password in the Old Password field.

Step 3 Enter the new password in the New Password field.

Step 4 Enter the new password again to confirm it, in the Confirm New Password field.

Step 5 Click **Update**. The AUS Database Password Change page refreshes to indicate that the AUS received the changes.

Summary

This section summarizes the information you learned in this chapter:

- The AUS provides a web-based interface for
  - Upgrading PIX Firewall software images.
  - Upgrading PDM images.
  - Managing and deploying PIX Firewall configuration files.
- The AUS requires CiscoWorks Common Services for its installation and operation.
- You can use the AUS to manage up to 1000 PIX Firewall devices.

Chapter Review Questions

To test what you have learned in this chapter, answer the following questions and then refer to Appendix A, "Answers to Chapter Review Questions," for the answers:

1 What are the three main tasks performed by AUS?

2 How many PIX Firewalls can be managed by an AUS server?

3 How much memory is required on the server for the installation of AUS server?

4 What is the minimum version of PIX Firewall supported by AUS?

5 Before you install AUS, what software component must you install on the server?

Lab Exercise—PIX Firewall Maintenance in Enterprise Networks

Complete the following lab exercises to practice enterprise PIX Firewall maintenance procedures. If you have not completed the lab exercises in Chapter 19, you can use the following initial configuration commands. You must also refer to the lab in Chapter 19 and add **pixfirewall** to the Firewall MC device list.

NOTE   Many of the settings shown in this initial configuration are default values and do not need to be entered on your PIX Firewall. Specific commands that must be entered are shown in bold for your convenience.

NOTE The instructions assume that workflow is not enabled in the Firewall MC. If you have workflow enabled, you must follow the appropriate submittal, approval, and deployment procedures for activities and jobs as required by your workflow settings.

NOTE The instructions assume that the username and password for access to Firewall MC and AUS are as follows:

Username: **pixuser**
Password: **cisco**

If your settings are different, use your username and password when configuring the AUS settings.

```
:
PIX Version 6.3(3)
interface ethernet0 100full
interface ethernet1 100full
nameif ethernet0 outside security0
nameif ethernet1 inside security100
enable password 8Ry2YjIyt7RRXU24 encrypted
passwd 2KFQnbNIdI.2KYOU encrypted
hostname pixfirewall
domain-name cisco.com
fixup protocol dns maximum-length 512
fixup protocol ftp 21
fixup protocol h323 h225 1720
fixup protocol h323 ras 1718-1719
fixup protocol http 80
fixup protocol rsh 514
fixup protocol rtsp 554
fixup protocol sip 5060
fixup protocol sip udp 5060
fixup protocol skinny 2000
fixup protocol smtp 25
fixup protocol sqlnet 1521
fixup protocol tftp 69
pager lines 24
mtu outside 1500
mtu inside 1500
mtu dmz 1500
ip address outside 192.168.1.2 255.255.255.0
ip address inside 10.0.1.1 255.255.255.0
ip audit info action alarm
ip audit attack action alarm
pdm history enable
arp timeout 14400
timeout xlate 3:00:00
timeout conn 1:00:00 half-closed 0:10:00 udp 0:02:00 rpc 0:10:00 h225 1:00:00
timeout h323 0:05:00 mgcp 0:05:00 sip 0:30:00 sip_media 0:02:00
timeout uauth 0:05:00 absolute
aaa-server TACACS+ protocol tacacs+
aaa-server RADIUS protocol radius
```

```
aaa-server LOCAL protocol local
http server enable
http 10.0.1.0 255.255.255.0 inside
no snmp-server location
no snmp-server contact
snmp-server community public
no snmp-server enable traps
floodguard enable
telnet timeout 5
ssh timeout 5
console timeout 0
terminal width 80
Cryptochecksum:aa0cc6e47d705ed128e041c2c2a8412b
: end
```

Objectives

In this lab exercise, you complete the following tasks:

- Install the AUS.

- Configure the PIX Firewall to use the AUS.

- Verify the operation of the PIX Firewall and the AUS.

- Add a PIX Firewall software and PDM image to the AUS.

- Assign images to a device.

Lab Topology

Figure 20-17 displays the topology you need for the lab exercises in this chapter.

Figure 20-17 *Enterprise PIX Firewall Maintenance Exercise Visual Objective*

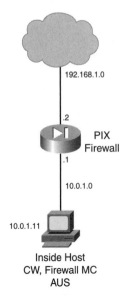

192.168.1.0

.2

PIX
Firewall

.1

10.0.1.0

10.0.1.11

Inside Host
CW, Firewall MC
AUS

Equipment required to perform the lab includes the following:

- A PIX Firewall with two interfaces
- Category 5 patch cables
- Host with the CiscoWorks Common Services 2.2 and Firewall MC 1.2.1 ready to install AUS

NOTE   Before starting this lab exercise, ensure that CiscoWorks Common Services 2.2 and Firewall MC 1.2.1 have been installed on your system.

Task 1—Install the AUS

Complete the following steps to install the AUS on the inside host:

Step 1   Run the AUS 1.1 installation file.

Step 2   Once the installation process starts, the Welcome Window opens.

Step 3   Click **Next**. The Software License Agreement window opens.

Step 4   Click **Yes** to agree to the Software License Agreement. The System Requirements window opens.

Step 5   Click **Next**. The Verification window opens.

NOTE   If a question window appears stating "The Service crmdmgtd is not stopped. Press YES to keep waiting or press NO to abort," click Yes.

Step 6   Click **Next**. A question window asks whether you want to change the AUS database password.

Step 7   Click **No**. Once setup is finished, the Setup Complete window opens.

Step 8   Click **Finish**. The AUS installation is now complete.

Step 9   If required by the installation routine, reboot the inside host.

Task 2—Configure the Firewall MC and PIX Firewall to Use the AUS

You must configure the PIX Firewall to use the AUS. Complete the following steps to configure the PIX Firewall to use AUS:

Step 1   Launch the Firewall MC.

Step 2   Click **Configuration > Device Settings > AutoUpdate Server > Server and Contact Information.**

Step 3   Use the Activity bar to select an existing activity or create a new activity.

Step 4   Use the object selector to select **pixfirewall**.

Step 5   Deselect **Inherit settings from Global** check box**.**

Step 6   Complete the following substeps to configure the server and contact information:

(1) Enter **autoupdate/AutoUpdateServlet** in the AUS URL field.

(2) Enter the IP address of your host (**10.0.1.11**) in the IP Address field.

(3) Verify that **443** appears in the Port field.

(4) Enter **pixuser** in the Username field.

(5) Enter **cisco** in the Password field.

(6) Enter **cisco** in the Confirm Password field.

(7) Click **Apply**.

Step 7   Click **Device AUS Settings** from table TOC. You should see the Device AUS Settings page.

Step 8   Deselect **Inherit settings from Global** check box**.**

Step 9   Complete the following substeps to configure the device settings:

(1) Select the **Enable Auto Update Server** check box.

(2) Enter **pixuser** in the Username field.

(3) Enter **cisco** in the Password field.

(4) Enter **cisco** in the Confirm Password field.

(5) Enter **2** in the Poll Period (minutes) field.

(6) Enter **35** in the Poll Retry Count field.

(7) Enter **2** in the Poll Retry Period (minutes) field.

(8) Click **Apply**.

Step 10 To verify that unique identity is set to use the host name, click **Unique Identity** on the TOC.

NOTE   You must configure the unique ID for the PIX Firewall for each PIX Firewall that is going to use the AUS. If you set the unique ID as the host name, you must enter the host name in the Unique ID field. If you set the unique ID to the serial number, you must enter the serial number for each PIX Firewall that is going to use the AUS.

Step 11 Complete the following substeps to configure the deployment of configuration files:

(1) Click **MC Settings > Deployment** in the TOC. The Deployment page appears.

(2) Deselect the **Inherit settings from Global** check box.

(3) Select the **Auto Update Server** radio button to change the deployment type.

(4) Click **Apply**. The Deployment page refreshes to indicate that the Firewall MC received the changes.

Step 12 Because you are now deploying the configuration to the AUS for distribution, it is necessary to configure the PIX Firewall to contact the AUS for future updates. Complete the following steps to generate the configuration and paste the AUS commands to pixfirewall:

(1) Select **Configuration > View Config**. The View Config page appears.

(2) Click **Generate Config** from the TOC. The Generate Config page appears.

(3) Scroll through the configuration generated by Firewall MC and locate following the lines:

```
auto-update device-id hostname
auto-update poll-period 2 35 2
auto-update server https://pixfirewall:cisco@10.0.1.11:443/
    autoupdate/AutoUpdateServlet
```

(4) Copy these lines and paste them into the configuration of the PIX Firewall.

Step 13 Submit the activity.

Step 14 Create and deploy a job that contains the previously created activity.

Task 3—Verify the Operation of the PIX Firewall and the AUS

Complete the following steps to verify that the PIX Firewall is able to successfully contact the AUS:

Step 1 Click the **Auto Update Server** icon, located in the VPN/Security Management Solution drawer, to launch the AUS. The AUS opens in another window.

Step 2 Minimize CiscoWorks in the background to avoid confusion when working with the AUS.

Step 3 Select **Reports**. The Reports page appears.

Step 4 Click **Event Report**. The Event Report page appears.

Step 5 You should see an event with CONNECT_SUCCESS on the event type along with the IP address of the PIX Firewall.

Task 4—Add a PIX Firewall Software and a PDM Image to the AUS

In this task, you add the PIX Firewall image file pix633.bin and the PDM image file pdm-301.bin using the AUS. You must obtain the image files from Cisco.com to complete these steps.

Complete the following steps to add software and PDM images to the AUS:

Step 1 Select **Files**. The File Summary page appears.

Step 2 Click **Add**. The Add File window appears.

Step 3 Click the **Browse** button. A Choose File window opens.

Step 4 Choose the location of the file **pix633.bin** and click **Open**.

Step 5 Select **pix-image** from the File Type drop-down menu.

Step 6 Click **OK**. The File Summary page refreshes to display the PIX Firewall image.

Step 7 Click **Add**. The Add File page appears.

Step 8 Click the **Browse** button. A Choose File window opens.

Step 9   Locate the file **pdm-.bin** and click **Open**.

Step 10   Select **pdm** from the File Type drop-down menu.

Step 11   Click **OK**. The File Summary page refreshes to display the PDM image
file.

Task 5—Assign Images to a Device

Complete the following steps to assign images to the PIX Firewall:

Step 1   Select **Assignments**. The Assignments page appears.

Step 2   Click **Assign Files to a Device**. The Device Assignment Summary
page appears.

Step 3   Select **pixfirewall** using the radio button next to it and click **Assign Files**.
The Assign Files to Device page appears.

Step 4   Select **pix633.bin** from the PIX Image drop-down menu.

Step 5   Select **pdm-301.bin** from the PDM drop-down menu.

Step 6   Click **OK**. The Device Assignment Summary page displays the new
image association.

PART VII

Special Topics

On completion of this chapter, you will be able to perform the following tasks:

- Describe the Firewall Services Module (FWSM) features and benefits.
- Explain the similarities and differences between the FWSM and the PIX Firewall.
- Describe a typical deployment scenario for the FWSM.
- Initialize the FWSM.
- Configure the switch VLANs.
- Configure the FWSM interfaces.
- Prepare the FWSM to work with PIX Device Manager (PDM).
- Install PDM on the FWSM.

Firewall Services Module

The Cisco FWSM is an integrated module for the Cisco Catalyst 6500 Series Switch and the Cisco 7600 Series Internet Router. The Cisco Catalyst 6500 provides intelligent services such as firewall capability, intrusion detection, and virtual private networking, along with multilayer LAN, WAN, and MAN switching capabilities. The Cisco 7600 Series Internet Router offers optical WAN and metropolitan-area network (MAN) networking with line-rate IP services at the network edge.

FWSM Overview

The Cisco FWSM is a high-performance firewall solution, providing up to 5 Gbps of throughput per module and scaling to 20 GB of bandwidth with multiple modules in one chassis. The FWSM is completely VLAN aware, offers dynamic routing, and is fully integrated within the Cisco Catalyst 6500 Series switches. The FWSM is based on Cisco PIX Firewall technology and, therefore, offers the same security and reliability as the PIX Firewall.

NOTE The 5 Gbps throughput is based on User Datagram Protocol (UDP) traffic.

FWSM key features include

- Switching and firewall capabilities on a single chassis
- Based on PIX Firewall technology
- Supports up to 100 firewall VLANs
- Supports entire PIX Firewall 6.0 feature set and some 6.3 features
- No failover license required
- 5 Gbps throughput, full duplex
- 1 million concurrent connections
- Multiple blades supported in one chassis

- Dynamic routing via Routing Information Protocol (RIP) and Open Shortest Path First (OSPF)

- High availability via intrachassis or interchassis stateful failover

- Management available via command-line interface (CLI), PIX Device Manager (PDM), PIX Management Center (MC), and Architecture for Voice, Video, and Integrated Data (AVVID) partners

- Supports secure, out-of-band management via IP Security (IPSec) on management VLAN

In addition to the entire PIX Firewall 6.0 feature set, the FWSM offers Inter-Switch Link (ISL) protocol support. It also supports the following features of PIX Firewall Software Version 6.3:

- Command authorization

- OSPF routing protocol

- Object grouping

- ILS/NetMeeting fixup

- URL filtering enhancement

- 802.1Q protocol

NOTE   ILS stands for Internet Locator Service.

FWSM and PIX Firewall Feature Comparison

With the addition of support for 802.1Q VLANs, OSPF routing protocol, and many other new features, PIX Firewall Version 6.3 has in many ways closed the gap in functionality between FWSM and the PIX Firewall. The FWSM has the following characteristics that differ from the PIX Firewall appliance:

- By default, FWSM denies all packets in all directions, including Internet Control Message Protocol (ICMP) pings from the management interface.

- The **conduit** command is not supported.

- ActiveX and Java filtering fixups are not supported.

- By default, the HTTP fixup is disabled.

- Bidirectional NAT is not supported.

- ISL protocol is supported.

- Faster performance is provided, even compared to a PIX Firewall 535.

- Support of up to 100 interfaces is provided, a significantly greater number, even compared to a PIX Firewall 535, which supports a maximum of 24 interfaces.

NOTE	All FWSM interfaces, including the console, are mapped via VLANs.

- No failover licensing is required.
- Virtual private network (VPN) functionality (IPSec, Point-to-Point Tunneling Protocol [PPTP] and Layer 2 Tunneling Protocol [L2TP]) packets flowing across the firewall is not supported.
- Intrusion detection system (IDS) syslog messages are not generated.
- The maximum number of access control lists (ACLs) supported is 128,000. PIX Firewalls support up to 2 million ACLs.

NOTE	The number 128,000 refers to the number of access control entry (ACE) nodes available on the network processor. The actual practical number of ACLs supported by the FWSM is approximately 80,000.

Catalyst 6500 Switch Requirements

The FWSM occupies one slot in a Cisco Catalyst 6500 switch. You can install up to four modules in the same switch chassis. The FWSM has the following requirements for the Catalyst 6500 switch:

- Supervisor 1a or 2 with Multilayer Switch Feature Card 2 (MSFC2) or Supervisor 720
- Native Cisco IOS Software release 12.1(13)E or higher (12.2(14)SX1 for Supervisor 720)
- Hybrid CatOS minimum software release 7.5(1) (excluding Supervisor 720)

Network Model

You can use the FWSM in a variety of topologies, depending on the needs of your network. For example, in a data center, you might want to provide access control or segregate your security domains. The security domain can be a collection of servers with the same security level. That domain can contain multiple subnets or server farms. When you configure the FWSM to function on the perimeter of the network, the module can provide access control to the inside network as a whole or segregate multiple security zones through VLAN interfaces of different security levels. The security zones can be in the same network or can define the boundaries of multiple networks.

The FWSM configuration has the following characteristics:

- Each firewall interface is a Layer 3 interface. It is uniquely associated with a VLAN, a security level, and an IP address.

- An interface is firewalled depending on where the interface is used. The module interfaces are firewalled, whereas all other interfaces in the system are considered outside the firewall. Each firewall interface has a fixed VLAN.

- You can configure the MSFC as a connected router on any one and only one firewall interface, but it is not necessary to configure the MSFC as a connected router. The FWSM views all networks or subnetworks beyond an interface as belonging to the same security level.

- Traffic from all the nonfirewall VLANs in the switch (those not recognized by the module) is routed through the MSFC without being stopped by the firewall.

Figure 21-1 shows a firewall configuration with the FWSM. The switch and the router beneath it represent a FWSM and a MSFC, respectively, within the same switch. This example uses the MSFC, which provides multiprotocol routing with multilayer switching for the Catalyst 6000 family switch Ethernet interfaces, as a router on the network inside the firewall. VLANs 100, 101, and 102 are configured as firewall VLANs. The MSFC is connected to only one of the controlled firewall interfaces. All router interfaces configured on the MSFC are considered the same security level as the firewall interface to which the MSFC is connected. In this example, VLANs 201 and 202, which are not configured as controlled, are considered inside the firewall, but traffic between them is routed by the MSFC without being protected by the firewall.

Figure 21-1 *Firewalling with the FWSM*

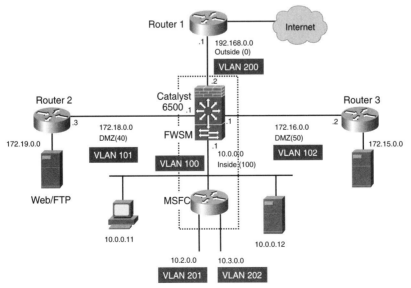

NOTE   The behavior described in this section applies only to Version 1 of the FWSM. Subsequent versions might behave differently.

How packets flow through FWSM depends on whether MSFC is used as the connected router on the inside. Figure 21-2 shows packet flow with MSFC as the connected router on the inside. In this figure, some of the VLANs carrying traffic are assigned to the FWSM. Only the traffic on those VLANs is protected by firewalls. The arrows trace a connection originating from VLAN 201 (effectively inside) and destined for the outside interface.

Figure 21-2 *Packet Flow with MSFC as a Connected Router on the Inside*

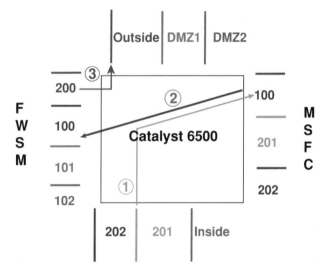

The following sequence of events occurs (the numbered arrows on Figures 21-2 and 21-3 correspond to the numbered sequence of events):

1 The packet from the inside interface (VLAN 201) is bridged to the MSFC interface.

2 The MSFC routes the packet to the firewall interface (VLAN 100).

NOTE   The MSFC should have the firewall interface as its next hop.

3 The firewall module rewrites the packet with the destination VLAN as 200. The packet from the firewall module is bridged to the outside interface.

NOTE The MSFC can be attached to only one interface on the FWSM. This setup prevents you from accidentally configuring a bypass route around the FWSM.

Figure 21-3 *Packet Flow with MSFC as a Connected Router on the Inside (Continued)*

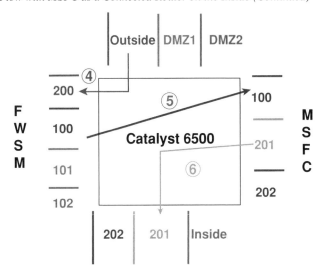

4 The return packet from the outside interface on VLAN 200 is bridged to the firewall interface.

5 The firewall rewrites the packet with the destination VLAN as 100. The packet from the FWSM is bridged to the MSFC interface.

6 The MSFC routes the packet back to the inside interface (VLAN 201).

Figure 21-4 shows the packet flow when MSFC is not used as a connected router on any firewall interface. The arrows trace a connection originating from VLAN 100 (inside) and destined for the outside interface.

Figure 21-4 *Packet Flow with MSFC Not Used as a Connected Router on Any Firewall Interface*

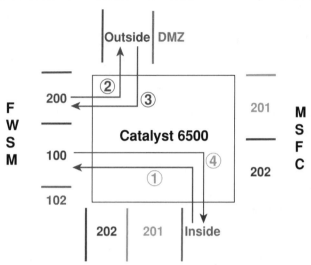

The following sequence of events occurs:

1 The packet from the inside interface on VLAN 100 is bridged to the FWSM interface.

2 Depending on the firewall configuration, the FWSM rewrites the packet with the destination VLAN as 200. The packet from the firewall module is bridged to the outside interface.

3 The return packet from the outside interface on VLAN 200 is bridged to the FWSM interface.

4 Depending on the firewall configuration and the earlier state maintained as a result of packet 1, the FWSM rewrites the packet with the destination VLAN as 100. The packet from the firewall module is bridged to the inside interface.

Configuring the FWSM

Before you can begin configuring the FWSM, you must complete the following tasks:

- Initialize the FWSM.
- Configure the switch VLANs.
- Configure the FWSM interfaces.

You can access the switch CLI through a Telnet connection to the switch or through the switch console interface. From the switch console, you can open a session into the FWSM to configure it.

Initializing the FWSM

Before you can use the FWSM, you must complete the following steps to initialize it:

Step 1   Enter the **show module** command to verify that the system acknowledges the new module and has brought it online. The syntax for the **show module** command is as follows:

> **show module** [*mod-num* | **all**]

You can specify the module number to view information on a single module or enter **all** to see information on all modules. If you supply no parameter, the system displays information on all modules.

Example 21-1 is sample output of the **show module** command.

Example 21-1   show module *Command*

```
Router# show module

Mod Slot Ports  Module-Type              Model               Sub Status
--- ---- -----  ------------------------ ------------------- --- --------
1   1    2      1000BaseX Supervisor     WS-X6K-S2U-MSFC2    yes ok
15  1    1      Multilayer Switch Feature WS-F6K-MSFC2        no  ok
2   2    6      Firewall Service Module  WS-SVC-FWM-1        no  ok
```

Step 2   Use the **session slot** command to establish a console session with the module. The syntax for the **session slot** command is as follows:

> **session slot** *mod* {**processor** *processor-id*}

Table 21-1 describes the **session slot** command arguments.

Table 21-1   session slot *Command Arguments*

Argument	Definition
mod	Slot number
processor *processor-id*	Processor ID

Step 3   At the login prompt, type **root** to log in to the root account.

Step 4   At the password prompt, type **root** as the root password.

Step 5   Use the **ip host** command to configure the IP host module used in the CLI prompt, **show** commands, and log messages. The syntax for the **ip host** command is as follows:

> **ip host** *hostname*

hostname is the module name to be used in CLI prompt, **show** commands, and log messages.

Step 6 Use the **ip address** command to configure the IP address and subnet mask. The syntax for the **ip address** command is as follows:

> `ip address` *ip-address netmask*

Table 21-2 describes the **ip address** command arguments.

Table 21-2 **ip address** *Command Arguments*

Argument	Definition
ip-address	IP address of the module
netmask	Netmask for *ip-address*

Step 7 Use the **ip broadcast** command to configure the IP broadcast address. The syntax for the **ip broadcast** command is as follows:

> `ip broadcast` *broadcast-address*

broadcast-address is the broadcast address for network of *ip-address*.

Step 8 Use the **ip gateway** command to configure the default gateway. The syntax for the **ip gateway** command is as follows:

> `ip gateway` *gateway-address*

gateway-address is the gateway of last resort to be used by the module.

Step 9 Use the **ip domain** command to configure the domain name for the module. The syntax for the **ip domain** command is as follows:

> `ip domain` *domain-name*

domain-name is the domain name for the module.

Step 10 Use the **ip nameserver** command to configure one or more IP addresses as Domain Name System (DNS) name servers. The syntax for the **ip nameserver** command is as follows:

> `ip nameserver` *name-server1* [*name-server2*][*name-server3*]]

Table 21-3 describes the **ip nameserver** command arguments.

Table 21-3 **ip nameserver** *Command Arguments*

Argument	Definition
name-server1	IP address of DNS servers
name-server2	IP address of the second DNS server if using a second DNS server
name-server3	IP address of the third DNS server if using a third DNS server

Example 21-2 shows initializing a firewall module in slot 9 of a Catalyst 6500 switch.

Example 21-2   *Initializing the FWSM*

```
Router# session slot 9 processor 1

The default escape character is Ctrl-^, then x.
You can also type 'exit' at the remote prompt to end the session
Trying 127.0.0.81 ... Open
Cisco Maintenance Image

login: root

Password:

Maintenance image version: 1.1(0.3)

FWSM(config)# ip host MYFWSM
MYFWSM(config)# ip address 172.26.26.200 255.255.255.0
MYFWSM(config)# ip broadcast 172.26.26.255
MYFWSM(config)# ip gateway 172.26.26.150
MYFWSM(config)# ip domain cisco.com
MYFWSM(config)# ip nameserver 172.26.26.132
```

Configuring the Switch VLAN

First, configure a VLAN on the route processor MSFC, and then configure the VLANs for the module. Configuring the VLANs in this order prevents the loss of switch configuration or the loss of synchronization in the definition of a firewall interface between the module and the route processor. VLAN IDs must be the same for the switch and the module. The route processor configuration for the module requires only a single VLAN for the firewall and a nonfirewall VLAN. After you configure the route processor VLAN, the controlled VLAN is sent to the module. You can then configure the module firewall functions.

Refer to the Catalyst 6000 Family IOS Software Configuration Guide on Cisco.com for details.

To enable a single controlled VLAN as the router interface on the route processor, complete the following steps:

Step 1   Use the **interface vlan** command to define a controlled VLAN on the MSFC (route processor). The syntax of the **interface vlan** command is as follows:

>   **interface vlan** *vlan_number*

>   *vlan_number* is the number of the VLAN.

Step 2   Use the **vlan** command to create VLANs. The syntax for the **vlan** command is as follows:

>   **vlan** *vlan_number* **no shut**

Step 3   Use the **firewall vlan-group** command to create a firewall group of controlled VLANs. The syntax for the **firewall vlan-group** command is as follows:

```
firewall vlan-group firewall_group vlan_range
```

Table 21-4 describes the **firewall vlan-group** command arguments.

Table 21-4   **firewall vlan-group** *Command Arguments*

Argument	Definition
firewall_group	Name of firewall VLAN group
vlan_range	Numerical range of VLAN numbers to be included in the group

Step 4   Use the **firewall module** command to attach the VLAN and firewall group to the slot where the module is located. The syntax for the **firewall module** command is as follows:

```
firewall module module_number vlan-group firewall_group
```

Table 21-5 describes the **firewall module** command arguments.

Table 21-5   **firewall module** *Command Arguments*

Argument	Definition
module_number	Number of the module
firewall_group	Name of firewall VLAN group

Step 5   Use the **end** command to update the VLAN database and return to privileged EXEC mode. The syntax for the **end** command is as follows:

```
end
```

Example 21-3 shows how to enable a controlled VLAN in global configuration mode. VLAN 100 is defined as the single controlled VLAN on the MSFC. VLANs 200, 100, 101, and 102 are then created in the switch and assigned to firewall VLAN group 3. Group 3 is attached to slot 3, the slot in which the FWSM is installed.

Example 21-3   *Switch VLAN Configuration*

```
Router(config)# interface vlan 100
Router(config)# vlan 200 no shut
Router(config-vlan)# vlan 100 no shut
Router(config-vlan)# vlan 101 no shut
Router(config-vlan)# vlan 102 no shut
Router(config-vlan)# exit
Router(config)# firewall vlan-group 3 100,101,102,200
Router(config)# firewall module 3 vlan-group 3
Router(config)# end
Router#
```

Configuring the FWSM Interfaces

To configure the module interfaces, complete the following steps:

Step 1   Use the **nameif** command to assign a module and security level to each interface on the module. The syntax of the **nameif** command is as follows:

```
nameif vlan_id if_name security_level
```

Step 2   Use the **ip address** command to configure an IP address and netmask for each module interface. The syntax for the **ip address** command is as follows:

```
ip address interface_name ip_address  [netmask]
```

After you initialize the FWSM, configure the switch VLANs, and configure the FWSM interfaces, you are ready to configure the FWSM to allow the desired traffic to protected networks. You need to create ACLs to allow outbound as well as inbound traffic because the FWSM, unlike the PIX Firewall, denies all inbound and outbound connections that are not explicitly permitted by ACLs. Configuring your firewall policy in the FWSM is similar to configuring in the PIX Firewall because the FWSM application software is similar to that of the PIX Firewall software.

Example 21-4 shows the commands you use to configure the interfaces on FWSM.

Example 21-4   *Configuring FWSM Interfaces*

```
fwsm(config)# nameif 100 inside security100
fwsm(config)# nameif 101 dmz40 security40
fwsm(config)# nameif 102 dmz50 security50
fwsm(config)# nameif 200 outside security0
fwsm(config)# ip address inside 10.0.0.1 255.255.255.0
fwsm(config)# ip address dmz40 172.18.0.1 255.255.255.0
fwsm(config)# ip address dmz50 172.16.0.1 255.255.255.0
fwsm(config)# ip address outside 192.168.0.2 255.255.255.0
```

For the most up-to-date copy of the PIX Firewall commands supported by the FWSM, check the Cisco documentation site at http://www.cisco.com/univercd/home/home.htm. At this page, select the link for the FWSM. This page contains the following:

- Commands that support the maintenance software
- Cisco IOS commands that support the FWSM
- New commands specific to the FWSM
- PIX Firewall commands that were changed for the FWSM
- PIX Firewall commands that are not used by the FWSM
- PIX Firewall commands used by the FWSM and their corresponding PIX Firewall software versions

Using PDM with FWSM

As you do with the PIX Firewall, you can use PDM to configure and monitor your FWSM. When running on the FWSM, PDM looks somewhat different because it does not have the Wizards menu or the VPN tab. Furthermore, the System Properties Interfaces table looks different. Running on the FWSM, the interfaces in the table are a combination of interfaces configured on the FWSM and the output from the **show vlan** command. PDM supports VLANs and syslog rate limiting but does not support OSPF. Use of PDM with the FWSM has the following limitations:

- FWSM currently supports only PDM Version 2.1.
- The Startup Wizard and VPN Wizard are not available.
- OSPF and VPN configuration commands specific to the FWSM are not supported by PDM.

To prepare the FWSM to use PDM, complete the following steps:

Step 1 Verify that the FWSM is installed in the switch.

Step 2 Verify that you have configured the firewall VLAN on the MSFC.

Step 3 Verify that the module is recognized by the switch.

Step 4 Verify that you have completed the basic FWSM configuration described earlier in this chapter.

Step 5 Telnet to the module and enter configuration mode.

Step 6 Execute the **setup** command and follow the instructions.

Step 7 Use the **copy tftp flash:ipdm** command to install the PDM image.

After you complete the previous steps, you can start using PDM to configure the FWSM. To access PDM, use the HTTP secure (**https**) command and enter the following address:

`https://IP address of FWSM`

The IP address is the address of one of the VLAN interfaces on the FWSM.

Troubleshooting the FWSM

This section provides troubleshooting information that you can use to determine the possible causes for the Catalyst 6000 FWSM not functioning properly.

Looking at the status LED is a quick method to determine the state of the FWSM. The status LED is located in the left corner of the module. Table 21-6 describes LED status colors.

Table 21-6   *FWSM Status Color Definitions*

Status Color	Description
Green	FWSM is operational.
Red	Diagnostic other than an individual port test failed.
Orange	One of the following conditions exists: FWSM is running boot and self-test diagnostics. FWSM is disabled. FWSM is shut down.
Off	FWSM power is off.

Resetting and Rebooting the FWSM

If you cannot reach the module through the CLI or an external Telnet session, enter the **hw-mod module** *module_number* **reset** command to reset and reboot the module. The reset process requires several minutes. The syntax for the command is as follows:

```
hw-module module module_number reset
```

module-number is the number of module you want to reset.

Example 21-6 shows how to reset the module, installed in slot 9, from the CLI.

Example 21-5   *Resetting and Rebooting FWSM*

```
Router(config)# hw-mod module 9 reset
Proceed with reload of module? [confirm] y
% reset issued for module 9
```

Memory Test

When the FWSM initially boots, by default it runs a partial memory test. To perform a full memory test, use the **hw-module module** *module_number* **mem-test-full** command. The syntax of the command is as follows:

```
hw-module module module_number mem-test-full
```

A full memory test takes more time to complete than a partial memory test and depends on the memory size. Table 21-7 lists the memory and approximate boot time for a long memory test.

Table 21-7   *FWSM Boot Time Matrix*

Memory Size	Boot Time
512 MB	3 minutes
1 GB	6 minutes

Summary

This section summarizes the information you learned in this chapter:

- The FWSM is a line card for the Catalyst 6500 family of switches and the Cisco 7600 Series Internet routers.
- The FWSM is a high-performance firewall solution based on PIX Firewall technology.
- The FWSM supports all features of PIX Firewall Software Version 6.0 and some features of 6.3.
- The FWSM offers support for 100 VLANs and OSPF.
- The FWSM supports interchassis and intrachassis failover.
- You can use PDM to configure and monitor the FWSM.

Chapter Review Questions

To test what you have learned in this chapter, answer the following questions and then refer to Appendix A, "Answers to Chapter Review Questions," for the answers:

1 What is the maximum throughput of the FWSM?

2 How many logical firewall interfaces are supported on FWSM?

3 Does FWSM support PDM? If yes, which version of PDM is supported?

4 What command do you use to enable Java and ActiveX filtering on the FWSM?

5 What is the maximum number of ACLs supported by FWSM?

On completion of this chapter, you will be able to perform the following tasks:

- Identify PIX Firewall technologies designed for small office/home office (SOHO) implementations.
- Identify PIX Firewall models best suited for SOHO networks.
- Describe VPN features best suited for SOHO networks.
- Describe PIX Firewall Dynamic Host Configuration Protocol (DHCP) and Point-to-Point Protocol over Ethernet (PPPoE) features.

CHAPTER 22

PIX Firewall in SOHO Networks

The need for secure connectivity to the Internet in today's business is universal. Just like their larger counterparts, small offices and businesses rely on their Internet connections for e-mail; for access to time-sensitive information on intranets, extranets, and the Internet; and, in some cases (such as those deploying VPNs), for access to central resources such as back-office applications.

The Internet has also paved the way for an increasing number of telecommuters. These users can access corporate resources from the comfort of their homes.

This chapter focuses on the PIX Firewall models and features designed to address the specific needs of the SOHO customer.

PIX Firewall Models

With the exception of several high-end features that are supported only on PIX Firewall models 515E, 525, and 535, all PIX Firewall models share the same function set and can be used in a SOHO environment. However, PIX Firewall models 501 and 506E are best suited for SOHO deployments. Several factors make these models the preferred options for SOHO deployment:

- **Physical size**—Whereas enterprise customers might prefer the ability to rack-mount PIX Firewall models such as the 515E, 525, or 535, the smaller size of the 501 and 506E models is a better fit for SOHO customers. The smaller size is made possible in part by removing the expansion slots that are available in 515E, 525, and 535 models.

NOTE   The PIX Firewall 501 includes a built-in, four-port switch, which is adequate for home office users and many small office deployments. This feature further reduces the footprint of networking equipment in SOHO environments by eliminating the need for a separate switch.

- **Noise**—PIX Firewall models 501 and 506E operate more quietly than models 515E, 525, and 535, which are primarily designed for operation in data centers. Noise levels are important to SOHO customers because the units are often installed close to users.

NOTE   PIX Firewall 501 includes a standard notebook-locking slot to provide physical security for SOHO customers who might be deploying the unit in unsecured areas.

- **Cost**—PIX Firewall models 501 and 506E can be obtained for a lower price than other 500-series PIX Firewall models. The lower price is made possible by the omission of several high-end features such as failover, VLANs, and Open Shortest Path First (OSPF) support (PIX Firewall 501) and the lower performance specifications on these models.
- **Licensing**—The PIX Firewall 506E includes an unrestricted license, and the PIX Firewall 501 can be purchased with 10-user, 50-user, or unrestricted licenses to match the requirements of the SOHO customer.

NOTE   The PIX Firewall 501 unrestricted license option is available on PIX Firewall Version 6.3 or higher.

PIX Firewall Features for SOHO Networks

With each new version of the PIX Firewall software, Cisco adds new features to address the needs of the entire spectrum of customers. Some new features such as OSPF and VLAN support introduced with PIX Firewall Version 6.3 aim at the large corporate and enterprise customers. However, recent PIX Firewall releases have also introduced many new features that specifically address the unique requirements of SOHO customers.

In addition to new features, PIX Firewall Version 6.3 provides up to six times the performance improvements for PIX 501 and 506E devices running earlier versions of the PIX Firewall software. PIX Firewall Version 6.3 also increases the number of site-to-site and remote access VPN tunnels supported on the PIX Firewall 501 from 5 to 10. It also introduces an unlimited user license option for the PIX Firewall 501. These enhancements make the PIX Firewall 501 more valuable for SOHO implementations.

Some of the other recent features of the PIX Firewall that are particularly useful for SOHO implementations include the following :

- PIX Device Manager (PDM)
- Easy VPN remote device functionality
- PIX Firewall PPPoE client support
- DHCP server support on all interfaces
- PIX Firewall DHCP relay
- PIX Firewall DHCP client

PIX Device Manager

PDM was introduced with PIX Firewall Version 6.0. Its current release (Version 3.01 at the time this book was written) is a much more capable and robust management console for the PIX Firewall with a graphical user interface (GUI). The expanded capability of PDM significantly reduces the learning curve for configuring and implementing the PIX in SOHO environments.

The VPN wizard function in PDM allows SOHO customers to implement site-to-site or remote access VPNs more easily and without errors. PDM configuration tasks and procedures are covered in detail in Chapter 6, "Cisco PIX Device Manager."

PIX Firewall as an Easy VPN Remote Device

PIX Firewall Software Versions 6.2 and higher let you use a PIX Firewall 501 or 506E as an Easy VPN remote device when connecting to an Easy VPN Server, such as a Cisco VPN 3000 Concentrator or another PIX Firewall. This functionality allows a small office LAN behind the PIX Firewall to connect through the Easy VPN Server and eliminates the need for software VPN clients on each user system.

PIX Firewall Version 6.3 and higher add load balancing and redundancy enhancements to the Easy VPN Remote functionality. Using the redundancy feature, a list of backup servers is configured on the PIX Firewall functioning as the Easy VPN Server. This information is pushed to the PIX Firewall Easy VPN Remote device. With the backup servers configured on the Easy VPN Remote device, it automatically tries the next server in the list if it cannot communicate with the primary server after 5 seconds.

NOTE	Load balancing is supported on the PIX Firewall Easy VPN Remote device. However, you must use the Cisco VPN 3000 Concentrator as the Easy VPN Server, which supports load balancing.

Two different modes of operation are supported when using the PIX Firewall as an Easy VPN Remote device:

- **Client mode**—The entire network behind the Easy VPN remote device is represented as a single IP address. The IP addresses of the hosts on this network are translated (network address translation [NAT]) to a single address visible to the Easy VPN Server. This mode reduces the need to allocate an entire network address to each Easy VPN Remote device. You must enable DHCP on the Easy VPN Remote device for client mode operation.

- **Network extension mode**—The entire network behind the Easy VPN remote device is visible to the Easy VPN Server. This mode requires the allocation of addresses for every host behind the Easy VPN Remote device. However, the remote hosts are visible and accessible from the Easy VPN Server.

You can configure Easy VPN Server and Remote device functionality on the PIX Firewall using the PDM or command-line interface (CLI) environments. The PDM VPN wizard is an excellent tool for configuring Easy VPN and other types of VPN connections. Refer to Chapter 16, "Site-to-Site VPNs," for instructions on using PDM and CLI commands to configure VPN connections.

PIX Firewall PPPoE Client

PIX Firewall Version 6.2 introduces PPPoE client functionality. It allows SOHO users of the PIX Firewall to connect to Internet service providers (ISPs) using Digital Subscriber Line (DSL) modems. The PPPoE standard and configuration procedures on the PIX Firewall are covered in depth in Chapter 5, "Getting Started with the PIX Firewall."

PIX Firewall DHCP Server

PIX Firewall supports DHCP servers and DHCP clients. DHCP is a protocol that supplies automatic allocation of reusable network addresses and configuration parameters to Internet hosts.

As a DHCP server, the PIX Firewall provides network configuration parameters, including dynamically assigned IP addresses, Domain Name System (DNS) and Windows Internet Naming Service (WINS) server information, and default domain name. Starting with PIX Firewall Software Version 6.3, you can enable DHCP server functionality on any interface. (Earlier versions only provide DHCP server functionality on the inside interface.) DHCP server functions and configuration procedures on the PIX Firewall are covered in depth in Chapter 5.

NOTE   The DHCP address is limited to 32 addresses with a 10-user license and 128 addresses with a 50-user license on the PIX 501. The unlimited user license on the PIX 501 and all other PIX Firewall platforms support 256 addresses.

Using Cisco IP Phones with a DHCP Server

Enterprises with small branch offices implementing a Cisco IP Telephony Voice over IP (VoIP) solution typically implement Cisco CallManager at a central office to control Cisco IP phones at small branch offices. This implementation allows centralized call processing, reduces the equipment required, and eliminates the administration of additional Cisco CallManager and other servers at branch offices.

Cisco IP phones download their configuration from a Trivial File Transfer Protocol (TFTP) server. When a Cisco IP phone starts, if it does not have both the IP address and TFTP server IP address preconfigured, it sends a request with option 150 or 66 to the DHCP server to obtain this information:

- DHCP option 150 provides the IP addresses of a list of TFTP servers.
- DHCP option 66, defined in RFC 2132, *DHCP Options and BOOTP Vendor Extensions*, gives the IP address or the host name of a single TFTP server.

Cisco IP phones can include both option 150 and 66 in a single request. In this case, the PIX Firewall DHCP server provides values for both options in the response if they are configured on the PIX Firewall.

Cisco IP phones can also include DHCP option 3 in their requests. PIX Firewall Version 6.0 (1) added support for this option, which lists the IP addresses of default routers.

PIX Firewall DHCP Relay

A new feature introduced with PIX Firewall Version 6.3 is the DHCP relay agent. The DHCP relay functionality can assist in the dynamic configuration of IP hosts on any of the PIX Firewall's interfaces. With this option enabled, DHCP requests received from hosts on a given interface are forwarded to a user-configured DHCP server on another interface. The DHCP relay option can work in conjunction with site-to-site or Easy VPN, enabling businesses to centrally manage their IP addresses.

DHCP Relay functions and configuration procedures on the PIX Firewall are covered in depth in Chapter 5.

PIX Firewall DHCP Client

You can configure the PIX Firewall as a DHCP client to dynamically obtain the IP address for its outside interface from a DHCP server. This setup is particularly useful for SOHO implementations that normally use DSL or cable modem connections. Many ISPs providing DSL or cable modem services do not assign static IP addresses for their service. The DHCP client feature, along with PPPoE, lets you use the PIX Firewall in such environments.

You can also use the **global** command with the **interface** option to enable port address translation (PAT) using the dynamically assigned IP address for outbound connections. Using these features together, you can have many users on a LAN behind the PIX accessing the Internet with a single dynamically assigned IP address. This setup eliminates the need for more expensive Internet services with static IP addresses.

Configuring the DHCP Client

Use the **ip address** command with the **dhcp** option to enable the DHCP client feature on the outside interface of the PIX Firewall. The syntax of the **ip address** command with **dhcp** is as follows:

```
ip address outside dhcp [setroute] [retry retry_cnt]
```

You can use the **setroute** option to configure the PIX Firewall to obtain its default route from the DHCP server. The optional **retry** sets the number of times the DHCP request is issued before terminating.

NOTE

When using the **setroute** argument of the **ip address dhcp** command, you should not configure the PIX Firewall with a default route (using the **route** *if_name* **0 0** *gateway_ip* command).

Summary

This section summarizes the information you learned in this chapter:

- PIX Firewall 501 and 506E are best suited for SOHO implementations.
- PIX Firewall Version 6.3 improves the functionality of PIX Firewall 501 and 506E devices for SOHO environments.
- PDM is the preferred configuration and management tool for SOHO installations.
- PIX Firewall provides Easy VPN remote device and server functionality to enable VPNs in SOHO environments.
- PIX Firewall support PPPoE and DHCP client functionality to interoperate with DSL and cable modem connections commonly used in SOHO implementations.

Chapter Review Questions

To test what you have learned in this chapter, answer the following questions and then refer to Appendix A, "Answers to Chapter Review Questions," for the answers:

1 How many site-to-site or remote access VPN tunnels are supported on the PIX Firewall 501 running Software Version 6.3?

2 Which mode of the Easy VPN Remote device allows access to the local LAN behind the remote device from the Easy VPN Server?

3 What is a common protocol used by ISPs to assign IP addresses for DSL and cable modem Internet connections?

4 What is the function of the DHCP relay agent introduced with PIX Firewall Version 6.3?

5 Which models of the PIX Firewall are best suited for SOHO installations? Why?

PART **VIII**

Appendixes

Answers to Review Questions

Chapter 1

1 What are the three types of network attacks?

Answer: The three types of network attacks are reconnaissance attacks, access attacks, and DoS attacks.

2 List the four primary threats to network security.

Answer: The four primary threats to network security are

- Unstructured
- Structured
- External
- Internal

3 What kind of threat do script kiddies pose to network security?

Answer: Script kiddies typically pose an unstructured threat to the network.

4 What are the four steps in the security wheel?

Answer:

Step 1—Secure the network.

Step 2—Monitor the network.

Step 3—Test security.

Step 4—Improve security.

5 What are the two main components of the Cisco vision for secure enterprise networking?

Answer: The Cisco AVVID framework and the SAFE Blueprint are the main components of the Cisco security and enterprise networking initiatives.

Chapter 2

1 What are the three types of firewall technologies?

Answer: The three types of firewall technologies are packet filtering, proxy server, and stateful packet filtering.

2 Which type of firewall technology provides the best overall security?

Answer: Stateful packet-filtering firewalls provide the best combination of security and performance.

3 Which type of firewall technology does the Cisco PIX Firewall use?

Answer: Cisco PIX Firewall is a stateful packet-filtering firewall.

4 What are the main technologies and benefits on the PIX firewall?

Answer: PIX Firewalls are stateful packet-filtering devices with the following technologies:

- Finesse, a non-UNIX, non-NT, secure, real-time, embedded operating system
- ASA
- Cut-through proxy
- Stateful packet filtering
- Failover capabilities

5 What are the main disadvantages of proxy servers?

Answer: Proxy-server firewalls create a single point of failure on the network, they are slow under stress, and new services are difficult to add.

Chapter 3

1 What is the maximum number of physical interfaces supported on the PIX Firewall 515E with a restricted license?

Answer: A maximum of three physical interfaces are supported on the PIX 515E with a restricted license. An unrestricted license supports a maximum of six physical interfaces.

2 Which model of the PIX family has only a single option for licensing?

Answer: The PIX Firewall 506E has a single license option providing unlimited user access. However, licensees for VPN encryption options are available for the 506E.

3 Which models of the PIX family support failover?

Answer: Failover is supported on the 515E, 525, and 535 models. PIX Firewall 501 and 506E do not support failover. FWSM also supports failover.

4 What is the maximum number of physical interfaces supported on a PIX Firewall 535 with an unrestricted license?

Answer: A PIX Firewall 535 with an unrestricted license can support up to 10 physical interfaces.

  5 How many VPN tunnels can you establish on a PIX Firewall 506E?

      Answer: PIX Firewall 506E can support up to 25 VPN peers simultaneously.

  6 What is the maximum 3DES throughput on a PIX Firewall 535 with VAC+?

      Answer: A PIX Firewall 535 with VAC+ provides up to 440 Mbps of throughput with 3DES encryption.

  7 What is the maximum throughput on the FWSM?

      Answer: FWSM provides a throughput of 5 Gbps.

  8 How many interfaces are supported on the FWSM via VLANs?

      Answer: FWSM supports up to 100 interfaces via VLANs.

Chapter 4

  1 How often should you review and revise your security plan?

      Answer: You should review and revise your security plan at least once a year or more frequently if required.

  2 What does *layered security* mean?

      Answer: Layered security is the deployment of several security measures to protect the network. In a layered security environment, if one security measure is compromised, the damage is likely to be limited.

  3 What types of security measures can you use in a layered security plan?

      Answer: A layered security plan can include the following. (This is not a comprehensive list and additional measures can be deployed.)

- AAA
- VPNs
- SSL encryption of web traffic
- SSH for secure remote management of network devices and servers
- Firewalls
- IDSs
- Cisco IOS routers with ACLs or a firewall feature set
- DMZs

4 If your security plan requires high-availability firewalls, which models of the PIX Firewall should you rule out?

Answer: PIX Firewall 501 and 506E do not support failover and are not suitable for implementation in high-availability scenarios.

5 What is the function of a DMZ?

Answer: By placing servers such as web servers, SMTP servers, and VPN concentrators on a separate, isolated network, you prevent direct access to internal hosts from the Internet. If these servers are compromised, security policies governing the traffic flow between the DMZ and the internal network can still prevent the internal hosts from being compromised.

Chapter 5

1 What are the six basic configuration commands for the PIX Firewall?

Answer: The six basic commands necessary to configure the PIX Firewall are **nameif**, **interface**, **ip address**, **nat**, **global**, and **route**.

2 What commands do you use to configure IP address translation?

Answer: You must use the **nat** and **global** command together to enable address translation. The **global** command specifies the pool of addresses that are used for translation, and the **nat** command enables translation using the address pool defined by the **global** command.

3 Which command do you use to disable NAT?

Answer: To disable address translation, you must use the **nat 0** command and specify the networks or ACLs that define the traffic that should be excluded from address translation.

4 Which logging command can adversely affect the performance of the PIX Firewall?

Answer: The use of the **logging console** command is not recommended on production PIX Firewalls. The overhead associated with this command can adversely affect the performance of the PIX Firewall.

5 On which interface does the PIX Firewall support DHCP server functionality?

Answer: DHCP server is supported only on the inside interface of the PIX Firewall for software versions before 6.3. PIX Firewall Software Version 6.3 supports DHCP on all interfaces.

Chapter 6

1 What version of the PDM is supported on PIX Firewall Version 6.3?

Answer: PIX Firewall Version 6.3 is supported only with PDM 3.0.

2 Can you use conduits and ACLs concurrently with PDM?

Answer: PDM does not support the use of conduits and ACLs in the same configuration. If you attempt to access a PIX Firewall with conduits and ACLs configured, the PDM warns you and opens in monitoring-only mode.

3 Which version of the PDM is supported on the FWSM?

Answer: PDM 2.11 supports FWSM.

4 What is the minimum recommended amount of RAM for a Windows client running PDM 3.0?

Answer: The minimum required RAM for Windows clients is 256 MB.

5 True or False: Configuration changes made by PDM are automatically saved to the PIX Firewall.

Answer: False. You must remember to apply and save any configuration changes made to the PIX Firewall's Flash memory. Otherwise, all changes are lost.

Chapter 7

1 Which protocol is easier to inspect, TCP or UDP?

Answer: TCP is a connection-oriented protocol featuring sequencing and acknowledgment of data. UDP is connectionless and provides no sequencing or handshaking. Consequently, it is more difficult to inspect and maintain the state of UDP transactions.

2 What are the four types of NAT provided by PIX Firewall?

Answer: PIX Firewall Versions 6.2 or higher provide the following types of NAT:

- Dynamic inside NAT
- Static inside NAT
- Dynamic outside NAT
- Static outside NAT

3 How many hosts can share a single outside IP address using PAT?

Answer: You can use a single registered IP address to connect up to 64,000 inside hosts to the Internet. However, a more practical limit is closer to 4000 inside hosts sharing a single PAT address.

4 How can you enable PAT using the IP address of the outside interface?

Answer: You can enable PAT using the IP address of the interface with the following commands:

```
pixfirewall(config)# nat (inside) 1 0.0.0.0 0.0.0.0
pixfirewall(config)# global (outside) 1 interface
```

5 What is the maximum number of perimeter interfaces supported on a PIX Firewall 535?

Answer: If you are running PIX Firewall Version 6.3, you can configure a maximum of 22 perimeter interfaces (24 interfaces total) by utilizing the 802.1Q VLAN capabilities of 6.3. Earlier versions of the PIX Firewall allow you to configure up to 8 perimeter interfaces (10 interfaces total).

6 List two methods that you can use to allow inbound connections.

Answer: You can configure inbound connections by using the **static** and **access-list** commands or by using the **static** and **conduit** commands. Using the **static** and **access-list** commands is the recommended method.

7 What form of the **nat** command allows you to use nontranslated IP addresses on the outside interface of the PIX Firewall?

Answer: You can use **nat 0** to disable address translation for a host or network. You can also use **nat 0** with the **access-list command** to disable address translation for specific traffic matching the access list criteria. This use is common in VPN configurations.

Chapter 8

1 What command takes precedence, a conduit or ACL?

Answer: If you have both conduit and ACL commands, ACL commands take precedence over conduits.

2 Which of the PIX models does not support Turbo ACLs?

Answer: Turbo ACLs are not supported on PIX Firewall 501.

3 What command binds an ACL to a specific interface?

Answer: The **access-group** command binds a previously defined ACL to an interface.

4 What is the maximum URL length that can be filtered with PIX Firewall 6.1 or earlier versions?

Answer: PIX Firewall Version 6.1 or earlier versions can only filter URLs that have 1159 bytes or less.

5 What are the new filter options introduced in PIX Firewall Version 6.3?

Answer: PIX Firewall Version 6.3 adds support for FTP and HTTPS filtering. Prior versions included support for HTTP filtering.

6 Which version of the PIX Firewall supports ACL editing (by line number)?

Answer: ACL editing is available only on PIX Firewall 6.3 or higher.

Chapter 9

1 What is the main benefit of object grouping?

Answer: Object grouping allows you to configure complex security policies with far fewer ACLs.

2 What type of objects can you group?

Answer: Object groups can comprise networks, protocols, services, and ICMP types.

3 What command do you use to start the configuration of object groups?

Answer: The **object-group** command is the primary command for configuring object groups.

4 You have created a network object group (MYNETWORK, 10.0.0.0 with subnet mask of 255.255.255.0) and a WEBSERVERS network object group with two hosts, 192.168.100.10 and 192.168.100.11. You now want to configure an ACL called ACLIN to allow inbound HTTP traffic from MYNETWORK to WEBSERVERS. Describe what is wrong with the following command and how it should be restated:

```
Pixfirewall(config)# access-list ACLIN permit tcp MYNETWORK WEBSERVERS eq
    HTTP
```

Answer: This command is incorrect because the keyword **object-group** does not precede the object group names. The correct command is as follows:

```
Pixfirewall(config)# access-list ACLIN permit tcp object-group MYNETWORK
    object-group WEBSERVERS eq HTTP
```

5 What is the maximum allowed level of hierarchical object grouping (levels of nesting)?

Answer: The maximum allowed level of hierarchical object grouping or nesting is 10.

Chapter 10

1 How many default routes can you configure on a PIX Firewall?

Answer: You can configure only a single default route on the PIX Firewall.

2 How many OSPF processes are supported on PIX Firewall Version 6.3?

Answer: You can configure up to two OSPF processes on PIX Firewall Version 6.3.

3 What OSPF LSA type can be filtered? Which type cannot be filtered?

Answer: PIX Firewall Version 6.3 supports filtering of Type 3 LSAs. Type 5 LSAs cannot be filtered.

4 What is the required command to configure an OSPF process with ID 5?

Answer: To enable an OSPF process with ID 5, issue the following command:

```
pixfirewall(config)# router ospf 5
```

5 What should you do to ensure that private network route updates are not sent to public areas in a NAT environment?

Answer: To prevent private network route updates from propagating to untrusted areas, you must configure the PIX Firewall as an ABR (not an ASBR), configure two separate OSPF processes, and filter Type 3 LSAs from your private network to the public network.

6 If you have overlapping network addresses, which dynamic routing protocol can you use on the PIX Firewall?

Answer: If you have overlapping address spaces on your network, you cannot enable OSPF on the PIX Firewall. Overlapping address spaces are not supported with OSPF. You can, however, run RIP under those conditions.

Chapter 11

1 You want to enable HTTP fixup protocol, but the developers at your company are using port 1180 for their development environment. How can you enable the HTTP fixup protocol on port 1180?

Answer: The default port for HTTP fixup protocol is port 80. Use the following command to add support for port 1180:

```
pixfirewall (config)# fixup protocol http 1180
```

2 Which version of PIX Firewall adds support for H.323 V3 and H.323 V4 fixup protocols?

Answer: PIX Firewall Version 6.3 introduced support for H.323 V3 and V4. Earlier versions support only H.323 V2.

3 What is the difference between the **no fixup protocol** and the **clear fixup** commands?

Answer: You use the **no fixup protocol** command to remove support for a specific protocol on a specific port or range of ports. The **clear fixup** command resets the PIX Firewall to its default settings for *all* fixup protocols.

4 Which version of PIX Firewall adds fixup protocol support for the skinny protocol?

Answer: Fixup protocol support for skinny is available on PIX Firewall Version 6.0 or higher.

5 What is the function of the **strict** option in FTP fixup protocol?

Answer: By specifying the **strict** option of the FTP fixup protocol, you can prevent web browsers from sending embedded commands in FTP requests.

Chapter 12

1 You are running Microsoft Exchange as your mail server. What should you do regarding the Mail Guard feature of the PIX Firewall?

Answer: The Mail Guard feature of the PIX Firewall does not support e-mail systems using the ESMTP such as Microsoft Exchange. Mail Guard should be turned off for the proper ESMTP operation of Exchange.

2 What type of attack is mitigated by the SYN Flood Guard feature of the PIX Firewall?

Answer: SYN Flood Guard protects the network against DoS attacks.

3 What two types of signatures are available on the Cisco PIX Firewall?

Answer: The PIX Firewall can work with two types of IDS signatures: information signatures and attack signatures.

4 What command do you use to enable the IDS functionality of PIX Firewall?

Answer: You enable the IDS function of PIX by using the **ip audit** command.

5 Which version of the Cisco Secure IDS software is required for shunning on the PIX Firewall?

Answer: Shunning with Cisco Secure IDS is supported with IDS Software Version 3.0 and higher.

6 How is DNS Guard enabled, and what is its major security benefit?

Answer: DNS Guard is enabled by default, and it is always functioning. There is no requirement to enable it manually. DNS Guard protects against UDP session hijacking and DoS attacks.

Chapter 13

1 What is the function of Virtual Telnet?

Answer: Virtual Telnet is an option used by the PIX Firewall to pre-authenticate users for services that do not support authentication on their own.

2 What is authentication?

Answer: The authentication process, typically consisting of a username and password, establishes who you are. Authentication can exist without authorization.

3 What is authorization?

Answer: Authorization requires authentication. After your identity is verified using authentication, the authorization process can determine what level of access is appropriate for your identity.

4 How does the cut-through proxy operation improve the performance of the PIX Firewall?

Answer: This process challenges a user initially at the application layer and then authenticates against standard TACACS+ or RADIUS databases. After the policy is checked, the PIX Firewall shifts the session flow and all traffic flows directly and quickly between the server and the client, eliminating the need for multiple challenges.

5 What are downloadable ACLs?

Answer: Downloadable ACLs are per-user ACLs configured on the CSACS server. This function allows you to dynamically modify the ACLs based on the identity of the user. It also provides scalability because you can configure the setting on a single CSACS and use it with multiple PIX Firewalls.

Chapter 14

1 What version of PIX Firewall software is required to enable LAN-based failover?

Answer: LAN-Based failover was introduced with PIX Firewall Software Version 6.2.

2 What version of the PIX Firewall software is required to enable stateful failover?

Answer: Stateful failover has been available since the introduction of PIX Firewall Software Version 5.0.

3   Which models of the PIX Firewall 500 series support failover?

Answer: Failover is supported on models 515E, 525, and 535. Legacy models 515 and 520 also support failover.

4   What type of interface is required for stateful failover?

Answer: Stateful failover requires a 100BASE-TX interface as a minimum. If you are using Gigabit interfaces on the PIX Firewall, stateful failover requires a 1000BASE interface.

5   Which version of the PIX OS supports virtual MAC addresses for the failover pair?

Answer: Virtual MAC address capabilities were introduced in PIX Firewall Software Version 6.2.

6   What are the four failover interface tests initiated when a failover occurs:

Answer: The four tests performed to test for failover include the link up/down, network activity, ARP, and broadcast ping tests.

7   When is the configuration of the primary PIX Firewall replicated to the secondary unit?

Answer: The configuration of the primary unit is replicated to the secondary unit in one of three ways:

- When the standby PIX Firewall completes its initial bootup, the active PIX Firewall replicates its entire configuration to the standby PIX Firewall.

- As you enter commands on the active PIX Firewall, they are sent across the failover cable to the standby PIX Firewall.

- Entering the **write standby** command on the active PIX Firewall forces the entire configuration in memory to be sent to the standby PIX Firewall.

Chapter 15

1   Which port is used for IKE negotiations?

Answer: IKE negotiations are performed using UDP port 500.

2   What is the benefit of using digital certificates and a CA for IKE?

Answer: A CA provides better security and scalability for IKE. You do not need to manually create and configure preshared keys for every new IPSec peer when using a CA.

3   What happens to the IP header when IPSec is configured in the tunnel mode?

Answer: In IPSec tunnel mode, the original IP header is encrypted and becomes a part of the ESP payload. The VPN device then adds a new unencrypted IP header to the packet to enable routing.

4   What are the advantages and disadvantages of IPSec tunnel mode?

Answer: The advantage of the tunnel mode is that the PIX Firewall acts as an IPSec proxy and performs all encryption. There is no need for client-based software. However, there is some additional overhead in this mode due to the addition of a new IP header.

5   What version of the PIX Firewall supports AES?

Answer: PIX Firewall Version 6.3 or higher provides support for 128-bit, 192-bit, and 256-bit AES encryption.

6   What is the function of IKE Phase 1?

Answer: IKE Phase 1 negotiations establish a secure channel between the IPSec peers. This secure channel is then used to negotiate IPSec SAs in Phase 2.

Chapter 16

1   What version of PIX Firewall supports the NAT- T standard?

Answer: PIX Firewall Version 6.3 adds support for NAT-T.

2   List the four IPSec configuration tasks.

Answer:

Task 1—Prepare to configure VPN support.

Task 2—Configure IKE parameters.

Task 3—Configure IPSec parameters.

Task 4—Test and verify VPN configuration

3   You would like to use AES. What version of the PIX Firewall do you need?

Answer: AES support is available only on PIX Firewall 6.3 or higher.

4   What is the command syntax for configuring IKE on an interface?

Answer: To configure IKE on a specific interface, use the following command:

```
pixfirewall(config)# isakmp enable interface-name
```

For example, to configure IKE on the outside interface, issue this command:

```
pixfirewall(config)# isakmp enable outside
```

5   What is the benefit of using the SHA algorithm versus MD5? What is the drawback?

Answer: SHA generally provides a higher level of security when compared to MD5. However, it tends to be slower than MD5.

6 What is the most secure encryption standard supported on the PIX Firewall Version 6.2?

Answer: The most secure encryption standard supported with PIX Firewall 6.2 is 168-bit 3DES. PIX Firewall 6.3 adds support for AES, which provides stronger encryption than 3DES.

7 You are creating a dynamic crypto map. What consideration must be given to the sequence number you choose for this map entry?

Answer: When creating a dynamic crypto map, you should make the sequence number the lowest priority entry by using the highest sequence number.

Chapter 17

1 What is the function of NAT-T?

Answer: NAT can break many protocols, including IKE and IPSec. NAT-T enables IPSec tunnels with NAT devices by encapsulating the IPSec packets inside UDP.

2 How do you enable NAT-T support on the PIX Firewall?

Answer: You configure NAT-T using the following command:

```
pixfirewall(config)# isakmp nat-traversal
```

3 Which version of PIX Firewall software supports NAT-T?

Answer: PIX Firewall Version 6.3 introduced support for NAT-T.

4 What does split tunneling mean?

Answer: Split tunneling allows the client to access certain networks through an encrypted IPSec tunnel, whereas access to other networks and the Internet is not encrypted.

5 How do you enable NAT-T support on the Cisco VPN Client?

Answer: NAT-T is autodetected and autonegotiated. As long as NAT-T support is enabled on the PIX Firewall, the clients automatically use NAT-T if necessary

Chapter 18

1 You want to upgrade the PDM image on your PIX Firewall to version 3.01 using a TFTP server with an address of 10.0.0.1 and a PDM image file named pdm301.bin. What command do you use to download this image to the PIX Firewall?

Answer: You must use the **copy tftp flash** command to copy the PDM image to the PIX Firewall. The exact command to use is as follows:

```
copy tftp://10.0.0.1/pdm301.bin flash:pdm
```

2 You are currently running PIX Firewall Version 6.0 and want to enable 3DES functionality by upgrading the activation key. What should you do to upgrade the activation key?

Answer: Because you are running PIX Firewall Version 6.0, you cannot use the **activation-key** command to enter a new activation key. This command is available only with PIX Firewall Version 6.2 or higher. For earlier versions of the PIX Firewall, you must reboot the device and enter the monitor mode. You must then download a new image file and write the image to the Flash memory. You are then presented with an opportunity to enter a new activation key. You can enter the new activation key, which provides the 3DES license to activate this feature.

3 What is the maximum number of Telnet commands allowed on the PIX Firewall?

Answer: You can open up to a maximum of five Telnet (and SSH) sessions simultaneously on the PIX Firewall.

4 What are the three different types of authentication databases that you can use with command authorization?

Answer: You can use command authorization with the following three user databases:

- Passwords
- Local user database
- CSACS

5 List the valid RSA key modulus sizes that you can specify in the **ca generate rsa key** command.

Answer: Valid modulus sizes are 512, 768, 1024, and 2048 bits.

6 What are the basic tasks required to configure command authorization with enable-level passwords?

Answer: The basic tasks to configure and use enable-level command authorization are as follows:

a. Use the **enable** command to create privilege levels and assign passwords to them.

b. Use the **privilege** command to assign specific commands to privilege levels.

c. Use the **aaa authorization** command to enable the command authorization feature.

d. Use the **enable** command to access the desired privilege level.

Chapter 19

1 What version of the PIX Firewall is supported on Firewall MC?

Answer: Firewall MC supports PIX Firewall Version 6.0 or higher. It provides support for most of the CLI commands, but some of the commands are not fully supported.

2 What Cisco software package must be installed before installation of Firewall MC?

Answer: Firewall MC relies on the CiscoWorks Common Services. If you try to install Firewall MC on a server without CiscoWorks Common Services pre-installed, the installation cannot proceed. Firewall MC versions up to and including 1.1.2 require CiscoWorks Common Services 1.0. Firewall MC Versions 1.1.3 or later require CiscoWorks Common Services 2.2.

3 Which protocol does Firewall MC use to securely communicate with the PIX Firewalls it manages?

Answer: All communications between Firewall MC and managed PIX Firewalls use the SSH protocol for increased security. You can also use SSL to secure communications between a client system accessing Firewall MC and the Firewall MC server.

4 Which models of the PIX Firewall can be managed by Firewall MC?

Answer: You can manage the following models using Firewall MC:

- PIX Firewall 501
- PIX Firewall 506/506E
- PIX Firewall 515/515E
- PIX Firewall 525
- PIX Firewall 535
- FWSM

5 List the basic user task flow for managing PIX Firewalls in Firewall MC:

Answer: The following activities are part of the basic user task flow in Firewall MC:

Task 1—Create a new activity.

Task 2—(Optional) Create device groups.

Task 3—Import devices.

Task 4—Configure building blocks.

Task 5—Configure settings.

Task 6—Configure access and translation rules.

Task 7—Generate and view the configuration.

Task 8—(Optional) Submit the activity for approval.

Task 9—Create a job.

Task 10—(Optional) Submit the job for approval.

Task 11—Deploy the job.

6 What command do you use to enable configuration access for Firewall MC on a PIX Firewall?

Answer: Similar to the PDM, you must enable HTTP access on the PIX Firewall, specify the interface, and identify the host or network that can access the firewall from a browser. The specific commands to allow this type of access are as follows:

```
http server enable
http ip_address [netmask] [if_name]
```

For example, to allow access on the inside interface of a firewall from the 10.0.1.0 network, you use the following commands:

```
pixfirewall(config)# http server enable
pixfirewall(config)# http 10.0.1.0 255.255.255.0 inside
```

7 How many PIX Firewalls can you manage with Firewall MC?

Answer: You can manage up to 1000 PIX Firewalls with the current version of Firewall MC.

8 You are importing a PIX Firewall into Firewall MC for management. The PIX Firewall is currently configured with several **conduit** commands. What must you do to successfully import and manage this firewall with Firewall MC?

Answer: Firewall MC does not support the **conduit** command, and you must remove all **conduit** commands from the PIX Firewall before it can be imported into Firewall MC. However, Firewall MC provides a utility to convert conduits into supported ACL commands.

Chapter 20

1 What are the three main tasks performed by AUS?

Answer: The three main tasks that you perform using AUS are as follows:

- Upgrading PIX Firewall software images
- Upgrading PDM images
- Managing and deploying PIX Firewall configuration files

2 How many PIX Firewalls can be managed by an AUS server?

Answer: AUS can support the management of up to 1000 PIX Firewall devices.

3 How much memory is required on the server for the installation of AUS server?

Answer: The server used to install AUS should have a minimum of 1 GB of RAM.

4 What is the minimum version of PIX Firewall supported by AUS?

Answer: The PIX Firewall should be running Version 6.2 or higher of the PIX software. AUS cannot manage earlier versions of the PIX Firewall.

5 Before you install AUS, what software component must you install on the server?

Answer: AUS relies on the components and service provided by the CiscoWorks Common Services 2.2. You must properly install these components on the server before you begin installing AUS.

Chapter 21

1 What is the maximum throughput of the FWSM?

Answer: FWSM supports up to 5 Gbps of throughput. However, this figure refers to throughput for UDP packets. Throughput for TCP packets is slower.

2 How many logical firewall interfaces are supported on FWSM?

Answer: FWSM can support up to 100 firewall VLANs or logical interfaces.

3 Does FWSM support PDM? If yes, which version of PDM is supported?

Answer: FWSM supports PDM Version 2.1. PDM 3.0 is not yet supported on FWSM.

4 What command do you use to enable Java and ActiveX filtering on the FWSM?

Answer: You cannot configure Java and ActiveX filtering on FWSM. Java and ActiveX filtering is one of the features of the PIX Firewall that is not supported on FWSM.

5 What is the maximum number of ACLs supported by FWSM?

Answer: FWSM supports a maximum of 128,000 ACLs. However, the 128,000 number refers to the number of ACE nodes available on the network processor. The actual practical number of ACLs supported by the FWSM is approximately 80,000.

Chapter 22

1 How many site-to-site or remote access VPN tunnels are supported on the PIX Firewall 501 running Software Version 6.3?

Answer: PIX Firewall 501 supports up to 10 IPSec tunnels when it is running Software Version 6.3 or higher. With earlier versions of the PIX Firewall software, it supports only up to five IPSec tunnels

2 Which mode of the Easy VPN Remote device allows access to the local LAN behind the remote device from the Easy VPN Server?

Answer: When you configure the Easy VPN Remote device in network extension mode, the hosts behind the remote device are visible and accessible to the Easy VPN Server. In client mode, the hosts are not directly accessible.

3 What is a common protocol used by ISPs to assign IP addresses for DSL and cable modem Internet connections?

Answer: ISPs commonly use PPPoE as an authenticated method of dynamically assigning IP addresses to client systems. PIX Firewall Software Version 6.2 or higher supports PPPoE.

4 What is the function of the DHCP relay agent introduced with PIX Firewall Version 6.3?

Answer: With DHCP relay enabled, requests received from hosts on a given interface are forwarded to a user-configured DHCP server on another interface. The DHCP relay option can work in conjunction with site-to-site or Easy VPN, enabling businesses to centrally manage their IP addresses.

5 Which models of the PIX Firewall are best suited for SOHO installations? Why?

Answer: PIX Firewall 501 and 506E are the most suitable models for SOHO implementations. They provide ample features and performance in small and compact form factors best suited to SOHO environments. They also omit high-end features not required in SOHO environments to significantly reduce the price of these models.

Security Resources

The purpose of this appendix is to provide you with a list of useful security resources available on the Internet.

Tables B-1 through B-14 provide information and links to the following related security resources:

- Professional development and security associations
- Legal resources
- Intrusion detection (network-based)
- Intrusion detection (host-based)
- Reconnaissance tools (UNIX)
- Reconnaissance tools (Windows)
- Simple Network Management Protocol (SNMP) discovery tools (Windows)
- Exploits by operating system
- Security portals
- Cracking tools
- Secure Shell (SSH)
- Cisco links
- Certificate authority (public-key infrastructure [PKI])
- Recommended reading

Table B-1   *Professional Development and Security Associations*

Association	URL
(ISC)^2: International Information Systems Security Certifications Consortium, Inc. CISSP certification	http://www.isc2.org
Information Systems Security Association (ISSA) (90-day trial membership available)	http://www.issa.org
SANS: Network security certifications and resources, including guidelines and security templates	http://www.sans.org
IEEE Computer Society Technical Committee on Security and Privacy	http://ieee-security.org

Table B-2   *Legal Resources*

Legal Resource	URL
U.S. Department of Justice Cybercrime	http://www.usdoj.gov/criminal/cybercrime/
InfoSysSec: Security Portal for Information System Security Professionals	http://www.infosyssec.org/infosyssec/seceth1.htm
FindLaw.Com: Searchable database of case law by court (Use keyword hacking)	http://laws.findlaw.com
International law enforcement resources	http://www.vaonline.org/law.html

Table B-3   *Network-Based Intrusion Detection*

Resource	URL
Cisco Secure IDS	http://www.cisco.com/en/US/customer/products/hw/vpndevc/ps4077/index.html
RealSecure (download eval)	http://www.iss.net/download
Snort: Free UNIX and Linux intrusion detection system	http://www.snort.org

Table B-4   *Host-Based Intrusion Detection*

Resource	URL
Cisco Security Agent	http://www.cisco.com/en/US/customer/products/sw/secursw/ps5057/index.html
BlackICE Pro	http://networkice.iss.com
TripWire for NT	http://www.tripwiresecurity.com

Table B-5   *Reconnaissance Tools (UNIX)*

Tool	URL
Security Administrator's Integrated Network Tool (SAINT)	http://www.saintcorporation.com/products/download.html
NetCat	http://www.atstake.com/research/tools/network_utilities/
Network Mapper (nmap)	http://www.insecure.org/nmap

Table B-6   *Reconnaissance Tools (Windows)*

Tool	URL
nMap NT	http://www.eeye.com/html/Research/Tools/nmapNT.html
eEye Retina	http://www.eeye.com/html
NetCat	http://www.atstake.com/research/tools/network_utilities/
Self-scan (check your own machine's vulnerabilities)	http://www.cablemodemhelp.com/portscan.htm
DNScape: DNS dump tool	http://www.newsbin.com/dnscape/index.htm

Table B-7   *SNMP Discovery Tools (Windows)*

Tool	URL
SolarWinds	http://www.solarwinds.net

Table B-8   *Exploits by Operating System*

Resource	URL
MITRE: Common Vulnerabilities and Exposures (CVE)	http://www.cve.mitre.org/cve
CERT advisories	http://www.cert.org
Insecure.Org	http://www.insecure.org/sploits.html
CyberArmy (links to top 50 hacking sites)	http://www.cyberarmy.com/t-50/index.shtml

Table B-9   *Security Portals*

Portal	URL
Security Focus	http://www.securityfocus.com
Packet Storm	http://www.packetstormsecurity.org
SearchSecurity.com	http://searchsecurity.techtarget.com
Web Security	http://www.w3.org/Security
Information Security Magazine (free subscription)	http://www.infosecuritymag.com
Cooperative Association for Internet Data Analysis (CAIDA)	http://www.caida.org/home/index.xml
Center for Internet Security	http://www.cisecurity.org
InfoSysSec: Security Portal for Information System Security Professionals	http://www.infosyssec.com

Table B-10 *Cracking Tools*

Tool	URL
L0pht Crack for NT	http://www.atstake.com/research/LC
LANguard: free security tools	http://www.languard.com/languard/lantools.htm
DMOZ cracking tools index	http://www.dmoz.org/Computers/Hacking/Cracking

Table B-11 *SSH*

Tool	URL
SSH communications security	http://www.ssh.com
PuTTY download page	http://www.chiark.greenend.org.uk/~sgtatham/putty/download.html
Teraterm Pro/SSH (Windows 3.1, Windows CE, Windows 95, and Windows NT 4.0): download the Free Teraterm Pro SSH v1.x Client	http://hp.vector.co.jp/authors/VA002416/teraterm.html
TTSSH security enhancement for Teraterm Pro	http://www.zip.com.au/~roca/ttssh.html

Table B-12 *Cisco Links*

Resource	URL
Improving security on Cisco routers	http://www.cisco.com/en/US/tech/tk648/tk361/technologies_tech_note09186a0080120f48.shtml
CCSP certification	http://www.cisco.com/en/US/learning/le3/le2/le37/le54/learning_certification_type_home.html
CCIE: security	http://www.cisco.com/warp/public/625/ccie/security/
Security advisories	http://www.cisco.com/en/US/products/prod_security_advisories_list.html
Cisco Secure Encyclopedia (CSEC) (requires Cisco.com account)	http://www.cisco.com/go/csec
Cisco SAFE Architecture (Security Blueprint)	http://www.cisco.com/go/safe
Cisco AVVID Framework	http://www.cisco.com/go/avvid
Cisco password recovery techniques	http://www.cisco.com/warp/public/474

Table B-13 *Certificate Authority (PKI) Resources*

Resource	URL
Configuring Microsoft Certificate Server (Windows 2000 Server)	http://www.cisco.com/univercd/cc/td/doc/ product/iaabu/ csvpnc/csvpnsg/idcmsft.htm

Table B-14 *Recommended Reading*

Resource	Author/Publishing Information/URL
Designing Network Security	Merike Kaeo, 1999, Cisco Press. ISBN: 1578700434.
Managing Cisco Network Security	Michael Wenstrom, 2001, Cisco Press. ISBN: 1578701031.
CCSP Cisco Secure PIX Firewall Advanced Exam Certification Guide	Christian Degu and Greg Bastien, 2003, Cisco Press. ISBN: 1587200678.
CCIE Security Exam Certification Guide	Henry Benjamin, 2003, Cisco Press. ISBN: 1587200651.
Internet Security Protocols: Protecting IP Traffic	Uyless D. Black, 2000, Prentice Hall PTR. ISBN: 0130142492.
Hacking Exposed: Network Security Secrets and Solutions, Second Edition	Joel Scambray, George Kurtz, and Stuart McClure, 2000, Osborne (McGraw-Hill Professional Publishing). ISBN: 0072127481.
The Cuckoo's Egg: Tracking a Spy Through the Maze of Computer Espionage	Clifford Stoll, 2000, Pocket Books. ISBN: 0743411463.
Take-Down: The Pursuit and Capture of Kevin Mitnick, America's Most Wanted Computer Outlaw	Tsutomu Shimomura and John Markoff, 1996, Hyperion. ISBN: 0786862106.
Cyberpunk: Outlaws and Hackers on the Computer Frontier	Katie Hafner and John Markoff, 1995, Touchstone Books. ISBN: 0684818620.
Network Intrusion Detection, Second Edition (Be sure to get the *new* Second Edition edition.)	Stephen Northcutt, Donald MacLachlan, and Judy Novak, 2000, New Riders Publishing. ISBN: 0735710082.
Intrusion Signatures and Analysis	Stephen Northcutt, et al., 2001, New Riders Publishing. ISBN: 0735710635.
Information Security Magazine	Free subscription available at http:// www.infosecuritymag.com.
Warriors of the Net (Multimedia presentation about IP routing, proxy operation, and firewalls)	http://warriorsofthe.net

INDEX

Numerics

A

R

S

X-Y-Z